The Books of Haggai and Malachi

The New International Commentary on the Old Testament

The Books of
HAGGAI and MALACHI

Mignon R. Jacobs

William B. Eerdmans Publishing Company
Grand Rapids, Michigan

Wm. B. Eerdmans Publishing Co.
2140 Oak Industrial Drive NE, Grand Rapids, Michigan 49505
www.eerdmans.com

Published 2017
Printed in the United States of America

26 25 24 23 22 21 20 19 18 3 4 5 6 7 8 9 10

ISBN 978-0-8028-2625-1

Library of Congress Cataloging-in-Publication Data

Names: Jacobs, Mignon R., author.
Title: The books of Haggai and Malachi / Mignon R. Jacobs.
Description: Grand Rapids : Eerdmans Publishing Co., 2017. | Series: The new international commentary on the Old Testament | Includes bibliographical references and index.
Identifiers: LCCN 2017025509 | ISBN 9780802826251 (hardcover : alk. paper)
Subjects: LCSH: Bible. Haggai—Commentaries. | Bible. Malachi—Commentaries.
Classification: LCC BS1655.53 .J33 2017 | DDC 224/.97077—dc23
LC record available at https://lccn.loc.gov/2017025509

With thanks for their support and encouragement
This book is dedicated to my brothers:
Edwin, Carlos, and Emil

The steadfast love of the Lord never ceases,
his mercies never come to an end;
they are new every morning;
great is your faithfulness.
"The Lord is my portion," says my soul;
"therefore I will hope in him."
(Lam 3:22–24 NRSV)

Contents

CONTENTS

List of Illustrations

TABLES

MAPS

FIGURES

General Editor's Preface

Long ago St. Paul wrote: "I planted, Apollos watered, but God gave the growth" (1 Cor. 3:6 NRSV). He was right: ministry indeed requires a team effort—the collective labors of many skilled hands and minds. Someone digs up the dirt and drops in seed, while others water the ground to nourish seedlings to growth. The same team effort over time has brought this commentary series to its position of prominence today. Professor E. J. Young "planted" it nearly fifty years ago, enlisting its first contributors and himself writing its first published volumes. Professor R. K. Harrison "watered" it, signing on other scholars and wisely editing everyone's finished products. As General Editor, I now tend their planting, and, true to Paul's words, through four decades God has indeed graciously "[given] the growth."

Today the New International Commentary on the Old Testament enjoys a wide readership of scholars, priests, pastors, rabbis, and other serious Bible students. Thousands of readers across the religious spectrum and in countless countries consult its volumes in their ongoing preaching, teaching, and research. They warmly welcome the publication of each new volume and eagerly await its eventual transformation from an emerging "series" into a complete commentary "set." But as humanity experiences a new century of history, an era commonly called "postmodern," what kind of commentary series is NICOT? What distinguishes it from other similarly well-established series?

Its volumes aim to publish biblical scholarship of the highest quality. Each contributor writes as an expert, both in the biblical text itself and in the relevant scholarly literature, and each commentary conveys the results of wide reading and careful, mature reflection. Ultimately, its spirit is eclectic, each contributor gleaning interpretive insights from any useful source, whatever its religious or philosophical viewpoint, and integrating them into his or her interpretation of a biblical book. The series draws on recent methodological innovations in biblical scholarship: for example, canon criticism, the so-called new literary criticism, reader-response theories, and sensitivity to gender-based and ethnic readings. NICOT volumes also aim to be irenic in tone, summarizing and critiquing influential views with fairness while defending their own. Its list of contributors includes male and female scholars from a number of Christian faith-groups. The diversity of contributors and their freedom to draw on all relevant methodologies give the entire series an exciting and enriching variety.

What truly distinguishes this series, however, is that it speaks from within that interpretive tradition known as evangelicalism. Evangelicalism is an informal movement within Protestantism that cuts across traditional denominational lines. Its heart and soul is the conviction that the Bible is God's inspired Word, written by gifted human writers, through which God calls humanity to enjoy a loving personal relationship with its Creator and Savior. True to that tradition, NICOT volumes do not treat the Old Testament as just an ancient literary artifact on a par with the *Iliad* or Gilgamesh. They are not literary autopsies of ancient parchment cadavers but rigorous, reverent wrestlings with wonderfully human writings through which the living God speaks his powerful Word. NICOT delicately balances "criticism" (i.e., the use of standard critical methodologies) with humble respect, admiration, and even affection for the biblical text. As an evangelical commentary, it pays particular attention to the text's literary features, theological themes, and implications for the life of faith today.

Ultimately, NICOT aims to serve women and men of faith who desire to hear God's voice afresh through the Old Testament. With gratitude to God for two marvelous gifts—the Scriptures themselves and keen-minded scholars to explain their message—I welcome readers of all kinds to savor the good fruit of this series.

ROBERT L. HUBBARD JR.

Author's Preface

A few words about my approach to this commentary may help you, the reader, to identify my perspective in writing it. My primary task was to interpret the texts, first, as prophetic literature and, second, as diverse intertextual voices within the Hebrew Bible / Old Testament canon. As I wrote, I placed several models of this approach before me. My primary influences were current and future pastors (students) and awareness of the questions they bring to the study of biblical texts; juxtaposed with these were the modern contexts that affect the ways we think and communicate about the biblical texts. At various points in this book, I discuss intertextual variations on the various interpretive options and allow these options to coexist. Given the richness of the text, the juxtaposed options may invite discussion and further reflection or may jar readers who want a single, decisive interpretation. The juxtaposition is intentional and allows readers to consider the options—even potentially competing options. I am aware that my faith commitments and theological stance shape this approach to writing a commentary. Readers are encouraged to participate in the study of the text and to see how their commitments influence their reading of the texts.

Second, anyone who writes a commentary (on prophetic literature especially) is tempted to take an interpretive or instructive stance within our modern context. My approach instead is to inquire about the significance of the text for both the ancient and the modern audience. Notably, it is not always possible to transpose ancient texts into modern contexts in a simple way. Recontextualizing the ideas and themes most often requires reconceptualizing. This task is not the primary concern of a commentary, even though it might offer specific theological stances for the reader. Admittedly, I have included some contemporary applications in discussions of various ideas and themes. In these cases and others where differing options are juxtaposed, I invite the reader to reflect further on the significance of an interpretation for today. The ethics of interpretation is also a compelling force in entering into discourse with readers who, like me, bring faith and interpretive commitments to this book. If the reading of this book draws the reader into additional reading and discussion of the biblical text and a commitment to understanding God's work, then the book begins to serve at least one of its purposes.

Third, readers will notice the use of divine names throughout the book. Note that I use the name provided in the Hebrew text to interpret that text. I do not use the English word *Lord* in place of Hebrew *Yahweh* but represent the name that appears in the Hebrew text. In various cases, to avoid the masculine pronoun, I use Deity (the Deity) or God. The use of *Deity* is also intended to distinguish the divine agent from human agents.

There are many people who have influenced me over the years and many factors that have shaped my understanding. Rolf P. Knierim, who is both a mentor and a friend, has shaped my approach to the text. My friends and family continue to be a blessing. My brothers are indeed the best brothers I could hope for. In many ways, my students have been among my dialogue partners, especially my teaching assistants and the students in my Hebrew Prophets and Exegesis of the Minor Prophets courses. Their questions and challenges served as a valuable contribution as I wrote and revised the book. I appreciate the fresh eyes that they brought to the texts and at times the filters they used to process textual and conceptual difficulties that they encountered. Their questions and filters allowed me to be more aware of my own.

I am grateful for the various avenues of support. I wish to thank the School of Theology at Fuller Theological Seminary and Dean Howard Loewen in particular. The sabbatical leaves allowed me time to complete this book. The work of others also allowed me to finish this book. Many thanks go to Jina Kang, my PhD student and research assistant, and Susan Wood, editor for faculty publications, for their assistance in editing the manuscript. I also wish to thank my editor, Bob Hubbard, for his support and steadfastness over the years that it took me to complete this volume. His encouragement provided the context for exploring my thoughts.

Last but most important, I thank God for all these and other gifts given to me all my life.

Abbreviations

AB	Anchor Bible
ABD	*Anchor Bible Dictionary*. Edited by D. N. Freedman. 6 vols. New York: Doubleday, 1992
ABRL	Anchor Bible Reference Library
AJBA	*African Journal of Biblical Archaeology*
AJBI	*Annual of the Japanese Biblical Institute*
AnBib	Analecta Biblica
ANET	*Ancient Near Eastern Tests relating to the Old Testament*. Edited by J. B. Pritchard. 3rd ed. Princeton: Princeton University Press, 1969
AnOr	Analecta orientalia
ARW	*Archiv für Religionswissenschaft*
ASV	American Standard Version
ATANT	Abhandlungen zur Theologie des Alten und Neuen Testaments
ATD	Das Alte Testament Deutsch
ATJ	*Ashland Theological Journal*
AzTh	Arbeiten zur Theologie
BASOR	*Bulletin of the American Schools of Oriental Research*
BBET	Beiträge zur biblischen Exegese und Theologie
BDB	Brown, F., S. R. Driver, and C. A. Briggs. *A Hebrew and English Lexicon of the Old Testament*
BEATAJ	Beiträge zur Erforschung des Alten Testaments und des antiken Judentum
BHK	*Biblia Hebraica*. Edited by R. Kittel. Leipzig: Hinrichs, 1905–1906
BHS	*Biblia Hebraica Stuttgartensia*. Edited by K. Elliger and W. Rudolph. Stuttgart: Deutsche Bibelgesellschaft, 1983
BI	*Biblical Illustrator*
Bib	*Biblica*

BibInt	*Biblical Interpretation*
BibLeb	*Bibel und Leben*
BJS	Brown Judaic Studies
BKAT	Biblischer Kommentar, Altes Testament
BN	*Biblische Notizen*
BR	*Biblical Research*
BRev	*Bible Review*
BT	*The Bible Translator*
BTB	*Biblical Theology Bulletin*
BZAW	Beihefte zur Zeitchrift für die alttestamentliche Wissenschaft
CAT	Commentaire de l'Ancien Testament
CBC	Cambridge Bible Commentary
CBET	Contributions to Biblical Exegesis and Theology
CBQ	*Catholic Biblical Quarterly*
CTR	*Criswell Theological Review*
CurBS	*Currents in Research: Biblical Studies*
CurTM	*Currents in Theology and Mission*
CV	*Communio Viatorum*
DJD	Discoveries in the Judaean Desert
EstBib	*Estudios bíblicos*
ESV	English Standard Version
ETL	*Ephemerides Theologicae Lovanienses*
EvQ	*Evangelical Quarterly*
EvT	*Evangelische Theologie*
ExpTim	*Expository Times*
FAT	Forschungen zum Alten Testament
FMSt	Frühmittelalterliche Studien
FOTL	Forms of the Old Testament Literature
GKC	*Gesenius' Hebrew Grammar.* Edited by E. Kautzsch. Translated by A. E. Cowley. 2nd ed. Oxford: Clarendon, 1910
GTJ	*Grace Theological Journal*
HAR	*Hebrew Annual Review*
HAT	Handbuch zum Alten Testament
HeyJ	*Heythrop Journal*
HTR	*Harvard Theological Review*
IBHS	*An Introduction to Biblical Hebrew Syntax*. B. K. Waltke and M. O'Connor. Winona Lake, IN: Eisenbrauns, 1990
ICC	International Critical Commentary
Int	*Interpretation*
ITC	International Theological Commentary
JAOS	*Journal of the American Oriental Society*
JBL	*Journal of Biblical Literature*

JBQ	*Jewish Bible Quarterly*
JETS	*Journal of the Evangelical Theological Society*
JJS	*Journal of Jewish Studies*
JNSL	*Journal of Northwest Semitic Languages*
JOTT	*Journal of Translation and Textlinguistics*
Joüon	Joüon, P. *A Grammar of Biblical Hebrew.* Translated and revised by T. Muraoka. 2 vols. Rome: Pontifical Biblical Institute, 1991
JPS	Jewish Publication Society Version
JSJSup	Journal for the Study of Judaism Supplement
JSOT	*Journal for the Study of the Old Testament*
JSOTSup	Journal for the Study of the Old Testament Supplement Series
JSP	*Journal for the Study of the Pseudepigrapha*
KAT	Kommentar zum Alten Testament
KJV	King James Version
MSJ	*The Master's Seminary Journal*
NAB	New American Bible
NCB	New Century Bible
NCBC	New Century Bible Commentary
NEB	New English Bible
NEchtB	Neue Echter Bibel
NIB	*The New Interpreter's Bible.* Edited by L. E. Keck. 12 vols. Nashville: Abingdon, 1994–2004
NICOT	New International Commentary on the Old Testament
NIV	New International Version
NJB	New Jerusalem Bible
NRSV	New Revised Standard Version
OBO	Orbis Biblicus et Orientalis
OBT	Overtures to Biblical Theology
OLP	*Orientalia Lovaniensia Periodica*
OTE	*Old Testament Essays*
OTG	Old Testament Guides
OTL	Old Testament Library
OtSt	Oudtestamentische Studiën
OTWSA	Ou Testamentiese Werkgemeenskap van Suid-Afrika
Presb	*Presbyterion*
RelSRev	*Religious Studies Review*
ResQ	*Restoration Quarterly*
RevExp	*Review and Expositor*
RevistB	*Revista Bíblica*
RIBLA	*Revista de interpretación bíblica latino-americana*
RSV	Revised Standard Version
RTR	*Reformed Theological Review*

SB Sources Bibliques
SBL Society of Biblical Literature
SBLDS Society of Biblical Literature Dissertation Series
SBLMS Society of Biblical Literature Monograph Series
SBLSCS Society of Biblical Literature Septuagint and Cognate Studies
SBLSP Society of Biblical Literature Seminar Papers
SBLSymS Society of Biblical Literature Symposium Series
SBT Studies in Biblical Theology
ScrB *Scripture Bulletin*
SEÅ *Svensk exegetisk årsbok*
SJOT *Scandinavian Journal of the Old Testament*
SSN Studia Semitica Neerlandica
ST *Studia Theologica*
SwJT *Southwestern Journal of Theology*
T & K *Texte and Kontexte*
TBT *The Bible Today*
TDNT *Theological Dictionary of the New Testament.* Edited by G. Kittel and G. Friedrich. Translated by G. W. Bromiley. 10 vols. Grand Rapids: Eerdmans, 1964–1976
TDOT *Theological Dictionary of the Old Testament.* Edited by G. J. Botterweck and H. Ringgren. Translated by J. T. Willis et al. 8 vols. Grand Rapids: Eerdmans, 1974–2006
ThWAT *Theologisches Wörterbuch zum Alten Testament.* Edited by G. J. Botterweck and H. Ringgren. Stuttgart: Kohlhammer, 1970–
TJ *Trinity Journal*
TLOT *Theological Lexicon of the Old Testament.* Edited by E. Jenni, with assistance from C. Westermann. Translated by M. E. Biddle. 3 vols. Peabody, MA: Hendrickson, 1997
TOTC Tyndale Old Testament Commentaries
Transeu *Transeuphratène*
TWOT *Theological Wordbook of the Old Testament.* Edited by R. L. Harris, G. L. Archer Jr., and B. K. Waltke. 2 vols. Chicago: Moody Press, 1980
TynBul *Tyndale Bulletin*
UF *Ugarit-Forschungen*
VC *Vigiliae Christianae*
VT *Vetus Testamentum*
VTSup Supplements to Vetus Testamentum
WBC Word Biblical Commentary
Williams, *Syntax* Williams, R. J. *Williams' Hebrew Syntax.* Rev. J. C. Beckman. 3rd ed. Toronto: University of Toronto Press, 2007
WW *Word and World*

ZAW	*Zeitschrift für die alttestamentliche Wissenschaft*

ANCIENT VERSIONS

1QS	Serek Hayaḥad (or Rule of the Community, Manual of Discipline)
CD	Cairo (Genizah copy of the) Damascus Document
LXX	Septuagint
LXXG	Septuagint
LXXV	Septuagint
MT	Masoretic Text
Tg.	Targum

Bibliography

Achtemeier, E. *Nahum–Malachi*. Interpretation. Atlanta: John Knox, 1986.

Ackroyd, P. R. "The Book of Haggai and Zechariah 1–8." *JJS* 3 (1952): 151–56.

———. *Exile and Restoration: A Study of Hebrew Thought of the Sixth Century BC*. OTL. Philadelphia: Westminster, 1968.

———. "The Jewish Community in Palestine in the Persian Period." Pages 130–61 in *Introduction: The Persian Period*. Edited by W. D. Davies and L. Finkelstein. Vol. 1 of *The Cambridge History of Judaism*. Cambridge: Cambridge University Press, 1984.

———. "Some Interpretative Glosses in the Book of Haggai: [Hag 2:5a, 9, 14, 17]." *JJS* 7 (1956): 163–67.

———. "Studies in the Book of Haggai." *JJS* 2 (1950–1951): 163–76.

Aharoni, Y. *The Land of the Bible: A Historical Geography*. Rev. ed. Philadelphia: Westminster, 1979.

Ahlström, G. W. *The History of Ancient Palestine*. Minneapolis: Fortress, 1993.

Alden, R. L. "Malachi." In *Daniel–Minor Prophets*. Vol. 7 of *The Expositor's Bible Commentary*. Grand Rapids: Zondervan, 1985.

Allen, N. "The Identity of the Jerusalem Priesthood during the Exile." *HeyJ* 13 (1982): 259–69.

Allison, D. C. "Elijah Must Come First." *JBL* 103 (1984): 256–58.

Althann, R. "Malachi 2:13–14 and UT 125:12–13." *Bib* 58 (1977): 418–21.

Amerongen, M. van. "Structuring Division Markers in Haggai." Pages 51–79 in *Delimitation Criticism: A New Tool in Biblical Scholarship*. Pericope: Scripture as Written and Read in Antiquity 1. Assen: Van Gorcum, 2000.

Amsler, S. *Les actes des prophètes*. Essais bibliques 9. Geneva: Labor et Fides, 1985.

———. "Les prophètes et la communication par les actes." Pages 194–201 in *Werden und Wirken des Alten Testament: Festschrift für Claus Westermann*. Edited by R. Albertz et al. Göttingen: Vandenhoeck & Ruprecht; Neukirchen-Vluyn: Neukirchener, 1980.

Amsler, S., A. Lacocque, and R. Vuilleumier, eds. *Aggée-Zacharie 1–8, Zacharie 9–14, Malachi.* CAT 11c. Geneva: Labor et Fides, 1981.

Anderson, J. S. *The Internal Diversification of Second Temple Judaism: An Introduction to the Second Temple Period.* Lanham, MD: University Press of America, 2002.

Assis, E. "Why Edom? On the Hostility towards Jacob's Brother in Prophetic Sources." *VT* 56 (2006): 1–20.

Aufrecht, W. E. "Urbanization and Northwest Semitic Inscriptions of the Late Bronze and Iron Ages." Pages 116–29 in *Urbanism in Antiquity.* Edited by W. E. Aufrecht, N. A. Mirau, and S. W. Gauley. JSOTSup 244. Sheffield: JSOT Press, 1997.

Aune, D. E. *Revelation 17–22.* WBC 52c. Nashville: Thomas Nelson, 1997.

Avi-Yonah, M. *The Holy Land from the Persian to the Arab Conquest.* Rev. ed. Grand Rapids: Baker, 1977.

Baillet, M., J. T. Milik, and R. de Vaux, eds. *Les 'Petites Grottes' de Qumran.* DJD 3. Oxford: Clarendon, 1962.

Baldwin, J. G. *Haggai, Zechariah, Malachi.* TOTC. Downers Grove, IL: InterVarsity; London: Tyndale, 1972.

———. "Mal 1:11 and the Worship of the Nations in the Old Testament." *TynBul* 23 (1972): 117–24.

Ballentine, S. E. "The Politics of Religion in the Persian Period." Pages 129–46 in *After the Exile: Essays in Honor of Rex Mason.* Edited by J. Barton and D. J. Reimer. Macon, GA: Mercer University Press, 1996.

Barrett, M. "The Message of Malachi: An Analysis of Dead Religion." *Biblical Viewpoint* 32.2 (1998): 33–43.

Barstad, H. M. *The Myth of the Empty Land: A Study of the History and Archaeology of Judah during the 'Exilic' Period.* Symbolae Osloeses Fasciculi suppletorri 28. Oslo: Scandinavian University Press, 1996.

———. "No Prophets? Recent Developments in Biblical Prophetic Research and Ancient Near Eastern Prophecy." *JSOT* 57 (1993): 39–60.

———. "On the History and Archaeology of Judah during the Exilic Period: A Reminder." *OLP* 19 (1988): 25–36.

Bartal, A. "Once Again—Who Was Sheshbazzar?" *Beth Miqra* 79 (1979): 357–69.

Barthélemy, D., ed. *Ezékiel, Daniel et les 12 prophètes.* Vol. 3 of *Critique textuelle de l'Ancien Testament.* OBO 50/3. Fribourg : Editions Universitaires; Göttingen: Vandenhoeck & Ruprecht, 1992.

Bartlett, J. R. "The Brotherhood of Edom." *JSOT* 2 (1977): 2–27.

———. "Edom." *ABD* 2:287–95.

Barton, J., ed. *The Biblical World.* London: Routledge, 2002.

Baumgarten, A. I. "The Paradox of the Red Heifer." *VT* 43 (1993): 442–51.

Becking, B., and R. Albertz, eds. *Yahwism after the Exile: Perspectives on Israelite*

Religion in the Persian Era. Studies in Theology and Religion 5. Assen: Van Gorcum, 2003.

Becking, B., and M. C. A. Korpel. *The Crisis of Israelite Religion: Transformation of Religious Tradition in Exilic and Post-exilic Times*. Leiden: Brill, 1999.

Bedford. P. R. "Discerning the Time: Haggai, Zechariah and the 'Delay' in the Rebuilding of the Jerusalem Temple." Pages 71–94 in *The Pitcher Is Broken: Memorial Essays for G. W. Ahlström*. Edited by S. W. Holloway and L. K. Handy. JSOTSup 190. Sheffield: JSOT Press, 1995.

———. *Temple Restoration in Early Achaemenid Judah*. JSJSup 63. Leiden: Brill, 2001.

Bellis, A. O. *Many Voices: Multicultural Responses to the Minor Prophets*. Lanham, MD: University Press of America, 1995.

Ben Zvi, E. "Inclusion in and Exclusion from 'Israel' in Post-monarchic Biblical Texts." Pages 95–149 in *The Pitcher Is Broken: Memorial Essays for G. W. Ahlström*. Edited by S. W. Holloway and L. K. Handy. JSOTSup 190. Sheffield: JSOT Press, 1995.

———. "Looking at the Primary (Hi)story and the Prophetic Books as Literary/Theological Units within the Frame of the Early Second Temple: Some Considerations." *SJOT* 12 (1996): 26–43.

———. "The Urban Centre of Jerusalem and the Development of the Literature of the Hebrew Bible." Pages 194–209 in *Urbanism in Antiquity*. Edited by W. E. Aufrecht, N. A. Mirau, and S. W. Gauley. JSOTSup 244. Sheffield: JSOT Press, 1997.

Bendor. S. *The Social Structure of Ancient Israel*. Jerusalem: Simor, 1996.

Bergant, D. "My Beloved Is Mine and I Am His' (Song 2:16): The Song of Songs and Honor and Shame." *Semeia* 68 (1994): 23–40.

Bergren, T. A. "The List of Leaders in 5 Ezra 1:39–40." *JBL* 120 (2001): 313–27.

Berquist, J. L. *Judaism in Persia's Shadow: A Social and Cultural Approach*. Philadelphia: Fortress, 1995.

———. "The Social Setting of Malachi." *BTB* 19 (1989): 121–26.

Berry, Donald K. "Malachi's Dual Design: The Close of the Canon and What Comes Afterward. Forming Prophetic Literature." Pages 269–302 in *Forming Prophetic Literature: Essays on Isaiah and the Twelve in Honor of John D. W. Watts*. Edited by J. W. Watts and P. R. House. JSOTSup 235. Sheffield: JSOT Press, 1996.

Beuken, W. A. M. *Haggai–Sacharja 1–8*. SSN 10. Assen: Van Gorcum, 1967.

Bianchi, F. "Le rôle de Zorobabel et la dynastie davidique en Judée du VIe siècle au IIe siècle av. J.-C." *Transeu* 7 (1994): 153–64.

Bickerman, E. J. "The Babylonian Captivity." Pages 342–58 in *Introduction, Persian Period*. Vol. 1 of *The Cambridge History of Judaism*. Cambridge: Cambridge University Press, 1984.

———. "The Edict of Cyrus in Ezra 1." *JBL* 65 (1946): 249–75.

Blake, R. D. "The Rhetoric of Malachi." PhD diss., Union Theological Seminary [New York], 1988.

Blenkinsopp, J. *Ezra–Nehemiah: A Commentary*. OTL. Philadelphia: Westminster, 1988.

———. *A History of Prophecy in Israel*. 2nd ed. Louisville: Westminster John Knox, 1996.

———. "The Judaean Priesthood during the Neo-Babylonian and Achaemenid Periods: A Hypothetical Reconstruction." *CBQ* 60 (1998): 25–43.

———. "Life Expectancy in Ancient Palestine." *SJOT* 11 (1997): 44–55.

———. "The Social Roles of Prophets in Early Achaemenid Judah." *JSOT* 93 (2001): 39–58.

Blomberg, C. L. "Elijah, Election, and the Use of Malachi in the New Testament." *CTR* 2 (1987): 99–117.

Boda, Mark J. "From Dystopia to Myopia: Utopian (Re)Visions in Haggai and Zechariah 1–8." Pages 210–48 in *Utopia and Dystopia in Prophetic Literature*. Edited by E. Ben Zvi. Publications of the Finnish Exegetical Society 92. Helsinki: Finnish Exegetical Society/University of Helsinki, 2006.

———. "From Fasts to Feasts: The Literary Function of Zechariah 7–8." *CBQ* 65 (2003): 390–407.

Boecker, H. J. "Bemerkungen zur formgeschichtlichen Terminologie des Buches Maleachi." *ZAW* 78 (1966): 78–80.

Bolin, T. M. "The Temple of YHWH at Elephantine and Persian Religious Policy." Pages 127–42 in *The Triumph of Elohim: From Yahwism to Judaism*. Edited by D. V. Edelman. CBET. Kampen: Kok Pharos, 1995.

———. "When the End Is the Beginning: The Persian Period and the Origins of the Biblical Tradition." *SJOT* 10 (1996): 3–15.

Boring, M. E. *Revelation*. Interpretation. Louisville: John Knox, 1989.

Bosshard, E., and R. G. Kratz. "Maleachi im Zwölfprophetenbuch." *BN* 52 (1990): 27–46.

Bossman, D. M. "Kingship and Religious System in the Prophet Malachi." Pages 127–41 in *Religious Writings and Religious Systems*. Brown Studies Series 1. Atlanta: Scholars Press, 1989.

Botha, P. J. "Honor and Shame as Keys to the Interpretation of Malachi." *OTE* 14 (2001): 392–403.

Botterweck, G. J. "Die Sonne der Gerechtigkeit am Tage Jahweh: Auslegung von Mal 3:13–21." *BibLeb* 1 (1960): 253–60.

———. "Ideal und Wirklichkeit der Jerusalemer Priester." *BibLeb* 1 (1960): 100–109.

———. "Jakob habe ich lieb—Esau hasse ich: Auslegung von Malachias 1,25." *BibLeb* 1 (1960): 28–38.

———, and H. Ringgren, eds. *Theological Dictionary of the Old Testament*. Translated by J. T. Willis, G. W. Bromiley, and D. E. Green. 8 vols. Grand Rapids: Eerdmans, 1974–2006.

Braaten, L. J. "God Sows: Hosea's Land Theme in the Book of the Twelve." Pages 104–32 in *Thematic Threads in the Book of the Twelve*. Edited by P. L. Redditt and A. Schart. Berlin: de Gruyter, 2003.

Braun, Roddy L. "Malachi: A Catechism for Times of Disappointment." *CurTM* 4 (1977): 297–303.

Brichto, H. C. *The Problem of "Curse" in the Hebrew Bible.* Journal of Biblical Literature Monograph 13. Philadelphia: Society of Biblical Literature, 1963.

Briend, J. "L'édit de Cyrus et sa valeur historique." *Transeu* 11 (1996): 33–44.

Bright, J. *A History of Israel.* 3rd ed. Philadelphia: Westminster, 1981.

Brown, W. P. *Obadiah through Malachi.* Westminster Bible Companion. Westminster John Knox, 1996.

Brueggemann, W. *First and Second Samuel.* Interpretation. Louisville: John Knox, 1990.

———. *1 Kings.* Knox Preaching Guides. Atlanta: John Knox, 1982.

Bulmerincq, A. von. *Einleitung in das Buch des Propheten Maleachi.* Vol. 1. Dorpat: Mattiesen, 1926.

Carroll, R. P. "The Elijah-Elisha Saga: Some Remarks on Prophetic Succession in Ancient Israel." *VT* 19 (1969): 400–415.

———. "Exile! What Exile? Deportation and the Discourse of Diaspora." Pages 62–79 in *Leading Captivity Captive*. Edited by L. L. Grabbe. JSOTSup 278. Sheffield: Sheffield Academic, 1998.

———. "The Myth of the Empty Land." *Semeia* 59 (1992): 79–93.

———. "Prophecy and Dissonance: A Theoretical Approach to the Prophetic Tradition." *ZAW* 92 (1980): 108–19.

———. *When Prophecy Failed: Cognitive Dissonance in the Prophetic Traditions of the Old Testament.* New York: Seabury, 1979.

———. "Whose Prophet? Whose History? Whose Social Reality? Troubling the Interpretive Community Again: Notes towards a Response to T. W. Overholt's Critique." *JSOT* 48 (1990): 33–49.

Carter, C. E. *The Emergence of Yehud in the Persian Period.* JSOTSup 294. Sheffield: Sheffield Academic, 1999.

———. "The Province of Yehud in the Postexilic Period." Pages 106–45 in *Second Temple Studies 2: Temple Community in the Persian Period.* JSOTSup 174. Sheffield: JSOT Press, 1994.

———, and C. Meyers, eds. *Community, Identity, and Ideology: Social Science Approaches to the Hebrew Bible.* Sources for Biblical and Theological Study. Winona Lake, IN: Eisenbrauns, 1996.

Cary, M., and G. B. Gary. "The Reign of Darius." Pages 173–227 in *The Persian Empire and the West*. Vol. 4 of *The Cambridge Ancient History*. Edited by

J. B. Bury, S. A. Cook, and F. E. Adcock. Cambridge: Cambridge University Press, 1974.

Cathcart, K. J., and R. P. Gordon. *The Targum of the Minor Prophets.* Vol. 14. Wilmington, DE: Glazier, 1989.

Chance, J. K. "The Anthropology of Honor and Shame: Culture, Values, and Practice." *Semeia* 68 (1994): 139–51.

Chary, T. *Aggie-Zacharie-Malachie.* SB. Paris: Gabalda, 1969.

Childs, B. S. *The Book of Exodus: A Critical, Theological Commentary.* OTL. Philadelphia: Westminster, 1974.

———. *Introduction to the Old Testament as Scripture.* Philadelphia: Fortress, 1979.

Chisholm, R. B. *Interpreting the Minor Prophets.* Grand Rapids: Zondervan, 1990.

Christensen, D. L. "Impulse and Design in the Book of Haggai: [Prosodic Analysis]." *JETS* 35 (1992): 445–56.

———. *Poetry and Prose in the Composition and Performance of the Book of Haggai: Verse in Ancient Near Eastern Prose.* Neukirchen-Vluyn: Neukirchener Verlag, 1993.

Claassen, W. T. T*ext and Context: Old Testament and Semitic Studies for F. C. Fensham.* Sheffield: JSOT Press, 1988.

Clark, D. J. "Discourse Structure in Zechariah 7:1–8:23." *BT* 36 (1985): 328–35.

———. "Elijah as Eschatological High Priest: An Examination of the Elijah Tradition in Mal. 3:23–24." PhD diss., University of Notre Dame, 1975.

———. "Problems in Haggai 2:15–19." *BT* 34 (1983): 432–39.

Clarke, F. "Tithing: A New Covenant Look at an Old Covenant Practice." *Searching Together* 16 (1987): 1–7.

Clements, R. E. *Prophecy and Covenant.* SBT 43. London: SCM, 1969.

Clendenen, E. R. "Old Testament Prophecy as Hortatory Text: Examples from Malachi." *JOTT* 4 (1990): 336–53.

———. "The Structure of Malachi: Textlinguistic Study." *CTR* 2 (1987): 3–17.

———. "Textlinguistics and Prophecy in the Book of the Twelve." *JETS* 46 (2003): 385–99.

Clines, D. J. A. *Ezra, Nehemiah, Esther.* NCBC. Grand Rapids: Eerdmans; London: Marshall, Morgan & Scott, 1984.

———. "Haggai's Temple, Constructed, Deconstructed, and Reconstructed." *SJOT* 1 (1993): 51–77.

———. *Interested Parties: The Ideology of Writers and Readers of the Hebrew Bible.* JSOTSup 205. Sheffield: JSOT Press, 1995.

———. "Regnal Year Reckoning in the Last Years of the Kingdom of Judah." *AJBA* 2 (1972): 9–34.

———, ed. *The Bible in Three Dimensions.* JSOTSup 87. Sheffield: JSOT Press, 1990.

Cogan, M. "Chronology, Hebrew Bible." *ABD* 1:1002–11.

Coggins, R. J. "The Exile: History and Ideology." *ExpTim* 10 (1999): 389–93.
———. *Haggai, Zechariah, Malachi.* OTG. Sheffield: JSOT Press, 1987.
———, A. Phillips, and M. Knibb, eds. *Israel's Prophetic Tradition: Essays in Honour of Peter R. Ackroyd.* Cambridge: Cambridge University Press, 1982.
Collins, C. J. "The (Intelligible) Masoretic Text of Malachi 2:16: Or, How Does God Feel about Divorce?" *Presb* 20 (1994): 36–40.
Collins, J. J. "The Message of Malachi." *TBT* 22 (1984): 209–15.
———, and G. W. E. Nickelsburg, eds. *Ideal Figures in Ancient Judaism: Profiles and Paradigms.* SBLSCS 12. Chico, CA: Scholars Press, 1980.
Collins, T. *The Mantle of Elijah: The Redaction of the Prophetical Books.* Sheffield: JSOT Press, 1993.
Conrad, E. W. "The End of Prophecy and the Appearance of Angels/Messengers in the Book of the Twelve." *JSOT* 73 (1997): 65–79.
———. "Messengers in Isaiah and the Twelve: Implications for Reading Prophetic Books." *JSOT* 91 (2000): 83–97.
———. *Zechariah.* Readings: A New Biblical Commentary. Sheffield: Sheffield Academic, 1999.
Cook, J. M. *The Persian Empire.* New York: Barnes & Noble, 1993.
Cook, S. L. *The Apocalyptic Literature.* Nashville: Abingdon, 2003.
Coote, R. B. *Elijah and Elisha in Socioliterary Perspective.* Semeia Studies. Atlanta: Scholars Press, 1992.
Craigie, P. C. *The Book of Deuteronomy.* NICOT. Grand Rapids: Eerdmans, 1976.
Crenshaw, J. L. "Theodicy in the Book of the Twelve." Pages 175–91 in *Thematic Threads.* Berlin: de Gruyter, 2003.
Cresson, B. C. "The Condemnation of Edom in Post-exilic Judaism." Pages 125–48 in *The Use of the Old Testament in the New and Other Essays: Studies in Honor of William Franklin Stinespring.* Edited by J. M. Efird. Durham, NC: Duke University Press, 1972.
Curtis, B. G. "After the Exile: Haggai and History." Pages 300–20 in *Giving the Sense: Understanding and Using Old Testament Historical Texts.* Edited by M. A. Grisanti and D. M. Howard Jr. Grand Rapids: Kregel, 2003.
———. "The Daughter of Zion Oracles and the Appendices to Malachi: Evidence on the Later Redactors and Redaction of the Book of the Twelve." Pages 872–92 in *SBL 1998: Seminar Papers.* SBLSP 37. Atlanta: Scholars Press, 1998.
Dandamaev, M. A. *A Political History of the Achaemenid Empire.* Leiden: Brill, 1989.
Davies, P. R., ed. *Second Temple Studies 1: Persian Period.* JSOT Sup 117. Sheffield: JSOT Press, 1991.
Davies, W. D., and L. Finkelstein, eds. *Introduction: The Persian Period.* Vol. 1 of *The Cambridge History of Judaism.* Cambridge: Cambridge University Press, 1984.

Deissler, A. *Zwölf Propheten III: Zefanja. Haggai. Sacharja. Maleachi.* NEchtB 21. Würzburg: Echter, 1988.

De Lange, Nicholas R. M. "Some New Fragments of Aquila on Malachi and Job." *VT* 30 (1980): 291–94.

Dempsey, C. J. *The Prophets: A Liberation Critical Reading.* Minneapolis: Fortress, 2000.

Demsky, A. "Double Names in the Exile and the Identity of Sheshbazzar." Pages 23–39 in *These Are the Names.* Edited by A. Demsky. Studies in Jewish Onomastics 2. Ramat Gan: Bar-Ilan University Press, 1999.

DeSilva, D. A. "The Noble Context: Honor, Shame, and the Rhetorical Strategy of 4 Maccabees." *JSP* 13 (1995): 31–57.

Deuel, D. C. "Malachi 3:16: 'Book of Remembrance' or Royal Memorandum? An Exegetical Note." *MSJ* 7.1 (1996): 107–11.

Deutsch, R. R. "Calling God's People to Obedience: A Commentary on the Book of Malachi." Pages 61–120 in *Joel & Malachi: A Promise of Hope—A Call to Obedience.* ITC. Grand Rapids: Eerdmans, 1987.

DeVries, S. J. *1 Kings.* WBC 12. Waco, TX: Word, 1985.

———. *From Old Revelation to New: A Tradition-Historical and Redaction-Critical Study of Temporal Transitions in Prophetic Prediction.* Grand Rapids: Eerdmans, 1995.

———. "Futurism in the Pre-exilic Minor Prophets Compared with That of the Post-exilic Minor Prophets." Pages 19–39 in *SBL 2001: Seminar Papers.* SBLSP 40. Atlanta: Society of Biblical Literature, 2001.

DeYoung, J. B. "The Function of Malachi 3:1 in Matthew 11:10: Kingdom Reality as the Hermeneutic of Jesus." Pages 66–91 in *Gospels and the Scriptures of Israel.* Sheffield: Sheffield Academic, 1994.

Dicou, B. *Edom, Israel's Brother and Antagonist: The Role of Edom in Biblical Prophecy and Story.* JSOTSup 169. Sheffield: Sheffield Academic, 1994.

Douglas, M. *Purity and Danger: An Analysis of Concepts of Pollution and Taboo.* London: Routledge & Kegan Paul, 1966.

Drinkard, J. F. "The Socio-Historical Setting of Malachi." *RevExp* 84 (1987): 383–90.

Driver, R. S. *An Introduction to the Literature of the Old Testament.* Rev. ed. New York: Scribner, 1922.

Dumbrell, W. J. "Malachi and the Ezra–Nehemiah Reforms." *RTR* 35 (1976): 42–52.

Durham, I. *Exodus.* WBC. Waco, TX: Word, 1987.

Eades, K. "Divine Action and Human Action: Comparative Study of Deuteronomy 26:1–11 and Haggai 2:10–19." Pages 103–23 in *Exegetical and Theological Studies.* Vol. 2 of *Reading the Hebrew Bible for a New Millennium.* Edited by W. Kim et al. Harrisburg, PA: Trinity Press International, 2000.

Edelman, D. *The Origins of the 'Second' Temple: Persian Imperial Policy and the Rebuilding of Jerusalem.* Bible World. London: Equinox, 2005.

Elazar, D. J. "Jacob and Esau and the Emergence of the Jewish People." *Judaism* 43 (1994): 294–301.

Elliger, K. *Das Buch der zwölf Kleinen Propheten.* Vol. 2. 4th ed. ATD 25.2. Göttingen: Vandenhoeck & Ruprecht, 1959.

Ellis, B. R. "An Annotated Bibliography for the Book of Malachi." *SwJT* 30 (1987): 48–50.

Eskenazi, T. C. "Current Perspectives on Ezra–Nehemiah and the Persian Period." *CurBS* 1 (1993): 59–86.

———. "Sheshbazzar." *ABD* 5:1207–9.

———, and K. H. Richards, eds. *Second Temple Studies 2: Temple and Community in the Persian Period.* JSOTSup 175. Sheffield: JSOT Press, 1994.

Evans, Craig A. "A Note on Targum 2 Samuel 5.8 and Jesus' Ministry to the Maimed, Halt, and Blind." *JSP* 15 (1997): 79–82.

Fischer, James A. "Notes on the Literary Form and Message of Malachi." *CBQ* 34 (1972): 315–20.

Fishbane, M. "Form and Reformation of the Biblical Priestly Blessing." *JAOS* 103 (1983): 115–21.

Fitzmyer, Joseph A. "More about Elijah Coming First." *JBL* 104 (1985): 295–96.

Floyd, M. H. "The מַשָּׂא (*maśśāʾ*) as Type of Prophetic Book." *JBL* 121 (2003): 401–22.

———. *Minor Prophets, Part 2.* FOTL 22. Grand Rapids: Eerdmans, 2000.

———. "The Nature of the Narrative and the Evidence of Redaction in Haggai." *VT* 45 (1995): 470–90.

———. "Zechariah and Changing Views of Second Temple Judaism in Recent Commentaries." *RelSRev* 25 (1999): 257–63.

Fohrer, G. *Die symbolischen Handlungen der Propheten.* 2nd ed. ATANT 54. Zurich: Zwingli, 1968.

Frankfurter, D. *Elijah in Upper Egypt: The Apocalypse of Elijah and Early Egyptian Christianity.* Minneapolis: Fortress, 1993.

Freedman, D. B. "An Unnoted Support for a Variant to the MT of Mal 3:5." *JBL* 98 (1979): 405–6.

Fried, L. S. "The Land Lay Desolate: Conquest and Restoration in the Ancient Near East." Pages 21–54 in *Judah and Judeans in the Neo-Babylonian Period.* Edited by O. Lipschits and J. Blenkinsopp. Winona Lake, IN: Eisenbrauns, 2003.

Froese, B. "Approaching a Theology of the Book of Malachi." *Direction* 25.1 (1996): 14–20.

Fuller, R. "The Blessing of Levi in Dtn 33, Mal 2, and Qumran." Pages 31–44 in *Konsequente Traditionsgeschichte: Festschrift für Klaus Baltzer zum 65. Ge-*

burtstag. Edited by R. Bartelmus, T. Krüger, and H. Utzschneider. OBO 126. Göttingen: Vandenhoeck & Ruprecht, 1993.

———. "Text-Critical Problems in Malachi 2:10–16." *JBL* 110 (1991): 47–57.

Gaiser, F. J. "Refiner's Fire and Laundry Soap: Images of God in Malachi 3:1–4." *WW* 19 (1999): 83–91.

Gammie, J. G. *Holiness in Israel*. OBT. Minneapolis: Fortress, 1989.

Garland, D. E. "A Biblical View of Divorce." *RevExp* 84 (1987): 419–32.

Gemser, B. "The Rîb- or Controversy-Pattern in Hebrew Mentality." Pages 120–37 in *Wisdom in Israel and in the Ancient Near East Presented to Harold Henry Rowley, in Celebration of His Sixty-Fifth Birthday, 24 March 1955*. Edited by M. Noth and D. Winton Thomas. VTSup 3. Leiden: Brill, 1955.

Gerstenberger, E. S. *Leviticus*. OTL. Louisville: Westminster John Knox. 1996.

Glatt-Gilad, D. A. "Yahweh's Honor at Stake: A Divine Conundrum." *JSOT* 98 (2002): 63–74.

Glazier-McDonald, B. "Intermarriage, Divorce, and the *bat-'el nekar*: Insights into Mal 2:10–16." *JBL* 106 (1987): 603–11.

———. "Malachi." Pages 232–34 in *The Women's Bible Commentary*. Louisville: Westminster John Knox, 1992.

———. *Malachi: The Divine Messenger*. SBLDS 98. Atlanta: Scholars Press, 1987.

———. "Malachi 2:12: *'er we'oneh*: Another Look." *JBL* 105 (1986): 295–98.

———. "*Mal'ak habberit:* The Messenger of the Covenant in Mal 3:1." *HAR* 11 (1987): 93–104.

Goldman, Y. *Prophétie et royauté au retour de l'exil*. OBO 118. Freiburg: Universitätsverlag; Göttingen: Vandenhoeck & Ruprecht, 1992.

Gordon, R. P. *Studies in the Targum to the Twelve Prophets: From Nahum to Malachi*. Leiden: Brill, 1994.

Grabbe, L. L. *Judaism from Cyrus to Hadrian*. 2 vols. Minneapolis: Fortress, 1992.

———. *Priests, Prophets, Diviners, Sages: A Socio-historical Study of Religious Specialists in Ancient Israel*. Valley Forge, PA: Trinity Press International, 1995.

———, ed. *Leading Captivity Captive*: *'The Exile' as History and Ideology*. JSOTSup 278. Sheffield: Sheffield Academic, 1998.

———, and R. D. Haak, eds. *'Every City Shall Be Forsaken': Urbanism and Prophecy in Ancient Israel and the Near East*. JSOTSup 330. Sheffield: Sheffield Academic, 2001.

Graesser, C. "The Seal of Elijah." *BASOR* 220 (1975): 63–66.

Graffy, A. A *Prophet Confronts His People*. AnBib 104. Rome: Pontifical Biblical Institute, 1984.

Grant-Henderson, A. L. *Inclusive Voices in Post-exilic Judah*. Collegeville, MN: Liturgical Press, 2002.

Gray, J. *I and II Kings: A Commentary*. Philadelphia: Westminster, 1963.

Gray, S. W. "Useless Fire: Worship in the Time of Malachi." *SwJT* 38 (1987): 35–41.

Greene, J. T. *The Role of the Messenger and Message in the Ancient Near East.* BJS 169. Missoula, MT: Scholars Press, 1989.

Gross, W. "Convertir el corazón de padres a hijos y el corazón de hijos a padres: El marco bíblico-teológico." *RevistB* 65 (2003): 215–28.

Hamerton-Kelly, R. G. "The Temple and the Origins of Jewish Apocalyptic." *VT* 20 (1970): 1–15.

Hamilton, M. W. "Who Was a Jew: Jewish Ethnicity during the Achaemenid Period." *ResQ* 37 (1995): 102–17.

Hamilton, V. P. *The Book of Genesis: Chapters 18–50.* NICOT. Grand Rapids: Eerdmans, 1995.

Hanson, P. D. *The Dawn of Apocalyptic.* Philadelphia: Fortress, 1975.

Hanson, R. S. "The Collection of Prophetic Books Ends with Three *massas*: But What's a *massa*?" *BRev* 7 (1991): 22–27.

Harland, P. J., and C. T. R. Hayward. *New Heaven and New Earth—Prophecy and the Millennium: Essays in Honour of Anthony Gelston.* Leiden: Brill, 1999.

Harrington, H. K. *The Purity Texts.* London: T&T Clark, 2004.

Harris, R. L., G. L. Archer Jr., and B. K. Waltke, eds. *TWOT.* 2 vols. Chicago: Moody Press, 1980.

Harrison, R. K. *Introduction to the Old Testament.* Grand Rapids: Eerdmans, 1969.

Hartley, John E. *Leviticus.* WBC 4. Dallas: Word, 1992.

Heath, E. A. "Divorce and Violence: Synonymous Parallelism in Malachi 2:16." *ATJ* 28 (1996): 1–8.

Heflin, J. N. "The Prophet Malachi, His World and His Book." *SwJT* 30 (1987): 5–11.

Heltzer, M. "A Recently Published Babylonian Tablet and the Province of Judah after 516 BCE." *Transeu* 5 (1992): 57–61.

Hendrix, J. D. "'You Say': Confrontational Dialog in Malachi." *RevExp* 84 (1987): 465–77.

Hentrich, T. "The Lame in Lev 21,17–23 and 2 Sam 5,6–8." *AJBI* 29 (2003): 5–10.

Hildebrand, D. R. "Temple Ritual: A Paradigm for Moral Holiness in Haggai II 10–19." *VT* 39 (1989): 154–68.

Hill, A. E. "Dating the Book of Malachi: A Linguistic Reexamination." Pages 77–89 in *The Word of the Lord Shall Go Forth: Essays in Honor of David Noel Freedman.* Edited by C. L. Meyers and M. O'Connor. Winona Lake, IN: Eisenbrauns, 1983.

———. *Malachi: A New Translation with Introduction and Commentary.* AB 25D. New York: Doubleday, 1998.

Hobbs, T. R. "Reflections on Honor, Shame, and Covenant Relations." *JBL* 116 (1997): 501–3.

Holtzmann, O. "Der Prophet Maleachi und der Ursprung des Pharisaerbundes." *ARW* 19 (1931): 1–21.

Homerski, J. "'Tag Jahwes' bei dem Propheten Maleachi." *Collectanea Theologica* 64 (1994): 5–17.

Horst, F. "Maleachi." In *Die zwölf kleinen Propheten: Hosea bis Micha. Nahum bis Maleachi.* Edited by T. H. Robinson and F. Horst. HAT 14. Tübingen: Mohr, 1964.

House, P. R. *The Unity of the Twelve.* JSOTSup 97. Sheffield: Sheffield Academic, 1990.

Houston, W. *Purity and Monotheism: Clean and Unclean Animals in Biblical Law.* JSOTSup 140. Sheffield: Sheffield Academic, 1993.

Huffmon, H. "The Covenant Lawsuit in the Prophets." *JBL* 78 (1959): 285–95.

Hugenberger, G. P. *Marriage as a Covenant.* VTSup 52. Leiden: Brill, 1994.

Hultgård, A. "The Ideal 'Levite': The Davidic Messiah and the Savior Priest in the Testament of the Twelve Patriarchs." Pages 93–110 in *Ideal Figures in Ancient Judaism: Profiles and Paradigms.* Edited by J. J. Collins and George W. E. Nickelsburg. SBLSCS 12. Chico, CA: Scholars Press, 1980.

Hunt, H. B., Jr. "Attitudes toward Divorce in Post-exilic Judaism." *BI* 12 (1986): 62–65.

———. "Malachi." *SwJT* 30 (1987): 5–49.

Hurowitz, V. A. "אכל in Malachi 3:11: Caterpillar." *JBL* 121 (2002): 327–30.

Isbell, C. D. *Malachi.* Grand Rapids: Zondervan, 1980.

Jacobs, M. R. "The Book of Malachi." Pages 474–77 in *Dictionary for Theological Interpretation of the Bible.* Grand Rapids: Baker Academic, 2005.

———. *Conceptual Coherence of the Book of Micah.* JSOTSup 322. Sheffield: Sheffield Academic, 2001.

———. "Love, Honor, and Violence." Pages 11–35 in *Pregnant Passion: Gender, Sex, and Violence in the Bible.* Edited by C. A. Kirk-Duggan. Semeia Studies 44. Atlanta: Society of Biblical Literature, 2003.

———. "Sin, Silence, Suffering, and Confession in the Conceptual Landscape of Psalm 32." Pages 14–34 in *Text and Community: Essays in Honor of Bruce M. Metzger.* Vol. 2. Edited by J. Harold Ellens. Sheffield: Sheffield Phoenix, 2007.

———. "Toward an Old Testament Theology of Concern for the Underprivileged." Pages 203–29 in *Theological and Hermeneutical Studies.* Vol. 1 of *Reading the Hebrew Bible for a New Millennium: Form, Concept, and Theological Perspective.* Edited by Wonil Kim et al. Harrisburg, PA: Trinity Press International, 2000.

Janzen, D. "Politics, Settlement, and Temple Community in Persian-Period Yehud." *CBQ* 64 (2002): 490–509.

Japhet, S. *I and II Chronicles: A Commentary.* OTL. Louisville: Westminster John Knox, 1993.

———. "Sheshbazzar and Zerubbabel: Against the Background of the Historical and Religious Tendencies of Ezra–Nehemiah, Part I." *ZAW* 94 (1982): 66–98.

———. "Sheshbazzar and Zerubbabel: Against the Background of the Historical and Religious Tendencies of Ezra–Nehemiah, Part II." *ZAW* 96 (1984): 218–29.

———. "The Temple in the Restoration Period: Reality and Ideology." *Union Seminary Quarterly Review* 44 (1991): 195–251.

Jemielity, T. *Satire and the Hebrew Prophets*. Louisville: Westminster John Knox, 1992.

Jenni, E. (*w*ith assistance from C. Westermann). *TLOT*. Translated by M. E. Biddle. 3 vols. Peabody, MA: Hendrickson, 1997.

Jenson, P. P. *Graded Holiness: Key to the Priestly Conception of the World*. JSOTSup 106. Sheffield: Sheffield Academic, 1992.

Jeyaraj, J. B. "Malachi and the Nations: Incense Everywhere." *Vidyajyoti* 59 (1995): 41–45.

Johnson, D. E. "Fire in God's House: Imagery from Malachi 3 in Peter's Theology of Suffering." *JETS* 29 (1986): 285–94.

Johnson, S. L. "Divine Love in Recent Theology." *TJ* 5 (1984): 175–87.

Jones, D. C. "Malachi on Divorce." *Presb* 15 (1989): 16–22.

———. "A Note on the LXX of Malachi 2:16." *JBL* 109 (1990): 683–85.

Jones, D. R. *Haggai, Zechariah and Malachi*. Torch Bible Commentary. London: SCM, 1962.

Jones, I. H. "Disputed Questions in Biblical Studies 4: Exile and Eschatology." *ExpTim* 112 (2001): 401–5.

Kaiser, W. C. "Divorce in Malachi 2:10–16." *CTR* 2 (1987): 73–84.

———. *Malachi: God's Unchanging Love*. Grand Rapids: Baker, 1984.

———. *Micah–Malachi*. The Communicator's Commentary 21. Waco, TX: Word, 1992.

———. "The Promise of the Arrival of Elijah in Malachi and the Gospels." *GTJ* 3 (1982): 221–33.

Kaufman, S. A. "An Emphatic Plea for Please." *Maarav* 7 (1991): 15–98.

Kelley, P. H. *Micah, Nahum, Habakkuk, Zephaniah, Haggai, Zechariah, Malachi*. Nashville, TN: Broadman, 1984.

Keown, G. L. "Messianism in the Book of Malachi." *RevExp* 84 (1987): 443–51.

Kessler, J. "*'t* (le temps) en Aggée I 2–4: Conflit théologique ou 'sagesse mondaine'?" *VT* 48 (1998): 555–59.

———. *The Book of Haggai: Prophecy and Society in Early Persian Yehud*. Leiden: Brill, 2002.

———. "Reconstructing Haggai's Jerusalem: Demographic and Sociological Considerations and the Search for an Adequate Methodological Point of Departure." Pages 137–58 in *"Every City Shall Be Forsaken": Urbanism and*

Prophecy in Ancient Israel and the Near East. Edited by L. L. Grabbe and R. Haak. JSOTSup 330. Sheffield: Sheffield Academic, 2001.

———. "The Second Year of Darius and the Prophet Haggai." *Transeu* 5 (1992).

Kittel, G., and G. Friedrich, eds. *TDNT*. Translated by G. W. Bromiley. 10 vols. Grand Rapids: Eerdmans, 1964–1976.

Klawans, J. *Impurity and Sin in Ancient Judaism*. Oxford: Oxford University Press, 2000.

———. "Pure Violence: Sacrifice and Defilement in Ancient Israel." *HTR* 94 (2001): 133–35.

Klein, R. W. *1 Chronicles: A Commentary*. Hermeneia. Minneapolis: Fortress, 2006.

———. "A Valentine for Those Who Fear Yahweh: The Book of Malachi." *CurTM* 13.3 (1986): 143–52.

———. "Were Joshua, Zerubbabel, and Nehemiah Contemporaries? A Response to Diana Edelman's Proposed Late Date for the Second Temple." *JBL* 127 (2008): 697–701.

Knierim, R. P. *Text and Concept in Leviticus 1:1–9: A Case in Exegetical Method*. FAT 2. Tübingen: Mohr Siebeck, 1992.

Knoppers, G. N. *1 Chronicles 1–9: A New Translation with Introduction and Commentary*. AB 12. New York: Doubleday, 2004.

Koch, K. "Haggais unreines Volk." *ZAW* 79 (1967): 52–66.

———. *The Prophets: The Babylonian and Persian Periods*. Translated by M. Kohl. Philadelphia: Fortress, 1984.

Korpel, M. C. A., and Josef M. Oesch, eds. *Delimitation Criticism: A New Tool in Biblical Scholarship*. Pericope: Scripture as Written and Read in Antiquity 1. Assen: Van Gorcum, 2000.

Krause, J. J. "Tradition, History, and Our Story: Some Observations on Jacob and Esau in the Books of Obadiah and Malachi." *JSOT* 32 (2008): 475–86.

Kressel, G. M. "An Anthropologist's Response to the Use of Social Science Models in Biblical Studies." *Semeia* 68 (1994): 153–61.

Krieg, M. *Mutmaßungen über Maleachi*. ATANT 80. Zurich: Theologischer Verlag, 1993.

Kruse-Blinkenberg, L. "Book of Malachi according to Codex Syro-Hexaplaris Ambrosianus." *ST* 21.1 (1967): 62–82.

———. "Peshitta of the Book of Malachi." *ST* 20.2 (1966): 95–119.

Kugler, R. A. "The Levi-Priestly Tradition: From Malachi to the Testament of Levi." PhD diss., University of Notre Dame, 1994.

Laniak, T. S. *Shame and Honor in the Book of Esther*. Atlanta: Scholars Press, 1998.

Lemaire, A. "Les formules de datation dans Ézéchiel à la lumière de données épigraphiques récentes." Pages 359–66 in *Ezekiel and His Book: Textual and Literary Criticism and Their Interrelation*. Edited by J. Lust. Leuven: Leuven University Press, 1986.

———. "Les formules de datation en Palestine au premier millénaire avant J.-C." Pages 58–62 in *Proche-Orient Ancien: Temps vécu, temps pensé*. Edited by F. Briquel-Chatonnet and H. Lozachmeur. Antiquités sémitiques 3. Paris: Maisonneuve, 1998.

Lemche, N. P. "On the Use of 'Systems Theory', 'Macro Theories' and Evolutionistic Thinking in Modern OT Research and Biblical Archaeology." *SJOT* 2 (1990): 273–86.

Lescow, T. *Das Buch Maleachi: Texttheorie—Auslegung—Kanontheorie; Mit einem Exkurs über Jeremia 8:8–9*. AzTh 75. Stuttgart: Calwer, 1993.

———. "Dialogische Strukturen in den Streitreden des Buches Maleachi." *ZAW* 102 (1990): 194–212.

Levin, S. "Zerubbabel: A Riddle." *JBQ* 24 (1996): 14–17.

Levin, Y. "Who Was the Chronicler's Audience? A Hint from His Genealogies." *JBL* 122 (2003): 229–45.

Levine, B. A. *Numbers 1–20: A New Translation with Introduction and Commentary*. AB 4. New York: Doubleday, 1993.

Lewis, J. P. "'Sun of Righteousness' (Malachi 4:2): A History of Interpretation." *Stone-Campbell Journal* 2 (1999): 89–110.

Lipschits, O. "Nebuchadnezzar's Policy in 'Huttu-Land' and the Fate of the Kingdom of Judah." *UF* 30 (1998): 467–87.

Locher, C. "Altes und Neues zu Maleachi 2,10–16." Pages 241–71 in *Mélanges Dominique Barthélemy: Études bibliques offertes a l'occasion de son 60e anniversaire*. Edited by P. Casetti, O. Keel, and A. Schenker. OBO 38. Fribourg: Editions Universitaires; Göttingen: Vandenhoeck & Ruprecht, 1981.

Lohfink, N. "The Deuteronomistic Picture of the Transfer of Authority from Moses to Joshua." Pages 234–47 in *Theology of the Pentateuch*, translated by L. A. Maloney. Minneapolis: Fortress, 1994.

Long, B. O. *1 Kings: With an Introduction to Historical Literature*. FOTL 9. Grand Rapids: Eerdmans, 1984.

———. "2 Kings iii and Genres of Prophetic Narrative." *VT* 23 (1973): 337–48.

———. "Social Dimension of Prophetic Conflict." *Semeia* 21 (1981): 31–53.

———. "Two Question and Answer Schemata in the Prophets." *JBL* 90 (1971): 129–39.

Lust, J. "The Identification of Zerubbabel with Sheshbassar." *ETL* 63 (1987): 90–95.

Malchow, B. V. "The Messenger of the Covenant in Mal 3:1." *JBL* 103 (1984): 252–55.

Malimi, I., and J. D. Purvis. "King Jehoiachin and the Vessels of the Lord's House in Biblical Literature." *CBQ* 56 (1994): 449–57.

March, E. W. "The Book of Haggai." *NIB* 7:707–32.

Margalith, O. "The Political Background of Zerubbabel's Mission and the Samaritan Schism." *VT* 41 (1991): 312–23.

Mariottini, C. F. "Malachi: A Prophet for His Time." *JBQ* 26 (1998): 149–57.
Marx, A. "L'impureté selon P: Une lecture théologique." *Bib* 82 (2001): 363–84.
Mason, R. *The Books of Haggai, Zechariah, and Malachi.* CBC. Cambridge: Cambridge University Press, 1977.
———. "The Messiah in the Postexilic Old Testament Literature." Pages 338–64 in *King and Messiah in Israel and the Ancient Near East: Proceedings of the Oxford Old Testament Seminar.* Edited by J. Day. JSOTSup 270. Sheffield: Sheffield Academic, 1998.
———. *Preaching the Tradition: Homily and Hermeneutic after the Exile.* Cambridge: Cambridge University Press, 1990.
———. "The Purpose of the 'Editorial Framework' of the Book of Haggai." *VT* 27 (1977): 413–21.
———. "The Use of Earlier Biblical Material in Zechariah 9–14: A Study in Inner Biblical Exegesis." Pages 136–40 in *Bringing Out the Treasures.* Edited by M. J. Boda and M. H. Floyd. JSOTSup 370; Sheffield: Sheffield Academic, 2003.
Mathews, K. A., and David S. Dockery. "Malachi." *CTR* 2 (1987): 3–144.
Mathys, H.-P. "Anmerkungen zu Mal 3,22–24." Pages 30–40 in *Vom Anfang und vom Ende: Fünf alttestamentliche Studien.* Edited by Hans-Peter Mathys. BEATAJ 47. Frankfurt am Main: Peter Lang, 2000.
Matthews, V. H. "Honor and Shame in Gender-Related Legal Situations in the Hebrew Bible." Pages 97–112 in *Gender and Law in the Hebrew Bible and the Ancient Near East.* Edited by V. H. Matthews, B. M. Levinson, and T. Frymer-Kensky. Sheffield: Sheffield Academic, 1998.
May, H. G. "'This People' and 'This Nation' in Haggai." *VT* 18 (1968): 190–97.
McCarter, P. K., Jr. *1 Samuel: A New Translation with Introduction, Notes, and Commentary.* AB 8. Garden City, NY: Doubleday, 1980.
McCarthy, D. J. "An Installation Genre?" *JBL* 90 (1971): 31–41.
McComiskey, T. E. *Zephaniah, Haggai, Zechariah, and Malachi.* Vol. 3 of *The Minor Prophets: An Exegetical and Expository Commentary.* Grand Rapids: Baker, 1998.
McEvenue, S. E. "The Political Structure in Judah from Cyrus to Nehemiah." *CBQ* 43 (1981): 353–64.
McKenzie, S. L., and H. N. Wallace. "Covenant Themes in Malachi." *CBQ* 45 (1983): 549–63.
Meier, S. M. *Speaking of Speaking: Marking Direct Discourse in the Hebrew Bible.* VTSup 46. Leiden: Brill, 1992.
Meinhold, A. "Gottesungewissheit: Zum Verhältnis von Form und Inhalt in Mal 1,2–5." *CV* 39 (1997): 128–54.
———. *Maleachi.* BKAT 14/8. Neukirchen-Vluyn: Neukirchener Verlag, 2000.
———. "Zur Rolle des Tages-JHWHs-Gedichts Joel 2,1–11 im XII-Propheten Buch." Pages 207–23 in *Verbindungslinien: Festschrift für Werner H. Schmidt*

zum 65. Geburtstag. Edited by A. Graupner, H. Delkurt, and A. B. Ernst. Neukirchen-Vluyn: Neukirchener Verlag, 2000.

Mendoza, C. "Malaquías: El profeta de la honra de Dios." *RIBLA* 35–36 (2000): 225–42.

Merrill, E. H. *Haggai, Zechariah, Malachi: An Exegetical Commentary*. Chicago: Moody Press, 1994.

———. "Remembering: A Central Theme in Biblical Worship." *JETS* 43 (2000): 27–36.

Merve, C. H. J. van der. "'Reference Time' in Some Biblical Temporal Constructions." *Bib* 78 (1997): 503–24.

Mettinger, T. N. D. *The Dethronement of Sabaoth: Studies in the Shem and Kabod Theologies*. Coniectanea Biblica: Old Testament 18. Lund: Gleerup, 1982.

Meyers, C. L., and E. M. Meyers. *Haggai, Zechariah 1–8*. AB 25B. Garden City, NY: Doubleday, 1987.

Meyers, E. M. "Priestly Language in the Book of Malachi." *HAR* 10 (1987): 225–37.

———. "Second Temple Studies in the Light of Recent Archaeology, Part I: The Persian and Hellenistic Periods." *CurBS* 2 (1994): 25–42.

———. "The Use of Tora in Haggai 2, and the Role of the Prophet in the Restoration Community." Pages 69–76 in *The Word of the Lord Shall Go Forth: Essays in Honor of David Noel Freedman in Celebration of His Sixtieth Birthday*. Edited by C. L. Meyers and M. O'Connor. Winona Lake, IN: Eisenbrauns and American Schools of Oriental Research, 1973.

———, and C. L. Meyers. *Haggai, Zechariah 1–8: A New Translation, with Introduction and Commentary*. AB 25B. New York: Doubleday, 1987.

———, and C. L. Meyers. *Zechariah 9–14: A New Translation with Introduction and Commentary*. AB 25C. New York: Doubleday, 1993.

Milgrom, J. *Leviticus 1–16: A New Translation with Introduction and Commentary*. AB 3. New York: Doubleday, 1991.

———. "Rationale for Cultic Law: The Case of Impurity." *Semeia* 45 (1989): 103–9.

Millar, W. R. *Priesthood in Ancient Israel*. Understanding Biblical Themes. St. Louis: Chalice, 2001.

Miller, J. M., and J. H. Hayes. *A History of Ancient Israel and Judah*. Philadelphia: Westminster, 1986.

Miller, P. D. *They Cried to the Lord: The Form and Theology of Biblical Prayer*. Minneapolis: Fortress, 1994.

———, P. D. Hanson, and S. D. McBride. *Ancient Israelite Religion: Essays in Honor of Frank Moore Cross*. Philadelphia: Fortress, 1987.

Mitchell, H. G. "Haggai." In *A Critical and Exegetical Commentary on Haggai, Zechariah, Malachi and Jonah*. Edited by H. G. Mitchell, J. M. P. Smith, and J. A. Bewer. ICC. Edinburgh: T&T Clark, 1912.

Moor, Johannes C. de, ed. *The Elusive Prophet: The Prophet as a Historical Person, Literary Character and Anonymous Artist.* OtSt 45. Leiden: Brill, 2001.

Motyer, J. A. "Haggai." Pages 963–1002 in *Minor Prophets.* Vol. 2. Edited by T. E. McComiskey. Grand Rapids: Baker, 1998.

Muenchow, C. "Dust and Dirt in Job 42:6." *JBL* 108 (1989): 597–611.

Murray, D. F. "The Rhetoric of Disputation: Re-examination of a Prophetic Genre." *JSOT* 38 (1987): 95–121.

Myers, J. M. "Edom and Judah in the Sixth–Fifth Centuries B.C." Pages 377–92 in *Near Eastern Studies in Honor of William Foxwell Albright.* Edited by H. Goedicke. Baltimore: Johns Hopkins University Press, 1971.

Neil, W. "Haggai." Pages 509–11 in vol. 2 of *The Interpreter's Dictionary of the Bible.* Nashville: Abingdon, 1992.

Nielsen, K. *Yahweh as Prosecutor and Judge.* JSOTSup 9. Sheffield: JSOT Press, 1978.

Noegel, S. B. *Puns and Pundits: Word Play in the Hebrew Bible and Ancient Near Eastern Literature.* Bethesda, MD: CDL, 2000.

Nogalski, J. D. "Intertextuality and the Twelve." Pages 102–24 in *Forming Prophetic Literature: Essays on Isaiah and the Twelve in Honor of John D. W. Watts.* Edited by James W. Watts and P. R. House. JSOTSup 235. Sheffield: Sheffield Academic, 1996.

———. *Literary Precursors to the Book of the Twelve.* BZAW 217. Berlin: de Gruyter, 1993.

———. *Redactional Processes in the Book of the Twelve.* BZAW 218. Berlin: de Gruyter, 1993.

———, and Marvin Sweeney. *Reading and Hearing the Book of the Twelve.* Atlanta: Society of Biblical Literature, 2000.

Noll, K. L. "Is There a Text in This Tradition? Readers' Response and the Taming of Samuel's God." *JSOT* 83 (1999): 31–51.

North, F. S. "Critical Analysis of the Book of Haggai." *ZAW* 68 (1956): 25–46.

Noth, M. *Leviticus.* OTL. Philadelphia: Westminster, 1977.

O'Brien, D. P. "Is This the Time to Accept . . . ? (2 Kings v 26b): Simply Moralizing (LXX) or an Ominous Foreboding of Yahweh's Rejection of Israel (MT)?" *VT* 46 (1996): 448–57.

O'Brien, J. M. "Historical Inquiry as Liberator and Master: Malachi as a Post-exilic Document." Pages 57–79 in *The Yahweh/Baal Confrontation and Other Studies in Biblical Literature and Archaeology: Essays in Honour of Emmett Willard Hamrick.* Edited by J. M O'Brien and F. L. Horton. Lewiston, NY: Mellen, 1995.

———. "Judah as Wife and Husband: Deconstructing Gender in Malachi." *JBL* 115 (1996): 241–50.

———. "Malachi in Recent Research." *CurBS* 3 (1995): 81–94.

———. *Priest and Levite in Malachi.* SBLDS 121. Atlanta: Scholars Press, 1990.

Ockinga, B. "The Inviolability of Zion: A Pre-Israelite Tradition." *BN* (1988): 54–66.

Ogden, G. S., and R. R. Deutsch. *Joel and Malachi: A Promise of Hope—A Call to Obedience.* ITC. Grand Rapids: Eerdmans, 1987.

———. "The Use of Figurative Language in Malachi 2:10–16." *BT* 39 (1988): 223–30.

O'Keefe, J. J. "Christianizing Malachi: Fifth-Century Insights from Cyril of Alexandria." *VC* 50 (1996): 136–58.

Olyan, S. M. "'Anyone Blind or Lame Shall Not Enter the House': On the Interpretation of Second Samuel 5:8b." *CBQ* 60 (1998): 218–27.

———. "Honor, Shame, and Covenant Relations in Ancient Israel and Its Environment." *JBL* 115 (1996): 201–18.

Orelli, C. von. *The Twelve Minor Prophets.* Translated by J. S. Banks. Edinburgh: T&T Clark, 1897.

Orton, D. E. *Prophecy in the Hebrew Bible: Selected Studies from Vetus Testamentum.* Leiden: Brill, 1999.

Otto, R. E. "The Prophets and Their Perspective." *CBQ* 63 (2001): 219–40.

Pasto, J. "When the End Is the Beginning. Or When the Biblical Past Is the Political Present: Some Thoughts on Ancient Israel, 'Post-exilic Judaism,' and the Politics of Biblical Scholarship." *SJOT* 12.1 (1998): 157–202.

Patterson, R. D. "Parental Love as a Metaphor for Divine-Human Love." *JETS* 46 (2003): 205–16.

Peckham, B. *History and Prophecy: The Development of Late Judean Literary Traditions.* ABRL. New York: Doubleday, 1993.

Penchansky, D., and P. L. Redditt, eds. *Shall Not the Judge of All the Earth Do What Is Right? Studies on the Nature of God in Tribute to James L. Crenshaw.* Winona Lake, IN: Eisenbrauns, 2000.

Petersen, D. L. "The Book of the Twelve/The Minor Prophets: Hosea, Joel, Amos, Obadiah, Jonah, Micah, Nahum, Habakkuk, Zephaniah, Haggai, Zechariah, Malachi." Pages 95–126, 224–25 in *Hebrew Bible Today: An Introduction to Critical Issues.* Edited by S. L. McKenzie and M. P. Graham. Louisville: Westminster John Knox, 1998.

———. *Haggai and Zechariah 1–8.* OTL. London: SCM, 1985.

———. "Israelite Prophecy: Change versus Continuity." Pages 190–203 in *Congress Volume: Leuven, 1989.* Edited by J. A. Emerton. VTSup 43. Leiden: Brill, 1991.

———. *Late Israelite Prophecy.* SBLMS 23. Missoula, MT: Scholars Press, 1977.

———. "Rethinking the Nature of Prophetic Literature." Pages 23–40 in *Prophecy and Prophets: The Diversity of Contemporary Issues in Scholarship.* Edited by Y. Gitay. Atlanta: Scholars Press, 1997.

———. *The Roles of Israel's Prophets.* JSOTSup 17. Sheffield: JSOT Press, 1981.

———. *Zechariah 9–14 and Malachi.* OTL. Louisville: Westminster John Knox, 1995.

Pfeiffer, E. "Die Disputationsworte im Buche Maleachi." *EvT* 19 (1959): 546–68.

Pfeiffer, R. H. *Introduction to the Old Testament.* New York: Harper, 1941.

Pierce, R. "Literary Connectors and a Haggai-Zechariah-Malachi Corpus." *JETS* 27 (1984): 277–89.

———. "A Thematic Development of the Haggai-Zechariah-Malachi Corpus." *JETS* 27 (1984): 401–11.

Poirier, J. C. "Purity beyond the Temple in the Second Temple Era." *JBL* 122 (2003): 247–65.

Polaski, D. C. "Malachi 3:1–12." *Int* 54 (2000): 416–18.

Pressler, C. *The View of Women Found in the Deuteronomic Family Laws.* Berlin: de Gruyter, 1993.

Prineas, M. "'Yet Once, It Is a Little While': Recovering the Book of Haggai in 'Lycidas.'" *Milton Quarterly* 33.4 (1999): 114.

Proctor, J. "Fire in God's House: Influence of Malachi 3 in the NT." *JETS* 36 (1993): 9–14.

Rackman, J. "Was Isaac Deceived?" *Judaism* 43 (1994): 37–45.

Radday, Y. T., and M. A. Pollatschek. "Vocabulary Richness in Post-exilic Prophetic Books." *ZAW* 92 (1980): 333–46.

Raitt, T. M. "The Prophetic Summons to Repentance." *ZAW* 93 (1971): 30–49.

Redditt, P. L. "The Book of Malachi in Its Social Setting." *CBQ* 56 (1994): 240–55.

———. "The Formation of the Book of the Twelve: Review of Research." Pages 58–80 in *SBL 2001: Seminar Papers.* SBLSP 40. Atlanta: SBL Press, 2001.

———. "The God Who Loves and Hates." Pages 175–90 in *Shall Not the Judge of All the Earth Do What Is Right? Studies on the Nature of God in Tribute to James L. Crenshaw.* Edited by David Penchansky and Paul L. Redditt. Winona Lake, IN: Eisenbrauns, 2000.

———. *Haggai, Zechariah, Malachi.* NCB. Grand Rapids: Eerdmans, 1995.

———. "Zechariah 9–14, Malachi, and the Redaction of the Book of the Twelve." Pages 245–68 in *Forming Prophetic Literature.* Sheffield: Sheffield Academic, 1996.

———. "Zechariah 9–14: The Capstone of the Book of the Twelve." Pages 305–32 in *Bringing Out the Treasure: Inner Biblical Allusion in Zechariah 9–14.* Edited by Mark J. Boda and Michael H. Floyd, with a major contribution by Rex Mason. London: Sheffield Academic, 2003.

Renker, A. *Die Tora bei Maleachi.* FMSt 112. Freiburg: Herder, 1979.

Reventlow, G. H. *Die Propheten Haggai, Sacharja, und Maleachi.* ATD 25/2. Göttingen: Vandenhoeck & Ruprecht, 1993.

Ribera, J. "El targum de Malaquías." *EstBib* 48 (1990): 171–97.

Rice, G. *Nations under God: A Commentary on the Book of 1 Kings.* ITC. Grand Rapids: Eerdmans, 1990.

Richardson, P. A. "Worship Resources for Malachi." *RevExp* 84 (1987): 479–86.

Robinson, B. P. "The Compassionate God of All Nations: Intimations of Universalism in the Old Testament." *ScrB* 30.1 (2000): 23–33.

Rofé, A. "The Onset of Sects in Postexilic Judaism: Neglected Evidence from the Septuagint, Trito-Isaiah, Ben Sira, and Malachi." Pages 39–49 in *Social World of Formative Christianity and Judaism*. Philadelphia: Fortress, 1988.

Rogerson, J. W. "The Social Background of the Book of Malachi." Pages 171–79 in *New Heaven and New Earth: Prophecy and the Millennium*. Leiden: Brill, 1999.

Rose, W. H. "Messianic Expectations in the Early Postexilic Period." Pages 168–85 in *Yahwism after the Exile: Perspectives on Israelite Religion in the Persian Era*. Studies in Theology and Religion 5. Assen: Van Gorcum, 2003.

———. *Zemah and Zerubbabel: Messianic Expectations in the Early Postexilic Period*. JSOTSup 304. Sheffield: Sheffield Academic, 2000.

Rude, T. "Malachi's Messenger Motif." *Biblical Viewpoint* 32.2 (1998): 27–32.

Rudolph, W. *Haggai, Sacharja 1–8, Sacharja 9–14, Maleachi*. KAT 13–14. Gütersloh: Mohn, 1976.

———. "Zu Maleachi 2,10–16." *ZAW* 93 (1981): 85–90.

Sacchi, P. *The History of the Second Temple Period*. JSOTSup 285. Sheffield: Sheffield Academic, 2000.

Saebø, M. "The Relation of Sheshbazzar and Zerubbabel—Reconsidered." *SEÅ* 54 (1989): 168–77.

Satlow, M. L. "Jewish Constructions of Nakedness in Late Antiquity." *JBL* 116 (1997): 429–54.

Scalise, P. J. "Malachi 3:13–4:3: A Book of Remembrance for God-Fearers." *RevExp* 95 (1998): 571–81.

Schaper, J. "The Temple Treasury Committee in the Times of Nehemiah and Ezra." *VT* 47 (1997): 200–206.

Schart, A. "Putting the Eschatological Visions of Zechariah in Their Place: Malachi as a Hermeneutical Guide for the Last Section of the Book of the Twelve." Pages 333–43 in *Bringing Out the Treasure*. London: Sheffield Academic, 2003.

Schnabel, E. J. "Israel, the People of God and the Nation." *JETS* 45 (2002): 35–57.

Schram, B. *The Opponents of Third Isaiah: Reconstructing the Cultic History of the Restoration*. JSOTSup 193. Sheffield: Sheffield Academic, 1995.

Schuller, E. M. "The Book of Malachi." *NIB* 7:843–77.

Schultz, R. R. *The Search for Quotation: Verbal Parallels in the Prophets*. JSOTSup 180. Sheffield: Sheffield Academic, 1999.

Seitz, C. "The Crisis of Interpretation over the Meaning and Purpose of the Exile: A Redactional Study of Jeremiah xxi–xliii." *VT* 35 (1985): 78–97.

Selms, A. van. "The Inner Cohesion of the Book of Malachi." Pages 27–40 in *Stud-*

ies in Old Testament Prophecy. Edited by W. C. van Wyk. OTWSA 13–14. Potchefstroom, South Africa: OTWSA, 1975.

Shemesh, Y. "Isaiah 31,5: The Lord's Protecting Lameness." *ZAW* 115 (2003): 256–60.

Shields, M. A. "Syncretism and Divorce in Malachi 2,10–16." *ZAW* 111 (1999): 68–86.

Simkins, R. A. "Return to Yahweh: Honor and Shame in Joel." *Semeia* 68 (1994): 41–54.

Smith, C. R. "The Book of Life [in OT and NT]." *GTJ* 6 (1985) 219–30.

Smith, G. A. *The Book of the Twelve Prophets*. Vol. 2. The Expositor's Bible. New York: Armstrong, 1905.

Smith, J. M. P. "Malachi." Pages 1–88 in A *Critical and Exegetical Commentary on Haggai, Zechariah, Malachi and Jonah*, by H. G. Mitchell, J. M. P. Smith, and J. A. Bewer. ICC 2. Edinburgh: T&T Clark, 1912.

Smith, M. S. *The Early History of God: Yahweh and the Other Deities in Ancient Israel*. San Francisco: Harper & Row, 1990.

Smith, R. L. *Micah–Malachi*. WBC 32. Waco, TX: Word, 1984.

———. "The Shape of Theology in the Book of Malachi." *SwJT* 30 (1987): 22–27.

Smith-Christopher, D. L. *A Biblical Theology of Exile*. OBT. Minneapolis: Fortress, 2002.

Smothers, Thomas G. "Malachi." *RevExp* 84 (1987): 371–506.

Snyman, S. D. "Antitheses in Malachi 1:2–5." *ZAW* 98 (1986): 436–38.

———. "Antitheses in the Book of Malachi." *JNSL* 16 (1990): 173–78.

Sommer, B. D. "Did Prophecy Cease? Evaluating a Reevaluation." *JBL* 115 (1996): 31–47.

Speck, J. van der. "Did Cyrus the Great Introduce a New Policy towards Subdued Nations? Cyrus in Assyrian Perspective." *Persica* 10 (1982): 279–82.

Sprinkle, J. M. "The Rationale of the Laws of Clean and Unclean in the Old Testament." *JETS* 43 (2000): 637–57.

Stansell, G. "Honor and Shame in the David Narratives." *Semeia* 68 (1994): 55–79.

Steck, O. H. "Zu Haggai 1:2–11." *ZAW* 83 (1971): 355–79.

Stiebert, J. *The Construction of Shame in the Hebrew Bible: The Prophetic Contribution*. London: Sheffield Academic, 2002.

———. "Shame and Prophecy: Approaches Past and Present." *BibInt* 8 (2000): 255–75.

Stuart, D. "Malachi." In *Zephaniah, Haggai, Zechariah, and Malachi*. Vol. 3 of *The Minor Prophets: An Exegetical and Expository Commentary*. Edited by Thomas E. McComiskey. Grand Rapids: Baker Books, 1998.

Stuhlmueller, C. *Haggai and Zechariah: Rebuilding with Hope*. ITC. Grand Rapids: Eerdmans, 1988.

———. *Rebuilding with Hope: A Commentary on the Books of Haggai and Zechariah*. ITC. Grand Rapids: Eerdmans, 1988.

———. "Sickness and Disease: An Old Testament Perspective." *Bible Today* 27 (1989): 5–9.

Sweeney, M. A. "Concerning the Structure and Generic Character of the Book of Nahum." *ZAW* 104 (1992): 364–77.

———. *Hosea, Joel, Amos, Obadiah, Jonah* and *Micah, Nahum, Habakkuk, Zephaniah, Haggai, Zechariah, Malachi.* Vols. 1–2. *The Twelve Prophets.* Collegeville, MN: Liturgical Press, 2000.

———. "The Place and Function of Joel in the Book of the Twelve." Pages 570–95 in *SBL 1999: Seminar Papers.* SBLSP 38. Atlanta: Society of Biblical Literature, 1999.

Swetnam, J. "Malachi 1,11: An Interpretation." *CBQ* 31 (1969): 200–209.

Swift, C. H. "Robbing God: The Lesson in Today's Life." *Christian Century* 34.50. December 13, 1971, 15.

Sykes, S. "Time and Space in Haggai–Zechariah 1–8: A Bakhtinian Analysis of a Prophetic Chronicle." *JSOT* 76 (1997): 97–124.

Syrén, R. *The Forsaken First-Born: A Study of a Recurrent Motif in the Patriarchal Narratives.* JSOTSup 133. Sheffield: JSOT Press, 1993.

Talmon, S. *King, Cult and Calendar in Ancient Israel: Collected Studies.* Jerusalem: Magnes, 1986.

Tate, M. E. "Questions for Priests and People in Mal 1:2–2:16." *RevExp* 84 (1987): 391–407.

Taylor, J. G. "And He Shall Purify: An Exposition of Malachi Chapters Two and Three." *Anvil* 15.1 (1998): 6–12.

———. *Yahweh and the Sun: Biblical Archaeological Evidence for Sun Worship in Ancient Israel.* JSOTSup 111. Sheffield: Sheffield Academic, 1993.

Thelle, R. I. *Ask God: Divine Consultation in the Literature of the Hebrew Bible.* BBET 30. Frankfurt am Main: Lang, 2002.

Thompson, H. O. *Haggai: A Bibliography.* Delhi: ISPCK, 1995.

Thompson, T. L. "The Messiah Epithet in the Hebrew Bible." *SJOT* 15 (2001): 57–82.

Tiemeyer, L.-S. "Giving a Voice to Malachi's Interlocutors." *SJOT* 19 (2005): 173–92.

Tigay, J. H. *Deuteronomy.* JPS Torah Commentary. Philadelphia: Jewish Publication Society, 1996.

Tilley, W. C. "A Biblical Approach to Stewardship." *RevExp* 85 (1987): 33–42.

Tillman, W. M. "Key Ethical Issues in Malachi." *SwJT* 38 (1987): 42–47.

Tollington, J. E. "Readings in Haggai: From the Prophet to the Completed Book, a Changing Message in Changing Times." Pages 194–208 in *The Crisis of Israelite Religion: Transformation of Religious Tradition in Exilic and Post-exilic Times.* Edited by B. Becking and M. C. A. Korpel. Leiden: Brill, 1999.

———. *Tradition and Innovation in Haggai and Zechariah 1–8.* JSOTSup 150. Sheffield: Sheffield Academic, 1993.

Torrey, C. C. "The Prophecy of Malachi." *JBL* 17 (1898): 1–15.

Tsumura, D. T. *The First Book of Samuel.* NICOT. Grand Rapids: Eerdmans, 2007.

Tucker, G. "Prophetic Superscriptions and the Growth of a Canon." Pages 56–70 in *Canon and Authority*. Edited by G. W. Coats and B. O. Long. Philadelphia: Fortress, 1977.

Tuell, S. S. "Haggai–Zechariah: Prophecy after the Manner of Ezekiel." Pages 263–86 in *SBL 2000: Seminar Papers.* SBLSP 39. Atlanta: Socity of Biblical Literature.

———. *The Law of the Temple in Ezekiel 40–48.* Atlanta: Scholars Press, 1992.

Tuttle, G. A. *Biblical and Near Eastern Studies: Essays in Honor of William Sanford LaSor.* Grand Rapids: Eerdmans, 1978.

Utzschneider, H. "Die Schriftprophetie und die Frage nach dem Ende der Prophetie: Überlegungen anhand von Mal 1,6–2,16." *ZAW* 104 (1992): 377–94.

VanderKam, J. C. *From Joshua to Caiaphas: High Priests after the Exile.* Minneapolis: Fortress, 2004.

Vargon, S. "The Blind and the Lame." *VT* 46 (1996): 498–514.

Vasholz, R. I. "Sarcasm in Malachi 1:8a." *Presb* 16 (1990): 129–30.

Veerkamp, T. "Vom profetischen und vom elitären Konservatismus." *T & K* 26.1 (2003): 14–35.

Vena, O. D. "Paul's Understanding of the Eschatological Prophet of Malachi 4:5–6." *BR* 44 (1999): 35–54.

Verhoef, P. A. *The Books of Haggai and Malachi.* NICOT. Grand Rapids: Eerdmans, 1987.

Viberg, Å. "Wakening a Sleeping Metaphor: A New Interpretation of Malachi 1:11." *TynBul* 45 (1994): 297–319.

Vuilleumier, R. "Malachie." In *Aggée, Zacharie, Malachie.* Edited by S. Amsler, R. Vuilleumier, and A. Lacocque. CAT 11c. Geneva: Labor et Fides, 1981.

Waldman, N. M. "Some Notes on Malachi 3:6; 3:13; Psalm 42:11." *JBL* 93 (1974): 543–49.

Wallis, G. "Wesen und Struktur der Botschaft Malaechis." Pages 229–37 in *Das ferne und nahe Wort: Festschrift Leonhard Rost zur Vollendung seines 70. Lebensjahres am 30. November 1966 gewidmet.* Edited by F. Maass. BZAW 105. Berlin: Töpelmann, 1967.

Wanke, G. "Prophecy and Psalms in the Persian Period." Pages 162–88 in *Cambridge History of Judaism.* Vol. 1. Cambridge: Cambridge University Press, 1984.

Watts, James W., and P. R. House. *Forming Prophetic Literature: Essays on Isaiah and the Twelve in Honor of John D. W. Watts.* Sheffield: Sheffield Academic, 1996.

Watts, John D. W. "A Frame for the Book of the Twelve: Hosea 1–3 and Malachi." Pages 209–17 in *Reading and Hearing the Book of the Twelve.* Edited by

James D. Nogalski and Marvin A. Sweeney. SBLSymS 15. Atlanta: Society of Biblical Literature, 2000.

———. "Introduction to the Book of Malachi." *RevExp* 84 (1987): 373–81.

Weinberg, J. *The Citizen-Temple Community*. Translated by D. Smith-Christopher. JSOTSup 151. Sheffield: Sheffield Academic, 1992.

Weinfeld, M. *Deuteronomy 1–11: A New Translation with Introduction and Commentary*. AB 5. New York: Doubleday, 1991.

Weis, R. "A Definition of the Genre *Maśśāʾ* in the Hebrew Bible." PhD diss., Claremont Graduate School, 1986.

Welch, A. C. *Post-exilic Judaism*. Edinburgh: Blackwood, 1935.

Wendland, E. "Linear and Concentric Patterns in Malachi." *BT* 36 (1985): 108–21.

Wenham, G. J. "The Akedah; A Paradigm of Sacrifice." Pages 93–102 in *Pomegranates and Golden Bells: Studies in Biblical, Jewish, and Near Eastern Ritual, Law, and Literature in Honor of Jacob Milgrom*. Edited by David P. Wright, David Noel Freedman, and Avi Hurvitz. Winona Lake, IN: Eisenbrauns, 1995.

———. *Genesis 16–50*. WBC 2. Dallas: Word, 1994.

———. "Method in Pentateuchal Source Criticism." *VT* 41 (1991): 84–109.

———. "Purity." Pages 378–94 in *Biblical World*. Edited by John Barton. Vol. 2. London: Routledge, 2002.

———. "The Theology of Old Testament Sacrifice." Pages 75–87 in *Sacrifice in the Bible*. Edited by R. T. Beckwith and M. J. Selman. Grand Rapids: Baker, 1995.

———. "The Theology of Unclean Food." *EvQ* 53 (1981): 6–15.

Westermann, C. *Basic Forms of Prophetic Speech*. Translated by H. C. White. Louisville: John Knox, 1991.

Weyde, K. W. *Prophecy and Teaching: Prophetic Authority, Form Problems and the Use of Traditions in the Book of Malachi*. BZAW 288. Berlin: de Gruyter, 2000.

Whedbee, J. W. "A Question-Answer Schema in Haggai 1: The Form and Function of Haggai 1:9–11." Pages 184–94 in *Biblical and Near Eastern Studies: Essays in Honor of William Sanford LaSor*. Edited by G. A. Tuttle. Grand Rapids: Eerdmans, 1978.

White, M. C. *The Elijah Legends and Jehu's Coup*. Atlanta: Scholars Press, 1997.

Williams, D. T. "The Windows of Heaven." *OTE* 5 (1992): 402–13.

Williamson, H. G. M. *Ezra, Nehemiah*. WBC 16. Waco, TX: Word, 1985.

———. *Ezra and Nehemiah*. OTG. Sheffield: JSOT Press, 1987.

———. "The Governors of Judah under the Persians." *TynBul* 39 (1988): 59–82.

———. "Persian Administration." *ABD* 5:81–86.

Wilson, R. *Prophecy and Society in Ancient Israel*. Philadelphia: Fortress, 1984.

Wisdom, T. "The Downward Spiral of Lost Love (Malachi 1)." *Biblical Viewpoint* 32.2 (1998): 20–26.

Wolf, H. *Haggai and Malachi: Rededication and Renewal.* Chicago: Moody, 1976.

Wolff, H. W. *Haggai: A Commentary.* Translated by M. Kohl. Minneapolis: Augsburg, 1988.

———. "Prophecy from the Eighth through the Fifth Century." *Int* 32 (1978): 17–30.

Wolff, R. *The Book of Haggai: A Study Manual.* Grand Rapids: Baker, 1967.

Woude, A. S. van der. "Der Engel des Bundes: Bemerkungen zu Maleachi 3,1c und seinem Kontext." Pages 289–300 in *Die Botschaft und die Boten: Festschrift für Hans Walter Wolff zum 70. Geburtstag.* Edited by J. Jeremias and L. Perlitt. Neukirchen-Vluyn: Neukirchener Verlag, 1981.

———. "Malachi's Struggle for a Pure Community: Reflections on Malachi 2:10–16." Pages 65–71 in *Tradition and Re-interpretation in Jewish and Early Christian Literature: Essays in Honour of Jürgen C. H. Lebram.* Edited by J. W. van Henten et al. Leiden: Brill, 1986.

Wright, D. P. *The Disposal of Impurity: Elimination Rites in the Bible and in Hittite and Mesopotamian Literature.* Atlanta: Scholars Press, 1986.

Wyrick, S. V. "Haggai's Appeal to Tradition: Imagination Used as Authority." Pages 117–25 in *Religious Writings and Religious Systems.* Edited by J. Neusner. Vol. 1. Atlanta: Scholars Press, 1989.

Yamauchi, E. M. *Persia and the Bible.* Grand Rapids: Baker, 1990.

———. "The Reverse Order of Ezra/Nehemiah Reconsidered." *Themelios* 5 (1980): 7–13.

Yaron, R. "The Schema of the Aramaic Legal Documents." *JJS* (1957): 33–61.

Yuval, I. J. *Two Nations in Your Womb: Perceptions of Jews and Christians in Late Antiquity and the Middle Ages.* Berkeley: University of California Press, 2006.

Zehnder, M. "A Fresh Look at Malachi ii 13–16." *VT* 53 (2003): 224–59.

Zipor, M. "'Scenes from a Marriage': According to Jeremiah." *JSOT* 65 (1995): 83–91.

The Book of
HAGGAI

INTRODUCTION

The book of Haggai is part of the Book of the Twelve, or the Minor Prophets. The book contains several chronological indications of a date at about 520 BCE, during the reign of Darius I, king of Persia. Consequently, the book is key to understanding the Persian period. Its status in the Haggai-Zechariah-Malachi part of the prophetic corpus, however, has been a point of contention. While some argue for its interdependence with Zechariah 1–8, others argue for its literary independence but conceptual connection. The focus of the book is the rebuilding of the temple in Jerusalem and the implications of obedience in this matter. It advocates a message of hope amid the challenges of a postexilic community forced by circumstances to make sense of its identity and traditions.

I. PROPHET AND DATE

A. THE PROPHET

The prophet's identity is known to us from the text's representation of the prophet's message and intertextual references to the prophet. Likewise, the appearance of the name in the versions leads to suggestions about the prophet's identity and role in his community. From the information in the book of Haggai, several assertions can be made about his identity, including that he prophesied during the second year of King Darius I (522/21–486 BCE), in approximately 520 BCE. According to the date formulas in the book (1:1, 15; 2:1, 10, 20), his prophetic activity was both short and effective. In four months, he convinced the reluctant community to work on the temple.

Any discussion about the prophet's identity must grapple with the message's conceptual framework as well as the social ethos that defines the people's role and actions. To the extent that the prophet is a product of this ethos, he reveals his conditioning in the thoughts represented in the book bearing his name. In this section, I discuss these matters: (1) the name of the prophet, (2) views about his identity, (3) his social location.[1]

The name *ḥaggay*, "Haggai," is derived from *ḥag*, meaning "feast, festival." For this reason *ḥaggî* ("my feasts") has been compared with *mal'ākî* ("my messenger") as a symbolic title.[2] One explanation for this rendering is that the prophecies in Haggai are all dated to festival days: the new moon and Feast of Tabernacles.[3] Likewise, comparisons of the name Haggai with other names indicating a day of birth are noteworthy—for example, *šabbətay*, "born on the Sabbath," Shabbethai (Ezra 10:15; Neh 8:7).[4] Several variations of the name appear in the Old Testament: *ḥaggî,* used of the descendants of Gad (Gen 46:16; Num 26:15); *ḥaggît,* the father of Adonijah (2 Sam 3:4; 1 Kgs 1:5, 11; 2:13; 1 Chr 3:2); *ḥaggiyâ,* sons of Merari (1 Chr 6:30 [MT 15]). These examples attest the popularity of the name or some version of it.

Second, his identity is as "the prophet Haggai" (*ḥaggay hannābî'*) in Hag 1:1, 3, 12; 2:1, 10; and Ezra 5:1; 6:14 (cf. 1 Esd 6:1; 7:3; 2 Esd 1:40). In these contexts, he is mentioned with other prophets—namely, Zechariah (Ezra 5:1; 1 Esd 6:1), Micah, Amos, Obadiah, Nahum and Habakkuk, Zephaniah, Zechariah, and Malachi (2 Esd 1:39–40). In three of the nine instances where his name is mentioned in the book of Haggai, it is without the designation *hannābî'*, "the prophet" (1:13; 2:14, 20). The word-event formula identifies Haggai as the instrument used by Yahweh to communicate with the community and

1. *Name of the prophet.* See J. Kessler, *The Book of Haggai: Prophecy and Society in Early Persian Yehud* (Leiden: Brill, 2002), 114–15; P. A. Verhoef, *The Books of Haggai and Malachi,* NICOT (Grand Rapids: Eerdmans, 1976), 4–5; C. L. Meyers and E. M. Meyers, *Haggai, Zechariah 1–8: A New Translation with Introduction and Commentary,* AB 25B (New York: Doubleday, 1987), 8–9; cf. P. L. Redditt, *Haggai, Zechariah, Malachi,* NCB (Grand Rapids: Eerdmans, 1995), 17; H. W. Wolff, *Haggai: A Commentary,* trans. M. Kohl (Minneapolis: Augsburg, 1988), 16, 37; J. G. Baldwin, *Haggai, Zechariah, Malachi,* TOTC 24 (Downers Grove, IL: InterVarsity; London: Tyndale, 1972), 27–28.

Views about the prophet's identity. See Verhoef, *Haggai and Malachi,* 7–8; J. Blenkinsopp, *A History of Prophecy in Israel,* rev. and enlarged (Louisville: Westminster John Knox, 1996), 201.

The prophet's social location. Kessler, *Haggai,* 25. Note his discussion regarding Haggai's political associations. Verhoef (*Haggai and Malachi*) cites those who assume that Haggai was among the "people of the land," those who remained in the land during the deportation as compared to the returnees. Cf. J. Blenkinsopp, "The Social Roles of Prophets in Early Achaemenid Judah," *JSOT* 93 (2001): 39–58.

2. See Malachi, Text and Commentary below for discussion of Mal 1:1.

3. See Verhoef, *Haggai and Malachi,* 4–5, for further discussion and bibliography.

4. H. W. Wolff, *Haggai,* 37; Verhoef, *Haggai and Malachi,* 4.

as "one sent by Yahweh" (1:12). Likewise, Haggai is designated messenger of Yahweh (*mal'ak yhwh*), affirming his role as one who transmits the message from its sender to its recipients (1:13).

According to Hag 1:14–15, the community worked on the house of Yahweh, their God. They began the work on the twenty-fourth day of the sixth month, about twenty-three days after receiving the message through Haggai. The last date formula, the twenty-fourth day of the ninth month, indicates that Haggai's prophetic activity lasted until some time afterward. The occurrences of Haggai's name in Ezra 5:1; 6:14 may suggest that Haggai's activity continued during the building of the temple. However, one should not draw this conclusion about the extent of Haggai's activity simply on the basis of the Ezra texts.[5] Based on his enthusiasm for building the temple, it has been suggested that Haggai was a cultic prophet who was closely associated with the priesthood and the cult.[6] This suggestion has been challenged on several grounds, including the recurrent designation of Haggai as prophet and the messenger formulas indicating the source of his message (Hag 1:2, 5, 7; 2:6, 11).[7] Haggai's cultic identity has also been challenged on the grounds of his tolerance for the neglected temple and unfamiliarity with cultic matters.[8] Yet another suggestion is that Haggai was of priestly lineage and not simply a cultic prophet.[9] Whether he was a cultic prophet or a political ideologist, his intolerance for the destroyed temple and his enthusiasm about rebuilding are evident.[10] In this respect, the identity of the prophet is evident by the concerns addressed to the audience. The significant aspect of his identity is that he is a prophet willing to address the issues of the temple, most likely to an audience with competing perspectives about the temple.

Third, the prophet's social location is distinguished by his function in the community and his association with groups or ideologies in that commu-

5. Verhoef, *Haggai and Malachi,* 6; Baldwin, *Hag, Zech, Mal,* 29. Kessler (*Haggai,* 44–51) discusses the extent of Haggai's ministry in relation to the redaction of the book, noting that the date formulas establish a close connection between the redaction of the book and the end of Haggai's ministry.

6. Blenkinsopp (*History of Prophecy,* 201) states this in relation to both Haggai and Zechariah and with particular reference to Hag 2:10–14.

7. H. W. Wolff, *Haggai,* 17.

8. Verhoef, *Haggai and Malachi,* 8; H. W. Wolff, *Haggai,* 17, 38.

9. For a discussion of the matter, see Baldwin, *Hag, Zech, Mal,* 28; Verhoef, *Haggai and Malachi,* 7. These authors note that this suggestion is based on the occurrences of the names Haggai and Zechariah in the superscription of several psalms as they appear in the LXX (Pss 137, 145–48).

10. Meyers and Meyers (*Haggai, Zechariah 1–8,* 63–64) and Kessler (*Haggai,* 70) deny that the prophet may have encountered ruins at the temple site.

nity.[11] Tensions had developed due to the coexistence of the two heterogeneous groups sharing the same heritage. In his discussion of the land, Carroll notes that at least two distinct groups laid claims to the Jewish identity during the restoration period (538–516 BCE): the people of the land and the returnees.[12] However, their experiences before the restoration, while they were separated temporally and geographically, may have defined their perspectives of each other religiously and sociopolitically.[13] For example, the returnees would have had a different perspective from individuals who had remained in the land regarding their status in the community—that is, whether someone was a leader who was also responsible to the Persian Empire or was an ordinary citizen or worker.[14]

From Carroll's perspective, the decisive and distinguishing element may have been the time of their deportation—that is, 597 or 587 BCE.[15] The rationale is that the first deportation took the educated, skilled, and young of the population, leaving behind the uneducated, unskilled, and poor. The 587 BCE deportation, therefore, consisted of those who were left. There were also the people scattered into Egypt and other countries who returned to the land when Gedaliah, appointed by Babylon, ruled over those who remained in the land (2 Kgs 25:22).[16] At issue is how the prophet's social

11. Regarding discussion of social location of the prophets, see D. L. Petersen, *The Roles of Israel's Prophets*, JSOTSup 17 (Sheffield: JSOT Press, 1981); R. Wilson, *Prophecy and Society in Ancient Israel* (Philadelphia: Fortress, 1984); Blenkinsopp, "Social Roles of the Prophets"; see Kessler, *Haggai*, 24–25, for additional bibliography.

12. R. P. Carroll, "The Myth of the Empty Land," *Semeia* 59 (1992): 81–85. Likewise, J. L. Berquist (*Judaism in Persia's Shadow: A Social and Cultural Approach* [Philadelphia: Fortress, 1995], 27–29) proposes that Jerusalem was "not an abandoned city during the reign of the Babylonian Empire." Rather, the city was occupied, and worship and life continued. The returnees or immigrants gradually reentered life and the administration of Jerusalem and Yehud (Aramaic *yəhûd;* Hebrew *yəhûdâ*; the designation of Judah as a province during the early Persian period [539–486 BCE]) but not without a power struggle and its ensuing dynamics. Cf. H. M. Barstad, *The Myth of the Empty Land: A Study of the History and Archaeology of Judah during the 'Exilic Period'*, Symbolae Osloeses Fasciculi suppletorri 28 (Oslo: Scandinavian University Press, 1996), 47–55.

13. Blenkinsopp, *History of Prophecy,* 198–99, 210; E. Ben Zvi, "Inclusion in and Exclusion from 'Israel' in Post-Monarchic Biblical Texts," in *The Pitcher Is Broken: Memorial Essays for G. W. Ahlström*, ed. S. W. Holloway and L. K. Handy, JSOTSup 190 (Sheffield: JSOT Press, 1995), 95–149. Meyers and Meyers, *Haggai, Zechariah 1–8,* xxix. Carroll, "Myth of the Empty Land," 81–85. Among the distinguishing characteristics of identity were issues of purity and adherence to the law.

14. See Berquist, *Judaism in Persia's Shadow,* 27–29. He notes the heterogeneity of the population in Yehud during Cyrus's reign: the returnees included priests and nonpriests, rural and urban workers—"urban, political orientations versus rural, agricultural segments."

15. Carroll, "Myth of the Empty Land," 81–85; cf. H. W. Wolff, *Haggai,* 51–52.

16. Cf. H. W. Wolff, *Haggai,* 17.

location is reflected in the vantage point of his message. If we use Carroll's argument to understand Haggai's social location, at least three possibilities should be considered.

First, Haggai may have been a descendant of the 597 BCE deportees who were taken to Babylon and considered "good figs"—the remnant to be restored (Jer 24; 29). As one returning to the land, he would have carried with him the tradition about the seventieth-year return and enthusiasm about restoring Jerusalem and the cult.[17] If so, Haggai's role in his social setting may have been theologically and politically motivated.[18] Alternatively, Haggai may have been among those under Zedekiah's rule who were subsequently deported in 587 BCE and dispersed among the population of Egypt.[19] The religious ideology characterized these deportees as "bad figs" who were to be destroyed (Jer 24 [esp. 24:9–10]; 29; 39–40; 52). If he were a part of this group, he would have been regarded as an outsider by descendants of those deported to Babylon in 597 BCE. Likewise, Haggai's experiences would have differed from those who remained in the land during the deportation.

Yet another view about Haggai's social location is that he remained in the land and was one of the so-called "people of the land" (*'am hā'āreṣ*), as compared to the returnees. This group experienced the desolation left behind by the Babylonians yet moved ahead with their lives. As one of this group, Haggai would have shared the legacy of living with the demolished temple while rebuilding houses and resuming other aspects of daily living. Two arguments support this understanding of Haggai as a non-deportee. First, his attention to the local economic problems suggests that he was familiar with the agricultural challenges of the land. Second, Haggai is not among the returnees listed in Ezra 2 (// Neh 7), and he refers to the people as people of the land in Hag 2:4 (*kol-'am hā'āreṣ*).[20] One challenge to the latter argument is that Haggai may have been excluded from that group because he was a child. Additionally, the use of the designation *'am hā'āreṣ* does not necessarily distinguish only between the returnees and the non-deportees.[21] Since Haggai is represented as an advocate of rebuilding the temple, it is apparent that he was influenced by the traditions and ideas regarding the need to rebuild. While that acquaintance may have been characteristic of the Babylonian deportees, it may not have been exclusive

17. Cf. Blenkinsopp, *History of Prophecy,* 210.

18. Theologically, to fulfill the message of Jeremiah; politically, to conform to the decree of the Persian Empire to restore various regions, particularly their religious practices.

19. Carroll, "Myth of the Empty Land," 81–84.

20. H. W. Wolff, *Haggai,* 17; contrast Verhoef, *Haggai and Malachi,* 7.

21. Verhoef, *Haggai and Malachi,* 7.

to them. Haggai's acquaintance with the local economy may simply attest the breadth of his understanding rather than indicating the extended duration of his experience in the land. Most likely, Haggai was among those returning to the land who, through experience, became aware of its economic challenges.

B. DATE OF THE PROPHETIC ACTIVITY

Understanding the date of the prophetic activity of Haggai depends in part on interpretations of the date formulas in the book and the coherence of the book. The formulas suggest that the book was produced in the sixth century—more specifically, the time of restoration (520–516 BCE). Thus, a significant question is the extent to which the nature and form of the date formulas cohere with others used in the same general time period. The date formulas most likely derive from the time of the prophetic activity rather than later redactional activity.[22] Table 1 identifies the formulas.

Table 1. Date Formulas in the Book of Haggai

Reference in Haggai	Date Formula
1:1	2nd year of King Darius, 6th month, 1st day
1:15	24th day of the 6th month
1:15–2:1	2nd year of Darius, 7th month, 21st day
2:10	24th day of the 9th month of the 2nd year of Darius
2:18	24th day of the 9th month
2:20	24th day of the month

22. H. W. Wolff, *Haggai,* 20; Kessler, *Haggai,* 49–57. Note the discussion relative to the tendency to consider Haggai and Zech 1–8 a continuous work. M. H. Floyd, "The Nature of the Narrative and the Evidence of Redaction in Haggai," *VT* 45 (1995): 474; Meyers and Meyers, *Haggai, Zechariah 1–8,* xliv–lxii; R. A. Mason, "The Purpose of the 'Editorial Framework' of the Book of Haggai," *VT* 27 (1977): 413–21.

II. HISTORICAL CONTEXT

An understanding of the historical context of the prophetic literature is important to the extent that prophetic activity is historical. In general, all prophecies are historical in that they are products of the historical moment when they were communicated (oral or written). Even so, identifying the precise historical context of prophetic activity is challenging at best and nearly impossible at times. What follows is a proposal regarding the historical context of Haggai's prophetic activity. The historical context of Haggai can be discerned through a reading of the text and the use of corroborative materials, including intertextual biblical materials.[23]

A. CHRONOLOGICAL INDICATORS

The use of various date formulas is well attested in Israelite prophetic literature. In the books of Jeremiah (28:1, 17; 36:9), Ezekiel (1:1), Haggai (1:1, 15), and Zechariah (1:7; 7:1), the date formulas may signal a movement toward precise dating begun in the late seventh century BCE. Scholars have noticed a distinctive shift in patterns from year-only date formulas (e.g., 1 Kgs 15:9; Isa 14:28) to month-day or year-month-day formulas (e.g., Jer 28:1, 17; 36:9, 22; 39:1, 2; 52:4, 5–6, 12; 2 Chr 3:2; Hag 1:1; Zech 7:1).[24] These date formulas may locate the prophecies within particular historical periods and assist in dating the prophetic history and text. In the book of Haggai, several date-formula patterns were used in narrating the receipt of prophecies (see table 1).

The first pattern includes the regnal year as part of the formula: namely, year + month + day (Hag 1:1; cf. Zech 7:1) or day + month + year (Hag 1:15; 2:10; cf. Zech 1:7). The chronological indicators in Hag 1:15 and 2:1, on the other hand, require special comment. Haggai 1:15 may comprise a single formula of the pattern day + month + year, the reverse of the pattern in Hag 1:1. Alternatively, the formula day + month in Hag 1:15a represents the concluding

23. While this is not a lesson in historiography, the challenges inherent in any historical reconstruction are also present in and inform this brief discussion.

24. Kessler, *Haggai,* 42–44. He also notes A. Lemaire, "Les formules de datation en Palestine au premier millénaire avant J.-C.," in *Proche-Orient Ancien: Temps vécu, temps pensé,* ed. F. Briquel-Chatonnet and H. Lozachmeur, Antiquités sémitiques 3 (Paris: Maisonneuve, 1998), 58–62; A. Lemaire, "Les formules de datation dans Ézéchiel à la lumière de données épigraphiques récentes," in *Ezekiel and His Book: Textual and Literary Criticism and Their Interrelation,* ed. J. Lust; Leuven: Leuven University Press, 1986); B. Porten, "The Calendar of Aramaic Texts from Achaemenid and Ptolemaic Egypt," in *Iran-Judaica II: Studies Relating to Jewish Contracts with Persian Cultures throughout the Ages,* ed. A. Netzer and S. Shekel (Jerusalem: Ben Zvi Institute, 1990), 13–32.

reference to 1:14 (the time when the "spirit came and stirred the people," while 15b + 2:1a comprises the year (1:15b) + month + day + (2:1) formula to introduce what follows (cf. 1:1). Whether the year element of the formula completes the indicator in Hag 2:1a or not, it is unnecessary to split 1:15 to achieve a complete formula. In other cases—Hag 2:20 and 2:18—the previously specified year (2:10) supplies that year element; the formula in 2:1 is to be interpreted in the same way as 2:20 (see table 1).[25]

The content introduced may determine which formula pattern occurs. Notably, date formulas that introduce the main units may not contain the year and the name of the king, although many scholars still base the book's main units on their presence (i.e., Hag 1:1, 15; 2:10).[26] On the other hand, some scholars do not consider Hag 2:1 to be a main unit because it does not follow the pattern of 1:15 or 2:10 but assumes the year from the previous indicator (cf. Jer 52:4 followed by 52:6, 12).[27] A further pattern of the date formulas incorporates an inference to a previously stated element: for example, the month + day formula (Hag 2:18) can be inferred from 2:1, while the comment

25. Cf. Meyers and Meyers, *Haggai, Zechariah 1–8,* 6, 36–37. They also note the possibility that a scribal error (haplography) may have resulted in the omission of the year in 2:1.

26. Others separate 1:15a and 1:15b by placing 1:15b with 2:1 as one chronological indicator: Redditt, *Haggai, Zechariah, Malachi,* 11, 23–24; M. H. Floyd, *Minor Prophets, Part 2,* FOTL 22 (Grand Rapids: Eerdmans, 2000), 255; W. P. Brown, *Obadiah through Malachi,* WBC (Louisville: Westminster John Knox, 1996), 124, 126. This is in contrast to Brown's proposal that there are five divisions—namely, 1:1–11; 1:12–15; 2:1–9; 2:10–19; 2:20–23 (p. 122).

27. For bibliography and further discussion of the extrabiblical data, see Kessler, *Haggai,* 42–44, 47–48. Meyers and Meyers (*Haggai, Zechariah 1–8,* 5) also note that the date formulas of Haggai and Zechariah are similar to those occurring in Ezekiel. See also R. Yaron, "The Schema of the Aramaic Legal Documents," *JJS* (1957): 60. Following the transition from year-only formulas to the more precise formulas, there appears to have been a further transition from a Judean (older) to a Persian (younger) pattern discernible by the sequence of the elements in the formulas. The older pattern (7th–6th c. BCE) appears in full and abbreviated forms, the latter being used when an element is omitted and inferred from a previously cited formula. The full pattern is year-month-day (e.g., Jer 39:2; 52:4, 31; Ezek 1:1; 8:1; 24:1; 29:1); and the abbreviated pattern month-day (Ezek 26:1; 32:17; cf. Ezra 10:9; Esth 3:12; 9:1) or year-month (Jer 28:1; 39:1; Ezra 3:8; 2 Chr 29:3). The more-recent pattern (late 6th c. BCE onward) seems to be a reversal of the older pattern and appears in full and abbreviated forms. The full pattern is day-month-year (e.g., Ezra 6:15), and the abbreviated pattern is day-month (Ezra 3:6; 6:19; 8:31; Neh 8:2; 2 Chr 7:10; 29:17; 35:1; Esth 3:13; 8:12; 9:15) or month-year (Ezra 7:8; 2 Chr 15:10). Kessler notes the pattern and texts as evidence to support Yaron's thesis that year-month-day is the traditional pattern from which a newer pattern emerged. Kessler explains the presence of the older pattern in Haggai as evidence of the transitional period and would most likely see Ezra, Nehemiah, Chronicles, and Esther as evidence of the more-recent pattern.

"the word came a second time, on the twenty-fourth of the month" (2:20) assumes the year indictor in 2:10 as its antecedent (the second year).

The second type of chronological indicator is the futuristic reference "in that day" (*bayyôm hahû'*; Hag 2:23). Floyd refers to these as "future event formulas" used of prophecies "whose fulfillment is envisioned as a development discontinuous with the present course of events."[28]

The third type of chronological indicator is the time-frame formula. This type states a general time frame, a specific historical time, or provides a futuristic reference. What shapes the choice of indicator is associated events and how they are perceived with regard to a goal or other significant events or processes. These time markers signal progression and the suitability of the time frame (Hag 1:2, 4) or ripeness for a particular activity—that is, "time to build" (*'et-bō'*),[29] "and now" (*wəʿattâ*), referring to the consequences of what has been said (Hag 1:5; 2:4, 15). The indicator "from this day . . ." (*min-hayyôm hazzê*; 2:18, 19), from the twenty-fourth of the ninth month (2:18), fits into this category as well as into the first type—the antecedent being the year reference in 2:10.

The chronological indictors are significant in that some reflect an element of "time watching," anticipating an event or occurrence, while others validate the prophetic claim that Yahweh is at work—for example: revelation and the ensuing occurrences (Hag 1:12–15); the past as Yahweh's doing (Hag 1:5–11); and the contrast between the past and the future as Yahweh's work (Hag 2:18–19).[30]

B. SOCIOPOLITICAL CONTEXT

The book of Haggai is a decisive source for reconstructing the Persian period, which is itself a point of reference for understanding the sociopolitical milieu of the book. This milieu is most often identified with reference to the rulers and major or salient events of a period. In this brief overview, however, I will

28. Floyd, *Minor Prophets 2,* 650; J. E. Tollington, *Tradition and Innovation in Haggai and Zechariah 1–8*, JSOTSup 150 (Sheffield: JSOT Press, 1993), 136–38; S. J. DeVries, *From Old Revelation to New: A Tradition-Historical and Redaction-Critical Study of Temporal Transitions in Prophetic Prediction* (Grand Rapids: Eerdmans, 1995), 52–55. See his discussion of the futuristic references and their occurrence in eschatological prophecies. M. R. Jacobs, *Conceptual Coherence of the Book of Micah*, JSOTSup 322 (Sheffield: Sheffield Academic, 2001), regarding Mic 4 and Isa 2.

29. M. V. Fox, *A Time to Tear Down and A Time to Build Up* (Grand Rapids: Eerdmans, 1999), 194–204. The classification of time is temporal and substantive (see discussion of 1:2–4 below).

30. See below for additional discussion of these texts.

characterize Judah in the Persian period based on its sociopolitical developments (the status of Yehud/Judah in the Empire, the leaders in the Empire, etc.; note that in this commentary, I use the term *Yehud* [Aramaic *yəhûd*; Hebrew *yəhûdâ*] to designate Judah as a province during the early Persian period [539–486 BCE]).[31] Although the prophet Haggai was part of this sociopolitical environment, he is discussed in §I.A above.

The superscription of the book of Haggai states that the word of Yahweh came through "the prophet" Haggai and situates the prophetic activity in the second year, sixth month, first day of Darius's reign—most likely Darius I (522–486 BCE)—see Hag 1:15; 2:10, 20. The transition from Babylonian to Persian rule was significant with regard to the events portrayed in the book of Haggai. Under Babylonian rule, the deported people were to live out their existence away from Jerusalem. The political system and ideology of the Babylonian Empire did not include the practice of restoring a people to its homeland. Instead, it depended on assimilation to facilitate the integration of foreign elements into its culture. Consequently, the Babylonian Empire deported the skilled and able-bodied and incorporated them into the life and functions of Babylonian society.[32]

After the death of Nebuchadnezzar, Babylon experienced internal instability that resulted in its collapse. The rise of Cyrus the Great (550–530 BCE) was the catalyst for the Babylonian collapse. When he became ruler of the Median Empire and later submitted to Persian control during a campaign in Asia Minor, he focused his attention on Babylonia, a kingdom already experiencing internal strife. In 539 BCE, Cyrus defeated the Babylonian army, slaughtered the people, and took control of the Empire.[33] Cyrus promoted an atmosphere of religious tolerance within the Persian Empire, allowing the various religious groups to maintain their own practices. In keeping with this tolerance for cultural and religious expression of the people living in Babylon, in 538 BCE, Cyrus issued a decree:

31. For further discussion of the Persian period (from 486 BCE onward), see part 2: Malachi, introduction, section IB.

32. The literature on the historical period is extensive. While comparison of the specific contributions of various scholars is not the focus of this section, I must note their contribution to my general understanding: Paolo Sacchi, *History of the Second Temple Period*, JSOTSup 285 (Sheffield: Sheffield Academic, 2000), 58–151; E. M. Meyers, "Second Temple Studies in the Light of Recent Archaeology, Part I: The Persian and Hellenistic Periods," *CurBS* 2 (1994): 1–32; G. W. Ahlström, *The History of Ancient Palestine* (Minneapolis: Fortress, 1993), 800–906; Blenkinsopp, *History of Prophecy*, 194–226. J. Bright, *History of Israel*, 2nd ed. (Philadelphia: Westminster, 1972); Berquist, *Judaism in Persia's Shadow*, 23–127; J. M. Miller and J. H. Hayes, *A History of Ancient Israel and Judah* (Philadelphia: Westminster, 1986), 437–75; Edwin M. Yamauchi, *Persia and the Bible* (Grand Rapids: Baker, 1990), 65–278.

33. Miller and Hayes, *History of Ancient Israel*, 439.

> Thus says King Cyrus of Persia: "The LORD, the God of heaven, has given me all the kingdoms of the earth, and he has charged me to build him a house at Jerusalem in Judah. Any of those among you who are of his people—may their God be with them!—are now permitted to go up to Jerusalem in Judah, and rebuild the house of the LORD, the God of Israel—he is the God who is in Jerusalem; and let all survivors, in whatever place they reside, be assisted by the people of their place with silver and gold, with goods and with animals, besides freewill offerings for the house of God in Jerusalem." (Ezra 1:2–4 NRSV)[34]

According to this Ezra version of the decree, Babylonian Jews were allowed to return to Yehud and to restore their religious practices. This restoration was part of Cyrus's administrative effort at imperial expansion and control. This effort encouraged and supported people's movement toward the colonies (and away from the center).[35] In part, the restoration facilitated the movement of the Persian army as it traveled throughout the Empire (see map 1). Cyrus also returned religious artifacts and supported temple building efforts. Consequently, people gradually returned to their countries. Cyrus entrusted leadership of Jerusalem to Sheshbazzar (538 BCE), governor of Judah.[36] The first returnees may have constituted a small group of Babylonian Jews, including various strata of the community.[37]

34. The extant form of the decree or Edict of Cyrus appears in Ezra 1:2–4 (in Hebrew), in 6:3–5 (in Aramaic), in 2 Chr 36:22–23, and in the "Cylinder of Cyrus." Cf. E. J. Bickerman, "The Edict of Cyrus in Ezra 1," *JBL* 65 (1946): 249–75; J. Briend, "L'édit de Cyrus et sa valeur historique," *Transeu* 11 (1996): 33–44; H. G. M. Williamson, *Ezra, Nehemiah,* WBC 16 (Waco, TX: Word, 1985), 6–19; Sacchi, *Second Temple Period,* 58–60; Kessler, *Haggai,* 61–62.

35. Berquist, *Judaism in Persia's Shadow,* 25–26.

36. Meyers and Meyers, *Haggai, Zechariah 1–8,* xxxix; Blenkinsopp, *History of Prophecy,* 197; Williamson, *Ezra, Nehemiah,* 7–19; D. J. A. Clines, *Ezra, Nehemiah, Esther,* NCBC (Grand Rapids: Eerdmans, 1984), 36–38. Sacchi (*Second Temple Period,* 64) posits that the community was organized under two leaders, namely, the "vassal king from the line of David and the high priest from the line of Zadok" (Ezek 45).

37. According to Ezra 2:64–65, approximately 50,000 people returned (i.e., 42,360 + 7,337 + 200 = 49,897). This reference may be the total number of people who returned gradually. Cf. H. W. Wolff, *Haggai,* 17, 51–52. While Berquist (*Judaism in Persia's Shadow,* 26–27) provides the number of people who returned because of Cyrus's edict, he also notes the challenges of using the books of Ezra and Nehemiah as sources for this information. The challenge of using Ezra as a basis for reconstructing history is well argued. For further discussion of the issues of population within Yehud during the Persian period, see discussion of the sparsely populated region (13,350–20,000): Verhoef, *Haggai and Malachi,* 29; C. E. Carter, *The Emergence of Yehud in the Persian Period,* JSOTSup 294 (Sheffield: Sheffield Academic, 1999), 147–48; Kessler, *Haggai,* 94–95.

Table 2. Persian and Yehudite Leaders (550–424 BCE)[38]

Persian Rulers	Governors	Biblical Reference to Governor (peḥâ)	High Priests
Cyrus (550–530)	Sheshbazzar (538)	Ezra 5:14 (*peḥâ*)	Jehozadak
		Ezra (*nāśî*, "prince")	
Cambyses (530–522)			
Darius I (521–486)	Zerubbabel (520–510?)	Hag 1:1, 14; 2:2, 21 (*paḥat yəhûdâ*)	Joshua
	Elnathan (510–490?)		Joiakim
Xerxes (486–465)	Yeho'ezer (490–470?)		Eliashib I
			Johanan I
Artaxerxes I (465–424)	Ahzai (470–?)		Eliashib II
	Nehemiah (445–433)	Neh 5:14; 12:26 (*peḥâ*)	Joiada I

38. Several sources were used in constructing this table, including Meyers and Meyers, *Haggai, Zechariah 1–8,* 14 (chart 12); A. E. Hill, *Malachi: A New Translation with Introduction and Commentary*, AB 25D (New York: Doubleday, 1998), 51, 71 (charts 1 and 4); Berquist, *Judaism in Persia's Shadow*, esp. pp. 8–9, 23–127; Yamauchi, *Persia and the Bible,* 65–278 (table, 265); Kessler, *Haggai,* 78–80. Others propose an earlier date for Zerubbabel; e.g., P. R. Ackroyd, *Exile and Restoration: A Study of Hebrew Thought of the Sixth Century BC*, OTL (Philadelphia: Westminster, 1968), 146–48 (during Cambyses's reign); Williamson, *Ezra, Nehemiah,* 44–45 (around 538 BCE); cf. H. G. M. Williamson, "The Governors of Judah under the Persians," *TynBul* 39 (1988): 59–82. See also W. H. Rose, *Zemah and Zerubbabel: Messianic Expectations in the Early Postexilic Period,* JSOTSup 304 (Sheffield: Sheffield Academic, 2000). For further consideration of the discussion regarding the dates of Zerubbabel and Artaxerxes I, see D. Edelman, *The Origins of the 'Second' Temple: Persian Imperial Policy and the Rebuilding of Jerusalem,* Bible World (London: Equinox, 2005); R. W. Klein, "Were Joshua, Zerubbabel, and Nehemiah Contemporaries? A Response to Diana Edelman's Proposed Late Date for the Second Temple," *JBL* 127 (2008): 697–701.

The newly restored community began its task of rebuilding the community. Sheshbazzar, appointed governor by Cyrus, began the work on the temple in 537/36 BCE[39] (i.e., the foundation of the temple on the site of the Solomonic one—Ezra 5:14, 16). Although the new temple[40] did not duplicate the old temple's dimensions, the altar was rebuilt in order to reinstitute sacrifices within the first year of the return (cf. Ezra 3:1–7). Sheshbazzar failed to rebuild the temple amid various pressures, including financial and personnel conflicts.[41] But the rebuilding of the temple is also attributed to Zerubbabel, who was appointed governor.

Several issues contribute to a lack of consensus about the identity and activity of Sheshbazzar. Discussions about his identity include the possibility of his non-Jewish ethnicity, his identity in relation to Shenazzar (1 Chr 3:18), and his identity in relation to Zerubbabel.[42]

Two main suggestions regarding Sheshbazzar and Zerubbabel have been put forth: First, Sheshbazzar and Zerubbabel were two different names for the same person. Having two different names was a part of the acculturation process of foreigners living in Babylonia. It is peculiar, however, that these are both Babylonian names; one would expect one Jewish and one Babylonian name if this is a situation of double names.[43] But the custom of double names supports the possibility that Sheshbazzar and Zerubbabel were the same person using different names.[44] Second, Sheshbazzar and Zerubbabel were different persons. Sheshbazzar may have been the appointed governor while Zerubbabel was the Davidic heir to the throne. They are both attributed with laying the foundation of the temple. But even this assertion is problematic due to the nature of the data source. Ezra credits Sheshbazzar with returning the temple vessels (Ezra 1) and laying the foundation of the temple (Ezra 5:16). Ezra 2–3 places Zerubbabel in Cyrus's reign; this assumes that Zerubbabel was present and active in Yehud around 538 BCE.[45] However,

39. The source of information is Ezra 1:8, 11; 5:14, 16.

40. The new temple is also referred to as the Second Temple.

41. Hill, *Malachi,* 68.

42. The arguments about these issues are varied and extensive. See Kessler, *Haggai,* 63–64, for a delineation of the arguments and accompanying bibliography.

43. See Kessler (*Haggai,* 63–64, 66) regarding the possibility that double names would be Zemah and Zerubbabel. Rose, *Zemah and Zerubbabel,* 23, 33. A. Demsky, "Double Names in the Exile and the Identity of Sheshbazzar," in *These Are the Names,* ed. A. Demsky, Studies in Jewish Onomastics 2 (Ramat Gan: Bar-Ilan University Press, 1999), 26–28. Demsky notes that Zerubbabel is a double name consisting of "seed" and "Babylon."

44. J. Lust, "Identification of Zerubbabel and Sheshbassar," *ETL* 63 (1987): 90–95; cf. Demsky, "Double Names in the Exile," 23–39; Williamson, *Ezra, Nehemiah,* 17.

45. Thus Williamson, *Ezra, Nehemiah,* 44–45 (approx. 538 BCE); see also Williamson, "Governors of Judah under the Persians," 59–82. Other options for Zerubbabel's time in Ye-

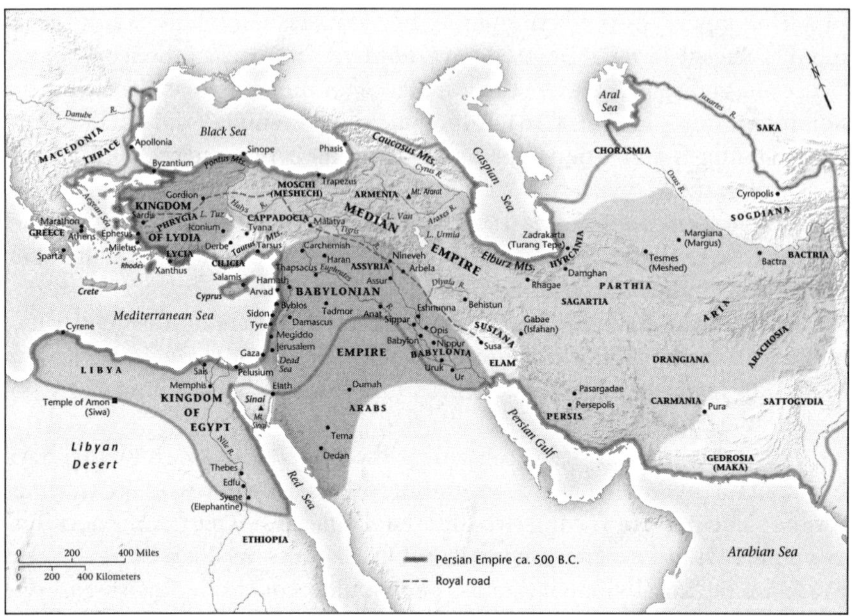

Map 1. Persian Empire

Ezra may represent, not a catalog of actual building activity, but an account of the progress in meeting the imperative of Cyrus's decree.

Thus, Meyers and Meyers contend that the refounding mostly presupposes that the foundation had not been completely demolished and that construction used some of the remaining materials. The implication is that Hag 2:18 speaks of ceremonial activity rather than laying an actual foundation.[46] Most likely Sheshbazzar was governor of Yehud and began the work of restoration—to lay the foundation for the temple—only to be succeeded by Zerubbabel, who completed the work and was thus credited for it.[47] In

hud include during Cambyses's reign. Kessler (*Haggai,* 71–72) notes that Ezra 3–4 inserted Zerubbabel as a "literary and theological device" to include Zerubbabel and Joshua, the high priest, "in the attempt at temple restoration" (p. 71).

46. Meyers and Meyers, *Haggai, Zechariah 1–8,* 63–64; Kessler, *Haggai,* 70.

47. Baldwin, *Hag, Zech, Mal,* 53; Verhoef, *Haggai and Malachi,* 26–27. Meyers and Meyers (*Haggai, Zechariah 1–8,* xxxiv) note that Zerubbabel was Sheshbazzar's successor and was successful where Sheshbezzar was not. S. Japhet, "Sheshbazzar and Zerubbabel: Against the Background of the Historical and Religious Tendencies of Ezra-Nehemiah, Part I," *ZAW* 94 (1982): 94; F. Bianchi, "Le rôle de Zorobabel et la dynastie davidique en Judée du VIe siècle au IIe siècle av. J.-C.," *Transeu* 7 (1994) 153–59; Hill, *Malachi,* 68–69; T. C. Eskenazi, "Sheshbazzar," *ABD* 5:1207–9; R. P. Carroll, *When Prophecy Failed*: *Cognitive Dissonance in the Prophetic Traditions of the Old Testament* (New York: Seabury, 1979), 164–67.

any case, Haggai's prophetic activity strongly encouraged the community to rebuild the temple in obedience to God.

During this period of Persian dominance, Cyrus died. Cambyses (530–522 BCE) assumed power over the Persian Empire and retained the administrative structure inherited from Cyrus. He changed the military focus from the eastern to the western border regions, thus directly affecting the coastal provinces of the west on his journey toward Egypt. This journey may have taken him via Acco and Gaza on the way to Egypt (see map 2).[48] Cambyses attacked Egypt at Pelusium and then captured Memphis in 525 BCE.[49] He succeeded in capturing Egypt but experienced ongoing problems with maintaining control of Egypt. The nature of the conquest is unclear; apparently, efforts were made to assimilate and destroy. Cambyses destroyed temples and decreased contributions to the remaining temples in Egypt.[50] Attempting to gain and retain control, Cambyses remained in Egypt (525–22 BCE). The circumstances of his death are a matter of debate. On his way back from Egypt and with news that his throne had been usurped, Cambyses died.[51] After Cambyses died, Gaumata[52] remained king until Darius I assumed the throne. There are no biblical references to Cambyses, perhaps because the restoration efforts had ceased during his time,[53] or for some reason the population did not maintain a literary record of its effort.[54]

48. Kessler, *Haggai,* 86. Alternatively, Berquist (*Judaism in Persia's Shadow,* 45–46, 48) proposed that Cambyses engaged the support of the Greeks in his military campaign by acquiring boats used to sail the Mediterranean Sea.

49. Yamauchi (*Persia and the Bible,* 93, 104–5) notes that, until Cambyses's campaign against Amasis (570–526 BCE), who was king during the twenty-sixth dynasty, Egypt had never been conquered. Neither the Assyrians nor the Babylonians subdued Egypt, and the Persian conquest would lead to perpetual struggle for control (pp. 96–97). Cf. Berquist, *Judaism in Persia's Shadow,* 45–46.

50. Yamauchi, *Persia and the Bible,* 104–5, 122; Berquist, *Judaism in Persia's Shadow,* 46.

51. There are various discussions about the circumstances surrounding his death and whether it was suicide or murder at the hand of Darius. Others suggest that the cause is unknown; see Meyer and Meyers, *Haggai, Zechariah 1–8,* xxxiii; Ahlström, *History of Ancient Palestine,* 817–19; Yamauchi, *Persia and the Bible,* 125–26, 143–45.

52. Yamauchi (*Persia and the Bible,* 125–26) notes the questions about the identity of the usurper, Gaumata (or Bardiya). Cf. Berquist, *Judaism in Persia's Shadow,* 46; Meyer and Meyers, *Haggai, Zechariah 1–8,* xxxvii–xxxviii.

53. Yamauchi (*Persia and the Bible,* 94) notes that Josephus (*Ant.* 11:88) "substitutes Cambyses for Artaxerxes (I) of Ezra 4:7" and most likely introduces "some confusing ideas in his . . . attempt to correct the passage."

54. Cf. E. Ben Zvi, "The Urban Centre of Jerusalem and the Development of the Literature of the Hebrew Bible," in *Urbanism in Antiquity,* ed. W. E. Aufrecht, N. A. Mirau, and S. W. Gauley, JSOTSup 244 (Sheffield: JSOT Press, 1997), 194–209; Kessler, *Haggai,* 95.

Darius I (521–486 BCE) continued the practices of religious and cultural tolerance in the Empire. Darius's effort at imperial expansion included gaining control over Egypt and other territories through negotiated loyalties rather than military conquest. Darius organized the Persian Empire into satrapies that were subdivided into provinces; he appointed governors over the satrapies and provinces.[55] Darius "charged the satrapal governors and local officials to codify and follow a law."[56] "The King's Law" included standard regulations throughout the Persian Empire and fostered local adaptation in accordance with various traditions. So, the Jewish people could codify their laws according to their traditions.[57] Along with the implementation of "The King's Law," Persian rule under Darius thrived on the loyalty of local leaders, through whom the Empire maintained control over various provinces. Thus, "Darius' administrative contracts with Yehud would have taken the form of the installation of local governors (such as Zerubbabel and his helpers) and rhetorical support for the Persian Empire (such as that offered by Haggai and Zechariah)."[58] The status of Yehud as a province is unclear, leading to arguments about whether the term *paḥat*, "governor," may be rightly applied to the leaders before Nehemiah (445–433 BCE).[59] This line of inquiry surrounds references to Zerubbabel's status as governor of Yehud (Hag 1:1, 14; 2:2, 21).[60]

C. CONCEPTUAL FRAMEWORK

The book of Haggai illustrates theological and social ambiguity in the people's conviction about the building of the temple—that is, about the time for building the temple (Hag 1:2–11) and about the reputation of the temple (Hag 2:3–9). In the people's opinion, it was not time to build the temple—a

55. For further discussion of Darius's reign, see part 2, Malachi, introduction, section IB.

56. Berquist, *Judaism in Persia's Shadow,* 55. See Meyers and Meyers (*Haggai, Zechariah 1–8,* xxxix) regarding Darius's command to codify Egyptian laws.

57. Berquist, *Judaism in Persia's Shadow,* 54–55; Yamauchi, *Persia and the Bible,* 257.

58. Berquist, *Judaism in Persia's Shadow,* 61.

59. For further discussion, see Kessler's delineation of the perspective (*Haggai,* 70–82). Cf. Rose, *Zemah and Zerubbabel,* 30–31;

60. At issue is Yehud's status within the Persian structure. One issue is whether Zerubbabel or Tattenai was the governor. It appears that they both were: Zerubbabel was governor of Yehud (provincial governor), while Tattenai was governor of the Eber-Nahara satrapy ("Beyond the River"), the satrapy containing several provinces (cf. Ezra 5:3, 6; 6:6, 13). Cf. Meyers and Meyers, *Haggai, Zechariah 1–8,* 13–16; Hill, *Malachi,* 68–69; Yamauchi, *Persia and the Bible,* 155–57. Another issue is the status of Yehud in relation to Samaria; cf. Kessler, *Haggai,* 72–80.

conviction that may have been based on their understanding of the appointed time for the restoration, which was at the end of the seventy-year period. The other aspect of their ambivalence was the reason for the temple. Was God's temple necessary for God's presence? Their experience in exile had called into question their previous ideology regarding the localized presence.[61] That the people in Babylon were assured by the exilic prophets of God's presence with them had prompted questions about the necessity for the temple (Isa 41:10; Jer 30:11; 42:11; 46:28). Additionally, economic factors may not have been conducive to rebuilding.

In fact, the economic hardships were articulated in the book of Haggai to illustrate God's displeasure with the lack of progress and to persuade the community to build the temple. God summons a drought to affect all inhabited and uninhabited regions as well as all aspects of human life and endeavors (Hag 1:10–11). Because God is in control of all of nature, he can use nature as an instrument to secure human obedience (cf. Deut 28). As to politics, the book of Haggai depicts God's universal authority through God's actions toward the nations (Hag 2:20–23), but it portrays God's particular concern about Jerusalem. Thus, the book is a validation of Yehud's significance—that is, it indicates that Yehud, however small in the Persian Empire, is central to God's plan and that God will subdue the nations and place God's servant in authority.

III. TEXT

The present translation of the book of Haggai is based on the Masoretic Text (MT), which is relatively well preserved. *BHS* identifies approximately forty-one variants in these two chapters, none of which significantly alters the primary reading of the text: 1:1bα, 2aβ, 4aβ, 6bβ, 7b, 9aα, 10aα, 10aβ (2×), 11aα, 11aβ, 12aγ, 13a, 15a; 2:1b, 2b, 4a (2×), 4b, 5aα, (2×), 6aβ, 6bβ, 7ab, 9bβ, 14b, 15aα, 16aα, 16b (3×), 17aα, 17b, 18b (2×), 19aα, 19aβ, 21b, 22aγ, 22bβ, and 23aα.[62] Several alterations are discussed but deemed unnecessary for understanding the text (e.g., 1:4, 7, 11; 2:4, 5, 16, 17, 18, 19, 22, 23). Among the ancient witnesses to the text of Haggai, none consistently deviates from the MT or supports only one other witness in all points of deviation. For example, the LXX deviates from the MT in 1:1, 2, 12; and 2:16 but also supports the MT (e.g., 2:10, 11). The fragmentary scroll of the Minor Prophets found at Wadi

61. This belief is associated with the representation of the temple as God's dwelling place.

62. For further discussion, see the Text and Commentary section below.

Murabbaʿat containing portions of the Haggai text (1:12–2:10; 2:12–23) is not superior to the MT but preserves readings that are markedly different from the LXX. The Murabbaʿat fragment exhibits two variants to the MT in 2:1 and 3.

There are several textual challenges attested in the versions and noted tendencies in the ways the versions handle the text. The LXX's variant readings include deviations of meaning (e.g., Hag 1:1, 8) and simple additions to clarify a feature of the text (e.g., 1:1; 1:12; 2:21). One of its tendencies is to expand the text via explanatory or reflective statements about a particular aspect of the text. The LXX's expansion statements also contribute to the difference in versification (e.g., MT 2:9, 14, 22 = LXX 2:10, 15, 23). Other tendencies include the harmonization (2:2) or omission of parts of the text (1:2; 2:5, 10; 2:6a) and an ordering of verses that results in different versification from the MT. The targum supports the MT in some instances (1:6, 7, 12, 15; 2:2, 5, 18), deviates from the MT reading in others (1:4, 12, 13; 2:17, 23), and shows support for the LXX at some points. Although the Vulgate usually supports the MT (1:9, 10, 11), it deviates from it in favor of several emendations (1:2, 4). In some instances, it supports the LXX over the MT (1:12); it also deviates from the LXX (1:9; 2:5, 7, 16). The Peshitta usually supports the MT but also shows a tendency to support the LXX and at times the targum over the MT: for example, like the LXX, the Peshitta deviates from the MT with reference to the designation of Zerubbabel (the great, the leader of Judah—1:1, 14; 2:2, 21). It does not, however, adopt the reading of the LXX (of the tribe of Judah). The Peshitta also supports the LXX and targum at 2:10 contra the MT, reading *bəyad* (by the hand) rather than *ʾel* (to). It also supports the LXX's omission of the second *ʿet* (1:2) and the pronominal suffix "their" from "houses" (1:4), as does the targum.

IV. INTERTEXTUAL INDICATORS

The connections between the book of Haggai and other Old Testament books are noteworthy. The elements that the book of Haggai shares with other biblical books range from vocabulary (words, phrases) to concepts signaled by but not limited to its vocabulary, to theologies and allusions. In this survey, I focus on the biblical books whose perspectives can be used to illuminate our discussions about Haggai: Ezra, Chronicles, Jeremiah, Isaiah, and Leviticus.

The book of Ezra reports Cyrus's decree identifying Persia's provisions for the return to Jerusalem (Ezra 1:2–4 [Hebrew]; 6:3–5 [Aramaic]; 2 Chr 36:22–23 [Hebrew]). The specific aspects highlighted are the conditions and provisions of the return and the religious rationale for the return. Although some scholars are of the opinion that the various versions of the decree reflect different goals, one can recognize conceptual connections among the versions.[63] Ezra 1 reports that Yahweh stirred the spirit of Cyrus, prompting him to make the decree (Ezra 1:1). According to the decree, Yahweh gave Cyrus "all the kingdoms of the earth" (cf. Hag 2:7, 22) and appointed him to "build him a house at Jerusalem in Judah" (cf. Hag 2:23 and Ezra 1:2). The people were permitted to return to Yehud and were provided with material resources, including silver and gold, livestock, and offerings (Ezra 1:4; cf. Hag 2:8). Among the returnees to Yehud/Judah were some leaders, including the priests and heads of families (cf. Ezra 3:12).

Ezra 6 also specifies that material resources be given to the people and further indicates that the vessels looted from the temple were to be returned (Ezra 6:5). Additionally, it specifies the dimensions of the rebuilt temple (60 × 60 cubits; Ezra 6:3). Each of the texts thus appears to have its own focus. Basic to understanding the book of Haggai is the fact that both perspectives of the decree tend to be fused: it provides for the return to the land and for restoration of the temple and its treasures (cf. 2 Chr 36:22–23).

The book of Chronicles presents some of the same history as the book of Ezra. Thus, the chronicler's perspective on the exile and restoration constitutes a part of the conceptual framework for understanding these events in the life of the community. A key text is 2 Chr 36:22–23, the report of Cyrus's decree. First, from the Chronicler's perspective the deportation was not simply a punishment of the people but served Yahweh's twofold purpose: to fulfill both Jeremiah's prophecy of the seventieth-year return (Jer 25:11–12; 29:10) and the sabbatical imperative concerning the land (Lev 26:34–35, 41–43). The deportation of the people to Babylon would remove the contaminating elements and thus purify the land. Part of the challenge of this perspective is that the land was not emptied of its inhabitants. Further, 2 Chr 36 seems to reflect conflicting viewpoints. In particular, 36:21 suggests that the deportation may have had restorative value for the land; while 36:22, usually identified as a gloss, appears to challenge this perspective.[64]

Second, regarding the restoration, the decree in 2 Chr 36 specifies the following elements: (a) the date of the proclamation—the first year of King

63. Miller and Hayes, *History of Ancient Israel*, 442–45; Kessler, *Haggai*, 60–62; H. G. M. Williamson, *Ezra and Nehemiah*, OTG (Sheffield: JSOT Press, 1987), 33–34.

64. S. J. DeVries, *1 and 2 Chronicles*, FOTL 11 (Grand Rapids: Eerdmans, 1989), 11–12, 423. DeVries does not accept Chronicles and Ezra–Nehemiah as a single work or as authored by the same person. He acknowledges that commonalities among the works show that they were generally accessible to the larger postexilic community. The effect of the placement of 2 Chr 36:22–23 is that it established Cyrus's decree as simultaneously the end of deportation and the beginning of the period of restoration.

Cyrus of Persia; (b) the source of the proclamation—Yahweh stirred the spirit of the king and thus prompted him to make the decree; (c) the intent of the proclamation—to enable the rebuilding of the temple in Jerusalem. It also provided for the people to go to Jerusalem. Thus, the foci of Ezra 1 and 6 are merged. The book of Haggai reflects on the circumstances of the people in Yehud, who were facing the question of rebuilding the temple. Keeping the Chronicler's perspective in mind, we can say that the intertextual framework shows the purposes of the Deity converging with the decree's ideological and economic approach to the rebuilding effort.

The book of Jeremiah provides the background of the exile and thus a perspective on the reason for it (i.e., disobedience), and it offers an understanding of the deportees in terms of the Deity's plans (whether they are good figs or bad figs; cf. Jer 24). In this theo-political message, the good figs are those whom Yahweh will use to actualize a return to Jerusalem (those exiled in Babylon), and the bad figs are those whom Yahweh has dedicated to destruction (those exiled in Egypt and other regions). From the perspective of Jer 27, God used Nebuchadnezzar, king of Babylon, as the instrument of destruction. In addition, Jer 25:11–12; 29:10 present the time frame and circumstances for the return (i.e., the seventieth-year return).

> For thus says the Lord: Only when Babylon's seventy years are completed will I visit you, and I will fulfill to you my promise and bring you back to this place. (Jer 29:10 NRSV)

In an atmosphere of competing ideologies regarding God's work in the world and plan for God's people, Jeremiah sheds light on questions about the status of the members of the community in relation to their compatriots and their neighbors—all of them are essential to God's plan for restoration. Jeremiah illuminates the internal tensions of Haggai's restored community which resulted in their competing perspectives about identity and role. Social stratification may have been a by-product of life in and around Jerusalem for those who were not deported. For segments of the community, the return may not have constituted a restoration as much as a reconfiguration of their ongoing existence in the community and the evidence of Persian imperial policies.

The community of Haggai's time consisted of those who had remained in the land plus those who were returning to the land. Both groups included people with memory of the Solomonic Temple before it was destroyed. Although we may be unable to delineate the precise ideology of the various groups based on their experience from 597 to 520 BCE, their resistance to rebuilding appears to have been fueled by both intra- and intergroup tensions. The message about rebuilding the temple addresses the community's skewed priorities, further reflecting the heterogeneous nature of the community.

Deutero-Isaiah (40–55) facilitates an understanding of the restoration community depicted in the book of Haggai. Of great significance is the portrayal of Cyrus in Isa 44–45.[65] Apparently, to Isaiah's Babylonian audience Cyrus is an essential part of God's involvement in their history. Thus, even a king outside the Davidic lineage and outside the covenant people is used by God to restore the people to the land:

> . . . who says of Cyrus, "He is my shepherd, and he shall carry out all my purpose"; and who says of Jerusalem, "It shall be rebuilt," and of the temple, "Your foundation shall be laid." (Isa 44:28 NRSV)

and

> Thus says the LORD to his anointed, to Cyrus, whose right hand I have grasped to subdue nations before him and strip kings of their robes, to open doors before him—and the gates shall not be closed. (Isa 45:1 NRSV)

Accordingly, Cyrus's success is not so much a success for the Persian Empire as a success for God's plan. The theo-political message indicates that Cyrus is God's instrument of change, but the message remains Yahwistic in its focus.

> Thus says the LORD, the King of Israel, and his Redeemer, the LORD of hosts: I am the first and I am the last; besides me there is no god. Who is like me? Let them proclaim it, let them declare and set it forth before me. Who has announced from of old the things to come? Let them tell us what is yet to be. Do not fear, or be afraid; have I not told you from of old and declared it? You are my witnesses! Is there any god besides me? There is no other rock; I know not one. (Isa 44:6–8 NRSV)

Whatever else has happened, Cyrus's rule is presented positively in relation to the community of the Babylon-based deportees and their descendants. The affirmation of a foreign ruler does not mean endorsement of Babylonian or Persian practices. By addressing idolatry, Isaiah may indicate that some had been involved with making and worshiping idols. Although the atmosphere in Babylon may have been conducive to adopting various religious practices, God still required unwavering commitment and prohibited idolatry (Isa 40:18–20; 44:9–20).

65. For a discussion of the literature associated with Cyrus's reign, see Berquist, *Judaism in Persia's Shadow,* 29–42.

Isaiah 56–66 also signals the tensions within the community over the issue of rebuilding the temple and making sacrifices. The theo-political aspects are also present, for example, in the claims of God's power over the nations, God's plan to use political leaders to rescue the community (cf. Isa 61:1–3), and the promised exaltation of Zion (Isa 60:13–15).[66]

The book of Leviticus portrays the deportation as the time away from the land necessary for the purification of the land (Lev 26:34–35, 41–43).

> Then the land shall enjoy its sabbath years as long as it lies desolate, while you are in the land of your enemies; then the land shall rest, and enjoy its sabbath years. As long as it lies desolate, it shall have the rest it did not have on your sabbaths when you were living on it. (Lev 26:34–35 NRSV)

Leviticus also sheds light on the place of the priests in the restoration community, specifically their responsibility to offer sacrifices, teach Torah, and distinguish between the holy and profane and clean and unclean (Lev 6–7; 10:10–11; 11 [esp. vv. 41–42]).[67] Even without a temple, the altar was a functioning part of the community, where sacrifices were offered and the cultic calendar observed (Ezra 3).[68]

These are some of the salient intertextual elements in the book of Haggai; many others are noted throughout the discussion below, including the Deuteronomistic blessing and curse (Deut 28; Hag 1:6–11; 2:15–19); traditions about the divine presence (e.g., Gen 28:15; Isa 41:10; 43:5; Jer 30:11; Hag 1:13; 2:4, 5); and the "new constitution of Ezekiel" (40–48), including the centrality of the Zadokite priests. Together, these intertextual nuances demonstrate the links between the book of Haggai and other parts of the Old Testament.

V. STRUCTURAL ANALYSIS

We can discern the structure of Haggai by examining its chronological indicators and the conceptual units marked off by these indicators (see table 1). While there is some consensus that the chronological indicators

66. See Berquist (*Judaism in Persia's Shadow*, 73–79) for an analysis of Isa 56–66 as the literary product of Darius's reign.

67. Sacchi (*Second Temple Period*, 439–45) identifies several texts as part of the sixth-century perspective on purity, including Lev 10:10–11 and ch. 11; Ezek 44:23.

68. The issues of purity were also part of the ideological current within the community (Hag 2:10–14).

are decisive to the structural composition of the text, there is disagreement about the extent of the units and their conceptual unity.[69] I propose that the book is an account of the restoration of the Jerusalem temple. It consists of three macro units, each focused on a phase of the restoration that is represented by the community's action and Yahweh's intervention: 1:1–15; 2:1–9; and 2:10–23. In this case, the superscription functions as an introduction to the first unit. The structural analysis is represented below, followed by an overview of the composition of each of the macro units and their subunits. A detailed discussion of the subunits is provided in the commentary below.

Structure

Superscription 1:1
I. Disputation Sequence about Building the Temple 1:2–15
  A. Disputation and Supporting Evidence 1:2–11
    1. The Competing Perspectives 1:2–4
      a. The People's Perspective 1:2
      b. Counterperspective 1:3–4
    2. The Supporting Evidence for Yahweh's Perspective 1:5–11
      a. Admonitions to Reflect on the Evidence 1:5–9
        (1) Admonition #1 to Reflect on Experiences 1:5–6
        (2) Admonition #2 to Reflect on Experiences 1:7–9
      b. Noted Consequences of the People's Deeds 1:10–11
  B. Outcome of the Disputation 1:12–15
    1. Report on the Community's Obedience 1:12
    2. Report on Yahweh's Assurance to the People 1:13
    3. Report on the Community's Transformation 1:14–15
II. Encouragement: Inquiry and Admonition 2:1–9
  A. Inquiry Regarding the Temple 2:1–3
  B. Expression of Encouragement 2:4–9

69. Several scholars share this interpretation of the structure, including the following: Floyd, *Minor Prophets 2,* 2, 253–55. Meyers and Meyers (*Haggai, Zechariah 1–8,* xlviiii, 3, 47) identify 1:1–15 as the first of two macro units in the book of Haggai (1:1–15; 2:1–23). They further divide this unit into two subunits, following the occurrences of the chronological indicators (1:1–11, 12–15). Others have variations of the proposed structure: Redditt (*Haggai, Zechariah, Malachi,* 13) identifies a fourfold structure following the chronological indicators (1:1–15a; 1:15b–2:9; 2:10–19; 2:20–23). Verhoef (*Haggai and Malachi,* 20–25) proposes a twofold structure: 1:1–15a and 1:15b–2:23. Haggai 1:1–15a is further subdivided into 1:1–11 and 12–15a. The second macro unit is further subdivided into three subunits: 1:15b–2:9; 2:10–19; and 2:20–23. D. L. Petersen (*Haggai and Zechariah 1–8,* OTL [London: SCM, 1985]) proposes 1:1–11; 1:12–15a; 1:15b–2:9; 2:10–15; 2:15–19; 2:20–23.

1. The Encouragement Proper (Admonition) 2:4–5
2. Basis of the Encouragement 2:6–9

III. Oracle concerning a New Era 2:10–23
- A. Present Status and Promise for the Future 2:10–19
  1. Illustration regarding the Status of the Community 2:10–14
     - a. Introductory Formula 2:10
     - b. Two-Question Sequence 2:11–13
       - (1) Yahweh's Command to the Prophet 2:11
       - (2) Questions Directed to the Priests 2:12–13
         - (a) First Question Directed to the Priests 2:12
         - (b) Second Question Directed to the Priests 2:13
     - c. Analogy regarding the Community's Status 2:14
  2. Admonition to Compare the Times 2:15–19
     - a. Admonition #1: Regarding the Past and Present 2:15–17
     - b. Admonition #2: Regarding the Present and Future 2:18–19
- B. Concerning Yahweh's Future Rule 2:20–23
  1. Yahweh's Dealing with the Kingdoms 2:20–22
  2. Yahweh's Appointed Servant: Zerubbabel 2:23

The first macro unit, 1:2–15, consists of two subunits: the disputation about building the temple (1:2–11) and the outcome of that disputation (1:12–15). The disputation in 1:2 begins with a message formula (*kô ʾāmar yhwh ṣəbāʾôt,* "thus says Yahweh of hosts") that signals the beginning of the Yahweh speech and concludes in 1:11 with the report of Yahweh's speech about the drought brought on the land and its inhabitants. As does a prophetic disputation in general, this one contains the interplay between competing perspectives. The participants in the disputation are the people (*hāʿām-hazzê,* "this people") and Yahweh. The people's perspective presented in 1:2 is a report from Yahweh concerning what the people said. The counterpoints challenging the people and supporting Yahweh's perspectives are contained in Hag 1:3–11.

Notably, 1:3 again identifies the instrument that conveys the content of the communication—"by the hand of Haggai the prophet" (*bəyad-ḥaggay hannābîʾ*)—without specifying the addressees (cf. Hag 1:1). The reference to "this people" in Hag 1:2 may therefore identify the participants in the dispute, while the audience of the dispute is the same as in 1:1, the governor and the high priest. The prophet delivers the message to the governor and high priest about the people, more specifically, about the people's perspective on building Yahweh's house (*bêt yhwh*). Yahweh's statement includes two admonitions—whose apparent intent is to prompt the hearers to reflect on their ways (Hag 1:5–6, 7–9)—and the noted consequences of the people's deeds (Hag 1:10–11). The message formula "thus says Yahweh of hosts" (*kô ʾāmar yhwh ṣəbāʾôt*) introduces both admonitions. In each case this formula is followed by the idiomatic expression *śîmû ləbabkem ʿal-darkêkem* meaning to reflect on your ways (lit., "set your heart toward your ways").

The second subunit in Hag 1:2–15 is 1:12–15, the outcome of the disputation, which notes the audience's response. Identified in Hag 1:12 are Zerubbabel and Joshua—without the appositives indicating their office—and the "entire remnant of the people" (*kōl šəʾērît hāʿām*). The subunit concludes with a chronological indicator marking the time frame of change from the circumstances depicted in Hag 1:2 to those depicted in 1:12–14—namely, a shift in the people's ways.

The second macro unit (Hag 2:1–9) begins with an abbreviated form of the chronological indicator.[70] It presupposes that the year was already named and thus omits it from the formulation (see table 1).[71] As does Hag 1:1, the 2:1 macro unit aso includes the prophetic-word formula "by the hand of Haggai" (*bəyad-ḥaggay*) plus the appositive "the prophet" (*hannābîʾ*). The command to Haggai to speak also identifies the intended hearers: Zerubbabel and Joshua (designated by name and title) and the remnant of the people. Haggai 2:1–9 consists of two subunits: an inquiry about the temple (2:1–3) and an admonition sequence (2:4–9). The addressees are named in both subunits. The messenger formula predominates in 2:4–9, appearing in each verse (twice in 2:9), as it underscores the reasons for the admonition not to be afraid. The formula sets off the reasons in 2:6 and concludes in 2:9.

The third macro unit (Hag 2:10–23) consists of two subunits (2:10–19 and 2:20–23). Its main concern is the new era and its connection to the present. Each subunit begins with a chronological indicator and the prophetic-word formula—"the word of Yahweh came to Haggai the prophet" (2:10, 20). In these two instances, the formula "to Haggai the prophet" (*ʾel-ḥaggay hannābîʾ*) is noteworthy as compared with the formula in Hag 1:1 and 2:1, "by the hand of Haggai the prophet" (*bəyad-ḥaggay hannābîʾ*). The difference between 2:10, 20, and 1:1, 2:1 is the role of the prophet—that is, the prophet is designated the instrument by whom the message is communicated (1:1; 2:1) rather than being identified as the recipient of the message (2:10). Undoubtedly, Haggai's role as instrument presupposes the receipt of the message. In the first and second macro units, the addressees are identified at the outset: Zerubbabel (governor) and Joshua (high priest) (1:1; 2:1–2). In the third macro unit, the addressee is the prophet who is given the instruction

70. Meyers and Meyers (*Haggai, Zechariah 1–8*, xlviiii, 3, 47) identify 2:1–23 as the second of two macro units in the book of Haggai. This unit is further subdivided into three units: 2:1–9, 10–19, and 20–23. They are explicit that these subunits are based on the presence of the chronological indictors.

71. See introduction, section IIA above.

to speak to the priests (*hakkōhănîm*). Zerubbabel is the addressee in the second subunit (2:20–23). As seen in table 3, each subunit in the book of Haggai specifies an addressee.

Table 3. Addressees in the Book of Haggai

Macro Units	Subunits	Stated Addressees
1:1-15	1:1-11	Zerubbabel (governor) and Joshua (high priest)
	1:12-15	Zerubbabel (governor), Joshua (high priest), and remnant of the people
2:1-9	2:1-3	Zerubbabel (governor) and Joshua (high priest)
	2:4-9	Zerubbabel (governor), Joshua (high priest), people of the land
2:10-23	2:10-19	Haggai (the prophet)(priests)
	2:20-23	Haggai (the prophet)(Zerubbabel [governor])

While Zerubbabel is identified as someone Haggai is commanded to speak to in only one part of the final subunit, Zerubbabel's centrality to the message of the book is evident in his appearance among the addressees of all but one of the subunits (2:10–19). Joshua the high priest is not identified in the final macro unit (Hag 2:10–23), but the priests are identified as those to whom Haggai is commanded to address his inquiry. His role as governor makes Zerubbabel integral to the rebuilding of the community in Jerusalem and essential to the hope for prominence.

VI. MESSAGE

The message of the book centers around the importance of obeying God in rebuilding the temple (Hag 1). This message is at once theological and political, reprimanding and encouraging. Theologically the message is the fulfillment of the prophecies of Jeremiah, Ezekiel, Micah, and Isaiah concerning the restoration of Jerusalem. The message represents the reality of the restoration, including rebuilding during the circumstances of the Persian Empire and consequent to the persistent ideology of Jerusalem's exalted status and God's universal reign from Jerusalem. The message stands at the boundary between disillusionment and commitment to the ideology of tradition. Politically, the rebuilding in Jerusalem is a result of Persia's policy and effort to expand and strengthen its Empire. Zerubbabel is part of the Persian political system on the one hand and a Davidic leader chosen by Yahweh on the other. Although they are illustrative of loyalty to the Persian Empire, restoring Jerusalem and building the temple are acts of obedience to Yahweh.

Fundamentally, the message of the book is one of hope that Yahweh is involved in the life of the community and has authority in the past, present, and future to safeguard the well-being of the community. God demands obedience and offers the divine presence as the blessing and reward for that obedience. Finally, God promises to overthrow the nations, possibly signifying the elevated status of God's people (Hag 2:20–23). In advocating for the actualization of God's plan, the message endorses the destruction of the nations, including the Persian Empire. This is as much a theo-political message as an eschatological one—theo-political in that it interprets the political reality in light of theological traditions, and eschatological because its futuristic language places the manifestation of that reality in the future and makes it contingent on God's success in subduing the nations. God's power is just as efficacious in moving the community from apathy to action as it is in controlling nature and the nations for God's purposes.

Although the primary aim of this commentary is interpretation and not lessons for today, the reader is encouraged to reflect on the several themes and their significance for modern audiences.

Misplaced Priorities. The text features a community whose priorities are upside down. Although the community is asked to rebuild the temple, the people are focusing their efforts on rebuilding their houses (1:2–11). The misplaced priorities resulted in negative consequences for their efforts and for nature (2:15–17), thus prompting questions about God's response to human behavior.

God's Presence. The affirmation of God's presence with God's people is one of the ways that hope is presented in the book of Haggai (1:13; 2:4–5). Affirmation of this sort appears intertextually in the Pentateuch (Gen 26:24; 28:15) and in the prophets (Jer 1:19; 15:20; 30:11; 42:11; 46:28). Even so, the book of Haggai poses theological challenges with regard to the manifestations of God's presence. The divine presence may be manifested in adversity. The futility is the people's efforts to achieve the desired outcomes of their labor (1:5–6; cf. Deut 28:1–3 vis-à-vis 28:15–30). The message is that God blesses the obedient and frustrates the efforts of the disobedient. Haggai's messages fit into this theme of retribution (Hag 1:7–11; 2:9, 14–19). The message does not distinguish between those in the community who were and were not obedient. Rather, it has a corporate view of the community in that the actions of some may determine the fate of all.

Competing Belief and Experiences. The book of Haggai affirms that God is with the people but also accommodates the idea of a localized presence—that God's presence will return when the temple is rebuilt. Was not God with the people when they were away from Jerusalem? While living in Babylon, the prophets assured the people that God was with them (Isa 41:10; 43:5; Jer 30:11; 42:11; 46:28). The tradition of the temple as God's dwelling place has two main facets. First, the temple is the place of God's localized presence in much the same way that God was present on Mount Sinai. Within this notion is the awareness that God's presence may be withheld or withdrawn. Thus, God's presence is not automatic. In Exod 32–33 God remained outside the camp in the tent of meeting lest God's presence consume the people. The nature of God's presence may be defined by the nature of the relationship between God and Israel. Thus, when Israel restores the temple, God will restore the blessings. The second tradition is seen in 1 Kgs 8:10–27, which both affirms and challenges the belief of the localized presence. God may choose to reside among the people, but God's presence is not limited to a physical structure or location.

God's Power. Trying to rebuild with relatively limited resources is no small task, especially if one's ambition far outpaces the resources. The affirmation to the people is that God owns the resources (Hag 2:6–8). The importance of this is that, despite how a situation appears—for example, the political power appears to have the resources—the reality is that God's power extends over the political and natural systems of the world (Hag 2:21–23). Even the most powerful forces from the human perspective are under God's control.

TEXT AND COMMENTARY

SUPERSCRIPTION (1:1)

[1]*In the second year of Darius the king, in the sixth month, on the first day of the month, the word of Yahweh came by the hand of Haggai the prophet to Zerubbabel son of Shealtiel, governor of Judah, and to Joshua son of Jehozadak, the high priest.*[a]

---

a. In the MT of Hag 1:1, *lēʾmōr* appears as the last element of the verse. The LXX adds "saying: speak . . .," while some other manuscripts add "indeed." The proposed LXX reading is most likely a harmonization of the text with 2:1, 10: *bəyad-ḥaggay hannābîʾ lēʾmōr*, "by the hand of Haggai the prophet saying." Verhoef (*Haggai and Malachi*, 51) argues that the LXX is not a variant reading but a "paraphrase in terms of 2:1." Cf. Kessler, *Haggai*, 103.

1 Superscriptions are typically located at the beginning of prophetic books, but each exhibits its own distinct form. A typical superscription provides the name of the prophet, designates the prophet's activity (with reference to the receipt of revelation and/or the intended recipient of the revelation), and situates the prophet's activity chronologically during the reigns of the kings of a particular period.[1] One form of superscription consists of the prophetic-word formula (*dəbar-yhwh*, "the word of Yahweh") plus a verbal clause (*ʾăšer hāyâ ʾel*, "that came to") plus the name of the prophet. This format with the relative particle is used to introduce both a prophetic book (Hos 1:1; Joel 1:1;

1. J. D. Nogalski, *Literary Precursors to the Book of the Twelve*, BZAW 217 (Berlin: de Gruyter, 1993), 76; S. M. Meier, *Speaking of Speaking: Marking Direct Discourse in the Hebrew Bible*, VTSup 46 (Leiden: Brill, 1992), 314; G. Tucker, "Prophetic Superscriptions and the Growth of a Canon," in *Canon and Authority: Essays in Old Testament Religion and Theology*, ed. George W. Coats and Burke O. Long (Philadelphia: Fortress, 1977), 56–70, esp. p. 62.

Mic 1:1; Zeph 1:1) and sections within a book (*'ăšer hāyâ dəbar-yhwh 'el*: Jer 14:1; 46:1; 47:1; 49:34).[2]

The formula also occurs with *wayəhî* in Jeremiah and Ezekiel when it introduces sections within the book without *'ăšer*; it sometimes includes *lē'mōr*, "saying"—*wayəhî dəbar-yhwh 'el* . . . ("the word of Yahweh came to . . . saying," Isa 38:4; Jer 32:26; 33:1, 19, 23; Ezek 3:16; cf. Jonah 1:1; 3:1). In other instances, the formula occurs as *hāyâ dəbar-yhwh 'el*, "the word of Yahweh came to" (Hag 2:10, 20; Zech 7:8; cf. without *lē'mōr*, Zech 1:7; 7:1).[3] Another form of the superscription does not use the prophetic-word formula and designates the revelation by use of other terminology: *dibrê*, "words" (Amos 1:1), *ḥăzôn*, "vision" (Isa 1:1; Obad 1:1), *maśśā'*, "oracle" (Hab 1:1; Nah 1:1; Mal 1:1).[4]

A third form of the superscription consists of the date formula plus the prophetic-word formula (Ezek 1:1; Hag 1:1; Zech 1:1). The combination of the elements and their function in their context has led some to designate them narrative introductions rather than superscriptions.[5] Apparently, the occurrence of various forms within a prophetic book is consistent within known patterns.

The superscription in Hag 1:1 (*In the second year of Darius the king, in the sixth month, on the first day of the month*) consists of a tripartite date formula, year + month + day (of the month), followed by an expanded prophetic-word formula. The date formulas in the book of Haggai reflect both the early preexilic and later postexilic forms of the formula. In Hag 1:1, the year + month + day pattern is reflective of the older pattern (see introduction, section II.A, above).

The second year is further qualified within Darius's reign. Although there is strong scholarly support for dating the reign to 522–486 BCE, the date of his reign is a subject of some question—in other words, whether or not the Babylonian system of postdating was used. While the majority reckon that 520 BCE would be the second year,[6] some propose 521–520 BCE, positing

2. Floyd, *Minor Prophets 2*, 643, 651.

3. In many instances the name of the prophet is replaced with the first-person pronominal suffix affixed to the preposition *'el*—*'ēlay*, "to me"—e.g., Jer 1:4, 11; 2:1; 13:8; 32:6; Ezek 3:16; 12:1; 24:15; 38:1; Zech 4:8; 6:9.

4. Floyd (*Minor Prophets 2*, 643) identifies one type that does not use the typical prophetic-word formula. There are also distinctions within this group: (a) construct phrase consisting of the terminology for the revelation plus the name of the prophet *dibrê*, "words of" (Amos 1:1; Jer 1:1) or *ḥăzôn*, "vision of" (Isa 1:1; Obad 1; Nah 1:1a); (b) non-construct phrase and use of *maśśā'* as the terminology for revelation (Hab 1:1; Zech 9:1; Nah 1:1a; Mal 1:1).

5. Floyd, *Minor Prophets 2*, 643, 319, 32.

6. For the 521–486/5 BCE date, see Meyers and Meyers, *Haggai, Zechariah 1–8*, 4; cf. Verhoef, *Haggai and Malachi*, 48; Floyd, *Minor Prophets 2*, 255.

that the antedating system was employed (nonuse of the accession year). Presumably, the concern of scholars who attempt to place the prophetic activity in 521 is their effort to depict Haggai as one "who was inciting Zerubbabel's rebellion against the Persian Empire."[7]

The biblical data mention Darius in the books of Ezra (4:5, 24; 5:5, 6, 7; 6:1, 14, 15), Nehemiah (12:22), Daniel (5:31; 6:1, 6, 9, 25, 28; 9:1; 11:1), Haggai (1:1, 15; 2:10), and Zechariah (1:1, 7; 7:1). Several variations in the designation appear in the biblical material, thus leading to questions about whether all of these references speak about the same person. The variations in the name include King Darius of Persia (Ezra 4:5, 24); Darius the Persian (Neh 12:22); and King Darius (Hag 1:1, 15; Zech 7:1; Ezra 5:6; 6:1, 13, 15; Dan 6:6, 9, 25). The Darius in Dan 9:1 appears to be a different person from the one mentioned elsewhere in the Old Testament; he is "Darius son of Ahasuerus, by birth a Mede, who became king over the realm of the Chaldeans" (Dan 9:1) and may be the predecessor of Cyrus (6:28 [MT 29]) as compared with Cyrus's successor and Artaxerxes's predecessor in Ezra (6:14).

In the Apocrypha, Darius appears in 1 Macc 1:1; 1 Esd 2:30; 3:1, 5, 7, 8; 4:47; 5:2, 6, 73; 6:1, 6, 7, 8, 23, 27, 34; 7:1, 4, 5. Of these, several designate him as king of the Persians (1 Macc 1:1; 1 Esd 2:30; 5:6); both Esdras texts identify the second year of his reign, including the resumption of work on the Jerusalem temple (1 Esd 2:30) and the identification of a group who gained the king's audience (1 Esd 5:6). Among those identified are Jeshua son of Jozadak and Joakim son of Zerubbabel son of Shealtiel.[8]

The absence of the epithet "king of Persia" with the name Darius in Haggai is variously interpreted, including suggestions about whether Darius's rule over Judah was accepted.[9] The variations in the designations may simply support the observation that Darius was widely known, thus making the epithet redundant. Likewise, to say that the absence of the epithet meant acceptance implies that, when the epithet is present, the identified king was not accepted. Consequently, one should be cautious in asserting the nature of the authority of Darius and the people's reception of his authority based on the epithet.

The expanded prophetic-word formula indicates the activity that took place in the specified time—*the word of Yahweh came.* The activity is fur-

7. Kessler, *Haggai,* 80.

8. Verhoef (*Haggai and Malachi,* 48) mentions the extrabiblical sources that attest Darius as king of Persia, namely: the Uruk King List from Kandalanu to Seleucus II and Receipt of Feudal Dues. Cf. *ANET,* 221, 566.

9. Contrast Kessler (*Haggai,* 115), who argues that the absence of the epithet implies the people's acceptance of Darius and his authority. He follows both Petersen (*Haggai and Zechariah 1–8,* 43) and Meyers and Meyers (*Haggai, Zechariah 1–8,* 5) in the use of this argument.

ther modified by specifying the mode of the activity, namely, *by the hand of Haggai,* plus an appositive designating Haggai as *hannābîʾ*, "the prophet," as the intermediary. The typical form of the word formula, *ʾel* plus name of the recipient or pronominal suffix, designates the recipient of the word (e.g., Gen 15:1, 4; 1 Sam 15:10; 2 Sam 24:11; 1 Kgs 6:11; 18:1; 21:28; 2 Chr 12:7; Isa 38:4; Jer 32:26; 33:1, 23; Zech 7:8; Jonah 3:1). The occurrences of the prophetic-word formula with *bəyad* (lit., by the hand of) in place of *ʾel* (to) is attested only in 1 Kgs 16:7 and Hag 1:1, 3; and 2:1. In these instances the formula *bəyad-. . .ʾel*, "by the hand of . . . to," designates the recipient of the word, and presupposes that the word came first to the prophet who then communicated it to the intended audience. When the prophetic word is directed first to the prophet, he is usually given instructions about what to do next (cf. Hag 2:10, 20).

Another expansion of the formula reveals the intended recipients of the *word of Yahweh,* namely, Zerubbabel[10] and Joshua, each with an appositive specifying his identity. In both cases the information about their lineage is given first, followed by their office. Zerubbabel, son of Shealtiel, is the governor of Judah (*paḥat yəhûdâ*); and Joshua, son of Jehozadak, is the high priest (*hakkōhēn haggādôl*; no regional identification is appended to the high priestly office in this case). Together, Zerubbabel and Joshua represent the political and religious leadership of Yehud (see table 2). Noticeably absent from the list of specified recipients are the people (cf. Hag 1:12, 14; 2:4). Haggai 1:1 confirms that the leadership of Yehud had changed since the loss of control to the Babylonians. The ruler of Yehud (520 BCE) is subject to the Persian king just like the other governors within the Empire. The contrast of this opening image and the last image of the book (Hag 2:20–23) exposes an irony. Who is in charge of Yehud? While the external reality is that the governor and his priest are the authorities in the restoration community, Hag 2 will show that they and the nations are subject to Yahweh, a higher authority. Yahweh not only controls all the nations and the foundation of existence but has selected Zerubbabel as an authority (cf. Hag 2:6–7; 21–23).

I. DISPUTATION SEQUENCE ABOUT BUILDING THE TEMPLE (1:2–15)

Haggai 1:2–15 focuses on building the temple and is delineated as a unit by the superscription (Hag 1:1) and date formula in 1:15. The messenger formula—"thus said Yahweh of hosts"—is followed by the direct speech signal

10. For further discussion of the historical context, *see* introduction, section II.

lēʾmōr, "saying." Haggai 1:2–11 is an extended disputation speech consisting of the competing arguments (1:2–4) and expanded argumentation (1:5–11). The unit Hag 1:12–15 identifies the repercussions of the disputation, including the prophetic claim about a change in the audience's behavior regarding the building of the temple.

A. DISPUTATION AND SUPPORTING EVIDENCE (1:2–11)

Consistent with the nature of disputation, the competing views form the basis of the encounter. Likewise, the presenting party represents one perspective (usually the Deity's) and depicts the competing perspective as a deviation from what should be. The text therefore posits a normative and a valid perspective, which may not be the same thing. The normative perspective often consists of attitudes and behavior patterns that are contrary to what God desires (cf. Mic 2:6–11; 6:2–8).[11] Conversely, the prophet is presented as being confident that the valid perspective should already be known and practiced by the people. This perspective often depends on traditions or history for its validity.

1. *The Competing Perspectives (1:2–4)*

2 *Thus says Yahweh of hosts: "This people says, 'The time has*[a] *not come, the time to build the house of Yahweh.'"*

3 *Then the word of Yahweh came by Haggai the prophet:* 4 *"Is it time for you yourselves to dwell in your roofed houses*[b] *while this house is desolate?"*

a. The repetition of *ʿet*, "time," in the MT has been a point of contention; the LXX's reading "The time has not yet come for rebuilding the house of the Lord" is shared by the Vulgate and Syriac.

b. The MT reading contains a series of second-person masculine-plural references that have been addressed in the versions (i.e., *lākem*, "for you," followed by the independent personal pronoun *ʾattem*, "you"). The LXX, targum, and Vulgate propose omitting the pronominal suffix, thus reading *bəbāttîm* ("in houses") in place of *bəbāttêkem* ("in your houses"), presumably because of its proximity to *ʾattem*, "you," or because of its redundancy when translated into other languages. The presence of the pronominal suffix in the MT (*bəbāttêkem*, "in your houses") may be viewed in contrast to the demonstrative *habbayit hazzê*, "this house," as illustrating the difference between the people's houses and Yahweh's house. Cf. Meyers and Meyers, *Haggai, Zechariah 1–8*, 23; H. W. Wolff, *Haggai*, 30; Verhoef, *Haggai and Malachi*, 44 n. 3; Kessler, *Haggai*, 104–5 nn. 8–9

11. Jacobs, *Conceptual Coherence*.

2 The messenger formula *Thus says Yahweh of hosts* is used in prophetic literature to identify the content of a speech as a quotation of the actual message given to the prophet by Yahweh and communicated to the recipients by the prophet.[12] Its occurrence elsewhere in the Old Testament confirms this use of the formula (e.g., Gen 32:4; 45:9; 2 Kgs 18:29; Num 22:16).[13] The basic form is followed by *lēʾmōr*, "saying." The formula is expanded by the epithet *ṣəbāʾôt*, "of hosts," and appears with the messenger formula throughout Haggai (1:2, 5, 7; 2:6, 11) and with the divine-utterance formula *oracle of Yahweh* (*nəʾum-yhwh*) in Hag 1:9; 2:4, 8, 9, 23; cf. 2:14. The frequency of the messenger formula indicates that what the speaker is saying is from Yahweh, regardless of how it is heard or how it affects the recipients.

Several suggestions regarding the significance of "thus says Yahweh of hosts" have been outlined and discussed by various scholars and will simply be mentioned here.[14] The epithet *Yahweh of hosts* (*yhwh ṣəbāʾôt*) may function in ways that are typical of its usage elsewhere. In general, the epithet is indicative of ideology regarding the divine presence and the cult. It usually highlights Yahweh's power in the preexilic tradition, where "the enthronement of Yahweh in Jerusalem was linked to the royal ideology of the Davidic dynasty."[15]

During the exilic period, as represented in the book of Ezekiel, the epithet "Yahweh of hosts" was largely unused, being replaced by the *kābôd*, "glory," that left the temple and the city and subsequently returned (Ezek 10:4, 18; 43:4–5; 44:4). Other examples of *kābôd* reflect ideas about the divine presence, especially in relation to guidance out of Egypt (Exod 16:10; 24:16, 17) and the tabernacle and tent of meeting (Exod 40:34, 35; Lev 9:6, 23; Num 14:10; 16:19, 42; 2 Chr 7:1–3). While there are notable patterns of occurrences, there are also instances that fall outside the pattern. Apparently, the preexilic notion of God's presence was reconceptualized in the postexilic community to signify the universality of Yahweh's reign. It also reclaimed the idea of the Deity's power despite the challenging political situation and recent history.[16]

12. Floyd, *Minor Prophets 2*, 650; C. Westermann, *Basic Forms of Prophetic Speech*, trans. H. C. White (Louisville: John Knox, 1991), 93–95.

13. Floyd, *Minor Prophets 2*, 650.

14. Meyers and Meyers (*Haggai, Zechariah 1–8*, 18–19) summarize the data regarding the occurrences of *ṣəbāʾôt* as presented in T. N. D. Mettinger, *The Dethronement of Sabaoth: Studies in the Shem and Kabod Theologies*, Coniectanea Biblica: Old Testament 18 (Lund: Gleerup, 1982).

15. Meyers and Meyers, *Haggai, Zechariah 1–8*, 19.

16. Kessler, *Haggai*, 122. Haggai's and Malachi's use of the epithet is consistent with the cultic connections as seen in the use of the epithet with Shiloh (1 Sam 1:3, 11) and the enthronement of Yahweh between the cherubim and in the temple in Jerusalem (1 Sam 4:4; Ps 48:8 [MT 9]).

a. The People's Perspective (1:2)

Using the narrative note *this people says,* the disputation begins with a citation of the people's views on the matter of rebuilding the temple. The people (*hāʿām-hazzê*) are not mentioned in Hag 1:1 as recipients of the message but are identified elsewhere in at least four ways: the remnant, Hag 1:12, 14 (*kōl šəʾērît hāʿām*) and 2:2 (*šəʾērît hāʿām*); people of the land, 2:4 (*kol-ʿam hāʾāreṣ*); people/nation, 2:14 (*hāʿām-hazzê wəkēn-haggôy hazzê*); and by the second masculine plural pronominal suffix "in their houses" (*bəbāttêkem,* 1:4). In the present text, the reference to "this people" (*hāʿām-hazzê*) may include the whole extent of the community and connote the quality of the relationship between the people and God. Usually "this people" is used of the entire community in whatever configuration that community exists (2 Sam 16:18; 1 Kgs 12:6, 9, 27; 14:2). In the book of Haggai, the designation "this people" most likely reflects the community rather than a particular segment of the community—for example, the returnees and the people of the land as two distinctive segments, or any other ethnic, religious, or sociopolitical grouping.[17] This is not a denial that the restoration community consisted of various groups but, rather, an assertion that the present designation may encompass all the groupings rather than attempt to isolate any one of them as the focal point of God's displeasure.

Throughout the Old Testament the designation *hāʿām-hazzê*, "this people," is variously used to identify the people of Israel. In many instances, the designation appears as a neutral or favorable reference without indicating tension between the people and the speaker (Exod 5:23 vis-à-vis Exod 17:4; 32:21, 31; 33:12; Num 11:11; 14:15; Deut 31:7; Josh 1:2; 7:7). In other instances, when used of the relationship between God and the people, the reference usually connotes a strained relationship, in response to which God is displeased. Outside the prophetic literature, there are numerous examples of this strained relationship (Exod 32:9; Deut 5:28; 9:13, 27; 31:16). Within the prophetic literature, the strained relationship between the people and the prophet is also indicated by use of "this people" (Isa 6:9–10; 8:6, 11–12; 28:14); however, when the speaker refers to the people who are being mistreated, the usual designation is "my people."[18] The usage here in Hag 1:2 at least suggests a strained relationship, and additional tension may be suggested by the people's competing agenda versus Yahweh's.[19]

The fact that the specified recipients are the leaders Zerubbabel and

17. Meyers and Meyers, *Haggai, Zechariah 1–8,* 19; Kessler, *Haggai,* 123.

18. Notable examples supporting this observation include Isa 3:15; 10:2; 40:1; Jer 8:11; 23:2 (cf. Exod 3:7; 5:1).

19. Verhoef, *Haggai and Malachi,* 54; Kessler, *Haggai,* 123.

Joshua (the people are not mentioned as recipients) has led to the idea that the leaders are being addressed about the people.[20] Usually the addressees in a disputation are the ones whose perspectives are being challenged (e.g., Mic 2:6–11; 6:2–8; Mal 2:1). The third-person form of the verb in Hag 1:2, *ʾāmərû*, "they say," introduces an alternative perspective; however, the second-person reference in Hag 1:4 is in confrontation with the addressees. The opposition to rebuilding the temple generates ideas among interpreters about religious factions in the community. These ideas stem in part from the nature of the opposition. One suggestion is that the opposing parties are the returnees and the people of the land.[21] Presumably, the returnees came back with a passion for rebuilding, while the people of the land were apathetic to the idea. Another suggestion is that the factions split along theological lines, and the prophet attempted to mediate between them by showing the significance of rebuilding the temple. The parties involved are variously interpreted: the priestly group versus the pro-Ezekiel group or the pro-Ezekiel group versus the pro-Deutero-Isaiah group.[22] One cannot deny that there were factions within the community; but whatever factions existed, they did not provide a basis for the focus in Hag 1:2. The proverbial "they" ("they say that. . .") represents the collective community—even if there were those who "said otherwise."

Although this verse comprises some textual challenges, the variant readings do not affect the nuance of the text. *The time has not come* identifies the perspective of the people (*hāʿām*), which will be challenged by God as a misconstrued perspective. The text first cites the perspective and then provides an explanation for it. The reference to *ʿet*, "time," may connote the time frame for a particular act. Here, it suggests the appropriateness of the time for a specific behavior. Some have argued that it could refer to the time of year, thus indicating that it was not an appropriate time for undertaking a building project. The inappropriateness of the time might cause a lack of work force for the construction.[23] The claim by itself does not reveal the nature of the inappropriateness. The formulation appears in Gen 29:7 (*lōʾ-ʿēt*, "not time") and suggests that timing may determine the appropriateness of an activity.

20. Kessler, *Haggai*, 123.

21. O. H. Steck, "Zu Haggai 1:2–11," *ZAW* 83 (1971): 375–76.

22. Kessler, *Haggai*, 123–24; J. Kessler, "*ʿt* (le temps) en Aggée I 2–4: Conflict théologique ou 'sagesse mondaine'?" *VT* 48 (1998): 555–59. Kessler also discusses R. G. Hamerton-Kelly, "The Temple and the Origins of Jewish Apocalyptic," *VT* 20 (1970): 1–15; P. D. Hanson, *The Dawn of Apocalyptic* (Philadelphia: Fortress, 1975), 225; H. W. Wolff, *Haggai*, 41. There are two groups that are divided by their views regarding the situation of the temple relative to the messianic age: (1) the temple is a prerequisite to the messianic age, and (2) the messianic age is a necessary condition for rebuilding the temple.

23. Thus Verhoef, *Haggai and Malachi*, 55–56; see Redditt (*Haggai, Zechariah, Malachi*, 18–19) on the lack of resources for the building project (monetary and work force).

By analogy, the people's objection in Haggai may not be to the building itself but to the timing of the building efforts.

The theological aspect of the claim should also be considered, given the people's experience of exile. Note the appearance in some of the Psalms of an "appointed time" or a time ripe for an event (Pss 102:13 [MT 14]; 119:126; cf. Hos 10:12; Sir 4:31). Another suggestion is that "time" has a theological or eschatological dimension, thus referring to the accumulation of factors leading to a particular event, such as the return from exile, as prophesied by Jeremiah. In this interpretation, the people may have been challenging the traditional perspective and claiming that, even though they had returned, the fulfillment of the prophecy had been deferred.[24] The reason for this thinking may have been their perceived needs versus the suggested priority of building the temple.

The interpretive aspects of "time" may be present in the delineation of God's actions toward the people, thus revealing that God has already been prompting them to see the significance of the building efforts. All the adversities are then interpreted as the result of God's attempt to reform their perspectives and their ways. Does the text represent a sequential relationship between what the people say and God's response? Insofar as the text represents the people's fostered conviction—not necessarily as a speech event with beginning and end but an ideology that informs their behavior—it presents a sequential relationship between this inner ideology and God's response. Likewise, the response from God is depicted as a continuous response in the people's lives with the single intent to confound and deplete their resources. Ironically, the depleted resources are those needed to rebuild the temple. By building their own houses, they have falsified their claim that it is not time to build Yahweh's house. Consequently, the depleted resources will verify their claim by bringing about the very conditions that merit the conviction.

It may be argued that the people's perspective reflects the influence of wisdom traditions regarding the discernment of appropriate times. Before we look at the biblical support for this assertion, let me note that recognizing connections to the sapiential tradition does not necessitate a textual emendation.[25] Kessler uses both grammatical and substantive arguments to support his assertion that the theological argument does not fit the current context.

24. Meyers and Meyers, *Haggai, Zechariah 1–8*, 19–21; see Kessler (*Haggai*, 123) and his citation of his previous work on the subject; Kessler, "*ʿt* (le temps)," 555–59. This includes a survey of the perspectives on the interpretation of *ʿet*. Verhoef, *Haggai and Malachi*, 55–56; Petersen, *Haggai and Zechariah 1–8*, 47.

25. Contrast Kessler, *Haggai*, 103–4, 126; Barthélemy, *Ezékiel, Daniel et les 12 prophètes*, 924.

Rather, as argued above, the context suggests people who used the wisdom tradition to support their behavior.[26]

Notably, one finds the construction *ʿet* plus the infinitive construct used to talk about appropriate times for specific actions/events—e.g., *ʿēt lāmût*, "a time to die"; *ʿēt lirpôʾ*, "a time to heal" (Eccl 3:1–8). These reflect the larger perspective of Eccl 8:4–8 (esp. v. 6): "For every matter has its time and way, although the troubles of mortals lie heavy upon them."[27] Within this wisdom perspective, there are times appointed by Yahweh for certain events such as punishment (Jer 46:21; 50:27, 31).[28] When adopted as a frame of reference for understanding *ʿet*, the theological perspective usually comprises the fulfillment of an appointed time or the conditions appropriate for a specific event. Although some texts use chronological indicators to signal the description of an eschatological period—*wəhāyâ bəʾaḥărît hayyāmîm*, "in the latter days," or some other variation (Isa 2:2; 27:6; Mic 4:1; Jer 49:39; Ezek 38:16); *bayyôm hahûʾ*, "in that day" (Isa 2:11; Mic 4:6; 5:10; Joel 3:18)—we find other eschatological texts without these chronological indicators (e.g., Isa 23:17; Jer 25:11–12; 29:10; Dan 9:2).[29]

The seventy-year period of exile was depicted as a set time frame in which Yahweh would act. Some therefore interpret Hag 1:2 as indicating the fulfillment of that time frame; and that fulfillment constitutes the necessity of rebuilding the temple. If we take the beginning of the seventy-year period as the destruction of the temple in 587/6 BCE, the end of the appointed period would be about 517 BCE.[30] Haggai's prophecy, dated to about 521/20 BCE, would then anticipate that fulfillment. Likewise, signs would accompany the appointed time—for example, the subjugation of Babylon and presence of blessings (Jer 25:11–14; 29:10; cf. Mic 4:1–4; Isa 2:1–4).[31] If the presence of

26. Kessler, *Haggai*, 127.

27. Meyers and Meyers (*Haggai, Zechariah 1–8*, 19–20) argue for an interpretation of the *ʿet* phrase as an infinitive construct, citing Lev 14:48; 1 Sam 9:6; Jer 36:29; Ps 126:6; Dan 11:10, 13; and 2 Chr 25:8 as precedents. They do not discuss the influence of the use of the formulation in wisdom literature. On the other hand, Kessler's (*Haggai*, 125–26) understanding of the phrase corresponds with its use in the wisdom tradition. Fox (*A Time to Tear Down*, 194–209, 278–79) identifies two types of time, temporal and substantive. He notes that, while the text speaks of the right time for a particular event, *ʿet* does not have the connotation of "appointed time" that is usually conveyed by *ʿittîm məzummānîm* (Ezra 10:14; Neh 10:35; Fox, *A Time to Tear Down*, 198 n. 12).

28. Cf. Kessler, *Haggai*, 125.

29. DeVries, *From Old Revelation*, 52–55.

30. Cf. Meyers and Meyers, *Haggai, Zechariah 1–8*, 20.

31. P. R. Bedford ("Discerning the Time: Haggai, Zechariah and the Delay in the Rebuilding of the Jerusalem Temple," in *The Pitcher Is Broken: Memorial Essays for Gösta W. Ahlström*, ed. S. W. Holloway and L. K. Handy, JSOTSup 190 [Sheffield: Sheffield Academic, 1995], 84) argues that blessings and the reestablishment of the divine reign would also have been signs to the people of the time to rebuild.

blessings is a prerequisite for the rebuilding efforts, then the people (as depicted in the book of Haggai) are justified in believing that the time is inappropriate for rebuilding. The drought and the futile attempts to benefit from the product of their labor are contraindications of the inauguration of the eschatological age. However, Haggai's reasoning counters and illuminates the people's perspective (Hag 1:5–11). Whether the people base their thinking on theological notions of the appointed time or not, their dominating conviction that "it is not time" stems from a more practical core.

Their contention is that it is not *time for rebuilding*. The very act of building presupposes that one already knows what is to be built and how. Their conviction shows that, to the extent that they are aware of the task ahead, they have assessed it and deemed it impossible for this point in time. The task is "to build" (*bānâ*) the house of Yahweh, not to repair the previous structure.[32] Likewise, given the administrative function of the temple in the life of the community, the idea of building a temple takes on added importance, including the establishment of an administrative center.[33] The task of building the city (*ʿîrî*, lit., "my city") was given to Cyrus (Isa 45:13) and the walls of the city to foreigners (Isa 60:10). In the case of Isa 45:13, the physical tasks were not assigned to Cyrus himself, but he would provide the opportunity for the city to be built. His 538 BCE decree undergirded the rebuilding efforts in the form of financial and political resources for the task.

In Isa 61:4 a triple representation of restoration is composed using several verbs plus their corresponding objects—*bānâ*, "build" + *ḥārəbôt ʿôlām*, "ancient ruins"; *qûm*, "raising up" + *šōməmôt riʾšōnîm*, "former devastations"; and *ḥādaš*, "renewing / repairing," + *ʿārê ḥoreb*, "desolate cities"—all of which create the imagery of transformation from ruin. Another aspect of the conviction to build appears in Jer 29:28, where the people are commanded to build their houses in Babylon. Additionally, Ezekiel is told to prophesy against a group of men who were advising the people not to build houses, presumably because of the inappropriateness of the time (*lōʾ bəqārôb bənôt bāttîm*, lit., "the building of houses is not near," Ezek 11:3). In Ezek 11:3, the people are introduced to the idea of building by their leaders, and the leaders are punished for the bad advice.

The conviction of the community is that it is not yet time to build *the house of Yahweh*. The Old Testament uses many designations for the temple, two of which occur in the book of Haggai: "house of Yahweh" (*bêt yhwh*, 1:2) and "this house" (*habbayit hazzê*, 1:4, 9). *Bêt yhwh* is a common designation (2 Chr 7:2; Isa 2:2; Jer 7:2, 19:14; 26:2; 27:16; 28:3; 36:6, 8, 10, 51:51; Mic 4:1), along with "the Temple of Yahweh" (*hêkal yhwh*; e.g., 1 Sam 1:9; 3:3; 2 Kgs

32. Cf. H. W. Wolff, *Haggai*, 42.

33. Cf. Meyers and Meyers, *Haggai, Zechariah 1–8*, 22–23.

18:16; 23:4; 2 Chr 27:2; Ezra 3:6, 10; Jer 7:4; 24:1; Ezek 8:16; 44:5; Zech 6:12, 13, 14, 15).[34] The temple is also designated "house of God" (*bêt-hā'ĕlōhîm*; e.g., Judg 18:31; 1 Chr 28:21; 2 Chr 3:3; 5:1; Dan 1:2; 5:3), which is the dominant reference throughout Ezra–Nehemiah (e.g., Ezra 3:8, 9; Aramaic, 5:2, 13, 14; Neh 6:10; 8:16; 11:11; 12:40; 13:7, 9). In some references, Yahweh is present with the appositive "your God": "house of Yahweh your [sing.] God" (*bêt yhwh 'ĕlōhêkā*, Exod 23:19; 34:26; Deut 23:18; 1 Chr 22:11; in Joel 1:14, *bêt yhwh 'ĕlōhêkem* [pl.]).

In the ideology of Israel, the house of Yahweh usually signified a localized presence of the Deity; it was where Yahweh lived. In the prophetic literature, this idea of the Deity's localized presence is also manifested in the people's belief that blessings accompany the divine presence (Mic 3:11). A competing perspective in the book of Haggai follows the exodus tradition, that the temple is not a prerequisite for the manifestation of the divine presence (cf. Hag 2:5 below).

b. Counterperspective (1:3–4)

3 The repetition of the prophetic-word formula (*the word of Yahweh came*) in 1:3 signals the beginning of a counterclaim to the people's perspective. Its presence emphasizes the fact that, while Haggai is communicator of the message, he speaks Yahweh's words.[35] This emphasis legitimates the prophet as one whose alliance is defined and determined by his role in God's revelation rather than by conforming to any external pressures from factions within the society.

4 Haggai 1:4 begins the counterclaim to the people's perspective with a question challenging the appropriateness of the time. On the one hand, they say that it is not time. This is their conviction and the grounds upon which they base their behavior—that is, their ways (cf. Hag 1:5, 7). The interrogative calls this conviction into question and thus suggests that there is a misunderstanding about the "time" for the activity that they have not undertaken. This also raises questions about the addressees: Are they already living in their houses? Who are they? Are they some of the returnees, who have built houses since their return, sometime between 538 and 521/20 BCE? Or are they a group of the non-deportees, "people of the land," who during their

34. Note additional reference to the temple of God in the Old Testament, including Mal 3:1. In the Apocrypha several references to the temple of God occur: Tob 14:4, 5; 1 Esd 1:2, 49; 2:7; 5:44, 53, 56, 57, 58; cf. Jdt 4:2; Wis 3:14. See New Testament references to the temple of God, including Matt 26:61; 2 Cor 6:16; 2 Thess 2:4; Rev 11:1.

35. Baldwin, *Hag, Zech, Mal,* 40; note here the use of the formula as anticlimactic, in a place where one would expect a response to the people's perspective.

time in the land, following the destruction, built houses and since then have been occupying them?[36]

The contrast is set up between their houses and Yahweh's, suggesting that, while they say it is not time to build, they have been building. Since they built what they deemed necessary, it is not the action of building itself to which they objected. This contrast will be seen again regarding the availability of resources. The people may not have the resources, but God has them all—the silver and the gold (Hag 2:8; cf. Ps 24:1–2). In Hag 1:4 the contrast illustrates the people's priority and is emphasized by the repetition of the second-person pronominal references (*lākem*, "you"; *ʾattem*, "you"; *bəbāttêkem*, "in your houses").

Here in Hag 1:4, however, the deemphasis on Yahweh in the people's priorities can also be seen in the reference to the temple as "this house" (*habbayit hazzê*)[37] instead of "Yahweh's house" (*bêt yhwh*) in Hag 1:2. So in 1:2 the people are convinced not to build Yahweh's house; in 1:4 the house is not identified as Yahweh's—neither by using a genitival relationship nor by use of the third-person pronominal suffix, "his house" (*bêtô*),[38] nor even using a first-person suffix, "my house" (*bêtî*),[39] which might be expected in direct speech that compares it with "your houses" (*bāttêkem*). The use of the first-person referent (*bêtî*) in contrasting the temple and the people's houses is also present in Hag 1:9.

Returning to the discussion of what is being contrasted: it is noteworthy that building multiple houses took time, commitment to the goal, the planning, and the execution of the plan. The people's effort and the outcome of that effort are presupposed by the existence of inhabitable houses. The contrast therefore illustrates ongoing commitment to one project and ongoing neglect of the other. The question in Hag 1:4 likewise suggests that, if it is not time to rebuild Yahweh's house, then it is also not time to inhabit theirs, because the conditions determining the appropriateness of the time apply to both.[40]

36. Cf. H. W. Wolff, *Haggai,* 42.

37. Notably, other references to the temple use the designation "this house," even in first-person speech (e.g., 1 Kgs 6:12; 8:27, 29, 31, 33, 38, 42, 43; 9:3, 8 [and the 2 Chr parallels]; 2 Kgs 21:7; Ezra 3:12; 5:3, 9, 13, 17; 6:12, 15. A variation of the reference is "this house of God" in Ezra 5:13, 17; 6:7, 8; 1 Esd 6:2, 7, 12, 16, 17; 7:24—"this house of the Lord."

38. Cf. Hag 1:9, *bêtî.* There is no reference to the temple using this noun + third-person-singular suffix, "his house," in which Yahweh is the referent of the pronominal suffix. There are references in the Apocrypha that mirror the construction (Tob 13:16; 1 Esd 8:25).

39. Other examples of *bêtî* used to refer to the temple: Hos 9:15; Jer 23:11; Ezek 23:39 (the people profaned the temple); Zech 1:16 (promise to build the temple); Zech 3:7; 9:8; Mal 3:10; cf. Ps 101:7.

40. Kessler (*Haggai,* 130) sees the people's conviction as a misuse of wisdom to support an unwise course of action.

The comparison of the people's and Yahweh's circumstances is further illustrated by use of the terms to describe their houses: the people's houses are "*roofed, paneled*" (*səpûnîm*),[41] and Yahweh's house is "desolate" (*ḥārēb*).[42] The availability of resources is presupposed by the fact that the people's houses are built and covered. There is much discussion about the term *səpûnîm* (*qal* passive participle in the masculine plural) derived from *sāpan*, "cover, cover in, panel." The term occurs as a noun, *sippun*, meaning "ceiling" (1 Kgs 6:15), as well as in several verbal forms.[43]

Many scholars translate *səpûnîm* in Hag 1:4 as "paneled" and associate that translation with luxury.[44] In these instances the paneling is believed to be refined or expensive wood associated with the temple or palaces (cf. 1 Kgs 6:9; 7:3, 7; Jer 22:14). Other scholars translate *səpûnîm* as "covered, roofed," noting the argument in Haggai as a decisive reason for their translation.[45] Wolff argues that cedar was the type of wood needed for the structural elements of the temple and palaces and does not in itself denote luxury.[46] Perhaps the dominant imagery in the context of Hag 1:4 is the relative completeness of the houses, thus favoring "roofed" as the translation but reserving the idea of luxury as a possible nuance of the argument.

The contrast is most likely between finished houses ready to be occupied and an unfinished house not yet constructed: *this house is desolate*. The unfinished nature is especially a concern because it is not a work in progress but a neglected work. Whatever the full range of its meaning, in the book of Haggai *ḥārēb*, "desolate," presumes the dismantled temple structure. Regarding the use of the term *ḥārēb*, Kessler supports the idea that the comparison is more than just the relative state of completion.[47] Without duplicating all his data,

41. The verbal form *sāpan*, "to cover," occurs in 1 Kgs 6:9; 7:3, 7, denoting the action of roofing one's house with cedar (*'erez*). Cf. Jer 22:14.

42. H. W. Wolff (*Haggai*, 42) favors the idea of "the final state of ruin."

43. Imperfect in 1 Kgs 6:9; infinitive absolute in Jer 22:14, usually translated "paneling with cedar," and the passive form of the participle (1 Kgs 7:3, 7).

44. Even some of those who translate the term "paneled" make distinctions in their use of the term. Kessler (*Haggai*, 104) uses "paneled" in his translation but argues for "roofed" as a better meaning for 1:4; cf. Verhoef, *Haggai and Malachi*, 43, 58–59. While Kessler uses "paneled" in his translation, he also argues that in the context of Haggai the term may be translated both "paneled" and "roofed." Redditt (*Haggai, Zechariah, Malachi*, 19) mentions "paneled" as an option as well as the alternative "roofed" houses. Brown (*Obadiah through Malachi*, 123) observes that the people were using the paneling intended for the temple to build their own houses. Modern translations tend to translate *səpûnîm* "paneled," e.g., NRSV and NIV 1 Kgs 7:7, "covered with cedar."

45. Meyers and Meyers, *Haggai, Zechariah 1–8*, 24. Baldwin, *Hag, Zech, Mal*, 40. Kessler (*Haggai*, 104) and Verhoef (*Haggai and Malachi*, 58–59) argue both sides.

46. H. W. Wolff, *Haggai*, 42.

47. Kessler, *Haggai*, 128–29.

we may summarize his view as follows: if relative completion of the structures were what the text was attempting to portray, several terms might have been used, including *nātaṣ*, "pull/break down" (Jer 4:26; 33:4; Ezek 16:39; Exod 34:13; Deut 7:5); *hālam*, "hammer, smite" (Ps 74:6); *pāraṣ*, "break through/down" (Neh 1:3; 2:13; 2 Chr 25:23; Isa 5:5); *hāras*, "throw down, break or tear down" (Ezek 30:4; 36:35; Jer 50:15).[48] In short, Kessler seeks to show that *ḥārēb* is a deliberate choice to convey a particular nuance—that of desolation.

Visually, the contrast would be inescapable, similar to seeing a demolished lot surrounded by new developments. The term *ḥārēb* is well attested in the Old Testament. A synonym is *šəmāmâ*, "desolate," used about the land and the cities as being uninhabited, burned, abandoned (e.g., Isa 1:7; 6:11; 17:9; Jer 4:27; 32:43; 33:10; Ezek 12:20; 33:28; Zeph 1:13). Similarly, *ḥārēb* and its synonym *šāmēm* are used to characterize the abandoned status of Jerusalem (e.g., Jer 26:9; 33:10; 51:62). The visual contrast is thus of relatively new houses against a backdrop of decades of rubble. Interpreting the finished houses as having been built subsequent to the return to the land (approximately 538–520 BCE) maintains the contrast; however, one cannot dismiss the suggestion that these were the non-deportees' homes,[49] which could have been built any time between 586 and 520 BCE. This latter interpretation would somewhat diminish the question of the meaning of *ḥārēb,* since the non-deportees' homes were finished as a prerequisite for occupation.

In the people's cultic ideology, the localized presence of the Deity persisted, and the temple was thus perceived as the Deity's residence. This raised additional questions about *yāšab* ("to sit or dwell") in relation to the houses. The crucial question was therefore not about building the people's houses but about inhabiting them while Yahweh's house was uninhabitable/nonexistent. A discernible progression of the argument of the dispute is achieved by juxtaposing the competing perspectives. On the one hand, the people, for whatever reason, are convinced of the inappropriateness of the time for building Yahweh's house (Hag 1:2). On the other hand, they have already built their own houses. While their hesitation to build Yahweh's house may be connected to their theological ideology about the seventy-year return, the condition of their houses reveals that there is quite a difference between their beginning a project and their enjoying the product of their labor—that is, committed sustained activity. There is sustained activity on both sides: their *work* of constructing houses vs. their *hesitation* about beginning the construction of the temple. The current state of *ḥārēb* is the result of the destruction and the decades of neglect.[50]

48. Kessler, *Haggai,* 128–29.

49. H. W. Wolff, *Haggai,* 42.

50. Carroll, "Myth of the Empty Land."

2. *The Supporting Evidence for Yahweh's Perspective (1:5–11)*

5 *So now thus says Yahweh of hosts: "Reflect on your ways!* 6 *You have sown much but reap little. You eat but never are satisfied. You drink but are never drunk. You wear clothes but are never warm; and the one who hires out himself*[a] *earns wages into a bundle with holes."*

7 *Thus says Yahweh of hosts: "Reflect on your ways.*[b] 8 *Go up the hills and bring wood and build the house so that I may take pleasure in it; and I will be honored," says Yahweh.* 9 *"You look for much but, behold,*[c] *there is little. You brought it to the house and I blew it away. Why?"—oracle of Yahweh of hosts—"Because my house is desolate while you are hurrying off to your own house.* 10 *Therefore, because of you,*[d] *the heavens*[e] *have withheld dew*[f] *and the earth withheld its yield.* 11 *And I called drought upon the land and upon the hills, and upon the grain and upon the new wine and upon the oil*[g] *and upon whatever the ground produces;*[h] *and upon human being and animal, and all hard labor."*

---

a. The juxtaposition of the *hithpael* participial forms of *śākar,* "to hire," leads two manuscripts to propose the finite verb *yiśtakkēr, hithpael* imperfect third person masculine singular of *śākar,* to replace the MT *miśtakkēr,* "the hired person, wage earner." The LXX has a finite verb, most likely to facilitate the reading "and he that earns wages has gathered." Some scholars propose an emendation by viewing the second *miśtakkēr* as dittography and deleting it to harmonize the pattern within the verse. Cf. Meyers and Meyers, *Haggai, Zechariah 1–8,* 26.

b. The issue is the place of the exhortation *śîmû ləbabkem ʿal-darkêkem.* The transposition or deletion is unnecessary.

c. The MT's reading *wəhinnê,* "and look," does not pose a difficulty in understanding the text. Nonetheless, the LXX emends the text to "and it was," assuming *wəhāyâ* or *wəhāyō.* This emendation is reflected in the versions—Peshitta and targum—as well as modern scholarship. Thus, Meyers and Meyers (*Haggai, Zechariah 1–8,* 3, 29) propose the infinitive absolute *wəhāyō,* "and/but there is," in place of *wəhinnê.* Others follow the MT "and look," e.g., Kessler, *Haggai,* 106 n. 21; Verhoef, *Haggai and Malachi,* 69.

d. A few options have been suggested for addressing the MT phrase *ʿal-kēn ʿălêkem.* First, with reference to the reading itself, the LXX omits *ʿălêkem,* "because of you," as possible dittography with the adjacent term, *ʿal-kēn,* "therefore." The targum and Murabbaʿat support the MT. Second, a few options are also available for translating the text. Meyers and Meyers (*Haggai, Zechariah 1–8,* 30) retain the MT and translate *ʿal-kēn,* "therefore," noting that the context allows for *ʿălêkem* to be translated "because of you" or "against you." Verhoef (*Haggai and Malachi,* 73) denies that "against you" is a viable translation of *ʿălêkem* in this context. Kessler (*Haggai,* 106 n. 24) notes that the MT may be a "Deuteronomism inspired by Deut 28:23" and, like the Vulgate, translates *ʿălêkem* as "above you" and the entire phrase as "for this reason, the skies above you." Cf. NRSV.

e. The MT *šāmayim* has been emended in a Hebrew manuscript to read *haššāmayim.* The emendation is most likely a facilitated reading to create consistency with the use of the definite article later in the verse—that is, *wəhāʾāreṣ,* "and the earth." Meyers and Meyers (*Haggai, Zechariah 1–8,* 31, 33) attribute the absence of the definite article on *šāmayim* to a deliberate omission to establish contrast between the cause (heaven's withholding dew) and the effect (the earth's withholding produce). The earth and all its associated elements are identified with the definite article. Furthermore, the last item of the series also omits the definite article. The latter omission is explained as a device to signal the last item as a summary element, in contrast to being one more item on the list.

f. The MT's use of *min*, "from," in the clause *kālə'û šāmayim miṭṭāl* is variously interpreted. One option that *BHS* identifies is the emendation *ṭālām*, "their dew" (noun + suffix), in place of *miṭṭāl* (lit., "from dew," preposition + noun). This involves deleting the preposition and adding the third-person masculine-plural pronominal suffix to *ṭal*, "dew." The resulting reading makes "heavens" the antecedent of the suffix and creates a parallelism with the pronominal suffix on *yəbûlâ*, "its yield" (noun + suffix), earth being the antecedent of the suffix. In this instance, the emendation avoids the use of *min* and the sense of depriving an entity of something. Thus, Kessler (*Haggai*, 106 n. 25) proposes that the pronominal suffix on *yəbûl* is doing double duty and is implied with *ṭal*. He does not, however, account for the preposition in his translation. At issue is the understanding of the preposition *min* in relation to the verb *kālā'*, "to withhold," which typically appears with *min* and would suggest that the heavens withheld something from dew. A second alternative, also identified by *BHS*, is the emendation of the text to *māṭār*, "rain" (e.g., targum). For Verhoef (*Haggai and Malachi*, 73) the emendations are unnecessary, since there are viable uses of *min* that fit this context—the explicative *min*, usually translated "namely." Cf. Gen 7:22; GKC §119w, n. 2—the Arabic *min el-beyan*. Meyers and Meyers (*Haggai, Zechariah 1–8*, 31) retain the MT and reflect their understanding of *min* as a partitive governing both *ṭal* and *yəbûlâ* and showing a partial rather than a total drought—"the heavens have withheld the dew in part and the earth has withheld some of its yield."

g. *BHS* identifies *wə'al-hayyiṣhār*, "and upon the oil," as a possible addition. The term *ḥōreb* is emended in some of the versions, and thus the LXX and Syriac read "sword," assuming *ḥereb*.

h. Several manuscripts add *kol*, "all," before the term *tôṣî'*, "to go/come forth," indicating the totality of the yield and perhaps to connect with the last clause of the verse where *kol* occurs. While it might appear that the extent of the drought is being highlighted, the addition of *kol* is unnecessary for an understanding of the text. Cf. Kessler, *Haggai*, 106 n. 29. Contrast Verhoef (*Haggai and Malachi*, 76–77), who proposes including *kol* to denote the extent of the drought. It has been argued that the absence of *kol* after *'al* may be accounted for by haplography, or else the final element of the verse is meant to be encompassing—i.e., *wə'al 'ăšer tôṣî'*, "and upon whatever. . . ." Regarding the uses of the relative pronoun, see Meyers and Meyers, *Haggai, Zechariah 1–8*, 4, 33; and GKC §138.

Having presented the two competing perspectives regarding the temple, the disputation continues by identifying the evidence to substantiate the need for the dispute and the reevaluation of the people's conviction. One would expect the evidence to substantiate the disputed element as in Mic 6:2–8, where the dispute appears to center on the people's conviction that God has wearied them. There, the Torah story itemizes various segments of God's acts on Israel's behalf in order to challenge their conviction, and it thus inquires whether specific acts resulted in the weariness of the people—namely, guidance out of Egypt, provision of leaders on their journey to the land, and entrance into the land. There, the dispute culminates in the realization that the people's misunderstanding led them to their conviction.[51] Unlike the Micah passage, which uses the Torah story to accomplish this purpose, the Haggai passage uses admonition to reflect on the people's ways.

a. Admonitions to Reflect on the Evidence (1:5–9)

Two admonitions are presented: an admonition about experiences in the harvest (1:5–6) and an admonition about experiences in building projects (1:7–9). Both subunits begin with the admonition to consider experiences as outcomes. The admonitions are connected to the adverse outcomes experienced by the community.

(1) Admonition #1 to Reflect on Experiences (1:5–6)

5 In Hag 1:5–6, the prophet clarifies the logical outcome of the message and admonishes the people to reflect on the conditions that they have experienced. In this admonition the prophet uses the futility of their work as an illustration. The term *wəʿattā*, "and now," signals the transition in the disputation from the participants' perspective to the argumentation. Some interpret *wəʿattā* as signaling the immediacy of the moment, calling the people to reflect sooner rather than later.[52] The particle is followed by the messenger formula and introduces the subsequent speech as the word of Yahweh (cf. Hag 1:2, 7; 2:6, 11).

The expression *śîmû ləbabkem*, "reflect on your ways" (lit., set your heart), occurs in several contexts (Hag 1:5, 7; 2:15, 18; Deut 32:46; Isa 41:22; Ezek 40:4; 44:5; Job 1:8; 2:3)[53] with various objects, including *ʿal-darkêkem*, "on your ways" (Hag 1:5, 7); *kol-haddəbārîm*, "all the words" (Deut 32:46). In Deut 32:46, the people are asked to reflect on all the words that are being brought as evidence against them.

In Hag 1:5, 7, *ʿal-darkêkem*, "on your ways," refers to the people's life course or pattern, including but not limited to behaviors and their consequences. Potentially, a life course includes convictions or beliefs that lead to and sustain the behavior patterns.[54] This concept is illustrated in Jer 2:33;

51. Jacobs, *Conceptual Coherence*.

52. H. W. Wolff, *Haggai*, 43.

53. Kessler, *Haggai*, 131. In keeping with Kessler's observation about sapiential influence, note similar expressions found in the wisdom tradition: *šît libbəkā*, "set your heart" (Prov 27:23; cf. Pss 48:13 [MT 14]; 62:10 [MT 11]); and *taṭṭeh libbəkā*, "incline your heart" (Prov 2:2).

54. H. W. Wolff (*Haggai*, 43) defines *derek* as people's goal and their success in achieving it—that is, "how they fare." He uses K. Koch, "דרך," *ThWAT* 2:307. Meyers and Meyers

4:18; 7:3, 5; 18:11; 22:21.[55] It is also used of the law to direct the people's way (Josh 1:8; cf. Ps 37:5; 119:15). When used of God, it connotes the divine will or the law and is often contrasted with human ways (Isa 55:8–9; 63:17; Pss 25:4; 27:11; 51:13; 67:2; 77:13; 86:11). Other texts manifesting the perspective that the people are judged and punished because of their ways are directly relevant to understanding Hag 1:5, 7 (Ezek 7:3–4, 8–9; 18:30; 24:14; 33:20). The people are asked to reflect on their ways because of the connection between their life course (especially their convictions and ensuing actions) and their present circumstances.

6 Haggai 1:6 identifies what the hearers ought to consider, which is their situation leading up to the moment of the dispute. The futility curse is employed as a situation analysis to highlight the correlation between their ways and their experiences of adversity. Futility curses typically depict the discontinuity between the anticipated outcome of one's efforts and the actual outcome. This pattern is established in the other futility curses found in the Old Testament (e.g., Lev 26; Deut 28; Mic 6:13–16; Amos 5:11–13; Hos 4:7–10 [esp. 10]; cf. Isa 17:10–11).[56]

The futility of their efforts is evident in five areas of their daily lives. The text uses a verb to indicate each effort and follows up each with its incongruous outcome. In Hag 1:6, the futility of the effort is not predicted but is identified as a past event with present consequences. Thus, the pattern in the first curse sets the stage for the other curses. The perfect form of the verb denoting the effort—*zəraʿtem, qal* perfect of *zāraʿ*, "you have sown"—is followed by the infinitive absolute denoting the incongruous outcome (*hiphil* of *bôʾ*, "to come"). For both verbs, the object is indicated by a substantive *harbê*, "much."[57] In the following three curses, the infinitive absolute indicates the effort—*ʾākôl*, "eat"; *šātô*, "drink"; *lābôš*, "clothe"—followed by the particle *wəʾên*, "nothing, is not," plus the infinitive construct indicating the outcome. The fifth and final curse in Hag 1:6 uses participles characterizing a person (*hammiśtakkēr*) and the action unique to that person (*miśtakkēr*).

The curses frustrate expectation by removing the anticipated realities. Yahweh's expectation was that they would build Yahweh's house; but they did not. The admonition to reflect thus highlights the people's experience as

---

(*Haggai, Zechariah 1–8,* 24–25) speak of welfare. Against Meyers and Meyers, Kessler (*Haggai,* 131) sees *derek* as used here to mean the "results that accrued from their choices." Cf. Verhoef, *Haggai and Malachi,* 60.

55. See also Ezek 7:3–4, 8–9; 18:30; Job 4:6; 22:3; cf. Ps 91:11.

56. Cf. Jer 12:1–13, which raises questions about the prosperity of the wicked, the apparent incongruity between the deeds and the outcomes. Jeffrey H. Tigay, *Deuteronomy,* JPS Torah Commentary (Philadelphia: Jewish Publication Society, 1996), 266–67.

57. *Hiphil* infinitive absolute of *rbh,* "to be many, great," used as an adverb versus *məʿāṭ*, "little."

being the fulfillment of Yahweh's effort and his success in frustrating their expectations (cf. Hag 2:16–17). The correlation between the people's infraction and Yahweh's punishment via curses is a discernible pattern in the prophetic literature—the type of infraction matches the announced judgment in kind, if not in extent (cf. Mic 2:1–4; 3:1–2).[58] In essence, Yahweh's message to them is that their frustrating Yahweh's expectations has resulted in Yahweh's frustrating their expectations; conversely, when they satisfy the Deity's expectations, the Deity will bless them (cf. Hag 2:19). The overarching idea is that the connection between behavior patterns and the futility of one's efforts is more than coincidental.[59] The curses itemized in Hag 1:6 encompass aspects of life that are basic to life or to obtaining the resources to sustain life.[60] The five areas addressed relate to the harvest: sowing, eating, drinking, clothing, and hired labor.

Sowing is one of the common activities identified in the futility curses and their analogous motifs (Lev 26:16; Deut 11:10–15; 28:38; Mic 6:15). In Hag 1:6 the extent of the effort—*you have sown much* (*harbê*, "much")—is incongruous with the yield (*məʿāṭ* "little"; cf. Deut 28:38 *rab*, "much," . . . *məʿāṭ*, "little"). The diligence of their great effort is highlighted and thus enhances the contrasting neglect of Yahweh's temple. In sowing their seed, they are aware of the "time" and, having followed the seasonal demands, expect yields consistent with their effort (cf. Hag 2:15–19). Congruity may be established in at least two ways: (a) if the availability of little is due to sloth (Prov 20:4), there is congruity; (b) in the larger futility motif, there is congruity if the behavior of the sower toward God is congruous with God's responses.

From the perspective of Deut 11:10–15, there is a correlation between obedience and the yield of the land; if the people keep the commandments, God will ensure rain and the yield of the land (cf. Deut 28:1–14).[61] Consequently, when they sow, the land will yield products for them and their animals sufficient to satisfy them—that is, their eating will result in being full. This sequence of effort and outcome, sowing and yield is established as a sequence that is guaranteed by God, not apart from God's favor and the laws regarding sowing and reaping (cf. Lev 25:3–7, 18–22). If there is abundance, that abundance is usually depicted as the blessing of God in response to the people's obedience. Thus, according to Isa 30:19–23, if the people heed God's voice and walk in God's way, God will give rain to water the seed, and a rich harvest will follow.

58. Jacobs, *Conceptual Coherence*.

59. Cf. Verhoef, *Haggai and Malachi*, 63.

60. Kessler, *Haggai*, 132.

61. The blessing that will result if the people are obedient to God (e.g., rain and vegetation to support livestock). Disobedience will lead to God's anger and acting to bring about adversity for the community (Deut 11:16–17).

I argue that *zāraʿ,* "to sow," in Hag 1:6 refers to planting seed as well as all tasks expended in securing life's basic means of sustenance (cf. Deut 28:1–14). I further argue that the results of sowing are a determining factor in all other aspects of the community's effort to sustain itself, including eating, drinking, being clothed, and spending wages.

As in Lev 26:26 and Mic 6:14, the expression *you eat without being satisfied* does not indicate an absence of food; food is available.[62] There is an assumption about eating and drinking and the results of these behaviors, however: both actions are expected to result in satisfaction.

As with the futility of eating, drinking will not accomplish its usual effect—*you drink without being drunk.* The verb and adjective of *šākar* is typically used to denote the intoxicating effect of wine or strong drink (Gen 9:21; 1 Sam 1:13–15; 2 Sam 11:13; 1 Kgs 16:9; 20:16; Isa 16:8; 29:9; Jer 25:27; 51:39; Lam 4:21; Nah 1:10; Hab 2:5). While recognizing this meaning and its validity in this context, some have argued that "being drunk" in the Bible may not have the negative connotation that it has in today's society.[63] Be that as it may, the present text suggests that the people's use of their own produce did not yield the desired effect. It may be due to the limitation of strong drink—insufficient to result in intoxication.

Added to the inadequacy of food and strong drink in producing their usual effects, the passage also highlights the ineffectiveness of clothing as a part of the people's futile efforts: *You wear clothes but are never warm.* Suggestions about the lack of desired effect from the clothing include the following: (a) the garments were made of poor quality (limited wool) and could therefore not serve their purpose; (b) the effect of the food shortage had taken its toll on the people, resulting in their malnutrition and its attending physical effects; (c) the people lacked the resources to procure the necessary materials for making clothes.[64] These are likely reasons, but in the larger framework of Hag 1:6, the focus is on the lack of warmth generated from the clothing. Usually *ḥōm* denotes the heat from various sources; for example, Gen 8:22 (heat or cold); Gen 18:1; 2 Sam 4:5; Isa 18:4; Jer 17:8; Job 24:19 (heat of the sun); 1 Sam 21:6 (of hot bread); Job 37:17 (used of garment). It is not that the people are without clothing and subject to the shame of nakedness (Isa 20:4; Ezek 16:37). In the curse in Deut 28:48, the cluster of results if the people are disobedient includes "hunger, thirst, and nakedness," summarized as the

62. Both Lev 26:26 and Mic 6:14 use the finite verbal forms and *lōʾ*, "not."

63. Meyers and Meyers, *Haggai, Zechariah 1–8,* 26. Verhoef (*Haggai and Malachi,* 61), on the basis of the Aramaic, argues that the term *šākar* simply means abundance rather than being drunk.

64. Verhoef, *Haggai and Malachi,* 61–62. Note his bibliographical references. Cf. Kessler, *Haggai,* 132.

lack of everything (*bəḥōser kōl*). Without going to the extent of nakedness, the sequence in Hag 1:6 reflects the cluster of circumstances resulting from God's curse on the people. They were wearing clothes (*lābaš*), but it was if they had none.

The enumeration of efforts continues regarding wages: *the one who hires out himself*. The verb *śākar*, "hire," means to hire someone to perform a particular function (Gen 30:16; Exod 22:15 [MT 14]; Deut 15:18; Judg 9:4; 18:4; 1 Sam 2:5; Neh 6:12, 13; 13:2; 2 Chr 25:6). The noun form means "wages" (Gen 30:28, 32; Exod 2:9; Deut 15:18; 1 Kgs 5:6; Ezek 29:19; Zech 8:10; 11:12; Mal 3:5). In many circumstances, the hired servant (*śākîr*) worked for daily wages and may have hired himself out, expecting to be paid at the end of the day (Lev 19:13; Deut 24:14–15; cf. Mal 3:5). Hired laborers had no economic reserve for procuring food or clothing. It would be challenging enough to be a hired worker, living from one wage to the next (Lev 19:13; Deut 24:15; cf. Jer 22:13; Mal 3:5).[65] To whatever extent the people's experience reflected this characterization, their situation was compounded by their inability to keep their wages—it was tantamount to putting their wages into a bag of holes (*ṣərôr nāqûb*).

One interpretation of this description of the hired person as working for a bag of holes is that it is a metaphor. The suggestion is that the metaphor describes inflation, when the money does not accrue because of the high cost of commodities. This interpretation means that reduced yield (Hag 1:6) and drought (1:11) were the catalyst for an ethos of low supply and high demand. Whatever the coinage available, this imagery holds.[66] In this economic situation, the depiction may not necessarily be of poor people but, instead, of working people with money who are unable to meet their needs.[67]

It has also been suggested that the reference to the hired worker is distinguishing between the farmer and those who work for employers.[68] The larger distinction, however, is between the common experiences and the unique experiences—for example, individuals earning a living in comparison with adversity that affects the whole population. Thus, sowing is a particular type of activity that leads to the common experience of limited resources to

65. Mignon R. Jacobs, "Toward an Old Testament Theology of Concern for the Underprivileged," in *Reading the Hebrew Bible for a New Millennium: Form, Concept, and Theological Perspective,* ed. Wonil Kim et al. (Harrisburg, PA: Trinity Press International, 2000), 1:214.

66. Regarding the nature of the container, pouch, or wrap, Verhoef (*Haggai and Malachi,* 62) doubts that coins were available in Haggai's time or that the switch to silver shekels had already taken place. See Kessler (*Haggai,* 133) for a discussion about coinage and for relevant bibliography; cf. Baldwin, *Hag, Zech, Mal,* 41.

67. Meyers and Meyers, *Haggai, Zechariah 1–8,* 27. Cf. E. H. Merrill, *Haggai, Zechariah, Malachi: An Exegetical Commentary* (Chicago: Moody Press, 1994), 23–24.

68. Meyers and Meyers, *Haggai, Zechariah 1–8,* 26.

satisfy oneself with eating and drinking as well as the particularized experience of limited money.

(2) Admonition #2 to Reflect on Experiences (1:7–9)

7 Introduced by the messenger formula in Hag 1:7 (*kô ʾāmar yhwh*), the admonition again urges the people to reflect on their ways. As in Hag 1:5–6, the admonition is juxtaposed to the ways that they are asked to reconsider. Unlike 1:5–6, however, the admonition of 1:7 is separated from the elements upon which they are to reflect by a command sequence that seems to address Yahweh's desire to have the temple built (1:8). The imperative compels behavior that will please Yahweh and presumably bring about a change in circumstances from the futility of effort to the receipt of blessings (cf. Hag 2:19). Haggai 1:9 picks up the language of the tension between *much and little* begun in 1:6 and ties it to concerns about the neglected status of Yahweh's house.

Following the admonition in Hag 1:7, 1:8a consists of a command, "go up the hill" (*ʿălû hāhār*), and several expansions presented as a linear progression from the command. Verse 1:8b reveals Yahweh's two assurances to the people, which are contingent on their obedience to the commands. The primary command to go (*ʿălû*) clearly requires a switch from the sustained inactivity (regarding building the temple) to activity (bringing wood). Thus, Yahweh's larger agenda for the people consists of three commands: go (*ʿălû*), bring wood (*hăbēʾtem ʿēṣ*), and build the temple (*bənû habbāyit*).

The command to *bring wood* (*ʿēṣ*) may have referred to various types of wood that were probably available in the region, including fig, palm, oak, cypress, olive, or sycamore. Sycamore was typically used in building houses, especially flat-roofed residences.[69] It was suitable for building both because of its availability through cultivation and because of its durability;[70] however, sycamores also have restrictive qualities, such as the length of beams, that limit its use in larger structures such as palaces. In agreement with Meyer and Meyers, Wolff does not think that the text is speaking of luxury when it refers to paneling. They argue that the type of wood used is a matter of practicality: cedar used in paneling provides longer beams; it is durable and ornate. Cedar, however, would not have been available from the trees surrounding Jerusalem.[71]

8 In comparison with Exod 25, Hag 1:8 is limited in materials requested

69. H. W. Wolff, *Haggai,* 42, 45; Meyers and Meyers (*Haggai, Zechariah 1–8,* 29) object to the idea that the prophet was referring to the sycamore. One of these objections is that sycamore trees grew in lowland and would thus not be found in the hills.

70. H. W. Wolff, *Haggai,* 42; Meyers and Meyers, *Haggai, Zechariah 1–8,* 27–28.

71. H. W. Wolff, *Haggai,* 42, 45; Meyers and Meyers, *Haggai, Zechariah 1–8,* 27–28.

for building the temple. This raises a question about the intended use of the wood requested, and several interpretations have been offered in response. One interpretation, due to the absence of an itemized list of materials, posits that sycamore would not have been available in the region. Furthermore, since only wood is mentioned, the project in mind was not the temple structure itself but the support elements and tools needed in building that structure, such as scaffolding, ladders, and ramps. In this view, the materials needed for the temple structure itself had already been collected and stored in Jerusalem during the first attempt to rebuild in 538 BCE, about eighteen years prior to Haggai's prophetic activity.[72]

Another interpretation of the request for wood without requesting other materials is that the request represents only the first step in the building project.[73] Along this line of thought, Kessler convincingly argues that the mention of wood is metonymy for all the materials needed to complete the work. He identifies the use of metonymy as a literary device in Hag 1:9; 2:8; and 2:22 as well.[74]

The basic expression "and build the house" (*ûbənû habbāyit*) is another way of identifying the temple in addition to more-specific expressions elsewhere in Haggai: house of Yahweh (*bêt yhwh*, 1:2); this house (*habbayit hazzê*, 1:4), house of Yahweh of hosts their God (*bəbêt-yhwh ṣəbā'ôt 'ĕlōhêhem*, 1:14).[75] The compound commands signal a progression, a deliberate effort to move toward a goal. The sequence also presupposes that the people know the specifics about building the temple and have all the resources for building, including the materials and the laborers. Another aspect of the command sequence deserves mention, given the futility of the efforts identified in Hag 1:6. Unlike those frustrated efforts, assuredly, these efforts to build will not be futile.

The first assurance, *so that I may take pleasure in it (wə'erṣeh-bô)*, recalls the relationship between the people's repentance and Yahweh's response in blessing. Although the expression "amend your ways" (*hêṭîbû darkêkem*) is not stated in Hag 1:8b, the extended command is analogous to passages in the book of Jeremiah (cf. 7:5; 18:11). In these passages, several assurances are contingent on the obedience of the people. First, if they amend their ways God will dwell among them as well as in Jerusalem (Jer 7:3–7). Second, God will change God's mind about the impending disaster planned against them (Jer 26:12–13) or the good intended for them (Jer 18:9–11), depending on

72. Meyers and Meyers, *Haggai, Zechariah 1–8*, 27–28.

73. H. W. Wolff, *Haggai*, 45.

74. Kessler, *Haggai*, 134. Hag 2:8, "silver and gold for all the treasures"; Hag 2:22, "throne for all powers and chariots for all weaponry."

75. See discussion of Hag 1:1, 4 above.

the situation. The content of the imperative in Hag 1:8b, as in 1:5, reflects this same sentiment.

The verb *rāṣâ,* "to take pleasure in," when used in the cult connotes the Deity's delight with the sacrifice.[76] The verb appears with both humans and the Deity as subject.[77] With God/Yahweh as subject, the verb occurs with several objects, including persons (2 Sam 24:23; Isa 42:1; Ezek 20:40–41) and values, ways, and deeds (Prov 16:7). Its use in the cultic system includes instances when the sacrifice might be deemed acceptable or unacceptable (e.g., Lev 1:3, 4; 7:18; 19:7; 22:23, 25, 27).[78] A sacrifice does not automatically elicit God's pleasure; rather, God's pleasure is reserved for sacrifices that are deemed acceptable. Conversely, there are times when God may be displeased with a sacrifice and reject it (Amos 5:22; Hos 8:13; Mal 1:8–10; Lev 7:18; 19:7; 22:23).[79]

The object of the verb in 1:8b is contained in the word *bô,* the preposition plus the third-person pronominal suffix. The referent of the suffix is the "house" identified in Hag 1:8a and may be the finished project or the building process. With the use of the imperfect and the nuance of sequential actions, the assurance carries the sense that the response is predicated on the existence of the temple rather than any further evaluation of its quality, whether better or worse, bigger or smaller, or more or less ornate than the first structure. While the people may be concerned about these aspects, the wording squelches worries about whether Yahweh may reject the temple, the fruit of their efforts (cf. Hag 2:3, 9). The assurance clarifies the fact that, although there are some offerings that Yahweh rejects, the temple will not be rejected. This sort of assurance is also found in Zech 1:3; Num 21:16 (cf. Mal 3:7–10).[80] The assurance is that Yahweh will do what is promised (without any further qualification) if the people follow Yahweh's command.[81]

The second assurance, *I will be honored* (*wəʾekkābēd*), is founded on the first and appears as the *niphal* imperfect first common singular form of

76. R. P. Knierim, *Text and Concept in Leviticus 1:1–9: A Case in Exegetical Method,* FAT 2 (Tübingen: Mohr Siebeck, 1992). Jacobs, *Conceptual Coherence*; G. Gerleman, "רצה," *TLOT* 3:1259–61.

77. Gerleman, "רצה," 3:1260. The object of the verb is usually introduced by the preposition (e.g., Ezek 20:41; Hag 1:8; Ps 49:13 [MT 14]).

78. Gerleman, "רצה," 3:1260–61.

79. Cf. Kessler, *Haggai,* 135. Verhoef (*Haggai and Malachi,* 66–67) discusses the use of *rāṣâ,* including several synonyms, namely: *ḥesed,* "loving kindness," *ḥānan,* "to show favor"; *rāḥam,* "love, have compassion"; *ʾāhēb,* "love,"; and *yəšûʿâ,* "deliverance." See discussion of Mal 1:8–10 in this commentary.

80. See discussion of Mal 3:7–10 in this commentary.

81. Cf. Kessler, *Haggai,* 134; Meyers and Meyers, *Haggai, Zechariah 1–8,* 93, regarding Zech 1:3.

the verb *kābēd*.[82] The *niphal* may be rendered passive, "I will be honored," or reflexive, "I will honor myself"; the passive meaning is adopted here.[83] That God will be honored by the completion of the temple is clear in the traditions about the temple in ruins, which would be a disgrace to God and the object of ridicule to those who pass by (e.g., 1 Kgs 9:8).[84] The assurance also reveals Yahweh's perspective on the current state of affairs—the neglected temple in the midst of inhabitable structures (cf. Hag 1:9). The demolished temple dishonors God (cf. Mal 1:6). God's honor, like God's pleasure, depends on the temple's existence rather than its reputation. Presumably, the people have specific instructions for building the temple and will execute those instructions. The assurance is brought to a close with the report formula, *ʾāmar yhwh*, "Yahweh has spoken," reaffirming the source of the message as Yahweh, not the prophet, who is the instrument of the message.

9 The call to reflect in Hag 1:7 is assumed by 1:9, and a question-and-answer schema punctuates the need for reflection on the correlation between the people's ways and their current experience.[85] It culminates in the analysis of the people's situation and God's response to them. It picks up the language of Hag 1:6—*much-little*—and highlights the incongruity between effort and effect. Two efforts are noted.

First, *you look for much*. Here the infinitive absolute form *pānōh*, "to turn," plus *ʾel*, "to," may mean "to look for, expect." The object of *pānōh*, *harbê*, "much," is used to indicate the expectation in contrast to the actuality of the situation—that is, *məʿāṭ*, "little."[86] In the occurrence of *pānōh* plus *ʾel* in Lev 26:9, God promises to look upon his people with favor, thus promising to keep the covenant with them and dwell with them (cf. Hag 2:4–5).

Arguably, Hag 1:9 describes the returnees from Babylonia, who may have overestimated the yield from their crops. The non-deportees would have

82. Keeping the imperfect of the *ketiv* maintains consistency with the imperfect form of *rāṣâ*. The MT lists the *ketiv wəʾekkābēd* (*niphal* imperfect first-person common-singular of *kābēd*) and the *qere wəʾikkābədâ* (*niphal* cohortative of *kābēd*). R. L. Smith (*Micah–Malachi*, WBC 32 [Waco, TX: Word, 1984], 153) proposes the passive meaning of the imperfect with the nuance of the cohortative.

83. See Verhoef (*Haggai and Malachi*, 67–68) for a discussion of the nuances of the various renderings of the *niphal* for *kābēd*, e.g.: "Yahweh will consider himself honored; God will reveal his honor."

84. Regarding the city/people, see 2 Chr 29:8; Jer 19:8; 25:9, 18; 44:12; Lam 2:15–16; Mic 6:16.

85. W. Whedbee, "Question-Answer Schema in Haggai 1: The Form and Function of Haggai 1:9–11," in *Biblical and Near Eastern Studies: Essays in Honor of William S. LaSor*, ed. G. A. Tuttle (Grand Rapids: Eerdmans, 1978), 188–89.

86. According to H. W. Wolff (*Haggai*, 46), in this context *pānâ* has the nuance of "to expect." Cf. Verhoef, *Haggai and Malachi*, 69; Kessler, *Haggai*, 136; Merrill, *Hag, Zech, Mal*, 25, 29.

known the tendencies of a semiarid climate. Drought with its resulting shortage of food and livestock would have been an unsurprising aspect of life for them. The returnees, on the other hand, may have perceived the drought as a disaster and responded accordingly.[87]

The language (*the house*) used to depict the second effort, in Hag 1:9, *you brought to the house,* is the same wording as in 1:8. Nonetheless, it suggests that the reference is to the people's homes rather than to the temple—thus the translation "you brought home" (NRSV). Usually the basis of this suggestion by the commentators is that the temple has not yet been built.[88] Thus, *habbāyit,* "the house," which is used of the temple in Hag 1:8 is given a different meaning in 1:9. In addition to "the temple" simply being a likely interpretation of "the house" in 1:9, Yahweh's response should also be considered, along with the assurances in 1:8b.

Attempts to understand Yahweh's response have generated much discussion. That Yahweh *blew away* or blew upon (*wənāpaḥtî bô*) what the people brought suggests an unfavorable response in contrast to Yahweh's promised pleasure in the temple—*so that I may take pleasure in it* (Hag 1:8b). There are several suggestions for understanding Yahweh's response based on one's understanding of the term *nāpaḥ,* "to blow." Its occurrences are varied even when it appears with the proposition *be*. Accordingly, it appears as a verb (*wayyippaḥ*) in Gen 2:7, with *yhwh 'ĕlōhîm,* "Yahweh God," as subject—"breathed into his nostrils the breath of life" (NRSV). The verb is used in a similar fashion in Ezek 37:7–9 to restore life and in Ezek 22:20–21 to blow fire on the people to consume them.[89]

Another suggestion about the nature of Yahweh's response is to interpret *nāpaḥ,* "breathe, blow," in light of Hag 2:13—a sign of Yahweh's displeasure. In this interpretation, the reference is to the temple and the displeasure is with what they brought—perhaps that they brought offerings to the temple in its desolate state.[90] In this view, the displeasure is not in the quantity of what they brought. Historically, offerings and sacrifices were being made to Yahweh during the restoration, when the temple had not yet been rebuilt.[91]

87. While they discuss this as a possibility, Meyers and Meyers (*Haggai, Zechariah 1–8,* 28–29) argue against this as a distinguishing factor between the groups in Hag 1:4–8 vis-à-vis 1:9–11. They cite Steck ("Zu Haggai 1:2–11"), who identifies the returnees with Hag 1:9–10 and the non-deportees with Hag 1:4–8.

88. H. W. Wolff, *Haggai,* 46; Petersen, *Haggai and Zechariah 1–8,* 52; Merrill, *Hag, Zech, Mal,* 27; Brown, *Obadiah through Malachi,* 122–24. Cf. Verhoef's (*Haggai and Malachi,* 71) discussion of Jerome, who rejects the idea that "the house" here refers to the temple.

89. Verhoef (*Haggai and Malachi,* 70) also mentions but rejects the suggestion that the term refers to the magical disappearance of an object.

90. Contrast H. W. Wolff, *Haggai,* 46.

91. Meyers and Meyers, *Haggai, Zechariah 1–8,* 29.

The perspective in Hag 1:9 could be that Yahweh sniffed at their offerings with contempt.[92] Presumably, the response is to the uncleanness of the altar and hence the sacrifice (cf. Hag 2:13–14; Mal 1:7)

Perhaps *I blew it away* refers to the effect of the wind (*rûaḥ*) on the elements in the open air or on elements inappropriately secured against the wind.[93] The imagery also emerges of people leaving their offerings at the site of the neglected temple. This understanding is supported by the rest of Hag 1:9. Even so, the wind is not listed as the culprit in this case. In other cases, where the wicked are the objects, the effect of the wind in blowing them away is clearly noted with the verb *nādap*, "drive, carry away" (Ps 1:4; Job 21:18), or *rādap*, "pursue, chase" (Isa 17:13; cf. Ps 35:5; 83:13). The first-person address indicates that Yahweh is the one who blows the objects away. On the other hand, the image is of Yahweh's blowing on products that the people brought home, and they dwindled or dried up, leaving even less than the little bit that the people brought home. This would be consistent with the loss of their resources signaled by the hole in the purse (Hag 1:6) and the loss of resources to blight (2:17). Both alternatives find support in the text and are therefore legitimate possibilities.

The question *why?* (*meh*) may be addressed to Yahweh, whose displeasure is manifested in the act of getting rid of what they brought. Why is Yahweh displeased when the people brought something to God, even with their economic hardship? Yahweh's question anticipates the people's question and assumes that they had not already noticed this connection. It assumes that they have misconstrued reality (cf. Hag 1:2) and what is required of them by Yahweh (cf. Mic 6:2–8). Haggai 1:8 anticipates 1:9 by establishing what would please Yahweh and by contrasting this with the reality of the people's experience. Once again, the contrast is between the house of Yahweh and the people's houses; thus, the correlation between Hag 1:4 and 1:9 is achieved. Yahweh's house is desolate, uninhabitable, while the people's houses are inhabitable and even inhabited. Again, the question of the people's identity is raised. In this instance, it could be that those who returned in 538 BCE had already built their homes. The alternative is that the most recent returnees are being targeted for their neglect of the temple. To address this difficulty, some have suggested a broader meaning of *bêtô*, "his house"—namely, "household of" or "family affairs."[94]

92. This idea is discounted by many, including Kessler, *Haggai,* 137; Verhoef, *Haggai and Malachi,* 71.

93. This could also refer to additional loss of materials after they were brought home. Kessler (*Haggai,* 137) favors this idea as being consistent with 1:4–7 and 1:9–11's image of the people's frustration. Cf. Whedbee, "Question-Answer Schema in Haggai 1," 187.

94. Thus Meyers and Meyers, *Haggai, Zechariah 1–8,* 30; Kessler, *Haggai,* 138. See Verhoef (*Haggai and Malachi,* 72), who mentions this possibility in his discussion about the

b. Noted Consequences of the People's Deeds (1:10–11)

The connective particle *ʿal-kēn*, "therefore," links Hag 1:9 and 10; but more importantly it transitions from the analysis of the situation to stating the reason for the situation. Again, the link between effort and effect is identified as more than incidental. Likewise, the transition moves from what the people have done to what Yahweh has done. Accordingly, Hag 1:10 explains Yahweh's response to the neglect and as such connects 1:4 with the question-and-answer schema in 1:9. It also reveals the reason for the futility of their efforts.[95] While there is disagreement about the significance of *ʿălêkem* in 1:10, I argue that the perspective of the message is that the heavens' behavior is caused by the people's ways (see footnotes to the translation).

10 The observation that *the heavens have withheld dew* provides nature's response to the situation. This is clearly analogous to the Deuteronomistic tradition of drought's being the result of God's curse. In essence, Deut 11:11–17 states that if the people obey Yahweh, then Yahweh will bring rain and thus ensure the success of their labor; but Yahweh will withhold rain if the people are disobedient (cf. Deut 28:23; Lev 26:19–20).[96] Even in the dry season, dew was an expected part of the ecological system in anticipation of the harvest (May to October). The absence of dew could be the difference between a failed or a successful harvest.[97] The withholding of dew (*ṭal*) and rain (*māṭār*) is also identified as a punishment (2 Sam 1:21; 1 Kgs 17:1). Deuteronomy 28:12 reflects the ancient perspective that rain and other elements were stored in the heavens, and God would open the heavens and release the rain in its season (cf. Job 37:9; 38:22; Jer 10:13; Zech 8:12; Ps 135:7). Thus, rain and other forms of moisture are perceived to be under God's control.[98] Withholding dew thus indicates a withholding of the last form of moisture expected—dew was expected even in seasons of drought.

The heavens' activity has a direct effect: *the earth withheld its yield*. Here nature achieves its effect, showing that some aspects of reality still function in a congruent manner. The congruity and incongruity, however, are explained as the work of Yahweh's hand. Haggai 1:10 provides the general statement that

---

various groups who may be addressed. He concedes that the groups may not be clearly distinguished but that the people as a whole are more concerned about their houses than God's.

95. Cf. H. W. Wolff, *Haggai*, 48.

96. The *ṭal*, "dew, moisture" (e.g., Gen 27:28, 39; Deut 32:2; cf. Judg 6:37–40). Cf. Kessler, *Haggai*, 139; Tigay, *Deuteronomy*, 112–14, 260, 266–67; John E. Hartley, *Leviticus*, WBC 4 (Dallas: Word, 1992), 462, 465; M. Noth, *Leviticus*, OTL (Philadelphia: Westminster, 1977), 198.

97. Meyers and Meyers, *Haggai, Zechariah 1–8*, 31; Verhoef, *Haggai and Malachi*, 73–74; Redditt, *Haggai, Zechariah, Malachi*, 21–22.

98. Tigay, *Deuteronomy*, 260, 396 n. 20.

is then expanded in 1:11. The noun form *yəbûlâ*, "yield" (*yəbûl* plus third singular suffix), is used of the produce of the land (Lev 26:4, 20) and is analogous to *təbû'â*, "yield" (e.g., Exod 23:10; Lev 19:25; 23:39; 25:3, 7, 22; Deut 14:22, 28; 16:15; 22:9; Neh 9:37). Both *yəbûl* and *təbû'â* are used of the yield specifically associated with God's blessing (Lev 25:21; 26:4, 20). The earth's yield is regulated by the moisture that the heavens provide; therefore, the earth's yield is consistent with the provisions that God allows the heavens to provide.

11 It is not that the heavens and the earth act of their own accord. Haggai 1:11 further explains the connection between the experienced hardship and a larger overarching reality. Yahweh commissioned the services of the heavens in order to achieve a particular outcome—the drought (*ḥōreb*).[99] Again, the message places the people's frustrated efforts to bring about the expected effects in contrast to the Deity's successful effort to bring about the desired effects in nature. The first-person speech highlights this contrast: *I called* (*wā'eqrā'*) for drought upon all aspects of life that would affect your livelihood and quality of life—whether the spontaneous growth of trees or herbage or the cultivated crops. The verb *qārā'*, "to call or summon," is used of people to indicate that they are required for a special task.[100] It is also used of events and objects such as famine (*rā'āb*, 2 Kgs 8:1), grain (*dāgān*, Ezek 36:29), and sword (*ḥereb*, Jer 25:29; Ezek 38:21; cf. Isa 13:3). In Hag 1:11 the object of *qārā'* is *ḥōreb*, "drought," using the same root *ḥārēb*, "to be dry," to indicate the state of dryness (cf. Judg 6:37–40).[101]

The entities affected by the drought are enumerated using *'al/wə'al*, "upon," to mark off the elements—*upon the land and upon the hills.* The first element, *hā'āreṣ*, "the land," sets the stage for all the other things in the region where the effects of the drought are being experienced. Likewise, it expands the general statement in Hag 1:10b that the earth is withholding its yield in response to the heavens. The second element, *hehārîm*, "the hills," recalls the destination in Hag 1:8, where the people are sent to get wood to build the temple. By their very nature, the hills exist at a higher elevation than the surrounding land and may have moisture that does not reach the lower land. Identifying both land and hills creates the image that all areas of the territory, cultivated or uncultivated, are subject to the drought.[102]

99. Tigay, *Deuteronomy,* 112.

100. For example, Gen 41:8; Exod 1:18; 7:11; 8:25; Lev 9:1; 10:4; Deut 25:8; 1 Sam 6:2; 1 Kgs 1:28; 2 Kgs 18:18; 1 Chr 22:6; Esth 3:12.

101. Cf. Meyers and Meyers, *Haggai, Zechariah 1–8,* 32; H. W. Wolff, *Haggai,* 48–49; Kessler, *Haggai,* 139.

102. Cf. Verhoef, *Haggai and Malachi,* 75–76. Verhoef identifies the contrast between the land and field as that of cultivated land versus uncultivated hill. Meyers and Meyers (*Haggai, Zechariah 1–8,* 32–33) understand the wording as describing the limited availability of flat land due to the topography of the territory.

The statement *upon the grain and upon the new wine and upon the oil* further identifies the effects of Yahweh's actions. These three elements, grain, wine, and oil, are typically identified with reference to drought and famine (Gen 41; Joel 1:10) or the diminution resulting from a curse (Deut 28:51). Deuteronomy 7:13 identifies these as elements of blessing: *dəgānəkā wətîrōšəkā wəyiṣhārekā*, "he will bless the fruit of your womb and the fruit of your ground, *your grain and your wine and your oil*, the increase of your cattle and the issue of your flock" (cf. Deut 11:14; Joel 2:19). References to the tithe also identify these three elements (Deut 12:17; 14:23; 18:4; 2 Chr 31:5; Neh 10:39; 13:5, 12).[103] These quotations show that this is a formula used to refer to the totality of the land's produce (cf. Hag 2:19).[104] This connotation is made explicit by the other element identified by *wəʿal*: *ʾăšer tôṣîʾ hāʾădāmâ*, "*whatever the ground produces.*" The relative clause summarizes the total effect of the drought on what the land produces.

The next two elements identify the effects of the drought on labor: *wəʿal-hāʾādām wəʿal-habbəhēmâ*, "upon human being and animal." Both humans and animals are to observe the Sabbath day of rest (Exod 20:10; Deut 5:14) and both are blessed and cursed in God's response to the obedience of the people (Deut 28:4, 11, 51; 30:9). In Hag 1:11, the final element in the sequence is marked as a summation of the labor: *kol-yəgîaʿ kappāyim*, "all hand labor" (Deut 30:9; Ps 1:3). This summarizing expression is similar to *kōl maʿăśê yādekā*, "all the work of your hands" (Deut 2:7) and *kōl mišlaḥ*, "all undertakings" (Deut 12:7, 18) regarding the objects of God's promised blessing. In Hag 1:11 the expression indicates that the drought targets the entire scope of activity—the yield of the land and all the work of the people's hands. Nothing has escaped Yahweh's successful effort—except the people who have not conformed to Yahweh's desire for them (cf. Hag 2:17; Amos 4:4–11).

Haggai 1:10–11 depicts the scope of the drought as God's act against the people. It also illustrates how God used nature as an instrument to impress upon the people the necessity of building the temple. The goal of the disputation sequence is therefore to convince the people that it is time to build the house of Yahweh. In its depiction, Hag 1:2–11 contributes to the perspective that, except for God's people, all aspects of nature (ecological and relational) conform to normal behavior (Mal 1:6; Isa 1:3; cf. Jer 8:7).[105]

103. Cf. H. W. Wolff, *Haggai*, 49; Verhoef, *Haggai and Malachi*, 76; Kessler, *Haggai*, 140. Meyers and Meyers (*Haggai, Zechariah 1–8*, 33) note that the typical terms are not used for these products, which would be *šemen*, "oil," and *yayin*, "wine." The wording illustrates the shortage as compared with the abundance in Hag 2:19.

104. Cf. Verhoef, *Haggai and Malachi*, 76; Kessler, *Haggai*, 140.

105. See discussion of Mal 1:6 in this commentary.

B. OUTCOME OF THE DISPUTATION (1:12–15)

12 Then Zerubbabel son of Shealtiel and Joshua son of Jehozadak, the high priest, and all the remnant of the people listened to the voice of Yahweh their God and unto the words of Haggai the prophet because Yahweh their God sent him;[a] *and the people feared Yahweh. 13 Then Haggai the messenger of Yahweh spoke to the people with a message of Yahweh:*[b] *"I am with you," utterance of Yahweh.*

14 And Yahweh stirred the spirit of Zerubbabel son of Shealtiel, governor of Judah, and the spirit of Joshua son of Jehozadak, the high priest, and the spirit of all the remnant of the people. And they came and worked on the house of Yahweh of hosts their God. 15 On the twenty-fourth day of the sixth [month][c] *in the second year of Darius the king. . . .*

---

a. The MT uses *ʾĕlōhêhem* as the appositive of *yhwh*, *yhwh* being the subject of the verb *šəlāḥô* (*šālaḥ*, "to send" + suffixed third-person masculine-singular object, "him"). While the MT specifies the direct object by the use of the pronominal suffix, it does not indicate an indirect object (i.e., to whom the prophet was sent). The LXX emends the text to specify the indirect object by adding "to them," assuming *ʾĕlōhêhem*. The Syriac, targum, and Vulgate also include the addition "to them." Kessler (*Haggai*, 107 n. 34) offers several reasons for retaining the MT, including stylistic reasons and the Deuteronomistic tradition as a context for the expression. Cf. Verhoef, *Haggai and Malachi*, 79, 82.

b. In place of the MT's *malʾak yhwh bəmalʾăkût yhwh*, the LXX reads "the Lord's messenger" followed by "messengers of the Lord." The *hapax* expression *bəmalʾăkût yhwh* may be translated "according to the mission of Yahweh" without emendation. Verhoef, *Haggai and Malachi*, 79, 84; cf. Kessler, *Haggai*, 107 n. 37.

c. There are some challenging aspects to this verse. First, the form of the number *baššiššî*, "in/on the sixth" (preposition + definite article + ordinal number) has been discussed as unusual because of the affixed preposition with definite article. However, there are instances of this or similar constructions: *haššiššî*, 1:1 (definite article + number); *lattəšîʿî*, 2:18 (preposition + number); *baḥămiššā laḥōdeš*, Ezek 1:1, 2; 8:1 (preposition + definite article + number); also *baššiššî*, in 8:1, referring to the month rather than the day of the month. Second, the sequence of the number in relation to the month following *laḥōdeš*, "the month" (preposition + definite article + noun), has often been viewed as unusual. Since the elements in the sequence vary, month + number followed or preceded by the day or year, the occurrence in Hag 1:15 is viewed as another form of the date formula (e.g., year + day + month—Hag 1:1; Ezek 1:1; 8:1; day + month + year—Hag 1:15; 2:10; Zech 1:7; month + year—Zech 1:1; *see* introduction above). The third challenge is connected to the sequence within the date formula to the extent that the relationship of 1:15a, 1:15b, and 2:1 is determined by efforts to maintain a uniformity of date formulas within the book of Haggai (cf. 1:1). As in the LXX, Vulgate, and Syriac versions, some scholars transpose 1:15b with 2:1 (Verhoef, *Haggai and Malachi*, 89; Kessler, *Haggai*, 108 n. 41). Meyers and Meyers (*Haggai, Zechariah 1–8*, 36) keep 1:15a+b separated from 2:1.

The final section of Hag 1 is a narrative framework that depicts the outcome of the dispute and verifies the effectiveness of God's actions in convincing the community to build the temple. We can discern three parts to this section:

report on the community's obedience (1:12); report on Yahweh's assurance to the community (1:13); report on the community's transformation (1:14).

1. Report on the Community's Obedience (1:12)

12 The reported response of the community represents all sectors of the population—that is, the leaders—Zerubbabel and Joshua—and the people—all the remnant of the people. Here Zerubbabel is identified as son of Shaltiel (*šaltî'ēl*) rather than Shealtiel (*šə'altî'ēl*) (cf. Hag 1:1), without the title "governor of Judah" (cf. Hag 2:2 vis-à-vis 2:4). Joshua is identified as son of Jehozadak (*ben-yəhôṣādāq*) and as the high priest (*hakkōhēn haggādôl*).[106] One suggestion concerning use of title is that, while Zerubbabel is the more prominent of the two figures, the epithet would have been a reminder of his allegiance to the Persian Empire at a juncture when loyalty to Yahweh was being highlighted.[107] On the other hand, the variations in his name that appear in Haggai may show that variations of this sort were typical and do not warrant theories about their significance in 1:12.

The others who heeded the Deity's injunction are identified as *kōl šə'ērît hā'ām, "all the remnant of the people."* Who are they? And are they the same as "this/the people" identified elsewhere (Hag 1:2, 14; 2:2, 4)? The use of *šə'ērît* in prophetic literature to refer to those who survive God's judgment is well attested (Isa 10:20; Jer 31:7–9; Mic 7:18; Zeph 3:12–13). As used here in Hag 1:12, *šə'ērît* may simply denote the rest of the community besides the leaders identified, without the specific nuanced meaning of "remnant."[108] The larger issue is the identity of the *šə'ērît* "remnant" (cf. Hag 1:14; 2:2). Some therefore propose that the *šə'ērît,* "remnant," refers to the returnees who were more keen than the non-deportees to build the temple. The returnees were descendants of the elite groups taken to Babylon who shared in the tradition of the promised restoration. This group of returnees would have been predisposed to hearing Haggai's message and may have been part of the contingency that eventually built the temple (Ezra 3:8; 4:1; 6:16).[109] Floyd distinguishes between those who responded and those who did not. He argues that, while

106. See table 2 in the introduction above.

107. H. W. Wolff, *Haggai,* 141.

108. Meyers and Meyers, *Haggai, Zechariah 1–8,* 34.

109. H. W. Wolff, *Haggai,* 51–52; compare Carroll ("Myth of the Empty Land"), who also distinguishes among the deportees. He argues that there are differences between the 587 and 597 BCE deportees. The major distinction is that the 587 deportees were designated the favored of Yahweh and would be brought back to the land following the purification of the land. However, the 597 BCE deportees were not of the same functional status and were deemed the "bad" elements of the community.

the leaders and the remnant responded, another segment of the community was too afraid to respond.[110]

To whatever extent one discerns distinctions among the people mentioned, the focus of the message appears to minimize those distinctions. Certainly, there is no clear pattern used to differentiate among the subgroups in the population; therefore, "the people" appear to refer to the ordinary citizens in contrast to the leaders, rather than specifying intragroup distinctions.[111]

As a collective, the leaders together with the people "listened to" *the voice of Yahweh their God* (*bəqôl yhwh ʾĕlōhêhem*; cf. Jer 7:28; 26:13; 42:6; 43:4; Zech 6:15). This expression formed by *šāmaʿ* plus *bəqôl yhwh* is typically used to indicate dis/obedience (Jer 3:13, 25; 7:28; 9:13 [MT 12]; 23:21; 26:13; 38:20; 42:21; Dan 9:10).[112] The Deity is identified here as Yahweh their God, denoting a relationship between the community and God.[113] Thus, obedience is placed within the larger context of the covenant relationship.[114]

The community also heeded the words of Haggai, *the prophet* (*hannābîʾ*; cf. Hag 1:1, 3; 2:1, 10). The text shows why the people heeded the words of Haggai: *because Yahweh their God sent him* (*kaʾăšer šəlāḥô yhwh ʾĕlōhêhem*).[115] The message to the people sometimes specifies that God sent the messenger (Jer 28:9; 44:1).[116] It is unnecessary to supply the indirect object—"to them." They respond to him as the intermediary sent by Yahweh. In addition, it seems that the consistency between his words and the words of Yahweh facilitated their recognition of his role as compared with instances when the prophet does not speak the words of Yahweh. Some prophets who are not sent by Yahweh prophesy lies in the name of Yahweh and thus mislead the people (cf. Jer 14:14; 23:25, 26, 32; 28:15; 29:31; Ezek 13:8, 19; 22:28; Zech 10:2; 13:3).

Having discerned that Haggai is in fact a prophet of Yahweh and that the words that he spoke to them are Yahweh's words, *the people feared Yahweh* (*wayyîrʾû hāʿām mippənê yhwh*). Although it is possible that "fearing Yahweh" entails reverence for Yahweh, in this context it seems more likely that fear denotes being horrified by Yahweh.[117] Notably, in the instances where *yārēʾ*, "to fear," occurs with *mippənê* and the person to be feared, it usually connotes

110. Floyd (*Minor Prophets 2*, 269–70) acknowledges that the whole community is being addressed. Cf. Berquist, *Judaism in Persia's Shadow*, 17, 27–29.

111. Redditt, *Haggai, Zechariah, Malachi*, 22; cf. Verhoef, *Haggai and Malachi*, 81.

112. Note also *šāmaʿ* plus *dābār*, "obey the word," in Jer 25:8, or with God as object, "obey God," in Jer 34:17; 35:14, 16.

113. Cf. Exod 6:7; 20:2; Jer 3:21; 7:28; 22:9; 30:9; Ezek 28:26; 34:30; Hos 3:5; Zech 9:16; 10:6; Isa 41:13.

114. Cf. Kessler, *Haggai*, 142–45.

115. See n. 1 above. Contrast Jer 43:1 with Jer 29:31.

116. Cf. Kessler, *Haggai*,146; Verhoef, *Haggai and Malachi*, 82–83.

117. Thus Verhoef, *Haggai and Malachi*, 83.

dread of the person (Exod 9:30; Eccl 3:14; Ps 33:8).[118] The hearers were told that the devastation they experienced was not coincidental. Rather, Yahweh their God caused it all to convince them to comply with Yahweh's wishes for a temple. The message creates an image of Yahweh as one who is in control of even the heavens and its yield, as well as the land and its yield. While it appears that no amount of human effort can change what Yahweh has put into motion—as in the drought and its all-encompassing effects—it also appears that Yahweh's actions in nature are affected by the people's behavior.

2. *Report on Yahweh's Assurance to the People (1:13)*

13 The report on the assurance given to the people reveals fear to be a component in the people's response. The narrative introduction states that Haggai again performed his role as intermediary between the recipients of the message and the sender of the message. His identity as intermediary is designated not by the word *bəyad* (by the hand of) but by the appositive *mal'ak yhwh*, "messenger of Yahweh." Less frequent is the variation found in Mal 2:7, *mal'ak yhwh-ṣəbā'ôt*, "messenger of Yahweh of hosts" (cf. 2 Esd 1:40).[119] The expression here refers to the one who carries a message and is consistent with the portrayal of Haggai as the intermediary between the sender and the recipients. Another expression follows: *bəmal'ăkût yhwh*. The meaning of this *hapax* (unique term) is unknown; therefore, one can find several suggestions by other scholars, including "message," with the understanding that Haggai, the messenger, spoke the message of Yahweh to the people.[120] Another alternative is to translate *bəmal'ăkût yhwh lā'ām* as "mission"—according to Yahweh's mission.[121] Finally, the expression has also been translated "commissioned of Yahweh."[122] In the latter option, the understanding is that Haggai spoke according to the mandate of Yahweh.

As the messenger, Haggai delivered Yahweh's words to the people in accordance with his commission. The message that he delivered to the people was Yahweh's assurance *'ănî 'ittəkem*, "*I am with you.*" It is a general assurance of Yahweh's presence (Gen 28:15) as well as a specification of what Yahweh's presence means in practical terms: for example, assuring success (Jer 1:19;

118. Kessler, *Haggai*, 147.

119. Kessler (*Haggai*, 148) identifies some other references to messengers without use of the expression "messenger of Yahweh" (which may also be what is occurring in this instance in Haggai): Isa 42:19; 44:26; 2 Chr 36:15–16. Cf. Edgar W. Conrad, "Messengers in Isaiah and the Twelve: Implications for Reading Prophetic Books," *JSOT* 91 (2000): 83–97.

120. Meyers and Meyers, *Haggai, Zechariah 1–8*, 35.

121. Verhoef, *Haggai and Malachi*, 84.

122. Kessler, *Haggai*, 107, 148.

15:20; 30:11; Hag 2:4); giving a reason not to be afraid (Gen 26:24; Isa 41:10; 43:5; Jer 1:8; 42:11; 46:28); providing assurance from one person to another (1 Sam 14:7; 2 Kgs 3:7).[123] Thus, the assurance provides support for the daunting task of building the temple and reports that the community feared Yahweh (Hag 1:12; cf. 2:4–5). The assurance closes with an oracle formula, *nəʾum-yhwh*, "utterance of Yahweh," again asserting that the words communicated to the people by the prophet are Yahweh's words.

3. Report on the Community's Transformation (1:14–15)

14 The report about the community's transformation is depicted as being the effect of the preceding events and interactions. This transformation includes: First, the role of Yahweh in the course of events—Yahweh stirred the spirit of all concerned. The whole community, the leaders and all the remnant of the people change perspective from their own to Yahweh's (cf. Hag 1:12). Second, the community's transformation consists of responding to Yahweh's expectation to build the temple—*the house of Yahweh of hosts their God* (*bəbêt-yhwh ṣəbāʾôt ʾĕlōhêhem*; cf. Hag 1:2, 4, 8, 9). This section then portrays the success of Yahweh's effort versus the people's effort to resist.

Haggai 1:14 describes the obedience to the command given in 1:8. Here, many scholars are puzzled about what happened. Was it the building that began or a dedication ceremony (cf. Hag 2:18; Ezra 3)? The work described may refer to the preparation, the rededication, or the actual building effort. It is the beginning community of 520 BCE.[124]

15 The date formula in 1:15 includes day, month, year: *bəyôm ʿeśrîm wəʾarbāʿâ laḥōdeš baššiššî bišnat šətayim*, "the twenty-fourth day of the month, in the sixth [month] in the second year," and specifies the regnal year, *lədārəyāweš hammelek*, of Darius the king. In its current position, the date formula may indicate the time during which the respondents to the prophecy were stirred and began to work on the temple. From this interpretive stance, the date formula concludes the first segment of the book. Likewise, it depicts a quick movement from the community's neglect of the temple to their work on the temple—within twenty-three days.

There are other alternatives for understanding this date formula, as noted above (see introductory section). Here, suffice it to say that some scholars begin Hag 2:1 with the year element of the formula instead of concluding

123. Cf. H. W. Wolff, *Haggai*, 50; Kessler, *Haggai*, 149–50; Verhoef, *Haggai and Malachi*, 84–85; Redditt, *Haggai, Zechariah, Malachi*, 22–23.

124. Cf. Meyers and Meyers, *Haggai, Zechariah 1–8*, 63–64; Baldwin, *Hag, Zech, Mal*, 53; Verhoef, *Haggai and Malachi*, 26–27.

chap. 1 with the year element. Regardless, the date formula describes the time when the community began to work on the temple and thus depicts the contrast between their past inactivity and adversity and their present response.[125]

II. ENCOURAGEMENT: INQUIRY AND ADMONITION (2:1–9)

This unit focuses on encouraging the community through an inquiry (2:1–3) and an admonition (2:4–9). The inquiry about the temple provides a foundation for the subsequent admonition. The admonition sequence further consists of the admonition itself and basis for the admonition—God's promise. The presence of the chronological indicator in this macrounit signifies that time is a key concept. It constitutes the time frame for the fulfillment of the prophecy and is also significant in highlighting the contrast between the present and the former condition of the temple.

A. INQUIRY REGARDING THE TEMPLE (2:1–3)

[1]*In the seventh [month] on the twenty-first day of the month, the word of Yahweh came by the hand*[a] *of Haggai the prophet:* [2]*Speak now to Zerubbabel son of Shealtiel, governor of Judah, and to Joshua son of Jehozadak, the high priest, and to the remnant of the people:*[b] [3]*"Who remains among you who has seen this house in its former splendor? And how are you seeing it now? Is it not as nothing in your eyes?"*

a. The MT *bəyad,* "by/through the hand," also appears in Hag 1:1, 3; the text reads *'el* in 2:10. While the LXX supports the MT reading, a Wadi Murabba'at fragment of 2:1 reads *'el,* "to." At issue is whether "the word of Yahweh came" to (*'el*) or through (*bəyad*) the prophet (cf. *bəyad,* 1:1). Verhoef (*Haggai and Malachi,* 94–95) notes that "the problem with the prepositional phrase . . . in this connection is that it is part of a direct speech followed by *lē'mōr* and *'əmār-nā'*." He retains the MT reading and incorporates the idea of reception as a nuance of that meaning (cf. Isa 20:2). This argument appears to mean that the other occurrences (Hag 1:1, 3; 2:10) did not introduce direct speech. However, all of the instances contain *lē'mōr*—that is, *hāyâ dəbar-yhwh . . . ḥaggay hannābî' lē'mōr* (Hag 1:1, 3; 2:1, 10). If *lē'mōr* indicates the onset of a speech, then an emendation to *'el* cannot be argued on the basis of its relationship or lack of relationship to direct speech.

b. The MT of Hag 2:2 reads *wə'el-šə'ērît hā'ām,* "and to the remnant of the people," as compared with *kōl šə'ērît hā'ām,* "all the remnant of the people," in Hag 1:12, 14. The LXX addition of "all" appears to harmonize with Hag 1:12, 14 and possibly 2:4 (*kol-'am hā'āreṣ,* "all you people of the land"). Some scholars follow the LXX and argue that the "loss of *kol*

125. See discussion of the date formula in the introduction above.

in the MT is due to haplography" (e.g., Meyers and Meyers, *Haggai, Zechariah 1–8,* 47, 49). Others retain the MT but reflect the presence of *kol* in their understanding of the text (e.g., Kessler [*Haggai,* 2] argues that both expressions [with/without *kol*] "carry the same meaning" [p. 164]; Verhoef [*Haggai and Malachi,* 95] retains the MT).

1 One of the first concerns about 2:1 and the unit it introduces is the relationship of the date formula to the date in 1:15 (twenty-fourth day of the sixth month). Haggai 2:1 dates this part of the prophetic activity to *the twenty-first day of the seventh month (baššəbîʿî bəʿeśrîm wəʾeḥād laḥōdeš),* presumably also during the second year of Darius, which is mentioned in 1:15. The significance of the seventh month in the history of Israel is twofold. First, it is the time for the Festival of Booths. Second and closely related to the first reason, the Solomonic Temple was dedicated in the seventh month (1 Kgs 8:2; 2 Chr 7:1–11).

The first, the Festival of Booths (Festival of Tabernacles), is an annual festival celebrated for seven days during the seventh month beginning on the fifteenth day of the month. According to Lev 23:33–44, the first day is to be a convocation, and like the Sabbath day, no work is to be done on the first and the eighth days (Lev 23:39). Then for seven days, offerings are to be presented by fire, followed by a day of convocation (the eighth day; Lev 23:36). It is a festival of remembrance (*zikkārōn*) regarding God's act on their behalf: that is, God brought them out of Egypt, after which they lived in booths (huts) while traveling.[126] During the Festival of Booths, they are instructed to live in booths in remembrance (Lev 23:42–43). Numbers 29:12–39 enumerates the offerings to be presented on each day of the festival (cf. Deut 16:13–17; 31:10–13; Ezek 45:25). These offerings are in addition to the regular burnt offering and its grain offering and the drink offering (Num 29:19, 22, 25, 28, 31, 34, 38, 39). From the perspective of Ezra 3:4, the people kept the Festival of Booths as prescribed by the law. The date formula therefore indicates that on the seventh day of the festival Haggai received a message from Yahweh. The eighth day is a day of rest (*šabbātôn*). The word-event formula appears here in Hag 2:1 indicating that the *word of Yahweh came by the hand of Haggai the prophet.*

The seventh month would be the equivalent of October 17, 520 BCE. According to Ezra 3:1–6, Joshua and Zerubbabel built the altar, observed the Festival of Booths, and offered sacrifices as specified by the law. They did this before the foundation of the temple was laid and probably timed the return to coincide with the seventh-month festival.[127] From the time of the Seleucids onward, the Festival of Booths became New Year's Day, or Rosh Hashanah

126. H. Eising, "זָכַר *zākhar,*" *TDOT* 4:78.

127. Clines (*Ezra, Nehemiah, Esther,* 63–64) observes that the text does not speak of a "foundation not yet being laid; but only of the temple not yet repaired" (p. 67).

(cf. Ezek 40:1). According to Hartley, the debate about the origins of Rosh Hashanah results in part from debates about the calendar (cultic versus civil). He proposes that the day was not regarded as the New Year in Lev 23, in contrast to Noth, who contends that it was.[128] Note that the seventh month was a significant time for beginning "new ventures" (Neh 7:73b; 8:2, 14–18; cf. 2 Chr 5:3; 7:8–10). Whether it was a historical or a literary device, the dating of these events during the seventh month achieved continuity between the past and the present.

The second reason that the seventh month is significant is its association with the dedication of the Solomonic Temple. During the time of Haggai, the people would have assembled for the seventh-month festival (month of Ethanim/Tishri). While at this point the text makes no explicit reference to that connection, the comparison between the past and present states of the temple would most likely have been in the foreground—if for no other reason, the contrast between the reputed opulence and splendor of the Solomonic Temple and the desolation of the current temple (cf. Hag 2:3) would have made the connection salient.[129] The Solomonic dedication included bringing the ark of the covenant and all that was in the Tent of Meeting to the holy of holies, offering sacrifices, and observing the Festival of Booths (1 Kgs 8:62–66). The ark was placed in the holy of holies "beneath the wings of the cherubim" (1 Kgs 8:6–7).

In the dedication speech, Solomon reflected on the concept of divine presence, noting that the temple (this house) cannot contain Yahweh; but the name of the Deity will dwell there (1 Kgs 8:28–30). Likewise, the prayer mentions the connection between the people's sin and the withholding of rain: repentance would bring about forgiveness and the restoration of rain. Even plague, blight, mildew, and locusts are identified as results of the people's sins (1 Kgs 8:35–40). Thus, to the extent that the seventh month recalled the dedication of the Solomonic Temple, it also probably recalled the speech, the essence of that dedication. The reminder would have established links as much to the reputation of the temple's former splendor as to the tradition concerning the reciprocity between sin and affliction, repentance/forgiveness and blessing.

2 In Hag 2:2 the prophet is commanded to address the recipients of the message. They were not identified in the word-event formula in 1:1. Here in 2:2 the command to the prophet is to speak. Because of the second-person

128. Hartley, *Leviticus,* 387. Noth, *Leviticus,* 172–73. "Even after the Babylonian spring year had been introduced for the official reckoning of year and month—probably shortly before the exile—the cultic beginning of the year kept its place in the 'seventh month'; and the only concession to the new calendar was the fixed dating on the first day of the month."

129. Cf. Kessler, *Haggai,* 164; Verhoef, *Haggai and Malachi,* 94.

address and the specific content, Verhoef follows the Murabbaʿat fragment in reading "by the hand of Haggai" (*bəyad-ḥaggay*) rather than *to Haggai* (*ʾel-ḥaggay*) to resolve the disagreement about reports versus direct speech. The recipients are those enumerated in Hag 1:12, namely: Zerubbabel son of Shealtiel, governor of Judah, and Joshua son of Jehozadak, the high priest, and the remnant of the people.

Zerubbabel's patronymic is a shortened form (*ben-šaltîʾēl*) as compared with the full/plene form in 1:1 (*ben-šəʾaltîʾēl*; see introduction, section I). Concerning the designation "remnant of the people" (*šəʾērît hāʿām*), Wolff argues that it refers to the returnees, those who in Hag 1:12 and 14 are also depicted as being obedient. For him this designation does not represent the entire people (cf. 1:4) but a segment of the population. He cites textual examples to support this argument (e.g., Zech 8:6, 11, 12; Neh 7:71; cf. Mic 5:7; 7:18).[130] Kessler sees no difference between the designation using "all," *kōl šəʾērît hāʿām* (Hag 1:14) and *šəʾērît hāʿām* (Hag 2:2); rather, he understands *šəʾērît hāʿām* (Hag 2:2) to be the entire community as opposed to the factions in Hag 1:1–3.[131]

If seen in connection with its usage in Zechariah and other books, the phrase "remnant of the people" refers to the survivors. Broadly speaking, the entire community may be designated a remnant (cf. Mic 4:6–7). This observation leads to a question regarding the use of the two designations: remnant of the people, people of the land. Here the prophet may be referring to (a) the leaders and (b) the rest of the people, or (c) the leaders and the entire remnant (all survivors, not simply the recent returnees). What does the latter suggestion mean in light of Hag 2:4, "all the people of the land"? (See below for further discussion; cf. Ezra 3:8, "rest of their people.") Most likely Hag 2:4 refers to all the people, including the residents who remained in the land while others were deported, and the returnees.

Yet another question suggests itself at this point: why the difference in focus? The scope of the addressees may also be manifested in the content of the address. Notably, the addressees are identified by use of the second masculine singular.

Furthermore, three elements form an inquiry about the temple: (1) Who can remember the glory of the temple? (2) What is its present state? (3) What is your evaluation of its present state?

Before looking at each of these constitutive components, we would do well to note the connection between Hag 1:2–4 and 2:3. While the perspective of 1:2–4 is that the people and Yahweh are at odds about the building of the temple, here in 2:3 the perspective is that the addressees must evaluate the situation. That situation is seen from two vantage points: the past, which

130. H. W. Wolff, *Haggai*, 76–77.

131. Kessler, *Haggai*, 64.

may influence their perception; and the present, insofar as it has affected their inclination toward the temple. Presumably, they have been stirred to activity (Hag 1:14), but the nature of that activity includes the need to understand their attitude and behaviors. The formula in 1:5 and 7 does not allude to Hag 2:3, but the force of the command to "reflect" may potentially achieve a similar outcome. As in 1:5 and 7, the addressees are asked to look at the past to see the connection with the present. Unlike 1:5 and 7, they are not asked to focus on their behaviors that affected the present status of the temple but on the temple itself, especially on issues of continuity and discontinuity.

3 The first question—*Who is left among you?*—is about people who can still recall the splendor of the former temple, the Solomonic Temple. This question signals a practical aspect. In 597 BCE, many were deported to Babylon who did not witness the destruction of the temple. The Solomonic Temple was destroyed in 587/6 BCE; some people were deported during that time while some remained in the land. If any who were deported between 597 and 586 BCE were old enough to remember the temple, returned, and were part of Haggai's audience in 520 BCE, they would be about seventy to eighty years old. There may have been others in the land who remained after the destruction of the temple and remembered the temple. According to Ezra 3:10–13, when the old people who had seen the former house (*habbayit hāriʾšôn*) on its foundation saw the new foundation, they wept. Among them were Levites, priests, and heads of families. Their weeping was in contrast to the jubilation of others—presumably those who had not witnessed the old/former temple. So while there may have been some left who knew the former temple, this group may have been relatively small.[132] While Verhoef acknowledges that some may have survived, he understands Ezra 3 to be speaking about the context of 536 BCE: it was possible that some people who had seen the preexilic temple were living in the time of Haggai.[133] Regardless of the date (536 or 520 BCE), both Ezra and Haggai note a comparison between the state of the preexilic temple and the postexilic temple.[134]

The group who saw the former temple is described in two ways: the people "who remain" (*hanniśʾār*) and those "who saw" (*ʾăšer rāʾâ*). The designation *hanniśʾār* (*niphal* participle of *šāʾar*) appears several times with the singular form of the participle (*niśʾār*) and also appears as a collective. Whether singular or plural, the *niphal* participle is usually indistinguishable

132. Cf. Kessler, *Haggai,* 165; J. Blenkinsopp, "Life Expectancy in Ancient Palestine," *SJOT* 11 (1997): 44–55; H. W. Wolff, *Haggai,* 77.

133. Verhoef, *Haggai and Malachi,* 95–96.

134. Cf. Meyers and Meyers, *Haggai, Zechariah 1–8,* 49–50; contrast Clines, *Ezra, Nehemiah, Esther,* 1.

from *šəʾērît,* "remnant." In the broadest sense, *nišʾār,* "the remainder, rest, what is left," also refers to food and to the residual after the harvest (e.g., 1 Sam 9:24; Isa 17:6).[135] Also in this broad sense it may describe those who survived and are therefore alive, in contrast to those who are dead (cf. Deut 3:11; Judg 4:16; 2 Kgs 10:17; cf. Josh 8:22); and in some cases it is used of descendants (e.g., Gen 45:7; Jer 11:23). With reference to destruction and war, *nišʾār* is sometimes used with *pālîṭ,* "place of escape," or with the same notion of *šəʾērît* (Gen 32:9; 2 Kgs 19:30; cf. Isa 66:19; Ezek 7:16; Ezra 9:14) and *śārîd,* "survivor" (Num 21:35; Deut 2:34; 3:3; Josh 8:22; 10:20; 2 Kgs 10:11; Obad 18). Both *pālîṭ* and *śārîd* are used together to denote the remnant or survivor in Jer 42:17.

Other terms associated with *šāʾar* are *nākâ,* "strike" (Gen 32:9; Num 21:35; 1 Chr 4:43), and *kārat,* "eradicate" (Isa 14:22). A lack of survivors is also referred to as *nišʾār* (e.g., Exod 14:28; Josh 8:17; Judg 4:16).[136] In addition to these general understandings, one can distinguish the "remnant" as those who were exiled, having survived judgment (cf. 2 Kgs 25:11; Jer 8:3; 52:15; Ezra 1:4; Mic 4:6), as well as those who survived judgment but remained in the land (Jer 24:8; 40:6; 41:10).

Here in Hag 2:3 it is likely that "remnant" refers to those who are old enough to remember the previous temple—that is, without any reference to whether they experienced exile.[137] All the Israelites living during that time, whether inside or outside the land, experienced the effects of the deportation. The fundamental characteristic is their link to the preexilic temple, not their experience after the deportations or destruction.

This brings the discussion back to the second characterization of the group mentioned in Hag 2:3—those "who saw" (*ʾăšer rāʾâ*) the former temple. It is not only that they survived but that they experienced the temple with their own senses—they saw it. Although the sensory perception is explicitly mentioned, the prophet is addressing more than this. Asking if there were any left *who saw* presupposes that they were cognizant of what they saw, which is distinct from those who heard about the temple and knew of it by reputation. Thus, the prophet is calling for eyewitnesses to the preexilic temple.[138] What was their function and influence in the restored community? One may gain some perspective from Ezra 3:10–13, which reports that the old people (*hazzəqēnîm*) who returned wept:

135. Note also the occurrences in the *hiphil* (Num 21:35; Deut 2:34; 3:3; Josh 8:22; 10:28; 2 Kgs 10:14). H. Wildburger, "שאר," *TLOT* 3:1284–92, esp. p. 1285.

136. Wildburger, *TLOT* 3:1286.

137. Cf. Kessler, *Haggai,* 164–65.

138. Meyers and Meyers, *Haggai, Zechariah 1–8,* 49–50; Verhoef, *Haggai and Malachi,* 96; H. W. Wolff, *Haggai,* 71.

> But many of the priests and Levites and heads of families, old people who had seen the first house on its foundations, wept with a loud voice when they saw this house, though many shouted aloud for joy, so that the people could not distinguish the sound of the joyful shout from the sound of the people's weeping, for the people shouted so loudly that the sound was heard far away. (Ezra 3:12–13 NRSV)

Why did the old people weep? As in Hag 2:3 this group is described as those who saw (*rāʾâ*) the former structure. They saw the former house on its foundation "with their eyes," *bəʿênêhem* (Ezra 3:12), and they saw this house in its glory (Hag 2:3). A few possible interpretations may inform our understanding of Hag 2:3. The first reason they wept may have been joy that the temple, after lying desolate, was being rebuilt. However, the text juxtaposes the weeping with jubilant shouting (Ezra 3:13), thus suggesting contrasting behaviors.[139]

The second reason for the weeping may be that the people knew they most likely would not witness the completion of the temple. They may have anticipated that, since the first temple took about seven years to be completed, the new temple would also take about that long (cf. 1 Kgs 6:38). If their work began in about 536 BCE and lasted until 516/5, it took about twenty years to complete. If the work began in 520, it took four or five years to complete. So, if indeed the weeping was regret that they would not see the temple, this notion was well founded, because any who saw and remembered the preexilic temple in 597–586 BCE would have been at least seventy-five or eighty years old in 520 BCE and at least seventy-nine to ninety years old in 515 BCE. These figures presume that those who saw the first temple were about seven years old at the time of their exile or the destruction of the temple. Presumably there were those who were born at the time of the exile or the destruction who were young enough to witness the return in 538 BCE; they would have been about sixty-six years old, and twenty-one years later in 515 BCE, they also would have been in their eighties.

The third reason for the weeping and the tension of the people in Hag 2 is that the current temple did not live up to the splendor of the former.[140] Their dashed expectations would have fueled their negative response. This brings the discussion back to the question of the remnant's function and influence in the community. The remnant was eyewitness to the glory (*kābôd*) of the former temple, identified in Hag 2:3 as "this house" (*habbayit hazzê*; cf. 1:2). The general sense of *kābôd* (masc.-sing. noun) is "glory, majesty, honor." It also denotes "wealth, respect" (Gen 31:1; 45:13; Isa 10:3; 61:6; 66:12) or the

139. Clines, *Ezra, Nehemiah, Esther,* 71.

140. Clines, *Ezra, Nehemiah, Esther,* 71; Blenkinsopp, *Ezra-Nehemiah*; Williamson, *Ezra, Nehemiah.*

impressive nature of an entity, for example: trees, woods (Isa 10:18; 35:2; Ezek 31:18), a chariot (Isa 22:18), the land (Isa 17:3; 66:11; Mic 1:15), or the temple (Jer 14:21; 17:12).[141] The latter nuance seems to be used here in Hag 2:3. The "glory" (*kābôd*) of "this house" is the focus of the question, though not the *kābôd* of its present state but of its former state. The text does not specify whether this is referring to its treasures or to its physical structure—that is, the dimensions of the temple. It seems unlikely that the reference is to the treasures since they were used to pay for the nation's security, and the temple was repeatedly plundered, leaving it stripped of much of its original opulence. Such depletion of the temple resources occurred during the reigns of several kings, including Rehoboam (to the king of Egypt; 1 Kgs 14:25–29), Jehoash (to the king of Aram; 2 Kgs 12:17–20), Ahaz (2 Kgs 16:17–18), Hezekiah (2 Kgs 18:13–16), Jehoiachin, and Zedekiah (2 Kgs 24:12–13; 2 Kgs 25:8–15).[142] Consequently, by 597 BCE when the first portion of Judah's population was deported, the resources may have been minimal compared to the time of Solomon.[143] Additionally, it would have been unlikely that the "aged group" would have seen the treasures. They would have been quite young when they were deported. Quite apart from their age, their status would have limited their access to the temple, since only the chief priest would have had access to the interior.[144]

Another argument that the comparison is not with the temple's former opulence is that Cyrus contributed treasures to the temple building project. According to Ezra 1:4–11, the people brought silver and gold vessels, and Cyrus returned the vessels that Nebuchadnezzar had taken when he invaded and destroyed Jerusalem (cf. Ezra 2:68–69; 5:14; 6:5; Neh 7:70–71).[145] What glory remained for the Solomonic Temple before Nebuchadnezzar, therefore, was not its opulence but its structure. Its structure and its dimensions were what any remaining person from the preexilic community would have seen (cf. Ezra 6:3).[146]

The second question in Hag 2:3—*How are you seeing it now?*—concerns the audience's present state, especially the aged group identified by *ʾattem*,

141. C. Westermann, "כבד," *TLOT* 2:590–602; cf. H. W. Wolff, *Haggai,* 77.

142. Verhoef, *Haggai and Malachi,* 96; cf. Kessler, *Haggai,* 165–67; H. W. Wolff, *Haggai,* 77.

143. Meyers and Meyers, *Haggai, Zechariah,* 72.

144. Meyers and Meyers, *Haggai, Zechariah 1–8,* 72; Kessler, *Haggai,* 166–67.

145. Clines, *Ezra, Nehemiah, Esther,* 43, 60–61. The items listed in 2 Kgs 25:13–14 are not listed in Ezra 1:4–11. The texts also differ in their representation of the treasures in that 1 Esd 2:14 records 5,469 total items. According to Neh 7:70–72 (MT 69–71), the governor and the heads of the ancestral houses contributed to the work.

146. Two dimensions are given: its height was to be sixty cubits and its width sixty cubits. Cf. Clines, *Ezra, Nehemiah, Esther,* 91.

"you," the second masculine plural personal pronoun. The question contrasts the present and the past. The fact that the community had recently begun its work on the temple (1:14) indicates that there was not much similarity between its former and its present state. For this reason, among others, scholars suggest that the question is strictly rhetorical.[147] The aged group is again asked to be an eyewitness to the state/condition of the temple. This is achieved by the repeated use of the verbal root *rāʾâ*, "to see," and the object (the temple), signaled by *ʾōtô* (third masculine singular pronomial suffix) whose antecedent is "this house" (*habbayit hazzê*, 2:3a).

The third and final question in Hag 2:3—*Is it not as nothing in your eyes?*—appears in 2:3bβ. Does it seem like nothing "in your eyes" (*bəʿênêhem*; cf. Ezra 3:12; Deut 4:9–11; 29:2–9; Josh 24:7; 1 Sam 24:10)? Again, as in the other two questions, the group's perception is the focal point. The question brings into focus the past completed temple and the present desolation. The community is not so much challenged to envision the future as to see the present reality. Possibly, the stark contrast between the past and present status led to discouragement, and so would have the contrast between the present and the projected future. How does one move from ruins or even partial destruction to the idealized image in the personal or collective memory of a far greater temple than perhaps there ever was? How does one move from the present reality to an idealized future, exalted temple?

Because memory often idealizes certain aspects of the past, it is conceivable that the people had a skewed recollection. For example, what could have been a more skewed view of the past than the people's hankering for Egypt and its water, food, and safety when they were confronted by challenging situations in the wilderness (Exod 16; 17; Num 11, 20; cf. Exod 14:10–14; 15:23–27; Num 14:1–12)? Added to idealization of the past was the tradition about the seventy-year return and the prophecy of restoration (2 Chr 36:15–23; Jer 24:1–7; 25:1–14; 29:10–14; cf. Mic 4:1–4; Isa 2:2–4). Most likely, the greater the remnant's awareness of their temple tradition was, the greater became their perception of the lackluster nature of the temple they were attempting to build. Why so much concern about this relatively small group of people in the community? Apparently their status—Levites, priests, heads of families—enhanced the value of their opinions in the community (cf. Ezra 3:10–14). As in the case of the spy report in Num 13:21–14:12, it was not the size of the group that determined their influence on the people. Rather, it was the power of these few to shape and define the perspective of the commu-

147. Kessler, *Haggai*, 166; Verhoef, *Haggai and Malachi*, 97. Meyers and Meyers (*Haggai, Zechariah 1–8*, 50) reason that the above-eighty age of the remnants makes it unlikely that this is an actual question; it is more of a rhetorical device than a question seeking a response.

nity, either to reflect their fears, concerns, and anxieties or to influence their ensuing cooperation and hope.

Another comparison comes into play here that is less salient but none-theless significant: reality versus the people's perception of reality, as suggested by the use of the idiom "in your eyes." This is significant in light of Hag 1:2–4's depiction of the people: their perception is faulty at best; they don't think it is time to build Yahweh's house. Meanwhile, their houses are already complete and inhabited (Hag 1:9). The community is inclined to misconstrue reality and thus may be in need of correction and encouragement.

B. EXPRESSION OF ENCOURAGEMENT (2:4–9)

4*And now be strong, Zerubbabel—oracle of Yahweh*[a]*—and be strong,*
Joshua son of Jehozadak, the high priest; and be strong, all people of the land—
oracle of Yahweh—and work, for I am with you—oracle of Yahweh of hosts, 5*that*
is, the word[b] *that I covenanted with you when you came out of Egypt*[c]*—and my*
spirit remains in your midst. Do not fear. 6*For thus says Yahweh of hosts, "Once*
again, in a little while[d] *and I am about to shake the heavens and the earth, and*[e]
the sea and the dry land; 7*and I will shake all the nations and all the treasure*[f] *of*
the nations will come. And I will fill this house [with] splendor," says Yahweh of
hosts. 8*The silver is mine, and the gold is mine—oracle of Yahweh of hosts.* 9*The*
latter splendor of this house will be greater than the former, says Yahweh of hosts;
and I will give peace in this place—oracle of Yahweh of hosts.[g]

---

a. *BHS* indicates that at least three elements in the verse may be later additions: (1) the divine-utterance formula in Hag 2:4a, *nəʾum-yhwh,* directly following *zərubbābel*; (2) the clause *ben-yəhôṣādāq hakkōhēn haggādôl waḥăzaq kol-ʿam hāʾāreṣ nəʾum-yhwh,* "son of Jehozadak, the high priest; and be strong, all people of the land—oracle of Yahweh"; (3) and *ṣəbāʾôt,* "hosts," found in the last formula in 2:4b. The second element provides the appositive for *yəhôšuaʿ*, "Joshua," an appositive also found in Hag 1:1, 12. Most likely the suggestion that the appositive is an addition and should be deleted is an effort to create balance with the preceding addressee, Zerubbabel, whose name is mentioned without his appositive. The omission would also eliminate the second exhortation addressed to the people of the land (*ʿam hāʾāreṣ*), resulting in an encouragement given to the leaders—Zerubbabel and Joshua—at the exclusion of the people. It would also mean that the people are not encouraged to work and are not reassured about the presence of Yahweh; therefore, I retain the MT reading.

b. *BHS* suggests that *ʾet-haddābār* should read *habbərît zōʾt,* "this covenant"; also perhaps *ʾet* forms an instance of dittography with *(ṣəbā)ʾôt,* at the end of the preceding word (v. 4).

c. The LXX omits *ʾet-haddābār ʾăšer-kārattî ʾittəkem bəṣēʾtkem mimmiṣrayim,* "the word that I covenanted with you when you came out of Egypt." It therefore reads: "Work, for I am with you, says the Lord Almighty; and my spirit remains in your midst." Perhaps the omission in the LXX and Syriac is due to the difficulty that its presence poses to the meaning of the text. This difficulty is generated in part by the presence of *'et* at the beginning of the clause. While most scholars retain the MT reading, their understandings of the text and its relationship to the preceding vary.

d. While it has been argued that the problematic nature of the MT clause (*ʿôd 'aḥat məʿaṭ hîʾ*) is due to its combined use of two idiomatic expressions—(1) *ʿôd 'aḥat,* "yet once," and (2) *məʿaṭ hîʾ,* "it is a little while"—there is no instance of *ʿôd 'aḥat* or *məʿaṭ hîʾ* as independent expressions (for further discussion, see Kessler, *Haggai,* 160 n. 11; Verhoef, *Haggai and Malachi,* 101–2). Even so, the LXX reads *eti hapax,* "yet once," assuming *ʿôd 'aḥat* and omitting the second part of the expression (*məʿaṭ hîʾ*). The Syriac also reflects the omission of *məʿaṭ hîʾ* and, like the LXX, signals an attempt to clarify the expression. Rather than seeing the MT as a fusion of two distinct expressions, some argue that the common expression *ʿôd 'aḥat,* "soon, in a little while," has been conflated to emphasize a particular perspective (cf. the use of *ʿôd* in Hag 2:19). Both Kessler (*Haggai,* 173) and Verhoef (*Haggai and Malachi,* 101–2) discuss the grammatical difficulties resulting from this apparent conflation into a common expression. In addition to the seeming awkwardness of *'aḥat* in the expression, the lack of accord between *'aḥat,* (feminine) and *məʿaṭ* (masculine) is problematic (note the uses of the term *məʿaṭ* in 1:6, 9). Meyers and Meyers (*Haggai, Zechariah 1–8,* 52) agree that a common expression was disrupted by the addition of two elements but concede that the MT reading is original, reflecting the prophet's concern to highlight the immediacy of Yahweh's action without giving a fixed time for the implementation of that action. Cf. GKC §141l; 142f–g.

e. The targum suggests *'et* in place of *wə'et.* Some modern translators also omit the *waw,* "and," in their translation; for example: Kessler, *Haggai,* 160; Verhoef, *Haggai and Malachi,* 91, 101; contrast Meyers and Meyers, *Haggai, Zechariah 1–8,* 47.

f. As it stands, *ḥemdat* (sing.) occurs with *bā'û* (the pl. verbal form). The textual apparatus suggests reading *ḥămûdôt* to fit with the plural verb. Some modern translators understand the *ḥemdat* (sing.) as a collective, which requires a plural verbal form (e.g., Verhoef, *Haggai and Malachi,* 92; Kessler, *Haggai,* 161). Others emend the text, thus reading *bā'û ḥămûdôt,* "treasures/desired things will come" (e.g., Meyers and Meyers, *Haggai, Zechariah 1–8,* 47; R. L. Smith, *Micah–Malachi,* 156).

g. Following *ṣəbā'ôt,* the LXX adds the following: "even peace of soul for a possession to every one that builds, to raise up this temple." The LXX thus provides an explanatory note regarding the nature of the promised peace and in so doing identifies the peace as a nonmaterial reward for those who build. This tendency to expand is also seen in Hag 2:14, 17.

4 Haggai 2:4 is noteworthy for several reasons. First, it is part of the unit 2:4–9 and subunit 2:4–5, which address the present circumstances of the community—that is, the community's disenchantment about the status of the temple vis-à-vis the former temple. Haggai 2:4 begins with the temporal indicator *wəʿattā,* "and now," focusing attention on the present in contrast to the past or the future but nonetheless connecting to both. The use of *wəʿattā* to achieve this contrast between time frames is attested elsewhere in prophetic literature (e.g., Isa 5:5; 28:22; 37:26; 48:16; Jer 27:6; Ezek 4:14; 7:3; Mic 4:7). Micah 4–5 employs the particle *wəʿattā,* "and now," to present the circumstances that would signal movement from the challenge of the present to the eschatological reality of the future. Thus, *wəʿattā* is used in Mic 4:9, 11, 14 in contrast to the

futuristic formula "in that day" (*bayyôm hahû'*, 4:6; 5:10).[148] While *bayyôm hahû'* is absent from Hag 2:4–9, the use of the phrase "once again, in a little while" may indicate a futuristic reference, though arguably not of the same period of time as *bayyôm hahû'* (Hag 2:23) and *wəʿattā* (Hag 1:5).

1. The Encouragement Proper (Admonition) (2:4–5)

The words of encouragement are addressed to the various segments of the community (Hag 2:4a) and provide the rationale for the encouragement (2:4bα), followed by the divine-utterance formula (2:4bβ). First, the exhortation to "be strong" (*ḥāzaq,* imperative sing. or pl.) is a typical usage in situations that offer encouragement: (1) The term *ḥāzaq* is often accompanied by other verbs, such as *'āmēṣ*, "to be firm, steadfast" (Deut 31:6–7, 23; Josh 1:6–7, 9, 18; 10:25; 1 Chr 22:13; 2 Chr 32:7; Pss 27:14; 31:24). (2) The term *ḥāzaq* also occurs with *ʿāśâ*, "to do" (Ezra 10:4; 1 Chr 28:10, 20; 2 Chr 19:11; 25:8). (3) In oracles promising divine assistance, *ḥāzaq* usually occurs with the admonition *'al-tîrā'û*, "do not fear" (Isa 35:4; 41:6; cf. Dan 10:19; Jer 46:28), or the support formula *ʿimməkā-'ānî* or *'ittəkā 'ānî*, "I am with you" (Isa 41:10; Jer 46:28; Deut 31:8, 23; 1 Chr 28:20; 2 Chr 19:11).[149] The formulas occur together in Isa 41:10; 43:5; Gen 26:24; Jer 1:8; 42:11. The affirmation "I am with you" may occur without the admonition "do not fear," while still indicating divine assistance or deliverance (Jer 1:19; 15:20; 30:11; cf. Hag 1:13). Here in Hag 2:4 the encouragement to the community to be strong is associated with the people's disposition toward the temple. Apparently, the people are discouraged because of their perceived inability to rebuild the temple to match the status of the former temple (Hag 2).

The first addressee identified in Hag 2:4 is Zerubbabel, whose name appears without his title (1:12; 2:23; contrast 1:1, 14; 2:2) or patronymic (contrast 1:1, 12, 14; 2:2). The repetition of the imperative *ḥāzaq*, "be strong," plus the addressee places emphasis on each segment of the community. The purpose of the repetition may be to single out each segment specifically in order to include all of them in the encouragement. This first segment of the encouragement concludes with the divine-utterance formula (see textual notes). Wolff posits that the focus of the reassurance is the community, Zerubbabel being responsible for their morale, with Joshua assisting him.[150] As the leader of the community, Zerubbabel was accountable to the Persian Empire, which

148. Jacobs, *Conceptual Coherence.*

149. A. S. van der Woude, "חזק," *TLOT* 1:403–6, esp. p. 405; Kessler, *Haggai,* 168; H. W. Wolff, *Haggai,* 79.

150. H. W. Wolff, *Haggai,* 78.

provided the resources for restoring the community. Likewise, he was responsible for overseeing the restoration efforts, especially the rebuilding of the temple.

The second addressee, Joshua, is identified by title and patronymic. The presence of the two designations with Joshua's name—juxtaposed as it is to Zerubbabel's name without them—has led to the suggestion that the verse reflects the elevation of the high priest over the governor;[151] however, there is nothing in this passage to support that claim. Perhaps the priest is mentioned and specified, not because the role is elevated, but because the priest is in greater need of encouragement than the governor. Understanding the temple tradition, and faced with the belief that what was being rebuilt would not approximate the former temple's structure or opulence, the priest may have felt the difficulty more keenly. If the priest were discouraged, undoubtedly his discouragement would influence the people. They needed to have a priest who was not only involved in the work but motivated to finish the work. This segment of the encouragement concludes without a divine-utterance formula.

The third addressee is designated *kol-ʿam hāʾāreṣ*, "all the people of the land." The book of Haggai designates the people using various terms: "this people," *hāʿām hazzê* (1:2); "the entire remnant of the people," *kōl šəʾērît hāʿām* (1:12, 14); and "remnant of the people" *šəʾērît hāʿām* (2:2). "People of the land" is well attested in the Old Testament to designate various groups. In the Pentateuch, it is used of the Canaanites and the general population of the region (Gen 23:7; Lev 20:2, 4; Num 14:9). As a general observation, in preexilic times *ʿam hāʾāreṣ*, "people of the land," may have referred to upper-class citizens.[152] Yet there are examples of the designation's being used to refer to the entire population of the land (Jer 1:18; 34:19; 37:2; 44:21; Ezek 39:13; cf. 2 Kgs 11:10–20; Ezek 45:22). In the postexilic period, various uses of the designation appear—for example, the non-Jewish population living in the land as compared with the returnees (Ezra 4:1, 4). Thus, the Samaritans may be regarded "the people of the land" in contrast to the *ʿam-yəhûdâ*, "people of Judah," or vis-à-vis the *bənê haggôlâ*, "sons of the *gola*/captivity" (Ezra 4:1b).[153]

> Then the people of the land discouraged the people of Judah, and made them afraid to build, and they bribed officials to frustrate their plan

151. Meyers and Meyers, *Haggai, Zechariah 1–8,* 50, in association with Zech 3:10; 6:9–15. Contrast H. W. Wolff, *Haggai,* 78.

152. A. R. Hulst, "עם," *TLOT* 2:896–919, esp. p. 902; cf. H. W. Wolff, *Haggai,* 78; Kessler, *Haggai,* 168.

153. Cf. H. W. Wolff, *Haggai,* 78; Hulst, *TLOT* 2:903; Clines, *Ezra, Nehemiah, Esther,* 74–75; Kessler, *Haggai,* 168. See additional bibliography on the "people of the land" in all of these sources.

> throughout the reign of King Cyrus of Persia and until the reign of King Darius of Persia. (Ezra 4:4–5 NRSV)

Some researchers have noted that "people of the land" is also a designation for those who were not accepted in the cultic community (Neh 10:28–29) and were forbidden as marital partners.[154] The qualifier *kol*, "all," in the designation "all the people of the land" may indicate a broader rather than a narrow sense of the term, whereby the non-returnees or non-Jewish people are also included in the designation. Here, when taken with reference to Hag 1:12, 14, the term may not distinguish and thus exclude some, but instead may include all the people living in the land—whether they recently returned or never left the land.[155] All the people in the land were thus being encouraged along with the governor and the high priest. This segment closes with the divine-utterance formula *nəʾum-yhwh*.

The second part of the encouragement exhorts the whole community to "work"; thus the complete text of encouragement is to "be strong and work," *ḥăzaq . . . waʿăśû*. Here *waʿăśû*, a *qal* imperative second masculine plural from the root *ʿāśâ*, "to work, do," is understood as encouragement to the community to engage in the work of building the temple.

The rationale for the encouragement is indicated by the *kî* clause that introduces the formula *ʾănî ʾittəkem*, "I am with you" (cf. Hag 1:13). Thus the whole text offering encouragement is: be strong and work because Yahweh of hosts is with you (pl.). The exhortation is similar to the use of the formula elsewhere in its focus on alleviating people's fears or providing reassurance of deliverance in the face of adversity. While one cannot simply presume that the need for the encouragement in the book of Haggai is the same as in Ezra, the opposition to the rebuilding there may have formed part of the people's memory here. In the book of Haggai, the cause for the discouragement seems to be the desolate state of the temple and the prospect of rebuilding a structure that will fall short of the impressive structure recalled in the temple tradition.

Another aspect of the discouragement was ambivalence about the need for a temple. This message may be reassurance about Yahweh's presence even without the temple structure: with or without the temple, Yahweh is with you. However, the assurance itself poses a challenge: Does Yahweh require a temple to be present with the people? The fact that they existed in exile and in the land without a temple for over fifty years may have called into

154. Verhoef, *Haggai and Malachi,* 98; H. W. Wolff, *Haggai,* 78; Clines, *Ezra, Nehemiah, Esther,* 74–75; Kessler, *Haggai,* 168.

155. H. W. Wolff, *Haggai,* 79; Kessler, *Haggai,* 168–69; contrast Floyd, *Minor Prophets 2,* 280–81; Meyers and Meyers, *Haggai, Zechariah 1–8,* 50–51.

question their belief about the localized presence of the Deity. The tension between their experience and their belief on this issue was heightened since they were also assured of Yahweh's presence with them while living in Babylon (Isa 41:10; 43:5; Jer 30:11; 42:11; 46:28). Along with the other reasons, their hesitation to rebuild may have been fueled by a change in their belief about the need for a temple to ensure the presence of Yahweh in their midst (cf. Isa 66:1–6).

5 Haggai 2:5 has been a point of much debate. Some commentators have suggested that the first word, *'et,* is used to indicate the presence of a direct object, in which case the clause would provide the object of the verb *wa'ăśû* (*qal* imperative second masculine plural of *'āśâ,* "to do") in the preceding verse, 2:4—"obey the word."[156] I will not duplicate here Verhoef's survey of the various options for understanding *'et*; however, it is worth mentioning the option of supplying a verb (e.g., *zākar,* "to remember") for which *'et* signals the object.[157] The attempt to supply a verb for *'et* recognizes a conceptual break between the two clauses in 2:4 and 2:5—"I am with you. . ." (*'ănî 'ittəkem,* 2:4) and "my spirit remains among you" (*wərûḥî 'ōmedet bətôkəkem,* 2:5). To bridge the conceptual gap, some have considered alternative uses of *'et* that fit its present context more closely. With the help of Barthélemy, Kessler identifies two alternative translations of *'et*—"concerning, regarding" (Ezek 43:7; 44:3) and "this is" (Ezek 47:17, 18, 19). Although Kessler uses "this is" in his translation, he expresses a clear preference for rendering *'et* as "concerning," and his understanding of the text reflects this alternative.[158] With this option, 2:5 would be providing an expansion of the affirmation of God's presence by locating the affirmation in the covenant.

As an affirmation, Hag 2:5 both expands 2:4bα "because I am with you" and grounds the assurance about the divine presence in 2:5aβ and 2:5b, also in the covenant. While rendering *'et* as "concerning, regarding," or "this is" may be valid, it is also valid to see *'et* as the continuation of the divine-utterance formula in order to provide an exposition. In this case, the text would read: "the utterance of Yahweh, namely, the word that I covenanted." Following Meyers and Meyers, we can affirm that the covenant language is similar to that of 1 Kgs 8:9:

156. Meyers and Meyers (*Haggai, Zechariah 1–8,* 47, 51) transpose the imperative of *'āśâ* from 2:4 to the beginning of 2:5 and propose that the interruption may be awkward in English but is attested in Hebrew.

157. While Verhoef (*Haggai and Malachi,* 99) notes that some scholars have supplied the verb *zākar,* thus reading "remember the word. . . ," he identifies the challenge of providing a word and attempts to address the place of *'et* in Hag 2:5 in some other way.

158. Kessler, 160 n. 8, 170; cf. Barthélemy, *Ezékiel, Daniel et les 12 prophètes,* 928. Verhoef (*Haggai and Malachi,* 99) also prefers to render *'et* as "concerning" but mentions "with" as another alternative used by some scholars.

> There was nothing in the ark except the two tablets of stone that Moses had placed there at Horeb, where the LORD made a covenant with the Israelites, when they came out of the land of Egypt. (NRSV)

Haggai 2:5 is thus an abbreviated reference to the Sinai covenant indicated by the term *haddābār*, "the word."[159]

This reference in Hag 2:4 and 5 is another basis for assurance about the divine presence. Accordingly, this word assures the community of Yahweh's presence on the basis of the covenant Yahweh made with the people. With this clearly established link to past generations, the assurance of Yahweh's presence is not dependent on the temple. When the people came out of Egypt, they had no temple, yet Yahweh was with them. This link to the past supports the ideology about the divine presence with the people apart from the temple, as several texts in Exodus also indicate. After Yahweh's displeasure with the people at Sinai and after God commanded them to leave Sinai to go to the land, God promised to go with them. God said, "My presence will go with you, and I will give you rest." And Moses said to God, "If your presence will not go, do not carry us up from here" (Exod 33:14–15 NRSV). The divine presence is also promised by variations of the formula "I am with you": *ʾānōkî ʿimmāk* (Gen 28:15); *ʿimməkā-ʾānî* (Isa 41:10); *ʾittəkā ʾānı* (Isa 43:5). In Exod 3:12 the formulation *kî-ʾehyê ʿimmāk* uses the first-person form of the verb *haya*, "to be," plus the preposition *ʿim*, "with," and the second masculine singular suffix (*ʾehyê ʿimmāk*). Other occurrences include the promise to the people regarding their occupation of the land (Deut 31:23)[160] and the assurance to Joshua (Josh 1:5; 3:7; negative formulation: 7:12). In addition to these, the exodus and Sinai traditions manifest the divine presence in several ways: the pillar of cloud and pillar of fire to guide the people (Exod 13:21–22; 14:20, 24; Num 10:11; 14:14; cf. Neh 9:12, 19); the dense cloud over Mount Sinai as a manifestation of Yahweh's presence (Exod 19:9, 16; 24:15–18); the cloud at the tent of meeting and tabernacle (Exod 33:9–10; Num 9:15–22; cf. Exod 40:34–38; Num 11:25). All of these examples demonstrate Yahweh's presence for the community.

Wolff observes that there may be a slight difference between the Hebrew prepositions used in the formulation "I am with you": *ʿim* connotes fellowship, while *ʾit* connotes spatial nearness—that is, "beside you." He concludes that Hag 2:4 (*ʾănî ʾittəkem*) is to be understood as assurance that Yahweh promises to be "at your side."[161] Thus by mentioning the exodus and Sinai traditions, the prophet Haggai is linking the exodus generation with

159. Meyers and Meyers, *Haggai, Zechariah 1–8*, 52.
160. The formulation is *wəʾānōkî ʾehyeh ʿimmāk*, "I will be with you."
161. H. W. Wolff, *Haggai*, 50.

the postexilic community as well as connecting the God of the exodus and the Sinai covenant with the God who now assures the people of the divine presence.[162] Neither communities had a temple, but they were assured of the presence. It is clear that, while the building of the temple is important to Yahweh, it does not dictate Yahweh's presence or the manifestation of that presence.

Haggai 2:5 continues the encouragement, reassuring the people of God's presence as well as recalling the covenant, and it includes two components: reassurance and an admonition. First, the reassurance about Yahweh's presence uses *rûḥî,* "my spirit," where a form of the first-person singular pronoun "I" usually appears (*ʾănî* or *ʾānōkî*)—*my spirit is standing in your midst.* Several texts refer to the spirit of Yahweh, including Judg 3:10; 6:34; cf. Num 11:29. In the prophetic texts, "my spirit" occurs in Isa 42:1; 44:3; 59:21; Ezek 37:14; Joel 2:28–29; Zech 4:6; 7:12. Furthermore, in the prophetic texts *rûaḥ yhwh,* "spirit of Yahweh," is the usual formulation (Isa 11:2; 40:13; 61:1; Ezek 11:5; 37:1; Mic 3:8) as compared with *rûaḥ ʾĕlōhîm,* "spirit of God" (Ezek 11:24; cf. Num 24:2; 1 Sam 10:10; 11:6).[163] It has been argued that *rûḥî,* "my spirit," in Hag 2:5 is analogous with the pillar of cloud in the exodus tradition,[164] especially because the spirit is depicted as standing in the midst of the people: *ʿōmedet* (feminine-singular particle of *ʿāmad,* "to stand"). In Exod 33:10 the pillar of cloud (*ʿammûd heʿānān*) was "standing" at the entrance of the tent (cf. Num 12:5; Deut 31:15). These images of the angel of Yahweh standing reveal the location as well as the angel's presence (Num 22:24, 26; Zech 1:11; 3:5; 1 Chr 21:16).[165] Other representations depict Yahweh standing (*niṣṣāb*): for example, by a wall (Amos 7:7) or by an altar (Amos 9:1). These texts that portray the divine presence as standing in particular locations thus personify that presence.[166]

The phrase "in your midst" (*bətôkəkem*) contrasts with the distance depicted by Yahweh's presence on the mountain or at the tent of meeting—away from the people (Num 12:5; Deut 31:15). In Lev 26:11 the promise to dwell in their midst (*bətôkəkem*) appears alongside the promise not to "abhor the people" (cf. Zech 2:10–11 [MT 14–15]). The divine presence among the people is also depicted by use of the verb *qārab,* "to come near, approach" (Num 11:20; 14:14; Pss 46:5, NRSV [MT 46:6]; 82:1; Jer 14:9; Hos 11:9; Joel 2:27; Zeph 3:17). Just as Yahweh could be in the midst of the people, evil could be also

162. Cf. Kessler, *Haggai,* 172.

163. H. W. Wolff (*Haggai,* 80) observes that the formulation "spirit of Yahweh" is used exclusively for prophetic proclamation; cf. Kessler, *Haggai,* 171.

164. Cf. Kessler, *Haggai,* 172; Verhoef, *Haggai and Malachi,* 100–101.

165. Cf. Ezek 3:23 the glory of Yahweh standing in the valley.

166. Cf. Meyers and Meyers, *Haggai, Zechariah 1–8,* 52; Kessler, *Haggai,* 171–72; Verhoef, *Haggai and Malachi,* 100; H. W. Wolff, *Haggai,* 80.

(e.g., Deut 13:5; 17:7; 19:19; 21:21); and when Yahweh was not in their midst, victory was not guaranteed (Deut 1:42). Apparently, there is little difference in meaning between the formulations *bətôk,* "midst," and *bəqereb,* "among," used to depict the divine presence. Both show the presence as close (immanent) rather than distant (transcendent). Haggai 2:5 thus depicts the spirit of Yahweh standing in the midst of the people, much as Yahweh in the pillar of cloud stood at the entrance of the tent of meeting. The presence is therefore manifested; its effect is discernible to the people.

What Yahweh therefore covenanted is presence and, more specifically, the manifestation of the presence, leaving no doubt about that presence. The people of postexilic community are guaranteed that Yahweh will be present with them without question. On the basis of that covenantal promise, they are exhorted to be strong (*ḥāzaq*) and work (*waʿăśû*; Hag 2:4). They are encouraged not to fear on the same basis. As discussed above, "do not fear" (*ʾal-tîrʾû*) offers encouragement and is sometimes seen in connection with "I am with you" as the motivation not to fear. Its use may suggest a situation that has generated fear. Thus, the admonition is to cease fearing, in spite of reasons to fear, and because of the divine presence (cf. Isa 41:10).

While Hag 2:5 further explains the affirmation regarding the divine presence, it appears between the two rationales for being strong. The first rationale is the divine presence (2:4). Haggai 2:6–9 provides the second rationale for the exhortation. A multilayered effect is achieved by the repetition of *kî* and the juxtaposition of the reasons for the exhortation to "be strong and work": (1) *because* I am with you . . . do not fear; (2) *because* in a little while. . . . The literary context juxtaposes the promise of divine presence with the formula "do not fear" in 2:5b. Likewise, the assurance is conceptually connected to both the exhortation and the formula. The second rationale for the exhortation addresses the issues of resources and any lingering concerns about the possibility of building a new temple to compare with the status of the former temple.

2. *Basis of the Encouragement (2:6–9)*

6 The exhortation continues by addressing the issues of resources for building the temple (Hag 2:6). The *kî* clause provides the time of Yahweh's provision by using the temporal indicator *ʿôd ʾaḥat məʿaṭ hîʾ*, *"once again, in a little while."* The phrase may consist of two parts—*ʿôd ʾaḥat* and *məʿaṭ hîʾ*. However, the typical expression is *ʿôd məʿaṭ*, "soon," denoting the imminence of an event. Thus in Exod 17:4 Moses expresses concern that the people are about to stone him (cf. Jer 51:33; Hos 1:4; Ps 37:10). This meaning of the expression is also observed in Isa 10:25; 29:17, where the phrase is lengthened by the adverbial particle to produce the phrase "yet a very little while" (*ʿôd məʿaṭ mizʿār*), emphasizing the relative shortness of the time. All instances of this formulation refer to the immediacy of the anticipated event. The expression *ʿôd ʾaḥat məʿaṭ hîʾ (once again, in a little while)* does not occur elsewhere in the Old Testament; however, *ʿôd ʾaḥat*, "once again," may be analogous to *yōsep ʿôd,* "once again" (*ʿôd* plus the verb *yāsap,* "to add, do again"; Num 22:15). The expression *ʿôd məʿaṭ* and *ʿet*, "time," occurs in Jer 51:33 to denote time as being accompanied by an event or the idea that time will produce an event.

The verbal aspect of the various actions characterized by this temporal expression is significant. One understanding is that *ʿôd* indicates continuous action, often with the participle (Gen 18:22; 29:9; Exod 9:2, 17; 1 Kgs 1:22, 42; Isa 5:25; 9:17, NRSV [MT 9:16]; 65:24; cf. Deut 31:27). Another is that the clause employing *ʿôd* is repeating an action after a period of cessation (Gen 4:25; 9:11, 15; 29:34; Exod 4:6; Lev 13:57; 1 Sam 10:22; Jer 22:12; 33:1; Ezek 5:4, 9; Zech 1:17).[167] The verb *yāsap* used with *ʿôd* also has the meaning of repeated action (Gen 8:10, 12; 18:29).[168]

Following the introductory clause plus the word-event formula, Hag 2:6–7 contains two components: (1) the temporal formula and (2) the designated action that will occur. The word-event formula "thus says Yahweh of hosts" (*kô ʾāmar yhwh ṣəbāʾôt*) is part of the *kî* clause and signals Yahweh as speaker. The presence of the temporal indicator is noteworthy in light of the other indicators in the book of Haggai that emphasize Yahweh's involvement and the efficacy of the proclamation. In Hag 2:6 *ʿôd* can be understood in at least two ways. First, "it refers to a waiting period that will still continue for a short while."[169] On theological grounds some try to avoid the repetitive nuance of *ʿôd*. Thus, Petersen notes that this "is a way of making indefinite the moment at which the cosmic shaking will occur," rather than indicating repeated action.[170] Petersen's understanding is that, prior to Haggai's proclamation and the ensuing events, there was no point in Israel's history that Yahweh shook the nations for their treasure.

The second and more viable understanding is that *ʿôd* has the repetitive nuance and can be translated as the adverbial "once"—thus, "once again." This option suggests that such a shaking of the nations has happened before and that shaking will take place again. Moreover, the events being

167. Kessler (*Haggai*, 174–75) notes that some of these repetitive nuances have an eschatological motif.

168. See also Exod 10:29; Num 22:15; Deut 19:20; 28:68; Ezek 36:12; Hos 1:6; Amos 7:8, 13; 8:2; Nah 1:15.

169. Kessler, *Haggai*, 174.

170. Petersen, *Haggai and Zechariah 1–8*, 62. Contrast this with Kessler, *Haggai*, 174–75.

anticipated will happen soon. Haggai 2:6 continues, specifying what Yahweh is about to do—namely, "to shake the heavens and the earth" (*marʿîš ʾet-haššāmayim wəʾet-hāʾāreṣ*; cf. Hag 2:20–23).[171] Several impersonal objects are identified, including "the heavens" (*haššāmayim*) and "the earth" (*hāʾāreṣ*), "the sea" (*hayyām*) and "dry land" (*heḥārābâ*). In addition to the fact that the order of the elements here reflects the order in Gen 1, here in Hag 2:6 Yahweh has the ability to shake these elements or cause them to shake. The nature of the objects being shaken further reveals Yahweh's supernatural power. These objects are expansive, essential parts of the created order, without which other realities cannot exist. The world in its current state would not exist without the heavens, earth, sea, and dry ground. So what does this shaking entail?

Answering this question calls for a look at the uses of the verb *rāʿaš*, "to quake." In several instances, the noun form of *rāʿaš* denotes an earthquake (1 Kgs 9:11, 12; Isa 29:6; Amos 1:1; Zech 14:5).[172] The verb is also used to describe the effect of God's action, in which case the impersonal subject is personified; for example, the earth or the foundation of the earth shakes (e.g., Jer 10:10). Confirming Kessler's observation, *marʿîš* in Hag 2:6 is one of seven *hiphil* forms of this verb (*rāʿaš*) in the Old Testament (i.e., Job 39:20; Ps 60:2 [MT 4]; Isa 14:16; Ezek 31:16; Hag 2:6, 7, 21).[173] The *hiphil* may also be used with human subjects (such as the king of Babylon) and *mamlākôt*, "kingdoms," as the object (e.g., Isa 14:16; cf. Hag 2:22). It is also used with God/Yahweh as subject and the earth as object (*hāʾāreṣ*—Ps 60:2 [MT 4]; Hag 2:6, 21); nations as object (*gôyim*—Ezek 31:16; Hag 2:7). It occurs in Jer 50:46 in the *niphal* to describe the sound effects of Babylon's being captured. Otherwise the verb *rāʿaš* occurs in the *qal* most often, with the earth/land as its object (Judg 5:4; 2 Sam 22:8; cf. Isa 13:13; 24:18), or hill/mountains (Jer 4:24).

The earth and mountains shake for various reasons, including the defeat of nations (Jer 50:46; 49:21; cf. Ezek 26:10, 15; 27:28); as a result of God's presence (Ezek 38:20; Joel 3:16 [MT 4:16]; Nah 1:5; Ps 18:7 [MT 8]), or as a result of God's anger (Pss 68:8 [MT 9]; 77:18 [MT 19]).[174] In addition to the shaking, the divine presence has the effect of destroying elements that appeared to be durable or even permanent, such as mountains melting (Ps 97:5; Mic 1:4; Nah 1:5). The imagery portrays a God who is capable of altering

171. *Hiphil* participle of *rāʿaš*, "to shake." Cf. Kessler, *Haggai*, 160 n. 12, 175. He cites GKC §116p and Joüon §119n as support for understanding the participle here as *futurum instans*.

172. Cf. Ezek 3:12; 38:19.

173. Kessler, *Haggai*, 176.

174. Kessler, *Haggai*, 176–77; Verhoef, *Haggai and Malachi*, 102–3; Meyers and Meyers, *Haggai, Zechariah 1–8*, 52–53.

the basic structure of the cosmos. The merisms—heaven and earth, sea and dry land—also depict the extent of Yahweh's action. According to Meyers and Meyers, the prophet speaks of an eschatological event "rooted in old pre-exilic ideas and not tied to current political expectations."[175] Evidently, the events described may recall the prophecies about Jerusalem/Zion's exaltation (cf. Isa 2:1–4; Mic 4:1–4). While this data indicates that the "shaking" of the heavens and earth may be a cosmic event, the shaking of the nations is also part of Yahweh's plan and may depict a universal event. Consequently, Yahweh is portrayed as having control over the universe and all nations (cf. Ps 47:8 [MT 9]; Jer 10:7).

7 The statement *I will shake all the nations* in Hag 2:7 repeats the verb *rāʿaš* and thus indicates the second aspect (if not phase) of Yahweh's plan: shaking all the nations (*hirʿaštî ʾet-kol-haggôyim*). Like the shaking of the created order, shaking the nations is presented as all-encompassing. All the nations will be subject to the action (cf. Hag 2:22). The formulation "all the nations" commonly signals a totality with reference to particular categories: all the nations among whom the people were scattered (Jer 25:15; 29:14, 18; 30:11; 43:5; 46:28; Zech 7:14); all the nations of the earth (Jer 26:6; Isa 52:10; Jer 33:9; 36:2; 44:8; Joel 3:2 [MT 4:2]; Obad 15); or all the nations, even the mightiest of them (Isa 40:17). Does Hag 2:7 suggest a nuance for the phrase "all the nations"? Does it refer to the specific category of nations where the people were scattered? Or is it referring to all the nations of the earth? Given the scope of the first use of the verb *rāʿaš* in 2:6, "all the nations" may mean the totality of the nations of the earth.[176]

It appears that the upheaval of the created order precedes the disruption of the societal and international order (cf. Joel 3:3 [MT 4]; Zech 12–14; Ezek 38–39).[177] As in other prophetic texts, the nations occupy a place in God's work on the people's behalf. The nations are used to bring judgment on God's people, and they themselves are instruments whose role terminates once it becomes obsolete (cf. Mic 4:11–12; Zech 12:3, 9; 14:2). The nations in the eschatological age will affirm the status of Zion by journeying there to receive Torah from Yahweh (Mic 4:1–4; Isa 2:1–4). Likewise, in Hag 2:7, the nations have a role designed by Yahweh's plans and for the benefit of Yahweh's people. What is the role of the nations in 2:7?

Haggai 2:7aβ reveals that the focus of the action on the nations is the nations' treasure. One option is to see the nations as the subject of the plural

175. Meyers and Meyers, *Haggai, Zechariah 1–8,* 53.

176. Cf. Kessler, *Haggai,* 179.

177. Kessler, *Haggai,* 179; R. Mason, "The Use of Earlier Biblical Material in Zechariah 9–14: A Study in Inner Biblical Exegesis," in *Bringing Out the Treasures,* ed. M. J. Boda and M. H. Floyd, JSOTSup 370 (Sheffield: Sheffield Academic, 2003), 136–40.

verb *ûbāʾû*,[178] in which case, as a result of shaking the nations will bring treasure (*ḥemdat*).[179] Another option is to understand the treasure as being the subject, treating the singular noun as a collective that "will come" (*bāʾû*).[180] Whether *ḥemdat* is seen as the subject or the object, it does not refer to an esteemed individual or precious person. Such an argument attempts to interpret the term as pointing to a messianic figure and ignores the connections within Hag 2:7 and 8—the treasure and splendor and the silver and gold.[181] Both options—the nations and the treasure—may be supported by the text; but unlike other cases where a subject is inferred for *bôʾ* with an inanimate object, here in Hag 2:7 the subject need not be inferred since a likely one appears in the verse: all the nations (*kol-haggôyim*). Kessler favors the implied subject but also argues that the subject is the nations.[182] Likewise, Meyers and Meyers not only propose "nations" as subject but presume that the context supports a third-person masculine-plural suffix "their"—thus "their treasures." They attempt to personify elements in Hag 2:7—namely, "their treasures" and "my glory." By doing so, they interpret *kābôd* in 2:7 as the divine presence in connection with at least two traditions: royal ideology (enthronement of God) and this prophecy's continuation of the revelation at Sinai (Exod 24:16, 17; 29:43; 40:34, 35; Lev 9:6, 23).[183] There is an undeniable connection between these two traditions that informs an understanding of *kābôd* in Hag 1:8 but not the occurrences of *kābôd* in 2:3, 7, 9, where the connection is to treasures and status rather than divine presence.[184]

Returning to the discussion of the treasure of the nations, one question remains in the foreground. What is the purpose of the treasure? Several noteworthy responses to the question have been offered. First, following the idea of the holy-war motif, the treasure (collective) is booty taken from the nations.[185] As Kessler notes, usually *ḥemdâ* is used to speak of booty (Dan 11:8; Hos 13:15; 2 Chr 32:27; 36:10).[186] Likewise, the anticipated splendor of

178. *Qal* perfect third masculine plural of *bôʾ*, "to come, go in." Meyers and Meyers, *Haggai, Zechariah 1–8,* 53.

179. Meyers and Meyers, *Haggai, Zechariah 1–8,* 53.

180. Verhoef, *Haggai and Malachi,* 103; Kessler, *Haggai,* 179–80. See n. 30.

181. See Verhoef (*Haggai and Malachi,* 103–4) for further discussion of the medieval trend to attribute messianic and Christological meanings to the verse. He does not endorse this interpretive trend, nor does Kessler (*Haggai,* 179).

182. Kessler, *Haggai,* 179–81.

183. Meyers and Meyers, *Haggai, Zechariah 1–8,* 53–54.

184. Cf. Verhoef, *Haggai and Malachi,* 104; see Kessler (*Haggai,* 181), who denies that these uses in Hag 2:7 and 9 refer to "a theophonic phenomenon" (e.g., Exod 40:34–35; 1 Kgs 8:10–11; Isa 6:3; Ezek 43:5; 44:4).

185. Verhoef, *Haggai and Malachi,* 103.

186. Kessler, *Haggai,* 180–88.

the temple plus Yahweh's ownership of all nations would exceed the resources that would be gained through plundering (cf. Isa 60:5; Ezek 39:9–10; Joel 3:5–7 [MT 4:5–6]; Mic 4:13; Zech 14:1).[187]

Second, the treasure is not given willingly but is obligatory, based on the vassal status of those who give tribute to their sovereign.[188] While the nations may not willingly yield their treasure, Hag 2:7 does not suggest that they will be paying tribute in recognition of Judah as a sovereign nation. Third, the treasure originally belonged to the temple—that is, it was looted in 597–587 BCE (2 Kgs 25:13–17) and returned by Cyrus (Ezra 1:5–11).[189] This is certainly a perspective seen in connection with Ezra 1:5–11, where Cyrus is said to have returned the vessels taken by Nebuchadnezzar. The extent of this return of the temple vessels would not take into account the fact that the surrounding nations in Ezra also gave resources to the exiles. Furthermore, the simple return of the vessels would hardly result in exceeding the splendor of the former temple (cf. Hag 2:9). If anything, the reacquisition would at best only approximate the former. Since the temple treasures were depleted over the centuries of Jerusalem's history, the reacquisition of the vessels lost in 597 BCE most likely would not equal the splendor of the former temple.

A fourth option regarding the treasure of the nations is that the nations would bring an offering when they come to worship Yahweh. This option picks up on the motif of pilgrimages to Jerusalem that usually occurs in eschatological prophecies about the exaltation of Zion (cf. Mic 4:1–4; Isa 2:1–4). Contextually, the shaking in Hag 2:7 and the overthrow of the nations in 2:20–23 do not support a motif of willingly recognizing Yahweh's sovereignty and a peaceful transformation.[190] Although the options for interpreting the "treasure" contribute to an understanding of the image and the result of the shaking, none of the options fully takes into account the image of Hag 2:7.

The final clause of Hag 2:7, *I will fill this house [with] splendor,* is attached to the word-event formula "says Yahweh of hosts" (*ʾāmar yhwh ṣəbāʾôt*). The speaker is still Yahweh in the sequence of actions signaled by the *waw*-consecutive forms—*wəhirʿaštî,* "I will shake"; *ûmillēʾtî,* "and I will fill." Here the verb *mālēʾ,* "to fill," is used to depict the totality of action matched by the effect of the shaking. It may also refer to the totality of the treasures—namely, every treasure of all the nations. Yahweh proclaims that Yahweh will fill this house (*habbayit hazzê*), the temple, communicating the Deity's direct involvement in contrast to designating an agent—for example, Cyrus (Isa 45:11–14; Ezra 1; 5:13–14). While agency is important to the prophetic proc-

187. Kessler, *Haggai,* 180–88.

188. Meyers and Meyers, *Haggai, Zechariah 1–8,* 53.

189. Petersen, *Haggai and Zechariah 1–8,* 68.

190. Cf. Kessler, *Haggai,* 188, for further discussion of this option.

lamation, in the context of encouragement, Yahweh's direct involvement is an essential element—that is, the promise of divine presence and the promise to achieve the splendor of the temple. Thus Hag 2:7 communicates that, even if the efforts of the community are limited in their ability to achieve or exceed the splendor of the former temple, Yahweh guarantees that splendor. The prophecy thus refocuses the disposition toward inactivity fostered by anticipated failure.

The promise is that Yahweh will fill the temple; but with what? The object of the verb *mālēʾ,* "to fill," is *kābôd,* "glory, splendor," which the syntax of the verse makes clear. At issue is the understanding of *kābôd.* The term appears elsewhere with the meaning "glory"—that is, presence (Gen 45:13; Job 29:20; Isa 4:2; Hos 9:11; 10:5).[191] Several factors regulate the meaning of *kābôd* in this context, including its relationship to "shaking" (2:7), the conceptual framework of the past splendor versus the present desolation (2:3, 9), and the reference to silver and gold (2:8). The claim that Yahweh will fill the temple will demonstrate Yahweh's commitment to exceed the expectation of the community. In contrast to the temple that anyone from preexilic times would have experienced and would now recall, the new temple will not be scantily adorned with vessels left after the most desirable ones are already taken or given away. Rather, Yahweh will exceed the community's experience and exceed even the expectations borne out of the tradition about the opulence of the Solomonic Temple. Here then, the one who encourages the community is the one who also guarantees the success of their work (cf. Hag 2:20–23).

8 Perhaps Hag 2:8 illustrates what the treasure entails. *The silver is mine, and the gold is mine*. Notably, in the enumeration of the treasures returned to the exiles, silver and gold predominate (cf. Hag 2:3). These are both used in the temple and are highly valued; and both belong to Yahweh. The order of these elements—silver and gold (*kesep wəzāhāb*)—has been explained relative to the content of what is being discussed, the time frame of the expression, and the economic conditions that the elements may reflect. First, it appears that the expression "silver and gold" is a merism for all treasures, and it signals Yahweh's ownership of all the earth's treasures (cf. Ps 24:1–2). Presumably, whether or not humans possess them, all the treasures belong to Yahweh (creator or champion in war).[192] Thus Petersen discusses two viable options for understanding Yahweh's claim: (1) that it is a justification for retrieving the treasure from the nations; (2) that Yahweh is clarifying to the community

191. Cf. Kessler, *Haggai,* 181.

192. See Kessler, 182; H. W. Wolff, *Haggai,* 82; and Verhoef (*Haggai and Malachi,* 105), who connects ownership of the treasures with war rather than with God as creator who owns everything.

that, even when the treasure is brought back to Jerusalem, Yahweh is the owner rather than the community. The treasure is to be used for the temple and not in any other project.[193]

Regarding the connection between Hag 2:8 and 2:7, one may also note the concept of treasures in the Old Testament context. A prime example of a conceptual framework for silver and gold is the exodus tradition: when leaving Egypt, the Israelites reportedly asked (*šāʾal*) and were given jewelry of silver and gold:

> The Israelites had done as Moses told them; they had asked the Egyptians for jewelry of silver and gold, and for clothing, and the LORD had given the people favor in the sight of the Egyptians, so that they let them have what they asked. And so they plundered the Egyptians. (Exod 12:35–36 NRSV)

Note that this is a conflated account that uses both the language of request-response and the language of war (*nāṣal*, "plunder, snatch away"). Plundering of treasures is typical of war and subjugation to a ruler.[194]

Another consideration regarding the mention of silver and gold is the relative time when the expression is used. It has been suggested that the order (silver and gold) is more typical of preexilic times,[195] while the reverse order (gold and silver) is more typical of postexilic texts.[196] Perhaps this observation does not account for the order in Hag 2:8, and a third factor may be considered, which is the relative economic value of silver and gold in various periods. Meyers and Meyers posit that the order reflects the relative value and limited availability of gold. In the preexilic economy up to postexilic times prior to the fifth century BCE, silver was more valuable. During the fifth century, gold became a more valuable commodity.[197]

9 Haggai 2:9 is the culmination of the unit begun in 2:3 and in a few ways is analogous to Isaiah's attention to the former and new things (cf. Isa 42:9; 43:9, 19; 46:9; 48:3, 6; 65:17). First, with respect to the culmination of the unit, 2:3 addresses the former splendor of the former temple, while 2:9

193. Petersen, *Haggai and Zechariah 1–8,* 69.

194. Cf. Kessler, *Haggai,* 182. He cites several examples, including Num 31:9; Isa 8:4; 10:13–14; Jer 15:13. B. S. Childs, *The Book of Exodus: A Critical, Theological Commentary,* OTL (Philadelphia: Westminster, 1974). See his "Excursus II: The Despoiling of the Egyptians," pp. 175–77.

195. See Exod 11:2; 12:35; Num 22:18; Deut 17:17; 29:17 (MT 16); Josh 6:19; 2 Sam 8:11; 1 Kgs 10:25; cf. Isa 60:9; Ezek 38:13; Dan 5:23; Zech 6:10, 11.

196. See 2 Kgs 14:14; 2 Chr 9:14; 24:14; Ezra 1:11; 5:14; 6:5; Esth 1:6; cf. Ezek 16:13; 28:4; Dan 5:2. Cf. Kessler, *Haggai,* 182, for further bibliography on this point.

197. Meyers and Meyers, *Haggai, Zechariah 1–8,* 54, 349. See Zech 6:9–15, esp. v. 11.

addresses the splendor of the house to be rebuilt. The promised status will use treasure acquired from all the nations and not simply the vessels that were looted from the temple.[198] Ironically, while the people are punished for not rebuilding the temple (Hag 1:6–11), it is clear that not everything is left up to humans' ability either to secure the resources or to ensure that the building meets the expectations of the community. God promises that the building will result in a structure that exceeds the splendor (*kābôd*) of the former (cf. Hag 1:9; 2:3)—*the splendor of this house.*

Does "splendor" refer to the dimensions or the treasures of the temple? The promise that the former temple will be exceeded could mean that the former will be surpassed in all respects. Yahweh's message to the community already admonished it to be strong and not to fear. In relation to 1:2–11, Hag 2:4–9 invokes human agency in accomplishing a divine plan and declares the ability of Yahweh to move humans into conformity with the divine plan and desire. This promise thus depicts Yahweh's power to achieve a plan. The shaking of all the nations, including the presumably immovable, thus attests Yahweh's supernatural power over all creation.

The final component of Hag 2:9, *I will give shalom in this place*, is also a promise—in this instance, it is a promise about "this place" (*bammāqôm hazzê*). Notably, the other references to the temple are "this house" (*habbayit hazzê*, Hag 1:4; 2:3, 7, 9a) and "Yahweh's house" (*bêt yhwh*, 1:2, 14; cf. "my house," *bêtî*, 1:9). Though juxtaposed to the promise about the temple, the reference to "this place" may not be speaking exclusively about the temple. Rather, the focus may be Jerusalem as the place where "peace" (*šālôm*) will be established. The establishment of peace in Jerusalem is a traditional part of eschatological prophecies (cf. Mic 4:1–14; Isa 2:1–4). The text does not address how the peace will come about, whether voluntarily—the nations coming to recognize Yahweh's sovereignty and yielding to it (Mic 4:1–4; Isa 2:1–4)—or involuntarily—the nations forced to follow Yahweh through threat of punishment (Zech 14; Isa 60). Table 4 identifies the elements of the peace tradition as they occur in various texts.[199] Despite noted differences with regard to some of the elements, most speak of the centralization of Jerusalem evident in pilgrimages there or the exaltation of Jerusalem. These elements are noticeably absent from Haggai.

Does Hag 2:9 speak about peace? The modern translations do not agree on this point. The NRSV translates *šālôm* as "prosperity" to harmonize with the wealth spoken of in 2:7–9a: "and in this place I will give prosperity." The NIV translates *šālôm* "peace": "And in this place I will grant peace."

198. Contrast Petersen, *Haggai and Zechariah 1–8*, 68.

199. Kessler, *Haggai*, 192–95. He summarizes several components of the eschatological tradition as seen in table 4.

Table 4. Comparison of the Peace Traditions in Prophetic Texts

Elements of the Tradition	Texts				
	Isaiah 2	Isaiah 60	Micah 4	Zechariah 14	Haggai 2
Geographical change (elevation of Jerusalem)	v. 2	——	v. 1	vv. 4, 8, 10	——
Decisive battle	——	——	——	vv. 2, 12–15	vv. 22
Nations' pilgrimages to Jerusalem	v. 3	vv. 3–9 ?	v. 2	vv. 16–19	——
Nations' wealth	——	vv. 3–9, 11	——	v. 14	v. 7
Established peace	v. 4 voluntary	vv. 12, 17–18 involuntary	vv. 3–4 voluntary	vv. 9, 12, 17–19 involuntary	v. 9 ? involuntary
Yahweh's instruction	v. 3	——	v. 2	——	——

Within the eschatological tradition delineated in table 4 in which through a sequence of events peace is established, most of the examples speak of peace vis-à-vis war. Haggai's adaptation of the tradition emphasizes the anticipated splendor of the new temple and deemphasizes the seditious elements such as war or radical upheaval. The divine promise addresses the perceived need of the community to be assured of Yahweh's presence amidst circumstances that appear to contradict that presence. God offers well-being in all of its dimensions, including prosperity, cessation of internal conflicts, and protection from the nations. Haggai's language makes the rebuilding of the temple the foremost element in the realization of God's promise to the community.

This unit admonishes reliance on God by affirming the Deity's presence, power, and unlimited resources. By depicting these characteristics, the passage presents a contrast between the community's futile reliance on its perception of timing and God's commands. The unit also allows a contrast between the community's unfounded fears about building the temple and the Deity's reassurance about providing for the community's needs out of the unlimited resources at the Deity's disposal.

III. ORACLE CONCERNING A NEW ERA (2:10–23)

The third and final macrounit (Hag 2:10–23) begins with a date formula and a prophetic-word formula denoting the addressees of the oracle. Haggai

2:10–23 focuses on the future by identifying the reality of the present and then articulating God's promise for a new era. The macrounit consists of two subunits, 2:10–19 (present and future) and 2:20–23 (Yahweh's future reign). The connection between the present and the future is signaled by the inquiry about ritual purity and the correlation between the process of purity and the present status of the nation (2:10–19). The future will unfold with Yahweh's reign over the nations and the appointment of Zerubbabel as Yahweh's authority (2:20–23). Each of the subunits begins with a chronological indicator and the prophetic-word formula "the word of Yahweh came to Haggai the prophet" (2:10, 20).[200]

A. PRESENT STATUS AND PROMISE FOR THE FUTURE (2:10–19)

The primary addressee of Hag 2:10–19 is the prophet Haggai, who is instructed to communicate with the priests regarding matters of purity. The communication will take a question-and-answer form, with Haggai leading the inquiry. The priests' role is to clarify the purity standards and thus demonstrate knowledge of those standards (2:10–13). The inquiry also serves as a basic illustration of the community's status before Yahweh (2:14). Given that status, the prophet admonishes the community regarding its obedience (2:15–19).

1. *Illustration regarding the Status of the Community (2:10–14)*

[10]*On the twenty-fourth [day] of the ninth [month] in the second year of Darius, the word of Yahweh came to Haggai the prophet, saying:* [11]*Thus says Yahweh of hosts, "Ask the priests for a ruling, saying,* [12]*'If a man carries consecrated meat in the edge of his garment and the edge of the garment touches the bread, or stew, or wine, or oil, or any food, will it become consecrated?'"*

And the priests answered: "No."

[13]*Then Haggai said, "If one unclean by a corpse touches any of these, will it become unclean?"*

Then the priests answered: "It will become unclean."

[14]*Then Haggai said, "So is this people, and so is this nation before me"—oracle of Yahweh—"and so are all the works of their hands; and whatever they bring there: it is unclean."*[a]

200. For further details about the addressees in the book of Haggai, *see* table 3 in the introduction, section V.

a. The LXX departs from the MT in two ways. First, where the MT reads "whatever they offer there it is defiled," the LXX reads "and whoever shall approach them shall be defiled." Second, where the MT ends, the LXX adds the following: "Because of their early burdens: they shall be pained because of their toils; and you have hated him that reproved in the gates." The last phrase of the LXX is similar to Amos 5:10 and may indicate the influence of a tradition—*śānə'û baššaʿar môkîaḥ wədōbēr tāmîm yətāʿēbû,* "They hate the one who reproves in the gate, and they abhor the one who speaks the truth" (NRSV). Notably, the LXX's addition explains about the people who are defiled, linking the defilement to their deeds.

a. Introductory Formula (2:10)

10 This subunit begins in Hag 2:10 with the date formula noting day, month, and year (twenty-fourth [day] of the ninth [month] in the second year of Darius [*bəʿeśrîm wə'arbāʿâ lattəšîʿî bišnat šətayim lədārəyāweš*]). This is the same year, three months later than the time mentioned in 1:15, when the community worked in response to the prophetic message, and two months after the date in 2:1 (seventh month, twenty-first day). As in Hag 1:1, verse 2:10 contains a word-event formula—"the word of Yahweh came to Haggai the prophet" (*hāyâ dəbar-yhwh bəyad-ḥaggay hannābî'*). Rather than the formulation *bəyad-ḥaggay*, "through Haggai," clearly indicating that the prophet is the agent (first but secondary) through whom Yahweh communicates, here in 2:10 the formulation is *'el-ḥaggay*, "to Haggai," the recipient of the message (first and primary). When the prophet is the first and primary recipient, the message is directed to him; but when the prophet is primary and secondary, he first receives the message, whose primary audience is someone else (see table 3).

b. Two-Question Sequence (2:11–13)

As a primary recipient of the word of Yahweh, Haggai is given a command. His obedience means that he engages in conversation with the priests. The content and mode of the conversation are included in the command, which is to inquire about a matter of purity. The three essential components are: (1) the command to inquire of the priests (2:11); (2) the inquiry (2:12–13); and (3) the analogy to be drawn (2:14) as the basis for speaking about the condition of the nation. The questions address the transmission of holiness and uncleanness.

(1) Yahweh's Command to the Prophet (2:11)

11 First, the prophet is told to request (*šə'al*) a ruling (*tôrâ*) from the priests. The command to the prophet presupposes the prophet's compliance in executing the command to communicate with the priests (*hakkōhănîm*) by means of inquiry. The request itself attests the status or influence of the priests in the community even at this time in history. It also presumes that the priests are sufficiently versed in the cultic tradition to provide a response that is at least consistent with the prophetic understanding. Thus, quite apart from the existence of the temple, the priests still had influence in the community. This authority would also be manifested in their performance of sacrifices at the altar.[201] The inquiry is a consultation during which the priests are to render judgment on the matter of defiled and consecrated items coming into contact with each other.[202]

Presumably, the inquirer is not ignorant of the response; rather, the inquirer already knows the answers to the questions.[203] Likewise, the request presupposes the inclination of the priests to respond; this is not a reprimand of the priests for being ignorant of the law (cf. Hos 4:6; Mal 2:7–9; Jer 18:18).[204] Responding to inquiries of this sort would have been part of their responsibility in teaching people and distinguishing between clean and unclean:

> You are to distinguish between the holy and the common, and between the unclean and the clean; and you are to teach the people of Israel all the statutes that the LORD has spoken to them through Moses. (Lev 10:10–11 NRSV)[205]

Clearly, the priests were given authority in cultic and some judicial matters to provide a final ruling. Being slack in their duties would have caused far-reaching repercussions for the community. The functioning priests would signal the availability of instruction; and their response to the inquiry would demonstrate their knowledge and fulfill their responsibility. Consequently, their responses to the questions revealed either their adherence to the law or their culpability in the community's delinquency.

Haggai 2:11 does not distinguish about whether the addressees were the Levitical priests or the whole tribe of Levi (cf. Deut 17:8–13; 18:1–8; 12:18–19; 14:27, 29). Numbers 18:1 notes that the tribe of Levi had "responsibility for offenses connected with the sanctuary," but the "responsibility for offenses connected with the priesthood" belonged only to the Aaronide priests. In Hag 2, although the high priest is identified by name, Joshua (Hag 2:2, 4), the inquiry is to be directed to the priests in general and not exclusively to him (cf. Hag 1:1, 12, 14).

201. Meyers and Meyers, *Haggai, Zechariah 1–8,* 77.

202. Cf. Petersen, *Haggai, Zechariah,* 72–73.

203. Contrast H. W. Wolff (*Haggai,* 17), who sees this inquiry as evidence of Haggai's ignorance of cultic matters.

204. Verhoef, *Haggai and Malachi,* 116.

205. See also Ezek 22:26; 44:23; Zech 7:2–4; Mal 2:5–9; cf. Deut 17:8–13.

(2) *Questions Directed to the Priests (2:12–13)*

12 Two questions are directed to the priests, one in 2:12 and the other in 2:13. Both questions present scenarios as the basis of the inquiry. What is the nature of the inquiry? The questions involve the responsibility to distinguish between sacred (*qōdeš*) and profane (*ḥōl*) and between clean (*ṭāhôr*) and unclean (*ṭāmēʾ*).[206]

(a) First Question Directed to the Priests (2:12)

The question begins with *hēn*, an interjection particle, "behold," or hypothetical particle meaning "if," used to establish the basis for a question (cf. Exod 8:26 [MT 22]; Jer 3:1).[207] The scenario that provides the basis for the question is carrying consecrated meat in the corner of one's garment. Several aspects of this scenario foster its plausibility and hence validate the questions. Yet along with these details, the larger issue of the communicability of holiness remains at the foreground.

The priests are asked about a situation in which a man (*ʾîš*) carries consecrated meat. Who would be carrying consecrated meat? The text designates the carrier as *ʾîš*, "a man," rather than *kōhēn*, "priest," indicating that a non-priest is intended. There are several types of offerings of well-being (*šelem*): thanksgiving, votive, and free-will offerings (Lev 7:15–18). The meat of the thanksgiving offering was to be eaten the same day; however, the meat of both the votive and the free-will offerings could be eaten up to two days after the sacrifice had been made. Meyers and Meyers therefore conclude that the offering of well-being, *šelem*, is the offering alluded to in Hag 2:12.[208] The layperson may eat of that meat and may have been allowed to take it home.[209] It is unnecessary to posit that the meat was taken home because, at the time this question was voiced, the temple was in ruins. Apart from the temple's existence, the allowance for eating the meat over a couple of days might have included eating the meat away from the place where it was offered, thus allowing for its transportation. Although Lev 7 does not address the transportation of the meat, it does specify eating in the holy place in the case of the *ʾāšām*, "guilt offering" (Lev 7:1–6).[210]

206. Petersen, *Haggai and Zechariah 1–8,* 71–80. Cf. K. Eades, "Divine Action and Human Action: Comparative Study of Deuteronomy 26:1–11 and Haggai 2:10–19," in *Exegetical and Theological Studies,* vol. 2 of *Reading the Hebrew Bible for a New Millennium,* ed. W. Kim et al. (Harrisburg, PA: Trinity Press International, 2000), 103–23.

207. H. W. Wolff (*Haggai,* 88) interprets *hēn* as an Aramaism parallel to *ʾim,* "if."

208. Meyers and Meyers, *Haggai, Zechariah 1–8,* 55–56; cf. Verhoef, *Haggai and Malachi,* 117.

209. Hartley, *Leviticus,* 100; Verhoef, *Haggai and Malachi,* 117.

210. Hartley, *Leviticus,* 99.

Leviticus speaks of the time frame for eating and disposing of the "leftovers" from the votive (*neder*) and free-will (*nədābâ*) offerings, along with issues of transmitting uncleanness (*ṭāmēʾ*; Lev 7:15–21).

The question deals with communicable states: *qōdeš,* "consecrated," and *ṭāmēʾ*, "unclean." Typically, the word pairs are (1) holy (*qōdeš*) and profane/common (*ḥōl*), and (2) unclean (*ṭāmēʾ*) and clean (*ṭāhôr*).[211]

> You are to distinguish between the holy and the common, and between the unclean and the clean. (Lev 10:10 NRSV)

The wording in Hag 2:12–13 pairs consecrated/holy with unclean, reflecting the first element of the pairs listed in Lev 10:10.[212]

The consecrated meat (*bəśar-qōdeš*) is being transported in the fold of a garment; the question is not about the effect of the meat on the fold of the garment. Presumably, contact with the consecrated meat affected the garment in much the same way that the splattering of blood from the sin offering affected a garment. The garment on which the blood was splattered must be washed in a holy place (Lev 6:27 [MT 20]). Likewise, specific instructions are given concerning the vessels in which the consecrated meat was boiled—clay vessels are to be broken; bronze vessels sterilized (Lev 6:28 [MT 21]). The special treatment of the garment and vessels that came into contact with the consecrated elements suggests that the consecrated elements left their effect on those objects. This is certainly the understanding of modern translations of Lev 6:18, 27 (MT 11, 20): "anything that touches them shall become holy" (NRSV); "whatever touches them will become holy" (NIV). At issue is the understanding of *yiqdāš*, "will become holy."[213]

Milgrom argues that, "just as *yiṭmāʾ* can only mean 'shall become impure,' so *yiqdāš* must be rendered 'shall become holy.' The formula, then, must signify that contact with a most sacred object brings about the absorption of its holiness" (e.g., Lev 11:24, 26, 27, 31, 36, 39; 15:10, 11, 21, 23, 27; cf. Hag 2:12–13).[214] Likewise, Durham observes that, because holiness is transmit-

211. Petersen (*Haggai and Zechariah,* 74–75) argues that the pairs lie along a spectrum from holy (*qōdeš*) to clean (*ṭāhôr*), profane/common (*ḥōl*), and unclean (*ṭāmēʾ*), with holy and unclean constituting the extremes and communicable states of the spectrum. Clean and profane are not contagious.

212. When the terms are used as a pair, the order is "unclean and clean" (cf. Lev 11:47; Deut 12:15, 22; 15:22; "holy and profane/common" (Ezek. 22:26; 42:20; 44:23).

213. The form *yiqdāš* is the *qal* imperfect third masculine singular of the verb *qādaš,* "to consecrate, set apart." Cf. Childs, *Exodus,* 521.

214. J. Milgrom, *Leviticus 1–16: A New Translation with Introduction and Commentary,* AB 3 (New York: Doubleday, 1991), 446. He further asserts that "the meaning of *kol-hannōgēaʿ . . . yiqdāš* is clarified beyond doubt when it is compared to its antonymic formu-

ted by touch, precautions were needed to prevent its transmission from the most-holy objects. Anyone or anything that came into contact with these objects became holy.[215] At least two types of measures were adopted to deal with the communicability of holiness via direct contact: (1) Preventive measures required consecrating persons before contact so that the consecrated might be handled by the consecrated. (2) Corrective measures included special cleansing for objects that came into contact with the consecrated meat or blood (Lev 6:27–28 [MT 20–21]).[216] In the case of people not designated for contact, contact brought immediate destruction. For example, when Uzzah attempted to prevent the ark from falling, he was immediately killed for touching the ark (2 Sam 6:6–8).[217]

All of the objects in the holy of holies that transmit holiness are deemed most holy (*qōdeš qādāšîm*, e.g., the altar, its implements, and the sin offering). On the one hand, Hartley translates Lev 6:18 (MT 11) "Anyone who touches these must be holy," and he translates *yiqdāš* the same way in Lev 6:27–28 (MT 20–23). On the other hand, he contends that holiness is not contagious but is acquired through consecration.[218] Milgrom examines what is entailed by the transmission of holiness and concludes: "Only whatever was eligible a priori as an offering is susceptible to *sancta contagion*. And as for the most sacred offering (Lev 6:11, 20), their contagion is communicable only to articles of food 'by absorption.'"[219] Summarily, Milgrom argues that while holiness is communicable, it is only communicable to other foods. Although Milgrom's argument may have some validity, it would mean that random contact would not result in the transmission of holiness. Kessler also concludes that Lev 6:27 (MT 20) indicates that "contact must be direct to transmit holiness."[220]

Returning to Hag 2:12—observe that, although the text specifies the food items (any food) that touch the consecrated meat, it also raises the question of the immediacy of the contact (direct vs. indirect). Leviticus 6 does

---

lation (*kol-hannōgēaʿ . . . yiṭmāʾ*)." See the occurrences of *qādaš* in Exod 29:21; Num 16:37–38 [MT 17:2–3]; 1 Sam 21:6).

215. Durham, *Exodus*, 406.

216. Durham, *Exodus*, 407.

217. Durham, *Exodus*, 407. Cf. Gordon Wenham, *The Book of Leviticus*, NICOT (Grand Rapids: Eerdmans, 1979), 121. Regarding Lev 6:18 (MT 11), he translates "Anyone (or anything) who touches them becomes holy." He also concludes that this is probably a warning to people in light of the fact that judgment is brought upon unclean persons who make contact with the holy.

218. Hartley, *Leviticus*, 97.

219. Milgrom, *Leviticus 1–16*, 446. Petersen (*Haggai and Zechariah*, 78) argues that the transmission of holiness from the most-holy objects differs for priests (who may touch) as compared with nonpriests (who should not touch).

220. Kessler, *Haggai*, 204; contrast Verhoef, *Haggai and Malachi*, 118.

not address transmission between like entities. Apparently, contact between dissimilar entities is just as likely to result in the transmission of holiness—for example, the garment of the priest[221] or the vessels in which the meat was boiled. Additionally, in the Exodus texts the dissimilarity of the objects affirms the conclusion that similarity is not a criterion for transmission (Exod 29:37; 30:29; 40:9). What is left is the question of immediacy. All the texts cited above that address the transmission of holiness involve direct contact.

Haggai's inquiry to the priests is therefore not about direct contact with the meat because the garment is in direct contact and presumably has become holy as a result of being in contact, not with a most-holy item (*qōdeš qādāšîm*), but with a holy item (*qōdeš*). The issue is whether indirect contact will also result in holiness. The other food items have indirect contact with the garment. The text designates that the meat is consecrated, *qōdeš,* and does not indicate whether the bread, stew, wine, or other foods are consecrated (*qōdeš*). But the absence of the specification is usually interpreted to mean that the items here are not consecrated (clean) but are neutral. The identified items are each preceded by the preposition "to" (*'el*); thus, *halleḥem wə'el-hannāzîd wə'el-hayyayin wə'el-šemen wə'el-kol-ma'ăkāl,* "bread, or stew, or wine, or oil, or any food." One need not examine the specificity of each item but should note the generality of the inquiry—any food product (edible items). The priests' response to the question of whether indirect contact between a consecrated item and another (food) item makes the other item consecrated is "no." The garment will not transmit holiness to the food—whatever the food may be (see fig. 1).

Perhaps food is mentioned because of its similarity to the consecrated object, thus emphasizing similarity as a nonfactor and the degree of contact relative to the consecrated object as essential. Haggai 2:12 does not mention the transmission of holiness from person to object or from object to person. The latter case seems to be in view in Ezek 44:19, where to prevent such transmission the priests remove their vestments before coming into contact with the people. The consecrated priestly vestment would be consecrated by contact with the consecrated priests or any other consecrated objects touched during their time in the inner court.

> When they go out into the outer court to the people, they shall remove the vestments in which they have been ministering, and lay them in the holy chambers; and they shall put on other garments, so that they may not communicate holiness to the people with their vestments. (Ezek 44:19 NRSV)[222]

221. Cf. Ezek 44:19.

222. Arguably, Hag 2:12 may represent a difference of opinion regarding the matter of

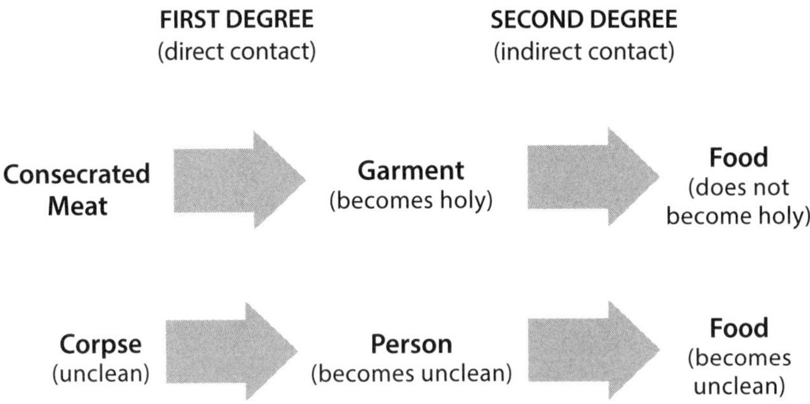

Figure 1. Degrees of Transmission according to Haggai 2:12–13

The priestly ruling in Hag 2:12 thus articulates an aspect of the law that is not yet explicitly addressed but may be inferred on the basis of analogy. Figure 1 illustrates the degrees of contact that affect the transmission of holiness according to the priestly ruling in Hag 2:12–13. In this case, holiness is transmitted from a holy object. The ruling is specific to the case introduced by *hēn*, and one must concede that at least in some cases holiness is transmittable via direct contact between a consecrated object and a neutral object.[223] The priestly response indicates that holiness may be transmitted but that it is limited to direct contact (or first-degree transmission); thereafter, holiness is not transmittable via indirect contact (second-degree transmission).

(b) Second Question Directed to the Priests (2:13)

13 Haggai speaks, continuing to obey the command given him to request a ruling from the priests (Hag 2:13). The question he asks them concerns con-

---

transmitting the consecrated state, in which case it competes with the perspective in Ezek 44:19. Alternatively, one may suggest that the garment is the consecrated object, and the contact with the people would represent a first-degree contact. Compare Kessler (*Haggai,* 204 n. 52), who also suggests that Ezek 44:19 was "redactional, dramatic, and literary, and inserted simply to set up the analogy in v. 14." Verhoef (*Haggai and Malachi,* 118) views Hag 2:12 and Ezek 44:19 as competing perspectives. Note also the New Testament occurrences of the concept of transmitting holiness through one's garments (e.g., Matt 9:21; 14:36; Mark 3:10; 5:28; 6:56).

223. Compare Meyers and Meyers (*Haggai, Zechariah 1–8,* 56), who assert that, "although defilement is contagious . . . holiness in contrast is not."

tact between the items of food in 2:12 and a person who has been defiled by contact with a corpse. The hypothesis is introduced by *ʾim*, "if," and refers to the second phase of the contact. The first phase is signaled by the phrase *ṭəmēʾ-nepeš*, which appears to be an abbreviated reference to someone who has been made "unclean by a corpse" (cf. Lev 22:4). Other instances of the expression *ṭəmēʾ-nepeš* used of a corpse include *ṭāmēʾ lānāpeš* (Num 5:2; 9:10) and *bəmēt bənepeš* (Num 19:13; cf. Lev 21:11).[224] Anyone who touches a corpse is unclean, needs to be purified (Num 19:13; 31:19), and is not allowed to participate in the Passover celebration (Num 9:6–7). Leviticus 22:4–6 speaks of short-term uncleanness that lasts until the evening, a category that includes persons who: (1) touch anything that is already unclean through contact with a corpse or carcass (Lev 5:2; 11:8, 11, 24–28, 32–40; 22:4; Num 19:11, 14–16); (2) have an emission of semen (Lev 15:16, 18; 22:4); (3) touch an unclean crawling animal (Lev 11:29–30; 22:5); (4) touch any unclean person (Lev 15:2–12; 22:5).[225]

This category may be compared with the long-term uncleanness that requires rites of purification and pronouncements: skin disease (Lev 13) and bodily discharges (Lev 15:1–12). Notably, Haggai is referring to a situation of short-term uncleanness that can be remedied by a bath (cf. Lev 22:6). The corpse itself is unclean, and contact with it results in uncleanness. Thus, the first phase, the basis of Haggai's question, is a situation that results in temporary uncleanness. The second phase is articulated in 2:13: the unclean person encounters another object. According to Num 19:22, "Whatever the unclean person touches shall be unclean, and anyone who touches it shall be unclean until evening" (NRSV).

The prophet's question thus pick up a ruling that is clearly known—whatever the cause or mode of uncleanness (*ṭāmēʾ*), the consequences of contact are the same. Likewise, it does not matter what is touched. The determining factor is that the person has been made unclean by contact rather than by his/her own disease or discharge. The uncleanness is thus short term and easily remedied. However, this sort of remedy and the extent of the uncleanness are not the issue here; Hag 2:13 focuses on the third phase—whether someone who is unclean due to contact with an unclean entity (a corpse in this case) can contaminate food (see fig. 1). Again, the query is specific to the food, and the specificity does not alter the ruling. The issue of immediacy of the contact, while present, is also of little importance in the issue of uncleanness. Whether direct or indirect, any contact between an unclean entity and a neutral entity renders the neutral entity unclean.

Although there is no third phase of transmitting holiness, all contact

224. H. W. Wolff, *Haggai*, 91; Verhoef, *Haggai and Malachi*, 118; Milgrom, *Leviticus 1–16*, 270–72.

225. See Hartley, *Leviticus*, 355; Milgrom, *Leviticus 1–16*.

with uncleanness results in the transmission of the uncleanness. The priests' answer to Haggai maintains that the food the unclean person touches will become unclean. The affirmative response is achieved by a repetition of the verb in the declarative rather than the interrogative: *yiṭmāʾ*, "it will be unclean."

c. Analogy regarding the Community's Status (2:14)

14 The two questions establish the basis for the prophetic declaration regarding the community's status before Yahweh. The first question (2:12) is the foundation for the second (2:13), and the second provides the analogy (2:14). Is the comparison made with the state or the process of uncleanness? The text does not appear to see these as mutually exclusive options. Uncleanness is perpetuated, and this now-defiled community—by whatever means—is perpetuating uncleanness.

Typically the priests make the declaration that something/someone is clean (*ṭāhār*) or unclean (*ṭāmēʾ*; cf. Lev 13:3, 11; 14:7); but in Hag 2:14, the prophet declares that "this nation" is unclean. To whom does this designation refer? The community is here described as both *hāʿām-hazzê*, "this people," and *haggôy hazzê*, "this nation." Considering the uses of *ʿām*, "people," and *gôy*, "nation," in the book of Haggai, Wolff concludes that "people" refers to the community, and "nation" refers to the foreign nations. Wolff is inclined to see the Samaritans as the individuals who are pronounced unclean;[226] however, the context in the book of Haggai does not seem to support Wolff's interpretation, which presumes that at this juncture, the prophetic proclamation changes focus from Jerusalem to Samaria.[227] The community in Yehud is the focus of the declaration. Thus, we need to see these two designations as contextual parallels referring to the same group of people.

The entities declared unclean are further enumerated and marked off by the adverbial particle *kēn*, "so, thus." The community is unclean, as is *every work of their hands* (*kol-maʿăśê yədêhem*). One cannot miss the echo from Deuteronomy and other books. In several instances, the work of the people's hands provokes Yahweh's anger against them. Thus, Moses observes that the people are inclined to evil and "will provoke God to anger" through the work of their hands (Deut 31:29). Similarly, God cautions the people not to provoke God to anger through the work of their hands and observes that they have already provoked God (Jer 25:6, 7).[228] The second-person formulation *kōl*

226. H. W. Wolff, *Haggai*, 93–94.

227. Cf. Kessler, *Haggai*, 206; Verhoef, *Haggai and Malachi*, 119.

228. Cf. 2 Kgs 22:17; Isa 2:8; Jer 25:14.

maʿăśê yādekā, "every work of your hands," promising blessing is also attested (Deut 16:15; 24:19; 28:12; 30:9).[229]

The final component pronounced unclean is *whatever they bring there (yaqrîbû šām)*.[230] The particle *kēn*, "so," precedes each of the previous three elements but not the fourth and last element, "whatever they bring there." Accordingly, the last element is not one of four items but is a new element that is outside the pattern. It is evident in its use of *ṭāmēʾ* (adjective) to characterize the community's offering that this final element in 2:14 continues the prophet's pronouncement and connects the analogy to the question in 2:13, which uses the verb *ṭāmēʾ* (to be/become unclean). The priestly ruling is logical in concluding that an unclean person would contaminate an object by contact with it (see fig. 1). Not surprisingly, what an unclean nation offers Yahweh is unclean, because everything it produces is unclean.[231] No indication of the duration of the uncleanness is provided, however. The analogy suggests that the uncleanness resulting from the situations depicted would be short term, but the pronouncement in 2:14 allows for an open-ended or long-term uncleanness. In the absence of a functioning temple, "there" may refer to the designated place in the community where sacrifices were offered—most likely the altar that was rebuilt by the returnees (in 536 BCE; Ezra 3:1–7).

2. *Admonition to Compare the Times (2:15–19)*

15*"And now[a] reflect carefully. From this day and onward, before putting stone upon stone in the temple of Yahweh,* 16*before they were[b]—One came[c] to a heap of twenty but there were ten; one came to the wine vat to draw[d] fifty measures[e] but there were twenty.* 17*I struck[f] you with blight and mildew and hail—i.e., every work of your hands—but nothing [brought] you to me,"[g] oracle of Yahweh.*
18*"Reflect carefully. From this day forward—from the twenty-fourth of the ninth [month],[h] from the day when the foundation of Yahweh's temple was laid—reflect carefully.[i]* 19*Is seed[j] still in the granary? And have even the vine and the fig and pomegranate[k] and olive tree not yielded fruit? From this day on, I will bless."*

a. *Wəʿattâ* is usually interpreted as a redactional element that signifies the onset of the unit Hag 2:15–19 and establishes the link between the date formula in 2:10 and the content of

229. The NRSV translates *kōl maʿăśê yādekā*, as "all your undertakings." Note also *kol-yəgîaʿ kappāyim* in Hag 1:11, which the NRSV translates "all their labors." Cf. Kessler, *Haggai*, 205.

230. This is the *hiphil* imperfect third masculine plural of *qārab* plus the adverb *šām*, "there." The verb *qārab* usually refers to the act of offering a sacrifice (cf. Lev 1:2, 3, 5, 14; 2:4; 3:1).

231. Contrast Petersen (*Haggai and Zechariah 1–8*), who posits that the uncleanness was derived from the altar itself.

2:15–19. Those who transpose 2:15–19 after 1:15a usually delete *wəʿattâ*. However, the particle may be considered part of the flow of the message, both as a temporal element that emphasizes the present and as a particle that signals the concluding comment to an argument. Cf. Verhoef, *Haggai and Malachi*, 121.

b. The form *mihyôtām* is an infinitive construct form of *hāyâ*, "to be," with the preposition *min* and the third masculine suffix "before they were." While keeping the MT reading, some posit that the antecedent of the suffix is "the days"—"how they (the days) will become." For example, Verhoef, *Haggai and Malachi*, 110, 125; Baldwin, *Hag, Zech, Mal*, 52. Merrill (*Hag, Zech, Mal*, 49) proposes an MT literal meaning "from their being," an idiomatic expression for "from the time they were." Alternatively, the LXX assumes *mâ-həyîtem*. One option is to emend the text in line with the LXX, thus reading *mâ-həyîtem*, "how were you?" This option is reflected in at least one modern translation—"How did you fare?" (NRSV); the NIV omits the phrase. Thus also H. W. Wolff, *Haggai*, 58, 64. Meyers and Meyers (*Haggai, Zechariah 1–8*, 47, 60) explain the MT reading as the result of fusing two terms, *həyîtem* and *mâ*. See also R. L. Smith, *Micah–Malachi*, 159; Brown, *Obadiah through Malachi*, 129; Redditt, *Haggai, Zechariah, Malachi*, 29. Finally, emending the text to *mi-həyîtem*, "who were you" or "in what capacity," is also an option that builds on the LXX.

c. Concerning *bāʾ*, the *qal* perfect third masculine singular, the apparatus suggests that the text probably reads *bôʾ*. The latter form could be an imperative (Gen 7:1; 38:8; Exod 6:11; 10:1; 1 Kgs 1:42; Isa 22:15), an infinitive absolute (Lev 14:48; 1 Sam 9:6; 1 Kgs 22:30; Jer 36:29; Hab 2:3; Ps 126:6; Dan 11:10, 13), or an infinitive construct (cf. Gen 19:31; Exod 2:18; 17:12; Lev 25:22). Regarding the verb *bôʾ* in 1:2, 6, and 9, *bôʾ* is most likely the infinitive absolute. In both 1:6 and 9, the verb occurs in the *hiphil*: 1:6, *hābēʾ*, the *hiphil* infinitive absolute; and 1:9, *hăbēʾtem*, the *hiphil* perfect second masculine plural. In 1:6, 9, the text depicts the frustrated expectation of the people. Kessler (*Haggai*, 198 n. 12) notes that the infinitive absolute fits the context well; however, his translation reflects the perfect. See Meyers and Meyers (*Haggai, Zechariah 1–8*, 19–20) and H. W. Wolff (*Haggai*, 58) regarding the use of the infinitive construct in Hag 1:2.

d. The verbal form *laḥśōp* is an infinitive construct of *ḥāśap*, "to draw, scoop," which serves as a complementary infinitive of *bôʾ*—thus: *came to the wine vat to draw*. Possibly because of the absence of a complementary infinitive in 2:16a after the first occurrence of *bôʾ* in the verse, the apparatus suggests that *laḥśōp* is an addition. Cf. Meyers and Meyers, *Haggai, Zechariah 1–8*, 60; Kessler, *Haggai*, 199.

e. The term *pûrâ* (feminine-singular noun) occurs also in Isa 63:3, where it is usually translated "winepress" (cf. the NRSV). Whatever the source of the reading, it is apparent that the verse is asymmetrical in several instances: (1) second verb (*laḥśōp*) in Hag 2:16b is absent from 2:16a; (2) word for measure in 2:16b (*pûrâ*) is absent from 2:16a. To correct this, Meyers and Meyers (*Haggai, Zechariah 1–8*, 60) have suggested the addition of a word for "measure" in 2:16a, namely, "heaps," thus reading: "twenty heaps, there were only ten." H. W. Wolff (*Haggai*, 58) reasons that, since *yeqeb* is the more common term, *pûrâ* is not an "interpretive gloss" (Cf. Kessler, *Haggai*, 199 n. 16; Verhoef, *Haggai and Malachi*, 126).

f. The apparatus suggests that Hag 2:17 is a gloss added in light of Amos 4:9, "I struck you with blight and mildew; I laid waste your gardens and your vineyards; the locust devoured your fig trees and your olive trees; yet you did not return to me, says the Lord" (NRSV). Thus H. W. Wolff, *Haggai*, 58; contrast Kessler, *Haggai*, 199; Meyers and Meyers (*Haggai, Zechariah 1–8*, 62), who retain the MT as original on the basis of its chiastic structure (absent from Amos 4:9). The MT is retained here, noting the similarity of expressions and conceptually parallel elements in Hag 1:17 and Amos 4:9.

g. How to interpret the phrase *wəʾên-ʾetkem ʾēlay* (lit., there was not you to me) is highly debated, with many proposing various emendations to the text. The versions are generally independent of the MT. The LXX reads: "but you did not return to me." Notably, the MT of Amos 4:9 reads *wəlōʾ-šabtem ʿāday.* Thus it appears that the LXX assumes the reading *wəlōʾ-šabtem ʾēlay*. Here H. W. Wolff (*Haggai,* 59) also notes that the Vulgate emended the text, reading *ʾitkem* (with or among you) instead of *ʾetkem*: "and there was no one among you who returned to me." This reading would probably assume *wəʾên ʾitkem šābîm ʾēlay* (there was none among you who return to me) and would pick up on the question in Hag 2:3 asking to distinguish among the people. In the case of the Vulgate, the distinction would be between those who would and those who would not return to Yahweh. Verhoef (*Haggai and Malachi,* 111, 128) assumes that there is no essential difference between the MT and the versions and translates as follows: "yet you did not turn to me." Petersen (*Haggai and Zechariah 1–8,* 92) translates "but you did not side with me." In discussing the options, S. Amsler ("Aggée, Zacharie 1–8," in *Aggée, Zacharie, Malachie,* ed. S. Amsler, A. Lacocque, and R. Vuilleumier, CAT 11c [Geneva: Labor et Fides, 1981], 28) notes but does not follow the emendation *ʾănî wəʾên ʾitkem*, "but I was not with you." The latter option would be the antithesis of Hag 1:13; 2:4.

h. As it stands, the phrase in Hag 2:18bα, *miyyôm ʿeśrîm wəʾarbāʿâ lattəšîʿî,* "from the twenty-fourth day of the ninth [month]," provides an explanation of 2:18a and particularly *min-hayyôm hazzê*, "from this day." Amsler (*Aggée, Zacharie,* 28) follows the apparatus in suggesting that the modifier is a gloss because the date is the same as in Hag 2:10. The occurrence of the date here in 2:18b is one of three in Haggai 2 (2:10, 18, 20) and may be one of several reasons for retaining the MT. Cf. Meyers and Meyers, *Haggai, Zechariah 1–8,* 63; cf. Kessler, *Haggai,* 200; H. W. Wolff, *Haggai,* 59.

i. There are two components of Hag 2:18bβ—namely, the modifier *ləmin-hayyôm ʾăšer-yussad hêkal-yhwh* and *śîmû ləbabkem.* The modifier is an additional explanation for the phrase "from this day." The apparatus suggests that the modifier is an addition. The LXX reads *kai apo*, "and from," assuming *wəmin.* There is no manuscript evidence that suggests precedence for omitting the formula. Cf. Meyers and Meyers, *Haggai, Zechariah 1–8,* 63; cf. Kessler, *Haggai,* 200; H. W. Wolff, *Haggai,* 59.

j. Concerning the MT reading *hazzeraʿ,* the *BHS* apparatus suggests reading *migraʿ*, "the diminution," in place of *hazzeraʿ* (masculine-singular noun), "the seed," or inserting *nigraʿ* (*niphal* perfect third masculine singular of *gāraʿ*, "to be diminished, reduced"; cf. Num 36:3–4; Deut 4:2; Jer 26:2).

k. The *BHS* apparatus suggests that the phrase *wəʿad-haggepen wəhattəʾēnâ wəhārimmôn* in Hag 2:19aβ is an addition. Many follow the LXX, reading "and still," assuming *wəʿōd,* in place of *wəʿad,* "and until" (cf. H. W. Wolff, *Haggai,* 59; Verhoef, *Haggai and Malachi,* 111; Meyers and Meyers, *Haggai, Zechariah 1–8,* 48). The more difficult reading is the MT; the LXX is a facilitated reading that attempts to harmonize with Hag 2:19a , where *haʿôd* occurs (cf. Hag 2:6). The MT is retained here with the translation "even" (cf. Barthélemy, *Ezékiel, Daniel et les 12 prophètes,* 933). Kessler, (*Haggai,* 200) retains the MT on the basis of Job 25:5 and 2 Sam 17:2, where *ʿad. . . lōʾ* occurs with the meaning "still not or not even yet."

15 A new unit begins in Hag 2:15, marked by the adverbial particle *wəʿattā,* "and now" (cf. 1:5; 2:4), and continues the unit begun in 2:10. The illustration in 2:10–14 makes it clear that the community is at odds with Yahweh. The particle *wəʿattā* has dual force—that is, "now (at this point in time)" or "so (consequently)." Notably, the traditions about blessings or curses usually employ them in connection with the people's deeds—for example, the work of their hands. Here, Hag 2 and its conceptual framework (cf. 1:6–11) present an image of a community poised for punishment because of its ways. So what is this community to do?

Like Hag 1:5, 7, the unit 2:15–19 admonishes the community to reflect—*śîmû-nāʾ ləbabkem*. In Hag 1:5, 7, the object of the reflection—*ʿal-darkêkem*, "upon your ways"—is immediately juxtaposed with the admonition. This object has a past-present orientation, pointing to what has already been done or is being done that is influencing the community's present circumstances. In Hag 1, the orientation connected their frustrated efforts to Yahweh's punishment of the community. The effort yielded little because Yahweh made it so. There are several challenges in this unit that will be discussed, including each component and its attenuating challenges.

In Hag 2:15 the admonition to reflect incorporates a temporal phrase, indicating a time frame to be considered, "from this day" (*min-hayyôm hazzê*) "and forward, on" (*wāmāʿəlâ*). The time frame is also indicated in 2:15b and 2:16 with the particle *min*, "from." Verse 17 likewise signals the perspective on what came before, giving other actions of Yahweh against the people in a failed effort to reform them. Haggai 2:16–17 may be seen as an interlude characterizing the period before the day on which the proclamation is being made.[232] Haggai 2:18 then resumes the focus on the present by repeating the admonition and the temporal phrase "from this day and onward." "From this day" refers to the twenty-fourth day of the ninth month cited in 2:10.

There are two modifiers to the temporal phrase: specification of the day via the date formula in 2:18b and specification of the event in 2:18bβ, which was laying the temple's foundation. The admonition focuses on the time frame and on the past and present circumstances presented, and it culminates in a declaration of promise: I will bless (*ʾăbārēk*; 2:19). The unit 2:15–19 divides into two distinctive parts, the two admonitions.

a. Admonition #1: Regarding the Past and Present (2:15–17)

Reflect carefully (śîmû-nāʾ ləbabkem) is like the formulation in 1:5, 7; but there, the object is introduced by *ʿal*. The admonition in 2:15 may be an abbreviated form that assumes the object—namely, the ways of the people and their experiences. At issue in 2:15aβ is the time frame referred to by the phrase *from this day and onward.* The term *māʿəlâ* in particular has various nuances: direction or location, "up, upward" (Exod 20:26; Ezra 7:9; Judg 1:36; cf. Pss 120, 121);

232. Cf. Verhoef, *Haggai and Malachi*, 122.

time, as in the clause "from that day forward" (1 Sam 16:13; 30:25; Ezek 39:22); age, as in the clause "from X years old and upward" (Exod 30:14; Num 1:3, 18; Ezra 3:8; 1 Chr 23:3, 24; cf. 2 Chr 31:16, 17).[233] Similar expressions use *hālə'â*, "beyond," to indicate from X-time and beyond, looking toward the future: "When an ox or a sheep or a goat is born, it shall remain seven days with its mother, and from the eighth day on it shall be acceptable as the LORD's offering by fire" (Lev 22:27 NRSV).

In various occurrences, *māʿəlâ* has the distinct meaning of forward rather than backward movement, and thus it should be interpreted with a prospective sense here in Hag 2:15 (cf. 2:18, 19), rather than a retrospective sense, as some have proposed.[234] The following phrase, *miṭṭerem, ṭerem* plus *min*, signals a retrospective view, an interlude or momentary digression to lay further ground for the promise to be articulated in 2:19.[235] The adverbial clause then sets the basis for the question in 2:16 by drawing the community's attention to the time *before putting stone upon stone in the temple of Yahweh.* What does it mean to put stone upon stone?

The phrase *stone upon stone (śûm-'eben 'el-'eben)* is sometimes interpreted as parallel to laying the foundation (Hag 2:18); both phrases referring to the "temple of Yahweh" (*hêkal-yhwh*). While Meyers and Meyers suggest there are at least two possibilities for understanding the phrase (part of the masonry work needed to construct the temple and a re-foundation ceremony), they believe that the text most likely refers to a re-foundation ceremony (cf. 2:18). They therefore propose that the significance of the re-foundation was to establish continuity with the preexilic temple and with the earlier building efforts begun during Cyrus's reign.[236] Likewise the date of the re-foundation is presented three times (2:10, 18, 20), denoting its prominence in Haggai's perspective on the community. Floyd affirms that Hag 2:18 speaks of the day when the foundation was laid but distinguishes between the beginning of the work reported in 2:15 (*stone upon stone* begun in 1:15a), which led to the laying of the foundation, and a ceremony celebrating that foundation.[237] Accordingly, there may be three different identifiable events.

233. BDB 751.

234. Retrospective view: Meyers and Meyers, *Haggai, Zechariah 1–8,* 58–59. They argue on the basis of the LXX and on the use of the admonition in 1:5 and 7 to call attention to the past. Likewise, they point to the unique occurrence of *miṭṭerem*. They propose that it is intended to clarify the use of *māʿəlâ* in 2:15a. Prospective view: Kessler, *Haggai,* 207; Verhoef, *Haggai and Malachi,* 121–22.

235. Meyers and Meyers, *Haggai, Zechariah 1–8,* 58–59; H. W. Wolff, *Haggai,* 39; Kessler, *Haggai,*198 n. 8, 207.

236. Meyers and Meyers, *Haggai, Zechariah 1–8,* 59; Petersen, *Haggai and Zechariah 1–8,* 88. See also the discussion in the introduction, section II, above.

237. Floyd, *Minor Prophets 2,* 289–90.

For some, it is problematic to have the affirmation of the beginning of the work in Hag 1:12–15a and again in 2:15–19. Amsler, therefore, proposes relocating 2:15–19 after 1:15a.[238] Likewise, Wolff, following a similar reasoning, relocates 2:15–19 and dates the beginning of the work to the twenty-fourth day of the sixth month (Hag 1:15) rather than the twenty-fourth day of the ninth month (of Hag 2:18).[239] Without giving precise information about what that work entailed, this reference in 2:15b to "stone upon stone" may in fact be indicating the beginning of the work on the temple that is confirmed in Hag 1:12–15a. The significance of the expression "stone upon stone" may be, not so much what was done, as the fact that something was done that changed Yahweh's response to the community. Thus, the recollection of the time before stone was laid upon stone is a vehicle for showing the contrast between the past inactivity and the present work on Yahweh's temple.

16 The second of these three verses provides an interlude concerning the past. With 2:15 as a basis, 2:16 describes an earlier time when the community situation was marked by frustration (cf. Hag 1:6–11). Two distinct interpretations of the opening formulation *mihyôtām* will be presented here. First, the formula can be read as an opening clause that establishes an additional basis for the description. The form *mihyôtām* is an infinitive construct form of *hāyâ*, "to be,"[240] with the preposition *min* and the third-masculine suffix, which is translated "before they were." In part, the difficulty with the MT is determining the referent of the suffix. In keeping with the third masculine plural suffix, the antecedent would be the stones in "stone upon stone"; thus the translation is "before they were," which depicts the time before the stones were placed together.

Second, the formulation (*mihyôtām*) can be read as a question, usually on the basis of the LXX. The LXX's "what were you?" seems to facilitate the reading by maintaining the second-person address form and assuming *mâ-həyîtem*. Another option is to emend the text in line with the LXX, thus reading *mâ-həyîtem*, "how were you?" This option is reflected in at least one modern translation: "How did you fare?" (NRSV); the NIV omits the phrase.[241]

What the community is asked to reflect on is its circumstances before

238. Amsler, *Aggée,* 27; cf. H. W. Wolff, *Haggai.*

239. H. W. Wolff, *Haggai,* 59–60, 63.

240. The infinitive construct form (*həyôt*) of *hāyâ* (to be).

241. H. W. Wolff, *Haggai,* 58, 64. Meyers and Meyers (*Haggai, Zechariah 1–8,* 47, 60) explain the MT reading as the result of fusing two terms: *həyiytem* and *mah.* R. L. Smith, *Micah–Malachi,* 159; Brown, *Obadiah through Malachi,* 129; Redditt, *Haggai, Zechariah, Malachi,* 29.

it began work on Yahweh's Temple. Like the admonition in Hag 1:5, 7, and 1:9–11, Hag 2:16 forges a connection between the community's response to the work of rebuilding the temple and whatever adversity they have been experiencing. Thus even in this formulation, the attempt to illustrate continuity is again evident—continuity between the former and present temples (2:3); between past actions and present circumstances (1:6–11; 2:16–17); between the present and the future blessing (2:19). Links thus suggest that all of the people's realities are interconnected and must therefore be addressed in the rebuilding effort (cf. 2:11–14). Two examples are cited to illustrate the past adversity, both addressing the frustrated expectations of the community.

One came to a heap of twenty. Concerning *bāʾ*, the apparatus suggests that the text probably reads *bôʾ*. The latter form (*bôʾ*) could be an imperative (Gen 7:1; 38:8; Exod 6:11; 10:1; 1 Kgs 1:42; Isa 22:15), or an infinitive absolute (Lev 14:48; 1 Sam 9:6; 1 Kgs 22:30; Jer 36:29; Hab 2:3; Ps 126:6; Dan 11:10, 13), or an infinitive construct (cf. Gen 19:31; Exod 2:18; 17:12; Lev 25:22). The verb *bôʾ* occurs in Hag 1:2, 6, 9; in 1:2 *bôʾ* is most likely the infinitive absolute. In both Hag 1:6 and 9, the verb occurs in the *hiphil*—1:6, *hābēʾ*, the *hiphil* infinitive absolute; and 1:9, *hăbēʾtem*, the *hiphil* perfect second person masculine plural. The text in 1:6 and 9 depicts the frustrated expectation of the people.[242]

No product or unit of measure is specified in 2:16 precisely because the focus is on frustrated expectations and not on the exact product or degree to which the expectations were frustrated. Even so, the characterization of the past is more precise here than in Hag 1:6–11. Here in 2:16, relative proportions are given, naming the expectation, which is a heap of twenty (*ʿărēmat ʿeśrîm*), and the reality, which is ten (*ʿăśārâ*); this is fifty percent less than expected. The heap (*ʿărēmat*) may refer to heaps of grain stored at the threshing floor (cf. Ruth 3:7; Jer 50:26).[243] The product is usually inferred from the context. Again as in Hag 1:6–11, according to 2:16 the resources are available but are quantitatively less than expected.

One came to the wine vat. The expectation did not match reality when one came to the wine vat (*yeqeb*). The wine vat was possibly the vessel that held the liquid pressed from the grapes (cf. Isa 5:2; Hos 9:2).[244] The verbal form *laḥśōp* is an infinitive construct of *ḥāśap,* "to draw, scoop," which serves as a complementary infinitive of the verb *bôʾ*—thus, *came to the wine vat to draw.* Possibly because of the absence of a complementary infinitive in Hag

242. Kessler (*Haggai,* 198 n. 12) notes that the infinitive absolute fits the context well; however, his translation reflects the perfect. See p. 105 n. d.

243. Cf. "Heap of stones," *gal* (Josh 7:26; 8:29; Hos 12:11); *gal-ʾăbānîm* (2 Sam 18:17).

244. H. W. Wolff, *Haggai,* 64–65; Verhoef, *Haggai and Malachi,* 125–26.

2:16a after the first occurrence of *bôʾ* in the verse, the apparatus suggests that *laḥśōp,* "to scoop," is an addition.[245] The expectation was fifty measures (*ḥămiššîm*), but the reality was twenty (*ʿeśrîm*)—that is, forty percent less than expected. The term *pûrâ* (feminine-singular noun) occurs also in Isa 63:3, where it is usually translated "winepress" (cf. the NRSV). Whatever the source of the reading, it is apparent that the verse is asymmetrical in several instances: (1) the second verb (*laḥśōp*) in 2:16b is absent from 2:16a; (2) the word for measure appears in 2:16b (*pûrâ*) but is absent from 2:16a. To correct for this, Meyers and Meyers have suggested the addition of a word for measure in 2:16a, namely, "heaps"—thus reading ". . . twenty heaps, there were only ten."[246] However, poetic symmetry or any other type of symmetry is unnecessary to an understanding of the verse; therefore, I retain the MT. Whatever the unit of measure, the verse describes dashed expectations experienced as a shortage of resources.

17 The recollection of the past in 2:17 is consistent with the description in 1:10–11. Likewise 2:17 is similar to Amos 4:9 both in its formulation and in its substance:

> I struck you with blight and mildew; I laid waste your gardens and your vineyards; the locust devoured your fig trees and your olive trees; yet you did not return to me, says the Lord. (NRSV)

God attempted to convince the people to return to God; but they did not return. The failure of God's efforts to persuade the people to conform to God's desire for them led to additional efforts to bring them into conformity. We see this persistent effort in the repetition of the refrain in Amos 4:6, 8, 9, 10, 11 (*wəlōʾ-šabtem ʿāday,* "yet you did not return to me"). Here in Hag 2:17, as in 1:10–11, the focus is on Yahweh's action. What has Yahweh done?

Yahweh speaks in the first person: *I struck you.* This action (*nākâ*) recalls at least two traditions: the exodus tradition and the Deuteronomistic tradition about blessing and cursing. In the exodus tradition and the associated plagues, God struck the Egyptians with gnats and struck down their firstborn (Exod 8, 12). Concerning the plagues, it took repeated efforts for Pharaoh to respond to God by releasing the people. Deuteronomy reports that Yahweh struck the community with curses when they were disobedient, and continued to do so until they were obedient (Deut 28:22, 27, 28, 35; cf. Lev 26:23–24). The formulation "I struck you" raises questions about how to understand Yahweh's action. The first possibility is to see "you" (*ʾetkem*) as the object of the verb, with an expansion, "every work of your hands" (*kol-maʿăśê yədêkem*) that

245. Cf. Meyers and Meyers, *Haggai, Zechariah 1–8,* 60; Kessler, *Haggai,* 199.

246. See p. 105 n. e.

functions as an appositive.[247] Another alternative is for the verb to have two objects: you and every work of your hands have been struck by blight and mildew and hail (cf. NRSV). Yet another alternative is to view the verb *nākâ* as doing double duty with two sets of objects and agents: "I struck you with blight and mildew; and I struck the work of your hands with hail."[248] I think the first alternative is being used to indicate that, as in Hag 1:10–11, Yahweh struck the entire community with all three agents—blight, mildew, and hail (*baššiddāpôn ûbayyērāqôn ûbabbārād*).

These agents, *blight and mildew and hail,* are listed in Deut 28:22 as punishment for the people's disobedience. Blight and mildew (*šiddāpôn ûbayyērāqôn*) typically occur together as a form of punishment (cf. Deut 28:22; 1 Kgs 8:37; 2 Chr 6:28; Amos 4:9). One cause of blight (*šiddāpôn*) is exposure to hot wind; the condition itself is the withering of a plant (cf. Gen 41:6, 23, 27; cf. 2 Kgs 19:26//Isa 37:27).[249] Mildew (*yērāqôn*) also affects plants; it results from an overexposure to moisture or drought that leads to plant disease. Blight and mildew may thus represent a merism referring to the effect of exposure to excess heat and moisture. The third element used by Yahweh was hail (*bārād*), which was also one of the plagues used to strike Egypt (Exod 9:18–35). The force of this form of precipitation may destroy vegetation and livestock (Exod 10:5–15; Ps 78:47–48; Isa 28:2, 17). Yahweh claims responsibility for all these agents used to strike the community.

In spite of these threatening acts, the community did not return to Yahweh—*but nothing [brought] you to me.* This is Yahweh's frustration with the people: they did not make the desired response. As seen in both the exodus tradition and the Deuteronomistic blessings and curses, Yahweh's actions were not random acts taken on a whim. Rather, the actions are presented as responses to human behavior. From the perspective of Hag 2:17 and 1:10–11, Yahweh is responsible for the failure of the crops and the destruction of the plants that survived the disease. The crops, no matter how limited, would be of poor quality because of Yahweh's doing. Thus, the text has juxtaposed Yahweh's acts on behalf of the community—encouraging them and assuring them of the divine presence—with Yahweh's punishment of the community. This God whom they are told has covenanted to be with them (2:5) is depicted as being in full control of their lives, even the very product of their labor (1:11). Moreover, God responds and repeats the punishment because the community has not responded.

Amos 4 uses a similar formulation, and the theme of God's people refus-

247. Verhoef, *Haggai and Malachi,* 126–27.

248. Kessler, *Haggai,* 199; Meyers and Meyers, *Haggai, Zechariah 1–8,* 62.

249. Cf. Verhoef, *Haggai and Malachi,* 127; Meyers and Meyers, *Haggai, Zechariah 1–8,* 61.

ing to return to God is common throughout the prophets (e.g., Mic 6:13–16). The admonition to reflect in Haggai appears on two fronts: (1) it is the basis of the first reflection, which prompts the people to respond to Yahweh and begin work on the temple; (2) it is the basis of the second reflection, which transitions from punishment to blessing.

b. Admonition #2: Regarding the Present and Future (2:18–19)

18 The repetition of the admonition (*śîmû-nāʾ ləbabkem*) signals the refocus on the present, further emphasizing the decisive transition from the past to the present—the twenty-fourth day of the ninth month (cf. Hag 2:10). It calls for reflection based on the particular time frame that begins today (from this day). *This day* (*min-hayyôm hazzê wāmāʿəlâ*) was "the day when the foundation of Yahweh's temple was laid," and the references in the date formula (the twenty-fourth day of the ninth month) highlight the importance of this day. At least two questions challenge one's understanding of the day's significance: what event happened on this day, and what is the relationship of this day's event to other events? I will address the first concern about the event with regard to 2:15 and 1:12–15 and to the issue of work done as compared with a re-foundation ceremony. Haggai 2:18bβ includes two components: the modifier "from the day when the foundation of Yahweh's temple was laid" (*ləmin-hayyôm ʾăšer-yussad hêkal-yhwh*) and the admonition to "reflect" (*śîmû ləbabkem*). The modifier is a further explanation of the phrase "from this day forward." Wolff provides two valuable perspectives for understanding the verse and the place of all its components. First he suggests that the preposition *lə* on *ləmin* carries the nuance of "namely."[250] The second component—*śîmû ləbabkem*—is thought to be an addition. It is one of three occurrences of the formula in Hag 2 (i.e., 2:15, 18a, 18b; cf. 1:5, 7). For Wolff, the repetition is necessitated by the gap that the "extensive amplification" creates between the demand and the object.[251]

The text says that *the foundation of Yahweh's temple was laid* (*yussad hêkal-yhwh*). As I noted in the discussion of 2:15, some commentators propose that both 2:15 and 2:18 refer to a re-foundation in a broad sense rather than a narrow sense. In the broad sense, a new foundation was not laid; the former foundation was restored.[252] It has also been suggested that a re-foundation ceremony is in view here, when a stone from the former foundation was used

250. H. W. Wolff, *Haggai,* 59; also Kessler, *Haggai,* 200; Verhoef, *Haggai & Malachi,* 111.

251. H. W. Wolff, *Haggai,* 59.

252. Verhoef, *Haggai and Malachi,* 129–30.

within the structure of the new one to achieve continuity between the past, present, and future. Yet another suggestion is that the rededication ceremony also included a purification rite similar to the *kalu* ceremony.[253] While some associate the defilement mainly with cultic infractions linked to the altar, apparently there was a more-pervasive problem than rejection of the altar[254]—that is, resistance to the current building efforts, or intergroup hostilities.[255] A purification ceremony would address the defilement noted by 2:14—a defilement of the entire community.

The second issue regarding the day that the foundation was laid is the relationship between Hag 2:18 and Ezra 3. From the perspective of Ezra 3:10–11, the re-foundation celebration for the temple would have happened about 537/36 BCE. Ezra 4:1–5 seems to be aware that the work on the temple had begun but was impeded.[256] If the work on the temple commenced in 537 BCE, then why is there a claim that the work began in response to Haggai's prophecy in 520 BCE (Hag 1:14–15a)? The most ready solution is to see the claim in Hag 1:14 as a recommencement after a period of cessation and a new celebration commemorating the renewed efforts.

The final element of 2:18 is the admonition to reflect (*śîmû ləbabkem*). This clause serves a dual function: It concludes the past-present reflection specifically relating to the temple, and it begins the present-future reflection specifically focused on the promise of blessing.

19 The verse concludes the unit 2:15–19 and contains two questions concerned with agriculture, thus establishing the final part of the contrast—before and after the blessing. The first question is about "seed" (*zeraʿ*): *Is seed still in the granary?* Understanding the question requires understanding both the "seed" (*hazzeraʿ*) and the location of the seed (*məgûrâ*). Some have translated *zeraʿ*, "grain,"[257] in contrast to *dāgān*, "grain," which is commonly used with *tîrôš*, "wine" (Deut 7:13; 12:17; 14:23; 18:4; 33:28; 2 Kgs 18:32; Isa 36:17; Jer 31:12; Hos 2:8 [MT 10]).[258] The term *dāgān* is the product in its edible form. This is not the picture presented in Hag 2:19. Rather, in combination with the other elements, *zeraʿ*, "seed," seems to be used in the same way as in Isa 30:23: "He will give rain for the seed with which you sow

253. Kessler, *Haggai,* 209, 214–16, including bibliography. Cf. Petersen, *Haggai and Zechariah 1–8,* 93.

254. Petersen (*Haggai and Zechariah 1–8,* 82–85, esp. p. 85) posits that the uncleanness of the temple complex and the altar rendered the people unclean. The rededication ceremony would address these sources of uncleanness.

255. Cf. Kessler, *Haggai,* 214–15.

256. Verhoef, *Haggai and Malachi,* 129.

257. Kessler, *Haggai,* 200.

258. Gen 42:1; 43:2, *šeber,* "grain." Jacob learns that there is grain in Egypt and sends his sons to purchase some.

the ground, and grain, the produce of the ground, which will be rich and plenteous" (NRSV). The concern is not about the abundance of resources being stored for community consumption or the balance of resources for food but about seed for planting.[259] The question is whether the seed that is for sowing in the ground remains in storage. If it remains stored, there is no potential for yield—it remains a seed; however, if it has been used for its purpose, it has the potential for yield (cf. John 12:24). Sowing the seed will manifest itself in future yield according to what God allows (cf. Hag 1:6–11; Deut 28:22).

Seed left in the granary will not yield a harvest. The term *məgûrâ*, "granary," is similar to *ʾôṣār*. Notably, the term usually selected for a storehouse for tithes is *bêt hāʾôṣār* (Mal 3:10; Neh 10:39 [MT 38]) or simply *ʾôṣār*, "treasury" (1 Kgs 7:51; 15:18; Jer 38:11; Joel 1:17). The term *ʾôṣār* is also used of Yahweh's storehouse for rain and wind (Deut 28:12; Job 38:22; Jer 10:13//51:16).[260] The image presents two alternatives: a full granary with no potential for yield, and an empty granary whose seed has been sown and has potential for yield. But the potential and the actual yield are two different matters.

The second part of Hag 2:19 also lists elements that are not necessarily ready for consumption but have potential for yield: *the vine, fig, pomegranate, and olive tree*. This potential state is signaled by the verbal clause *"have even . . . not yielded"* (*wəʿad . . . lōʾ nāśāʾ*)—using the *qal* perfect third masculine singular form of the verb *nāśāʾ*, which usually means "bear, carry" but here appears with the secondary meaning "to bear fruit, produce" (cf. Ezek 36:8).[261] If the trees enumerated have not yet yielded fruit, what is the cause? Presumably, the question is rhetorical and is meant to indicate that the trees have not yet produced their yield. But why not? If seen in connection with Hag 1:10–11, the reason is quite clear. Any withholding of rain and the ensuing effects of limited resources are Yahweh's doing. The plants identified all have potential for yielding produce—grapes, figs, pomegranates, and olives—that can be consumed or refined into other products (e.g., wine, oil). One cannot escape the comparison between the two images of the crops, "blight and mildew" (Hag 2:17) as compared with these plants' potential for yield. So why name these plants?

Meyers and Meyers posit that these plants were part of the "late summer harvest and may represent an actual agricultural sequence, terminat-

259. Meyers and Meyers (*Haggai, Zechariah 1–8*, 64) assume that the question is about these different types of resources.

260. BDB 69–70.

261. The compound subject precedes the singular verb, and the deletion of the first three elements, "vine, fig tree, pomegranate" (*haggepen wəhattəʾēnâ wəhārimmôn*), would result in *ʿēṣ hazzayit*, "olive tree," the masculine-singular subject plus the singular verb *nāśāʾ*—"has the olive tree not yielded?"

ing with the late olive harvest."[262] They note that the products from these three constituted the "basic food crops of Palestine" (i.e., wine, olives, grain).[263] Some comparison with the triad of elements is evident here as elsewhere (Deut 7:13; 12:17; 33:28; Isa 36:17). Concerning the fig (*tə'ēnâ*) and pomegranate (*rimmôn*): vines and figs occur together in several passages (Judg 9:9–11; Amos 4:9; Hos 9:10; Nah 3:12; 1 Kgs 5:5; Isa 34:4; 36:16; Mic 4:4; Prov 27:18);[264] pomegranates appear with vines and figs (Deut 8:8);[265] pomegranates and figs are among the products that connote abundance in the land (Deut 8:7–8; Num 13:23).[266] Meyers and Meyers also argue that the pomegranate is a luxury item that can indicate abundance.[267] Even if that is so, the mention alone does not point to abundance; wine was also produced from the pomegranate.[268] Here, it is on the list of plants that have not produced any fruit. As seen in his translation, Petersen offers another perspective: "Will the seed in the granary still be diminished? Will the fig, the pomegranate, the olive tree continue not to bear fruit?"[269] He interprets these questions as the logical progression from Hag 2:17: that is, these plants are also affected by the blight and mildew.

The transition from fruitless plants to abundance is seen as being controlled by God. According to Deut 28, when Yahweh opens the window of the heavens, the resources will be given in abundance (cf. Mal 3:10–11). Likewise in Hag 2:19 and the larger context of the book, Yahweh's blessing is key for the community. Yahweh assures the nation that, *from this day on, I will bless.* The promise to bless echoes the promises to the patriarchs. In Gen 12:2, "I will bless" occurs with the object of the verb specified, "I will bless you" (*'eʿeśkā*—referring to Abram; cf. Gen 12:3; 17:6; 17:20; 26:3, 24). Haggai 2:19 uses *'ăbārēk* (first common singular) as compared with *yəbārekkā*, "he will bless you" (third masculine singular plus second masculine singular suffix). The verb *bārak* with the specified object depicts (1) the connection between blessing and prosperity (Deut 7:13), (2) Yahweh's promised blessing on all of Israel's undertakings (Deut 15:10, 18; 28:8), and (3) the blessing in the land that is contingent upon obedience (Deut 30:16).

In Hag 2:19, a modifier, *from this day on,* restricts the promise and suggests a contrast between the past and the present: "from this day forward, the twenty-fourth day of the ninth month." What of the days prior to this day?

262. Meyers and Meyers, *Haggai, Zechariah 1–8,* 64.

263. Meyers and Meyers, *Haggai, Zechariah 1–8,* 65.

264. BDB 1061.

265. BDB 941.

266. Petersen, *Haggai and Zechariah 1–8,* 94.

267. Meyers and Meyers, *Haggai, Zechariah 1–8,* 65.

268. Petersen, *Haggai and Zechariah 1–8,* 94.

269. Petersen, *Haggai and Zechariah 1–8,* 96.

Arguably, the imagery in Hag 2:15–19 contrasts pre- and post-blessing time frames. Before being blessed the people experienced adversity at the hand of Yahweh. There is no neutrality presented wherein Yahweh's presence is passive or undetectable. Whether or not this observation may be generalized in regard to other passages (such as in the case of Deut 28 and Lev 26), the book of Haggai clearly supports it and ties the blessings/curses to the work on the temple. As Meyers and Meyers observe, Haggai incorporates the temple typology that was common in the Near East, in which temple construction was linked to prosperity.[270] The temporal modifier in Hag 2:19 marks the beginning point of the blessing and does not specify the nature of the blessing. The particle *wāmāʿəlâ*, "and onward," is absent; but the formulation may be an abbreviation of the one in Hag 2:15, 18.

I will bless may be compared with Hag 2:17, "I struck you." Since no direct object is mentioned, some modern translators supply an object: "From this day on I will bless *you*" (NRSV and NIV). However, the nature of the blessing may be inferred from the juxtaposition of the promise (Hag 2:19b) with the enumeration of plants in 2:19aβ, and from the perspective in 1:6–11 (cf. Lev 25:21; 26:3–4; Ps 128:1–5). The influx of wealth already mentioned in Hag 2:7 would add to the prosperity envisioned for Judah. Even so, the promise may address the immediate situation without necessarily giving a guarantee concerning all future situations (cf. Deut 28:22). The question arising from Hag 2:19 is whether this expression of the promised blessing guarantees the continuation of blessing. If so, then the blessing would be perpetual, lasting from its beginning point to an undetermined future.[271] Likewise, to the extent that the blessing is linked to the temple, the continuation of that blessing would also be linked to the temple. Neither of these possibilities may be excluded from an understanding of the book. By admonishing the community to reflect on its situation, Haggai also reminds them of the correspondence between obedience and blessing, disobedience and adversity. The Deity's power over nature is manifested in accordance with God's plan and in response to the community.

B. CONCERNING YAHWEH'S FUTURE RULE (2:20–23)

20*And the word of Yahweh came to Haggai a second [time], on the twenty-fourth [day] of the month:* 21*Speak to Zerubbabel, governor of Judah:*[a] *"I am*

270. Meyers and Meyers, *Haggai, Zechariah 1–8,* 65–66.

271. Verhoef (*Haggai and Malachi,* 136) argues against this perpetual blessing; he states, "The promised blessing did not materialize." However, he affirms the correlation between blessings and obedience.

about to shake the heavens and the earth. [22]*And I will overthrow the throne of kingdoms and I will destroy the strength of the kingdom*[b] *of the nations; and I will overthrow a chariot and its rider; and horses and their riders will go down, each by the sword of his brother.*[c] [23]*In that day"—utterance of Yahweh of hosts—"I will take you, Zerubbabel, son of Shealtiel,*[d] *my servant"—utterance of Yahweh—"and I will place you as a signet ring because I have chosen you"—utterance of Yahweh of hosts.*

---

a. There are two expansions of the MT found in the LXX. First, "the son of Shealtiel" in line with Hag 1:1, 12; 2:2. This addition is identified by some commentaries but not incorporated into their translation. Thus, H. W. Wolff, *Haggai,* 98; Kessler, *Haggai,* 219; Amsler, *Aggée, Zacharie,* 40. Regarding the term *hāʾāreṣ* in Hag 2:21b, the LXX-V adds "and the sea and dry land." This appears to be a harmonization with Hag 2:6.

b. Following the apparatus on Hag 2:22aβ, some commentaries propose the deletion of *mamlākôt,* "kingdom."

c. The apparatus suggests that *ʾîš bəḥereb ʾāḥîw* is probably a gloss. LXXA adds, "I will overthrow all their power, I will bring down their borders, I will strengthen my chosen ones."

d. The apparatus suggests that the patronymic *ben-šəʾaltîʾēl* (son of Shealtiel) may be a gloss.

1. Yahweh's Dealing with the Kingdoms (2:20–22)

20 The final unit of the book of Haggai begins with a word-event formula—*the word of Yahweh came to Haggai a second [time] (wayəhî dəbar-yhwh šēnît ʾel-ḥaggay)*—plus the date formula denoting the specific day, *the twenty-fourth [day] of the month* (2:20). Haggai 2:10, 20 depict Haggai as the recipient of the word of Yahweh as compared to the instrument or vehicle of that word (cf. 2:10–14; see table 3). As recipient, Haggai is given further instruction to speak to Zerubbabel, governor of Judah (cf. 2:1).

21–22 The words that Haggai is commanded to speak to Zerubbabel follow in 2:21: *I am about to shake the heavens and the earth* (cf. 2:6). Having addressed this to an audience that includes Zerubbabel (2:1–9), Yahweh now addresses it to Zerubbabel on this second occasion. The heavens and the earth and the universe are the objects of Yahweh's action; as in Hag 2:6–7, cosmic upheaval progresses to international upheaval. Haggai 2:22 discontinues the use of *rāʿaš,* "shake," with reference to the kingdoms; instead, the verb *hāpak,* "to turn, overturn," is used to depict the action taken against the kingdoms. As a transitive verb, *hāpak* means "turn, turn about, overturn" (2 Kgs 9:23; 21:13); the overthrow of cities (Gen 19:21–29; Deut 29:23 [MT 22]; Amos 4:11; Lam 4:6; of Sodom and Gomorrah; cf. Jer 20:16; Jonah 3:4 of cities). As an intransitive, *hāpak* means "change, change into, transform" (Exod 7:15; Lev 13:16, 20; Jer 31:13; Amos 5:7).[272] The feminine-singular noun *mahpēkat,* "overthrow," always occurs in this form and is used as a verbal noun of Sodom or both Sodom and Gomorrah (cf. Isa 13:19; Jer 49:18; 50:40; Amos 4:11).[273] The root, *hāpak,* occurs with *šāmad,* "destroy" (Deut 28:20, 24, 25, 45, 61), with reference to Yahweh's punishment of Israel for disobedience.[274]

The message to Zerubbabel is *I will overthrow the throne of kingdoms.* The verb *hāpak* is therefore associated with what God did to Sodom because of its wickedness. Here in Hag 2:22a, the verb with the object "throne of kingdoms" (*kissēʾ mamlākôt*) is a unique formulation. The collective sense is achieved by pluralizing the genitive (kingdom).[275] While the reason for the overthrow is not specified in Haggai, the nature of the action may be inferred from the action taken against cities and nations including Israel. The "throne" (*kissēʾ*) is used as a metonymy for authority.[276] The seat of authority or rule in Israel is also designated "the throne of Israel" (1 Kgs 2:4; 8:25; 2 Chr 6:10). Equating the throne of the king with the throne of Yahweh, Jerusalem is also prophesied to be Yahweh's throne (*kissēʾ yhwh*), where all the nations will gather (Jer 3:17; Ezek 43:7; cf. 1 Chr 29:23). Likewise, Yahweh's throne is eternal (Ps 9:7 [MT 8]), established in the heavens (Ps 103:19; Isa 66:1). Thus, while the throne of Israel and its rulers are temporary and vulnerable to destruction, as is any other throne of the nations, Yahweh's throne is inviolable and will not be destroyed. Even so, Yahweh will destroy the thrones of the nations.

At issue is whether the message to Zerubbabel is about Yahweh's plan for the Persian Empire. At the time, the Persian Empire ruled over many nations, including Yehud (cf. Ezra 1:2). Zerubbabel was the governor of Yehud and came from the Davidic line. While the Persian Empire might have been included in the promised overthrow, it would not have been the sole focus of the proclamation—Egypt and Greece would also be included.[277] As in Hag 2:6–7, the scope of the promised action is universal. The promise is

272. BDB 245–26. Note *mahpēkat,* "overthrow," used of Sodom or both Sodom and Gomorrah (cf. Isa 13:19; Jer 49:18; 50:40; Amos 4:11). Meyers and Meyers, *Haggai, Zechariah 1–8,* 66; Kessler, *Haggai,* 223; Verhoef, *Haggai and Malachi,* 143; H. W. Wolff, *Haggai,* 102–3; Petersen, *Haggai and Zechariah 1–8,* 99.

273. BDB 246.

274. Kessler, *Haggai,* 224.

275. GKC §124r; the compound idea is used to express a plural (substantive "throne" [*nomen regens*] + genitive "kingdoms" [*nomen rectum*]). Kessler, *Haggai,* 223–24; Verhoef, *Haggai and Malachi,* 144; H. W. Wolff, *Haggai,* 103.

276. Cf. Kessler, *Haggai,* 223.

277. Thus H. W. Wolff, *Haggai,* 103; contrast Meyers and Meyers, *Haggai, Zechariah 1–8,* 67.

to dissolve the authority of the kingdoms, thus rendering them ineffective (cf. Jer 24:9; 25:26).

I will destroy the strength of the kingdom, continues the depiction of Yahweh's action: *šāmad,* "to destroy," with *ḥāzaq*, "strength," as the object. "Strength" (*ḥāzaq*) is parallel with "throne" (*kissēʾ*) and is used as a metonymy for power. Other occurrences of *šāmad* depict the destruction of persons (esp. Israel, Deut 1:27; 6:15); of other persons (Deut 2:21; Isa 13:9); and of nations (Isa 23:11; Mic 5:13 [MT 14]; Num 33:52; Amos 9:8).[278] The term *ḥāzaq* denotes God's strength used to bring Israel out of Egypt (Exod 13:3, 14, 16). It is also used of national strength in Amos 6:13. Yahweh has the strength to deliver and destroy the power of all kingdoms of the nations—all their domains and sources of power (cf. 2 Chr 20:6).[279] In this portrayal of Yahweh's future reign, disclosed to Haggai, the Deity will succeed in subduing the kingdoms. Presumably, these will include the Persian Empire; Egypt, which continues to resist Persian control; and the Greeks and any emerging powers.

The total destruction of the nations is further detailed in terms of the nations' power: *overthrow a chariot and its rider; and horses and their riders.* Yahweh promises to destroy the sources of the nations' security. Here the language echoes that of the destruction of Pharaoh and his army at the Sea of Reeds (Exod 14) and the imagery of the annihilation of the nations. First, with respect to Pharaoh and his army, Exod 14 depicts a scene in which Pharaoh took his chariots and horses in pursuit of Israel; the chariot (*rekeb*) and driver (*pārāš*) are mentioned as a pair (Exod 14:17, 23, 26, 28). Likewise, the pair horse (*sûs*) and chariot (*rekeb*) appears in references to war activity and implements (Josh 11:4, 6; 1 Kgs 10:26; cf. 1 Sam 13:5; 2 Sam 1:6). These were basic to the nations' defense and in some cases were seen as being the locus of Israel's corruption and its misplaced confidence (Mic 1:13; 5:10; Nah 2:13). The list suggests that all elements necessary for effective use of the chariots will be destroyed so that the possibility of warring against distant regions is reduced to a minimum, if not removed completely.

Moreover, the nations' chariots are their defense. Thus, to destroy these would leave the nations defenseless and vulnerable. The image is of internal chaos and eventual decline—that is, the people within the nations warring against each other. This scenario contrasts with the transformation from war to peace depicted in Mic 4 (see table 4). Yahweh takes responsibility for this destruction as the one who has the power to accomplish this total cataclysm. Shaking the heavens and earth and destroying nations demonstrate Yahweh's power over creation and political structures. Nothing lies beyond Yahweh's

278. BDB 1029.
279. GKC §124r.

power; however, this Deity who has and uses this power relates to the community on its relatively small scale to move it into conformity with Yahweh's wishes (Hag 1:6–11; 2:6–9) and to encourage the community in the face of discouragement (Hag 2:2–5). Therein lie the message of hope and the politically charged claim of Yahweh's unmatched power.

2. *Yahweh's Appointed Servant: Zerubbabel (2:23)*

23 The final part of Hag 2:20–23 refocuses on Zerubbabel, whom Yahweh calls "my servant," the one whom Yahweh has chosen. The oracle opens with the temporal indicator *bayyôm hahûʾ*, "in that day," followed by the formula *nəʾum-yhwh ṣəbāʾôt,* "utterance of Yahweh of hosts."[280] The phrase *bayyôm hahûʾ* is typically used as a reference in prophecy to a time in the future (Deut 31:17). Some of these references are to an imminent or proximate future (Isa 4:2; 7:21; 10:20; 12:1–6; 22:20, 25; 28:5; 31:7; Jer 4:9; 30:8; Joel 3:18 [MT 4:18]; Mic 2:4; Zech 3:10). In other cases the formula has a distinct eschatological sense as a reference to a time frame signaled by the formula *bəʾaḥărît hayyāmîm,* "in the latter days/days to come"—a remote future (Isa 2:2, 11; Mic 4:1–4, 6; 5:10 [MT 9]; 7:11, 12; Amos 8:9).[281] Tollington considers the use in Hag 2:23 to be an eschatological motif and also observes that the phrase denotes the imminence of the actions noted, "for otherwise they could not be related to a change in Zerubbabel's status brought about by Yahweh at that particular time."[282] Kessler notes a distinction between the other chronological reference, "from this day" (*min-hayyôm hazzê*), which points to a "historical future," and "in that day" (*bayyôm hahûʾ*), which points to an "eschatological future."[283] Even so, he classifies Hag 2:6–9 as referring to an eschatological intervention.

The distinction between the historical and eschatological future is helpful if (1) the two are seen as overlapping rather than being mutually exclusive categories; (2) their uses are not oversimplified in connection with the formula "in that day" (*bayyôm hahûʾ*) in the book of Haggai and elsewhere. What is evident is that the term *bayyôm hahûʾ*, "in that day," in futuristic prophecies envisions a time that is distant from the present and is characterized by a decisive change in circumstances. Whether that temporal distance is imminent

280. DeVries (*From Old Revelation,* 158) looks at instances in which the temporal formula occurs with the utterance formula: Isa 22:25; Jer 7:22; 19:6; 30:3; 31:1; 51:52; Zech 12:4.

281. DeVries, *From Old Revelation,* 52–55, 92–93, 212–14.

282. Tollington, *Tradition and Innovation,* 136–37. Cf. DeVries, *From Old Revelation,* 212; Verhoef (*Haggai and Malachi,* 145), who affirms the eschatological context.

283. Kessler, *Haggai,* 227.

or remote is often discerned through the nature of the changes in relation to the historical conditions that will effect the changes.

Concerning the future, Yahweh promises "to take you [*'eqqāḥăkā*],[284] Zerubbabel." When Yahweh "takes" a person/group, it is for a specific purpose or mission (see: of a group—Exod 6:7; Deut 4:20; Isa 66:21). Thus, David was taken from his sheep and made ruler over Israel (2 Sam 7:8; Amos 7:15; Ps 78:70). When used to represent future action, as in 1 Kgs 11:37, the purpose is explicit: "I will take you, and you shall reign over all that your soul desires; you shall be king over Israel." While some of these uses may refer to the purpose of the "taking," others uses refer to the relationship into which one is taken (cf. Exod 6:7; Num 3:12; Deut 4:20).[285] Rose argues that the explicit language of mission is absent from Hag 2:23.[286] Tollington proposes that the exclusion of the title "governor of Judah" is deliberate to deemphasize his political role.[287] Haggai 2:23 does not fit readily into either of these classifications. Rather, it designates Zerubbabel as *'abdî,* "my servant," suggesting that the relationship already existed at the time of the proclamation.[288]

The designation *'abdî,* "my servant," is used of various individuals, including Abraham (Gen 26:24), Moses (Num 12:7, 8), David (2 Sam 3:18; 1 Kgs 11:13; Isa 20:3; 37:35), and Nebuchadrezzar (Jer 25:9; 27:6). It is also used of nations (e.g., Isa 41:8; 44:1; Jer 30:10) and prophets (Jer 7:25; 29:19; Ezek 38:17).[289] The reference *'abdî,* "my servant," is not unique to Zerubbabel or to descendants of the Davidic line. Likewise, the designation itself, while connoting a relationship with Yahweh, does not indicate that Zerubbabel's relationship is extraordinary as compared with others such as Abraham, Moses, and David. It likewise does not indicate that Zerubbabel is the fulfillment of an ideal ruler. Nonetheless, the fact that Zerubbabel is of the Davidic line may be significant to the postexilic community. That community may perceive him as the embodiment of the ideal.[290] According to Sacchi, the returnees in 521/20 BCE brought with them Ezekiel's view of a new David (Ezek 34:23; 37:24–26). What was distinct about the returnees' vision was that they expected David to be the messiah king rather than the ancestor of the messiah king. They thought that this new David would not only fulfill expectations about the Davidic line but would also be an ideal figure, though not necessarily of the Davidic line. Thus, Zerubbabel may

284. *Qal* imperfect first person singular plus second masculine singular suffix.

285. Rose, *Zemah and Zerubbabel,* 217–18.

286. Rose, *Zemah and Zerubbabel,* 216–17.

287. Tollington, *Tradition and Innovation,* 137.

288. Contrast Meyers and Meyers, *Haggai, Zechariah 1–8,* 68.

289. Rose, *Zemah and Zerubbabel,* 210–11; Tollington, *Tradition and Innovation,* 139–41; Cf. Petersen, *Haggai and Zechariah 1–8,* 103.

290. Petersen, *Haggai and Zechariah 1–8,* 103, Ezek 34:23; 37:24–26.

have held more authority than Joshua (the high priest) during the rebuilding phase.[291]

Zerubbabel's significance as the servant may lie more in his appointed role in Yahweh's plan for the future than in his lineage—*I will place you as a signet ring*. While he is already a servant, he is to be placed like a signet ring (*ḥôtām*) in Yahweh's plan. There is no shortage of Old Testament uses of the term *ḥôtām* and likewise no singular usage (Gen 38:18; Exod 28:11, 21, 36; 39:6, 14, 30; 1 Kgs 21:8; Job 38:14; Jer 22:24).[292] Its occurrence in Jer 22:24–27 is significant to this discussion of Hag 2:23.

> As I live, says the Lord, even if King Coniah son of Jehoiakim of Judah were the signet ring on my right hand, even from there I would tear you off and give you into the hands of those who seek your life. (Jer 22:24–25 NRSV)

Coniah the king is the focus of the oracle in which Yahweh swears that nothing will stop Yahweh from punishing the king.

There are several options for understanding the signet ring and hence Zerubbabel's role. First, it was sometimes a sign of the royal authority worn by the king. In some instances, however, it was given to another person in designating authority (cf. Gen 41; Esth 3, 8). In these cases, the ring was taken back when the authority was taken back.[293] As a symbol of authority and trust, the ring might be given to a subordinate to act in place of the sovereign and in accordance with the sovereign's plans. Thus, in Hag 2:23 it would mean that Yahweh had entrusted Zerubbabel with Yahweh's authority and approved Zerubbabel's effort. To the extent that it is Yahweh's plan to complete the temple, the success of Zerubbabel's work is guaranteed.[294] This interpretation sees the fulfillment of Zerubbabel's role as being imminent, within the historical context of the postexilic period.

Another understanding of the signet ring (*ḥôtām*) is that it symbolized the close relationship between the ring and its owner, who wore it and seldom if ever removed it.[295] While Jer 22:24–27 reflects the precious value of the ring, its value may be less of a focus in Hag 2:23. Without doubt, the language of the text already signals a valued relationship by using the formulations "my servant" (*ʿabdî*) and "because I have chosen you" (*kî-bəkā bāḥartî*). Within

291. Sacchi, *Second Temple Period*, 382–83. By the dedication ceremony in 516/15 BCE, his authority may have already faded.

292. Rose, *Zemah and Zerubbabel*, 218.

293. Rose, *Zemah and Zerubbabel*, 223.

294. H. W. Wolff, *Haggai*, 105–6.

295. Rose, *Zemah and Zerubbabel*, 224–39; Meyers and Meyers, *Haggai, Zechariah 1–8*, 70.

the larger context of Hag 2, the concern to encourage the community and assure it of God's presence is certainly an important aspect of the oracle. Zerubbabel's role is to be the extension of Yahweh's authority in the community. His status suggests a reconceptualization of the role of the Davidic line compared to the Jer 22:24–30 use of King Coniah, son of Jehoiakim of Judah, as an object lesson. The Jeremiah text depicted God's determination to exile Coniah and to ensure that no one from the Davidic line ruled. Jeremiah 22, following vv. 24–25 quoted above, goes on to state:

> Thus says the LORD: Record this man as childless, a man who shall not succeed in his days; for none of his offspring shall succeed in sitting on the throne of David, and ruling again in Judah. (Jer 22:30 NRSV)

Did choosing Zerubbabel change the resolve to exclude a Davidic heir? Or did the restoration community demonstrate the fulfillment of that prophecy—no other Davidic heir ruled (as monarch), even though someone ruled as an appointee of a foreign monarch (in this case, the Persian king). Carroll argues that the perspective of Hag 2:23 on Zerubbabel illustrates the tendency of Haggai and Zechariah "to adjust or correct earlier prophecies."[296]

Jeremiah 22:3–4 shows the conditional aspect of the resolve. The key will be obedience to God's standards (acting righteously, in 22:3): "For if you will indeed obey this word, then through the gates of this house shall enter kings who sit on the throne of David." Disobedience would lead to the destruction of Jerusalem (Jer 22:5–9). In light of Jeremiah, both interpretations about the significance of Zerubbabel are possible; but the reconceptualization may be expedient for encouraging confidence in God's work and presence. The interpretation does not necessarily signify that the community has acted righteously. Rather, the exile is evidence that they have not. The promise regarding Zerubbabel reveals the altered standards for installing someone from the line of David. By changing the preconditions, Yahweh extends hope to the community. Choosing to place Zerubbabel in authority is thus removing the prerequisite of the community's obedience and making the choice to appoint a leader solely Yahweh's prerogative according to Yahweh's purpose.

Zerubbabel's role, though connected to his status of governor, was the result of Yahweh's action—Yahweh chose (*bāḥar*) him (cf. Isa 42:1). The se-

296. Carroll, *When Prophecy Failed,* 164; R. P. Carroll, "Prophecy and Dissonance: A Theoretical Approach to the Prophetic Tradition," *ZAW* 92 (1980): 118–19. Berquist (*Judaism in Persia's Shadow,* 68) contends: "Coniah was a puppet ruler with some administrative responsibilities but little autonomy (2 Kings 24:10–16). As signet, Coniah was a tool for a world empire, and Hag 2:23 places Zerubbabel in this role." Cf. Rose, *Zemah and Zerubbabel,* 221–24.

lection of an individual brings to mind the motif of Yahweh's choice as being independent of the qualities of the "chosen" one(s)—for example, the people (Deut 7:6–7; 12:5, 11; 14:2; 16:6; Isa 49:7) or God's servants (1 Sam 10:24). It also brings to mind Moses's call/commission, in which God's choice is independent of what humans consider adequate qualifications (Exod 3, 6). Here, Hag 2:23 designates Zerubbabel as the extension of Yahweh's authority because Yahweh has selected him. On that basis he has the authority, and he retains that authority as long as Yahweh chooses to retain him in the role. So, while Zerubbabel may have authority and may be the embodiment of hope for a particular future, he is subject to Yahweh's higher authority.

In the larger context of Haggai 2, God's affirmation of Zerubbabel is part of encouraging the people to complete the temple because Yahweh promised provision and leadership in the rebuilding efforts. Although appointed by the Persian Empire, Zerubbabel has been chosen by God. As powerful as it is, the Persian Empire operates under Yahweh's power; its status and existence are subject to Yahweh's plan and actions. For a people living under Persian rule and at the same time attempting to make sense of its tradition that they are the center of God's rule on earth, Hag 2:20–23 affirms the traditions and in so doing affirms Yahweh's power. This is as much a theological message as it is a political message (see introduction, VI. Message).

The Book of
MALACHI

INTRODUCTION

In the Hebrew Bible, the book of Malachi is the last of the Book of the Twelve, or the Minor Prophets, and the final book of *Nebi'im*, the "Prophets," which is the second section of the Hebrew Bible, directly preceding the book of Psalms in the *Ketubim*, "Writings" (the third section of the Hebrew Bible). In most English versions, Malachi is the last book of the prophetic literature and of the Old Testament and thus directly precedes the New Testament. There is no biographical information about the prophet in the book and no consensus about whether the designation *mal'ākî* is the name of a person or a title. The question-answer schema is one of the distinctive features of the book and contributes to our understanding of its genre and structure. The message of the book is Yahweh's love for Israel and the fractured state of the Yahweh-Israel relationship.

I. HISTORICAL CONTEXT

The date of the prophecies in the book of Malachi is contested, due in part to the absence of: an account of the prophetic call, biographical information, many historical allusions.

A. CHRONOLOGICAL INDICATORS

Although it contains no date formulas such as those in the books of Haggai (1:1, 15) and Zechariah (1:1; 7:1), the book of Malachi has chronological pointers to the eschatological dimensions of the prophecy—that is, from the speaker's perspective, a time that lies in the future, whether imminent or remote. Included among these indicators are references to "the day."[1] Table 5 lists the appearances of "the day" in Malachi. The presence of this phrase does not resolve the question of the date of the oracles, but it does facilitate discussion about the eschatological time period—that is, the characteristics of that time and the identity of the agent/figures who will be involved. Regarding the characteristics of that time, the account of "the day" describes precursory events (cf. Joel 2); but unlike Joel, where the natural realm is affected during the precursory events, in Malachi the coming of a forerunner and the ensuing actions define the precursory event.

Table 5. References to "the Day" in the Book of Malachi

Reference in Malachi	Hebrew Formulation	NRSV Translation
3:2	*yôm bôʾô*	*the day* of his coming
3:17	*layyôm ʾăšer ʾănî ʿōśê*	on *the day* when I act
4:1 (MT 3:19)	*hinnê hayyôm bāʾ*	See, *the day* is coming
4:3 (MT 3:21)	*bayyôm ʾăšer ʾănî ʿōśê*	on *the day* when I act
4:5 (MT 3:23)	*lipnê bôʾ yôm yhwh*	before *the day of* Yahweh comes

Unique to the book of Malachi is the expression "the day when I act" (*bayyôm ʾăšer ʾănî ʿōśê*, 3:17; 4:3 [MT 3:21]). The expression *hinnê hayyôm bāʾ*, "see, the day is coming," continues the account of the messenger's and Yahweh's coming. The expression also occurs in Zech 14:1 (*hinnê yôm bāʾ*).[2] The expression "day of Yahweh" (*yôm yhwh*) culminates the account of "the day" and signals the future aspects of other occurrences of the phrase (e.g., Isa 13:6, 9; Jer 46:10; Ezek 30:3; Joel 1:15; 2:1, 11, 31 [MT 3:4]; 3:14 [MT 4:14]; Amos 5:18, 20; Obad 15; Zeph 1:7).[3]

B. SOCIOPOLITICAL CONTEXT

Several dates have been proposed for the prophetic oracles in the book of Malachi. Without reiterating the arguments for these proposals here, I offer a brief

1. See the introduction to the book of Haggai for discussion regarding the types of chronological indicators.

2. Compare Isa 39:6 (*hinnê yāmîm bāʾîm*); Ezek 30:9; Matt 24:42; Acts 2:20.

3. For occurrences of the "day of the Lord" in the New Testament, see 1 Cor 5:5; 1 Thess 5:2; 2 Thess 2:2; 2 Pet 3:10.

sketch of the options to illustrate the range of the perspectives.[4] Commentators' views on the date of the Malachi prophecies are, from the most ancient to the most recent (605–333 BCE): (1) before or during the time of Haggai and Zechariah;[5] (2) before either Ezra or Nehemiah;[6] (3) after Ezra but before Nehemiah;[7] (4) contemporary with Ezra and Nehemiah;[8] (5) during Nehemiah's first governorship;[9] (6) between Nehemiah's first and second governorship;[10]

4. For a comprehensive outline of the perspectives and advocates, see A. E. Hill, *Malachi: A New Translation with Introduction and Commentary,* AB 25D (New York: Doubleday, 1998), 77, 393–95 (appendix A). Hill builds his categories on those proposed by A. von Bulmerincq, *Einleitung in das Buch des Propheten Maleachi* (Dorpat: Mattiesen, 1926), 1:87–97.

5. J. M. O'Brien (*Priest and Levite in Malachi,* SBLDS 121 [Atlanta: Scholars Press, 1990], 147) proposed 605–500 BCE; cf. J. M. O'Brien, "Historical Inquiry as Liberator and Master: Malachi as a Post-exilic Document," in *The Yahweh/Baal Confrontation and Other Studies in Biblical Literature and Archaeology: Essays in Honour of Emmett Willard Hamrick,* ed. J. M. O'Brien and Fred L. Horton (Lewiston, NY: Mellen, 1995), 57–79. Another possibility here is 520 BCE, which is proposed by A. C. Welch, *Post-Exilic Judaism* (London: Blackwood, 1935).

6. This is the most popular view about dating the oracles of Malachi, although the rationale for the proposal may vary. See G. A. Smith, *The Book of the Twelve Prophets,* vol. 2, The Expositor's Bible (New York: Armstrong, 1905); J. M. P. Smith, "Malachi," in *A Critical and Exegetical Commentary on Haggai, Zechariah, Malachi and Jonah,* by H. G. Mitchell, J. M. P. Smith, and J. A. Bewer, ICC (Edinburgh: T&T Clark, 1912); von Bulmerincq, *Einleitung in das Buch des Propheten Maleachi*; R. H. Pfeiffer, *Introduction to the Old Testament* (New York: Harper, 1941); A. E. Hill, "Dating the Book of Malachi: A Linguistic Reexamination," in *The Word of the Lord Shall Go Forth:Essays in Honor of David Noel Freedman,* ed. C. L. Meyers and M. O'Connor (Winona Lake, IN: Eisenbrauns, 1983), 77–89; Hill, *Malachi*; K. Koch, *The Prophets: The Babylonian and Persian Periods,* trans. M. Kohl (Philadelphia: Fortress, 1984); B. Glazier-McDonald, *Malachi: The Divine Messenger,* SBLDS 98 (Atlanta: Scholars Press, 1987); Edwin M. Yamauchi, *Persia and the Bible* (Grand Rapids: Baker, 1990); E. H. Merrill, *Haggai, Zechariah, Malachi: An Exegetical Commentary* (Chicago: Moody Press, 1994); J. L. Berquist, *Judaism in Persia's Shadow: A Social and Cultural Approach* (Philadelphia: Fortress, 1995); David L. Petersen, *Zechariah 9–14 and Malachi,* OTL (Louisville: Westminster John Knox, 1995).

7. See R. K. Harrison, *Introduction to the Old Testament* (Grand Rapids: Eerdmans, 1969); J. Bright, *A History of Israel,* 3rd ed. (Philadelphia: Westminster, 1981); R. B. Chisholm, *Interpreting the Minor Prophets* (Grand Rapids: Zondervan, 1990).

8. See S. R. Driver, *An Introduction to the Literature of the Old Testament,* rev. ed. (New York: Scribner's Sons, 1922); J. G. Baldwin, *Haggai, Zechariah, Malachi,* TOTC 24 (Downers Grove, IL: InterVarsity, 1972); A. Deissler, *Zwölf Propheten III: Zefanja, Haggai, Sacharja, Maleachi,* NEchtB 21 (Würzburg: Echter, 1988).

9. D. R. Jones, *Haggai, Zechariah and Malachi,* Torch Bible Commentary (London: SCM, 1962); R. L. Smith, *Micah–Malachi.*

10. See C. von Orelli, *The Twelve Minor Prophets,* trans. J. S. Banks (Edinburgh: T&T Clark, 1897); P. A. Verhoef, *The Books of Haggai and Malachi,* NICOT (Grand Rapids: Eerdmans, 1976).

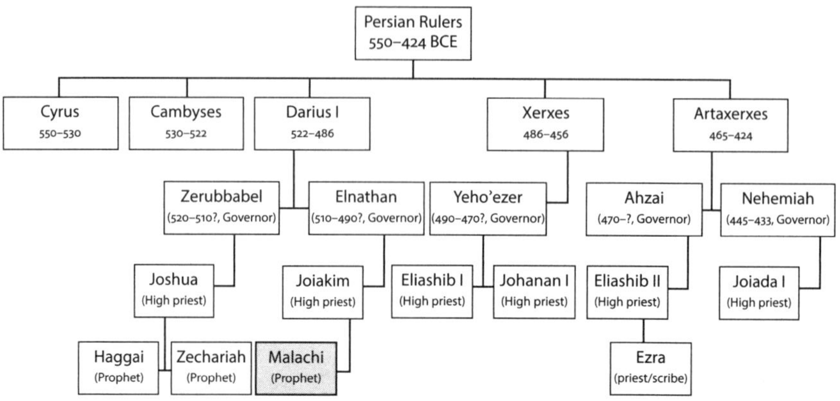

Figure 2. Proposal concerning the Date of Malachi[11]

(7) during Nehemiah's second governorship;[12] and (8) during the late Persian or Hellenistic period.[13] At issue is understanding the historical context of the prophecies and the first audience of the message. But proposing the date of Malachi with reference to Ezra–Nehemiah has its own challenges, including their dates, their chronological sequence, and the effectiveness of their reforms.[14] In this commentary, I consider 515–400 BCE to be the possible context for the oracles in Malachi but propose 515–458 BCE as the most likely date—after the dedication of the temple and before the times of Ezra and Nehemiah (see fig.

11. This proposal places the oracles of the book of Malachi (515–458 BCE) after the completion of the temple (515 BCE) and before Ezra (458 BCE). See above discussion for the various options concerning the possible date of the oracles.

12. See H. Wolf, *Haggai and Malachi: Rededication and Renewal* (Chicago: Moody Press, 1976); W. C. Kaiser, *Malachi: God's Unchanging Love* (Grand Rapids: Baker, 1984); J. Nogalski, *Redactional Processes in the Book of the Twelve,* BZAW 218 (Berlin: de Gruyter, 1993); P. L. Redditt, "The Book of Malachi in Its Social Setting," *CBQ* 56 (1994): 240–55.

13. See C. C. Torrey, "The Prophecy of Malachi," *JBL* 17 (1898): 1–15; O. Holtzmann, "Der Prophet Maleachi und der Ursprung des Pharisaerbundes," *ARW* 19 (1931): 1–21.

14. One of the issues has been the date of Ezra. There are at least three proposals, including the following: (1) during the seventh year of Artaxerxes I (458 BCE; Ezra 7:7–8); (2) in the twenty-seventh or the thirty-seventh year of Artaxerxes I (438 or 428 BCE; assuming the corruption of the text of Ezra 7:8); (3) during the seventh year of Artaxerxes II (398 BCE; Neh 12:26). For further discussion of these proposals, see D. J. A. Clines, *Ezra, Nehemiah, Esther,* NCBC (Grand Rapids: Eerdmans, 1984), 14–24; H. G. M. Williamson, *Ezra, Nehemiah,* WBC 16 (Waco, TX: Word, 1985), xxxix–xliv; Yamauchi, *Persia and the Bible,* 253–56; Hill, *Malachi,* 72; Paolo Sacchi, *History of the Second Temple Period,* JSOTSup 285 (Sheffield: Sheffield Academic, 2000), 135–37.

2).[15] This date takes into account the possibility of earlier failed attempts at reform, which then led to the issues seen in Malachi (i.e., quality of the covenant relationship) which had persisted from Ezra's and Nehemiah's time, such as: exogamous (mixed) marriages, nonpayment of taxes and/or tithes, and priestly malpractice.

I will not attempt to date the historical background of Malachi more precisely here; this commentary builds on a postexilic date of approximately 515–458 BCE. This and similar proposals are based on the oracles in the book and their insights into the practices and ideology of the community as compared with those presented in Ezra–Nehemiah and the practices in the Persian Empire. Some of these indicators are the presence of the temple (Mal 1:10; 3:1, 10), the reference to the leader as *peḥâ,* "governor" (Mal 1:8); the annihilation of Edom (1:4); and the malpractice of the priests. Alternatively, Hill proposes the use of the "typological categorization of Biblical Hebrew" to determine the date of the oracles. He concludes that the date 515–458 BCE is the most viable range, and 500 BCE is the most likely date.[16] The term *Yehud* is used for Judah during the postexilic period to identify the status of the region as one of the provinces in the Persian Empire's political organization.[17]

In accordance with the proposal to date Malachi sometime between 515 and 458 BCE, I will include key Persian rulers and Yehudite leaders in this brief survey, and I will highlight circumstances that may shed light on the issues depicted in the book of Malachi (see table 2 above). First, the policies of Cyrus and Darius inform the subsequent events in the Persian Empire, including the relocation of expatriates to their homeland, the reinstitution of religious practices, and the fostering of loyalties to the Persian Empire. It was also during Darius's reign that the Empire was organized into twenty satrapies.[18] One satrapy was Babylon and Beyond the River, which was later divided into "the protectorate Babylon" and "the protectorate Beyond the River" (Eber-Nahara), which included the province of Yehud. As illustrated in

15. See Hill, *Malachi,* 77–84, 395–400.

16. Hill, *Malachi,* 81–83. In contrast, Verhoef (*Haggai and Malachi,* 159–60) suggests that the Malachi prophecies be dated to the period after 433 BCE.

17. Hill, *Malachi,* 62–63; Yamauchi, *Persia and the Bible,* 178–79; Berquist, *Judaism in Persia's Shadow,* 10, 60–61. See also M. Avi-Yonah, *The Holy Land from the Persian to the Arab Conquest,* rev. ed. (Grand Rapids, Baker, 1977); Y. Aharoni, *The Land of the Bible: A Historical Geography,* rev. ed. (Philadelphia: Westminster, 1979).

18. As noted above in the introduction to Haggai, the status of Yehud has been the topic of several discussions, especially it relates to the status of its governor. Although there has been discussion about who divided the region into satrapies and how many satrapies there were, suffice it here to say that the region was divided, and Yehud was one of the provinces. See Yamauchi, *Persia and the Bible,* 178–79; Berquist, *Judaism in Persia's Shadow,* 10, 60–61; Hill, *Malachi,* 60–62.

map 2, Yehud was adjacent to Samaria (on the north), Ammon (on the east), Idumea (or Edom, on the south), and Ashdod (on the west).[19]

Darius's expansion efforts can be seen in the appointment of loyal leaders (satraps) over the satrapies, and governors over each province. Darius supported the building of the administrative and religious infrastructure within the provinces. Zerubbabel was one of the Persian-appointed governors. In spite of internal and external challenges, Zerubbabel and Joshua, the high priest, resumed work on the temple (520 BCE) and completed that work in 516/15 BCE.[20] As a political appointee, Zerubbabel was accountable to the Persian Empire in building the temple and maintaining the region as a viable region of the Empire.[21] Divided loyalties, however, may have been manifested in the religious institution of the temple. Joshua, the high priest, would have felt pressure from both the community and the Persian Empire as contending factions in administering the temple. The negotiation of these loyalties along with the codification of the law and the emergence of a canon of Scripture would have helped to define Yahwism in Yehud.

Several issues during Darius's reign may have set the foundation for later dynamics in Yehud, including the priesthood and the apparent neglect of the temple by the people. First, regarding the prominence of the priesthood, note that the temple was one of the administrative arms of the Persian Empire in that it enhanced the region's ability to pay its taxes.[22] Darius may have financed the building of the Jerusalem temple. The appointed priests' loyalties and efforts to appease the Persian Empire, therefore, would have fostered tensions between them and the devout Yahwists. The significance assigned to the Jerusalem temple by the people may also have resulted from religious and political tension, such as their disenchantment over its diminished status as compared with the Solomonic Temple and over the apparent inability to exalt Jerusalem (cf. Hag 2:7; Ezek 40–48).[23] Second, the well-being of Yehud's religion was not the foremost concern of the Persian Empire, but perhaps the temple's role in collecting taxes and the province's strategic location for

19. Hill, *Malachi,* 61.

20. Apparently, Tattenai, the governor of the Eber-Nahara satrapy, was responsible for one element of opposition to the rebuilding (cf. Ezra 5:3–6:12). Yamauchi, *Persia and the Bible,* 156–58; Hill, *Malachi,* 70.

21. Berquist, *Judaism in Persia's Shadow,* 63–64; Kessler (*The Book of Haggai,* 86–87) argues that Persian interest in Yehud was limited prior to Cambyses's conquest of Egypt. Yehud's location became strategic during that time.

22. D. Janzen, "Politics, Settlement, and Temple Community in Persian-Period Yehud," *CBQ* 64 (2002): 492. Janzen sees no Persian sponsorship, administrative overlap, or economically elite class.

23. Cf. Berquist, *Judaism in Persia's Shadow,* 87, 92; Hill, *Malachi,* 75–76; Sacchi, *Second Temple Period,* 118–20.

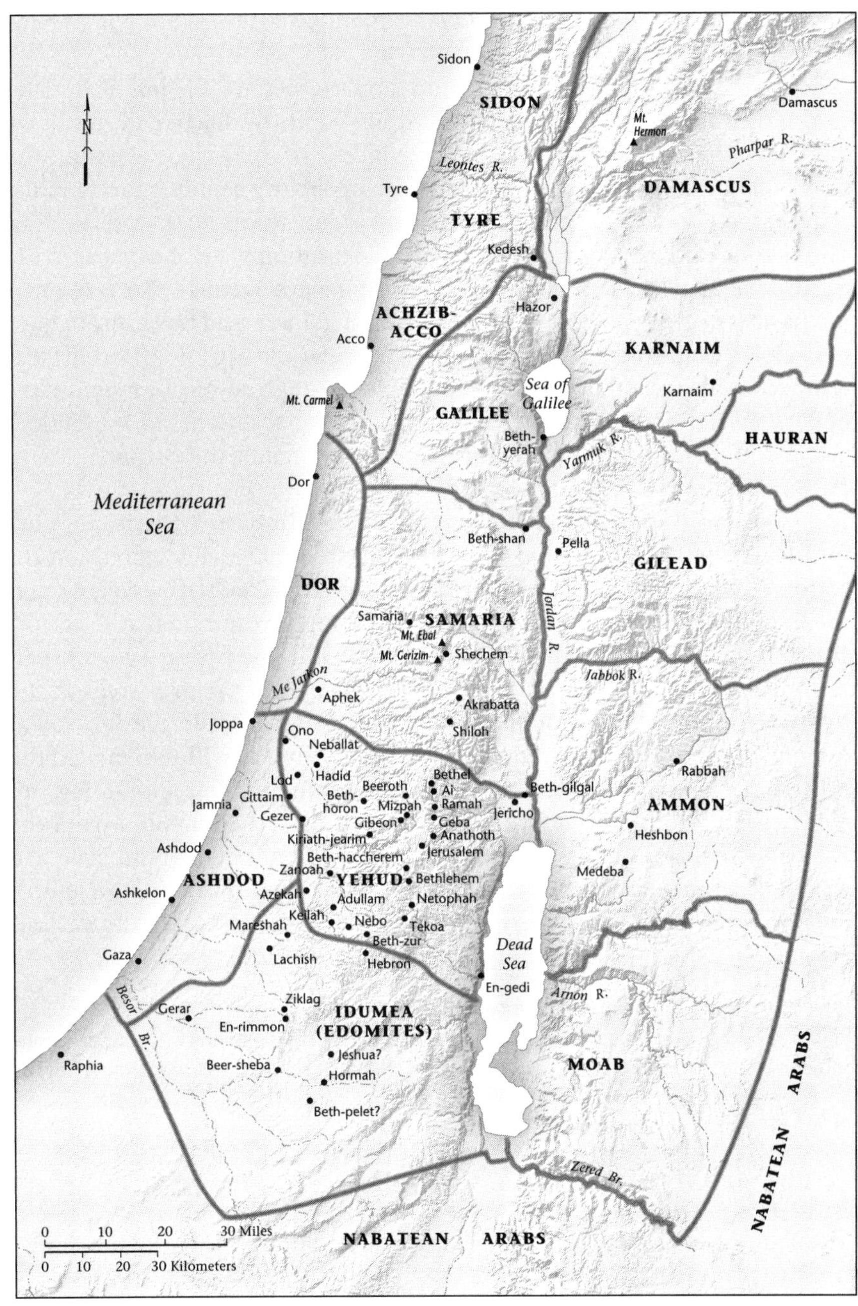

Map 2. Yehud among the Persian Provinces

maintaining control of the region and gaining access to Egypt would have contributed to its value.[24]

Third, the division of regions into satrapies defined the political structure of the Empire geographically and administratively. Each of the satrapies had a governor, and the constitutive provinces had a governor. Possibly, the governor of the satrapy executed the Persian policies, including the administrative measures for collecting taxes and providing troops to the Persian Empire.[25] The political structure determined the taxation system, which is to say the provinces' contribution to the Empire's finances. Darius's efforts to build the palaces at Persepolis would have resulted in increased taxes throughout the Persian Empire, as seen during Xerxes's reign (486–465 BCE), which was characterized by centralization of the Empire through political appointments of Persian leaders over the satrapies and continued taxation. These practices also led to increasing taxes on non-Persians to finance the construction of Persepolis, the site of great palaces.[26]

Perhaps due to decreased revenue in the Empire, financial support for local temples ended, and Persia manifested increased aggression toward non-Persians.[27] Babylonian leaders were replaced with Persians, and the Babylonian satrapy was separated from the Beyond the River satrapy. Persia also experienced further loss of control in the northeastern Mediterranean.[28] The destruction of temples throughout the provinces of the Persian Empire also characterized Xerxes's reign. While the Jerusalem temple was not destroyed, financial support for it was withdrawn, and the economic challenges were exacerbated by famine in the region (Hag 1:6; Neh 5:1–5). The priests and others who had directly benefited from the Empire's financial support could no longer rely on it and would have had to find other means of support while continuing their service to the temple and community.[29] Further compounding the problem were the various

24. See Berquist (*Judaism in Persia's Shadow,* 80–81), who cites the suppression of competing perspectives and the place of the temple in the life of the community (i.e., separate, and sometimes in the service of the political powers). Hill (*Malachi,* 54–55) also notes the apathy toward Yahwism as a lingering effect of Darius's policies. Contrast Kessler, *The Book of Haggai,* 86.

25. Yamauchi, *Persia and the Bible,* 178.

26. Yamauchi, *Persia and the Bible,* 23; Berquist, *Judaism in Persia's Shadow,* 106.

27. Berquist, *Judaism in Persia's Shadow,* 88–89.

28. Yamauchi, *Persia and the Bible,* 193–94; Berquist, *Judaism in Persia's Shadow,* 88–89, 92–93. The persistent tension with Greece would continue beyond Xerxes's reign.

29. Berquist, *Judaism in Persia's Shadow,* 93–96. Looking at Mal 1:6–2:9, he presents the prophetic critique of priestly malpractice—namely, the priests' disrespect for Yahweh, which resulted in their neglect of "proper or acceptable" worship. See Sacchi (*Second Temple Period,* 118), who contends that the priests were poor and sought economic sustenance even through intermarriage with the Samaritans and Ammonites.

layers of taxes—the satrap tax (national) and the provincial tax (local; cf. Neh 5:15; cf. 5:3, 7–8).[30] Likewise, disillusionment about the temple may have contributed to malpractice in pursuits such as sacrifices and tithes (Mal 1:8; 3:8) and in turn may have informed the book of Malachi's focus on priestly corruption (Mal 1:6–2:9).

The reign of Artaxerxes I (465–424 BCE) was characterized by ongoing tensions with Greece and Egypt. Consequently, Artaxerxes I appointed governors in Yehud who would support Persian policies and rebuild the walls and thus facilitate stability in the province. One stabilization effort was the reinstatement of funding for religious practices, including the temple in Jerusalem. Once Persia attained a measure of control over Egypt and Greece, however, Yehud was no longer as important to the Persian agenda; consequently, economic support declined again. Increasingly, trading with Greece became central to Yehud's economic viability. Even so, the Yehudite economy weakened while increased taxation of the provinces and other factors led to the inability of the local landowners to pay their taxes and to the eventual seizure of local property by Persian landlords.[31]

In summary, as the historical context of the oracles of the book of Malachi, this overview permits us a glimpse of the Persian Empire, the economy of the community, and the allegiance to the Persian Empire manifested by the governors. Even the Yehudite leaders were part of the Persian agenda and most likely had competing loyalties. The place of the temple as both an administrative and a religious center is an example of the province's competing allegiances to both home and Empire. In addition, the possibility that economic factors contributed to intermarriage may have influenced perspectives on intermarriage within the provinces and in Yehud in particular. Thus, the community had to deal with several challenges: the reality of restored worship; ordinary existence within a political system in which Yehud was only one of numerous colonies rather than the center of the political sphere; and the challenge of understanding its own history and traditions (e.g., as articulated by prophets). The prophetic message would have addressed disenchantment regarding Yehud's place given the political and economic ethos and Yehud's significance in relation to the Deity. An emphasis on the practices of the priests and community would then address how to foster a viable relationship with the Deity Yahweh, who sustained the ancestors and would sustain the current generation.

30. Hill, *Malachi,* 65, 75.

31. Berquist, *Judaism in Persia's Shadow,* 106.

II. TEXT

My translation of Malachi is based on the Masoretic Text as presented in *BHS*, which identifies about 75 variants within the three chapters (1:1–3:24) of the book (1:1–4:6 in English).[32] These variants may be found in the following verses: 1:1, 2, 3, 5, 7, 8 (2×), 9 (2×), 10, 11 (2×), 12 (3×), 13 (5×), 14 (3×); 2:2, 3, 4 (2×), 5 (2×), 7, 9 (2×), 10, 11–12 (6×), 13 (3×), 15 (4×), 16 (4×), 17; 3:1, 2, 3–4, 5 (4×), 7 (2×), 8 (5×), 9 (2×), 13, 16 (2×), 19 (3×), 22, 23/24. Of these, the variants in Mal 2:15–16 are perhaps the most challenging, because they are multivalent, yielding various readings and explanations for the grammar, syntax, and concepts of the text.[33]

A few comments about the witnesses illustrate their tendencies as represented in Malachi. Specific discussions of the primary variants accompany my translation and are included in the text and commentary section. The ancient witnesses include Qumran manuscripts, the LXX (and other Greek versions), the targum (Aramaic), the Peshitta (Syriac), and the Vulgate (Latin).

The Qumran manuscripts include 5QapMal, commentary on Mal 1:13–14,[34] and a quotation of Mal 1:10 in the *Damascus Document* (CD). A group of fragments, 4Q12^{a-g}, includes Mal 2:10–4:6 [MT 2:10–3:24].[35] Among the variants are 2:16, "But if you hate [her], send [her] away," as compared with some modern versions: "I hate divorce/putting away" (e.g., NRSV, ASV).

The LXX is the most frequently cited ancient witness in the *BHS* apparatus of Malachi, which includes about thirty citations—1:1, 7, 8, 13; 2:2, 3 (3×), 4, 9, 10, 12 (2×), 13, 15 (2×), 17; 3:2, 5 (2×), 8 (4×), 9, 13, 16, 19 (2×), 22. Although the LXX usually preserves the MT reading, at least two tendencies may be noted regarding the LXX of Malachi: expansions (e.g., 1:1, 7; 2:2, 4; 3:2, 5, 8; 4:1 [MT 3:19]) and paraphrasing (e.g., 1:3, 7, 9, 10; 2:2, 3, 4, 10, 11, 12, 13, 16; 3:5, 6–7, 8, 9, 10, 11, 15, 16; 4:1 [MT 3:19], 5 [MT 3:23]; 4:6 [MT 3:24]).[36] Some LXX manuscripts rearrange 4:4–6 [MT 3:22–24] as follows: 4:5, 6, 4 [MT 3:23, 24, 22].[37]

The Aramaic version (*Targum of the Prophets—Tg. Neb.*) is cited in the

32. *BHK* has identified some of the same variants but also has different variants and a single reference to Targum Jonathan.

33. See discussion in the text and commentary section of Mal 2:15–16.

34. M. Baillet, J. T. Milik, and R. de Vaux, eds., *Les 'Petites Grottes' de Qumran,* DJD 3 (Oxford: Clarendon, 1962), 180; see R. Fuller, "Text-Critical Problems in Malachi 2:10–16," *JBL* 110 (1991): 47–57.

35. CD VI 11.

36. Verhoef, *Haggai and Malachi,* 169–70; Hill, *Malachi,* 5.

37. Hill (*Malachi,* 5) notes that "later Jewish liturgical tradition introduced the repetition of Mal 3:23 [Eng. 4:5] after the reading of 3:24 [Eng. 4:6]."

BHS apparatus at 1:12; 2:15, 17; 3:8. The Aramaic version tends to rely on the MT and in some instances seems to paraphrase it (e.g., 1:9, 10, 11; 2:3, 15; 3:6).

The Latin version (Vulgate) is noted in the *BHS* apparatus concerning 1:8; 2:3, 9, 15, 17; 3:8. The Vulgate tends to support the MT reading (e.g., 1:7, 12, 13, 14; 2:2, 4, 7, 11; 3:16).[38] In at least three instances, it deviates from the MT (1:3, 10; 2:3) and sometimes reflects the LXX (e.g., 1:9, 13; 2:3, 9, 12, 16; 3:2).[39]

The Syriac version (Peshitta) is cited in several instances, including 1:3, 12, 13 (2×); 2:2, 17; 3:8, 16. The Peshitta tends to reflect the LXX (e.g., 1:3, 10, 13, 14; 2:2, 3, 4, 11, 13; 3:6). Likewise, the Peshitta agrees with the targum on 1:2, 13; 2:3, 12; it deviates from the MT by expansions in 1:4, 9, 12, 14; 2:2, 16; 3:11.[40]

These witnesses preserve ancient interpretations of the book of Malachi. Brief notes on the variants are included with the translation of the text, as well as specific readings of these witnesses.

III. INTERTEXTUAL INDICATORS

In reading through the book of Malachi, one notes several words, phrases, or allusions that reveal the writer's knowledge of earlier biblical texts.[41] Through shared vocabulary and perspectives on various traditions, the book of Malachi reflects a number of traditions evident in the Old Testament.[42] Likewise, scholars doing research on intertextuality have examined Malachi's dependence on pentateuchal sources (P and D) and the book's apparent silence about Nehemiah's policies on divorce. Delineated below are some of the intertextual indicators, most of which are examined in greater detail in the discussion of the text in the commentary section below. This itemization of

38. For further discussion of the examples, see Hill, *Malachi,* 10; Verhoef, *Haggai and Malachi,* 170.

39. Hill, *Malachi,* 10; Verhoef, *Haggai and Malachi,* 170;

40. Hill, *Malachi,* 10; Verhoef, *Haggai and Malachi,* 170.

41. See K. W. Weyde (*Prophecy and Teaching: Prophetic Authority, Form Problems and the Use of Traditions in the Book of Malachi,* BZAW 288 [Berlin: de Gruyter, 2000], 52), who notes elements that may reflect literary dependence.

42. The examination includes the occurrence of words, phrases, and allusions in addition to usage (form and function) within the literary contexts. Cf. E. M. Meyers, "Priestly Language in the Book of Malachi," *HAR* 10 (1987): 225–37; D. K. Berry, "Malachi's Dual Design: The Close of the Canon and What Comes Afterward: Forming Prophetic Literature," in *Forming Prophetic Literature: Essays on Isaiah and the Twelve in Honor of John D. W. Watts,* ed. J. W. Watts and P. R. House, JSOTSup 235 (Sheffield: Sheffield Academic, 1996), 269–302; J. D. Nogalski, "Intertextuality and the Twelve," in *Forming Prophetic Literature,* 102–24; Hill, *Malachi,* 79, 401–12; Weyde, *Prophecy and Teaching,* 49–51.

intertextual elements is not meant to be exhaustive but to reflect the richness of the intertextual dimension exhibited by the oracles in Malachi. These intertextual references include priests and Levites, the tithe, marriage and divorce, and sacrifices, all of which point to issues of in/fidelity to the covenant and insist on acceptable behavior toward Yahweh.

Priests and Levites. The priests and the Levites were entrusted with the task of instructing the people. But they had not fulfilled this responsibility (Mal 2:6–9). They exhibited malpractice in their instruction and the performance of their duties, such as sacrifices (Mal 1:7, 12) and instruction (Mal 2:8). Regarding their identity, the book of Malachi calls the priests sons of Levi (Deut 31:9) rather than sons of Aaron (Lev 1:5), but in other instances Malachi makes no apparent distinction between the priests and Levites (cf. Deut 18:1 and Num 3:9).[43] In the commentary section below, I will examine these descriptions in more detail.

The tithe. Several texts describe the nature of tithes, including Gen 14:20 regarding the quantity (cf. Gen 28:22). According to Num 18:21–26, the tithe was a means of support for the Levites (cf. Mal 3:10), and the Levites were to present an offering to God from the tithes that they received. As priests, they were not allocated land but were to maintain themselves via the tithe. Even so, they were to give a tithe of the tithe that they received (Num 18:21–26). The nature of a tithe was connected to its type, frequency, or quantity. Several types of tithes are noted, including general tithes from the produce of the land and livestock designated for the Levites (Lev 27:30–32; Num 18:21); tithes from produce (annual and seasonal, Deut 14:22–27); the third-year tithes designated for the underprivileged, including the Levites (Deut 14:22–29; 26:12).[44] Malachi alludes to Lev 27:30 vis-à-vis Deut 14:22–27. Presumably the concern about tithes was analogous to the concerns in Neh 5; 13:10–12.

Marriage and divorce. Malachi's perspective may address practices seen in Ezra–Nehemiah, where Jewish men were required to divorce their foreign wives. The emphasis appears to be on the potential threat to fidelity to Yahweh that was posed by those who did not serve Yahweh. The prohibition on Israelite men's intermarriage to women from other nations was to prevent breaking the people's covenant with God (cf. Exod. 34; Deut. 7). Malachi says, however, that God would rather that the people stay married than be divorced. "When seen in the intertextual framework of the OT, Mal 2:16 challenges the Deut 24:1–4 representation of divorce as a recognized practice within the community (cf. Deut 22:13–19, 28–29)."[45]

43. Hill, *Malachi,* 70.

44. M. R. Jacobs, "The Book of Malachi," in *Dictionary for Theological Interpretation of the Bible* (Grand Rapids: Baker Academic, 2005), 474–77.

45. Jacobs, "Malachi."

In the book of Ezra, the emphasis in the topic of divorce was on correcting the practice of intermarriage.

> Shecaniah son of Jehiel, of the descendants of Elam, addressed Ezra, saying, "We have broken faith with our God and have married foreign women from the peoples of the land, but even now there is hope for Israel in spite of this. So now let us make a covenant with our God to send away all these wives and their children, according to the counsel of my lord and of those who tremble at the commandment of our God; and let it be done according to the law." (Ezra 10:2–3 NRSV)

and

> Of the descendants of Nebo: Jeiel, Mattithiah, Zabad, Zebina, Jaddai, Joel, and Benaiah. All these had married foreign women, and they sent them away with their children. (Ezra 10:43–44 NRSV)

The question of Jewish identity was a concern in the book of Nehemiah. The people of Yehud were intermarrying with people of the surrounding Persian provinces (see map 2). But the threat to the covenant relationship with Yahweh remained the primary reason for the concern about divorcing the foreign women:

> In those days also I saw Jews who had married women of Ashdod, Ammon, and Moab; . . . And I contended with them and cursed them and beat some of them and pulled out their hair; and I made them take an oath in the name of God, saying, "You shall not give your daughters to their sons, or take their daughters for your sons or for yourselves. Did not King Solomon of Israel sin on account of such women? Among the many nations there was no king like him, and he was beloved by his God, and God made him king over all Israel; nevertheless, foreign women made even him to sin. Shall we then listen to you and do all this great evil and act treacherously against our God by marrying foreign women?" (Neh 13:23–27 NRSV)

Since the priests were also intermarried, they were charged with defiling the priesthood (Neh 13:28–31).[46]

Sacrifices. The concern about acceptable worship was an extension of the concern about Yahweh's receiving honor from the people. From Malachi's perspective, the community deviated from God's requirement (e.g., Mal

46. Cf. 1 Esd 8:92; 9:7, 36. The concern about apostasy is seen in Exod 23:23–33; 34:12–16, with a prohibition against intermarriage in Exod 34:16.

2:6–9). For example, God required sacrifices that met a specified standard (cf. animal sacrifice, Lev 22:18–25; firstborn sacrifice, Deut 15:19–23). Malachi 2:8 identifies the unacceptable nature of the sacrifices that included blind, lame, and blemished animals (cf. Deut 15:19–23; 17:1).[47] To be acceptable or pleasing, the sacrifices brought to Yahweh needed to be without blemish. No compromises could be made on the quality of the sacrifice.

The New Testament contains several quotations and allusions to the book of Malachi. Table 6 lists the intertextual links between Malachi and the New Testament.[48] Among these are God's election of Israel (Mal 1:2–3; Rom 9:13); leading by example and lifestyle and the effects of the leaders' conduct on the community (Mal 2:7–8; Matt 23:3). The identity of the prophet Elijah as a forerunner also appears in the New Testament (Mal 4:5–6 [MT 3:23–24]; Matt 17:10–12//Mark 9:11–13).[49]

Table 6. Intertextual Links between Malachi and the New Testament[50]

Malachi Text	NT Text	Topic
Mal 1:2-3 Yet I have loved Jacob but I have hated Esau.	Rom 9:13 I have loved Jacob, but I have hated Esau.	Yahweh's love for Israel
Mal 1:6 If I am a master, where is the respect due me?	Luke 6:46 Why do you call me "Lord, Lord," and do not do what I tell you?	Appropriate honor
Mal 1:11 For from the rising of the sun to its setting my name is great among the nations.	2 Thess 1:12 So that the name of our Lord Jesus may be glorified in you, and you in him, according to the grace of our God and the Lord Jesus Christ.	Glorification of the Lord's name
Mal 2:7-8 For the lips of a priest should guard knowledge, and people should seek instruction from his mouth.... But you have turned aside from the way; you have caused many to stumble by your instruction; you have corrupted the covenant of Levi.	Matt 23:3 Therefore, do whatever they teach you and follow it; but do not do as they do, for they do not practice what they teach.	Leading by example and leaders' impact

47. See. Lev 3; Num 19.

48. See the list in K. Aland et al., eds., *The Greek New Testament,* 4th rev. ed. (New York: United Bible Societies, 1993). For a brief summary of the content of the texts, see Hill, *Malachi,* 84–88.

49. Other elements appear in Mal 1:1, 12, and 1 Cor 10:21; Mal 3:5 and Jas 5:4; Mal 4:2 (MT 3:20) and Luke 1:78.

50. To facilitate the reader's use of this list with modern translations, all the quotations in table 6 are from the NRSV. The table is arranged sequentially according to the Malachi text. Allusions and quotations (words and phrases) thus appear together in the table.

Malachi Text	NT Text	Topic
Mal 2:10 Have we not all one father?	1 Cor 8:6 Yet for us there is one God, the Father.	God as father
Mal 3:1 See, I am sending my messenger to prepare the way before me.	Matt 11:10 This is the one about whom it is written, "See, I am sending my messenger ahead of you, who will prepare your way before you." (// Mark 1:2; Luke 7:27)	The messenger/ forerunner
Mal 3:2 But who can endure the day of his coming...?	Rev 6:17 For the great day of their wrath has come, and who is able to stand?	Enduring the day the Lord
Mal 3:3 He will purify the descendants of Levi and refine them like gold and silver.	1 Pet 1:7 So that the genuineness of your faith—being more precious than gold that, though perishable, is tested by fire....	Purification/ testing
Mal 3:7 Return to me, and I will return to you.	Jas 4:8 Draw near to God, and he will draw near to you. Cleanse your hands, you sinners, and purify your hearts, you double-minded.	Return to God/ repentance
Mal 4:5 (MT 3:23) Lo, I will send you the prophet Elijah before the great and terrible day of the Lord comes.	Matt 11:14 And if you are willing to accept it, he is Elijah who is to come. Matt 17:10-12 And the disciples asked him, "Why, then, do the scribes say that Elijah must come first?" He replied, "Elijah is indeed coming and will restore all things; but I tell you that Elijah has already come, and they did not recognize him, but they did to him whatever they pleased." (//Mark 9:11-13)	Elijah as messenger
Mal 4:5-6 (MT 3:23-24) Lo, I will send you the prophet Elijah.... He will turn the hearts of parents to their children and the hearts of children to their parents, so that I will not come and strike the land with a curse.	Luke 1:17 With the spirit and power of Elijah he will go before him, to turn the hearts of parents to their children, and the disobedient to the wisdom of the righteous, to make ready a people prepared for the Lord.	The task of Elijah as messenger

IV. STRUCTURAL ANALYSIS

A. GENRE

Among the recurrent issues in interpreting the book of Malachi are the structure of the book, identifying its definitive generic elements, the function and place of 4:3–6 (MT 3:21–24), and the book's independent status.[51]

Proposals for the genre of the book of Malachi include diatribe, disputation, and others.[52] In this commentary I recognize the scholarly discussions about the book's poetry and prose and affirm the presence of poetic elements in the prose composition. There have been several attempts to understand Malachi as a single-genre book. Notably, E. Pfeiffer promoted the idea that the book has one genre and argued that it is a prophetic disputation consisting of a tripartite unit; that is, an assertion accompanied by a question-and-answer schema (the question plus a response).[53] He contended that the book consists of seven units: 1:2–5; 1:6–2:9; 2:10–16; 2:17–3:5; 3:6–12; 3:13–4:3 (MT 3:13–21); and 4:4–6 (MT 3:22–24). According to Petersen the book consists of diatribe-like discourses.[54] O'Brien classifies the book as a covenant lawsuit with the following structural units: prologue (1:1–5), accusations (1:6–2:9; 2:17–3:5; 3:6–12; 3:13–4:3 [MT 3:13–21]), an admonition (4:4 [MT 3:22]), and an ultimatum (4:5–6 [MT 3:23–24]).[55] Lescow proposes that the extant form of the book of Malachi is a product of redactional activity that transformed the original Torah speeches for didactic and homiletic purposes (e.g., 1:6–2:9). He sees 3:22–24 as an appendix or conclusion to the prophetic corpus.[56] Weyde proposes that the book reflects the didactic saying with the question-and-answer schema reflective of priestly instruction.[57]

Verhoef understands the book as resembling the covenant treaty.[58] Hill classifies it as oracular prose and notes that "the literary structure of Malachi is a combination of prosaic and rhetorical features approaching

51. Jacobs, "Malachi," pp. 474–77.

52. For an overview of these discussions (19th to 20th century), see Weyde, *Prophecy and Teaching,* 14–45; J. M. O'Brien, "Malachi in Recent Research," *CurBS* 3 (1995): 81–94.

53. E. Pfeiffer, "Die Disputationsworte im Buche Maleachi," *EvT* 19 (1959): 546–68 (esp. 554).

54. Petersen, *Zechariah 9–14 and Malachi.* He disagrees with the idea that the book consists of seven units. Instead he proposes that the text of Malachi is one of three oracles in the Zechariah-to-Malachi unit.

55. J. M. O'Brien, *Priest and Levite.*

56. T. Lescow, "Dialogische Strukturen in den Streitreden des Buches Maleachi," *ZAW* 102 (1990): 194–212.

57. Weyde, *Prophecy and Teaching,* 46–48.

58. Verhoef, *Haggai and Malachi,* 180–83.

poetic discourse but distinctive of prophetic style."[59] I propose that the book of Malachi is a disputation and that the genre need not include verbatim quotations of the various parties whose views are represented in the disputation.[60]

B. STRUCTURE

The structure of the book has long been a point of discussion; several options will be overviewed briefly here. The Masoretes' effort to identify the book's structure is evident by the placement of the paragraph markings. Accordingly, major paragraph marks (indicated with *pes*) separate the book into four pericopes and their subunits (minor paragraphs—indicated with *sameks*): pericope I: 1:1–2:9 (1:1–13; 1:14–2:9); pericope II: 2:10–12; pericope III: 2:13–3:21 (2:13–16; 2:17–3:12; 3:13–18; 4:1–3 [MT 3:19–21]); pericope IV: 4:4–6 [MT 3:22–24].[61] Hill uses a thematic outline while also offering a rhetorical outline and an outline that situates the book of Malachi in relation to Haggai and Zechariah.[62]

The adversative formulas in the book of Malachi ("but you say")—1:2, 6, 7, 12, 13; 2:14, 17; 3:7, 8, 13—while significant for the tone of the book and the structure of a few major units, are not decisive in regard to its macrostructure.[63] As displayed in table 7, the formulas have various functions, including marking the question-and-answer schema. In Weyde's delineation, three of the functions of the adversative formulas are (1) "to motivate and develop accusations against the addressees which occur in the previous context" (e.g., 1:13a; 3:14 and 1:7b, 12b; 2:17b); (2) to cite what the addressees "say after having experienced Yahweh's destruction of Edom" (i.e., Mal 1:5b); (3) to inquire about the "motivation for a previous statement" (Mal 1:2, 6, 7; 2:17a; 3:7, 8; 3:13; cf. 2:14).[64]

Regarding the relationship of Malachi in the Haggai-Malachi corpus, several opinions have been offered by commentators. The first is that Malachi

59. Hill, *Malachi,* 25–26.

60. Compare A. Graffy, *A Prophet Confronts His People,* AnBib 104 (Rome: Pontifical Biblical Institute , 1984), who discredits Malachi because of the lack of direct quotations.

61. Hill, *Malachi,* 27.

62. Hill, *Malachi,* xxxv–xxxix. He includes a thematic and rhetorical outline as well as an outline of the "interrogative elements" in the Haggai-Zechariah-Malachi corpus. His commentary follows this thematic outline: 1:1; 1:2–5; 1:6–2:9; 2:10–16; 2:17–3:5; 3:6–12; 3:13–21 [4:3]; appendixes—3:22 [4:4]; 3:23–24 [4:5–6].

63. The occurrence of *tōʾmrû* in Mal 1:5 is omitted from table 7 below.

64. Weyde (*Prophecy and Teaching,* 6–9) discusses the different functions of "the quotations introduced by the verb *ʾāmar* ['to say']."

is interdependent with Zechariah, as evidenced by the presence of the term *maśśā'* in both Malachi (1:1) and Zechariah (9:1a and 12:1).[65] Second, some scholars see Malachi as interdependent with both Haggai and Zechariah—the latter corpus being unified by its representation of the restoration community.[66] Additionally, Mal 3:22–24 functions as the conclusion to the Book of the Twelve, or the *Nebi'im*—the prophetic corpus.[67] Third, some regard Malachi as being independent from Zech 9–14.[68] In agreement with Floyd, I affirm the independent status of the book of Malachi and consider Mal 3:22–24 to be an integral part of the microunit 2:17–3:24.

Table 7. Adversative Formulas in the Book of Malachi

*Signal the start of a macro-unit

Reference	Formula	Accompanying verb	Analysis of the verb	Response to the Challenge
1:2*	*wa'amartem bammâ*	*'ahabtānû*	Qal perfect 2ms +1cp (object suffix) *How have you loved us?*	1:2—Question + Declarative statement: *Is not Esau Jacob's brother? Yet I love Jacob and hate Esau*
1:6*	*wa'amartem bammê*	*bāzînû*	Qal perfect 1cp + object *How have we despised your name?*	1:7—Declarative statement: *by offering defiled food on my altar*
1:7	*wa'amartem bammê*	*gē'alnûkā*	Piel perfect 1cp + 2ms (object suffix) *How have we defiled you?*	1:7—Declarative statement: *when you say, "YHWH's table is despised"*
1:12	*be'emārekem*			1:12—Declarative statement: when you say the Lord's table is despised
1:13	*wa'amartem*			1:13—Exclamatory statement: *"what a weariness," you say* (NRSV)

65. Petersen, *Zechariah 9–14 and Malachi,* 23–29; R. Mason, *The Books of Haggai, Zechariah, and Malachi,* CBC (Cambridge: Cambridge University Press, 1977), 159–61.

66. R. Pierce, "Literary Connectors and a Haggai-Zechariah-Malachi Corpus," *JETS* 27 (1984): 277–89; T. Lescow, *Das Buch Maleachi* (Stuttgart: Calwer, 1993), 145–56, 168–74; Hill, *Malachi,* 14.

67. Weyde, *Prophecy and Teaching,* 6–9.

68. B. S. Childs, *Introduction to the Old Testament as Scripture* (Philadelphia: Fortress, 1979), 491–92; Baldwin, *Hag, Zech, Mal,* 77–81; R. L. Smith, *Micah-Malachi,* 296–97; Verhoef, *Haggai and Malachi,* 155; Floyd, *Minor Prophets 2,* 568–69.

Reference	Formula	Accompanying verb	Analysis of the verb	Response to the Challenge
2:14	*wa'amartem*			2:14—Question + citation of a question + declarative statement: You ask, *"Why does he not?" Because the Lord was a witness* (NRSV)
2:17a*	*wa'amartem bammâ*	*hôgā'enû*	Hiph perfect 1cp *How have we wearied [him]?*	2:17—Declarative statement: *When* you say, *"all evildoers are good in the eyes of YHWH"*
2:17b	*be'emārekem*			
3:7	*wa'amartem bammê*	*nāšûb*	Qal imperfect 1cp *How shall we return?*	3:8—*Question: Will a human/person rob God?*
				3:10—*Command: Bring the full tithe to the storehouse*
3:8	*wa'amartem bammê*	*qeba'anûk*	Qal perfect 1cp + 2ms (object suffix) *How have we robbed you?*	3:8—Declarative statement: *Tithe and offering*
3:13	*wa'amartem mâ*	*nidbarnû*	Niphal perfect 1cp + prepositional phrase *What have we said against you?*	3:14—Declarative statement: *You say that it is vain to serve God*

I view Malachi as being a prophetic disputation with three major units (1:2–5; 1:6–2:16; 2:17–4:6 [MT 3:24]) and their constituent subunits.

Structure

Superscription 1:1

I. Introduction: Disputation regarding Yahweh's Love for Israel 1:2–5
   A. Yahweh's Declaration of Love for Israel 1:2aα
   B. Israel's Challenge to Yahweh's Claim 1:2aβ
   C. Yahweh's Response to Israel's Challenge: Presentation of Evidence 1:2b–5
      1. Rhetorical Question 1:2bα
      2. Statement of the Comparison 1:2bβ–5

a. Declaration of Love for Jacob 1:2bβ
b. Declaration of Hatred for Esau 1:3–5
(1) The Statement 1:3a
(2) Evidence Substantiating the Claim 1:3b–4
(3) Effect of the Evidence on Israel 1:5
II. Disputation Sequence:
Behaviors and Beliefs regarding Honor 1:6–2:16
A. The Priests' Cultic Malpractice 1:6–2:9
1. Charges regarding Corrupt Sacrifices 1:6–14
a. Charge against the Priests 1:6–9
(1) Yahweh's Declaration and Challenge regarding Honor 1:6a–bα
(a) General Declaration regarding Honor in Relationships 1:6a
(b) Challenge about Specific Relationships 1:6bα
(2) The Priests' Response: Question Challenging Yahweh's Claim 1:6bβ
(3) Interchange regarding Cultic Malpractice 1:7–9
(a) Statement of the Argument (Yahweh) 1:7aα
(b) Refutation (Priests) 1:7aβ
(c) Presentation of the Evidence (Yahweh) 1:7b–9
b. Announcement of Judgment on the Priests 1:10–14
(1) Expressed Desire to Terminate Cultic Practices 1:10
(2) Rationale for the Expressed Desire 1:11–13
(a) Exaltation Abroad 1:11
(b) Dishonor/Malpractice at Home 1:12–13
(3) Pronouncement of the Curse 1:14
2. Regarding Priestly Instruction 2:1–9
a. Yahweh's Command to the Priests 2:1–4
(1) The Introductory Statement 2:1
(2) The Command—as Curse for Their Malpractice 2:2–3
(3) Conclusion: Rationale for the Command 2:4
b. Covenant of Levi as Basis of Instruction 2:5–9
(1) Nature of the Covenant 2:5a
(2) Contrasting Priests' Responses to the Levitical Covenant 2:5b–9
(a) First Recipients' Adherence 2:5b–7
(i) Nature of the Adherence 2:5b–6bα
(ii) Effects of the Adherence 2:6bβ–7
(b) Current Priests' Violation 2:8–9
(i) Nature of the Violation 2:8
(ii) Consequences (Announcement of Judgment) 2:9

B. Charges regarding the People's Malpractice: Unfaithfulness 2:10–16
  1. Marriage Leading to Apostasy: Unfaithfulness 2:10–12
    a. General Statement regarding
       the People's Unfaithfulness 2:10
    b. Statement Substantiated 2:11
    c. Announcement of Judgment for the Unfaithfulness 2:12
  2. Attention to Marriage and Divorce 2:13–16
    a. Description of the People's Futile Behavior
       (regarding Offerings) 2:13
    b. Cited Rationale for the Futility: Yahweh's Disfavor 2:14–16
      (1) Report of the People's Question 2:14a
      (2) The Prophet's Response to the People's Question 2:14b–16
        (a) The Violation of the Marriage Covenant 2:14b–15
        (b) Response to Divorce 2:16

III. Disputation Sequence:
   Words Exemplifying Beliefs 2:17–4:6 (MT 2:17–3:24)
 A. Words Spoken against Yahweh—Yahweh's Justice 2:17–3:12
  1. Report of a Charge: Misrepresenting God 2:17
    a. Declaration of the Charge 2:17aα
    b. Response/Challenge to the Charge 2:17aβ–b
      (1) The People's Question 2:17aβ
      (2) The Substantiation of the Charge 2:17b
  2. Yahweh's Response to the Misrepresentation 3:1–12
    a. Announcement of Impending Judgment 3:1–7aα
      (1) Sending and Coming—the Messenger and Yahweh 3:1–4
        (a) Announcement regarding the Sending 3:1
        (b) Effects of the Coming 3:2–4
      (2) Yahweh's Own Coming (Further Delineated) 3:5–7aα
        (a) The Target of the Judgment 3:5
        (b) The Reason the Wicked Continue to Exist 3:6
        (c) The Time Span of the Disobedience 3:7aα
    b. Admonition regarding the Impending Judgment—
       Return to Yahweh 3:7aβ–12
      (1) Declaration of the Admonition 3:7aβ
      (2) Expansion of the Admonition 3:7b–12
        (a) Report of the People's Question regarding
            Returning to Yahweh 3:7b
        (b) Reported Response to the People's Question
            (Robbing Yahweh) 3:8–12
          (i) Reported Interchanges 3:8
            (a) First Interchange (God) 3:8aα
            (b) Second Interchange (God and the People) 3:8aβ–b

(ii) Effects of the People's Actions 3:9–12
(a) Announcement of Judgment regarding Robbing God 3:9
(b) Command to the People: The Tithe as a Way to Return 3:10
(c) Announcement: Promise regarding the Return 3:11–12

B. Words about Reward for Serving Yahweh 3:13–4:6 (MT 3:13–24)
1. Words against Yahweh 3:13–15
a. Charge against the People: You Spoke Harshly against Yahweh 3:13a
b. Challenging the Charge 3:13b–15
(1) The People's Question: How? 3:13b
(2) Yahweh's Response: Quoting the People's Words 3:14–15
2. Counterperspective and Yahweh's Response 3:16–4:6 (MT 3:16–24)
a. Report concerning Those Who Fear Yahweh 3:16
(1) The God-Fearers' Reaction to the Words against Yahweh 3:16a
(2) Yahweh's Reception of Their Behavior: The Book of Remembrance 3:16b
b. Yahweh's Extended Response to the Yahweh-Fearers 3:17–4:6 (MT 3:17–24)
(1) Their Relationship with Yahweh 3:17–4:3 (MT 3:17–21)
(a) Yahweh's Special Possession 3:17
(b) Ability to Differentiate between the Righteous and the Wicked 3:18–4:3 (MT 3:18–21)
(i) The Ability Identified 3:18
(ii) Specification of the Contrast 4:1–3 (MT 3:19–21)
(a) The Arrogant and Evildoers 4:1 (MT 3:19)
(b) Those Who Fear the Name of Yahweh 4:2 (MT 3:20)
(c) The Wicked 4:3 (MT 3:21)
(2) Prescription regarding Averting Judgment 4:4–6 (MT 3:22–24)
(a) Prescription: Call to Remembrance— Law of Moses 4:4 (MT 3:22)
(b) Expansion: Yahweh's Provision— Elijah the Promised Prophet 4:5–6 (MT 3:23–24)
(i) Announcement of the Prophet's Coming 4:5 (MT 3:23)
(ii) Purpose of the Coming 4:6 MT (3:24)

This commentary will follow the structural analysis above, using the literary units as the organizational elements. Each chapter of the commentary and the constituent sections will address text-critical issues as deemed necessary to the understanding of the text. Intertextual indicators are noted throughout, with attention to the uses of the traditions or perspectives represented by the various occurrences.

V. MESSAGE

At its core, the book of Malachi portrays a fractured relationship in which the behaviors of both parties evidence the status of the relationship. In particular, Malachi illustrates the dissonance and impasse that have resulted from the clash between the expectations and the experience in the Yahweh-Israel covenant relationship. Through the disputation sequences, the prophet portrays both sides of the relationship and the dominance of the Deity's perspective on efforts to sustain the relationship. The question-answer schema contributes to the literary construction and overall tone of the book.

Each unit of the book contributes to the coherence of the central message of the book: that God loves Israel. Fundamentally, Malachi is the prophet's portrayal of a disagreement about Yahweh's love for Israel. Each unit explores questions about love in the Yahweh-Israel relationship (see fig. 3). Through Malachi's exploration of the dimensions of Yahweh's love, various realizations emerge, including the nature of God's love (as seen in the effort to confirm that love), the relational context of the love (the parties are still in the relationship), and the concurrent reality that the relationship is broken (the quality of the relationship).

Yahweh is persistent, and Israel is reluctant to sustain the type of relationship required of them. The dynamics of the relationship raise questions about the divine choices to love and hate: Does God select some to be loved and others to be hated? How is God's choice manifested? How does God decide whom to love or hate?

The depicted malpractice within the community is thus illustrative of the fractured relationship, and the book analyzes this relationship through the lenses of the present community's postexilic conditions. Even the announced judgment is part of the relationship dynamics in which Yahweh seeks for Israel "to return" to God. The message thus reflects theological as well as sociopolitical realities, including the nature and verifiability of God's love; the justice of God; the responsibility of priestly leadership in the care for the community; and the status of Jerusalem and Judah/Yehud among the other nations or political entities[69]—issues that will be discussed in the commentary that follows. Section III of this Malachi commentary identifies key themes as

69. See Jacobs, "Malachi," for survey of the theological and hermeneutical issues.

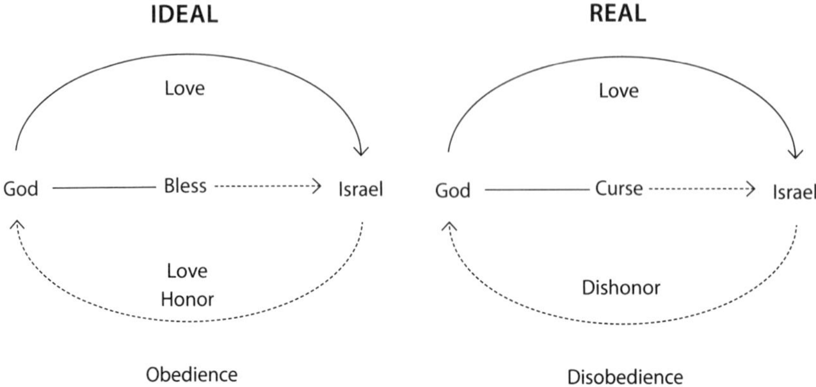

Figure 3. The Dynamics of the Yahweh-Israel Relationship

they are manifested intertextually. Here, I will further delineate the themes as related to the book of Malachi.

Dishonoring God. The audacity of giving to the Deity what one would not give to a human leader illustrates the brokenness of the relationship and lack of reverence for God. The leaders are held responsible for these distorted practices in the community. To the extent that the priests (the leaders of the community) do not teach the people, they are misleading the people (Mal 2:6–9). The misguiding is evident in matters of faith, relationship, and understanding God's faithfulness.

Stealing from God. A broken community lives in ways that reflect the brokenness—for example, withholding tithes. The purpose of the tithes was to provide for the community's underprivileged and the priests and to maintain the work on the temple. Withholding tithes will disrupt the community far beyond the well-being of a single individual. Just as various segments of the community may be withholding tithes, so the negative impacts will encompass all segments of the community. God's response illustrates God's power over nature (rain, crops, etc.) and highlights the interconnectedness of human behavior and nature (cf. Mal 3:10–12; Hag 1:10–11).

Divorce. Some see this statement as a reaction to the practices of Ezra and Nehemiah, who required the Israelite men to divorce their foreign wives (Ezra 10:2–3, 43–44; Neh 13:23–31). If this is a response to the requirement of divorce for those who married foreign women, Mal 2:16 is saying that God would rather have the people stay married than be divorced. The emphasis is not on the nationality of the wives and the possibility that they may bring other customs into Israel or expose Israel to other religions. Israel has already been exposed. The emphasis is on God's response to divorce.

The Day of Yahweh. The prophetic perspective is that a time of judgment is coming in which the righteous and wicked will witness God's actions (Mal 3:17–4:5 [MT 3:17–23]). Even when it seems that the wicked are winning, God keeps track and will act against the wicked. God is also aware of those who honor and reverence the Deity and will bless them.

TEXT AND COMMENTARY

SUPERSCRIPTION (1:1)

[1]*An oracle, the word of Yahweh to Israel by the hand of Malachi.*[a]

a. The MT has been variously rendered: the LXX reads "his messenger" (*aggelou autou*) in addition to the clause "place it upon your heart" (*thesthe de epi kardia hymon*). The latter clause is analogous to Hag 2:15, 18. The targum qualifies the term *mal'ākî*, "my messenger," with the clause "whose name is Ezra, the scribe," and in this way identifies the messenger.

1 The superscription consists of several elements: specified message and modifier, designated audience, and identification of the instrument of the message. Concerns regarding these elements involve the meaning of *maśśā'*, "oracle," and *mal'ākî*, "my messenger."

The superscription designates the message *maśśā' dəbar-yhwh, an oracle*, and modifies it with *the word of* Yahweh. The phrase denotes the nature of the message and qualifies the noun *maśśā'*, "oracle," as being Yahweh's word.[1] The phrase occurs three times in the prophetic books: Zech 9:1a ; 12:1a; and here in Mal 1:1a. In Zech 12:1a and Mal 1:1a, *maśśā' dəbar-yhwh* is followed by a prepositional phrase that identifies the audience of the message, thus: Zech 12:1a—*'al-yiśrā'ēl*, "concerning Israel"; and Mal 1:1a—*'el-yiśrā'ēl*, "to Israel."[2]

In Mal 1:1, *to Israel ('el-yiśrā'ēl)* denotes the recipient of the *maśśā'*, referring to the people with whom Yahweh has a covenant relationship. The ref-

1. W. C. Kaiser, "מַשָּׂא," *TWOT* 2.600–602. Cf. M. H. Floyd, "The מַשָּׂא (*maśśā'*) as a Type of Prophetic Book," *JBL* 12 (2002): 401–22.

2. Note how *Israel* is used in Malachi. Here in the superscription, it is much too soon to say whether it refers to the Northern Kingdom Israel or to Israel the people. Other references in the book suggest that the reference in the superscription is a designation of the people.

erences and allusions to the covenant further confirm the recipients' identity (e.g., Mal 1:2–5). The election tradition is signaled through reference to the Deity's love for Jacob and hatred of Esau, the progenitors of the nations of Israel and Edom, respectively. Other confirmations of the recipient(s) include references to the ancestors who disobeyed (Mal 2:10; 3:17) and to the statutes and ordinance of Moses (Mal 4:4). However, other passages in Malachi identify segments within Israel as being the focus of particular parts of the message—for example, the priests (1:6–8; 2:1–9), Judah (Mal 2:11; 3:4), and the general "you," which presumably encompasses all individuals (Mal 2:17; 3:6). Finally, although the covenantal relationship and the use of traditions shape the focus of the message and the configuration of its audience's identity, the book's greater geopolitical awareness is also evident. It does refer to the national borders (Mal 1:5), and to Judah and Jerusalem (Mal 2:11) in contrast to the other nations (Mal 1:9, 11).

Notably, in Mal 1:1a, *maśśāʾ dəbar-yhwh* is further extended by the particle *bəyad, by the hand of*, referring to the instrument by whom the *maśśāʾ* (oracle) was delivered; such a particle in not found in Zech 9:1a (or 12:1). This may be a conceptual rather than a stylistic difference; in Zech 12:1a, "concerning Israel" (*ʿal-yiśrāʾēl*) indicates the focus and hence the subject of the *maśśāʾ*.[3] Other references use the formulation "by the hand of" (*bəyad*) and name the prophet who serves as the intermediary of Yahweh's message to the people (Hag 1:1; 2:1; Jer 50:1; contrast Hag 2:10). The phrase *by the hand of* (*bəyad*) denotes the instrument through which the *maśśāʾ* was delivered to its recipient, Israel (cf. Jer 50:1; Hag 1:1; 2:1, 10). Most modern translations interpret *malʾākî* as the name of a person, "Malachi" (e.g., NRSV, NIV, NEB, KJV). The term *bəyad* usually precedes a proper name, and when the phrase appears in the book of Malachi, most scholars translate *malʾākî* as the proper name "Malachi," noting the tradition (cf. Hag 1:1; 2:1, 10; Jer 50:1).[4] Some modern scholars follow the LXX because of its consistency with the third-person report in the introduction. They explain the first-person suffix in Mal 1:1 as a harmonization with 3:1, where "messenger of the covenant" (*malʾak habbərît*) appears.[5]

3. See other uses of the prepositional phrase to indicate the subject of the message—that is, "concerning. . .": Isa 1:1, "concerning Judah and Jerusalem"; Amos 1:1bα, "which he saw concerning Israel"; Mic 1:1b, "which he saw concerning Samaria and Jerusalem."

4. E.g., Verhoef, *Haggai and Malachi*, 155–56, 191; Glazier-McDonald, *Malachi: The Divine Messenger*, 29; Hill, *Malachi*, 135–36.

5. R. Vuilleumier, "Malachie," in *Aggée, Zacharie, Malachie*, ed. S. Amsler, A. Lacocque, and R. Vuilleumier, CAT 11c (Geneva: Labor et Fides, 1981), 223–24; Petersen, *Zechariah 9–14 and Malachi*, 165.

I. INTRODUCTION: DISPUTATION REGARDING YAHWEH'S LOVE FOR ISRAEL (1:2–5)

2*"I have loved you," says Yahweh.*
But you say, "How have you loved us?"
"Is not Esau Jacob's brother?" declares Yahweh.[a] *"So I have loved Jacob.*
3*But Esau I have hated. I put his mountains to desolation and made his inheritance into a desert for the jackals."*[b]

4*If Edom says, "We are beaten down, but we will return and rebuild the ruins," thus says Yahweh of hosts, "They will rebuild, but I myself will destroy. Then they will call them the territory of wickedness and the people whom Yahweh has cursed forever.* 5*Then your eyes will see and you yourself will say, 'Great is Yahweh beyond the territory of Israel.'"*[c]

---

a. *BHS* suggests that the formula (*nəʾum-yhwh*) be deleted on the basis of its meter, which apparently does not conform to the meter of the verse; however, its presence conforms to the representation of the message as Yahweh's words uttered to the nations. While it occurs only once in Malachi, it is attested in the Book of the Twelve (e.g., Hag 1:9, 13; 2:4; Zech 1:3, 4; 10:12; 11:6). Commentators who retain the MT without adapting *BHS*'s suggestion include Verhoef, *Haggai and Malachi,* 193; Petersen, *Zechariah 9–14 and Malachi,* 167; Glazier-McDonald, *Malachi: The Divine Messenger,* 31; and Hill, *Malachi,* 151. On the other hand, some scholars delete the formula, such as Vuilleumier, "Malachie," 223.

b. Regarding *lətannôt,* "for the jackals," the reading *nātattî* has been proposed. The LXX reads *eis domata eremou,* "in dwelling of the wilderness," assuming the Hebrew term *nəôt* (cf. Peshitta). The Hebrew term *nəʾôt,* "pastures," appears in Jer 9:10 (MT 9); 23:1. Cf. Verhoef, *Haggai and Malachi,* 203; Petersen, *Zechariah 9–14 and Malachi,* 165.

c. Assuming dittography of the *lamed* with the preceding word, *BHS* suggests that *gəbûl* be read in place of *ligbûl.*

The first prophetic speech in the book, 1:2–5, contains several elements typical of disputation speeches (claim and counterclaim and an attempt to refute the counterclaim).[6] Note that disputation speeches are usually a representation of divergent perspectives on a particular subject.[7] This speech form occurs in other prophetic books, including Mic 2:6–11 and Nahum.[8] The text of Malachi attributes the perspectives to named or unnamed agents (e.g., Israel, a prophet, etc.), including summary views, and not necessarily to reported speech that is linked to a particular speech act.[9]

6. D. F. Murray, "The Rhetoric of Disputation: Re-examination of a Prophetic Genre," *JSOT* 38 (1987): 95–121. Hill (*Malachi,* 145–46) identifies the two elements as the charge and countercharge along with the refutation. Graffy, *A Prophet Confronts His People.*

7. Floyd, *Minor Prophets 2,* 638.

8. M. Sweeney, "Concerning the Structure and Generic Character of the Book of Nahum," *ZAW* 104 (1992): 364–77; Jacobs, *Conceptual Coherence.*

9. See Hag 1:2–4 regarding the nature of the priests' and community's response.

A. YAHWEH'S DECLARATION OF LOVE FOR ISRAEL (1:2aα)

2 Malachi 1:2 is the beginning of the oracle that was referenced in the superscription of 1:1. Yahweh's claim forms the foundation of the book and provides the context for understanding the relationship depicted throughout the book—a fractured relationship with the resulting dynamics and efforts at repair. This relationship is characterized by reluctance (on the part of Israel) and determination (on the part of Yahweh).

The speaker, Yahweh, articulates the claim *I have loved you (ʾāhabtî ʾetkem).*[10] The object of Yahweh's love is manifested in the second-person plural suffix *-kem,* "you," the antecedent of which is found in Mal 1:1a—namely, Israel. The people later identified as "Jacob" is the object of Yahweh's love (Mal 1:2b). Yahweh's claim to the community establishes a link between the community (present addressees) and its ancestor Jacob. The continuity established between past and present shows that, whatever relationship Yahweh had with the ancestor, Yahweh also intends for the present community—or Yahweh envisions this same relationship. But herein lie the blessing and the challenge: Yahweh expects the current generation to conform to the commitment made by the previous generation under different circumstances.

The way the Old Testament depicts several types of love (*ʾahab*) can facilitate our understanding of Yahweh's claim: they are subcategories of human-human love in its various manifestations and divine-human love. First, regarding the types of human-human love, the love between a man and a woman is prevalent, as seen in the following examples: Isaac-Rebekah (Gen 24:67); Jacob-Rachel (Gen 29:18, 20, 30); Samson-Delilah (Judg 16:4); Elkanah-Hannah (1 Sam 1:5); Michal-David (1 Sam 18:20, 28);[11] Rehoboam-Maacah (2 Chr 11:21); Ahasuerus-Esther (Esth 2:17); Solomon's love for many women (1 Kgs 11:1). Male-female love is usually identified as emotive love and a preferential regard for one person over another, especially in situations where co-wives are involved (Rachel and Leah, Hannah and Peninnah). In such situations, the husband's love for one wife might be quantitatively different from his love for the other, and God responds by making the loved wife infertile (Gen 29:30–31; 1 Sam 1:2, 15). Thus, God responds to the preferential love of a husband for one of his wives by creating difficulty for the beloved wife. In some instances the preference is stated (e.g., Rachel, Maacah, Esther).[12]

10. *Qal* perfect first common singular of *ʾāhēb,* "to love."

11. Usually the man is said to love the woman; but in this case the woman is said to love the man.

12. In these instances, the love for one woman is represented vis-à-vis the love for another by use of the particle (*min*); thus the construction *wayyeʾəhab . . . mikkol-nāšāyw*—"He loved . . . more than all of the wives" (2 Chr 11:21; verb + particle + object).

The concept of love in situations of violence against a woman is challenging, but these situations also demonstrate the selective aspects of the love—for example, Shechem-Dinah (Gen 34:3)[13] and Amnon-Tamar (2 Sam 13:1, 4). However, in these examples the choice of one woman is not defined in terms of the nature or quality of the love compared with other loves.

Parent-child love is also usually seen with the nuance of preferential love of one child over another: Isaac-Esau (Gen 25:28); Rebekah-Jacob (Gen 25:28); Jacob-Joseph (Gen 37:4); and David-Amnon (2 Sam 13:21). The law recognizes the human tendency to prefer the offspring of the "loved wife" and to hate the offspring of the "hated wife" and thus prescribes that someone's love not be the decisive factor in the way that the firstborn children of co-wives are treated (Deut 21:15–16).[14] The firstborn of the husband, whether by the loved or the hated wife, is to be heir. In this instance the traditions demonstrate the presence or potential presence of different levels of love and hate manifested toward wives and children.

The love within friendship is another form of love—for example, the love between David and Jonathan (1 Sam 18:1–3; 20:17). This type of love is not constituted by a familial bond but by the establishment of relational bonds—compare Saul's love for David. Another category is the love depicted between daughter- and mother-in-law, such as Ruth and Naomi (Ruth 4:15). Yet another is the love of a people for a leader—for example, Judah for David (1 Sam 18:16)—or a slave's love for his master (Exod 21:5). While there are various types of human relationships, the law presumes that love can be commanded of individuals toward each other and toward God. Thus:

> You shall not take vengeance or bear a grudge against any of your people, but you shall love your neighbor as yourself: I am the Lord. (Lev 19:18 NRSV)

and

> The alien who resides with you shall be to you as the citizen among you; you shall love the alien as yourself, for you were aliens in the land of Egypt: I am the Lord your God. (Lev 19:34 NRSV)[15]

13. Shechem's regard for Dinah is identified here because the text also uses *'āhēb*, "to love," to characterize Shechem's love for Dinah. For further discussion of that topic, see M. R. Jacobs, "Love, Honor, and Violence," in *Pregnant Passion: Gender, Sex, and Violence in the Bible,* ed. C. A. Kirk-Duggan, Semeia Studies 44 (Atlanta: Society of Biblical Literature, 2003), 11–35.

14. Cf. C. Pressler, *The View of Women Found in the Deuteronomic Family Laws* (Berlin: de Gruyter, 1993).

15. Cf. Deut 10:19.

Finally, the nature of male-female love is sometimes used to portray God's love for Israel and in some instances also the tension between God and the reluctant beloved (Israel; see Ezek 16; Jer 3–4).

The second type of love, Divine-human love is seen, again, in God's love for Israel, but also in a person's love for the Deity—for example, Solomon's (1 Kgs 3:3). This human love for the Deity is usually characterized much like God's love for Israel (e.g., 1 Kgs 10:9; 2 Chr 9:8; Deut 7:13). The claim that God loves Israel also appears in Jer 31:1–6, using covenant language paired with the promise of restoration:

> At that time, says the LORD, I will be the God of all the families of Israel, and they shall be my people. Thus says the LORD: The people who survived the sword found grace in the wilderness; when Israel sought for rest, the LORD appeared to him from far away. I have loved you with an everlasting love; therefore I have continued my faithfulness to you. (Jer 31:1–3 NRSV)

It was also Yahweh's love and oath to Israel's ancestors that kept Yahweh faithful to Israel to the point of preparing them for and bringing them into the land promised to their ancestors (Deut 7:8; cf. Deut 23:5 [MT 6]). Likewise, God's love for Israel is characterized as parent-child love (Hos 11:1).

Obedience to the law is also designated "love" (Deut 7:9); and love for the Deity is commanded. Its presence or absence may be determined by obedience (Deut 7:13; cf. Exod 20:5–6).

> You shall love the LORD your God with all your heart, and with all your soul, and with all your might. (Deut 6:5 NRSV)[16]

Yahweh is also said to love types of behavior and inanimate objects; for example, righteous deeds and individuals who seek righteousness (*ṣədāqôt*, Ps 11:7; Prov 15:9); righteousness and justice (*ṣədāqâ ûmišpāṭ*, Ps 33:5); justice (*mišpāṭ*, Pss 37:28; 99:4; Isa 61:8); Judah and Mount Zion (Ps 78:68).

Clearly, the initial love in Divine-human relationships was not the result of anything that the humans did or who they were. On the other hand, the withdrawal of Divine love may result from the human failure to obey or to please God. Just as human-human love is manifested in selecting one person over another, so the connection between loving (*'āhēb*) and choosing (*bāḥar*) is a prevalent aspect of Divine-human relationships (Deut 4:37; 7:7–8; 10:15). Even so, a human being does not define or compel God's love. Thus, while God claims to love Israel, the love is regulated by God's choice to love and by God's terms for manifesting it.

16. Cf. Deut 11:1; 13:3; Josh 22:5; 23:11.

B. ISRAEL'S CHALLENGE TO YAHWEH'S CLAIM (1:2aβ)

The counterclaim is introduced by the narrative element *but you say (wa'ămartem),* a phrase that also appears in other counterclaims in the book (i.e., Mal 1:6, 7, 13; 2:14, 17; 3:7, 8, 13 and 14 [without *wa*]). The purpose of the counterclaim is to challenge the validity of the claim. It is not necessarily that the people verbalized this question or challenge at some point in time. Rather, the counterclaim reveals their belief or attitude toward the issue addressed. Here the counterclaim is challenging the fact of Yahweh's love for Israel by asking for evidence of that love.

The question *how have you loved us?* is directed to Yahweh using the second- and first-person address reflected in the assertion—*I have loved you* (1:2). The interrogative particle *bammâ* appears in Mal 1:2 and 2:17 and is used in disputations or other speeches to suggest that there is no valid answer to the question. The form occurs elsewhere in Malachi as *bammê* (Mal 1:7; 3:7, 8), showing no significant distinction in the meaning of the two spellings of the particle. Both have the meaning "wherein, by what means, how."[17] In Mal 3:13 the counterperspective is signaled by the interrogative particle *mâ*.

The question (*how have you loved us?*) may be requesting evidence of Yahweh's love for them, the people. Arguably, the people at this stage in their history are questioning whether Yahweh loves them and are leaning toward the idea that Yahweh does not love them. This would not be the first time that the people's perception of their circumstances led them to the conclusion that Yahweh does not love them but instead hates them. Deuteronomy 1:27 recalls the people's reluctance to enter the land because of their perception that Yahweh hated them and sought to destroy them. Yahweh's response to them thus illustrates the difference between love and hate and addresses the notion that Yahweh hates them. It is as though they are being told: you think that I hate you, but let me show you what hate looks like.

The second consideration in the counterclaim is the type of love, as discussed in regard to the claim (see also 1:6). For now, suffice it to say that the issue here is an established relationship in which love should be natural rather than a relationship in which love would be surprising. The response makes Yahweh's love for the people in his claim and their doubt of his love more specific. Their concern is not whether Yahweh loves, nor is it about another people whom Yahweh loves or may have loved. Rather, their challenge

17. BDB 553. Modern commentators and translators reflect the various renderings. Those who prefer "in what manner" include Verhoef, *Haggai and Malachi,* 193; Vuilleumier, "Malachie," 223. Those who translate with "how" include Hill, *Malachi,* 145; Petersen, *Zechariah 9–14 and Malachi,* 165; Merrill, *Hag, Zech, Mal,* 390, 391; Baldwin, *Hag, Zech, Mal,* 222; and the NRSV and NIV.

reveals their skepticism about Yahweh's claim to love them and their implied counterclaim that there is no evidence of Yahweh's love.

The people doubt Yahweh's love mainly because their experiences were incongruous with their ideas of being loved by the Deity. What were the incongruous aspects? For one thing, if Yahweh loves them, why were they subjected to adversity? Why was Yahweh not acting on their behalf to ensure that they escaped suffering? Why were they not living an ideal political existence? Their counterclaim does not seek information but lays bare the shattered belief of a people and—in whatever manner, skeptical or cynical—dares Yahweh to back up the claim with evidence. They are focused on themselves as the objects of Yahweh's love and demand proof that is particular to them. Instead, Yahweh's response seems to diverge and focuses on Esau as an example of the antithetical aspect of love: hate.

We might have been expecting a Torah story itemizing Yahweh's key acts of benevolence on behalf of Israel (e.g., Mic 6:3–5),[18] but instead we read a list of malevolent deeds toward Edom. Where we might expect a recounting of Yahweh's acts since the judgment that resulted in exile, we find a focus on the distant past, relating directly to the ancestors—a focus on the collective experiences rather than the specific experiences of the current generation (cf. Isa 43:5–6; 51:5; 65:9; Jer 24:6; 28:3; 30:3; 32:37, 42). Compare:

> I will let you find me, says the Lord, and I will restore your fortunes and gather you from all the nations and all the places where I have driven you, says the Lord, and I will bring you back to the place from which I sent you into exile. (Jer 29:14 NRSV)

The reference in Malachi to the distant past seems evasive, since the experiences of the current and recent generations produced skepticism about Yahweh's love. Recollections about the Torah story usually focus on the collective experiences of past generations. The difference here, however, is that this recollection does not focus directly on acts of benevolence toward the chosen people but on the act of choosing from which the benevolence ensued.

C. YAHWEH'S RESPONSE TO ISRAEL'S CHALLENGE: PRESENTATION OF EVIDENCE (1:2b–5)

Yahweh's response begins with the rhetorical question, *Is not Esau Jacob's brother?* The fact that Esau and Jacob were brothers is made clear in Gen 25:22–24, which identifies them as twins within Rebekah's womb. While the

18. Jacobs, *Conceptual Coherence.*

term *ʾāḥ* is used of kin generally, here in Mal 1:2 it has the specific meaning of brother, male sibling. It also has this nuance in several other passages that depict the relationship between Esau and Jacob. Thus in Num 20:14–21 Moses sent messengers from Kadesh to Edom to request passage through the land. He used the relationship between Israel and Edom as the basis of his request and gave Edom Israel's biography to show the adversities that Israel had suffered. Despite this tailored argument, Edom refused to grant Israel passage through the land, forcing Israel to go around Edom. The situation illustrates the animosity between the nations, and the memory of their progenitors is still evident. The Deity's response to the challenge to provide evidence of love for Israel also presumes the people's knowledge of the relationship between Jacob and Esau as a component of their current tradition and identity.

Yahweh also declares, *so I have loved Jacob*. The story of Esau and Jacob depicts a situation of preferential love and trickery as well as juxtaposition of the divine and human wills in contention with each other (Gen 27). The narrative depicts Isaac's disfavor toward Esau as heir to the covenant that had been made with him (Isaac). Whatever Esau's behavior was subsequent to the choice of Jacob, it appears that Esau acted in ways that corresponded to that preference for Jacob.[19] Without being mutually exclusive, the multivalence of the Genesis narrative shows that neither God nor Rebekah favored or perceived Esau as being Isaac's heir. Genesis clearly states that Isaac loved Esau and Rebekah loved Jacob, but it does not report God's regard for either Jacob or Esau (Gen 25:28). Thus, the claim in Mal 1:2 represents the tradition in a way that illuminates the Deity's role in Jacob's place in his family and the history of his people. While the claim depicts the favored one as being loved and the disfavored one as being hated, it does not qualify the nature or extent of this love.

1. Rhetorical Question (1:2bα)

The question-answer schema is evident in this rhetorical question. The basis of the question is the nature of the divine-human relationship. The question introduces the disputational tone of the relationship. On the one hand, it suggests that the people dispute whether the Deity loves them. On the other

19. D. J. Elazar, "Jacob and Esau and the Emergence of the Jewish People," *Judaism* 43 (1994): 294–301. Elazar suggests that part of the preference for Jacob rather than Esau may have been Esau's character, which became evident in his choice to sell his birthright and to marry foreign women. Cf. J. Rackman, "Was Isaac Deceived?" *Judaism* 43 (1994): 37–45. Rackman proposes that Isaac was planning to bless Jacob but was trying to find a way of doing so without offending Esau.

hand, the question is a challenge to the Deity to verify the existence of God's love.

2. Statement of the Comparison (1:2bβ–5)

The comparison is between Jacob and Esau and promotes the idea that God selected to love Jacob and to hate Esau. The declaration clearly identifies the sibling relationship of the two human agents who are identified. The central agent in the declaration is the Deity, and the declaration responds to the question about how the Deity has loved the community.

a. Declaration of Love for Jacob (1:2bβ)

Loving and hating are the two divine actions that are highlighted. The community to whom the message is being delivered is presumably the object of the Deity's love. The immediate juxtaposition of the contrast regarding Esau may have been for the purpose of demonstrating the difference between love and hate as manifested in the Deity's behavior.

b. Declaration of Hatred for Esau (1:3–5)

3 Yahweh's response also provides a contrast between love (*'āhēb*) and hate (*śānē'*). These concepts are typically placed together to depict antithetical behavior—"love evil and hate good" (2 Sam 19:6; 2 Chr 19:2; Mic 3:1–2; Ps 52:3 [MT 5]; cf. Prov 12:1; 13:24; 14:20).

(1) The Statement (1:3a)

Following the declaration of love for Jacob, Yahweh declares, *but Esau I have hated.* As with the concept of love, hate is depicted within various types of relationship that fall into the two categories of human-human and divine-human. Among the human-human relationships, the male-female (husband-wife) relationship is most prevalent. Jacob loved Rachel and hated Leah (Gen 29:18; 29:33). The text also quantifies Jacob's regard for each of the sisters: he loved Rachel more than Leah (Gen 29:30). In this instance, the quantification constitutes the difference between love and hate. Furthermore, the qualitative differences may be signaled by Jacob's behavior toward the beloved. Similarly, one may note Delilah's challenge to Samson that his behavior does not demonstrate love (Judg 16:15). She claims that he does not love her because, if he did, he would behave differently toward her. As with the Jacob narrative (Gen 29), assertions about love or hate are built on the evaluation of behavior; Israel's evaluation of Yahweh's behavior results in doubt (Mal 1:2). The evaluation itself has criteria by which "love" and "hate" are measured. For Israel, the criteria possibly included deliverance from suffering, granting of prosperity, and possibly even the inauguration of a messianic age that coincided with the restoration of the temple and affiliated cultic and administrative realities.

In the parent-child relationship, preferential love is also represented as a quantification of love: for example, Jacob loved Joseph more than he loved his other sons (Gen 37:3–4). The sibling relationship also manifests hate, usually because of a perception of a parent's preference for someone's sibling. Joseph's brothers hated him (Gen 37:4–5, 8) because their father favored him. Furthermore, Jacob's love for Joseph is an outgrowth of his love for Joseph's mother, Rachel. Thus the love-hate dynamics within the human-human relationships are seen to perpetuate themselves. Likewise, Esau is said to hate Jacob because Isaac conferred the blessing on him (Gen 27:41). In both of these instances, behaviors or events accompany and represent the claim of hate. Similarly, Yahweh's love and hate are manifested in behaviors and events: Yahweh follows the proclamation of hate for Esau by stating how that hate has been manifested. The correspondence of the hate and malevolent action demonstrates that, even in the divine-human relationship, hate is the source of adversarial relationships between the person doing the hating and the person who is hated.

Some are reluctant to regard God's inclination toward Jacob and Esau as qualitatively different; instead, they argue that the difference is simply quantitative—loving Jacob more than Esau (cf. Gen 29:30).[20] The reluctance is understandable because the Genesis narrative contains no assertion that God hated Esau. There, the distinction between them appears to be a choice for Jacob, who moves in a conciliatory effort toward Esau. By comparison, Mal 1:3 asserts that Yahweh hated Esau, thus re-signifying the behaviors narrated in Genesis. Petersen asserts that "what Rebekah and Jacob had done earlier is now attributed to Yahweh, though of course, one might say that the oracle in Gen 25:23 already foreshadows the Deity's position on the relationship between Jacob and Esau."[21]

20. Petersen, *Zechariah 9–14 and Malachi,* 169. Cf. E. Assis, "Why Edom? On the Hostility towards Jacob's Brother in Prophetic Sources," *VT* 56 (2006): 1–20; B. Dicou, *Edom, Israel's Brother and Antagonist: The Role of Edom in Biblical Prophecy and Story,* JSOTSup 169 (Sheffield: Sheffield Academic, 1994); J. J. Krause, "Tradition, History, and Our Story: Some Observations on Jacob and Esau in the Books of Obadiah and Malachi," *JSOT* 32 (2008): 475–86.

21. Petersen, *Zechariah 9–14 and Malachi,* 169.

Usually, at the foundation of this interpretation of the contrast is the theological belief that God does not hate but may prefer one person to another. In part, this ideology depicts God's preservation of those who receive less love. Clearly, however, Mal 1:3 states that Yahweh loves and hates. The Deity's action toward the object is only one factor differentiating love from hate. The nature of the commitment to love versus hate determines the Deity's behavior to a person/people. One also notes a tolerance for the object of hatred—a toleration for its existence rather than a constructive effort toward its advancement and well-being. The most accurate understanding of the theological ideology is that the Deity does hate and love and does so in such a way that less love is equated with hate and is manifested in malevolent actions.

(2) Evidence Substantiating the Claim (1:3b–4)

In this context, the presentation of this and the subsequently identified actions echoes the Torah story, which usually manifests Yahweh's deeds on behalf of the people (cf. Mic 6:1–5). It is clear that Yahweh attributes the acts of malevolence to Yahweh just as much as those of benevolence. This attribution uses the first-person account, *I put his mountains to desolation.* In Mal 1:3 as elsewhere, Yahweh takes ownership for the adversities that have characterized a person's or nation's existence. Two actions demonstrate Yahweh's hatred for Esau and for the nation of Edom. Using one verb (*wāʾāśîm*)[22] in the *qal* first common singular with two objects (*hārāyw* and *naḥălātô*), Yahweh claims responsibility for the devastation experienced by Esau. Additionally, the use of the third masculine singular suffixes referring to Esau clarifies that the actions were taken against Esau, against "his mountains" (*hārāyw*) and "his inheritance" (*naḥălātô*). While the actions are reported in sequence, that does not mean that this is a chronological reporting of the actions. The concern is not about which happened first or second but that Yahweh effected both actions against Esau.

Employing language typically used to depict the destruction or abandonment of lands or cities, the text portrays the mountains as being turned into a waste (*šəmāmâ,* e.g., Exod 23:29; Lev 26:33; Josh 8:28; Isa 17:9; 64:10 [MT 9]; Jer 4:27). A typical characteristic of mountains is their durability; they outlast humans and are thus able to witness God's work throughout history (Mic 6:1–2).[23] The mountains to which the speech refers most likely include Mount Seir of Edom. Furthermore, Esau's inheritance will be *made . . . into a desert for the jackals,* an image that is consistent with the desolation

22. The clause is formed by the *waw*-consecutive first-person form of *śîm,* "to put, place," plus its two objects, each signaled by *ʾet,* the sign of the direct object.

23. Jacobs, *Conceptual Coherence.*

of the mountains. According to Deut 2:4–5, Israel is told not to do battle with Edom. The cited rationale is that Yahweh would not give any of Edom's land to Israel because that land had already been given (*nātan*) to Esau as a possession (*yəruššâ*). Similarly, the prohibition on engaging in battle against Moab and Ammon is articulated on the basis of Yahweh's having given the land to someone other than Israel—that is, Lot's descendants (Deut 2:9, 19). Thus it appears that in some instances Yahweh safeguards the possessions of the particular nations to whom they were given—even protects them from Yahweh's favored people. In these instances, Yahweh safeguards others against Yahweh's favorite by forbidding battle and guaranteeing that the favored will be unsuccessful in taking a particular land. From a historical perspective, one may ask whether Edom experienced such destruction as is depicted in several texts, including Jer 9:10 (MT 9); 23:10; Joel 1:19, 20; 2:20. Without specifying the mode or human agency of the destruction, Mal 1:3 depicts the annihilation of Esau/Edom. That destruction confirms Yahweh's hatred: despite Yahweh's choice to make Esau/Edom valuable, he is still nonessential to the Deity's plan.

4 Yahweh's choice—rather than Edom's own determination—defines Edom's existence, as Yahweh illustrates by the following scenario (Mal 1:4). In the statement *if Edom says* (*kî-tō'mar 'ĕdôm*), the *kî* clause represents the protasis (condition), which is followed by Edom's words. The particle *kô*, "thus," introduces the apodosis (consequence). The protasis provides the basis for the subsequent assertion.[24] The force of the protasis is contested mainly because of the condition that it depicts. Thus it has been argued on grammatical grounds that the "condition here is *irreal* in that it . . . is incapable of fulfillment."[25] The disagreement over this point appears in the LXX as well as modern translations. Thus the LXX reads, ". . . because one will say, 'Edom has been overthrown'" (*dioti erei . . . katestraptai*). The NIV reads, "Edom may say"; the NEB "when." The NRSV sees the conditional nuance of the *kî* clause, thus reading, "If Edom says."[26] The *kî* clause also introduces the name Edom (*'ĕdôm*) into the disputation and by virtue of the conceptual and historical contexts links Esau and Edom. Genesis 25:30 cites an etiological basis for the connection between Esau and Edom—"Esau said to Jacob, 'Let me eat some of that red stuff, for I am famished!' (Therefore he was called Edom)." This link is also forged by equating the two names (Gen 32:3; 36:1, 8, 19, 43; cf. Obad 8). Historically, the land of Edom is also known as land of

24. The *qal* imperfect form *tō'mar* has two possibilities: third feminine singular or second masculine singular form of *'āmar*, "to say," whose subject is *'ĕdôm*.

25. Hill, *Malachi*, 156. He cites the following as support for his assertion: *IBHS* §§38.2a, d, c; 39.3.4e; Williams, *Syntax*, §446.

26. Cf. Hill, *Malachi*, 156.

Seir (Gen 32:3; 36:8). Several clans occupied that land, including the clans of Eliphaz and of Reuel, Esau's son (Gen 36:16–17). Furthermore, Edom was a nation ruled by kings even before Israel had kings (Gen 36:31). The condition that some believe to be *irreal* is the restoration of Edom, not its destruction.

The reported words *we are beaten down* precede the idea of restoration. Malachi 1:4 depicts the hypothetical situation in which Edom is doing what Israel was hesitant to do, namely, to rebuild (cf. Hag 1:2–11). According to Jeremiah's prophecy of the seventy-year return to the land, God promised to bring the people back to Jerusalem (Jer 25:11–12). In that prophecy, the question of agency comes to the fore. Likewise, in Mal 1:4 questions of agency arise, such as, who is going to restore Edom? In the latter instance, Edom would instigate its own return and restoration, and its plans for itself are different from God's plan for it. First, the nation recognizes that it has been beaten down (*ruššašnû*; *pual* perfect first common plural of *rāšaš*). In its other occurrence, in Jer 5:17, the verb *rāšaš* is used in the *poel* imperfect third masculine singular (*yərōšēš*), indicating that someone will beat down the fortified city in which the people have placed their trust. Elsewhere, Edom is also characterized as the fortified city (Ps 60:9 [MT 10]//108:10 [MT 11]), suggesting that it has a means of self-protection. Edom's ability to protect itself does not secure it from all destruction; thus, it might consider what would happen if it were beaten down.

Given the eventuality of its destruction, Edom plans to return and rebuild: *but we will return and rebuild the ruins*. The intention is represented by the first common plural forms *wənāšûb* and *wənibnê*. The sequence of actions presumes the first action, "to return" (*šûb*), as being necessary to the second, "to build" (*bānâ*). Verhoef acknowledges that the literal meaning of the clause is "we will return and rebuild" but argues that the main idea is presented by the second verb, *bānâ* (to build), while the first, *šûb* (to return), indicates "the manner of the action."[27] Notably, many modern translations follow this option, such as the NIV and NRSV, "but we will rebuild the ruins." The issue is whether the verb *šûb* functions as an independent or an auxiliary verb. As an independent verb, *šûb* would indicate a repatriation of the land.[28] This possibility must be considered, especially in light of the use of *šûb* to speak of return to Yahweh (Mal 2:6; 3:7; 4:6 [MT 3:24]). More fitting to the idea of repatriation, however, is the juxtaposition of Edom and Israel within the disputation—namely, Edom's willingness to return to its land in light of Judah's consent to return (with encouragement and support). While some refused to return, others returned to rebuild Jerusalem (Hag 1:14; 2:18; Zech 1:16; 8:3).

27. Verhoef, *Haggai and Malachi,* 205; cf. GKC §120d; Petersen, *Zechariah 9–14 and Malachi,* 171.

28. Cf. R. L. Smith, *Micah–Malachi,* 304. Hill (*Malachi,* 156) cites but does not favor this interpretation.

As an auxiliary verb, *šûb* may be used with *bānâ* to represent the idea of rebuilding.[29] Hill cites the use of *šûb* in Yahweh's response as further support for seeing it as an auxiliary verb.[30] Notably, *šûb* is not repeated in Yahweh's response. At this point the LXX reads: "But let us return and rebuild the desolate places" (*kai epistrepsomen kai anoikodomesomen*). One may then ask, if the idea of rebuilding is represented by the compound verb in the protasis (condition), why is it altered in the apodosis (consequence)? Yet another question is whether the idea of rebuilding is represented elsewhere with an auxiliary verb. Since the occurrence here in Mal 1:4 is unique, it should be given attention in this context. Even if the focus is on the rebuilding, the return is acknowledged as a prerequisite and as an indication that this refers to a restoration of the Edomite territory—the land given to the Edomites, which they occupied until its destruction (see map 2). Whatever Yahweh's preference for Israel versus Edom, Yahweh intended to honor the commitment to Edom and would not allow Israel to dispossess Edom (Deut 2:4–5).[31] Nevertheless, the preferential treatment of safeguarding Edom included only limited protection from the Deity. Accordingly, Ezekiel prophesied Edom's destruction:

> Thus says the Lord GOD: I am against you, Mount Seir; I stretch out my hand against you to make you a desolation and a waste. I lay your towns in ruins; you shall become a desolation, and you shall know that I am the Lord. (Ezek 35:3–4 NRSV)

That the two nations to whom Yahweh had given land were destroyed speaks to the similarities between Edom and Israel. However, the difference between the two nations is their response to their destruction and Yahweh's plan for each nation. One initiates its own return (Edom); the other's return is orchestrated and prophesied (Judah/Israel). That contrast is crucial to Yahweh's argumentation. So while it is grammatically feasible to see *šûb* as a compound verb that functions as an auxiliary verb, its use as an independent verb is favored here because of its significance to the framework of the text—namely, the contrast between the fate of the two nations, lands, judgments, and future prospects.

Rebuilding is possible for any nation, and other nations may have attempted to rebuild after a period of desolation. Pointing to the Isaiah text here is simply to highlight the contrast between Edom's plan and Yahweh's plan—

29. GKC §120d; *IBHS* §39.3.1b.

30. Hill, *Malachi*, 156.

31. P. C. Craigie, *The Book of Deuteronomy*, NICOT (Grand Rapids: Eerdmans, 1976), 108.

hypothetically speaking (Isa 34). From the apodosis in Mal 1:4, it is clear that Edom may be successful in its rebuilding; and without that possibility, the apodosis makes little sense. As evidence of Yahweh's love for Israel, Yahweh's continued preferential treatment of Israel (Jacob) over Edom (Esau) is highlighted as a perpetual historical phenomenon.

Because of the aforementioned issue that the condition presented is *irreal,* I think that a brief note about the historical viability of the condition may be helpful in understanding Mal 1:4. Several passages prophesy and depict Edom's destruction, as shown in the discussion of Mal 1:3.[32] Regarding the possible time frame and circumstances of Edom's demise[33] and restoration,[34] the text's statement that "we will return" (*wənāšûb*) presupposes that the Edomites were away from their land, much as was Israel, their northern neighbor. While we cannot determine historical validity based solely on the use of this language, we can make some observations on the basis of the expression. The return could mean that the Edomites, like the Israelites from Judah, were subjected to something similar to the Babylonian deportation of conquered peoples. Like some Israelites who fled to Egypt, some Edomites fled their land to escape the destruction. One must therefore contend with references to Edom's being a place of refuge for those fleeing Judah (587 BCE; Jer 40:11). Presumably, the two nations were not simultaneously destroyed, since Edom was able to receive refugees from Judah. Even though the simultaneous destruction of Edom and Judah is unlikely, a deportation of the Edomite population could have taken place in at least two periods: during Nabonidus's campaigns (552 BCE) or during the gradual infiltration of the Nabateans.[35]

Looking at the possibility of return, the other part of the scenario in 1:4 is that the Edomites planned to *rebuild the ruins (wənibnê ḥŏrābôt).* The prospect of rebuilding assumes the destruction of Edom (cf. Mal 1:3)—in other words, that it was desolate (*ḥŏrābôt*). The feminine noun (*ḥārəbâ* sing.; *ḥŏrābôt* pl.) is used of cities or towns, including Jerusalem and other cities/towns of Israel and Judah (Isa 44:26; Jer 25:18; Ezek 36:10, 33) and of Edom (Ezek 25:13). Much like Judah, Edom would be rebuilding what was ruined, presumably at the site of the ruins. However, Isaiah and Ezekiel prophesy the destruction of the nation and focus on its total demise.

32. Cf. Jer 9:10 (MT 9); 23:10; Joel 1:19, 20; 2:20; Ps 65:12 [MT 13]. Verhoef, *Haggai and Malachi,* 203.

33. Verhoef, *Haggai and Malachi,* 203–4.

34. Verhoef, *Haggai and Malachi,* 204; Hill, *Malachi,* 168–70.

35. Petersen, *Zechariah 9–14 and Malachi,* 170–72. See bibliographical references in: Hill, *Malachi,* 167; Glazier-McDonald, *Malachi: The Divine Messenger,* 30–44; Weyde, *Prophecy and Teaching,* 87–70.

> And the streams of Edom shall be turned into pitch, and her soil into sulfur; her land shall become burning pitch. Night and day it shall not be quenched; its smoke shall go up forever. From generation to generation it shall lie waste; no one shall pass through it forever and ever. (Isa 34:9–10 NRSV)

and

> I will make Mount Seir a waste and a desolation; and I will cut off from it all who come and go. I will fill its mountains with the slain; on your hills and in your valleys and in all your watercourses those killed with the sword shall fall. I will make you a perpetual desolation, and your cities shall never be inhabited. Then you shall know that I am the Lord. (Ezek 35:7–9 NRSV)

In Isaiah and Ezekiel, Edom's destruction will be permanent, while in Mal 1:4, Edom's hypothetical presumption is that the ruins are temporary. Another contrast involves the agents—the Deity and the human agents representing two distinct and competing perspectives. On the one hand, the Deity intends the land to be desolate. On the other hand, human beings strive to rebuild it. Likewise, the Deity decides that the desolation will be permanent, while the people attempt to make the desolation temporary.

The messenger formula, *thus says Yahweh of hosts* (*kô ʾāmar yhwh ṣəbāʾôt),* introduces the apodosis (consequence) of the *kî* + *kô* formulation and designates the message as Yahweh's (Mal 1:4–5). Other instances of the formula include *ʾāmar yhwh* (Mal 1:2, 13; 3:13; Hag 1:8); *ʾāmar yhwh ṣəbāʾôt* (Mal 1:6, 8, 9, 10, 11, 13, 14; 2:2, 4, 8; 3:1, 5, 7, 10, 11, 12, 17; 4:1 [MT 3:19]); with *kô ʾāmar yhwh ṣəbāʾôt* (Mal 1:4; cf. Hag 1:2, 5, 7; 2:6, 11; Zech 1:3, 4, 14, 17; 3:7; 6:12; 7:9; 8:2, 4, 6, 7, 9, 14, 19, 20, 23); and *kô-ʾāmar yhwh* (e.g., Amos 5:16; 7:17; Mic 3:5; Zech 1:16; 8:3). The frequency of the occurrence is noteworthy because it is an indication of the centrality of the divine message and an affirmation of the Deity's participation in the sequence of events.[36]

The messenger formula also introduces the apodosis as a viable possibility inasmuch as it is the Deity's perspective. The deterrent to Edom's behavior is not that the rebuilding is *irreal* or impossible; rather, the claim for the condition depicted *is* possible. At issue is how Yahweh will respond to Edom—a response that will be born out of Yahweh's choice regarding Israel. Does the text represent a dichotomy in which love for one people necessarily

36. Cf. Hill, *Malachi,* 157–58. See Part One: Haggai of this commentary for a discussion of *ṣəbāʾôt.*

means hatred of all others? Most likely it does not represent mutually exclusive categories defined by the limitation of divine love. Perhaps, if anything, it reflects the Deity's choice about whom to love rather than a limited quantity of love, sufficient for only one object or people.

Yahweh's planned action is contrasted to Edom's: *they will/may rebuild, but I myself will destroy.* The juxtaposition of the two efforts may reflect the futility curse pattern that was already noted above, in the discussion of Hag 1:6–11 (cf. Mic 6:9–11; Deut 28:38–44);[37] however, the anticipated efforts by Edom deviate from that pattern. The imperfect form of the verb *bānâ* (to build) is preceded by the third masculine plural independent pronoun *hēmmâ,* "they." The actors and actions are emphasized by pairing the independent pronouns and verbs *hēmmâ* + *yibnû* (they [Edom] will build) followed by *'ănî* + *'ehərôs* (but I [Yahweh] will destroy). *They will/may rebuild:* The verb *yibnû* is the *qal* imperfect third masculine plural form of *bānâ,* "to build," and its implied subject is Edom. Modern translations and commentators differ in their understanding of *yibnû.* Some continue the conditional nuance—see the NEB: "If they rebuild" (carrying on the conditional element from the first part of Mal 1:4). The NIV and NRSV interpret *yibnû* as a volitional jussive, thus rendering "they may rebuild."[38] Others see a jussive, "let them build" (NJB). Hill cites two reasons for preferring the jussive reading: it fits the "rhetorical nature of the disputation and emphasizes the authority and power of Yahweh as sovereign of the nations."[39] Although I portray the jussive here to show possibility and to maintain the contrast, the text's portrayal of possibility does already underlie the dynamics of the divine-human interaction.

Yahweh frustrates Israel's effort when Israel refuses to rebuild. When Israel attempts to rebuild, Yahweh enables, supports, encourages, and even guarantees Judah's success in its rebuilding efforts (Hag 2). In contrast, in Mal 1:3–4 Yahweh will allow the Edomites to rebuild but destroy the product of their labor. Consequently, their efforts may be successful, but the frustration will come when they lose what they have restored. Analogy to the curses is evident in the destructive force of Yahweh's involvement, not necessarily in the futility of efforts to accomplish a task. Unlike Deut 28, the Malachi text does not specify the connection between the curse and the Edomites' action; that connection may be part of the tradition of the futility curses. Nonetheless, Yahweh's commitment to Edom's destruction raises questions regarding Yahweh's response to the nations: Are nations other than Israel subject to

37. See Part One: Haggai of this commentary.

38. Cf. Verhoef, *Haggai and Malachi,* 194, "Edom's intention vs. Yahweh's resolution"; R. L. Smith, *Micah–Malachi,* 304; Petersen, *Zechariah 9–14 and Malachi,* 165.

39. Hill, *Malachi,* 158.

these curses because of their disobedience to Yahweh? And on what basis are other nations accountable to Yahweh?

In the election-of-Israel tradition, the curses against the nations may be due to their treatment of Israel—"I will bless those who bless you, and the one who curses you I will curse; and in you all the families of the earth shall be blessed" (Gen 12:3). However, the possibility of Yahweh's curse on Edom appears to be outside this particular aspect of the Deuteronomistic tradition, even though it is central to the election tradition. Perhaps the first reason for the divine response to Edom is Yahweh's choice and the ensuing behavior put in place to maintain and represent the nature and vitality of the constitutive relationships. Any subsequent behavior—that is, wickedness by Edom—may be significant to Yahweh's response to the nation; but in Mal 1:4 the connection to the election tradition is the fundamental basis for Yahweh's treatment of Edom. In the election tradition, Israel did not secure Yahweh's love by being good any more than Edom secured Yahweh's hatred by being wicked. The dynamics of divine-human will are inescapable in this understanding of Yahweh's behavior toward Edom. That is to say, one cannot ignore the representation of Edom as not being in control of its existence. Yahweh has defined what happens to the nation, and here also Yahweh is in control. The contrast between "they" (Edom) and Yahweh ("I") conveys this control.

The destruction of Edom is consistent with other images of Edom's destruction in the prophetic texts. According to Yahweh, *I myself will destroy.* The verb *ʾehərôs* is the *qal* imperfect first common singular of *hāras*, "throw down, break, tear down," and appears here in the first-person singular form, with Yahweh as the implied subject. The verb *hāras* is used elsewhere to describe the destruction of cities (Isa 14:17; 2 Sam 11:25; 2 Kgs 3:25; 1 Chr 20:1); of implements of national security, including walls and strongholds (Ezek 13:14; 26:12; Lam 2:2; Mic 5:10); and of altars (Judg 6:25; 1 Kgs 18:30; 14:10, 14). Without a specified object, *hāras* (tear down) appears in Jer 24:6 and 42:10 (cf. Jer 45:4). Its connection with *bānâ* (to build) also appears in several texts (Jer 1:10; cf. Ezek 36:26; Ps 28:5; Prov 14:1; Job 12:14).[40] In Mal 1:4 the objects of the verbs are not expressed, but the image is inescapable. Yahweh will tear down (referring to what Edom builds up). Although reference to Edom may point to the physical structures of the city, it could also indicate the administrative, social, and religious infrastructure of the nation. Whatever the content of the reference, the image shows a difference between the efforts of two agents—human (Edom) and divine (Yahweh). Elsewhere Yahweh is also depicted as being responsible for Edom's devastation; thus, Edom is characterized as the object of the Deity's judgment (Isa 34:5). Likewise, Yahweh planned to ravage Edom and its warriors.

40. Cf. Hill, *Malachi,* 158.

> Therefore hear the plan that the Lord has made against Edom and the purposes that he has formed against the inhabitants of Teman: Surely the little ones of the flock shall be dragged away; surely their fold shall be appalled at their fate. . . . Look, he shall mount up and swoop down like an eagle, and spread his wings against Bozrah, and the heart of the warriors of Edom in that day shall be like the heart of a woman in labor. (Jer 49:20–22 NRSV)[41]

The transition within the 1:2b–5 subunit is introduced by *waw* + verb construction, *then they will call them the territory of wickedness.* The verb *wəqārəʾû* is the *qal* converted perfect third masculine plural of *qārāʾ,* "call," followed by the object.[42] The passive nuance of the third masculine plural is a viable option for this term: "they will be called."[43] That the proverbial "they" will call them (the Edomites) a name reveals that Edom will gain a particular reputation that ensues from Yahweh's actions against it. This is analogous to the theme of the temple, which was reputable due to its destroyed, desolate status.

> This house will become a heap of ruins; everyone passing by it will be astonished, and will hiss; and they will say, "Why has the Lord done such a thing to this land and to this house?" (1 Kgs 9:8 NRSV)[44]

Likewise, Jeremiah reflects analogous circumstances leading to or perhaps constitutive of Edom's reputation:

> Edom shall become an object of horror; everyone who passes by it will be horrified and will hiss because of all its disasters. (Jer 49:17 NRSV)

As to the naming of Edom—*territory of wickedness*—the same sort of naming is depicted elsewhere using the preposition *lə* plus the verb *qārāʾ*. It is used of a nation, city, or place (Gen 31:47; Exod 33:7; Deut 2:11, 20; cf. Gen 1:5, 8, 10); or of a person or animal (Gen 35:18; cf. 2:19). In some cases the name is a phrase: Yahweh is my banner (Exod 17:15); Yahweh is peace (Judg 6:24). The formulation *qārāʾ* plus the noun *šēm*, "name," serves a similar function, particularly as an etiological element; for example: the quarreling or cessation

41. Cf. Ezek 25; 35; Joel 3:19 (MT 4:19).

42. The object is indicated by the preposition *lə* affixed to the third masculine plural suffix *lāhem*, "them." Hill (*Malachi,* 158) sees this as the indirect object.

43. Cf. Verhoef, *Haggai and Malachi,* 194; Petersen, *Zechariah 9–14 and Malachi,* 165; GKC §144f–g.

44. Cf. Lam 2:15.

of quarrels leading to the naming of the wells (Sitnah and Rehoboth in Gen 26:21–23); and the naming of locations (Marah in Exod 15:23; Massah and Meribah in Exod 17:7; cf. 1 Kgs 7:21; 2 Kgs 14:7). Typically, an event gives rise to an entity's name and thus the name reflects the incident—in other words, gives rise to its etiology. The connection between the name "territory of wickedness" in Mal 1:4 and Edom is not readily apparent, since neither the preceding nor the subsequent elements depict actions characterized as "wicked." Thus far it has been said of Edom that the Deity selected it as an object of hate and dealt with it accordingly. It is also depicted as a nation that may be diligent in its futile attempt at self-preservation. So why would it be called "territory of wickedness" (*gəbûl riš'â*)?

The first element of the name is "territory," *gəbûl*, which can mean "border." Malachi 1:4 does not refer to "the land of Edom" (*'ereṣ 'ĕdôm*—Gen 36:17, 21, 31; Num 20:23; Judg 11:18; 1 Kgs 9:26; 1 Chr 1:43; 2 Chr 8:17; Isa 34:6) or to "the land of Seir, the region of Edom" (*'arṣâ śē'îr śədê 'ĕdôm*—Gen 32:3 [MT 4]; cf. 36:21). Joshua 15:1 and 21 refer to the border of Edom (*gəbûl 'ĕdôm*) to indicate a point of demarcation—that is, the southern boundary of Judah (cf. Num 33:37). Usually "region of Edom" is also indicated by *śədê 'ĕdôm* (Judg 5:4; Gen 32:3 [MT 4]; cf. Num 21:20, of Moab).[45] The term *gəbûl* may signify Edom as a geopolitical entity vis-à-vis a border or point of demarcation (see map 2). In comparison, the use of *gəbûl* in Mal 1:5 (*ligbûl yiśrā'ēl*) may illustrate the use of the term to denote the point of demarcation, that is, border.

The epithet "territory of wickedness" seems incongruous with the descriptive sequence about Edom. Intratextually (within this text), Edom is presented as one whom Yahweh hates because Yahweh has chosen to hate. Yahweh's hatred, like the Deity's love, is compelled by Yahweh's choice. Just as Jacob/Israel did nothing to merit Yahweh's love, so Esau/Edom did nothing to merit Yahweh's hate.[46] Yahweh's love and hate is an anomaly with regard to the peoples being described. The descriptor *riš'â,* "wicked, wickedness," may refer to the nature and practices of a country (cf. Mal 3:15; 4:1 [MT 3:19]).[47] Notably, *riš'â* is used to characterize both "the nations" (Deut 9:4) and Israel (Ezek 5:6).

Understanding the epithet thus depends on understanding the traditions regarding Edom. Why call it a territory of wickedness? What would have solicited this name? The election tradition is not the source of the name but the nation's behavior subsequent to its election. Edom's election as an object

45. Cf. Petersen, *Zechariah 9–14 and Malachi,* 171; he cites Num 32:33.

46. Contrast Hill, *Malachi,* 159.

47. M. Weinfeld, *Deuteronomy 1–11: A New Translation with Introduction and Commentary,* AB 5 (New York: Doubleday, 1991), 406. Hill (*Malachi,* 159) understands the wickedness to be idolatry, referring to Zech 5:6. Note that Zech 5:6 uses *'ayin* rather than *rāša'*.

of the Deity's hatred is no more based on its wickedness than Israel's election is based on its goodness. The prophetic tradition attests the wickedness of Israel, who is elect and beloved (e.g., Amos 3; Mic 3; Isaiah). Thus, retribution does underlie the epithet's connection between the perceived devastation and the nation's behavior (wickedness), but retribution is not the sole basis. The use of *riš'â* in Deut 9:1–5 places it in contrast to one of its antonyms, *ṣedeq*, "righteousness." The nations' loss of their lands and Israel's gain are connected; however, the nations' "wickedness" (*riš'â*) is the reason for their loss, not Israel's righteousness (*ṣədāqâ*). Seeing Mal 1:4 in this light would mean that Edom's devastation is a consequence of Edom's wickedness—a sequence exemplified elsewhere (e.g., Gen 18:16–33; 1 Kgs 8:32).[48] Instead, Edom's devastation is due to the prior choice by the Deity to treat it in a particular way and thus to determine the course of its existence.

The second part of Edom's epithet in 1:4 focuses on the people (*hā'ām*), and the modifier is introduced by the relative particle (*'ăšer*)—*the people whom Yahweh has cursed forever*. The relative clause identifies Yahweh as part of the modifier of the verb *zā'am*, "to injure, to curse, to be indignant," and creates a wordplay: *hā'ām—zā'am*. While many scholars translate *zā'am* "curse," one must be aware of the context in understanding the term.[49] Thus Hill joins those who translate *zā'am* "curse" on the grounds that it depicts the "national judgment" and the nature of curses in general.[50] Glazier-McDonald cites Num 23:7 and Prov 24:24 as instances where *zā'am* occurs in parallelism with other terms: *'arar*, "curse," and *qābab*, "to utter a curse against."[51] Petersen translates *zā'am* "curse" in both Mal 1:4 and Zech 1:12, "which you have cursed for these past seventy years." He identifies the language of lament as the context of the occurrence (cf. Ps 7:11).[52] One fundamental question to ask is: who is the subject of the verb? Those who translate *zā'am* "curse" understand Yahweh as the subject and the people as object: Yahweh cursed the people.[53] On the other hand, could the people (masculine singular) be

48. Compare Ezek 18:5–20. Cf. Verhoef, *Haggai and Malachi*, 205; C. van Leeuwen, "רָשָׁע," *TLOT* 3:1263–64.

49. The verb *zā'am* appears in several texts, such as Num 23:7; Zech 1:12; Prov 24:24; 25:23. The noun form used of "anger, wrath" appears in Isa 10:5; 13:5; 26:20; 30:27; Jer 10:10; 15:17; 50:25; Ezek 21:31; 22:24; and Nah 1:6.

50. Hill, *Malachi*, 159; cf. Petersen, *Zechariah 9–14 and Malachi*, 167; Glazier-McDonald, *Malachi: The Divine Messenger*, 31, 34.

51. Glazier-McDonald, *Malachi: The Divine Messenger*, 34. She cites the inflected forms *'eqqōb*, "I will curse"; *qabbō*, "he curses"; *yiqqəbuhû*, "he will curse him."

52. Petersen, *Haggai and Zechariah 1–8*, 136, 147; Petersen, *Zechariah 9–14 and Malachi*, 167.

53. Hill, *Malachi*, 159; cf. Petersen, *Zechariah 9–14 and Malachi*, 167; Glazier-McDonald, *Malachi: The Divine Messenger*, 31, 34.

the subject of the verb ("to anger," the third masculine singular)? In the latter case, Yahweh would be the object: the people angered Yahweh. It may be unnecessary to reconfigure the word order to achieve an understanding of Edom's name. Many modern translations read "anger, wrath"; thus, the NIV: "the people always under the wrath of . . .";[54] and the NRSV: "the people with whom the LORD is angry." In Zech 1:12, where it again occurs in a relative clause, *zāʿam* is also translated "anger, wrath."[55]

The other part of the epithet is the temporal indicator *ʿad-ʿôlām*, "forever." As in Zech 1:12, there is a temporal modifier in Mal 1:4—namely, *ʿad-ʿôlām*, thus designating the perpetuity of the entity or condition.[56] Other examples of actions or conditions that are considered perpetual include emotions (such as anger); covenant, *ḥesed* (Ps 18:50 [MT 51]), and judgment; wiping out the name of the nations (Ps 9:5 [MT 6]); Yahweh's enthronement and rule (Ps 9:7 [MT 8]; 10:16; 29:10); and blessing (Ps 45:2 [MT 3]). Zechariah indicates a seventy-year period as the temporal framework for Yahweh's cursing of Jerusalem. If the term *zāʿam* in Mal 1:4 is rendered "curse" with Yahweh as subject, the epithet describes Edom as the people whom Yahweh has cursed forever. This would be consistent with Jer 49:13 with respect to the perpetuity of the judgment and its effect.[57]

> For by myself I have sworn, says the LORD, that Bozrah shall become an object of horror and ridicule, a waste, and an object of cursing; and all her towns shall be perpetual wastes. (Jer 49:13 NRSV)

How does this understanding fit the present context? First, it aligns well with the depiction of Yahweh's judgment on Edom in Mal 1:3–4. Does the label "perpetual" allow any possibility of suspending the judgment, or a break in the perpetuity? The use of *ʿôlām* with reference to the indefinite future may include the life span of a person—for example: a slave forever (Exod 21:6; Deut 15:17); give thanks forever (Ps 30:6 [MT 7]); and sing forever (Ps 89:1). According to Glazier-McDonald, "One of the characteristics of a curse is its unqualified and irrevocable execution and it is this characteristic to which the *ʿad-ʿôlām* alludes."[58] On the other hand, the usage in Zech 1:12 challenges the notion that a curse is irrevocable. Rather, many factors contribute to the

54. Verhoef, *Haggai and Malachi,* 194, 205.

55. Cf. Meyers and Meyers, *Haggai, Zechariah 1–8,* 116–17; Baldwin, *Hag, Zech, Mal,* 223.

56. BDB 761–63.

57. Cf. Hill, *Malachi,* 159–60; Verhoef, *Haggai and Malachi,* 205; Petersen, *Zechariah 9–14 and Malachi,* 167.

58. Glazier-McDonald, *Malachi: The Divine Messenger,* 34 (transliteration provided in place of the Hebrew characters).

extent of a curse: the one making the curse, the one who is to be cursed, and the duration of the curse. Thus, Yahweh may curse for a specified period or for an indefinite period. Even the indefinite, however, may refer to a period that has a conceivable end within given historical parameters.

(3) Effect of the Evidence on Israel (1:5)

5 What Yahweh has done to Edom will be a public matter that will lead Israel to acknowledge Yahweh. *Then your eyes will see* is a portrayal of Israel's response to Yahweh's malevolence toward Edom. Those who sought proof of Yahweh's love will see this evidence. Presumably, the Deity could have presented direct evidence of love toward Israel. Instead, the presentation illustrates Yahweh's hatred for Edom and by implication attests Yahweh's love for Israel. The Deity illustrates what the absence of love looks like and thus challenges Israel to reconsider whether what they have experienced is representative of hate or love. This is indeed a quandary for Israel, who, like Edom, suffered the devastation of its land and infrastructure and the persistent adversity that ensued from being ravaged by other nations. So on the one hand, Israel has Yahweh's claim of love and, on the other, the reality of its history. At best, Israel could draw the conclusion that Yahweh's display is a version of love measured by the Deity's standards. Israel's experience of devastation would suggest that love does not exclude devastation and would thus challenge Israel to understand the nature of a love that manifests in much the same way as hatred for Edom.

The observation *then your eyes will see (wəʿênêkem tirʾênâ)*[59] may signal that the addressees will have a firsthand experience. That experience may include—but not be limited to—the visual observation of an event, place, or entity (Prov 23:33; Isa 33:17, 20; Jer 42:2; cf. Deut 4:9; 7:19; 11:7; 28:34, 67; 2 Chr 34:28), or the mental understanding of occurrences or circumstances: "see and know" (*yirʾû wəyēdəʿû*—Isa 41:20; 44:18; cf. 1 Sam 12:17; 24:11; Jer 2:19). Some modern versions include an object, thus reading: "our own eyes shall see this" (NRSV). Since no object is specified, what the addressees will see is ambiguous. First, they may see Yahweh's love for Israel. The initial declaration and the counterclaim focused on that love; the final element in the substantiation of Yahweh's claim may be summarized in this depiction.[60] Second, the unspecified object may be Edom's plight depicted in the previous verse (Mal 1:4). These two options are complementary aspects of the declaration.

59. The *qal* imperfect third feminine plural form of the verb *rāʾâ*, "to see," whose subject is the feminine plural form of the noun "eye" (*ʿayin*) plus second masculine plural suffix "your" (*kem*).

60. Cf. Hill, *Malachi,* 160.

Whether the declaration equates the exodus event with Edom's devastation is not suggested by this text.[61] Rather, Edom's plight functions in the claim as the antithesis of Yahweh's love for Israel and not merely an object lesson. Accordingly, the unspecified object is the entirety of what Yahweh has done in the larger history of Edom, Israel, and their ancestors.[62]

In addition, Israel will see and affirm Yahweh's greatness, *and you yourself will say, "Great is Yahweh."* In the context of the claim and counterclaim, this shows a progression from the addressees' perception of what Yahweh has done to their affirmation of Yahweh. The dichotomy between the addressees and Yahweh is once again clearly delineated by the use of the second-person pronoun *'attem*. Just as the people contested Yahweh's love for them (Mal 1:2),[63] so they will affirm Yahweh's greatness. The affirmation is signaled by the verb *tō'mrû*—the *qal* imperfect second masculine plural form of *'āmar,* "to say." The statement *Great is Yahweh* appears to be a direct quote of the addressees' affirmation given in response to their witnessing Yahweh's involvement in Edom's and Israel's existence and circumstances. The term *yigdal* is the imperfect verbal form of *gādal,* "to be great" (cf. Ps 104:1), rather than the adjective (*gādôl*) found in many other affirmations of the greatness of Israel's Deity. The designation *'ēl gādôl* is found in several texts (Deut 7:21; 10:17; Ps 95:3). Another designation *gādôl yhwh* may be used in affirming the supremacy of Yahweh as compared with others (Ps 135:5 and Jer 10:6) or simply to affirm Yahweh's greatness (Pss 48:1 [MT 2]; 96:4; 99:2). Likewise, that affirmation is also expressed by *gādôl* in connection with *'ĕlōhîm,*[64] including references to the divine name—*gādôl šəmî* (my name, Mal 1:11), *gādôl šəmô* (his name, Ps 76:1 [MT 2]; Jer 10:6). The verbal form (*yigdal, qal* imperfect third masculine singular) may denote that the Deity is great or is manifested as great (cf. Ps 70:4 [MT 5]).[65] The form *yigdal* may also be understood as a jussive denoting volition—"may Yahweh be great."[66] Basic to these affirmations are the tradition of the Deity's sovereignty in Zion and/or the universal scope of that Deity's power. In the context of Mal 1:5, the affirmation further attests the scope of the Deity's greatness.

61. Contrast Hill, *Malachi,* 160.

62. Cf. Baldwin, *Hag, Zech, Mal,* 224; R. L. Smith, *Micah–Malachi,* 306; Verhoef, *Haggai and Malachi,* 206. He supplies the third singular object, thus reading, *"your own eyes will see it."*

63. Cf. Hill, *Malachi,* 161.

64. Cf. Hill, *Malachi,* 161.

65. See Verhoef, *Haggai and Malachi,* 206. Hill, *Malachi,* 161; P. D. Miller, *They Cried to the Lord: The Form and Theology of Biblical Prayer* (Minneapolis: Fortress, 1994), 358–59. Miller notes the content of what those commanded are to say. While his examples pertain directly to the use of *kî,* Ps 70:4 (MT 5) is also cited as an example of that content.

66. Hill, *Malachi,* 145, 161.

Accordingly, the affirmation of Yahweh's greatness is modified by the phrase *beyond the territory of Israel (mēʿal ligəbûl yiśrāʾēl)*. The understanding of the particle *mēʿal* (followed by the preposition *lə*) has elicited disagreements about the phrase—that is, whether to translate the preposition "above" or "beyond" the borders of Israel and how to understand any distinction between the particular and universal aspects of the affirmation. The *gəbûl yiśrāʾēl*, "territory/border of Israel," is a common phrase designating the geographical border or territory of Israel (see map 2).[67]

First, the adverbial particle is usually rendered "above or over" (e.g., Gen 1:7; 1 Sam 17:39; Ezek 1:25; Jonah 4:6; 2 Chr 13:4).[68] In this alternative, the phrase affirms the particularistic view of Yahweh's sovereignty over Israel as one who loves Israel. Some understand this interpretation as referring to the manifestation of that love more so than to the devastation of Edom; they appeal to the structure of the first disputation as support for this interpretation.[69] Notably, the LXX *hyperanō* and Vulgate *super* support this first rendering of *mēʿal* as "above." The second alternative appeals to the universal aspect of the affirmation, whereby Israel will acknowledge Yahweh's encompassing greatness, recognizing that this greatness transcends the geographical boundaries of Israel.[70] This interpretation takes into account the perspective offered in Mal 1:2–4 of Yahweh's dealings with Edom—choosing to hate Edom, devastating it, and sustaining that devastation. All of these actions demonstrate that Yahweh acts beyond the confines of Israel's geographical territory.[71] Thus, Yahweh's greatness is not restricted to Israel. Moreover, any understanding of the extent of Yahweh's greatness also concerns the nature of that greatness. While the previous depiction includes the adverse manifestation of Yahweh's power against Edom, the affirmation highlights Yahweh's greatness.

What is it about Yahweh's actions on behalf of Israel and against Edom that are considered great? It appears that this greatness includes the ability to subjugate a nation. In this respect, greatness is the power to destroy a nation and to perpetuate its desolation. Yahweh's greatness is seen further in the ability to work outside the geographical region of Israel; while the Deity's power may be localized, it is not geographically restricted. The manifestation of power also reveals that Yahweh's dealing with Israel is regulated by the Dei-

67. See 1 Sam 7:13; 11:3, 7; 27:1; 1 Kgs 1:3; 2 Kgs 10:32; 14:25, where its use with *kol*, "all," necessitates the English plural form "borders."

68. Without the following *lə* particle in Gen 49:25; Num 7:89; cf. Exod 20:4. Verhoef, *Haggai and Malachi*, 206. Note also the use of *ʿal*, "above," in Gen 1:20 and 7:17.

69. Verhoef, *Haggai and Malachi*, 206; Hill, *Malachi*, 161.

70. Cf. Petersen, *Zechariah 9–14 and Malachi*, 173; R. L. Smith, *Micah–Malachi*, 304, 306; Glazier-McDonald, *Malachi: The Divine Messenger*, 31.

71. Cf. Floyd, *Minor Prophets 2*, 583; Petersen, *Zechariah 9–14 and Malachi*, 173.

ty's choice. Yahweh's response to the challenge compels further thought about how the devastation and restoration are in fact acts of love toward Israel.

II. DISPUTATION SEQUENCE: BEHAVIORS AND BELIEFS REGARDING HONOR (1:6–2:16)

This unit, Mal 1:6–2:16, involves two sets of addressees: the priests (Mal 1:6–2:9) and the community (Mal 2:10–16). In light of Mal 1:2–5, the macrounit 1:6–2:16 defines the perspective about the issue of honor in the Yahweh-Israel covenantal relationship. At issue are the dashed expectations of both parties in the relationship. Each party legitimizes its perspective about and behavior toward the other. Fundamentally, Mal 1:6–2:16 illustrates an impasse, in which each party potentially withholds what is due the other.

A. THE PRIESTS' CULTIC MALPRACTICE (1:6–2:9)

Malachi 1:6–2:9 is unified by its concern over the honor due the Deity, which is distinctively absent from the relationship between Yahweh and the priests. The unit consists of two subunits addressed to the priests: 1:6–14 (focused on the cultic malpractice regarding sacrifices) and 2:1–9 (focused on the cultic malpractice regarding instruction). While the question-answer schema is evident in 1:6–14 and 2:1–9, the conceptual elements dominate in decisions about how to delineate these subunits. The unit 1:6–14 is characterized by a dialogue pattern that culminates in the Deity's declaration of a curse. Malachi 2:1–9 consists of the Deity's perspective regarding the nature of the curse on the priests and their descendants.

1. Charges regarding Corrupt Sacrifices (1:6–14)

Two units form Mal 1:6–14, namely, 1:6–9 and 1:10–14. Clearly Mal 1:6–14 consists of an accusation against the priests and a punishment for their cultic malpractice in the offering of sacrifices (1:6–9). Malachi 1:6 introduces the unit and identifies the addressees and the issues. The highlighted issue is the expected honor due to the Deity and the manifested dishonor received by the Deity. The introduction consists of an assertion about honor within particular relationships and proceeds to questions about the honor due the Deity. The essence of the accusation is that the name of Yahweh is dishonored when it ought to be honored (Mal 1:11, 14).

a. Charge against the Priests (1:6–9)

6 *"A son honors [his] father and a slave his master. So if I am 'father,' where is my honor? And if I am master, where is my reverence?" says Yahweh of hosts to you the priests who despise my name.*

But you say, "How have we despised your name?"

7 *"By presenting defiled food upon my altar."*

But you say, "How have we defiled you?"[a]

"By saying the table of Yahweh is despised."

8 *"When you present a blind [animal] for sacrifice, is there no evil? And when you present a lame and sick [animal], is there no evil? Offer it to your governor! Would he be pleased with you*[b] *or show you favor?" says Yahweh of hosts.*[c]

9 *"So now entreat God so that he may be gracious to us. This is from your hand. Will he show favor to you?" says Yahweh of hosts.*[d]

---

a. Regarding the textual difficulties of *gēʾalnûkā* in Mal 1:7aβ, the textual apparatus suggests *gēʾalnûhû*, the third masculine singular suffix, thus reading "polluted it." The LXX reads *elisgesamen autous*, a third-person masculine plural, where the MT reads a second masculine singular. Notably, the LXX third masculine plural reading represents the Hebrew third masculine plural suffix (*-hem*) rather than the third masculine singular suffix (*-hû*). The NRSV adapts the third-person reading, thus, "polluted it." In this case, the NRSV emends both the LXX and MT in order to achieve agreement of the verbal object with its presumed antecedent ("my altar" in 1:7a). The switch from the first- to the second-person singular is in part normative with the dialogue. Cf. R. L. Smith, *Micah–Malachi*, 309; Hill, *Malachi*, 178.

b. Regarding *hăyirṣəkā*, a few LXX manuscripts read "if he will receive it" (*ei prosdexetai auto*), while others read "if he will receive you" (*ei prosdexetai se*). The Vulgate reading assumes *hăyirṣêhû*, with the third masculine singular ending: "would he be pleased with it." If one follows the suggestion, the referent of the suffix would be the sacrifice rather than the person making the sacrifice. On the basis of Mal 1:10–13, J. M. P. Smith follows the Vulgate in reading a third masculine singular instead of second-person singular ("Malachi," 28).

c. *BHS* suggests that the formula *ʾāmar yhwh ṣəbāʾôt* be deleted on the basis of meter (cf. Mal 1:2).

d. *BHS* suggests that the formula *ʾāmar yhwh ṣəbāʾôt* be deleted as in other occurrences in the book of Malachi (e.g., Mal 1:2).

Here the question-answer format presents an interchange between Yahweh and the priests, who challenge the Deity to substantiate the accusations (1:6b–7). However, the use of questions and answers does not necessarily mean that an actual interchange occurred between the Deity and the addressees: as noted in Mal 1:8–9, the Deity both articulates and responds to the questions himself, without a noted response from the priests.[72]

72. As a diatribe, the book of Malachi would reflect proposed contentious interactions between the identified agents.

(1) Yahweh's Declaration and Challenge regarding Honor (1:6a–bα)

6 Malachi 1:6 consists of a statement about honor in typical relational dynamics and a question implying divergence from normative dynamics in relationships. Verse 1:6 identifies two types of relationship and inquires about the normative dynamics expected between Yahweh and the priests. The text highlights the norm of a subordinate honoring a superior by illustrating with a subordinate son and slave who honor their superiors, their father and master. The direction in which this honor is given contrasts with the assertion *"I have loved you,"* in which love is directed from the superior (the Deity) to the subordinate (Israel). While mutuality is possible in normative behavior, Mal 1:6 focuses on the directional aspect of honor—that is, from a subordinate to a superior, from the people to Yahweh. The statement presumes that honor exists in particular relationships, highlighting the normative aspects without giving a prescription or command regarding honor. Two types of relationship provide the basis for understanding the divine-human relationship, and more specifically, the Yahweh-Israel covenant relationship: the parent-child (familial bond) and the slave-master (functional bond).

(a) General Declaration regarding Honor in Relationships (1:6a)

The first element of the declaration and challenge is the statement *a son honors [his] father*. Malachi 1:6 mentions only the son (*bēn*) and father (*'āb*); however, the Decalogue mentions both parents: "honor your father and your mother" (Exod 20:12; Deut 5:16). According to Hill, the honor (*kābôd*) that is typical in the familial relationship is "ascribed" honor—the type that usually exists in a relationship constituted by birth.[73] The Decalogue prescribes honor for parents, specifying long life in the land as a motivating factor for obedience. As a fact upon which to base further assertions, Mal 1:6 presumes the normativity of honor. Because the text makes an assertion in order to support the claim that honor is missing from a relationship, Mal 1:6 considers honor to be typical without hinting at instances when sons dishonor their fathers (Deut 21:18–20; Mic 7:6). Accordingly, it portrays dishonor as a deviation from the norm; it suppresses examples of dishonor to emphasize the image of priestly dishonor and to define honor as the norm.[74]

The terminology of the text provides additional insights on the relation-

73. Hill, *Malachi*, 218.

74. J. K. Chance, "The Anthropology of Honor and Shame: Culture, Value, and Practice," *Semeia* 68 (1994): 145–46, 148. He argues that texts tend to present the normative perspective; thus one needs to understand the difference between value and practice, and the heterogeneity of those practices in any given culture.

ship used to illustrate the Yahweh-Israel relationship. The term *yəkabbēd* is the *piel* third-person singular form of *kābēd*, meaning "to honor, to be heavy, weighty and glorify." The term *kābēd* is used to depict the authority or importance of a person in a relationship.[75] Notice that one synonym of *kābēd* that is also used is *yārēʾ*, "to fear, reverence" (Isa 25:3; cf. Gen 22:12; Lev 19:14), specifically in reference to the name of Yahweh (Ps 102:15 [MT 16]) and the connection to Yahweh's reward (Ps 111:5). The antonyms *bāzâ*, "to despise, regard with contempt," and *qālal,* "to be dishonored," are also linked to Yahweh's response—that is, to curse those who dishonor the Deity (1 Sam 2:30; cf. Mal 1:12; 2:9; Isa 3:5).[76] Other antonyms include *nāʾaṣ*, "contemn, spurn," in reference to the word of Yahweh (Jer 23:17), and *zālal*, "make light of, despise," regarding Jerusalem's change from being honored to being despised (Lam 1:8). The assertion "a son honors his father" may be understood as a "popular saying" that was based on the Decalogue (Exod 20:12; Deut 5:16).[77] Malachi may have used a popular saying to convince the hearers/readers to assent to its perspective on the nature of honor.

The second clause of the assertion—*and a slave his master*—does not contain the verb *kābēd*, "to honor," or any other verb. It is linked to the preceding clause by the conjunction *waw*, "and," which forms the parallel: *A son honors [his] father and a slave his master*. Consequently, some have supplied a verb, usually *yārēʾ*, "to fear, reverence," in view of *môrāʾî*, "my fear," in Mal 1:6 and in accordance with the LXX's use of the verb "fears" (*phobethestai*) in 1:6a.[78] Most likely the verb *kābēd*, "honor," carries over from the first assertion; thus, the understanding is that a slave honors his master (*ʿebed ʾădōnāyw*). Honor is normative in the relationship of a "slave and his master." Concerning the understanding of *ʿebed,* "servant, slave," Hill denies that *ʿebed* refers to a "slave in bondage." Rather, in connection with the term used to speak of Moses (Mal 4:4 [MT 3:22]), he prefers "servant," a subordinate who trusts his superior.[79] Notably, Israel (Lev 25:55), David (1 Kgs 8:66), and others (1 Sam 3:9) are referred to as Yahweh's servant (*ʿebed).*

75. Verhoef, *Haggai and Malachi,* 211. He identifies both the literal (heavy) and figurative (riches, honor) aspects as well as the positive and negative aspects.

76. Specifically, the *niphal* and *hiphil* of *qālâ* mean "to be dishonored or to dishonor" (Deut 25:3; 27:16; 1 Sam 18:23; Isa 3:5; 16:14). Cf. G. Stansell, "Honor and Shame in the David Narratives," *Semeia* 68 (1994): 57–58, 65–66. In his discussion of 1 Sam 18:23 and 2 Sam 6:16 and 20–23, Stansell locates the term *qālal* and *qālâ*, "to be slight, trifling," and *bāzâ*, "to despise," within the semantic field of honor and shame.

77. Hill, *Malachi,* 174.

78. E.g., R. L. Smith, *Micah–Malachi,* 307.

79. Hill, *Malachi,* 174. Cf. Petersen, *Zechariah 9–14 and Malachi,* 173, 177. He notes that while the honor in the parent-child relationship is prescribed, the same cannot be said of the servant-master relationship.

Since "servant" and "slave" are both viable translations of *'ebed,* it is unnecessary to harmonize interpretations here. Whether the Hebrew word refers to a laborer or a slave, the subordinate status is in view. However, an additional observation may help elucidate the comparison and, hence, the charge against the priests. While the typical father-son relationship is highlighted, it appears that a slave's love (*'ahab*) for a master would be an exception rather than a norm (cf. Exod 21:1–6; Deut 15:12–17). In Mal 1:6 the language of honor, though implied, is a normative part of the slave-master relationship. To the extent that the circumstances compel a slave to recognize the authority of the master, honor or respect is normative. Its compulsory nature makes honor the norm in the slave-master relationship.[80] Mal 1:6 identifies two types of relationship in which honor is the norm: biological and functional. Notably, the text does not speak of love as a normative part of these relationships, even though Yahweh's love for Israel is the issue at hand. It implies that honor is the normative response to the Deity's love.

Building on the assertions about the honor that relational and functional subordinates give their superiors, Yahweh poses two sets of questions. The first set focuses on the father-son relationship and asks about the relationship itself. *So if I am "father," where is my honor?* Here the controlling premise is *if I am "father,"* with the understanding that Yahweh is father (*'āb*) to the addressees, with "father" denoting a title.[81] This picture of Yahweh as father and Israel as son is well attested in the Old Testament, as seen in the affirmation of Israel as son (Exod 4:22–23; Deut 14:1) and in analogies depicting God as parent and Israel as a child (e.g., Deut 1:31; 8:5; Hos 11:1).[82] Thus, the question regards Yahweh as "father," entitled to be treated as "father." It brings to mind the charge in Isa 1:2–3, where Israel is characterized as children (*bānîm*) whom Yahweh raised and who were rebellious. Likewise, in Isa 1:2–3 Israel is presented as a deviant, outside the norm of Yahweh's relationships, while other peoples function naturally in their relationships with Yahweh.[83]

80. Hill (*Malachi,* 218) classifies this as an instance of "acquired" honor—i.e., that earned or achieved through social position. Cf. Verhoef, *Haggai and Malachi,* 212. He cites several examples of this compulsory honor—the Code of Hammurabi §§197–99, 205, 210, 282; Exod 21:20, 21, 26, 27.

81. Hill, *Malachi,* 175; D. Stuart, "Malachi," in *The Minor Prophets,* ed. Thomas E. McComiskey (Grand Rapids: Baker, 1998), 3:1297.

82. Verhoef, *Haggai and Malachi,* 212. Hill (*Malachi,* 175) includes the personal pronoun to clarify the relational aspect, "[your] father."

83. Stuart ("Malachi," 1297) identifies this formulation as *a fortiori* (if *x* is something, then *y* is, by definition, more so).

(b) Challenge about Specific Relationships (1:6bα)

The question—*where is my honor?*—is the second part of the first set of questions (an apodosis of the preceding condition) addressed to the priests about their relationship with Yahweh.[84] The term *kābôd* in this instance refers to the honor or respect that is due someone.[85] The question suggests that dishonor characterizes Yahweh's experience with Israel. The text here speaks not about a relationship of indifference but one of dishonor—behavior that is an affront to the expected relationship (cf. 2:9).

Even parents and masters receive the honor due them by virtue of the relationship. The next question (*If I am master, where is my reverence?*), like the previous one, expresses the expectation for the relationship. Here in Mal 1:6, the first-person speech serves as a protasis (conditional statement) and identifies the speaker (Yahweh) as master (*'ădōnîm*)—plural form of *'ādôn* (cf. 1 Kgs 22:17; Isa 19:4; 2 Chr 18:16).[86] The resulting construction parallels *'āb* ("father," singular) and *'ădōnîm* ("lord, master," plural). Similarly, in Isa 1:3 the "lord, master" is identified with a plural construct form with the third person masculine singular suffix (*bəʿālāyw*, "his master").[87] Isaiah 1:3 therefore contends that even the animals recognize their relationship to their human owner and master but that Israel (human) does not know Yahweh (the Deity). The question *where is my reverence?* constitutes the apodosis in Mal 1:6c. It picks up the same particle *'ayyê* (where) used in the parallel question about Yahweh as father (Mal 1:6). The identified element is not a person, as in most phrases containing the particle *'ayyê* (where), but an intangible entity, *môrā'î* (my fear/reverence)—*my reverence* (cf. Mal 2:5).[88] In its other occurrences, *môrā'î* typically means "fear" but can also mean "respect" (Gen 9:2; Deut 4:34; 11:25; 26:8; 34:12; Ps 9:20 [MT 21]; 76:11–12 [MT 12–13]; Isa 8:12–13;

84. Hill, *Malachi,* 175.

85. With the first-person suffix on the term, *kəbôdî* may be translated "honor due me." There are various rendering of *kəbôdî* according to one's understanding of the first common singular suffix: "my honor" (Hill, *Malachi,* 170); "honor due to me, or due me" (Verhoef, *Haggai and Malachi,* 208, 213; Glazier-McDonald, *Malachi: The Divine Messenger,* 44; NRSV); "honor due" (Petersen, *Zechariah 9–14 and Malachi,* 173).

86. Verhoef, *Haggai and Malachi,* 208, 212. Verhoef argues that the plural forms are majestic plurals with God as the subject. Cf. Hill, *Malachi,* 175.

87. The noun used is *baʿal* rather than *'ādôn.*

88. A similar use of *'ayyê* is also found in Mal 2:17. The particle is used with an object or person/being, inquiring about his/her/its location; for example, of Sarah (Gen 18:9); of the lamb to be sacrificed (Gen 22:7); of the temple prostitute (Gen 38:21); of Yahweh/God (Jer 2:6, 8; Mic 7:10; cf. Ps 42:3 [MT 4]; 42:10 [MT 11]; 79:10; 115:2; Job 35:10); of the word of Yahweh (Jer 17:15; cf. Gen 19:5; 2 Sam 17:20; 2 Kgs 18:34; 19:13; Isa 19:12; 33:18). Of intangible elements, it is used of a boast (Judg 9:38); fury (Isa 51:13); of zeal and might (Isa 63:15); of steadfast love (Ps 89:49 [MT 50]); of hope (Job 17:15).

Jer 32:21).[89] More specifically, fear is equivalent to the terror that God instills rather than a sense of reverence ensuing from being in God's presence.[90] In light of the servant-master relational context, it seems best to render *môrā'* as "fear" rather than the somewhat milder "respect."[91] Thus the parallel is *kābôd* (honor) and *môrā'* (fear), reflecting the full gamut of expected dispositions within these relationships. Consequently, in whatever way the relationship is conceived or represented, Yahweh does not receive the honor due, considering the relational/functional dynamics. This is not a matter of greater or lesser agents—divinity being greater than a human father or master.[92] The point is that every type of relationship compels a particular type of regard between/among those involved; but Yahweh is not getting the requisite honor. The assertion presents a contrast between what is expected and what exists in the relationship—the ideal and the real.

The messenger formula, *says Yahweh of Hosts ('āmar yhwh ṣəbā'ôt),* has several functions here in Mal 1:6. First, it concludes the segment of the disputation in which Yahweh is challenging the addressees about their regard for the Deity. Second, the formula verifies that the content of the preceding speech is Yahweh's word and perspective (cf. Mal 1:8, 9, 10, 11, 13, 14; 2:2, 4, 8).[93] The presence of the formula also juxtaposes the human and the divine agents. On the one hand, the human agents appear to have questioned whether Yahweh loves them. On the other hand, Yahweh contends that the humans have withheld the honor and the fear due to the Deity by virtue of the existing relationship. Third, the formula also identifies the recipients of the message as the priests—*to you the priests who despise my name.*

Ironically, the priests (*hakkōhănîm*)—designated as leaders in the covenant community to teach the people the ways of Yahweh and present the people's offerings and sacrifices to Yahweh—are accused of dishonoring the Deity. The priests should know that the Yahweh-Israel relationship compels honor for the Deity. One of the primary questions at this point is who is being identified as "priests" (*hakkōhănîm*). First, the reference may be to the Aaronide/Zadokite priesthood. In Lev 10:10–11, Aaron is given the responsibility of teaching Torah and discerning between the holy (*qōdeš*) and

89. Hill, *Malachi,* 175–76; Verhoef, *Haggai and Malachi,* 213–14. All of the noted texts associate *môrā'* with dread, or signs and wonders.

90. Fuhs, "יָרֵא *yārē',*" *TDOT* 6:290–315.

91. Verhoef (*Haggai and Malachi,* 214) prefers to translate *môrā'* in Mal 1:6 as "respect," on the grounds that it is parallel with honor. Notably, a few modern translations render *môrā'* "respect," including the NIV and NRSV.

92. Contrast Stuart ("Malachi," 1297), who argues that Mal 1:6 implicitly assumes that God deserves honor or fear because God is greater than any lord or master.

93. Cf. Hill, *Malachi,* 176. Hill argues that it may be more accurate to render *'āmar* (*qal* perfect) "said Yahweh" instead of "says Yahweh."

profane (*ḥōl*), between the unclean (*ṭāmēʾ*) and clean (*ṭāhôr*). It may also be that Mal 1:6c refers to the priests in general, while Mal 2:8–9 refers to the Aaronide/Zadokite priesthood in particular. Malachi 1:6 does not signal whether a distinction is intended here between the priests and the Levites. Thus, Petersen looks at the priests in light of the Ezra–Nehemiah representation of the priesthood concerning issues of legitimacy.[94] However, it is unnecessary to distinguish between the groups, since the book of Malachi appears to use the terms interchangeably.[95] Whatever the case, it is clear that the priests committed malpractice in their duties (Deut 33:10). That irony creates the crescendo in Mal 1:6c, when the priests are identified, not only as those who are being addressed by Yahweh, but also as those who are dishonoring Yahweh. Consequently, it is not simply that the people under their care have violated cultic practices but that the priests as leaders of the people have been practicing such violations.

The first-person account characterizes the priests with reference to their actions against Yahweh—namely, those who despise (*bôzê*) Yahweh's name. Usually *bāzâ*, "despise, show contempt," is used with inanimate objects and persons, such as the following: of Esau despising his birthright (Gen 25:34); of persons who despise the word of Yahweh (Num 15:31; 2 Sam 12:9);[96] of despising the Deity, including mutual disregard (people vs. Yahweh—1 Sam 2:30; 2 Sam 12:10; Ezek 17:18; cf. Mal 2:9). Notably, *nāʾaṣ*, "contemn," occurs with the Deity as object in several cases (Num 16:30; Isa 1:4), and with the word of Yahweh as object (Isa 5:24; Jer 23:17). Its occurrence with the Deity as object can also represent a punitive response to those who despised Yahweh; they are not granted access to the land (Num 14:23; cf. 14:11). Isaiah 52:5 uses the verb *nāʾaṣ*, "contemn," with *šəmî*, "my name," as the object, referring to the name of Yahweh, in much the same way that Mal 1:6 uses *bāzâ*, "despise," with *šəmî* as the object. Similarly, other texts speak about dishonoring the Deity using various terms for dishonor.[97] In Mal 1:6 the modifier (those who despise) not only extends the identity of the addressees (the priests) but also exemplifies the converse of what Yahweh seeks from them. The descriptor offers a preliminary response to the question "where is my honor?" leaving further response to the rest of the book of Malachi. The answer here is that the honor is not to be found in the relationship with the priests. Rather, that relationship involves dishonor in the form of despising Yahweh's name.

94. Petersen, *Zechariah 9–14 and Malachi.*

95. J. M. O'Brien, *Priest and Levite*, 143–44.

96. Note also the use of *bāzâ* with an oath and juxtaposed to breaking the covenant (Ezek 16:59; 17:16); of wisdom (Prov 1:7; Eccl 9:16); of persons despising each other (1 Sam 17:42; 2 Sam 6:16; cf. Isa 53:3; Jer 22:28).

97. Terms used for actions against the "holy name" include *ṭāmēʾ*, "to defile" (Ezek 43:7–8); *ḥālal*, "to pollute" (Lev 22:2, 32).

(2) *The Priests' Response: Question Challenging Yahweh's Claim (1:6bβ)*

The reported response from the priests is introduced with *wa'ămartem*, the adversative *waw* plus the second person masculine plural form of *'āmar*, "to say" (Mal 1:2, 7, 13; 2:14, 17; 3:7, 13; cf. 3:14 without *waw*). *But you say, "How have we despised your name?"* The response addresses the descriptor used to identify the priests, challenges Yahweh to substantiate the implicit assertion, and to a certain extent denies Yahweh's assertion. As in the previous question, the challenge calls for evidence to substantiate the claim (cf. Mic 6:1–8). Likewise, the challenge does not concern all instances in which Yahweh's name may have been despised but the ways in which the priests in particular have despised the name. First, to despise (*bāzâ*) the name is a particular formulation designating an action that results in the defamation of Yahweh's character or reputation. Leviticus 22:2, 32 cautions the Aaronides against "polluting" the holy name. To commit any of the infractions listed in Lev 22 would be to pollute Yahweh's name.[98] Likewise, Ezekiel identifies practices that defile Yahweh's name:

> He said to me: "Mortal, this is the place of my throne and the place for the soles of my feet, where I will reside among the people of Israel forever. The house of Israel shall no more defile my holy name, neither they nor their kings, by their whoring, and by the corpses of their kings at their death. When they placed their threshold by my threshold and their doorposts beside my doorposts, with only a wall between me and them, they were defiling my holy name by their abominations that they committed." (Ezek 43:7–8 NRSV)

The priests' question in Malachi (*how have we despised your name?*) seems to presume that the priests are innocent of the charge. It is also possible that the prophetic voice represents the priests as feigning innocence.[99] The priests' question could signal their innocence of the charge that they have committed a cultic infraction by despising the name of Yahweh.[100] Their presumed innocence would give occasion for the Deity to substantiate the charge; however, one should also consider the context of Mal 1 as indicative

98. Note that the list includes infractions related to being clean or unclean.

99. The prophetic voice represents the priests rather than quoting the actual words of the priests—thus Weyde (*Prophecy and Teaching*, 126), regarding Mal 1:7b. Contrast L.-S. Tiemeyer ("Giving a Voice to Malachi's Interlocutors," *SJOT* 19 [2005]: 173–92), who argues that the responses are the words of the addressees.

100. Tiemeyer ("Giving a Voice to Malachi's Interlocutors," 180) contends that the priests' question reflects their innocence of the charge against them, not necessarily that either the priests or God was lying about the charge.

not so much of ignorance or innocence but of disregard and disrespect, exemplified by the charge in 1:6.

(3) Interchange regarding Cultic Malpractice (1:7–9)

7 The confrontation thus continues with Yahweh's and the priests' responses. While the textual issues contribute to various interpretations, Mal 1:7 presents a clear picture of the nature of the priests' dishonor through cultic infractions.

(a) Statement of the Argument (Yahweh) (1:7aα)

The priests are further accused of despising Yahweh's name by *presenting (nāgaš) defiled food* on the altar (Mal 1:7a). The clear reference to Yahweh further illuminates the gravity of the charge. Here "food" (*leḥem*) is used of animal sacrifice, as in Lev 21:6, 8, "food of their/your God," and Hag 2:12.[101] In Lev 22:21–25 (esp. v. 25) the "food" presented to Yahweh is disqualified as unacceptable "for you" if it is corrupt (*mošḥāt*) or blemished (*mûm*). In Mal 1:7a) the food is deemed to be defiled (*məgō'āl*). Apparently, the term *məgō'āl* is derived from *gā'al*, a late usage that appears mainly in prophetic texts depicting a defiled city (Lam 4:14) or the corrupting practices of the city leaders (Isa 59:3; Zeph 3:1–4).[102]

(b) Refutation (Priests) (1:7aβ)

Consistent with the pattern of the text, the accusation/charge is followed by a question that appears to challenge the charge. From this perspective the first question—how Yahweh's name is being despised (*bāzâ*)—is answered. The response shows the connection between Yahweh's name and Yahweh's altar: defiling (*gā'al*) the altar is despising Yahweh's name.

Presumably, the priests recognize and do not debate the fact that they have defiled something. The follow-up question *How have we defiled you? (bammê gē'alnûkā)* responds to the charge that the priests have presented defiled food on the altar and directly links the cultic malpractice with defiling Yahweh. Neither the presentation nor the content of the question suggests the priests' ignorance of the connection. Rather, they debate the connection be-

101. Note other instances of "food" used in reference to offerings: Lev 3:9–11, 16; Num 28:2, 24.

102. Weyde, *Prophecy and Teaching*, 122–23. Weyde cites Ezra 2:62//Neh 7:64 as examples of the late use to characterize those excluded from the priesthood because of their uncleanness. He also cites Isa 59:3, saying that "the addressee of the accusation is uncertain" (p. 122 n. 45).

tween the accusation of despising the name and presenting polluted food on the altar. Thus, the priests ask how they have polluted Yahweh, implying that it is the altar—if anything—that they have polluted.[103] In this depiction, the priests' question suggests that they see no connection between their activity on the altar and polluting Yahweh's name. Hence, those whose role presumes their knowledge of the connection are perhaps feigning ignorance of the connection. Yahweh's charge is that the priests have despised the name and the altar; their question ties the name and the altar to Yahweh by inquiring how they have defiled Yahweh.[104] Table 8 displays these connections.

Table 8. Synecdoche for the Deity in Malachi 1

1:6b	1:7aα	1:7aβ	1:7b
My/your Name →	My altar →	you →	Yahweh's table
Despise (*bāzâ*)	Defile (*gā'al*)	Defile (*gā'al*)	Despise (*bāzâ*)

The charge against the priests together with the priests' response presupposes the possibility of defiling Yahweh and may explain the announcement of judgment against their descendants (to defile them, Mal 2:3): tit-for-tat. Likewise, the connection of the various elements (name, altar, table) equates the two terms used to characterize each of the elements. So *to despise* and *to defile* connote the same outcome, if not the same process.

(c) Presentation of the Evidence (Yahweh) (1:7b–9)

The question-answer pattern continues with the Deity's response to the priests' question about defiling the Deity. As in Gen 3, where the man's response belies the state of the speaker, here in Mal 1:7b the priests betray their awareness of their behavior through their perspective: *the table of Yahweh is despised.* Would the priests voice such a perspective about Yahweh's table and by implication the sacrificial system and the Deity? Some argue that the prophetic voice here represents in words what the priests' actions already demonstrate.[105] Whether voiced or implied, the perspective attributed to the

103. See Petersen, *Haggai and Zechariah 1–8*, 83–84. He posits that the defilement spoken of in Hag 2:14 is derived from the altar. As such, the sacrifices themselves were not necessarily defiled when they were brought to the altar; their contact with the altar rendered them unclean.

104. See textual notes on Mal 1:7 above.

105. Regarding 1:7b, Tiemeyer ("Giving a Voice to Malachi's Interlocutors," 180–82) argues for the accuracy of the priests' words as represented by the prophet.

priests agrees with the Deity's perspective that the priests have despised Yahweh, albeit by means of the name, altar, and table (cf. Mal 1:12).

While Mal 1:7aα and 1:7b equate the altar (*mizbēaḥ*) and the table (*šulḥān*), the two are distinguished elsewhere (cf. Mal 1:8a, 13aβ). "Altar" (*mizbēaḥ*) is typically used when referring to "food" offered in fire to the Deity (cf. Lev 3:11; 21:21; 22:22, 25). The "table" (*šulḥān*), on the other hand, usually refers to the table of the Presence (Num 4:7) or the bread of the Presence (cf. Exod 30:27–29; 31:8–10; 35:13–15; 40:3–5; Num 4:7, 13 [the altar]; 2 Chr 29:18; Num 3:31 [table and altar]). The usage in Ezek 40–48 seems to differ from that of the Pentateuch.[106] Thus, the table is a place of slaughtering the sacrifice (Ezek 40:38–39) and presenting the burnt offering (Ezek 44:14–15).[107] Consequently, the structure of the argument in Mal 1:6–7 treats the altar and table as equivalent, and Ezek 40–48 attests that equivalence in the cultic tradition.

8 Using two points in its argumentation, Mal 1:8 continues Yahweh's response to the priests' question by providing evidence. First, it focuses on the priests' presentation of unacceptable sacrifices (to the Deity). Second, it illustrates the nature of the priests' malpractice and hence their dishonor of the Deity with a rhetorical question about the governor (a human). Regarding the presentation of an unacceptable sacrifice, the sarcastic tone highlights the priests' insolence in this practice. If no one else, they ought to know the requirements for evaluating and presenting pleasing sacrifices to Yahweh.

The law stipulates that the sacrifice be without blemish (cf. Lev 22:18–25; Deut 15:19–23). Leviticus 22:18–25 identifies a burnt offering (*ʿōlâ*) that is acceptable to present to Yahweh as being a "perfect male" (*tāmîm zākār*)—that is, one without blemish (*mûm*). By comparison, an unacceptable offering is any animal with a blemish (*mûm*), including blindness (*ʿawweret*), injury, or disproportional limbs (Lev 22:21–25; cf. Mal 1:12).[108] Deuteronomy 15:21 stipulates any blemish (*mûm*) that renders the "firstling of the herd or flock" an unacceptable sacrifice to the Deity: being lame (*pisséaḥ*) or blind (*ʿiwwēr*) is to have a severe blemish (*mûm rāʿ*). While the blemished firstling may be unacceptable to the Deity, it is acceptable for human consumption, whether the person eating is unclean (*ṭāmēʾ*) or clean (*haṭṭāhôr*; cf. Deut 12:15–16).[109] The stipulations thus distinguish between what is acceptable for humans and what is acceptable for the Deity. Like Deut 15:21–23, Mal 1:8 identifies blindness (*ʿiwwēr*), lameness (*pisséaḥ*), and other severe blemishes (e.g., sickness

106. See Ezek 41:22, where the altar (*mizbēaḥ*) and table (*šulḥān*) appear to be equated.

107. Cf. Weyde, *Prophecy and Teaching,* 127.

108. Cf. Hartley, *Leviticus.*

109. Craigie, *Deuteronomy,* 218–19, 239–40. Cf. Tigay, *Deuteronomy*; J. M. Sprinkle, "The Rationale of the Laws of Clean and Unclean in the Old Testament," *JETS* 43 (2000): 640.

[*ḥōlê*]) as characteristics of an unacceptable sacrifice. Although it is typically used of people (e.g., Gen 48:1; 1 Sam 19:14; 1 Kgs 14:5; 2 Kgs 8:7),[110] the term *ḥālâ*, "to be sick, to entreat," is used of an animal in Mal 1:8 and 13 to denote the diseased. Nowhere is the "sick" listed among criteria for "unacceptability" of the sacrifice; its inclusion in Mal 1:8 provides another example of a blemish.

The refrain *there is no evil (ʾên rāʿ)* further highlights the absurdity of the cultic practices by contrasting the priests' behavior with their apparent lack of concern. The qualification for sacrifices accounts for Yahweh's displeasure. While human beings may consume a lame or blind animal, not even they would consume a sick animal. The offense of offering lame, blind, or sick animals is that the priests would be obliterating the distinction between themselves (humans) and Yahweh (the Deity) by treating Yahweh as "one of them." They have not accorded Yahweh the distinction due the Deity.

The second facet of the argument focuses on another relationship and thus extends the accusation in Mal 1:6 regarding dishonor. Malachi 1:6 identifies relationships where honor or fear is normative, such as in father-son and master-slave relationships. Malachi 1:8 adds to the list of relationships without naming the subordinate: governor-subordinate. The exhortation—*offer it to your governor*—proposes that the priests do something preposterous. It dares them to present (*qārab*) to their human ruler what is unacceptable to the Deity. The priests are part of the province ruled by a governor (*peḥâ*), whom they are presumably expected to honor. While it may not have been the practice to present the governor (or political official) with sacrifices, the analogy shows that the priests, who are leaders in the community, would not offend their governor or ruler by giving him substandard gifts. The rhetorical question elucidates the fact that a human ruler would not find the lame and sick presentations acceptable. In other words, just as the priests would respect their leader, so they ought to respect the Deity simply by virtue of the honor due the Deity.

The pairing of the rhetorical questions rests on the perspective that the governor would not be pleased with the priests if they offered him substandard products. *Would he be pleased with you or show you favor?* Furthermore, the question unites the political and religious spheres under the heading of honor. The prophet envisions the priests, the leaders of the community, as being imprudent if they disrespected their governor. As with Mal 1:6, the image is a deviation from the norm; all others receive honor, but Yahweh receives none.

9 Following the sentiment of Mal 1:8, verse 9 furthers the argument by

110. Other examples of the term *ḥālâ*, "to be sick," used in reference to a person include 1 Sam 19:14; 30:13; 1 Kgs 14:1; 17:17; 2 Kgs 8:29; 13:14; 20:12; 2 Chr 22:6; cf. Ezek 34:4, 16 (figuratively of people).

intensifying the "dare." In Mal 1:9 the prophet facetiously invites the priests to seek God's favor: *So now entreat God so that he may be gracious to us.* Several elements of this inquiry are noteworthy: the formulation, the dynamics of the invitation, and the suggested outcomes of the entreaty. Regarding the formulation, the repeated use of the root *ḥālâ* in Mal 1:8 (*ḥōlê*) and 1:9 (*ḥallû*) is significant albeit ambiguous. Petersen opts for the reading *wiḥannenu*, "he may be gracious to us," positing use of the Hebrew term *ḥānan* rather than the MT's reading *wîḥānēnû*.[111] The difference is not in meaning but in orthography. It is based on the precedence of other occurrences, including in Gen 43:29; Exod 33:19 (*wəḥannōtî*); Isa 27:11; Ps 67:1 (MT 2); and 123:2. The use of the form in Num 6:25 (*wîḥunnekā*) most closely resembles the morphology in Mal 1:9; both are imperfect forms with a suffixed object and a connecting (anatyptic) vowel. The difference is that the form in Num 6:25 has a *dagesh forte,* which is evidence of the assimilated *nun* of the root *ḥānan*, "to show favor, be gracious."

> The LORD bless you and keep you; the LORD make his face to shine upon you, and *be gracious to you*; the LORD lift up his countenance upon you, and give you peace. (Num 6:24–26 NRSV)

Similarly, a *dagesh forte* also appears in Ps 67:1 (MT 2; *yəḥānnēnû*) and in 123:2 (*šeyyəḥānnēnû*), which have a first person common plural pronominal suffix. The form used in Isa 27:11 is an imperfect with *dagesh forte, yəḥunnennû;* however, in this instance the suffixed object appears in the third person masculine singular form. The root occurs in the formula expressing God's characteristics (Exod 34:6, *ʾēl raḥûm wəḥannûn*). The effect of the first common plural is that the speaker includes himself along with the addressees. The LXX departs from the MT in its reading "and beseech him" (*kai deēthete autou*), presumably to exclude the prophet from the group.[112]

The phrase "to entreat the favor of" (*ḥālâ*) + *pənê* + the Deity (*yhwh* or *yhwh ʾĕlōhêkā*) occurs in several passages throughout the Old Testament (e.g., 1 Kgs 13:6; Jer 26:19; Ps 119:58).[113] Furthermore, the formulation "to entreat Yahweh" (*ləḥallôt ʾet-pənê yhwh*) usually connotes seeking Yahweh's favor with the intent of persuading Yahweh to respond in accordance with the human's request or desire (Zech 7:2; 8:21, 22; cf. Dan 9:13).[114] The imperative

111. Petersen, *Zechariah 9–14 and Malachi,* 176.

112. Verhoef, *Haggai and Malachi,* 209.

113. The formulation also occurs in Exod 32:11; 1 Sam 13:12; 1 Kgs 13:6; 2 Kgs 13:4; 2 Chr 33:12. Other instances that refer to entreating a human being include Ps 45:13; Job 11:19; Prov 19:6. Cf. Weyde, *Prophecy and Teaching,* 134 n. 100.

114. Cf. Hill, *Malachi,* 181–82; Verhoef, *Haggai and Malachi,* 219–20.

form occurs in 1 Kgs 13:6 (of "Yahweh your God," *yhwh ʾĕlōhêkā*) and Mal 1:9 (of "God," *ʾēl*), each with the particle of entreaty (*nāʾ*), each asking the addressee to seek the Deity. Likewise, in both instances a person or group is asked to entreat the favor of the Deity on behalf of the speaker, and the desired outcome is specified: "so that my hand may be restored to me" (1 Kgs 13:6a) and "that he may be gracious to us" (Mal 1:9).[115] When a leader—such as Moses (Exod 32:11), or a king (1 Sam 13:12; 2 Kgs 13:4; cf. Jer 26:19)—is speaking on behalf of others to the Deity, the leader usually includes the "people" as part of the requested outcome. Presumably, the one who entreats the Deity has access to the Deity and is authorized to speak or act on behalf of the people. Likewise, Mal 1:9 is an example of a person asking a group (the priests), though facetiously, to speak on behalf of others (the community).

The content of the entreaty varies: explicit content (Exod 32:11), implicit content, and content deduced from the context (cf. 2 Kgs 13:4; 2 Chr 33:12).[116] The implicit content of the entreaty is juxtaposed with the explicitly desired outcome of the entreaty. Malachi 1:9 is implicit and is deduced from the context. The goal of the entreaty is that Yahweh would be gracious. A similar thought occurs in 2 Sam 12:22, "Perhaps Yahweh will be gracious to me (*ḥānan*)"; and Jonah 3:9, "Perhaps God will relent and change his mind (*yāšûb wəniḥam*)."[117] Unlike the latter texts, which use *mî-yôdēaʿ* (lit., "who knows") plus a verb, Mal 1:9 uses the verb *ḥānan*, in the expression *wîḥānēnû*, "that he may be gracious to us." Yet the nuance of uncertainty is also present in Mal 1:9.

The voice of the prophet continues with an accusation against the priests. *This is from your hand.* This is your doing. The referent is the entire situation involving displeasing and defiling Yahweh. Rather than a question representing the priests' perspective, the prophet asks, *will he show favor to you?* Consequently, the prophet invites the priests to entreat God but suggests that God may not respond favorably toward them.

The unit reaches a climax with another way of dealing with the dishonor. The priests deny the dishonor, and Yahweh disputes their attempt to show ignorance. The Deity further argues that they will be disregarded (just as they have disregarded the Deity). In all this argumentation about dishonor, nothing is said about the priests' love for the Deity or the Deity's

115. In both instances the jussive third masculine singular form of the verb indicates the desired outcome of the entreaty—*wətāšōb* (*waw* + *qal*, third feminine singular, of the verb "to return"; 1 Kgs 13:6a) and *wîḥānēnû* (*waw* + *qal*, third masculine singular of the verb "to be gracious"; Mal 1:9).

116. Weyde, *Prophecy and Teaching*, 134–35. He also speaks of "implicit content."

117. To reflect uncertainty about the identified outcome, 2 Sam 12:22 and Jonah 3:9 use the expression *mî-yôdēaʿ* (lit. "who knows"), formed by *mî* (who) plus an imperfect form of the verb *yādaʿ* (to know). See *IBHS* §18.2–3. See discussion on Mal 1:10 below.

love for them, which is presumably the subject from 1:2 that guided the focus of the discourse. The image that emerges is of the Deity loving Israel but Israel disregarding the relationship by insulting Yahweh in its cultic practices. Those responsible for the temple, the cult, and access to the Deity profane the temple, the cult, and the Deity and are not remorseful about their behavior. Rather, the priests are insidious in their practices and appear to justify those practices. On what basis do they justify them? Perhaps on the basis that Yahweh does not live up to their expectations. Perhaps because Yahweh does not accept their sacrifice even when they present it (whether or not the sacrifice meets the requirement; cf. Mal 1:13). The connection between 1:9 and 1:10 is the acceptability of the offering or activity and the repeated reference to the priests' hands as the source of the offering or activity.

b. Announcement of Judgment on the Priests (1:10–14)

10*"Would that one among you would close the doors and not kindle my*
altar in vain. I have no delight in you," says Yahweh of hosts;[a] *"nor will I accept*
offerings from your hand. 11*For from the rising of the sun to its setting, the name*
of Yahweh is great among the nations, and in every place where incense is offered
in my name and pure offerings; for my name is great among the nations," says
Yahweh of hosts. 12*"But you are profaning it when you say, 'The table of the*
Lord is despised and its fruit (its food)[b] *is despised.'*[c] 13*But you say, 'Ah, what*
hardship!' But you ignite it,"[d] *says Yahweh of hosts. "And you brought that which*
was stolen[e] *or lame or sick; and you brought the offering. Shall I accept it from*
your hand?" says Yahweh. 14*"Cursed be the one who deceives, who has a male*
in his herd, but who vows and sacrifices what is corrupt to the Lord; for I am a
great king," says Yahweh of hosts, "and my name is revered among the nations."

---

a. *BHS* suggests that the formula *'āmar yhwh ṣəbā'ôt* is an addition.

b. *'Oklô*, "its food," should probably read *kullô*, "all of it." This would provide an explanatory note, that the entirety of the food was despised.

c. *Wənîbô nibzê* should probably read *wənibzê* (*nîbô* may have arisen due to dittography with *wənibzê*); compare the Peshitta and targum. In translations that honor the MT, "its fruit is despised" means its food, referring to the food on the table.

d. Instead of *'ôtô*, read *'ôtî* (*Tiq soph*). This is the sign of the direct object with a third masculine singular pronominal suffix referring to the food in 1:12 (thus Petersen, *Zechariah 9–14 and Malachi*, 174; Hill, *Malachi*, 171; Verhoef, *Haggai and Malachi*, 209). This represents a continuation of the focus on the despised elements of the table. The alternate reading in the first common singular represents a shift from the food to the speaker and the one to whom that food is offered, namely, Yahweh. The NRSV follows the alternate reading. It is unnecessary to adapt the emendation; however, the alternative offers a different concept, how Yahweh is regarded. Cf. J. M. P. Smith, "Malachi," 31: "you esteem me lightly"; lit., "you snort (or sniff) at me"; Stuart, "Malachi," 1304: "you mistreat me."

e. Probably read *'et-haggāzûl*, providing the sign of the direct object and the definite article. This is the *qal* passive participle. The result is a harmonization of the text with the following object, each with the sign of the direct object and the definite article (*wə'et-happisséaḥ* and *wə'et-haḥôleh*). The first is a masculine adjective, *pisséaḥ*, "lame," the second a *qal* participle from *ḥālâ*, "to be weak, sick."

Malachi 1:10–14 is a subunit of 1:6–14; it represents the Deity's response to the situation alleged in 1:6–9. That response is to reject the sacrifices, if not all of the cultic practice performed in the temple (1:10), and to offer the rationale for that rejection (1:11). The response includes a representation of the priests' perspective on the matter of presenting unacceptable sacrifices (1:12–13) and the articulation of a curse (1:14). Notably, Mal 1:14 connects to 1:6 by mentioning the honoring of the Deity's name.

(1) Expressed Desire to Terminate Cultic Practices (1:10)

10 The sentiment in Mal 1:10 is noteworthy because of what it envisions about cultic practices. One problem is how to interpret the expression *mî gam-bākem* (lit., *who even among you?*)[118] and the relationship of this expression to the stated actions. The LXX renders *dioti* (presuming *kî* rather than *mî gam*) and a passive verb rather than an active, thus: "Because even among you the doors shall be shut."[119] Recognizing that *mî* (who?) may have a desiderative sense[120] and keeping in view the persons and practices that Yahweh disfavors, I translate *mî gam-bākem* here as *would that one among you*. Accordingly, the Deity's expressed desires about the cultic practices are focusing on the nature of the priests' malpractice. Their dishonor is emphasized again by presenting two parts to the charge: Yahweh's desire for specific actions (1:10a) and Yahweh's disfavor (1:10b). The desire expressed to the priests is that one of them (*one among you*) would halt the dishonor by ceasing cultic practice. In Mal 1:10 the desire and uncertainty are about whether there is even one priest who *would* terminate the contaminated practices.

The desired actions (1:10a) include restricting access (1:10aα) and not performing (1:10aβ), the latter resulting from the former. The desired restriction of access, *would close the doors* (1:10aα), is multivalent; it does not specify

118. Note the KJV: "Who is there even among you. . .?"

119. Note also that the ancient versions' perspectives differed from the MT in varying degrees: the Vulgate omits *gam*. The targum includes explanatory comments that clarify the doors: "the doors of the house *of my sanctuary* that you might not *bring detestable sacrifices* upon my altar."

120. See *IBHS* §18.2–3 regarding the "exclamatory question," usually with a nonperfective verb. Examples of *mî* plus imperfect appear in 2 Sam 15:4; 23:15; Job 9:12.

which doors (*dəlātayim*).[121] The possibilities included the gates to the temple courtyard, where the tables for slaughtering the sin, burnt, and guilt offerings were located (Ezek 40:39–41);[122] the doors to the inner sanctuary of the holy of holies (*dəbîr* 1 Kgs 6:31); and the doors to the large room of the temple (*hêkal*), where the altar of incense (1 Kgs 6:20–21, 33) and table for the bread of the presence were (1 Kgs 7:48).[123] Any of these is a viable option. Closing the doors restricts access to all areas of the temple and may already signal the cessation of "acceptable" cultic practices.

The chronistic view of Ahaz's unfaithfulness may shed light on the implications of closing the doors. In 2 Chr 28 Ahaz's evil ways resulted in punishment for the nation. Reeling from defeat and desperate for help, Ahaz sacrificed to the gods of Damascus, desecrated the temple, cut up the temple vessels, erected altars throughout Jerusalem, and offered sacrifices to other gods on the high places that he erected. In the midst of this, Ahaz shut the doors of the house of Yahweh (*yisgōr ʾet-daltôt bêt-yhwh*, 2 Chr 28:24) and thus relocated the cultic activity away from the temple. The closing of the doors terminated the sacrifices to Yahweh and perpetuated the sacrifices to other gods—that is, paying homage to the gods that he perceived as being his source of help (28:23).

Further depicting Ahaz's unfaithfulness, 2 Chr 29 reports Hezekiah's review of the situation, including the termination of the cultic practices:

> They also *shut the doors* of the vestibule and *put out the lamps*, and *have not offered incense or made burnt offerings* in the holy place to the God of Israel. (2 Chr 29:7 NRSV)

The account also depicts Hezekiah's action of reopening the doors of the house of Yahweh and commanding the priests and Levites to restore the cultic practices (i.e., to consecrate the temple and offer sacrifices on behalf of the community).[124] In the Chronistic account, closing the doors was the pinnacle

121. The door of the temple would be *daltôt hêkal*; cf. 2 Kgs 18:16; door of the gate, *daltôt haššəʿārîm* (1 Chr 22:3). There are other terms, such as "opening/entrance" (*petaḥ*) or even "gate" (*šaʿar*), that may denote the point of entrance or, in the case of "door" and "gate," a device for opening and closing.

122. Thus Weyde, *Prophecy and Teaching*, 142–43; Petersen, *Zechariah 9–14 and Malachi*, 182–83; Baldwin, *Hag, Zech, Mal*, 227. Note also this designation in the book of Ezekiel, e.g.: 40:39–41, where the tables were for slaughtering the various offerings (i.e., burnt, sin, and guilt offerings); 41:23–24, the doors to the holy place. Ezekiel uses "table" where others refer to the "altar."

123. Petersen, *Zechariah 9–14 and Malachi*, 182–83.

124. Two views reflect different perspectives on the events and scope: The Deuteronomistic view (2 Kgs 16) reports that Ahaz had a bronze altar erected that was patterned after

of malpractice, while reopening them was the beginning of reparation for the unfaithfulness of the previous generation. Malachi 1:10aα illustrates Yahweh's desire to terminate the sacrificial system because of the dishonor rendered to Yahweh. The Chronistic account and Mal 1:10 have in common the termination of "legitimate" or acceptable practice to Yahweh; shutting the doors is simply the culmination rather than the beginning of the problem. Just as the priests were exhorted to entreat Yahweh's favor with the express desire of securing Yahweh's compassion, so Yahweh explains the desired outcome by tightening the focus on the futility of the priestly practice and Yahweh's disdain for the priests' practices. The desire focuses on actions related to cultic implements (doors and altar).

Regarding the second action in Mal 1:10aβ, the Deity desires the cessation of fire on the altar: *and not kindle my altar in vain (wəlōʾ-tāʾîrû mizbəḥî ḥinnām).* The doors (*dəlātayim*) and altar (*mizbēaḥ*) are focal points for the concept of futile practices. The verb form "kindle" (*tāʾîrû*),[125] which is used to convey the action or desired nonaction, is not used elsewhere with the altar as the object or in a prophetic critique of cultic practices. The usage that is closest to the meaning in Mal 1:10aβ appears in Isa 27:11 (cf. Isa 50:11).[126] Because of the range of meanings for *ʾûr*, Mal 1:10aβ has been variously interpreted.[127] One interpretation is that Yahweh desires that the priests not perform their services "for free."[128] Another interpretation is that they should not perform their activity unless there is a benefit—that is, the benefit of the Deity's favor. In the context of Mal 1:10, *ʾûr* refers to fire on the altar (cf. Mal 1:7). To kindle [the fire] "in vain" (*ḥinnām*) signals the futility of an activity or offering that is unacceptable to God (cf. Ezek 6:10).

The second of the two aspects of Mal 1:10b is Yahweh's expressed disfavor toward the priests and their offering: *I have no delight in you.* The noun

---

the altar in Damascus and moved or removed some of the temple elements (esp. 16:10–16). It does not report the closing of the temple. By comparison, the Chronistic view (2 Chr 28–29) includes the closing of the temple, the cessation of cultic practices there, and the building of multiple altars. Second Chronicles 29 depicts the priests' and Levites' duties under Hezekiah, including cleansing the house of Yahweh and disposing of the unclean elements brought out of the inner part of the house (29:15, 16). The priests cleansed the inner part of the house of Yahweh, removed the unclean elements, and took them to the court (29:18–28, slaughtering the sacrifice and sprinkling the blood; performing the music). See S. Japhet (*I and II Chronicles,* OTL [Louisville: Westminster John Knox, 1993], 896, 908–9, 918) regarding the historical accuracy of the Chronistic account.

125. The *hiphil* of the verb *ʾôr* has several nuances, including "to illuminate" (e.g., Ps 97:4; 105:39); "to give light or shine" (e.g., Num 6:25; Ps 31:16; 67:1; of God's face).

126. The noun form *ʾûr* may occur with *ʾeš* (fire) to denote the light or flame of the fire.

127. Among the meanings are "without compensation" (Gen 29:15; Num 11:5), "without cause" (1 Sam 19:5; 25:31; Job 2:3; Lam 3:52), and "without benefit or profit."

128. See Hill (*Malachi,* 185) for further discussion of rabbinic interpretations.

is derived from the verb *ḥāpēṣ*, "to delight" (cf. Gen 34:19; Num 14:8; Deut 21:14; 25:7, 8). There are several categories of objects used with Yahweh as subject of the verb *ḥāpēṣ*, including delighting in sacrifices and people (Isa 62:4; 65:19; Jer 31:20).

> You shall no more be termed Forsaken, and your land shall no more be termed Desolate; but you shall be called My Delight Is in Her, and your land Married; for *the LORD delights in you*, and your land shall be married. (Isa 62:4 NRSV)

On the other hand, there are also objects in which Yahweh does not delight, including solemn assemblies and sacrifices (Isa 1:11). In the book of Malachi, the root *ḥāpēṣ* occurs in several places (i.e., 1:10; 2:17; 3:1, 12).[129] Referring to the priests, Yahweh thus declares that Yahweh has *no delight in you (ʾên-lî ḥēpeṣ bākem)*. Just as Mal 1:6 depicts a progression in identifying the entities, so also one sees a progression here in 1:10b. Just as the text equates despised and defiled; the name and the Deity; the altar and the table; so also Yahweh declares unacceptable the priests and their offering. The fire on the altar is discouraged because of Yahweh's displeasure. The other instance where the noun *ḥēpeṣ* is used in reference to individuals as compared with sacrifices or offerings is Eccl 5:3, "no pleasure in fools"—*ʾên ḥēpeṣ bakkəsîlîm*—that is, those who reneged on their oath (cf. Mal 1:14). In this case, the progression moves from the individuals to their offerings—you or anything that you offer (Mal 1:10).

The final statement in Mal 1:10 again affirms Yahweh's displeasure—*nor will I accept offerings from your hand*. The use of the verb *rāṣâ* (to accept or be pleased with) to refer to Yahweh's response (rejection/acceptance) to offerings is well attested in prophetic critiques of cultic practices. Thus Hag 1:8 indicates that the building of the house would please and honor Yahweh.[130] On the other hand, Amos 5:22 identifies the offerings that Yahweh would not accept or be pleased with (e.g., burnt and grain offerings), also noting the Deity's rejection of the peace offerings and fattened animals. Similarly, Hos 8:13 reveals that Yahweh would not be pleased with their "choice sacrifice." Malachi 1:10b identifies *minḥâ*, "offering," and does not qualify what offerings, thus implying all the offerings of their hands vis-à-vis the work(s) of their hands (*maʿăśê yədêkem*; cf. Hag 2:14). The reference to their hands is analogous to the use in Hag 2:14, where the contamination flows from their

129. See discussion of Mal 2:17 (*qal* perfect third masculine singular verb, *ḥāpēṣ*), 3:1 (masculine plural absolute adjective, *ḥăpēṣîm*), and 3:12 (masculine singular absolute noun, *ḥēpeṣ*).

130. For further discussion of Hag 1:8, see part 1: Haggai, in this commentary.

hands. The expression "works of your hands" (*ma'ăśê yədêkem*) occurs in the critique of the community's sins leading to the announcement of God's judgment (e.g., Deut 31:29; Jer 25:6–7). In Jer 44:8 and 2 Chr 34:25, the works are further described as the offerings made to other gods.[131]

(2) Rationale for the Expressed Desire (1:11–13)

(a) Exaltation Abroad (1:11)

11 Malachi 1:11 provides the rationale for God's expressed desire that the cultic practices cease. The use of the *kî* clause connects 1:11 to 1:10 and lays the foundation for 1:12 by contrasting the nations and those who should honor Yahweh. *For from the rising of the sun to its setting, the name of Yahweh is great among the nations.* This statement denotes both temporal and spatial dimensions, depicting the identified activity as all-encompassing.[132] The formulation is attested in several texts, including Ps 50:1–2; 113:3; Isa 41:25; and 45:5–7.

> From the rising of the sun to its setting
> the name of the Lord is to be praised. (Ps 113:3 NRSV)

Likewise the scope or dimension of God's activity in summoning the earth includes no gaps:

> The mighty one, God the Lord,
> speaks and summons the earth
> from the rising of the sun to its setting. (Ps 50:1 NRSV)

The temporal expression in Mal 1:11 denotes the all-encompassing nature of the activity or status. In this case, it is the status of the Deity's name: the name is great (*gādôl*).

The adverbial modifier *among the nations (baggôyim)* affirms the spatial dimension. This presumes no activity by the nations to make Yahweh's name great; rather, Yahweh's name is inherently great. Nonetheless, Mal 1 restricts the affirmation by mentioning an exception—the people of God disregard the name of Yahweh. This observation presumes that Yehud is regarded as one of the nations. In view of Mal 1:5—*beyond the territory of Israel (mē'al ligbûl yiśrā'ēl)*—1:11 may also connote spatially differentiated activity (Yahweh's name is esteemed) outside Yehud versus inside Yehud (see map 2). The

131. See the expression "work(s) of their hands" (*ma'ăśê yədêkem*), in 2 Kgs 22:17; Jer 32:30.

132. Contrast Verhoef (*Haggai and Malachi*, 223), who denies the temporal dimension.

first part of the affirmation addresses the scope of the greatness of the Deity's name. In the context of Mal 1:6–14, it is important to remember that Yahweh is the speaker in this affirmation, which fact shows the Deity's perspective about the dishonor resulting from the priests' behaviors and attitudes. Moreover, the fact that Yahweh is honored everywhere but among Yahweh's people compounds the dishonor.

The second part of the affirmation correlates greatness with the nation's activities done in Yahweh's name—that is, presenting incense and clean offerings. Accordingly, the adverbial phase *in every place (ûbəkol-māqôm)* further specifies and thus clarifies the scope of the activities done in the name of Yahweh. However, this affirmation does not highlight simply the activity or the location; the activity only affirms Yahweh's status when it is done in the name of Yahweh.

The activity, *incense is offered,* is expressed by use of the verb *qāṭar*, "to make sacrifices smoke," and governs two objects—*muqṭār*, "incense," and *minḥâ,* "offerings." The *waw* constitutes a compound object of the verb *muggoš*, the *hophal* form of *nāgaš*, "to approach," where incense and pure offerings are offered.[133] Verhoef omits the conjunction; thus, his translation is "in every place incense is offered to my name, a pure offering."[134] The omission of the conjunction understands offering incense in Yahweh's name to be equal to a pure offering. Conceivably, this interpretation also designates the extent of the place—among the nations or wherever incense and/or a pure offering is offered—thus broadening the scope and circumstances of the name's greatness.[135]

The word *ṭāhôr,* a form of which appears in the *pure offerings (minḥâ ṭəhôrâ)*, is used of an entity's ceremonial status. It usually denotes that someone/something is pure or clean, meets the requirements for sacrifice, and thus is worthy of inclusion in the prescribed activity.[136] The person offering the sacrifice and the quality of the sacrifice contribute to the status of the offering as pure (cf. Lev 11; Deut 14:3–19). Consequently, any unclean person makes his/her offering unclean. On the other hand, being clean transforms an un-

133. Lev 6:22 [MT 15] uses *toqṭār*, the imperfect *hophal* form of the verb *qāṭar*.

134. Verhoef, *Haggai and Malachi,* 209. Elsewhere, Verhoef argues for the inclusion of the conjunction—thus, "incense is offered to my name, and a pure offering" (p. 225). Compare Hill (*Malachi,* 188) for a review of the various interpretations of the expression, including *muqṭār* as a verb (smoke is made to rise), omitting *muggoš*, omitting *muqṭār,* and reordering the words of the text in various ways.

135. See Hill's (*Malachi,* 171) translation "even a pure offering." Others reflect the compound object of the passive verb: Petersen (*Zechariah 9–14 and Malachi,* 174), "In every place incense and a pure offering are presented to my name"; Stuart ("Malachi," 1304), "Everywhere, incense will be offered to my name, and a pure offering, for my name will be great."

136. See discussion of Hag 2:10–13 in part 1: Haggai, in this commentary.

clean sacrifice into a clean one. The expression *pure offerings (minḥâ ṭəhôrâ)* is unique to Mal 1:11 and refers to the ceremonial status of the offering in contrast to the blemished (*mûm*), displeasing sacrifices that the priests of Jerusalem offered to Yahweh (cf. Lev 22:20; Deut 15:21). Human contributions may affirm the greatness of Yahweh's name. Nations may contribute in the form of incense and pure offerings. Consequently, wherever someone offers these contributions in Yahweh's name, there is the possibility of honoring Yahweh. Restrictions do not depend on the place or person but on the quality and possibly the intent. It makes sense to close the doors of the temple to prevent contaminating the practices and further dishonoring Yahweh. The rationale is that Yahweh does not need the polluted cultic practices for Yahweh's name to be honored. In spite of priestly corruption, Yahweh's name remains great; it is not dependent on priestly acknowledgment but is only affirmed by it.

The final part of Mal 1:11 reaffirms the greatness of Yahweh's name and thus establishes a stark contrast with the priests' contempt for Yahweh's name (1:12): *for my name is great among the nations.* Of the five occurrences of the root *gādal* in the book of Malachi, four are used in affirmation of Yahweh: 1:5, *great is Yahweh (yigdal yhwh);* 1:11 (2×), *my name is great (gādôl šəmî);* 1:14, *for I am a great king (kî melek gādôl 'ānî).* The attributions in 1:11 and 14 are part of the broad recognition of political and international entities. An additional nuance appears in the use of the durative sense, indicating that the name continues to be great.[137] This nuance contrasts with the sentiment in 1:12. The activities affirm the greatness but do not establish it; Yahweh's name is great apart from the worship or cultic activities done in Yahweh's name.

(b) Dishonor/Malpractice at Home (1:12–13)

Immediately juxtaposed with the claims about the universal reputation of Yahweh's name is the charge that the priests profane (*ḥālal*) the name. The claim is cryptic; the contrast is stark. The charge is appalling; the universality is challenged. The name is temporally great, without human contribution, but the behavior of the priests is significant. Perhaps the manifestation of greatness is seen through the regard accorded to the Deity by humans—groups and nations.

12 The second masculine plural independent pronoun *wə'attem* (you) refers to the priests, who have been the focus of the prophetic critique. In this case, the contrast is between the nations and the priests. *But you are profaning it.* How is the name of Yahweh profaned? The verb *məḥalləlîm*[138] is used in

137. Hill, *Malachi,* 187; *IBHS* §14.3.2.

138. *Piel* masculine plural particle of the verb "to profane, desecrate." See *IBHS* §37.6b for discussion of the durative sense.

Mal 1:12 with *ʾôtô* (it), the direct object marker and third person masculine suffix, to indicate the object.[139] The antecedent of the suffix is the name of Yahweh, identified in 1:11 as that which is great among the nations. How can it be despised through speech? Perhaps *when you say* does not refer simply to a speech act but to the priests' tendencies, including their beliefs and actions. This sentiment regarding the table of Yahweh and the associated offerings also occurs in Mal 1:7.

Regarding the mode of profaning Yahweh's name and substantiating the charge, the speaker cites the priests' words: the table is defiled. These words are introduced using the verbal form *beʾəmārəkem*, "when you say," suggesting the equivalence between their actions and their words or sentiment (cf. 1:7).[140] Whether the priests vocalize this perspective or it is surmised from their behavior, the quotation is used as evidence of their malpractice and failure to affirm the greatness of Yahweh's name. The priests reportedly conveyed two sentiments regarding the table of the Lord: first, that the table was defiled (*šulḥan ʾădōnāy məgōʾāl hûʾ*). In contrast to the pure offerings in 1:11, mention of the defiled table echoes 1:6 (the name is despised [*bāzâ*]) and 1:7 (Yahweh is defiled [*gāʾal*], and the table is despised [*bāzâ*]). Malachi 1:12, *by saying the table of Yahweh is despised (beʾəmārəkem šulḥan yhwh nibzê hûʾ),* echoes 1:7 in using the formulation *beʾəmārəkem šulḥan yhwh*. The charge's equivalent treatment of the components and implements of the cultic offerings makes them all vital to honoring Yahweh.

The priests' sentiment regarding the Lord's table extends to the fruit of the table (its fruit—*nîbô*): *its fruit (its food) is despised (nibzê).*[141] Here in 1:12 *ʾoklô,* "its food," further clarifies the meaning of "its fruit" and need not be deleted as an error.[142] This reading expresses more than the possibility of despising the table but actual disregard for the table of the Lord.[143] This is not an instance where Yahweh rejects (*zānaḥ*) the altar. Compare this with:

> The Lord has scorned his altar, disowned his sanctuary; he has delivered into the hand of the enemy the walls of her palaces. (Lam 2:7 NRSV)

God may profane (*ḥālal*) the temple in order to punish Israel. But in those instances, the choice to desecrate or profane is Yahweh's, as are the mode

139. *BHK* presents *ʾōtî* (me) as the object. *BHS* reads *ʾôtô* (it). The *BHK* reading directly connects the name and the being of Yahweh; but Mal 1 has already made that connection.

140. The infinitive construct form of *ʾāmar,* "to say," plus the preposition *bet.*

141. The LXX reads "and his food stuff placed thereon is despised."

142. Cf. Petersen (*Zechariah 9–14 and Malachi,* 176): "its food may be despised"; NRSV: "the food for it may be despised."

143. Contrast with *can* or *may* be despised; thus Baldwin, *Hag, Zech, Mal,* 230; Petersen, *Zechariah 9–14 and Malachi,* 175; and the NRSV.

and instrument of the desecration (Ezek 24:21, *məḥallēl,* of the sanctuary; Isa 47:6, *ḥillaltî,* of Yahweh's heritage). In Mal 1:12 the profaning of the table by the priests seems to be outside Yahweh's control.

13 The charge against the priests continues with their practices and sentiments. As in the previous instances of quoting the priests, *wa'ămartem,* "but you say," serves as a narrative element (cf. 1:2)

"Ah, what hardship!" is the priests' comment about their reason for dishonoring Yahweh. The priests claim to be weary, perhaps of presenting offerings to the Deity. The expression *what hardship (mattəlā'â)* is formed by the interrogative particle (*mâ*) plus the feminine noun *təlā'â* (hardship). This noun occurs in several passages denoting difficulty or hardships suffered—for example, Exod 18:8 (of the hardships encountered en route from Egypt); Num 20:14 (hardships en route to the land); and Lam 3:5 (of the hardships that God brought on Israel).[144] Particular to these is the difficulty or adversity experienced and perhaps the resulting exhaustion (esp. Exod 18:8). These do not refer to a nuisance[145] but an experience of difficulty or adversity. The priests consider the table of the Lord (*'ădōnāy*) and the requirements to be burdensome, even oppressive, thus leading them to slight the table and Yahweh.

Their action is depicted as an affront to Yahweh and is identified as cultic malpractice (cf. 1:11).[146] Two issues have influenced the understanding of the charge *but you ignite it*: the reading of *'ôtô* (it) and the understanding of the verb *nāpaḥ* (breathe or blow). Some modern translations conclude that *'ôtô* refers to Yahweh (in other words, that it means "me") and translate "sniff at me" (cf. the NRSV), thus following the LXX (*'ôtî*). I retain the MT reading to signify that the priests are accused of slighting "it," the table of the Lord (*šulḥan 'ădōnāy*).

The verb *nāpaḥ,* "breathe or blow," is used in several texts in the context of fire (blow the fire, Job 20:26; Ezek 22:20; Isa 54:16), to breathe (Gen 2:7), or to blow (Hag 1:9). Many interpret the verb as "sniff" to denote insolence and disregard for the cultic practices by translating *wəhippaḥtem 'ôtô* as "you sniff it."[147] However, the verb may be rendered best as "you ignite it,"[148] to illustrate the contrast between the perceived burden and the persistent practice. The priests perceive or even complain about the cultic practices as being adverse and burdensome, but they persist in them. This discrepancy between

144. See Neh 9:2, "all the hardship that has come upon us" (NRSV).

145. Thus Petersen, *Zechariah 9–14 and Malachi,* 174, 184–85.

146. The antecedent of *'ôtô* in Mal 1:12 is Yahweh's name, the specific concern in 1:11; but the antecedent of the pronoun in 1:13 is the table and the food mentioned in 1:12.

147. Thus Hill, *Malachi,* 171, 191; Verhoef, *Haggai and Malachi,* 209, 233.

148. Cf. Petersen, *Zechariah 9–14 and Malachi,* 174, 185; Weyde, *Prophecy and Teaching,* 152–53.

attitude and behavior may be at the root of the problem leading to Yahweh's express desire that they shut the doors (cf. Mal 1:10). It may also be the condition depicted in Mal 1:14—a lack of integrity.

Furthermore, the priests who ought to assess the sacrifices bring unacceptable sacrifices themselves. According to Lev 22 they are to screen an offering before it is presented to the Deity. Thus, the priests' assessment of an offering as acceptable (enough) to bring to Yahweh conflicts with Yahweh's assessment of the priests' evaluation as flawed and dishonoring to the Deity. Regarding the latter, the priests may be careless in their assessment or perhaps deliberate in offering corrupt sacrifices and downplaying the significance of the sacrifice and the cult.

Malachi 1:13 characterizes the animals presented (*bôʾ*)[149] as offerings (*minḥâ*; cf. Mal 1:10) as lame, sick, or stolen. In comparison with the list of characteristics in Mal 1:8—blind (*ʿiwwēr*), lame (*pissēaḥ*), and sick (*ḥōleh*)—Mal 1:13 adds *stolen* (*gāzûl*).[150] *And you brought that which was stolen or lame or sick.* The inclusion of the characteristic stolen expands the requirements beyond physical traits—lame (*pissēaḥ*) and sick (*ḥōlê*) (cf. Deut 15:21). That Yahweh cannot accept stolen goods introduces the matter of possession, which will be picked up in Mal 1:14. Whether the stolen animal is perfect is irrelevant since the infraction of stealing renders it unacceptable. Anyone who steals is required to restore the stolen goods and to present a guilt offering to the priests, who will then make atonement for the thief (Lev 6:1–7 [MT 5:20–26]).[151] If stolen goods are being presented, they may mean that the person presenting them has not realized his guilt and thus has compounded his sin; or they may mean that he is committing one sin (by presenting the stolen goods) to atone for another sin. What matters is not the offering of a sacrifice in itself but the offering of a sacrifice that is acceptable to Yahweh and does not offend Yahweh.

The rhetorical question broaches the issue of whether Yahweh will accept the sacrifice. *"Shall I accept it from your hand?" says Yahweh.* The question is not whether sacrifices in general are brought to the Deity; rather, the question is how Yahweh will respond to what is brought. In light of the rhetorical question in Mal 1:8, this question is not surprising. In both Mal 1:8 and 1:13, the question deals with the acceptability of an offering to a human ruler on the one hand and to the Deity on the other. The sequence in 1:13 signals the sheer absurdity of accepting an offering that should not even be presented since it does not meet the basic legal criteria for acceptability.

149. The verb *bôʾ* in the *hiphil*, "to bring," occurs with reference to the offering.

150. This is the *qal* passive particle of *gāzal*, "to seize, rob." Note its occurrence in Mic 2:2; 3:2 with the objects "field" and "skin," respectively. It occurs with *miyyad*, "from hand," in 2 Sam 23:21 and 1 Chr 11:23.

151. Cf. Hartley, *Leviticus*; Milgrom, *Leviticus 1–16*; Weyde, *Prophecy and Teaching*, 153.

Could it be that the Deity entertains the idea of accepting unacceptable offerings from the priests' hands? Could the question also include the possibility that Yahweh may concede to the malpractice of the priests and hence the community for the sake of the relationship? Given the tone of the text, it is unlikely that Yahweh's question suggests ambivalence or doubt about accepting the unacceptable. Instead, the question in Mal 1:13 shows that Yahweh has already decided that accepting the unacceptable is not an option.

(3) Pronouncement of the Curse (1:14)

14 According to Yahweh, the priests (and community) claim hardship, yet they are not completely lacking in resources. The problem is that they vowed one thing and did another: they promised a male sacrifice and instead gave something that was corrupt, stolen, lame, or sick. The deception was the incongruity between their vow and their action. In addition to their deception, another reason for the curse against them is that they offended Yahweh. Malachi 1:14 closely intertwines several aspects of the curse: the formulation, the person who deceived, and the nature and consequence of the deceit.

Cursed be the one who deceives articulates the punishment on the addressees. First the formulation of the curse uses *'ārûr* followed by a participle to establish the person who is cursed.[152] Other expressions of a curse include use of the relative clause: "cursed is the person who..." (*'ārûr hā'îš 'ăšer,* Deut 27:15; Josh 6:26; 1 Sam 14:24, 28);[153] "cursed is anyone who does not..." (e.g., Deut 27:26; Jer 11:3). The pronouncement in Deut 27:15–26 and 28:16–19 clearly uses the curse or the *'ārûr* formula plus a designation for the persons or entity. Deuteronomy 27:15–26 pronounces a curse based on the actions of a person rather than on the basis of his/her identity—for example, anyone who makes an idol (Deut 27:15) and anyone who deprives the underprivileged of justice (Deut 27:19).[154] In this regard, the curse lasts as long as the behavior is practiced (cf. Josh 6:26; Judg 5:23; Jer 11:3; 17:5; 48:10).

While using the *'ārûr* formula, Mal 1:14 expands the description of the cursed person by detailing the nature of the action: *but who vows and sacrifices what is corrupt to the Lord.* It thus identifies the cursed person as one who cheats or deceives (*nôkēl*).[155] The specific deception relates to the individual's vow to Yahweh regarding a sacrifice. He or she vows (*nādar*) but does not

152. Of the forty occurrences of the *qal* passive particle (*'ārûr*), thirty-eight are a part of an *'ārûr* formula (e.g., Jer 20:14–15; v. 14, "regarding the day" [*hayyôm*], and v. 15, "of the man" [*hā'îš*]; 48:10 [2×]).

153. Note the use in Jer 17:5, "cursed is the man who" (*'ārûr haggeber 'ăšer*).

154. See Num 24:9: cursing any who curse Israel.

155. The term *nākal,* "deceitful or slick," is rare, occurring only in Gen 37:18; Num 25:18; and Ps 105:25.

follow through. Although the person vows to present a male (*zākār*) sacrifice, he or she offers "a corrupt [offering]" (*mošḥāt).* Seeing it in connection with several texts illumines the nature of the curse. In Lev 22:18–20 any person could present a free-will offering or an offering in payment of a vow (*neder*). In either case, the offering must be a blemish-free (*tāmîm*) male (*zākār*) bull, sheep, or goat (*babbāqār bakkəśābîm ûbāʿizzîm*). A blemished (*mûm*) offering is unacceptable (*lōʾ lərāṣôn*). Leviticus 27:9–12 addresses the situation of substituting a different offering in place of the one that was vowed: there should be no substitution, whether good or bad, and if one is substituted for another, then both offerings—the one vowed and the substitute—"shall be holy" (*yihyê-qōdeš*). The priest is responsible for assessing whether an offering is an unclean (*ṭəmēʾâ*) animal that should not be presented to Yahweh.

So it is neither the offering of the sacrifice that is condemned nor the fact that it is offered to the Lord (*laʾdōnāy*). According to Deut 15:21 one should not present to Yahweh a blemished (*mûm*) offering—lame or blind. The fact that someone owns a male sacrifice and vows it but then presents a blemished offering is deemed deceitful. Malachi 1:14 does not specify the gender or type of animal (cf. Lev 22:18–20); if it is blemished or corrupt, the type of animal or its gender is irrelevant. The curse is therefore pronounced on a person who deceives by substituting an unacceptable offering for the male he or she vowed.

Changing from second-person address to third-person is common for the curse formula and may be signaling a general "anyone" rather than distinguishing between the presence or absence of the addressees.[156] Furthermore, the general sense may include the priests and the people—the priests because they are responsible for assessing the worthiness of the sacrifice and the lay people because they have broken a vow. Given the context, Mal 1:6–14 most likely refers to the priests and the people for their respective parts in the process of offering a blemished animal to Yahweh.

In Mal 1:14b, the *kî* clause *for I am a great king* provides the rationale for the curse. The priests are cursed because they dishonor Yahweh by offering unacceptable sacrifices. The contrast between what they would do for the governor and what they do for Yahweh is again a cause of concern (cf. Mal 1:8). The formulation *for I am a great king* could be categorized as a recognition formula—to identify the Deity's status and reputation. It functions as a reminder to the addressees and perhaps as a defense of the Deity's status as "a great king" (*melek gādôl*). Such a defense fits the caustic tone of the pas-

156. See Weyde (*Prophecy and Teaching,* 154) for a discussion about the use of the third-person formulation to indicate the absence of addressees. Weyde also notes the instances where the curse appears with the second-person formulation; for example, Gen 3:14; 4:11; Deut 28:16 (2×), 19 (2×); and Josh 9:23.

sage. Furthermore, the defense illuminates the Deity's apparent challenge to those who show no honor: give a semblance of respect. In the face of their disrespect, the Deity reminds the hearers of the Deity's status as king. As in Mal 1:6, the Deity's position in the relationship does not match the treatment given in the relationship. Perhaps Israel's disregard matches its perception of Yahweh's status. Malachi 1:14 echoes 1:11's assertion about the universal and transtemporal presence and honor of Yahweh. The attention to the governor in 1:8 shows awareness of the honor a leader should receive.[157] Here in 1:14, Yahweh's kingship is juxtaposed with its status among the nations. So rather than being a contrast between instances of misplaced honor, here the contrast is between the international reputation and the fractured covenant relationship, between affirmation and honor (received from the masses) and disregard and dishonor (received from the chosen group).

Two parts of the verse's last clause are illuminated: that the name is feared or reverenced (*nôrāʾ*) and that it is reverenced among the nations (*baggôyim*). Reference to the name is prominent in the book of Malachi (cf. Mal 1:6, 11, 14; 2:2, 5; 3:16; 4:2 [MT 3:20]—all but 3:16 referring to "my name" [*šəmî*]). Malachi 1:11 claims that Yahweh's name is great among the nations (*baggôyim*). The reverence for Yahweh's name among the nations picks up the idea from Mal 1:5 that Yahweh's greatness extends beyond the territory of Israel.

While affirming Yahweh's identity, the claim attests the Deity's quest for the elusive honor of his own people. This claim's boastful self-affirmation evidences a susceptibility formed by sensitivity to being dishonored. The one who claims universal recognition still desires the attention of a reluctant people. While saying *Shall I accept it?* the Deity cares enough to highlight the displeasure of not receiving the best offerings. Whatever else we may assert about the claims of wide recognition, it is clear that the Deity is entangled, determined to receive honor, and perhaps frustrated by the inability to secure that honor. This verse reads like the story of someone who wants to walk away from a relationship but continues to discuss all the problems while remaining in it. Highlighting the reverence received from other nations does not blind Yahweh to the dishonor from Israel. It is not simply being revered that is a problem for the Deity; the problem is that the people from whom Yahweh desires honor do not give it. Further compounding the aggravation is the fact that the nations do what the selected group fails to do. The nations revere Yahweh, but the priests

157. The instances in 2 Kgs 18:19, 28//Isa 36:4, 13 use the definite article in reference to an earthly ruler, "the great king" (*hammelek haggādôl*)—the Assyrian king Rabshakeh. For uses without the definite article referring to an earthly ruler, see Eccl 9:14. The designation "a great king" (*melek gādôl*) occurs with various designations of the deity: Mal 1:14 (*yhwh ṣəbāʾôt*); Ps 47:3 (*yhwh ʿelyôn*); and 95:3 (*yhwh*).

who ought to know better despise Yahweh's name. In part, the dishonor fuels the Deity's emotions toward Israel and the quest for Israel's love and honor.

2. *Regarding Priestly Instruction (2:1–9)*

Malachi 2:1–9 is the second subunit of the macrounit that is 1:6–2:9. To review, the first dealt with priestly malpractice in the area of sacrifices (1:6–14); the second now deals with priestly instruction (2:1–9). A few transition elements contribute to the continuity of the macrounit. First, the addressees in 2:1–9 are identified as the priests (*hakkōhănîm*; 2:1). Second, the references to *kābēd,* "honor," which were introduced in 1:6 and continued in 1:11 and 14, further the continuity of the unit (cf. Mal 2:2, 5). Third, the theme of the curse introduced in 1:14 is sustained in 2:2–3. Both 1:6–14 and 2:1–9 portray the priests as violating their responsibilities and thus dishonoring Yahweh. Although the priests offer sacrifices and teach the people, their performance is unacceptable because it violates the stipulations about their duties.

a. Yahweh's Command to the Priests (2:1–4)

1*So now, this is the command to you, O priests!* 2*"If you will not listen and if you will not set your heart to give honor to my name," said Yahweh, "then I will send the curse on you and I will curse your blessings.*[a] *Indeed, I have cursed it because you do not set [it] to heart.* 3*Look, I am rebuking*[b] *your seed*[c] *and I will spread dung on your face—dung of your feasts.*[d] *And he will take you to it.*[e]
4*And you will know that I sent to you this command to do*[f] *my covenant with Levi," said Yahweh of hosts.*

---

a. The MT has the feminine plural noun (*bərākôt*) with a second masculine plural suffix, *birkôtêkem,* "your blessings," followed by a verbal form with the third feminine singular suffix, *'ārôtîhā,* "I cursed it." The LXX reads the singular noun, thus presuming *birkatkem,* "your blessing," rather than the plural form *birkôtêkem,* "your blessings," of the MT. The singular form of the LXX may be an attempt to clarify the MT by harmonizing the third feminine singular noun with the third feminine singular suffix on the following verbal form (*'ārôtîhā*)—thus the reading "I cursed it" (cf. Vuilleumier, "Malachie," 233–34).

Some scholars and modern translations harmonize the reading by proposing a third feminine plural suffix, thus "I cursed them," referring to the blessings (see the NIV, NRSV)—Verhoef, *Haggai and Malachi,* 236, 240. Petersen (*Zechariah 9–14 and Malachi,* 175, 176) believes that he is following the MT when he inaccurately observes, "The LXX presupposes a singular pronominal suffix as opposed to the plural one in MT" (p. 176). Instead, both the MT and LXX have a plural suffix on the noun and a singular suffix on the verbal form.

b. Although the MT reads *gō'ēr,* "to rebuke," *BHS* proposes *godēa',* the masculine singular participle from the verb *gāda',* "hew down, cut off." The LXX reads *aphorizō,* "to separate," which *BHS* equates with *gāraʿ*, "restrain, withdraw." Petersen (*Zechariah 9–14 and Malachi*, 175–76) assumes the verb *gāraʿ*; thus his translation: "I am removing your progeny."

c. The LXX reads *ōmos*, "shoulder," probably assuming *hazzərōaʿ*, "the arm," in place of the MT *hazzeraʿ*, "the seed." Some modern translations follow the LXX, e.g., NEB, NJB: "I will cut off your arm."

d. *BHS* proposes that *pereš ḥaggêkem*, "dung of your feasts," is a gloss to be deleted, possibly based on the understanding that *pereš* refers to the waste products of the animals; several modern translations render this phrase as "sacrifice or offering," e.g., NRSV: "dung of your offering"; NJB: "solemn sacrifice."

e. The last clause of Mal 2:3 (*wənāśāʾ ʾetkem ʾēlāyw*) is also difficult in that it transitions from a first-person (*wəzērîtî*) to a third-person (*wənāśāʾ*) account. *BHS* suggests that the clause is an addition and offers the following reading: *wənāśāʾtî ʾetkem mēʿālay*, "I will take you from my presence" (cf. 2 Sam 13:17). This reading retains the first-person address and the imagery depicting the humiliations (cf. Mal 1:10). The LXX reads *eis to auto*, "to the same," in place of the MT *ʾēlāyw*, "to him, it." *BHS*'s suggestion is the most plausible option for understanding the verse; however, it is also possible that the subject of the verb *nāśāʾ* is impersonal: "someone" with *pereš*, "dung," the referent of the third singular suffix. Cf. Verhoef, *Haggai and Malachi*, 243. Petersen (*Zechariah 9–14 and Malachi*, 176) contends that the MT is corrupt in that the words are incorrectly divided. Consequently, he proposes an emendation, reading a masculine plural verbal form plus the prepositional phrase offered by *BHS* "from me"; thus: "you shall be carried away from me."

f. *BHS* proposes *ləḥayyôt*, "to live" (*lamed* plus infinitive construct of the verb *hāyâ*). The alternate reading is *mihyôt* ("from being," *min* plus the infinitive construct form of *hāyâ*). Yet another reading is *ləhaḥet*, "to be dismayed."

The essence of the command in 2:2–3 is to present the options: either correct the malpractice or be cursed. Retribution forms the basis of the relationship between the priestly practices and the subsequent experiences. Nonetheless, even though the priests are called to amend their ways, such action on their part will not necessarily avert punishment because the cause-effect sequence is already in motion (Mal 2:2–3). The mention of a command introduces the charge against the priests' malpractice regarding instruction and sets the stage for the ensuing consequences.

(1) The Introductory Statement (2:1)

1 The statement *So now, this is the command to you, O priests!* builds on the previous unit's portrayal of the priests and addresses their skewed knowledge of their responsibility. The particle *wəʿattā*, "and now," in 2:1 signals a new thought and a continuation of pronouncements from the preceding discussion addressed to the priests (cf. 1:9).[158] The priests are confirmed

158. Hill, *Malachi*, 196; Petersen, *Zechariah 9–14 and Malachi*, 187; Verhoef, *Haggai and Malachi*, 237.

as the addressees by the use of *ʾălêkem,* "to you" (preposition *ʾel* plus the second masculine plural suffix *kem,* "you") in addition to the vocative *hakkōhănîm,* "priests." The statement draws attention to "this command" (*hammiṣwâ hazzōʾt*), the singular form.[159] A similar formulation occurs in Deut 15:15 ("I command you this word," *haddābār hazzê*) and Jer 7:23, where the charge is articulated directly following the introductory clause: "this word I commanded them" (*haddābār hazzê ṣiwwîtî ʾôtām*).[160] "This command" (*hammiṣwâ hazzōʾt*) in Mal 2:1 does not point to a new command, nor is it a verdict against the priests.[161] Presumably, the priests know the command because the content of the command is presupposed. "This command" apparently refers to a charge given to the priests regarding their role as priests (e.g., Exod 32:26–29; Num 25:11–13; Deut 33:8–11).[162] The command is therefore a charge regarding a responsibility that is presupposed rather than being articulated or reiterated.

(2) The Command—as Curse for Their Malpractice (2:2–3)

Malachi 2:2–3 illustrates the ongoing tension in the relationship between the priests and Yahweh. The "if . . . then" structure portrays the conditions (protasis) and the outcomes (apodosis).

2 In 2:2 the protasis establishes negative conditions by using the *ʾim-lōʾ* formula with the particle of contingency (*ʾim*) and the particle of negation (*lōʾ*) plus the verb indicating the negated action. The first element of the protasis—*if you will not listen (ʾim-lōʾ tišməʿû)*—uses the *qal* imperfect form, indicating a future orientation. The absence of an object further suggests general or overall behavior. Whether they listened is not a part of this first element of the protasis but is a question that arises with the indication that the curse has already commenced against the priests (2:3).

The second element of the protasis, *if you will not set your heart to,* is an idiomatic expression that also occurs in Hag 1:5, 7; 2:15, 18, where the *qal* imperative *śîmû,* "set," is used to call for reflection or consideration.[163] The use in Mal 2:2 occurs with the particle of negation (e.g., Jer 12:11; Isa 42:25; 57:1, 11). Jeremiah 12:11 and Isa 42:25 depict situations in which nobody reflects on

159. Modern versions differ in their rendering of *hammiṣwâ hazzōʾt;* for example: the ASV and KJV translate "commandment," ESV and NRSV "command," JPS "charge," and NIV "admonition."

160. Jer 7:23—*ʾet- haddābār hazzê ṣiwwîtî ʾôtām,* "the word I commanded them"; cf. NRSV "this command I gave them."

161. See Glazier-McDonald (*Malachi: The Divine Messenger,* 64–65) for discussion of *hammiṣwâ hazzōʾt* as indicative of the verdict beginning in 2:1.

162. See discussion of Mal 2:5–7 below.

163. See part 1: Haggai, in this commentary, for further discussion of the occurrences.

a noted tragedy. The idiomatic expression *śîm* + *ʿal* + *lēb* here specifies the object (cf. Hag 1:5, 7), which is your deeds (*darkêkem*), while in Hag 2:15 and 18 the temporal aspects of the circumstances are defined. The specified object in Mal 2:2 is the act of giving glory to Yahweh's name (*lātēt kābôd lišmî*).[164] The second element of the protasis thus shows the alternative of honoring or not honoring Yahweh's name. The protasis focuses on the negative result—that is, what will happen if the priests do not honor Yahweh's name. The condition (protasis) does not explain what the behavior is that would constitute honoring the name.

The conditional formulation reveals that adherence to the command is necessary to avoid the curse. But it also indicates that the priests have already been cursed. So, would adherence be effective in ending the implementation of the curse or discontinuing a curse that had already been implemented? Perhaps there is an interruption in the thought process—to create a more accurate representation rather than to suggest an unrealistic way of avoiding what already exists. An interruption in the thought does not mean that the initial intent was to mislead. Rather, the apparent stream of consciousness that characterizes the conditional statement is a device for updating the content while emphasizing the inevitability of the curse. Here the inevitability means that it already exists, not that it is imminent.

The idea of cursing the priests is startling because the curse is against those who are responsible for blessing others. God can curse whomever God chooses to curse. In general, a curse is a malevolent expression of the intent to bring about a particular future occurrence. So then, what does it mean to curse the priests? Moreover, what does it mean to curse the blessings? Presumably cursing and blessing are mutually exclusive or at least suggest different processes and outcomes. So what does it mean to curse the blessings? This may be a reference to the "extent of the blessings," including two components: the pronouncement (content) of the blessings and the material benefits or privileges of the priestly status/role.[165]

The apodosis ("then. . .," 2:2aβ) identifies the outcome of the condition specified in the protasis ("if. . .," 2:2a). But is this a real condition? What is the effect of 2:2b juxtaposed with the conditional statement in 2:2a? As in the protasis, so in the apodosis there are two elements, each beginning with the first common singular converted perfect form of the verb (with Yahweh as speaker). In the first element of the apodosis, the pattern is: verb "I will send" (*wəšillaḥtî*) + indirect object "on you" (*bākem*) + direct object "the curse"

164. Notably the *qal* infinitive construct form *lātēt,* "to give," functions as a complementary infinitive plus the direct object and indirect object *šəmî,* "my name," referring to Yahweh.

165. Hill (*Malachi,*199) suggests that the reference includes both components.

(*hammәʾērâ*). The converted perfect form *wәšillaḥtî* denotes a future action, "I will send," echoing the language of sending fire (cf. Amos 1:4, 7, 10, 12; 2:2, 5; Hos 8:14) and of the Deity's act of judgment on a nation (e.g., Jer 9:16 [MT 15]; 24:10; 49:37; Ezek 5:17; 7:3; 14:21 [perfect form]; 28:23; 39:6).[166] Among the occurrences of the first-person form of *šālaḥ*, "to send," plus object in prophetic literature, Mal 2:2 stands out by labeling the punishment "the curse" (*hammәʾērâ*). However, the pattern of the verb *šālaḥ* plus an object is found in Deut 28:20, where the object is also in the definite form (*hammәʾērâ*).[167] In other instances that identify a curse, particular elements are affected—for example, crops, nature, and the well-being of the community.

The second element of the apodosis uses the verb *ʾārar*, "to curse," plus an object to specify the negative outcome of the condition. Here in Mal 2:2 the verb *wәʾārôtî* is used plus the object "your blessings" (*birkôtêkem*), referring to the priests. Is this an elaboration of the curse, or is this another outcome of the negative condition? The curse would be a curse on the blessings. Keeping in mind that this could be a curse on their pronouncement, it is a startling reversal of the priests' actions and intent. Where else does the Deity reverse the intention of the priests or God's messenger (cf. Num 22:6; 23:8)? Possibly the curse is on both their pronouncements and the privileges/benefits of their status, and thus both their status and the performance of their duty are suspended.

3 The announcement of the penalty takes into account the current priests (2:2) and their descendants (2:3). The use of "the seed" (*hazzeraʿ*) declares the Deity's intent to punish both those who have sinned and subsequent generations. In 2:3 rebuking (*gōʿēr*) is the mode of the penalty. This is one of several occurrences in the Minor Prophets. In some instances *gōʿēr* (rebuke) is used of Yahweh's action against the adversary (*haśśāṭān*, Zech 3:2) and action against the devourer (*ʾōkēl,* Mal 3:11).[168] In the book of Proverbs a positive response to the rebuke (*gәʿārâ*) is perceived as beneficial (Prov 13:1; 17:10).[169] Despite these occurrences of the root, some scholars emend Mal 2:3, positing the root *gādaʿ*, "to hew or cut off" (e.g., Deut 7:5;

166. Genesis 27:45 uses *wәšālaḥtî* of the promise to return Jacob to his family. Other forms used to designate sending various types of adversity include particles (*mašlîaḥ*, Exod 8:21 [MT 17]; *šōlēaḥ*, 9:14); the first-person form of the imperfect used of the Deity (*ʾăšallaḥ,* Exod 23:27); and the converted perfect form *wәšālaḥtî* used of the Deity, who will send an agent to drive out the Canaanites (Exod 23:28; 33:2).

167. Cf. Mal 3:9; Prov 3:33; 28:27—God's curse against a person.

168. It also occurs in Isa 50:2; 51:20; 54:9; 66:15. Other uses of the root *gāʿar* include verbal forms in Pss 68:30 (MT 31); 119:21 and a feminine noun form *gaʿărāt* Ps 76:6 (MT 7); 80:16 (MT 17); 104:7; Eccl 7:5.

169. The perspective is also conveyed using the synonym *yākaḥ*, "to reprove, chide," used in Prov 15:10; 24:25; 25:12; 27:5; 30:6. This root is also found in Isa 37:3, 4.

12:3), and the object "arm" (*hazzərōaʿ*), rather than the MT reading "seed" (*hazzeraʿ*; cf. 1 Sam 2:31).[170]

> See, a time is coming when I will cut off your strength and the strength of your ancestor's family, so that no one in your family will live to old age. (1 Sam 2:31 NRSV)

The image of terminating the addressees and their lineage influences the interpretation of Mal 2:3aα as argued by those who read the text "I will cut off your descendants or strength."[171] By contrast, the penalty announced in Mal 2:3aα is not to annihilate the line but to terminate the function or role of the priests' offspring.[172] One may also note Jer 22:24–30, which announces the termination of the Davidic reign—"for none of his *offspring* shall succeed in sitting on the throne of David, and ruling again in Judah." Moreover, the intention of and delight in extending the curse across generations are evident in Deut 28:20–68.[173]

> All these curses shall come upon you, pursuing and overtaking you until you are destroyed, because you did not obey the Lord your God, by observing the commandments and the decrees that he commanded you. They shall be among *you and your descendants* as a sign and a portent forever.. . . If you do not diligently observe all the words of this law that are written in this book, fearing this glorious and awesome name, the Lord your God, then the Lord will overwhelm both *you and your offspring* with severe and lasting afflictions and grievous and lasting maladies. . . . And just as the Lord took delight in making you prosperous and numer-

170. There are two main options for the translation of Mal 2:3aα. First, the MT "to rebuke" is retained. Among those who follow this option are Weyde, *Prophecy and Teaching,* 159; Verhoef, *Haggai and Malachi,* 236, 240; Hill, *Malachi,* 171, 200. Some modern translations follow the MT reading "to rebuke": e.g., NRSV, KJV, ASV, NIV. The second option for the verb in 2:3aα is "to hew, cut off," which the apparatus suggests with the object "arm/strength" rather than "seed" of the MT. J. M. P. Smith ("Malachi," 36–37) emends the text to read "going to hew off the arm for you" and argues for consistency with the version and harmony of the images in the verse, namely the face and the arm. Petersen (*Zechariah 9–14 and Malachi,* 175–76) proposes "to remove."

171. Cf. Petersen, *Zechariah 9–14 and Malachi,* 175–76.

172. Contrast Glazier-McDonald (*Malachi: The Divine Messenger,* 67), who proposes that "seed" refers to grain (cf. 3:11).

173. Weyde (*Prophecy and Teaching,* 163–64) discusses the "formal and terminological" connection between Mal 2:2–3 and Deut 28, including Yahweh's sending (*šālaḥ*), curse (*məʾērâ*), rebuke (*migʿeret*)—derived from *gāʿar,* "to rebuke," the verb used in Mal 2:3.

> ous, so the Lord will take delight in bringing you to ruin and destruction. (Deut 28:45–46, 58–59, 63)[174]

While the curse on the current generation is the first part of the announced punishment for not glorifying Yahweh, the second part of the punishment is the rebuke of the priests' descendants (Mal 2:3). Then, as if the rebuke or insulting of the descendants were not devastating enough, the punishment includes another dimension of humiliation.[175] The specific humiliation is the act of spreading or smearing (*zārâ*) the descendants' faces with dung (*pereš*)—not just any dung or excrement but that of the sacrificial animal (e.g., the bull used as the sin offering). Waste elements and dung in particular were supposed to be disposed. In all of the word's occurrences outside Mal 2:3, the dung of the sacrifice along with the entrails, blood, and skin was to be burned outside the camp (Exod 29:14; Lev 4:8–12; 8:16–17; 16:27–28; cf. Num 19:5).[176] Malachi 2:3 resignifies the treatment of dung in association with the priests who were to dispose of it. The image of smearing dung uses the term *zārâ*, "to spread, scatter," a term used in judgment against a people/nation (cf. Jer 31:10; 49:32, 36; 51:2; Ezek 5:10, 12; 12:14–15; 20:23; 22:15; 29:12; 30:23, 26; Zech 2:2, 4).[177] The spreading of dung on faces signals the priests' uncleanness and disqualification from priestly functions. Summarily, the priests' blessings are cursed and the refuse of their sacrifices is used to humiliate them. In both instances (Mal 2:2, 3), the resignification is the result of disfavor toward the priests. Smearing dung on their faces will entail humiliating and contaminating them rather than purifying them. They defiled Yahweh, and Yahweh will make them ineligible as priests. Thus, they will be denied the opportunity to dishonor Yahweh further through cultic means.

(3) Conclusion: Rationale for the Command (2:4)

4 Malachi 2:4 articulates the purpose or rationale for the judgment against the priests and their descendants. The recognition formula (*yāda‘* + *kî*—you [they]

174. In these texts the continuation of the curse is not a residual effect but a deliberate act of the Deity in sustaining the curse—a curse on subsequent generations.

175. See Mal 1 regarding honor and shame in the book of Malachi.

176. Various terms are used for dung, but they still convey the presence of humiliation: for example, of eating one's dung (*ḥere’*) and drinking one's urine (*šên*)—2 Kgs 18:27. The term *dōmen*, "dung," occurs in several texts to denote refuse, for example, 2 Kgs 9:37; Jer 8:2; 16:4; 25:33; Ps 83:11. Cf. Milgrom, *Leviticus 1–16*, 239; B. A. Levine, *Numbers 1–20: A New Translation with Introduction and Commentary*, AB 4 (New York: Doubleday, 1993), 462; A. I. Baumgarten, "The Paradox of the Red Heifer," *VT* 43 (1993): 442–51.

177. Other texts that use *zārâ* with the nation/people as object include Lev 26:33; 1 Kgs 14:15; Ps 44:11; 106:27.

will know that . . .) affirms that the insults and humiliation are signs that the command comes from the Deity. Similar formulas appear in other confirmations of judgment on a nation/people. They identify the Deity as bringing the judgment and confirm the connection between the Deity and the specific judgment. In Ezekiel the recognition formula has various foci, including identity of the Deity, "Then you will know that I am Yahweh" (Ezek 7:3–5; 28:23; 39:6); justification of the Deity's actions (Ezek 14:21–23); and benevolence toward the people (Ezek 13:23; cf. Isa 49:23). In particular, the use of the verb *šālaḥ*, "to send," in the recognition formula affirms a specific action as being the Deity's:

> See now, I am going to raise my hand against them, and they shall become plunder for their own slaves. Then you will know that the Lord of hosts has sent me. . . . Many nations shall join themselves to the Lord on that day, and shall be my people; and I will dwell in your midst. And you shall know that the Lord of hosts has sent me to you. (Zech 2:9, 11 [MT 13, 15])[178]

Malachi 2:4 confirms the threat to invalidate the priests. However, the rationale affirms the Deity's intent to sustain the covenant of Levi (*bərîtî ʾet-lēwî*). The fact that Mal 2:1 addresses the priests (*hakkōhănîm*) and 2:4 comments on the covenant of Levi (*bərîtî ʾet-lēwî*) provokes a question about the significance of the designations. Are two different groups intended? Is this an indictment on the priests on the one hand and an affirmation of the Levites on the other (cf. 2:8), given that the covenant seems to include the priests?[179] Apparently, even though there are two designations, both groups are included in the covenant and its requirement to teach. However, the Levites may here be presented as exemplary in contrast to the priests with their deplorable behavior.[180]

b. Covenant of Levi as Basis of Instruction (2:5–9)

5 *"My covenant was with him, life and peace; and I gave them to him, reverence, and he reverenced me. And he was in awe before my name.* 6 *The true instruction was in his mouth and wrong was not found on his lips. He walked with*

178. Cf. Zech 4:9; 6:15; Num 16:28.

179. Cf. J. M. O'Brien, *Priest and Levite*; E. Meyers, "Priestly Language in the Book of Malachi," *HAR* 10 (1986): 225–37.

180. See Petersen (*Zechariah 9–14 and Malachi,* 192 n. 52), who argues that Mal 2, like the Chronicler's history, elevates the Levites by designating them "messengers of Yahweh" (*mal'ak yhwh;* Mal 2:7; cf. Hag 1:13).

me in peace and in uprightness; and he turned many from iniquity. [7]*Because the lips of a priest keep knowledge; and they seek instruction from his mouth because he is a messenger of Yahweh of hosts.* [8]*But you yourself have turned aside from the way. You caused many to stumble in the Torah. You corrupted the covenant of Levi," says Yahweh of hosts.* [9]*"So indeed I myself will make you despised and humiliated before all the people, inasmuch as you are not keeping my ways but [you are] showing partiality in the Torah."*

A reminder of the priests' responsibility follows the command (2:1) and uses a historical perspective on the covenant with Levi to illustrate ideal priestly conduct (2:5–7), present what Levi practiced (2:5–6), and summarize the priests' responsibility (2:7). The reminder includes attention to priestly malpractice (2:8) and the consequences of malpractice (2:9). As in 2:2–4, so in 2:9 judgment will not be averted. Just as the priests publicly dishonored Yahweh, so Yahweh will publicly dishonor the priests. In this respect, the people who were subjected to the corrupt practices of the priests' instruction (2:7) will witness the priests' demise (2:9).

(1) Nature of the Covenant (2:5a)

5 Malachi 2:5–7 continues on the topic of God's covenant with Levi, further describing that covenant, including the nature of the covenant (2:5) and the varied responses to the covenant (2:6–7). Clearly noted is the influence of the priests' behavior on the community.

In presenting an account of the past, 2:5 implies that Yahweh made a covenant with Levi—*my covenant was with him.* The verb *hāyətâ,* the *qal* perfect, indicates past action.[181] The two parties in the covenant are Yahweh, identified by the first-person singular pronominal suffix "my" on the term *bərîtî* (my covenant), and Levi, identified by the prepositional phrase *'ittô,* "with him." While there is no explicitly named covenant (*bərît*) with Levi, several texts do attest the special relationship between God and Levi/the Levites. That relationship may be in view here regarding Yahweh's covenant with Levi and may include promises, loyalty, and so forth. Passages that articulate that special relationship are Exod 32:26–29, a blessing was given in response to their actions during the apostasy at Sinai;[182] Num 25:11–13, granting Phinehas the covenant of peace; Deut 10:8–9, God's designating the

181. Compare with *lihyôt* (*lə* plus *qal* infinitive construct form) in 2:4, pointing to possibility in contrast to the past action in 2:5. Hill, *Malachi,* 206.

182. Many note that there is no account of a covenant with Levi in the Old Testament and see these texts as possible articulations of the covenant—e.g., Baldwin, *Hag, Zech, Mal,* 234; Verhoef, *Haggai and Malachi,* 244; R. L. Smith, *Micah–Malachi,* 317; Hill, *Malachi,* 206.

tribe of Levi to carry the ark of the covenant; and Deut 33:8–11, a blessing on the Levites for their devotion to God. That Moses and Aaron belong to the tribe is also noteworthy (Exod 2:1–10; 4:14). Consider also the fact that God's promise to David in 2 Sam 7 is not designated a *bərît* in that context but is recognized as a covenant elsewhere (e.g., Ps 89:3, 28 [MT 4, 29]).[183] Similarly, Jer 33:21 designates the promises made to David and the Levites covenants (*bərît*). Malachi 2:5 may also use *bərît* to designate the promises and blessing of the Levites.

The covenant is further characterized as *life and peace* (*haḥayyîm wəhaššālôm*). These designations function as an appositive to the covenant.[184] In essence, the covenant was for life, existence, and peace, denoting prosperity and well-being. In Prov 3:2, long life and well-being (*ḥayyîm wəšālôm*) will be the result of keeping the commandments.[185] Likewise, well-being and long life are a reward for obedience.[186]

> Keep his statutes and his commandments, which I am commanding you today for your own well-being and that of your descendants after you, so that you may long remain in the land that the Lord your God is giving you for all time. (Deut 4:40 NRSV)

God gave life and peace to Levi—*I gave them to him, reverence.* In this instance, "fear" (*môrā'*) is an object of the verb *nātan*, "to give," and is part of the covenant along with life and peace.[187] The clause *I gave them to him* in-

183. Weyde, *Prophecy and Teaching,* 184–86. He further notes the similarities to 2 Samuel 7, God's promise to David, where the term *bərît* is not used to designate the special relationship between God and David (the Davidic covenant). That covenant is referenced in 2 Sam 23:5 (*bərît ʿôlām,* everlasting covenant); Ps 89:3, 28, 34, 39 (MT 89:4, 29, 35, 40; *bərît or bərîtî*).

184. Thus Petersen, *Zechariah 9–14 and Malachi,* 175; cf. Hill, *Malachi,* 171. Compare other options for understanding how they function: (a) covenant of life and peace—e.g., Baldwin, *Hag, Zech, Mal,* 235; JPS, NRSV; (b) my covenant with him was life and peace—e.g., Verhoef, *Haggai and Malachi,* 246; (c) life and peace I gave to him—e.g., Floyd, *Minor Prophets 2,* 597; Weyde, *Prophecy and Teaching,* 186; R. L. Smith, *Micah–Malachi,* 309; NEB.

185. Proverbs 3:2 (years of life, *šənôt ḥayyîm*) and Mal 2:5 are the two texts where life and peace/well-being (*ḥayyîm wəšālôm*) appear together in the Old Testament. Isaiah 38:17 uses *šālôm* and *nepeš,* saving life, for a person's well-being. Cf. Rom 8:6.

186. Several other passages in Deuteronomy use the verb *'ārāk,* "to live long," to convey long life and the verb *yāṭab,* "to go well," to denote well-being (e.g., Deut 5:16, 29, 33; 6:2, 18; 12:25, 28; 22:7).

187. Glazier-McDonald, *Malachi: The Divine Messenger,* 45; Verhoef, *Haggai and Malachi,* 246; Hill, *Malachi,* 171, 207. Other options for understanding include, "I gave them to him in fear," e.g., R. L. Smith, *Micah–Malachi,* 309; "reverently he fears me," e.g., LXX;

terrupts the sequence but also conveys the idea that God placed fear in Levi as part of the covenant design. Fear is both a gift and an obligatory response to the covenant.[188] The three elements may then be classified as rewards for obedience (life and peace) and as a gift and obligation (fear).

(2) Contrasting Priests' Responses to the Levitical Covenant (2:5b–9)

The characterization of Levi continues by highlighting his behavior, specifically qualities connected to the exemplary behavior of the Levites whom Moses commended (Deut 33:8–11). Some of the Levites' commendable behaviors are observing Yahweh's word and keeping the covenant, teaching, and offering sacrifices on Yahweh's altar.[189] According to Ezek 44:15–27, the Levitical priests (Zadokites) are responsible for the sanctuary, including the sacrifices, teaching (*yārâ*) the people to distinguish between the holy and the common, and presiding in judicial matters. The priests' responsibility includes both pedagogical and judicial functions and requires the integrity of the priests. The unit Mal 2:5b–9 contrasts the positive response of the first recipient of the covenant (2:5b–7) with the response of the current generation of priests (2:8–9).

(a) First Recipients' Adherence (2:5b–7)

This first part of the contrast between the past and present priests depicts their behavior and its effects on the community.

(i) Nature of the Adherence (2:5b–6bα)

The past actions continue with reference to Levi's responses to the covenant—*he reverenced me (wayyîrāʾēnî)* and *he was in awe before my name (ûmippənê šəmî niḥat hûʾ)*. These actions contrast with the attitude of those who dishonored Yahweh by despising the name (Mal 1:6) and by oppressing the underprivileged (Mal 3:5). The report about Levi also illuminates the positive aspect of the Yahweh-fearers (Mal 3:16; cf. 1:14). In addition, Levi's

---

"that he might fear me," e.g., Baldwin, *Hag, Zech, Mal,* 235; RSV; "this called for reverence," e.g., NRSV. Petersen (*Zechariah 9–14 and Malachi,* 175) omits *môrāʾ* and thus reads "these I allocated to him and he feared me."

188. Among those who see fear as an obligation rather than a gift are Verhoef, *Haggai and Malachi,* 246; and the NEB.

189. Deut 33:9 uses *šāmar,* "to watch, preserve, keep," and *nāṣar,* "watch, keep, guard," of the word and the covenant, respectively. See Lev 10:11, where Aaron and his sons Eleazar and Ithamar are informed of their duties, including teaching the statues (*kol-haḥuqqîm*) to the people of Israel.

being in awe before Yahweh's name indicates prudence as compared with the current haughtiness or arrogance. The term "awe" (*ḥātat)* connotes fear and dismay and is typically used of human interactions (cf. Deut 1:21; 1 Sam 17:11).[190] The synonyms *yārēʾ* and *ḥātat* appear together in contexts that offer encouragement (e.g., Deut 31:8; Josh 8:1; Isa 51:7).[191] Only in Mal 2:5 do they occur together without denoting encouragement. The Levites were in awe of Yahweh and not because of a terrifying situation. Here the roots denote the proper gift and obligation (*môrāʾ*) and the proper response to the covenant with Yahweh: awe (*ḥātat*).

6 The presentation of the exemplar Levite focuses on integrity. The first two characteristics highlight speech as compared with the second two, which concern lifestyle. Regarding speech, *the true instruction was in his mouth.* The noun *ʾĕmet* (trustworthiness, faithfulness, truth) characterizes *tôrâ,* which in this instance refers to the teaching process and the quality of the content. Used in a construct genitive formulation, *ʾĕmet* is usually translated "true"—for example, true instruction (*tôrat ʾĕmet*—Mal 2:6); true God (*ʾĕlōhê ʾĕmet*—2 Chr 15:3); truthful witness (*ʿēd ʾĕmet*—Jer 42:5); true justice (*mišpaṭ ʾĕmet*—Ezek 18:8); truthful lips (*śəpat-ʾĕmet*—Prov 12:19). That the Levites' role included teaching allowed them the opportunity to influence others and left room to tailor the instruction. The teaching process, usually denoted by the verb *yārâ,* "to direct, teach," encompassed both negative and positive elements. The critique of negative teaching practices includes the priests' teaching for a price (Mic 3:11); false prophets, and priests who follow the false prophets' directions (Jer 5:31). Concerning the positive aspect of teaching, 2 Kgs 12:2 (MT 3) reflects the influence of a priest on a king: "Jehoash did what was right in the sight of the LORD all his days, because the priest Jehoiada instructed him" (NRSV).[192] Like 2 Kgs 12:2 (MT 3), Mal 2:6 reflects a positive outcome of instruction, when true instruction (*tôrat ʾĕmet*) is an exemplary behavior, and identifies both the quality of the instruction and the instructor from whose mouth it comes.

True instruction is a product of a true instructor's/priest's mouth—that is, it is *in his mouth (bəpîhû)*.[193] The product of the mouth reflects the character of the person or group. Negative traits are also associated with mouths. In depicting the enemies and asking for God's guidance, Ps 5:9 (MT 10),"there

190. The *niphal* form of *ḥātat,* "to be dismayed," also occurs in Josh 1:9; 8:1; 10:25; 1 Sam 17:11; Isa 30:31; 51:7; Jer 1:17; 10:2; 17:18; 23:4; 30:10; Ezek 2:6; 3:9; 1 Chr 28:20; 2 Chr 20:15; or "shattered," 1 Sam 2:10; Isa 7:8.

191. There are 36 instances of these verbs occurring together, all in the context of encouragement.

192. Contrast 2 Chr 15:3—the absence of teaching and the law.

193. Cf. Isa 53:9, "no deceit in his mouth" (*bəpîw*).

is no truth in his mouth," uses *bəpîhû* to characterize the enemies. Other examples include Mic 6:12 (tongues of deceit in their mouths—*bəpîhem*) and Pss 36:3 (MT 4); 10:7 (regarding deceit [*mirmâ*] in the mouth). In the book of Malachi, negative behaviors and attitudes involve forms of contamination (Mal 1:6–7, 12), but the behavior of Levi serves as a salient contrast. The product of his mouth is "true instruction." Identifying the mouth as the source of good practices, Zeph 3:13 says of the remnant, "no tongues of deceit are in their mouths" (*bəpîhem*).

Continuing with the speech function to characterize the exemplary Levi, Mal 2:6 indicates that *wrong was not found (ʿawlâ) on his lips (biśpātāyw)*. Typically *ʿawlâ*, "wrong," is used of iniquity and wickedness and in some instances is paired with bloodshed to speak about building Jerusalem/Zion (cf. Mic 3:10; Hab 2:12).[194] It is also used in depictions of a person or the Deity as not doing "wrong" (Zeph 3:5, 13; Ps 119:3).[195] In Job 27:4, *ʿawlâ* is used parallel with *rəmiyyâ* (deceit) to denote false speech that the speaker will not utter. Typically, *rəmiyyâ* denotes speech as a mode of deceit. These examples help one to understand the nuances of *ʿawlâ* in Mal 2:6.[196]

The absence of wrong expressed as *lōʾ-nimṣāʾ*, "not found," denotes a positive trait.[197] The absence of negative traits to indicate a positive character is also attested in Ps 32:2: in his spirit there is no deceit (*ʾên bərûḥô rəmiyyâ*).[198] This and other instances identify the absence of deceit (*mirmâ*) as exemplary or ideal (Zeph 3:13). Note also the power of the speech organs—mouth (*peh*) and lips (*śəpātayim*)—to reveal wisdom or folly and to produce decisive results (Prov 15:7; 18:6–7; cf. 10:21). Regarding the Deity, Deut 32:4 uses *ʿāwel* to denote the absence of wrong or deceit and the presence of righteousness and uprightness. Accordingly, Mal 2:6 expresses the exemplary characteristics of speech—namely, the presence of true instruction and the absence of wrong.

The second set of characteristics of the exemplary Levi pertains to his lifestyle or conduct—*He walked with me in peace and in uprightness*. The verb *hālak*, "to walk," signals the lifestyle, and the prepositional phrases further de-

194. Other occurrences include Isa 59:3; 61:8; Ezek 28:15; and Ps 43:1.

195. Active formulations with the active form of the verbs *ʿāśâ* and *pāʿal* are: *lōʾ-yaʿăśû ʿawlâ*, "they do not do wrong"; *lōʾ yaʿăśê ʿawlâ* or *lōʾ-pāʿălû ʿawlâ*, "he does not do wrong."

196. Compare various translations: Hill (*Malachi*, 209), "no deceit"; Verhoef (*Haggai and Malachi*, 248), "nothing unjust"; Petersen (*Zechariah 9–14 and Malachi*, 175, 191), "perversity."

197. The *niphal* perfect third masculine singular form of *māṣāʾ*, "to find." See the negated *niphal* form in Exod 12:19; 22:7; Deut 18:10; 22:20; 1 Sam 10:21; and 13:19.

198. Mignon R. Jacobs, "Sin, Silence, Suffering, and Confession in the Conceptual Landscape of Psalm 32," in *Text and Community: Essays in Honor of Bruce M. Metzger*, ed. J. Harold Ellens (Sheffield: Sheffield Phoenix, 2007), 2:14–34.

note the behavior of Levi as exemplary. Regarding the phrase "he walked with me" (*hālak 'ittî*), the preposition *'et* may denote accompaniment and thus signal the companionship of two parties. The expression "to walk with" is used mostly of human companions (e.g., Gen 12:4; 14:24; Num 10:29; 23:13; Judg 1:3; 7:4);[199] in at least two instances, humans walked with the Deity: Enoch (Gen 5:22, 24) and Noah (Gen 6:9).[200] Other expressions include walking in the way of others (*hālak bəderek*) or following their pattern of behavior (cf. 1 Kgs 16:2; 22:43, 52; 2 Kgs 8:18)[201] or walking according to God's principles (1 Kgs 11:33).[202] Notably, in Mal 2:6 Levi walked with the Deity and not with others who might have distracted him from true instruction (cf. Ps 1).

Two nouns characterize his walk (*hālak*): peace (*šālôm*; cf. 2:5) and uprightness (*mîšôr*),[203] both with the bound preposition *bet*. Used of the judicial action of judging (*šāpaṭ*), the prepositions *bet* and *min* may qualify the nature of an action or ruling (e.g., Ps 67:4 [MT 5]; cf. 45:6 [MT 7]). Accordingly, *mîšôr* is used parallel with *ṣedeq*, "righteousness," of the quality of judgment rendered by the shoot of the stump of Jesse:

> He shall not judge by what his eyes see, or decide by what his ears hear; but *with righteousness* he shall judge the poor, and decide *with equity* for the meek of the earth. (Isa 11:3–4 NRSV)[204]

Exemplary traits include the quality of one's behavior toward the underprivileged.

(ii) Effects of the Adherence (2:6bβ–7)

The quality of Levi's life affected the behavior of other people and, more directly, his actions on their behalf altered their life course: *he turned many from iniquity.* This speaks of his influence on others through the action of his teaching or instruction (2:6a). That he turned (*hēšîb*)[205] them suggests that they

199. Cf. 2 Kgs 3:7; Jer 51:59; Prov 1:11, 15. Note also expressions using *hālak*: e.g., Exod 33:16 (humans with God); Num 22:13–14; Job 34:8; 2 Chr 25:13 (of humans); Job 31:5 (with "falsehood" as object).

200. In the Genesis texts, the verb occurs in the *hithpael* stem—*wayyithallēk* in Gen 5:22, 24 and (*hithallek*) in Gen 6:9. Cf. Weyde, *Prophecy and Teaching,* 191.

201. See "walk in the customs or practices" (*bəḥuqqôt*): e.g., 2 Kgs 17:8, 19.

202. See 2 Chr 17:4, referring to God's commandments (*miṣwōt*).

203. The noun also means "plain or level place," regarding the topography of the land (e.g., Deut 3:10; 1 Kgs 20:23; 2 Chr 26:10; Isa 40:4; 42:16; Zech 4:7).

204. See Isa 33:15: "who walk righteously and speak uprightly, who despise the gain of oppression."

205. *Hiphil* perfect third masculine singular form of *šûb,* "to return." Note the occur-

were already involved in iniquity and returned from it (*mēʿāwōn*). Iniquity (*ʿāwōn*) includes sin, misdeeds, and the guilt resulting from the misdeeds (cf. Zech 3:4, 9).[206] Who are the many (*rabbîm*) that he turned? One possibility is that "many" refers to the "lay members of the community" rather than the priests themselves.[207] The priests are a stumbling block to many (*rabbîm*, 2:8); deviating from Yahweh was done by some of the "many." Accordingly, Levi was an exemplar in relationship to the community and the priests.

7 The interpretation of 2:7 and its place in Mal 2 have prompted questions about the integrity of the text and how to understand the *kî* clause. First, this text's clear conceptual connections with the argument of the unit support its integrity.[208] Second, there are two options for understanding the *kî* clause: (1) *kî* may be used as a conjunction ("for") to introduce a subordinate clause;[209] and (2) *kî* may be a causal adverb used logically ("because")[210] or emphatically ("indeed, verily").[211] The emphatic and logical sense function together in 2:7 to provide a rationale for the behavior of "the many" (*rabbîm*) in 2:6. The function of *kî* is tied to understanding the grammar of the text, especially the subject of the verb *yišmərû*, "they seek or safeguard." Who is "they"? In this case, the lips and mouth continue to be the focal point of the exemplar priests. Consequently, most interpreters consider the subject of the masculine plural verb (*yišmərû*) to be the feminine dual "lips" (*śiptê*) of a priest.[212] For example, taking "lips" as the subject of the verb, the LXX reads "for the priest's lips should keep knowledge."

The description of the behavior is related to the Levites, *because the lips of a priest keep knowledge.* As in 2:6, which highlights the speech organs, here in 2:7 the speech organs (*śiptê kōhēn*) are used to identify behavior. According to the traditions about the Levites, their responsibilities included keeping or safeguarding (*šāmar*) Yahweh's words, teaching (*yārâ*) the ordinances and laws (Deut 33:9–10), and presiding (*šāpaṭ*) in judicial matters (Ezek 44:24).

---

rence of the root in the prophetic criticism of the people's failure to return to Yahweh: e.g., Amos 4:6, 8, 9, 10, 11; Hag 2:17; Zech 1:4; Mal 3:7.

206. Note instances where iniquity is used parallel with *ḥaṭṭaʾt* (Hos 4:8; 8:13; 9:9; 13:12).

207. Hill (*Malachi*, 209–10) notes the discussion about the "many" as a technical term for "the religious community" reflected in "later Qumran documents." Cf. Verhoef, *Haggai and Malachi*, 249 n. 19.

208. For further discussion, see J. M. P. Smith, "Malachi"; Verhoef, *Haggai and Malachi*, 249.

209. Thus the NRSV, "for the lips"; see also JPS, NIV, NAB.

210. R. L. Smith, *Micah–Malachi*, 309.

211. Several interpreters prefer the emphatic use: "verily"—Verhoef, *Haggai and Malachi*, 236, 249; "surely"—Hill, *Malachi*, 210; "indeed"—Petersen, *Zechariah 9–14 and Malachi*, 175.

212. Thus Verhoef, *Haggai and Malachi*, 249–50; Petersen, *Zechariah 9–14 and Malachi*; Weyde, *Prophecy and Teaching*, 195–96; modern translations, e.g., NRSV, NIV.

These affirmations of the Levites' function are usually taken as the basis for understanding Mal 2:7.

Nonetheless, two other interpretive traditions also have implications for the discussion of Mal 2:7. The first, the wisdom tradition, reads the priest's lips as the subject of the verb (*yišmərû*) and the first part of 2:7 as a description of the ideal priest. Thus the *kî* clause provides the rationale for the priest's impact on the community. Together with the noted role of the mouth in 2:6a, 2:7aα qualifies the priest's speech or the product of his speech organs. The occurrence of the feminine dual form with both masculine and feminine verbs may add to the ambiguity rather than clarify Mal 2:7a. Note that in Ps 31:18 (MT 19), *śiptê šāqer*, "lying lips," is the subject of the feminine plural verb *tē'ālamnâ*, "to be dumb"; and in Prov 10:21, *śiptê ṣaddîq*, "lips of the righteous," is the subject of the masculine plural verb *yirʿû*, "feed, shepherd."[213] In this first tradition, the ideal priest seeks or safeguards knowledge or should do so (cf. NIV).[214] The wisdom tradition attests the role of the lips in safeguarding and imparting knowledge and provides a framework for understanding the depiction of the priest in Mal 2:7.[215]

> The *lips* of the wise *spread knowledge*;
> not so the minds of fools. (Prov 15:7 NRSV)

COMPARE

> An intelligent mind *acquires knowledge*,
> and the ear of the wise *seeks knowledge.* (Prov 18:15 NRSV)

If gender within the subject-verb agreement is the basis for the decision about the interpretation of Mal 2:7, one must remember that in many instances the feminine form of the verb precedes the dual noun (lips),[216] whereas the mas-

213. Note that, regarding the occurrence of the construct phrase with the masculine verb, *rabbîm*, "many," also occurs in Prov 10:21. For more, see "the lips of the righteous" (*śiptê ṣaddîq*—Prov 10:32); "lips of the wise" (*śiptê ḥăkāmîm*—Prov 14:3; 15:7); lips of the fool (*śiptê kəsîl*—Prov. 18:6). Cf. Richard Clifford, *Proverbs*, OTL (Louisville: Westminster John Knox, 1999), 116, 151 and 67. Clifford notes that the lips and heart are the typical elements used to denote the source of character. The heart is the source of knowledge (Prov 15:7).

214. Thus Verhoef, *Haggai and Malachi*, 249–50; Petersen, *Zechariah 9–14 and Malachi*, 175; Glazier-McDonald, *Malachi: The Divine Messenger*, 45.

215. Regarding keeping knowledge, Prov 5:2 uses the masculine plural verb (*yinṣōrû*) with the feminine dual (*śəpātêkā*, "your lips")—so that you may hold on to prudence, and your *lips* may *guard knowledge* (Prov 5:1–2). This interpretation follows the MT. See Clifford (*Proverbs*, 67) for discussion of the textual difficulties.

216. Psalm 71:23 (lips will sing for joy); 119:171 (my lips will pour forth praise). The

culine plural form follows it.[217] There is enough precedent to interpret "lips of a priest" as the subject of the verb *yišmərû*—thus, *the lips of a priest keep knowledge.*[218] This interpretive tradition notes the accusation of the priests in Hos 4:4–6 as an additional indication of the negative influence on the community when the priests do not fulfill their responsibility.[219]

The second tradition interprets the subject of the verb *yišmərû* as *rabbîm* (many) in 2:6bβ.[220] Taking into consideration the usual grammatical need for agreement between the subject and the verbs *yišmərû* and *yəbaqšû*, Hill proposes, "Surely [*from*] the lips of the priest they safeguard knowledge, and Torah they seek *from* his mouth" (italics added). The significance of this interpretation for the conceptual flow of the unit is that it identifies the actions of the community in relation to the priest as being based on what his speech reveals about him.

Because of the exemplar Levi, the Israelites all *seek instruction from his mouth.* Most likely the subject of the verb *bāqaš* (seek) is *rabbîm* (many), which is a reference to the members of the community mentioned in 2:6bβ. The reciprocity of the agents is evident in their relationship to *tôrâ* (instruction). On the one hand, the exemplary Levite emanates true instruction and thus influences the community. On the other hand, the community seeks (*bāqaš*) instruction from him—that is, from the priest's mouth (*mippîhû*). It is not only the priest's behavior that reflects wisdom but also the community's search for instruction. The typical formulation *šamar* plus *tôrâ* is used in several contexts to denote keeping or safeguarding *tôrâ* in instances of: a prescription (1 Chr 22:12; cf. Deut 31:12); good behavior (Deut 17:19; 30:9–10; Ps 119:44, 55; Prov 28:4; 29:18); or an accusation or a concern about neglect (e.g., Deut 28:58–59; Jer 16:11; Ps 119:136). A similar expression occurs in Hag 2:11, "ask instruction"—*šāʾal* plus *tôrâ.*[221] Note also the expression "seeking knowledge" (*bāqaš* plus *daʿat*—Prov 15:14; 18:15), where knowledge (*daʿat*) may refer to God's law or covenantal requirements.[222] Although Mal 2:7 does not reflect the typical expressions because it pairs

---

dual form followed by the feminine participle, 1 Sam 1:13 (lips moving). Other exceptions include Prov 10:13.

217. Other instances of the dual (not in a first element in a construct chain) with the masculine plural verb appear in Job 15:6 (lips testify); Ps 63:3 (MT 4; lips will praise you); 140:9 (MT 10; let the mischief of their lips overwhelm).

218. Contrast Hill, *Malachi,* 211.

219. Cf. Weyde, *Prophecy and Teaching,* 195–97.

220. Thus Hill (*Malachi,* 211), who argues that "the preference for masculine over feminine forms, especially in late Biblical Hebrew" may explain the feminine subject of a masculine verb in 2:7.

221. See discussion of Hag 2:11 in this volume.

222. Weyde, *Prophecy and Teaching,* 196–97.

bāqaš with *tôrâ* and *šamar* with *da'at*, it reflects the active engagement of instruction and knowledge. The action signifies a change—conveyed through the community's turning away from iniquity (2:6bβ)—and the motivation for the change (2:7b).

The priest's status in relation to the Deity is the reason for the community's reliance on him—*because he is a messenger of Yahweh (mal'ak yhwh) of hosts.* Conversely, this status bespeaks reliability and trust, which is what the community presupposed when they placed their trust in him and relied on him to be a messenger of Yahweh (*mal'ak yhwh*) for them. This dependence makes the charge against the priests dramatic (cf. 2:8) because it not only demonstrates the influence of the priests' behavior but betrays the priests' violation of the community's trust. Like Levi (the exemplar), the priests are supposed to keep/preserve knowledge; judging from the impact on the community, they have not done so.

Although the expression "messenger of Yahweh" (*mal'ak yhwh*) occurs frequently in the Old Testament,[223] the designation *mal'ak yhwh-ṣəbā'ôt* is unique to Mal 2:7. Elsewhere in prophetic literature the designation angel/messenger of Yahweh (*mal'ak yhwh*) refers to an angelic or supernatural being—that is, a mediator of Yahweh's will to human beings (Isa 37:36; Zech 1:11, 12; 3:1, 5, 6; 12:8).[224] The "messenger of Yahweh" in Hag 1:13 refers to the prophet. The use in Mal 2:7 most likely connotes a human mediator and furthers the idea of companionship between Yahweh and priests.[225] Perhaps the play on words seen in the designation *mal'ākî* reflects the prophet's attempted identification with the Levites and his inclusion among them (cf. Jer 1:1; Ezek 1:3).[226]

Some scholars have suggested that Mal 2:7 reflects an elevated role of the priests in postexilic times, a placement of priests on a par with prophets.[227]

223. The *mal'ak yhwh*, "angel of Yahweh," was a supernatural being and appeared in Gen 16:7, 9, 10, 11; 22:11, 15; Exod 3:2; Num 22:22, 23, 24, 25, 26, 27, 31, 32, 34, 35; Judg 2:1, 4; 5:23; 6:11, 12, 21, 22; 13:3, 13, 15, 16, 17, 18, 20, 21; 1 Kgs 19:7; 2 Kgs 1:3, 15; 19:35; 1 Chr 21:12; 15, 16, 18, 30.

224. Cf. Zech 1:9; 2:2 (MT 1:19)—the messenger.

225. Weyde (*Prophecy and Teaching*, 197–98) argues that the messenger priest is also found in Eccl 5:6 (MT 5). Here "the messenger" (*hammal'āk*) was a priest in a situation where someone may have reneged on a vow. Weyde includes a discussion by scholars who have noted the connection between Mal 2:7 and Eccl 5:4–6.

226. Hill, *Malachi*, 213.

227. R. Fuller, "The Blessing of Levi in Dtn 33, Mal 2, and Qumran," in *Konsequente Traditionsgeschichte: Festschrift für Klaus Baltzer zum 65. Geburtstag*, ed. R. Bartelmus, T. Krüger, and H. Utzschneider, OBO 126 (Göttingen: Vandenhoeck & Ruprecht, 1993), 39; Cf. Petersen, *Zechariah 9–14 and Malachi*, 192. For further discussion of the development of the concept of the ideal Levite, see A. Hultgård, "The Ideal 'Levite': The Davidic Messiah and the Savior Priest in the Testament of the Twelve Patriarchs," in *Ideal Figures in Ancient*

Others suggest that the priests rendered the prophets obsolete as messengers of Yahweh.[228] They argue that, due to the shift in the political structure, the absence of a monarchy, and the devaluation of the prophets' efforts among the populace, the prophetic function diminished.[229] Another perspective is that Mal 2:7 does not replace the prophetic or angelic aspects of the messenger but denotes the participation of the priests in the intermediary role as "interpreters of Yahweh's will."[230] Similarly, one should note that the role of the priest had come to incorporate the functions of the prophet and sage, thus combining knowledge of the law with the instruction and guidance of the people (cf. 1 Chr 15:22; 2 Chr 35:3).[231] The exemplar or ideal Levite has a positive relationship with the Torah and influences the community toward positive change. Accordingly, the community recognizes, accepts, and trusts the exemplar priest as a messenger of Yahweh.

(b) Current Priests' Violation (2:8–9)

8 In contrast to Levi, the current priests' behavior is not commendable. The perspective shifts from the ideal to the reality of the priestly behavior and influence. Two aspects of 2:8 signal the shift: the adversative use of *waw* and the emphatic use of the personal pronoun (*ʾattem*) plus the second-person plural form of the three verbs (cf. Mal 1:12).[232] The second-person pronoun signals the shift and resumes the address from 2:1, "to you, priests" (*ʾălêkem . . . hakkōhănîm*). Three verbs that characterize the priests contribute to the overall contrast between the priests and Levi: *you turned aside (sartem) from the way; you caused many to stumble (hikšaltem);* and *you corrupted (šiḥattem) the covenant of Levi.* Each description corresponds to one characteristic of the exemplary Levi: his walk (2:6bα), his influence (2:6bβ), and his maintenance of the covenant (2:4–5, 6a). The consequence of the current priests' violations is punishment. Yahweh will shame them because they have dishonored Yahweh (2:9).

Judaism: Profiles and Paradigms, ed. J. J. Collins and George W. E. Nickelsburg, SBLSCS 12 (Chico, CA: Scholars Press, 1980), 93–110.

228. Cf. J. M. P. Smith, "Malachi," 40; Carroll, *When Prophecy Failed,* 204–5.

229. Glazier-McDonald, *Malachi: The Divine Messenger,* 71–72. Among the texts cited in support of this argument are Isa 44:26; 2 Chr 36:15–16; Jer 23:33; Ezek 13:10–12, 17–19, 22; Zech 13:2–6.

230. Thus Hill, *Malachi,* 212–13. Verhoef (*Haggai and Malachi,* 250) argues that the description in Mal 2:7 is of a priest in the "classical period" rather than of the decline of the prophetic office.

231. Thus Weyde, *Prophecy and Teaching,* 200–201.

232. A similar construction is seen in Mal 1:12 with the participial form of the verb. The effect is to contrast the behavior of two groups or individuals.

(i) Nature of the Violation (2:8)

The statement *but you yourself have turned aside (sûr) from the way (min-hadderek)* resumes the second-person address to the priests. "The way" (*derek*) refers to the principles and commands governing their behavior, including the appropriate sacrifices and regard for Yahweh. "The way" is not identified as "the way of Yahweh" (*derek yhwh*) but may refer to it (cf. Judg 2:22; Jer 5:4, 5).[233] Clearly, it does not mean that the priests have turned from the way of evil. Their turning aside (denoting alienation) contrasts with Levi's walking with the Deity (denoting intimacy). The formulation "turning aside," using the verb *sûr*, appears in two contexts denoting the apostasy of the people. First, the usage in Exod 32:8 refers to the people's haste in abandoning Yahweh's command to them: "quickly turned aside from the way that I commanded them" (*sārû mahēr min-hadderek ʾăšer ṣiwwîtim*; cf. Deut 9:12, 16). Consequently, they made a golden calf to lead them. The way (*derek*) is what Yahweh commanded and what they chose to abandon. Second, in Judg 2:17 (*sārû mahēr min-hadderek*), the current generation had abandoned the ways of their ancestors, affirming that the ancestors obeyed Yahweh's commandments and that the current generation did not; rather, "they quickly turned aside from the way." In these texts, the adverbial particle (*mahēr*) qualifies "turning aside" (*sûr*), thus indicating readiness to abandon what they knew and the path that had been set before them. Furthermore, these texts specify the behavior that demonstrates the turning away from the way—making and worshiping images (Exod 32:8) and not obeying the commandments as the ancestors had done (Judg 2:17b). All other occurrences of a similar formulation regarding turning aside illustrate a negative event, a deviation from what is good or favorable (cf. Deut 11:28; 31:29; Isa 30:11).[234] Note the similar concept of causing people to err or go astray (*tāʿâ*; cf. Jer 23:13; 23:32; 50:6; Mic 3:5),[235] which is also a deviation from what is acceptable or good.

As compared with the texts that speak of turning aside, Mal 2:8 does not use *mahēr* to qualify the behavior of the priests, nor does it mention the commandments or the path of the ancestors. Rather, it refers to the way (*hadderek*) without qualifiers or specification of the behavior that constitutes the turn.[236] Immediately juxtaposed to the turning aside is the effect of that

233. See Ps 119:14–32 regarding *derek*, the way of faithfulness, status, commandments, and so on, in contrast to the way of evil and the wicked (Pss 1:6; 146:9). One example of keeping the way is to practice righteousness and justice (*laʿăśôt ṣədāqâ ûmišpāṭ*, Gen 18:19).

234. Cf. Lam 3:9,11 regarding Yahweh's actions against Jerusalem.

235. Cf. Ezek 14:11; of not going astray: Ezek 44:10; 48:11; going astray in the same way as the ancestor: Amos 2:4.

236. For example, Ps 1:6—way of the righteous and way of the wicked.

behavior on the community. The juxtaposition of the exemplary Levi and the current priests accentuates the significance of the turning. In addition, this second part of the statement about the priests's turning aside increases our understanding of the course from which they have deviated and the impact of their behavior: they have turned, not from iniquity or from evil, but from uprightness (cf. Mal 2:6; Ps 25:8–10).

Just as the behavior of the Levite influenced many, so the behavior of the priests influenced many (*rabbîm*): *You caused many to stumble in the Torah.* By violating the covenant and because of their influence in the community, the priests have caused the apostasy of others. Thus their behavior affects more than their lives and impacts those whom they lead. They have caused the community to stumble (*kāšal*).[237] The verb denotes falling down, stumbling, or staggering and may have the nuance of moral downfall (cf. Hos 5:5; 14:1). In some of the occurrences of *kāšal* plus the preposition *bet*, *kāšal* is associated with the way (*derek*) and portrays a falling away from the way or path (e.g., Jer 18:15).[238] This association is evident in the priests' deviation from the way (Mal 2:8a) and the effects of their deviation (2:8aβ).

Using the formulation *kāšal* plus the preposition *bet*, Mal 2:8aβ specifies that the stumbling occurs in relation to the Torah (*battôrâ*), but the expression "stumble in the Torah" has yielded several interpretations. First, some people understand *tôrâ* as instruction or teaching and maintain that the preposition indicates agency: "by your instruction/teaching."[239] This interpretation assumes the presence of a second masculine plural suffix referring to the priests. Second, some interpreters understand *tôrâ* as the law of Yahweh and the preposition as an adversative circumstance—"from/against the law/torah"[240] or "at the law."[241] It is also possible to perceive the *tôrâ* as "law" (including the principles and related instructions) and the preposition as "over": in other words, stumble "over the law or Torah."[242] Finally, some observe that the definite form (*battôrâ*) denotes not only instruction concerning the law but the law itself. The preposition *bet*, "in," may connote the instability of the

237. *Hiphil* perfect second masculine plural: *hikšaltem*. See. Ezek 44:12: the priests became a stumbling block to Israel.

238. Several texts use *kāšal* with the preposition *bet* and in association with the way (e.g., Jer 31:9; Prov 4:19; Ezek 33:12), and they associate the abandonment of wickedness with the improbability of stumbling. Cf. Weyde, *Prophecy and Teaching*, 204, esp. nn. 383 and 384.

239. Thus Glazier-McDonald, *Malachi: The Divine Messenger*, 45, 70: "through your instruction"; Verhoef, *Haggai and Malachi*, 236; Weyde, *Prophecy and Teaching*, 204; cf. Baldwin, *Hag, Zech, Mal*, 236. Modern versions that reflect this perspective include the NAB, NJB, NIV, and NRSV.

240. Thus Petersen, *Zechariah 9–14 and Malachi*, 175: "fall away from torah."

241. Thus the KJV. The ASV reads "stumbles in the law."

242. Thus Hill, *Malachi*, 215.

walk, and falling down over issues of Torah. For example, the verb (*kāšal*) indicates stumbling resulting from the priests' behavior.

> Those who are wise understand these things; those who are discerning know them. For the ways of the Lord are right, and the upright walk in them, but transgressors *stumble in* them. (Hos 14:9 NRSV)

Thus, Mal 2:8 depicts the priests as causing the moral decay of the community. Their influence and power do not concern solely their cultic practices and their status; the passage suggests that the negative influence is also the result of the community's regard for their instruction. The potential for the community to turn away from iniquity does not simply stem from the integrity of the Levites but from a cooperative relationship between them and the community. Likewise, the community's stumbling is a product of its reliance on the priests for instruction and guidance in Torah. The priests' instruction has become a stumbling block or impediment to the community, preventing the people from steadily following the Torah (cf. Ezek 44:12).[243]

The third element of the priestly violation in 2:8 pertains to the covenant of Levi: *You corrupted the covenant of Levi.* As in Mal 1:12, here in 2:8bβ comparisons with other individuals, groups, or nations continues. For example, 2:8 compares the postexilic priests with the covenant of Levi by stating that they have corrupted (*šāḥat*) the covenant of Levi. The root *šāḥat* occurs two other times in the book of Malachi: (1) referring to the priests' presenting corrupt or blemished (*mošḥāt*) sacrifices to Yahweh (Mal 1:14) and (2) referring to the destruction of agriculture by pests (*yašḥit*, 3:11). Several examples of accusations about the people's behavior illustrate the first usage (e.g., Ezek 16:47; 22:30; 28:17; Zeph 3:7; Hos 9:9).[244] The verb *šāḥat* also denotes destruction brought about by the Deity, the second usage (Lam 2:5, 6, 8). In none of these instances is *šāḥat* used with the object "covenant of Levi" or any covenant. Nevertheless, the priests seem to have done nothing acceptable to the Deity; it appears that in the Deity's perspective all is wrong with the priests and, by comparison, there is always someone else doing better than the priests (e.g., the nations, 1:11). To whatever extent the depiction of the priests coheres with the reality of their practices, the Deity holds them in contempt. Their behavior undermines Yahweh's goal to maintain the covenant of Levi (2:4); the priests have corrupted it and nullified it for themselves.[245]

243. See Jer 6:21: God as a stumbling block to the people.

244. D. Vette, "שחת," *TLOT* 3:1319. Other examples include Jer 6:28; 51:25; Exod 32:7; Isa 14:20; and Amos 1:11.

245. Verhoef (*Haggai and Malachi*, 252) interprets *šāḥat* as annulled, thus indicating the destruction of the covenant.

Their behavior shows that they consider the covenant to be void for their lives and practice. As in Exod 32:7–8; Deut 9:12, and 16, here also in Mal 2:8 the concept of acting corruptly is paired with turning aside from the way.

> Then the LORD said to me, "Get up, go down quickly from here, for your people whom you have brought from Egypt have *acted corruptly*. They have been quick to *turn from the way* that I commanded them; they have cast an image for themselves." (Deut 9:12 NRSV)[246]

Acting corruptly (*šāḥat*) was evidence of turning aside and committing idolatry. There is no indication of idolatry in Mal 2:8, but it may be indicated in Mal 2:11.

The object they corrupted in the covenant of Levi (*bərît hallēwî*) may be the promise referred to in Deut 10:8–9 and 33:8–11. Being accountable for their behavior toward the covenant of Levi in some way refers to their lineage and their share in the responsibility of the Levites. Arguably, in this context the priests and the Levites (*hallēwî*) are individuals with a common heritage regarding responsibilities. If they are distinct, it is not with regard to their responsibilities but the way they approach and execute those responsibilities.[247] This understanding of the priests and Levites clarifies the nature of the judgment announced against the priests and thus also the correspondence between their behavior and their punishment (2:9).

(ii) Consequences (Announcement of Judgment) (2:9)

9 The announcement of judgment against the priests is presented as a direct consequence of their behavior (cf. 2:8). The announcement includes a twofold description of judgment (focused on humiliation) and a two-part rationale for the judgment (focused on deviation from responsibilities).

Two elements of the judgment against the priests are announced: *So indeed I myself will make you despised and humiliated before all the people*. The contrast between Yahweh, the speaker (*ʾănî*), and the object of the action is signaled by *ʾetkem*, "you"—second masculine plural, continuing the addressees from 2:8—namely, the priests. Together with the personal pronoun, the verbal form *nātattî* conveys emphasis, *I myself will make you* (lit., set, place you).[248] What the priests have done to Yahweh, Yahweh will do to the priests.

246. See Deut 31:29: "You will act corruptly, turning aside from the way that I have commanded you."

247. Cf. Floyd, *Minor Prophets 2*, 599.

248. The *qal* perfect first common singular form of *nātan*, "to give, put, place," with the Deity as the subject.

The first element of the announced judgment reveals that the priests will be despised (*bāzâ*), just as they despised Yahweh (Mal 1:7, 12). The use of *nibzîm*, the *niphal* participle, connects Yahweh's behavior with the priests' behavior toward Yahweh—measure for measure. The reason for Yahweh's action is to punish, perhaps to make the priests experience what the Deity experienced in being publicly dishonored. It is as if to say, "I made the covenant with Levi that the priests ought to have honored and kept; but they deviated from the covenant and thus dishonored me." The punishment here in Mal 2:9 does not state that Yahweh is breaking or annulling the covenant. Rather, the priests are the individuals who ought to have kept the covenant made with Levi—Levi being the "father" of the priests.

The second element of the judgment is open humiliation (*šəpālîm*) of the priests, which includes an audience who witnesses it.[249] Honor (1:6) is the antithesis of being despised (*nibzîm*, 1:7, 12) and humiliated (*šəpālîm*; cf. 1 Sam 2:30; 2 Sam 6:22; Prov 29:23). Malachi 2:9 pairs "despised" and "humiliated" (*nibzîm ûšəpālîm*), which reflects the pairing in 1 Sam 2:22–31, where Eli's family, the priests at Shiloh, despised Yahweh by neglecting the cultic-sacral laws.[250]

Malachi 2:9 thus echoes the scope of the public dynamics in which Yahweh's relationship with the priests is played out; the attention of other people factors into the Yahweh-priests relationship. Why is the relationship with others and the nations an issue (cf. Mal 1:5, 11)? An outsider was already part of the argument when Esau provided an object lesson for the text to speak about Yahweh's love for Israel. The issue here is the contrast between "others" and the agents in the disputation (the priests). Humiliation is hardly a private process. Part of the dynamics of debasement or humiliation is the exposing of an individual's behavior to others.

Here in Mal 2:9 the audience of the humiliation is not the nations but the people or community—the many (cf. 2:7, 8). As in 1 Sam 2:22–31, the people are included because of the priests' effects on the community. Furthermore, the success of the humiliation depends on the audience. Those with a vested interest in the loss of status or demise of the debased party make the best witnesses. Yahweh humiliates the priests in view of all the people (*kol-hāʿām*) so that all are aware. Furthermore, the humiliated party must have something

249. The masculine plural adjective *šəpālîm* is derived from the verb *šāpēl*, "to become low, to debase or humiliate." See 2 Sam 6:22 (masculine singular form) and Job 5:11 (masculine plural form).

250. Cf. Weyde, *Prophecy and Teaching*, 206; David Toshio Tsumura, *The First Book of Samuel*, NICOT (Grand Rapids: Eerdmans, 2007), 166–67; W. Brueggemann, *First and Second Samuel*, Interpretation (Louisville: John Knox, 1990), 23; P. K. McCarter, *1 Samuel: A New Translation with Introduction, Notes, and Commentary*, AB 8 (Garden City, NY: Doubleday, 1980), 94.

to lose—status, relationship, reputation, or something else. The humiliation by Yahweh signals to the community the fractured relationship between the priests and Yahweh and Yahweh's disapproval of the priests. What humiliation for those who purport to act on Yahweh's behalf to be rejected publicly by Yahweh! The text does not specify how the humiliation will be accomplished, but it notes why Yahweh will humiliate those who were entrusted with leading the community in matters concerning the will of Yahweh, who were entrusted with safeguarding the relationship between Yahweh and Israel.

The priests are punished for violating Yahweh's trust—*inasmuch as you are not keeping my ways.* In 2:9 the phrase *kəpî ʾăšer* introduces the two-part motivation for the punishment: deviating from the ways of Yahweh and from their relationship to the Torah. The first element connects the punishment with the priests' deviation from the way, using the same language as 2:8 regarding their turning aside from the way. Here in 2:9 the plural form occurs with the personal suffix referring to Yahweh—my ways (*dərākay*). The priests' relationship with the Deity requires behavior according to the rules of the relationship. To violate those rules is to violate the relationship. Such violation then becomes motivation for the announcement of judgment against the priests.

Although the priests and the Levite are part of the same group—those who have been entrusted with sacred practices and guiding the community—here the priests are distinguished from the Levite in terms of time and behavior. First, the Levite is the ancestor, their predecessor in time. It is from his way that the priests have deviated, the way defined by their obligation to Yahweh. Second, the priests' behavior is the antithesis of the Levite's maintaining of the covenant. Instead of continuing in the way of the Levite, the priests turned aside from the way, despised Yahweh, and corrupted the covenant. The Levite's exemplary conduct included walking with the Deity in uprightness and peace and being a positive influence on the community (2:6–7). As in other texts noting the current generation's deviation from the ways of the ancestors or predecessors, the ancestor followed Yahweh, and the illustration of the ideal does not include examples that would distract from its argument. Not all the ancestors behaved in an exemplary fashion, but Mal 1:6, like other such texts, makes no reference to instances when the ancestors were corrupt or deviated from the way of Yahweh.

By its attention to "the ways," Mal 2:9 refocuses on the accusation that the priests have turned aside (2:8). Similar formulations referring to Yahweh's commands, precepts, and so on clarify the motivation for Yahweh's actions against the priests (1 Kgs 2:3; 3:14; 8:57–58; 11:38).[251] In these and other references, not following the commandments, precepts, and ordinances indicates

251. See 1 Kgs 11:33, the charge about not walking in the ways of Yahweh.

not walking in Yahweh's ways. Clearly, the motivation also encompasses the effect of the priests' deviation, and consequently, both their deviation and its impact on the community form the basis of the punishment they will receive.

The second element of the reason for punishment involves relationship to the Torah (*battôrâ*; cf. 2:8): *but [you are] showing partiality in the Torah.* Two observations about function and form may inform our understanding of this charge. The function of the clause is to explain the mode of their deviation by noting the particular area of behavior. As such it also functions to identify a second aspect of the priests' behavior as compared with the exemplary Levite. Regarding form, the expression *wənōśəʾîm pānîm* has yielded various interpretations about the significance of *nāśāʾ* plus *pānîm*. In the judicial realm, *nāśāʾ* plus *pānîm* usually has the negative connotation of "showing partiality" (e.g., Deut 10:17; 16:19; Prov 18:5).[252] Deuteronomy 10:17 uses the expression *lōʾ-yiśśāʾ pānîm*, "does not show partiality," to characterize Yahweh's fairness. Added to the challenge of understanding the phrase is the question of whether the negative particle (*ʾên*) in 2:9b) applies to 2:9bβ, thus yielding two negated actions—not keeping and not *nōśəʾîm pānîm* (lit.: lifting faces in Torah).[253] When interpreted as showing partiality, the *waw* is an adversative and the negative particle (*ʾên*) applies only to the first element—not keeping (see the NRSV, KJV, and ASV—"respect of persons").[254] In this interpretation, "but showing partiality" in Torah signifies that the priests have deviated from Yahweh by doing what Yahweh does not do.

To grant favor or be gracious is another way of interpreting the expression *nāśāʾ* plus *pānîm* (cf. Gen 19:21; Deut 28:50; 1 Sam 25:35; Mal 1:8).[255] Accordingly, Hill argues that the presence of the negative particle rules out the possibility of understanding *nōśəʾîm pānîm* as showing partiality. He thus proposes that *ʾênkem* applies to the second element—"[you are not] acting graciously"—seeing a correspondence between the question in Mal 1:8, "will [God] lift up your face?" and the affirmation in 2:9 that the priests are "not lifting up the faces [of the people] in Torah."[256] A third interpretation also applies the negative particle (*ʾên*) to both elements in 2:9 and translates *nōśəʾîm pānîm* "to regard or consider." In this interpretation, the priests are charged with not keeping Yahweh's ways and not regarding Torah.[257] The latter would mean

252. See the use in Deut 1:17 of the expression *lōʾ-takkîrû pānîm*, "do not show partiality"; the expression *hakkēr-pānîm* also denotes showing partiality (cf. Prov 24:23).

253. Compare *ûnəśuʾ pānîm*, which denotes status—for example, of dignitaries (2 Kgs 5:1; Isa 3:3; 9:14); and favored/honorable (Job 22:8). Cf. Weyde, *Prophecy and Teaching*, 208.

254. Thus Verhoef, *Haggai and Malachi*, 237, 253; Weyde, *Prophecy and Teaching*, 209; Petersen, *Zechariah 9–14 and Malachi*, 174.

255. Cf. Prov 6:35; 2 Kgs 3:14.

256. Hill, *Malachi*, 217–18.

257. Glazier-McDonald, *Malachi: The Divine Messenger*, 73.

that they do not favor or consider Torah in their ruling or teaching; rather, they disregard Torah. Given the function and form of *wənōśəʾîm pānîm*, this interpretation seems to fit the context of the announcement of judgment without including the people as the object of the action. Despite the insights gained from this perspective, it overlooks the fact that the priests are already depicted as being engaged with Torah: their behavior does not simply lack regard but shows a negative regard for Torah.

I favor the first interpretation for the reasons noted above and for contrast with the exemplary Levite in 2:6, who provides true instruction as compared with the priests' skewed interpretation and application of Torah. Malachi 2:9 concludes the unit by announcing the punishment and delineating the reasons for the specific punishment on the priests.

B. CHARGES REGARDING THE PEOPLE'S MALPRACTICE: UNFAITHFULNESS (2:10–16)

Malachi 2:10–16, the second subunit of 1:6–2:16, picks up the relational theme evident in 1:6–14 and 2:1–9 regarding acceptable behavior within the specified relationship. Malachi 2:10–16 begins with rhetorical questions about the people's common lineage using relational terms: "one father" and "one god." This presupposes that the text is speaking of one creator because the audience still has an "intragroup perspective" defined by the covenant relationship: that is to say, the shared bond is not across groups (Judah and other nations) but is within the group (various segments within Judah, including generational segments). Building on the relationship concept, 2:10–16 uses *bāgad* (to act treacherously or unfaithfully) to refer to a compromise or violation of the relationship (2:10, 11, 14, 15, 16) and thus includes an intergenerational focus (the past and the present).

Several challenges confront an interpretation of 2:10–16, which will be discussed in the analysis of the various units below, but I present them here in preparation for further discussion. The first challenge is to identify the speaker in 2:10; the possibilities include the prophet, the community, and even the individuals who were involved in an exogamous marriage. Second, the language of the text has received considerable attention because of its multivalence and its significance in depicting relationship issues. One challenge involves the textual difficulties in 2:15–16 (see textual notes). Another is determining whether the relationships are literal or figurative. If they are figurative, then the text is speaking about practices that result in apostasy but not necessarily about marriage or divorce.[258] On the other hand, if in-

258. Petersen, *Zechariah 9–14 and Malachi*, 195.

terpreted literally, the text is speaking about marriage, women, divorce, and negative repercussions for subsequent generations. These practices would exhibit the unfaithfulness of the nation.[259] In the latter case and quite apart from chronological relationships, intertextual challenges arise from the coexistence of Deut 24:1–4; Ezra 9:1–15; and Neh 13:23–30—texts that also address issues of marriage and divorce.

The third challenge is the relationship between 2:10–12 and 2:13–16 with reference to the content and addressees. Notably, Mal 2:10–16 addresses the nation's unfaithfulness, which is manifested in two ways: (a) the marriages and subsequent dynamics (2:10–12), and (b) the dissolution of the marriages (2:13–16).

1. Marriage Leading to Apostasy: Unfaithfulness (2:10–12)

10Do we not all have one father? And has not one God created us? Why do we act treacherously to each other, defiling the covenant of our ancestors? 11Judah acted treacherously and made an abomination in Israel and in Jerusalem; for Judah defiled the holiness of Yahweh which he loves and married a daughter of a foreign god. 12May Yahweh cut off the man who does it—witness[a] *or respondent—from the tents of Jacob, although one brings*[b] *an offering to Yahweh of hosts.*

a. The MT reads *'ēr wə'ōnê—'ēr* (the masculine singular noun meaning "awake," derived from *'ûr*, "to awake, arouse"). The term *wə'ōnê* combines a *waw* plus the *qal* participial form of *'ānâ*, "to answer." The closest translation of this formulation is "waketh and him that answereth" (ASV); J. M. P. Smith, "Malachi," 50–51; R. L. Smith, *Micah-Malachi*, 319. Several proposed ways of emending the text are noteworthy: The LXX reads *heōs*, assuming the preposition *'ad*, "until he is cast down." Several propose emending *'ēr* to read *'ēd*, "witness," for example: the NRSV ("any to witness or answer"); Hill (*Malachi*, 221, 235) and Floyd (*Minor Prophets 2*, 605): "witness or respondent." D. R. Jones (*Haggai, Zechariah and Malachi*, 195) proposes "Er and Onan" (*'ēr wə'ônān*), recalling Judah's sons in Gen 38 and suggesting that the brothers represent those who married foreign women (cf. Gen 38:3, 4, 6–9; 46:12; Num 26:19; 1 Chr 2:3). On the basis of the targumic reading, Baldwin (*Hag, Zech, Mal*, 239) proposes "son and grandson." Petersen (*Zechariah 9–14 and Malachi*, 194, 201) rearranges the text and proposes the reading "involving nakedness and improper cohabitation." His reading is clearly an attempt to continue the image of the foreign deity and to introduce sexual infractions as indicators of the violation. Glazier-McDonald (*Malachi: The Divine Messenger*, 95–98) proposes "the aroused one and the lover." Among modern translations and commentators, one finds "master or scholar" (KJV); "whoever he may be" (Verhoef, *Haggai and Malachi*, 270–71).

b. The MT reads *ûmaggîš* (*hiphil* masculine singular participle) compared with *maggîšê*—the plural construct form (Mal 3:3). *BHS* suggests *ûmmimaggîšê* (*waw* + *min* + *hiphil* masculine plural participle) compared with the LXX, "and from the presenters." Floyd (*Mi-*

259. Floyd, *Minor Prophets 2*, 603.

nor Prophets 2, 605) argues that the offender will be excluded from participation in the cult. Lescow (*Das Buch Maleachi,* 110) notes the exclusion of the priest from offering sacrifices. Modern translations vary in their interpretation; for example, the NRSV assumes three participles, each denoting a characteristic of the offender: "any to witness or answer, or to bring an offering." The ASV and KJV refer to "him that offereth an offering."

The opening declaration in 2:10–12 builds on the intragroup perspective already seen in 1:2–5—us versus them, Israel versus Edom—and focuses on Yahweh's particular relationship with Israel. While it is the focus, this particular relationship does not exclude all other realities; that is, Yahweh's relationship with Israel does not negate Yahweh's relationship with others. Nevertheless, Israel's relationship with God is to be exclusive and in line with Yahweh's expectations for Israel. Part of the expectation is adherence to prescriptions about the intergroup covenants and marriage (e.g., Exod 34). Thus, Mal 2:10–12 addresses the breaking of the covenant relationship by engaging in proscribed practices such as intergroup relationships leading to worship of deities other than Yahweh. Malachi 2:10–12 both identifies and evaluates the infraction relative to the cult (2:10–11b) and notes the consequences (2:12). As in 1:6–14 and 2:1–9, one can identify an accusation (2:10–11) and a punishment (2:12) within 2:10–12.[260]

a. General Statement regarding the People's Unfaithfulness (2:10)

10 The progression of the argument in 2:10 highlights the elements that bind the addressees and speaker together. Who is the speaker? Among the options are the prophets and the people themselves. Regarding the prophet as speaker, one can argue that he speaks representing the sentiment of the people in much the same way as in Mal 1:6–14.[261] Regarding the people as speaker, some argue that the people are questioning the nature of the malpractice.[262] Finally, the speaker might be a group of men who, having married foreign wives, seek to justify these marriages on the basis of having a common human heritage.[263] In the present discussion, however, I interpret the speaker as the prophet addressing the community.

The sequence of *hălô'* (which is the interrogative particle plus the par-

260. Floyd, *Minor Prophets 2,* 602.

261. Verhoef, *Haggai and Malachi,* 265; Glazier-McDonald, *Malachi: The Divine Messenger,* 83; J. M. O'Brien, *Priest and Levite,* 67; Hill, *Malachi,* 224, 255.

262. Petersen, *Zechariah 9–14 and Malachi,* 195.

263. See Weyde (*Prophecy and Teaching,* 220–21) for further discussion of this and other interpretive options.

ticle of negation) followed by *maddûaʿ*, "why," reflects a similar sequencing in Jer 14:19–22 and Hab 1:12–13, where the questions form the basis for an accusation or assertion.[264] Malachi 1:6 begins with a claim and uses questions to establish the basis for another claim. The sequencing introduces the subject matter and establishes the framework for discussing it by identifying the issues involved. Malachi 2:10 puts the focus on the common heritage and the implication of the heritage for intragroup behavior.

The first *hălôʾ* conveys the rhetorical question *do we not all have one father?* The question is addressed to the community and requires no discussion or interaction. The particle *hălôʾ* introduces the question and conveys the single expected or acceptable response: "yes." Even so, the designation "one father" (*ʾāb ʾeḥād*) is multivalent. One possibility is that "one father" refers to one of the patriarchs, Abraham or Jacob, both of whom were connected to the covenant as the common heritage of the people (2:10).[265] Given the focus on the relationship between Yahweh, the community, and the priests, one can see how the text might refer to the patriarch Abraham as the progenitor. Given the opening exchange about Jacob and Esau, it is significant that the covenant was reaffirmed with Jacob (cf. Mal 1:2; 2:12; 3:6).[266] So Jacob may be the patriarch in view.

Another possibility for understanding "one father" is to broaden the reference beyond the shared heritage of the covenant to the fundamental human connection of all people. However, the nature of the marital relationships—including Yahweh as witness to the marriages—suggests that the scope of the community is Judah/Yehud, not the entire world community.[267]

Finally, one father (*ʾāb ʾeḥād)* may not refer to human ancestry or heritage but to the Deity.[268] This interpretation further clarifies the designation as an attempt to address the people and so to accuse them of their infractions. Understanding the reference as the Deity rather than the patriarchs builds on 1:6 (God as father/parent) and the numerous Old Testament portrayals of God as father (e.g., Exod 4:22, 23; Deut 32:6, 18; Isa 63:16; 64:8; Jer 2:27; 3:4).[269] In addition to the interpretation of "father" in the natural sense (as parent), "father" may be interpreted in the covenantal sense.[270]

264. Weyde, *Prophecy and Teaching,* 219.

265. Baldwin, *Hag, Zech, Mal,* 237.

266. Cf. Baldwin, *Hag, Zech, Mal,* 237.

267. Cf. Glazier-McDonald, *Malachi: The Divine Messenger,* 86.

268. Compare the New Testament's use of "one father" to refer to God: Matt 23:9; John 8:41; Heb 2:11.

269. Thus Verhoef, *Haggai and Malachi,* 265. Verhoef cites "the antithetical reference to daughters of a foreign god" in 2:11 and common usage to support his argument.

270. The "covenantal" rather than "spiritual" sense is used to include the various di-

> Do you thus repay the Lord, O foolish and senseless people? *Is not he your father, who created you,* who made you and established you? (Deut 32:6)

As in Deut 32:6, Mal 2:10aα most likely uses "one father" as a reminder of the shared bond uniting the people of the community with one another. Whether a similar bond is shared with all peoples is not at issue in Mal 2:10a. This first question thus highlights the covenant that is the source of potential unity for the people. But, as seen in 1:6 and 2:5–9, the existence of an ideal does not guarantee the expected behavior.

Like the first question, the second question in Mal 2:10 continues to focus on the people's common heritage: *and has not one God created us?* The designation "one god" (*'ēl 'eḥād*) in the Old Testament is unique to Mal 2:10.[271] The concept of God as creator is the particular aspect of the Deity used to establish the argument and the basis for the charge against the community. By noting that God "created us" (*bərā'ānû*), the question in Mal 2:10aβ, like the previous question, narrows the focus to the people of the community and includes the prophet among them through the use of the first common plural suffix (us).[272] The commonality formed by having the same creator cannot be disrupted; nonetheless, the universal bond of all humans is not the issue in Mal 2:10.[273] Rather, the prophet uses the rhetorical question as the basis for his statement and charge against the hearers.

The first two questions in 2:10a reflected on the common heritage of the people. In contrast, the question in 2:10bα accuses the community of treacherous behavior, making a few assumptions and charges. *Why do we act treacherously to each other?* This question already assumes the treachery (*nibgad*) between the speaker and hearers.[274] The second aspect of the question constitutes the focus of Mal 2:10b. In part, the problem is that this mistreatment is intragroup behavior. *Bāgad,* "to act faithlessly or treacherously," is used in association with several dimensions of the relationship and the laws or expectations pertaining to them. Used of marital relationships, it typically signifies mistreatment of a spouse and points to "an objectively measurable

---

mensions of the relationship, including spiritual, social, and geopolitical. Compare Verhoef, *Haggai and Malachi,* 265–66; Petersen, *Zechariah 9–14 and Malachi,* 196.

271. Malachi 2:15 uses the word "one," referring to God in 2:10. The New Testament references include 1 Cor 8:6; Eph 4:6 (one God and Father of all); 1 Tim 2:5.

272. On God's creation of Israel in particular, see Deut 32:6; Isa 43:1.

273. For examples of the uses of *bārā'* in reference to the creation of human beings, see Gen 1:27; 5:1, 2; Deut 4:32; 32:6; Isa 45:12.

274. The verbal form *nibgad*—the *qal* imperfect first common plural of *bāgad*—includes the prophet (speaker) and the community (hearers).

offensive behavior (cf. Exod 21:8; Mal 2:14)."[275] Used of social relationships, *bāgad* signifies the breach in the relationship, and the kinship of God's people in particular (Mal 2:10, 16; cf. Ps 73:15).[276] Furthermore, *bāgad* in the social realm includes violating the covenantal requirements, ordinances, commandments, ritual laws, and so on (1 Sam 14:33; Lev 7:26; 17:10; Ps 78:57). The formulation *bāgədû bî*, "faithless to me," is used of God's relationship to God's people (Jer 5:11; cf Jer 3:20; Hos 5:7; 6:7; cf. Isa 24:16). In Mal 2:10bβ, the general reference to the breach of their relationship builds on the idea of a common intragroup heritage. That heritage defines the nature of the responsibility and the expectations about how people ought to be treated. Evidently, the shared heritage does not guarantee "good" behavior since "bad" behavior characterizes the way community members treat each other—that is, "a man against his brother" (*ʾîš bəʾāḥîw*). The focus on the community suggests that all are included in the violation of the grounds of the relationship.

Malachi 2:10 concludes with the rhetorical question and points to the consequence of the people's behavior toward each other. Malachi 2:10bβ identifies the misdeed in covenant terms: *defiling the covenant of our ancestors.* Continuing to include himself, the prophet accuses the community of defiling (*ḥālal*) "the covenant of the ancestors" (*ʾăbōtênû*).[277] While Mal 1:6–14 focuses on the priests for their violation of the cult, Mal 2:10 focuses on the community for its malpractice with reference to the covenant (*bərît*). Malachi 2:5 identifies the covenant of Levi; 2:10 mentions the covenant of the ancestors, indicating the full-scale breach within the community—cultic and social. The speaker maintains the connection between the current hearers and the past generations. Just as the priests turned aside from Yahweh's ways (2:8), so the community has gone astray from their ancestors' ways.

Because a number of behaviors can desecrate the priests or high priests, the law cautions against any desecration, including marrying a divorcée, rape victim, or prostitute (Lev 21:7, 14); or approaching a corpse (Lev 21:2, 11). The laws also recognize that mishandling the sacrifices can desecrate the offering and Yahweh's name (Lev 22:1–16).[278] In addition, the behavior of the community can desecrate the name of Yahweh—for example, child sacrifice (Lev 18:21), false oaths (Lev 19:12), or disobeying the commandments (Lev 22:32). In the prophetic literature, acts of desecration also include violating the Sabbath by not keeping the ordinance of God (Ezek 20:13, 16, 21, 24), idolatry (Jer 16:18),[279]

275. M. A. Klopfenstein, "בגד," *TLOT* 1:199. Other uses include political-diplomatic relationships (Judg 9:23; Isa 21:2).

276. See Jer 12:6 (family); Job 6:15 (compatriots); cf. Hab 1:13; Ps 25:3.

277. Cf. Deut 4:31–32 regarding the "covenant with your ancestors" (*bərît ʾăbōtêkā*).

278. F. Maas, "חלל," *TLOT* 2:428.

279. Jeremiah 16:18 uses *ḥālal* and *tôʿăbôt*, "abominations," of the act of defiling the land; see Mal 2:11 for use of the two terms.

and destruction of the temple (Isa 43:28; 47:6; Ezek 24:21; Lam 2:2). The Psalter attests the use of *ḥālal* regarding reneging on a vow (Ps 55:20 [MT 21]) or in relating to the Deity; God desecrates Judah's king and denounces the covenant with him (Ps 89:39 [MT 40]), but the psalmist tries not to desecrate God's covenant (Ps 89:34 [MT 35]).[280]

What is "the covenant of the ancestors"? The answer depends on whether one understands the term "ancestors" to be a reference to Abraham, Jacob, or Levi. Given the focus in 2:10 on the people's ancestors, this covenant may have a broader referent than the priests' covenant. The covenant of the ancestors may point to the patriarchal and Sinaitic covenants. The common heritage was established through the Abrahamic covenant, which included land, progeny, and divine blessing (cf. Isa 41:8–9).[281] The Sinaitic covenant built on the deliverance from Egypt and the laws of relationship and conduct—toward the Deity and the community.[282]

When depicting the people's and their ancestors' behavior, Mal 2:10 glosses over any variation between the ancestors and the present generation. It does not consider whether the ancestors defiled the covenant; nor does it attempt to identify groups in the community that are not defiling the covenant. Its corporate view of practices contrasts with the view that focuses on the priests, and illustrates that all within the community have responsibilities. Already assuming a response, the rhetorical question presumes that there is no valid reason for their acting treacherously given their shared heritage (i.e., covenant of the ancestors). By defiling the covenant, the community calls into question the foundation of its relationship with Yahweh (cf. Exod 19:5–8); it has breached the relationship though perhaps it has not annulled it.

b. Statement Substantiated (2:11)

11 Following the question in Mal 2:10 about the people's behaviors, 2:11 provides a response from the speaker's perspective. The response affirms the treachery or faithlessness but gives no reason for it. One might argue that the question "why" (*maddûaʿ*) does not solicit a reason but betokens the absence of any valid reason for the behavior. The concern is covenant faithfulness, and whatever threatens that faithfulness is an abomination.

Moving from the first common plural reference (we and us), Mal 2:11 names Judah (*yəhûdâ*) as the political, national, and covenantal entity, the

280. Maas, *TLOT* 2:429–30.

281. Cf. Baldwin, *Hag, Zech, Mal,* 237.

282. Cf. Glazier-McDonald, *Malachi: The Divine Messenger,* 87–88; Verhoef, *Haggai and Malachi,* 267; Hill, *Malachi,* 227.

party that has breached the relationship. Judah acted treacherously. First, the general charge is that the nation has behaved in a deplorable manner. To behave treacherously (*bāgad*) is analogous to falsehood and violence or violation of a relationship. The community as a whole is accused of the breach, and the nature of the breach is specified. The second element of the charge further denotes the severity of the infraction by labeling it an abomination—an abomination the community committed in Israel and in Jerusalem (*tôʿēbâ,* feminine singular). Several acts are labeled abominations in the Old Testament, including cultic and social practices. Leviticus 18 lists proscribed behaviors identified as abominations.

> But you shall keep my statutes and my ordinances and commit none of these abominations, either the citizen or the alien who resides among you. (Lev 18:26 NRSV)

The term is used elsewhere to indicate dangerous behavior—that is, behavior that has the potential to destroy the community, including but not limited to cultic offenses (cf. Deut 18:12; 22:5; 25:16; Prov 6:16–19).[283] The term *tôʿēbâ* is also used parallel to *ṭāmēʾ*, "be/become unclean," regarding the corruption of the land (Jer 2:7). Deuteronomy 17:1–7 identifies two types of actions labeled abominations: blemished sacrifices (17:1) and transgression of the covenant by serving other gods (17:2–7), which is punishable by stoning. The explanatory statement in 2:11b specifies abominable actions, which are punished by destruction or being cut off from the community (Lev 17:4; 18:29). Such a punishment becomes the subject of Mal 2:12.

Malachi 2:11 locates the atrocity in "Israel and Jerusalem" (*bəyiśrāʾēl ûbîrûšālāim*). Some contend that "Israel" refers to the inhabitants of the Northern Kingdom who during the restoration era were living in Jerusalem.[284] The typical formulation "Judah and Jerusalem" (*yəhûdâ wîrûšālāim*) signifies the nation and its capital (Mal 3:4; cf. 2 Kgs 23:1; 1 Chr 6:15; 2 Chr 11:14; 20:17; 24:18; 36:4, 10).[285] In Mal 2:11a, "Israel" refers to the people of God, the covenant community, a relational entity juxtaposed with a geopolitical and cultic entity, Jerusalem. The use of Judah, Israel, and Jerusalem indicates that the focus is on the covenant community identified by the place it inhabits (cf. Zech 1:19 [MT 2:2]).[286]

283. E. Gerstenberger, "תועב," *TLOT* 3:1430–31. The term also includes guarding against that which is foreign or "strange."

284. Thus Hill, *Malachi,* 229; cf. Glazier-McDonald, *Malachi: The Divine Messenger,* 89.

285. These and other references indicate that Judah and Jerusalem is a frequent designation in the Chronicler's perspective. Compare the occurrences in the prophetic literature: Isa 1:1; 2:1; Jer 19:7; 27:20; 29:2; Joel 3:1, 6.

286. See the Zech 1:19 (MT 2:2) reference to the horns that have scattered Judah, Israel, and Jerusalem.

The evaluation identifies Judah's actions in terms similar to the charges brought against the priests (Mal 1:7): *for Judah defiled the holiness of Yahweh which he loves.* "Judah defiled" (*ḥillēl*) is the same charge as in 2:10, using the form of a rhetorical question. The object of the defilement is the *qōdeš yhwh*, "holiness of Yahweh," and is modified by the phrase *ʾăšer ʾāhēb*, "which he loves." At issue is whether *qōdeš*, the masculine noun, refers to the temple[287] or to something that is holy to Yahweh, including the people or the covenant.[288] A reference to the people of Yahweh might reflect the postexilic terminology of Ezra 9:1–2, including the perspective that intermarriages are abominations with negative repercussion for the holy seed (*zeraʿ haqqōdeš*).[289] Alternatively, the expression *qōdeš yhwh* may refer to the character of Yahweh, the holiness of Yahweh—which is most likely the meaning in Mal 2:11.[290] Apart from Mal 2:11, the formulation *ḥillēl* with the object *qōdeš yhwh* only occurs in Lev 19:8, where it refers to the peace offering.

> All who eat it shall be subject to punishment, because they have profaned what is holy to the LORD; and any such person shall be cut off from the people. (Lev 19:8 NRSV)[291]

Several instances reflect the antithetical parallel of *qōdeš* ("holy," noun) and *ḥālal* ("profane," verb) where the noun (either singular or plural) is the object of the verb (e.g., Lev 22:15; Ezek 22:26; Zeph 3:4). In some instances, the expression refers to the sanctuary (e.g., Ezek 23:39; 24:21; 28:18).[292] In Mal 1:11–12, however, the expression *qōdeš yhwh* refers to the holiness of Yahweh rather than the temple.

Also challenging is the final phrase of Mal 2:11—*ʾăšer ʾāhēb*, typically translated "which he loves or loved."[293] In Pss 47:4 (MT 5); 78:68, Yahweh is the subject of the verb, and *ʾăšer* refers to the pride of Jacob and Judah/Mount Zion, respectively: "but he chose the tribe of Judah, Mount Zion, which he loves" (78:68). In Mal 2:11 the issue is the subject of the *qal* perfect third mas-

287. Thus the modern versions NIV, NJB, and NRSV; Baldwin, *Hag, Zech, Mal,* 238; Verhoef, *Haggai and Malachi,* 268; Glazier-McDonald, *Malachi: The Divine Messenger,* 82; R. L. Smith, *Micah–Malachi,* 319; Fuller, "Text-Critical Problems," 51; Floyd, *Minor Prophets 2,* 604.

288. See the LXX reading *ta hagia kuriou*, "what is holy to Yahweh."

289. Weyde, *Prophecy and Teaching,* 233–34.

290. Hill, *Malachi,* 231; Petersen, *Zechariah 9–14 and Malachi,* 198.

291. See Lev 22:15—do not defile the *qodšê bənê yiśrāʾēl*, "holy things of the children of Israel."

292. See other occurrences of the antithetical terms in Lev 10:10; Num 18:32. Hill, *Malachi,* 230; Weyde, *Prophecy and Teaching,* 230.

293. See notes on Mal 2:11 above.

culine singular verb *ʾāhēb* and the antecedent of the relative pronoun *ʾăšer*. Among the options for the subject is Yahweh or Judah. With Yahweh as subject, the antecedent of the relative pronoun is *qōdeš yhwh*, "the holiness of Yahweh."[294] Regarding Judah as subject, Hill proposes that *ʾăšer ʾāhēb* be read "he [Yehud] loved," thus presenting the causal relationship between the defiling of Yahweh's holiness and the loving and marrying a daughter of a foreign deity.[295] The proposed reading creates a contrast between Yahweh loving Jacob (1:2–5) and Judah loving the daughter of a foreign deity.[296] In this case, *ʾăšer* is interpreted as the conjunction "because." While making insightful use of the behavior labeled as treacherous, Hill's interpretation attributes to Judah loving the daughter of a foreign god—Judah loved and married the daughter of a foreign god.

Petersen's interpretation is noteworthy because of his effort to highlight idolatry in Mal 2:11. Accordingly, he suggests an emendation of the text (*ʾăšer ʾāhēb*) and hence the reading "he loves Asherah." Noting the occurrences in 1 Kgs 15:9–13 and 18:19 as the basis for understanding the inclusion of both Israel and Judah in the indictment against their treachery, Petersen appeals to epigraphic evidence and the association of the goddess Asherah with Sidon in the sixth century.[297] Fundamental to his argument is understanding "daughters of a foreign god" as a reference to Asherah.

As it stands, Mal 2:11bα indicates that the treachery is the defilement of Yahweh's holiness, a charge similar to that brought against the priests in Mal 1:12. While 2:11bα is not a direct reference to Asherah or to a goddess, it sets the stage for the indictment against practices leading to idolatry (2:11bβ) thus signaling the connection between defiling the covenant and worshiping other gods (cf. Deut 17:2–7).

The last phrase in 2:11bβ, *and married a daughter of a foreign god*, refers to the second of two ways in which Judah has committed an abomination: the defilement and the marriage, which are connected by *waw*. The formulation *a foreign god (ʾēl nēkār)* is rare in the Old Testament, occurring in Deut 32:12 and Ps 81:9 (MT 10).[298] But the formulation *ʾĕlōhê hannēkār*, "foreign gods,"[299] also denotes the concept of foreign deities and the judgment on individuals who follow them (Josh 24:23; cf. Josh 24:20; Judg 10:16). First Samuel 7:3 sees putting away foreign gods as essential to whole-hearted repentance and devotion to Yahweh (cf. 2 Chr 33:15). God punishes those who neglect Yahweh by worshiping other deities (Deut 31:16; Jer 5:19).

294. Those who identify Yahweh as the subject include Baldwin, *Hag, Zech, Mal,* 238; Verhoef, *Haggai and Malachi,* 268; Weyde, *Prophecy and Teaching,* 229.

295. Hill, *Malachi,* 231. See notes on Mal 2:11 above.

296. Hill, *Malachi,* 231.

297. Petersen, *Zechariah 9–14 and Malachi,* 198–200. See notes on Mal 2:11 above.

298. Cf. Weyde, *Prophecy and Teaching,* regarding Dan 11:39, *ʾəlôah nēkār.*

299. Also *ʾəlôah nēkār* without the definite article.

Intergroup or exogamous marriages are discouraged if not prohibited in Israel, perhaps because of the potential threat to Israel's covenant with Yahweh. Yehud, the community, is depicted as someone who married (*bāʿal*) the daughter of a foreign god (*bat-ʾēl nēkār*), highlighting the presence of other deities and covenants with the worshipers of other deities. The singular formulation (*ʾēl nēkār*) may denote a particular foreign deity, but none is identified in the text of Malachi. The conceptual framework is that marriage to foreigners leads to idolatry because the foreigners' religious practices influence the Israelites toward idolatry (Exod 34:12–16). Thus Deut 7:1–5 cautions Israel not to make covenants with the Canaanites because they will turn Israel away from God to "serving other gods" (*ʾĕlōhîm ʾăḥērîm*). Idolatry is also signaled by the concept of the people following "their gods" rather than Yahweh, sacrificing to those deities (cf. 1 Kgs 16:31; 21:25, Ahab-Jezebel)[300] and thus violating the covenant with Yahweh (Ezra 10:2). The underlying concern is the wife's allegiance to a foreign god—*daughter of a foreign god*—without attention to whether Israelites might influence the worship of other gods. Anyone who worships a foreign deity could dishonor and defile Yahweh. Although the phrase "daughter of a foreign god" may be most closely associated with foreign women, it does not need to refer to them.[301] The reference *ʾēl nēkār* is not to a god or a goddess or necessarily a reference to a foreigner.[302] Rather, the designation "daughter of a foreign god" (*bat-ʾēl nēkār*) can suggest allegiance to a deity—thus, "people of Chemosh" (*ʿam-kəmôš,* Num 21:29)—in much the same way that *ʿam-yhwh* signifies people of Yahweh (Judg 5:11; 2 Sam 6:21; cf. Deut 32:19).[303]

The abomination referred to in Mal 2:11 is marriage to women of a foreign god. The issue is that exogamous marriages were a catalyst for idolatry. The disruption in society caused by marriages to foreign women is also the focus of Ezra, where the marriages are the means of violating the covenant with Yahweh. As in Mal 2:10, where the prophet as speaker includes himself in the behavior, so in Ezra 10:2, Ezra, the priest, includes himself, using *māʿal* to depict the behavior ("to act treacherously," a synonym of *bāgad*).

> We *have broken faith* with our God and *have married foreign women* from the peoples of the land, but even now there is hope for Israel in spite of this. (Ezra 10:2 NRSV)

300. See 1 Kgs 18–21 and 1 Kgs 11 regarding King Solomon.

301. Glazier-McDonald (*Malachi: The Divine Messenger,* 92–93) interprets the text as a reference to foreign women. But one should observe that "foreign women" is usually designated by the formulation *nāšîm nokrîôt*; e.g., 1 Kgs 11:1; Ezra 10:2, 10.

302. Petersen, *Zechariah 9–14 and Malachi,* 199–200.

303. See *bat-bābel,* "daughter of Babylon," in Zech 2:7 (MT 11); *bat-ṣîôn,* "daughter of Zion," in Zech 2:10 (MT 14).

> Then Ezra the priest stood up and said to them, "*You have trespassed* and *married foreign women*, and so increased the guilt of Israel." (Ezra 10:10 NRSV)

In Ezra 10:10 the charge is directed to the people without Ezra's self-inclusion.[304] Whether the prohibited marital union is labeled *mā'al* or *bāgad*—both denote a breach of the relationship.[305] Ezra specifies that the spouses are foreign women (*nāšîm nokrîôt*), of the people of the land; Mal 2:11 is ambiguous regarding their nationality and looks at their allegiance, which is to a foreign god (*bat-'ēl nēkār*).

c. Announcement of Judgment for the Unfaithfulness (2:12)

12 The announcement of punishment addresses the violation depicted in Mal 2:11. Thus, Yahweh's judgment is not arbitrary but specific to those who commit the noted infraction—defiling the covenant through marrying a daughter of a foreign god. The emphasis on the infraction makes the identity of the offender irrelevant in assigning punishment.

The announcement identifies the target and the range of individuals who may be offenders. *May Yahweh cut off the man who does it—witness or respondent.* The mode of punishment is being cut off (*kārat*) or ostracized from the community.[306] The formulation *yakrēt yhwh lā'îš* is similar to other texts where the object is *'îš*, "man" (e.g., Lev 17:4, 9; cf. Num 9:13). In Num 9:13, "cut off" (*kārat*) is used with the preposition *min*, which refers to the entity from which the offender would be removed—from the people (*'am*, with the suffix indicating "their" or "your" people). Likewise, these texts clearly identify the object of punishment as a person (*nepeš*) and denote the offense (cf. Lev 17:10; 20:5, 6).[307] Both Lev 18:29 and 19:8 denote the offenders by their actions. The formulation "to cut off" also appears in Ezek 14:1–11, which articulates the punishment for any in the community who committed idolatry yet sought the prophet to inquire of Yahweh.[308] Yahweh will punish them

304. See Blenkinsopp's (*Ezra-Nehemiah*, 187) discussion about the switch from first to third person, including the compilation of possible sources; cf. Hos 1–3.

305. Both Ezra 10:2 and 10 use *mā'al*, "act unfaithfully, treacherously"—10:2, *mā'alnû bē'lōhênû*, "act unfaithfully toward our God."

306. The *hiphil* jussive third masculine singular form *yakrēt* is used in Ps 109:15 with Yahweh as subject.

307. Leviticus 7:20, 21, 25, 27; 22:3; 23:29; Num 15:30, 31 (native-alien); 19:13 (cf. Lev 20:17, 18). Cf. Weyde, *Prophecy and Teaching*, 237. Weyde also cites the passive forms of the verb in Leviticus and Ezekiel.

308. The articulation of the punishment includes a formula for recognition—that "you will know that I am Yahweh" (Ezek 14:8).

(including the prophet) by cutting them off from among the people. These texts focus on the preservation of the community by removing the offenders whose behavior—mostly idolatry—threatens the unity of the community. The contrary actions of idolatry and seeking Yahweh's assistance stand out in Yahweh's response. In Mal 2:12 the announcement of punishment functions in much the same way regarding the offender in relation to the community; however, neither the offense nor divorce is mentioned with the punishment (cf. Ezra 10).

The formulation *the man who does it* identifies the target of Yahweh's action, with reference to the behavior being punished (denoted here by the third feminine suffix "it"). Designated by the gender-specific marker, *lāʾîš,* "the man," refers to any male of the community who defiled the covenant of Yahweh by entering into exogamous marriages.[309] The *ʾăšer* clause modifying *lāʾîš* identifies him. The imperfect form of the verb *yaʿăśennā*[310] denotes the action as ongoing and narrows the focus from all individuals to any male who commits a particular act: "it," defiling Yahweh through exogamous marriage.

The idiomatic expression *witness or respondent (ʿēr wəʿōnê)* further describes the offenders' behavior by revealing the range of people who are being punished. Nevertheless, the expression has been a topic of debate due in part to the formulation *ʿēr wəʿōnê.*[311] At issue are the functions of the guilty individuals and the dimensions of life being referenced. Without repeating all the perspectives here, I will simply note the interpretive possibilities. First, it has been suggested that *ʿēr wəʿōnê* indicates "son and grandson."[312] This interpretation signals the generational dimension of life and suggests that the punishment is transgenerational.

A second interpretation is that *ʿēr wəʿōnê* refers to Er and Onan, Judah's sons who married the foreign woman Tamar (Onan, after Er's death; Gen 38). In this interpretation, the people of Yehud (in the Persian period) are like Er and Onan, who were killed for practicing exogamous marriage.[313] The argument falls apart when one considers that Judah's and

309. Contrast the NRSV: "anyone." Several commentators support a gender-inclusive reference. Verhoef (*Haggai and Malachi,* 270) argues that "the man" refers to the guilty, namely, "every member of the covenant people who acted accordingly." See also R. L. Smith, *Micah–Malachi,* 319; Petersen, *Zechariah 9–14 and Malachi,* 194, 200. Others recognize the gender-specific aspect of the announcement: Glazier-McDonald, *Malachi: The Divine Messenger,* 82; Floyd, *Minor Prophets 2,* 605.

310. The *qal* imperfect third masculine singular plus third feminine singular pronominal suffix.

311. See p. 236 n. a above for further details concerning the various perspectives.

312. Baldwin, *Hag, Zech, Mal,* 239.

313. Thus D. R. Jones, *Haggai, Zechariah and Malachi,* 195; M. Krieg, *Mutmaßungen*

Tamar's descendants Perez and Zerah played a vital role in the history of God's people.[314] The progeny was an issue for Er and Onan not because of their exogamous marriage but because of their reprehensible behavior.[315] In considering the agents represented by *ʿēr wəʿōnê*, Weyde cites the use of word pairs to refer to the object of Yahweh's punishment in total—"head-tail," Isa 9:14; "name-remnant," Isa 14:22; "righteous-wicked," Ezek 21:3.[316] This evidence supports the notion of the comprehensive scope of the punishment (*kārat*).

Floyd proposes that the punishment applies to both the judicial and the cultic realms, so the cutting off excludes the guilty party from participation in both realms.[317] The two sectors are identified by the terms "witness and respondent" in the first part of the announcement (Deut 17:6; 19:15) and by the reference to bringing an offering in the second part.

However one interprets the offenders, the focus is on the infraction. While the range of individuals included in the punishment may signal the comprehensiveness of the punishment (Isa 9:14; 14:22, etc.), in Mal 2:12 this range of people contributes to the perspective that Yahweh does not show partiality in executing punishment. The nature of the infraction dictates the punishment—not the identity of the offender. Potentially, the announcement targets all offenders in the society, whether priest or layperson, young or old, slave or free.[318] In essence, the guilty men would cease to function as members of the community in spite of any attempt to appease the Deity (cf. Mal 2:17; 3:5; cf. Zech 13:1).[319]

The punishment also identifies the community from which they will be cut off: *from the tents of Jacob*. The combination of *kārat* plus the preposition *min* occurs frequently in the Old Testament, sometimes with a specified location, name, or people—for example, "from Israel" (*miyyiśrāʾēl*—Exod

über Maleachi, ATANT 80 (Zurich: Theologischer Verlag, 1993), 183–85; Weyde, *Prophecy and Teaching,* 245–46, 276–77.

314. Perez is an ancestor of David (Ruth 4:18–22) and Jesus (Matt 1; Luke 3:23–33).

315. See Jacobs (*Gender, Power and Persuasion*) regarding the significance of their behavior at the time of their death. It is argued that the cause of their death was not Tamar but their actions and God's decision to punish them.

316. Weyde, *Prophecy and Teaching,* 245 n. 105. The totality is expressed by listing entities—male, both "bond and free" (*ʿāṣûr wəʿāzûb*), 1 Kgs 14:10; 21:21; 2 Kgs 9:8. Cf. Verhoef, *Haggai and Malachi,* 271. Other examples of word pairs with the verb are Num 15:30 (native-alien); Ezek 14:13, 17; 25:13; 29:8 (humans-animals); Ezek 21:4 (righteous-wicked); Ezek 35:7 (all who come and go).

317. Floyd, *Minor Prophets 2,* 605.

318. Note the various interpretations of the LXX and targum.

319. Zechariah 13:2 uses *kārat,* "to cut off," and *ʿābar* in parallelism to denote cleaning the land by removing the bad elements, the idols and prophets, and the unclean spirits.

12:15; Num 9:13; Isa 9:14). The formulation "cut off from" usually designates removal from the community—from the people.[320] In 1 Sam 2:33 the cutting off is from the altar (*mizbēaḥ*).[321] In Mal 2:12, the offender is cut off from "the tents of Jacob" (*mēʾohŏlê yaʿăqōb*), an expression that also appears in a few other passages, including Jer 30:18:

> Thus says the Lord: I am going to restore the fortunes of *the tents of Jacob*, and have compassion on his dwellings; the city shall be rebuilt upon its mound, and the citadel set on its rightful site. (Jer 30:18 NRSV)

Perhaps the phrase "tents of Jacob" (*mēʾohŏlê yaʿăqōb*) signifies the heritage, not simply the location, and echoes an earlier existence of the people when they were not yet settled in the land promised to them (cf. Gen 25:27). On the one hand, the text uses "Judah" to identity the community, a term that most likely brings into focus political and national identity (Mal 2:11). By referring to the community as "Jacob," 2:12 reconnects to the thought and charge in Mal 1:2–5 and the covenantal relationship that defines the reason for the fractured Yahweh-Israel relationship. "Tents of Jacob" refers to the community and its heritage and is not limited to association with its early development and nomadic lifestyle; it is the equivalent of the community whose ancestor is Jacob—thus "tents of Ham" (Ps 78:51), "tents of Edom" (Ps 83:6 [MT 7]). The reference to the "tents of Judah" would also denote the covenant community and political entity (Zech 12:7). To be cut off from the tents is to be removed from the community and the legacy it signifies.

The announcement of the punishment continues with attention to cultic practices: *although one brings an offering to Yahweh of hosts.* The *waw* expands the object of the verb "to cut off" (Mal 2:12a), noting another action of the person to be punished. Having indicated the total range of those to be punished, 2:12bβ identifies a competing action. Judah/Yehud has defiled Yahweh by marrying a woman who worships a foreign god, yet Judah continues to bring offerings to Yahweh.[322] Given what has been presented about an offering (*minḥâ*) and malpractice in that regard, one can hardly be surprised by

320. To be cut off from the people is a punishment for a wide range of infractions; cf. Exod 12:19; 30:33, 38; 31:14; Lev 7:20, 21, 25, 27.

321. Usually denoted with the preposition *min* to indicate expulsion from the named entity—for example, the city or Israel. In particular, the expression "tents of Jacob" (*mēʾohŏlê yaʿăqōb*) occurs in Num 24:5. Tents may also be qualified by other nouns to denote the dwelling place and influence of someone or something; thus, the tents of bribery (Job 15:34); of the wicked (Ps 84:10 [MT 11]); of the righteous (Ps 118:15).

322. Glazier-McDonald, *Malachi: The Divine Messenger,* 99; Weyde, *Prophecy and Teaching,* 247; cf. Verhoef, *Haggai and Malachi,* 271–72.

the inefficacy of bringing an offering to Yahweh in order to win the Deity's favor (cf. Mal 1:10, 13; 2:13; 3:3). Accordingly, violating Yahweh in one practice influences Yahweh's response to the worshiper; all areas of the person's life contribute to Yahweh's response (cf. Ezek 14:1–14). Consequently, an offering does not automatically secure Yahweh's favor. In particular, an exogamous marriage could deter Yahweh's favorable response. Here, Mal 2:12 does not mention the quality of the offering since the behavior regarding the one offering (the *minḥâ*) is determinative. This final phrase in 2:12 aims not only at the priests who are responsible for the sacrifice (Mal 1:10, 13; cf. Lev 2)[323] but, potentially, whoever offended Yahweh—whether the priests who present the offering or the lay members for whom the offering is presented (cf. Mal 2:13; 3:3).

Important to the perspective of Mal 2:10–12 is the nature of the punishment and the ramifications for anyone who is in an exogamous marriage. The punishment is exclusion from the covenant community, with no prescribed action of divorce. Hence, the removal of the men involved in the practice and by implication their wives would remove the practices and any threat to the covenant of Yahweh. The perspective here in Mal 2:12 is different from that seen in Ezra 9:1–10:17 (cf. Neh 13:23–31).[324] The relevant texts in Ezra and Nehemiah seem to reflect a different way of handling the matter: keeping the offender within the community but requiring that he divorce. While the latter texts prescribe that all the men who are married to foreign wives divorce the wives, Mal 2:12 announces that Yahweh will cut off the offender from participation in the community, without the option of dissolving the marriages as part of the punishment (cf. 2:16).[325] Both approaches punish exogamous marriage, though the social implications differ for each community.

323. Cf. E. Gerstenberger, *Leviticus,* OTL (Louisville: Westminster John Knox, 1996), 37–43. Regarding the Leviticus discussion of the cereal offering, Gerstenberger looks at the involvement of the priest and the laypersons and the priestly-congregational structure characteristic of the early Second Temple period (beginning in 516/15 BCE). He argues that, while the cereal offerings belonged to the laypersons and the farmers as offerings to the deity, the practice changed. Among these variations, "the cereal offering was taken out of the familial sphere and integrated into the most sacred priestly system. Although an offering portion may have always been burned in Israel (cf. Gen 4:3–5; Amos 5:21–22), the cereal offering now belongs on the one hand to the sacrosanct expiatory offering, and on the other to the priestly income, and is completely expropriated from familial use" (p. 43).

324. Cf. Floyd, *Minor Prophets 2,* 605.

325. See G. P. Hugenberger (*Marriage as a Covenant,* VTSup 52 [Leiden: Brill, 1994], 17) for discussion about the relationship of Malachi to Ezra and Nehemiah on the subject of divorce. See also Blenkinsopp, *Ezra-Nehemiah,* 187.

2. Attention to Marriage and Divorce (2:13–16)

13*"And this second thing you do:*[a] *tears cover*[b] *the altar of Yahweh—weeping and groaning; because*[c] *there is no turning to*[d] *the offering or receiving a favor from your hand.* 14*But you say, 'Why?' Because Yahweh was a witness between you and the wife of your youth whom you yourself treated treacherously even though she is your companion and the wife of your covenant.* 15*He did not make one but also the residue of his spirit. So what does the One*[e] *seek? Godly offspring. So safeguard yourself in your spirit and do not treat the wife of your youth treacherously.*[f] 16*Because he [the One] hates*[g] *divorce," says Yahweh God of Israel;*[h] *"for he who covers*[i] *his garment with violence," says Yahweh of hosts. "So keep yourself in your spirit and do not act treacherously."*

---

a. The LXX reads "I hate" (presuming *śānēʾtî*, the first-person form of *śānēʾ*, "to hate") rather than the ordinal number *šēnît*, "second." This appears to be a harmonization with Mal 2:16. There are two options for translating *šēnît*: (1) "again, the second time"—J. M. P. Smith, "Malachi," 51; Baldwin, *Hag, Zech, Mal,* 239; (2) "second act or thing"—Verhoef, *Haggai and Malachi,* 272; Glazier-McDonald, *Malachi: The Divine Messenger,* 99–100; Petersen, *Zechariah 9–14 and Malachi,* 194; Floyd, *Minor Prophets 2,* 605; NRSV, NIV.

b. The MT has the infinitive construct form, *kassôt* from *kāsâ*, "to cover." The apparatus suggests the imperfect second masculine plural form *təkassû*, "you cover." The LXX reads *ekaluptete,* "cover," providing a subject for the verb. Modern translations that follow this reading include the NRSV: "you cover"; compare with the ASV; and commentators: Petersen, *Zechariah 9–14 and Malachi,* 194; Verhoef, *Haggai and Malachi,* 272; Glazier-McDonald, *Malachi: The Divine Messenger,* 82.

c. The translation of *mēʾên* (preposition *min* plus negative adverb *ʾên*, "there is not") and its function in Mal 2:13 includes various perspectives. *BHS* proposes reading *mēʾēn*, the *piel* perfect third masculine singular from the verb *māʾēn*, "to refuse," and inserting Yahweh, or reading *ʿôd*, the adverb. The LXX and Qumran (4Q12[a]) assume *min* plus *ʾāwen*, "trouble"; the LXX reads *ek kopon*, "because of trouble," thus "weeping and groaning because of trouble"; 4Q12[a], *mēʾāwen* (cf. Fuller, "Text-Critical Problems," 52). Modern translations interpret *mēʾên* in the causal sense, "because," and seem to insert or assume Yahweh; NRSV: "because he no longer regards" (cf. ASV, KJV, NIV). Among those who interpret it as causal are Verhoef (*Haggai and Malachi,* 272–73), who also assumes Yahweh as subject; R. L. Smith, *Micah–Malachi,* 319; and Hill, *Malachi,* 238.

d. Yahweh is the one who does not carry out the actions, which are portrayed by use of two infinitive construct forms—*pənôt* from *pānâ*, "to turn," and *lāqaḥat* (*le* plus the verb *lāqaḥ,* "to take").

e. As a whole, Mal 3:15 poses many difficulties, making a compelling translation elusive. Without presenting the list of difficulties, I will highlight several translations to illustrate the range of interpretations. One issue has been whether to translate *wəlōʾ-ʾeḥād ʿāśâ* as a question (JPS, NIV, NJB, NRSV) or as a statement (LXX). Examples from *modern translations*: (1) "Did not one God make her? Both flesh and spirit are his. And what does the one God desire? Godly offspring" (NRSV); (2) "And did not he make one? Yet had he the residue of the spirit. And wherefore one? That he might seek a godly seed" (KJV). Examples from *commentaries*: (1) "No one with a residue of spirit would act that way. What does the one do?" (Verhoef, *Haggai and Malachi,* 263); (2) "Surely the one made everything? Even a residue of spirit belongs to him. What does the one seek?" (Hill, *Malachi,* 221); (3) "Did He not make [you/them] one, with a remnant of the spirit belonging to it? And what was the One seeking?" (Hugenberger, *Marriage as Covenant,* 133); (4) "Has not (the) One made (us), his vigorous remnant?" (Petersen, *Zechariah and Malachi,* 194). Intending to provide an understanding of 2:15, R. R. Deutsch renders "He has not made (or created) one only, but has completed him by adding another human being" ("Calling God's People to Obedience: A Commentary on the Book of Malachi," in *A Promise of Hope: A Call to Obedience,* ITC [Grand Rapids: Eerdmans, 1987], 96).

Concerning the MT clause (*ûmâ hāʾeḥād*), the LXX reads *allos.* Verhoef (*Haggai and Malachi,* 276) reads "What does the one do?" R. L. Smith (*Micah–Malachi,* 319), "Why does the One seek godly offspring?" The NIV separates the clause from the verb *məbaqqēš,* thus reading, "And why one?"

f. In place of the MT *yibgōd* (the third masculine singular), the LXX, targum, and Vulgate presume *tibgōd,* the second masculine singular. Several interpreters retain the MT: for example, Hill, *Malachi,* 249; Verhoef, *Haggai and Malachi,* 263; Glazier-McDonald, *Malachi: The Divine Messenger,* 109; Petersen, *Zechariah 9–14 and Malachi,* 194. Contrast R. L. Smith, *Micah–Malachi,* 319.

g. *BHS* suggests *śānēʾtî* (first common singular), "I hate," in place of *śānēʾ* (third masculine singular), "he hates."

h. *BHS* indicates that the phrase in Mal 2:16 is an addition—the messenger formula "Yahweh" plus the epithet "God of Israel" (*ʾĕlōhê yiśrāʾēl;* cf. Exod 5:1; 32:27; Josh 7:13; Judg 6:8; Isa 37:21). In Zeph 2:9 the formula plus epithet "Yahweh of hosts, the God of Israel" occurs (*yhwh ṣəbāʾôt ʾĕlōhê yiśrāʾēl*). The epithet "Yahweh God of Israel" (*yhwh ʾĕlōhê yiśrāʾēl*) appears a number of times in the Old Testament (e.g., Jer 11:3; 13:12; 21:4; 23:2; 25:15; 34:13; Ezek 44:2).

i. At issue is understanding the MT *wəkissā,* the *piel* perfect third masculine singular form of the verb *kāsâ,* "to cover." One proposal is the infinitive form *wəkassê.* There is no consensus among the ancient versions about how to interpret the verb: the LXX reads, "Then ungodliness will cover. . ."; the Peshitta reads, "Let him not conceal"; and the targum reads, "You shall not conceal."

Malachi 2:13–16 consists of the question-answer schema already noted in several instances in the book (e.g., 1:2–5, 6–7). Continuity with the preceding unit is manifested in the recurrence of the "one" motif—one father (*ʾāb ʾeḥād,* 2:10), one god (*ʾēl ʾeḥād,* 2:10, 15), "the One" (2:16).[326] Nevertheless, the difficulties in 2:16 require discussion (see translation and notes). Attention to covenants continues, from "the covenant of our ancestors" (2:10) to *the wife of your covenant* (2:14) along with faithlessness and treachery defined by the parameters of a covenant (Mal 2:10, 11 vis-à-vis 2:14, 15, 16).

Marriage is both an element of continuity and discontinuity, and the dissolution of marriage is the concern of Mal 2:13–16. Because it mentions *the wife of your youth,* the unit addresses the males and only by inference the fe-

326. Cf. Floyd, *Minor Prophets 2,* 608.

males of the community. The people are shown the connection between their weeping on the altar and the Deity's rejection of their offerings. The imagery of covering the altar suggests an abundance of tears and groaning, not literal tears literally overflowing the physical structure. The abundance of tears echoes the abundance of violence in 2:16. Likewise, Yahweh's rejection of the people's offering parallels the rejection of the priestly offerings (1:6–14). The people ask for an explanation about God's rejection (2:14). God's justification for rejecting them is that they have been faithless or treacherous (2:14–16). Verse 16 identifies the nature of the faithlessness by mentioning hatred and "covering one's garment with violence." Note that the image of faithlessness is usually spoken of in reference to the wife's infidelity (cf. Hosea). Malachi 2:13–16 does not address marital infidelity or polygyny; however, 2:16 admonishes the men to be faithful to their responsibility by picking up the theme again from 2:15.

a. Description of the People's Futile Behavior (regarding Offerings) (2:13)

13 The description of the people's behavior serves as a foundation for addressing the Deity's disfavor and the admonition about the people's practices. Malachi 2:13 begins the unit by noting another of Judah's actions and the futility of the people's practice, as shown by the Deity's rejection.

The reading *this second thing you do (wəzō't šēnît ta'ăśû)* is difficult to understand, which leads us to several suggestions regarding its interpretation. The ordinal number "second" (*šēnît*) extends the series of accusations from Mal 2:11. The first accusation was for defiling Yahweh's holiness by means of the exogamous marriages. Those who interpret 2:11 as "defiling" Yahweh's sanctuary note a progression from the sanctuary now to the altar (*mizbaḥ*).[327] The second action is signaled by the verb *kassôt*, the infinitive absolute "to cover" the altar (cf. 2:16).

The behavior at the altar is depicted as an external demonstration: *tears cover the altar of Yahweh.* The behavior identified as weeping and groaning suggests the presence of sorrow or remorse. The image that emerges from the use of the verb *kassôt*, "to cover," with Yahweh's altar (*mizbaḥ yhwh*) is an abundance of tears. One understanding is that "tears" (*dim'â,* a feminine singular collective noun) functions as the indirect object of the verb, the object being the altar of Yahweh. In this understanding the second masculine plural of the verb is usually supplied in place of the infinitive construct form (*kassôt*): thus, "*you* cover Yahweh's altar

327. Thus Hill, *Malachi,* 237.

with tears."[328] The other understanding is that the tears function as the subject: "tears cover the altar."[329] Psalm 6:6 (MT 7) notes the distress of the speaker by citing the abundance of tears paired with sighing (*ʾănāḥâ*). Whose tears? The tears in Mal 2:13 may come from the divorced women in Yehud.[330] This interpretation, however, does not recognize the rationale for the tears: that Yahweh is not pleased with the ones whose tears flood the altar. Most likely, the tears come from the community and are the effect of Yahweh's displeasure with them 2:13.

The terms *weeping and groaning (bəkî waʾănāqâ)* further explain the tears. These two elements may be the source of the tears or activity associated with the tears. The less frequent term "groaning" (*ʾănāqâ*) occurs in Pss 12:5 (MT 6); 79:11; and 102:20 (MT 21) in the context of distress. The pair "tears" (*dimʿâ*) and "weeping" (*bəkî*) usually appears as a result of distress (e.g., Isa 16:9; 22:4; Jer 9:1; 13:17; 31:16; Lam 1:16; Ezek 24:16). The use of tears with weeping and groaning is unique to Mal 2:13 and denotes (in this context) distress over Yahweh's response to the community.

Another suggestion is that the tears are part of a lament rite associated with other deities—for example, Tammuz and Ba'al, deities for whom ritual lamentation was performed annually.[331] Accordingly, Petersen suggests that the weeping in Mal 2:13 may point to the inappropriate veneration of a male deity at Yahweh's altar.[332] If the weeping is associated with improper veneration and thus connected to 2:10–12, it may be better to see the veneration as the misappropriation of the lamentation rites to Yahweh or perhaps even the misuse of Yahweh's altar to carry out a ritual to another deity. But as interesting as this possibility is, the text does not support it; rather, the text provides the motivation for the tears: Yahweh's disfavor.

The Deity's disfavor is signaled by the clause *because there is no more turning to the offering*. The particle *mēʾên* is used in the causal sense to introduce the reason for weeping and groaning and to connect the people's and Yahweh's actions. The tears of the people cover Yahweh's altar because Yahweh is rejecting their practices. Yahweh's response to the community appears in two expressions governed by the particle *mēʾên* (*pənôt ʾel-hamminḥâ* and *lāqaḥat rāṣôn*). These expressions belong to the large framework of the Dei-

328. Thus Verhoef, *Haggai and Malachi,* 262; Glazier-McDonald, *Malachi: The Divine Messenger,* 82; R. L. Smith, *Micah–Malachi,* 319; Petersen, *Zechariah 9–14 and Malachi,* 194.

329. Thus Hill, *Malachi,* 237.

330. Among those who cite it as one of many interpretations are Verhoef, *Haggai and Malachi,* 272; and R. L. Smith, *Micah–Malachi,* 323.

331. Petersen, *Zechariah 9–14 and Malachi,* 201–2; cf. Glazier-McDonald, *Malachi: The Divine Messenger,* 100.

332. Petersen (*Zechariah 9–14 and Malachi,* 201–2) also sees the people as worshiping Asherah, the female deity.

ty's response to sacrifices; both include a verb plus its object. First, while the formulation *no turning to (pənôt ʾel),* uses the infinitive construct to denote a reason, the action suggests that Yahweh is the subject. The verb *pānâ* plus *ʾel* is used of showing regard for someone or something and may be negated to reflect disregard for the entity. Thus Moses asked God not to regard the people's offering (*minḥātām,* Num 16:15), and Solomon requested Yahweh's favorable regard when he prayed (*təpillat,* 1 Kgs 8:28).[333] The formulation, apart from cultic practices, has the same meaning of regarding or not regarding (cf. Deut 9:27; 2 Sam 9:8).[334] In Mal 2:13, the reason for not regarding "the offering" (*hamminḥâ*) is that Yahweh does not look favorably at it. Although it does not use the verb *rāṣâ,* "be pleased with, or accept," Mal 2:13 conveys the perspective of nonacceptance as in Mal 1:10, 13.

The second, parallel construction of the verb plus its object reveals that Yahweh does not receive the offering as favorable (*or receiving a favor from your hand*). Some propose that "favor" (*rāṣôn*) in this context refers to the "condition"—that is, with favor.[335] Yahweh does not receive the offering with favor (*rāṣôn*), nor is Yahweh pleased with the offering. This interpretation focuses on the offering and regard for the offering. But this interpretation may reduce the scope to disfavor. One should therefore consider the significance of the parallel construction for understanding the Deity's actions.

Another interpretation sees "a favor" (*rāṣôn*) as having the general meaning of "any favor," thus broadening the scope of the nonacceptance: Yahweh will not receive as acceptable anything from their hand. To receive the offering as "a favor" connotes garnering the Deity's favor.[336] Here in Mal 2:13 the offering may be an object that Yahweh will not receive on their behalf, one of the elements among many that they offered to win Yahweh's favor. In Leviticus, the noun (*rāṣôn*) is used to convey the acceptable nature of the offering or sacrifice on behalf of the one who offers it (cf. Lev 19:5; 22:19, 20, 21, 29; 23:11). The issue in Mal 2:13 is that Yahweh will not receive any offering as acceptable—not necessarily because of the quality of the offering—because of its source: from their hand (cf. Hag 2:14).

As in Mal 1:10 and 13, the expression *miyyedkem, from your hand* (singular noun plus the second plural suffix), highlights the source of the people's offering and their responsibility for it.[337] Whether the last clause in 2:13

333. Cf. Ps 102:17 (MT 18); Lev 26:9. See usage in Hag 1:9 (discussion above).

334. The formulation may be used of both the Deity and a human agent.

335. Thus Verhoef (*Haggai and Malachi,* 273) proposed the reading "or accept them with pleasure from your hands"; cf. R. L. Smith, *Micah–Malachi,* 319; Petersen, *Zechariah 9–14 and Malachi,* 194.

336. See the LXX: "or receive anything from your hands as favor."

337. Contrast those who translate *miyyedkem* as plural, "your hands": Verhoef (*Haggai and Malachi,* 273); cf. R. L. Smith, *Micah–Malachi,* 319; Petersen, *Zechariah 9–14 and Malachi,* 194.

echoes the last clause of 2:12 is worth considering. The last clause in both 2:12 and 2:13 attests the futility of the community's offerings. Both instances bring to the foreground the question of who is involved; the question should be considered in light of the reference to Judah and the tents of Jacob (including both priests and laypersons). The quality of an offering alone does not suffice in garnering God's favor; rather, the quality of the individuals who bring the offering (their regard for Yahweh) determines Yahweh's response.

b. Cited Rationale for the Futility: Yahweh's Disfavor (2:14–16)

(1) Report of the People's Question (2:14a)

14 With 2:13 as the basis for Yahweh's rejection of Judah's offering, 2:14 tightens the focus on the cause of Yahweh's disfavor. The prophet introduces the people's dissenting voice with the formula *waʾămartem, but you say,* and their question, *"Why?" (ʿal-mâ).* The question represents the people's bewilderment with Yahweh's disfavor regarding their offering.

(2) The Prophet's Response to the People's Question (2:14b–16)

(a) The Violation of the Marriage Covenant (2:14b–15)

Yahweh's response to their inquiry is introduced by the expression *ʿal kî,* "because," and echoes the charge in 2:11 that they have acted faithlessly (2:14b). Yahweh was a witness (*hēʿîd*)[338] to the union (*between you and the wife of your youth*), and their subsequent treachery has prompted the actions against them. Who is this wife? Her identity involves the designation "wife of your youth" (*ʾēšet nəʿûrêkā*). Taken literally, "wife of your youth" suggests that Judah or the men of Judah married when they were young and that the spouse someone married early in his life is considered the wife of his youth. Typically the expression "wife of" (*ʾēšet*) is followed by the name of the man (e.g., Gen 36:10; 38:12; 1 Sam 4:19; 2 Sam 11:26; 1 Kgs 14:5, 6; 2 Kgs 22:14),[339] or in other instances the designation is "another man," a nameless person or friend (*mēʾēšet rāʿ*—Prov 6:24, 26), for adultery or prostitution (Hos 1:2). A forsaken wife of someone's youth is used as a metaphor for Israel's position when called by the Deity (Isa 54:6). The formulation "wife of your youth" occurs in Prov

338. The use of the verb that indicates being a witness or bearing witness to an act or event. It may also refer to testifying (cf. 1 Kgs 21:13).

339. Cf. Deut 22:22; 25:5.

5:18 and twice in Mal 2:14 and 15[340] and may refer to a man's primary wife or at least the one taken in his youth (first love) as compared with a wife taken later.

The men are accused of mistreating the wives: *whom you yourself treated treacherously* (*bāgad*). This is not simply a matter of being unfaithful—which would likely use the root *nāʾap,* "to commit adultery" (cf. Mal 3:5; Exod 20:14). Rather, the term *bāgad* may signify that the husband is not living up to the responsibility of the covenant with his wife. The accusation is not limited to marital infidelity but may extend to caring for his wife, including basic sustenance and shelter (e.g., Exod 21:8 regarding female slaves). Whether care meant not divorcing her is another matter since the law permitted a man to divorce his wife except in a case of unsubstantiated slander (Deut 22:13–19) or marrying a fiancée whom he had previously raped (Deut 22:26–29).

Malachi 2:14 further reiterates the nature of the union—the woman is *your companion (ḥăbertəkā)* and *wife of your covenant (wəʾēšet bərîtekā)*—perhaps denoting the responsibility and the relational bond. These two characteristics contrast with the treacherous behavior committed against the wife. Describing her as a companion (*ḥăberet*)[341] uses a term that was typically used of a male companion or of equals, thus possibly indicating parity within the relationship in addition to the contractual agreement.[342] The occurrences of *ḥābēr,* "friend, companion," suggest mutuality and an affinity formed through shared experience or values.[343] That affinity usually binds persons and influences them to protect each other (Eccl 4:10). In Mal 2:14, her being *the wife of your covenant* shows the contradiction in the man's behavior. The husband does not affirm the bond with his wife but violates it.

The third of the three designations in 2:14, *the wife of your covenant,* further highlights the nature of the union in contrast to the man's atrocious behavior. Just as a question arises whether divorcing a wife other than the one "of your youth" would generate the same response, so also, here, a question arises regarding the significance of the designation *the wife of your covenant (ʾēšet bərîtekā)* in comparison with the other designations. Is Yahweh a witness to the covenant between a husband and any or all of his wives, regardless of how or when they were acquired? What about a captive wife (Deut 21:10–14) or a wife acquired as the result of rape (Exod 22:16–17 [MT 15–16];

340. See "husband of her youth" (*baʿal nəʿûrêhā*), Joel 1:8; "partner of her youth," Prov 2:17.

341. For further discussion of the root, see Hill, *Malachi,* 242.

342. Baldwin, *Hag, Zech, Mal,* 239–40; cf. Hill, *Malachi,* 242.

343. Other occurrences include companion or friend (*ḥābēr*), denoting affinity or shared values, Ps 119:63 (God-fearers); Prov 28:24 (of a thief). Regarding the unity of a group of persons acting together, a company or companions, see Judg 20:11 (*ḥăbērîm*); Isa 1:23 (*ḥabrê gannābîm,* companion of thieves); Ezek 37:16 (*ḥăbērô,* the associate of Israel); Eccl 4:10 (of mutual support). Cf. Song 1:7 (*ḥăbērêkā*); 8:13 (*ḥăbērîm*).

Deut 22:28–29) or even a hated wife (Deut 21:16–17)?[344] Deuteronomy has different perspectives on the dissolution of these marriages. Glazier-McDonald interprets "wife of your youth" as being synonymous with "wife" and having no additional significance.[345] Regarding "wife of your covenant" as compared with the "wife of one's youth," both Hill and Glazier-McDonald equate "wife of your youth" and "wife of your covenant."[346] Malachi 2:14 is concerned with the obedience of the covenant community even in matters of marriage. Whether the marriage is formed by a covenant between a man and a woman or by a contract, the focus is the covenant community's concept of marriage, including endogamy (cf. Deut 7:3).

Besides the use of the term "wife of your covenant" to refer to the marital covenant, it may be used to refer to the covenant between Yahweh and the community as compared with the wife who makes a covenant with other gods (Mal 2:11).[347] The contrast is between the wife endorsed by the covenant with Yahweh and the wife prohibited because she is perceived to be a threat to the covenant with Yahweh. As important as it is, the covenant between a man and a woman is not the exclusive focus here. Rather, the focus is on the violation of the community covenant by a man who takes a wife who does not support or adhere to the Yahweh-Israel covenant.

15 Picking up on the relationship between the man and his wife in Mal 2:14b, 2:15 looks further at the basis of the violation. Malachi 2:15 is a reminder to husbands to honor their covenant of marriage. The first part of this verse poses various interpretive challenges.[348] I understand it to be an affirmation of the connection between a man and woman: *He did not make one but also the residue of his spirit.* In this sense *'eḥād*, "one," refers to the man, and "the residue of his spirit" (*ûšə'ār rûaḥ lô*) refers to the man's flesh. Some have noted that the idea of woman as a residue of man is part of a larger understanding of the Gen 2:20–24 creation account and the man's affirmation that the woman is "flesh of my flesh" (*bāśār mibbəśārî*).[349] Notably, Mal 2:15 is the only place

344. Craigie, *Deuteronomy,* 282, 295.

345. Glazier-McDonald, *Malachi: The Divine Messenger,* 101; Petersen, *Zechariah 9–14 and Malachi,* 194.

346. Hill, *Malachi,* 243; Glazier-McDonald, *Malachi: The Divine Messenger,* 101; cf. Hugenburger, *Marriage as a Covenant,* 278–79, 342–43.

347. Cf. Glazier-McDonald, *Malachi: The Divine Messenger,* 101.

348. The nature and extent of the difficulties have led to the assessment that Mal 2:15 is unintelligible or obscure; see, e.g., Baldwin, *Hag, Zech, Mal,* 240; Verhoef, *Haggai and Malachi,* 275.

349. Hill (*Malachi,* 246) proposes that a contemporary proverb may lie behind the affirmation. "It is possible that the saying reflects postexilic attitudes (or theological teaching regarding the female as the 'residue' of the spirit of the man). . . . Perhaps the prophet seeks to elevate the status of the woman in Israelite society by appealing to a tradition that gives equal standing to male and female as creatures of God" (p. 246).

in the Old Testament that uses the formulation *šəʾār rûaḥ*. Typically, the noun *šəʾār*, "remainder, remnant," is used of survivors of a nation (e.g., Israel in Isa 10:20, 21; 11:11, 16; 28:5).[350] Among the understandings of the formulation *rûaḥ* are "spirit of God," the "breath of life" (cf. Gen 2:7), and "intelligence/sound judgment."[351] The *rûaḥ* here is the life force or what is essentially human. The *rûaḥ* is the aspect of a man that is shared only with a woman (not with the animals). The highlighting of creation in Mal 2:15 is on the oneness and unity of kind and purpose. If the creation motif is operative in Mal 2:15, it supports all unions on the basis of the union of Adam and Eve, a man and a woman. Instead, Mal 2:15 has in mind the particular unions of the covenant community and uses the largest common basis to argue for those unions and for godly offspring.

As with 2:15a, one must also ask about the function of the agent in the question *so what does the One seek?* Does the designation *hāʾeḥād*, "the One," refer to a human or a divine agent? Several interpreters understand it to be a human agent. In the first proposal, "the one" refers to Abraham, who married Hagar and made her a co-wife of Sarah. Accordingly, Abraham sets a precedent for taking a second wife but with the sole purpose of seeking godly offspring.[352] A second proposal regarding a human agent is that "the one" refers to a man of sound judgment. This man would not violate his wife by breaching the marital covenant but would be with his wife primarily for procreative purposes. Furthermore, such a man would not divorce his legal wife in order to marry a foreign woman (because a foreign woman would not yield godly offspring).[353] Similar to this view is the proposal that this man (because he is misguided) seeks to produce offspring through sexual union in an exogamous marriage.[354]

Finally, my perspective is that the Deity is the agent who is designated

350. Some emend the MT *šəʾār*, "remainder, remnant," to read *šəʾēr*, "flesh"—for example, Baldwin, *Hag, Zech, Mal,* 240; Deutsch, "Malachi," 96; NIV, and NRSV. Contrast Petersen (*Zechariah 9–14 and Malachi,* 194), "a vigorous remnant."

351. Concerning the idea that the "residue of spirit" is the breath of life, Verhoef thinks that God had leftover breath of life after making Adam and Eve, and could have made more wives for Adam. He favors the view that "residue of spirit" refers to sound judgment (*Haggai and Malachi,* 276).

352. For further discussion of this option, see Verhoef, *Haggai and Malachi,* 277.

353. Thus Verhoef, *Haggai and Malachi,* 277. In Verhoef's survey of the various interpretations, he mentions an option in which God is the subject, and "one" is flesh. The suggestion is that God could have given Adam more than one wife but opted to give only one for the purpose of progeny—that the man and his wife would be one flesh and produce "godly offspring." Also noted is the idea that God united Adam and Eve as one flesh for the sole purpose of procreation.

354. Glazier-McDonald, *Malachi: The Divine Messenger,* 106–8.

hā'eḥād, "the One," recalling the references in Mal 2:10—one father (*'āb 'eḥād*) and one God (*'ēl 'eḥād*).[355] In this interpretation, the same One who unites the community also clarifies what constitutes favorable actions and results. The LXX reads, "What does the deity seek?" thus clarifying the phrase (*mâ hā'eḥād məbaqqēš*).

Just as the question has produced various interpretations, so has the response. Yahweh's response to the question *what does the One seek?* is godly offspring (*zera' 'ĕlōhîm*; cf. Mic 6:8). This reference may point to human offspring (procreation) as well as to the nature of the offspring (covenant keepers).[356] The response brings to mind Ezra 9:2 about the results of the intermarriages: the mixing of the holy seed (*zera' haqqōdešû*). Here in Mal 2:15 offspring is also an issue and may clarify the negative judgment on intermarriage. The Deity wants godly *offspring* (*zera' 'ĕlōhîm*). Does this desire concerning the offspring refer to ethnic identity? Or does it refer to allegiance to Yahweh, to someone who remains in the ways of Yahweh by keeping the commandments, ordinances, and so on? The response, "godly seed/offspring," is not a statement about ethnically pure offspring. Rather, the issue is fidelity to the Deity and a concern about producing children who are faithful to Yahweh. Presumably, people who have an allegiance to foreign gods will not produce offspring who are faithful to Yahweh (cf. Exod 34:16). As with the observation about the positive influence of putting forth true instruction (2:6–7), so Mal 2:15 speaks about influence—in this case the influence of the parents (wives) on their offspring.

In light of the concern to produce godly offspring, the people are admonished to be careful: *So safeguard yourself (wənišmartem bərûḥăkem)*. This warning is not simply for self-preservation but for the well-being of the wife. The covenant with the wife of one's youth is one witnessed by Yahweh. Thus, Yahweh endorses the marriage with the wife of one's youth. The repetition of the phrase "wife of your youth" serves as a reminder that the focus is on sustained marriages. To the extent that they foster worship of other gods, marriages are not included in this exhortation. The ending exhortation repeats the focus seen earlier, in Mal 2:14—do not let anyone be treacherous to the wife of his youth. Preserving the community and detering further erosion in the covenant community are the goals of the admonition.

(b) Response to Divorce (2:16)

16 The use of the *kî* clause at the beginning of Mal 2:16 connects the content to the preceding verses. Conceptually, 2:16 provides the reason for the ad-

355. Hill, *Malachi*, 246.
356. Cf. Hugenberger, *Marriage and Covenant*, 140–41.

monition in 2:15 after the accusation that the community has acted treacherously (2:10, 11, 14, 15): *because he [the One] hates divorce.* Who is the subject of the verb? And how does the verb function in the clause? First, we note that *šālaḥ* (to dismiss, send) denotes divorce when used of a man's dismissal of the woman, giving her a certificate of divorce (cf. Deut 24:1–4; Jer 3:8; cf. Gen 21:14).[357] There are wives whom a husband is not permitted to divorce (*šālaḥ*):[358] a wife he has slandered (Deut 22:19); a wife he sexually violated before becoming engaged to her (Deut 22:29); a "prisoner-of-war" wife with whom he is dissatisfied (Deut 21:14). A man who divorces (*šālaḥ*) his wife may not remarry her after she has become the wife of another man (Deut 24:4; Jer 3:1). Why is Mal 2:16 talking about divorce? It is because of the violated relationships within the covenant community that have resulted from marrying worshipers of deities other than Yahweh. In that context, divorce is viewed as a path toward idolatry; taking a wife who does not share the covenant of Yahweh takes one further along the path.

Regarding the interpretive possibilities of Mal 2:16, one suggestion is to read "I hate," with Yahweh as the speaker and subject, followed by the object, which is divorce (the infinitive construct form of *šālaḥ*).[359] Without the emendation, Yahweh is still the subject of the verb *śānēʾ*, "to hate." Elsewhere, Yahweh is portrayed as hating—for example, Esau (Mal 1:3), and your festivals (Isa 1:14; Amos 5:21). All of these denote rejection of the hated entity. With Yahweh as subject, this hate of the practice contradicts the laws of divorce (Deut 24:1–4).[360] Also at stake is the program to divorce the foreign wives seen in Ezra 9–10, which seems to have a different perspective on the matter (cf. Mal 2:12). Presumably, the divorces permitted in Deut 24:1–4 include the "wife of your youth." The prohibition against divorcing a woman whom a husband once sexually violated is an attempt to hold him responsible (of caring for her well-being). In contrast to Mal 2:10–16, Deuteronomy's view of divorce does not include the issue of idolatry (not even in the law regarding the captive wife). The difference in focus therefore dictates the nature of the concern. Divorce is permissible, yet hating it does not nullify it as an option.

A second suggestion is that the subject of *śānēʾ* is not Yahweh but the

357. The expression "certificate" or "bill of divorce," *sēper kərîtut,* occurs in Deut 24:1 and 3 in the context of indictment against Israel's practices; see also Isa 50:1; Jer 3:8; cf. Matt 5:31; 19:7; Mark 10:4.

358. In Deut 22:19, 29, the *piel* infinitive construct form is used to denote divorce. This form is also used in Mal 2:16. Note that the noun *kərîtut,* "divorce," appears in Deut 24:1, 3 (certificate of divorce).

359. Thus Baldwin, *Hag, Zech, Mal,* 241; Verhoef, *Haggai and Malachi,* 278; R. L. Smith, *Micah–Malachi,* 319. Most modern versions also emend the text to read "I hate," for example: the ASV and NRSV. Contrast the KJV: "he hates."

360. Hill, *Malachi,* 250.

man, and "divorce" is not the object of the verb (a noun) but is the second (verb) of a three-verb sequence of interconnected actions: "the one who hates, divorces, and covers his garment with violence."[361] In relation to the closing admonition, this interpretation would signify that one is to guard one's spirit because the spirit influences behavior, especially the way one behaves toward others. In this interpretation, hatred is manifested in treachery and other behaviors detrimental to relationships.

There are three possibilities for understanding the *waw* in the clause *for he covers his garment with violence (wəkissā ḥāmās ʿal-ləbûšô)*. The first possible interpretation is that the *waw* functions as a simple conjunction and thus supplies an additional practice that Yahweh hates.[362] The second alternative sees the *waw* as causal, indicating the rationale for the declaration.[363] The final alternative is to interpret the *waw* consequentially as the outcome of a prior action: "then, so he covers.. . ."[364] I support the first option, with the understanding that covering a garment with "violence" (*ḥāmās*) may connote wearing signs of one's violation. Thus, arrogant individuals manifest such violence; it is as though they are wearing it as a necklace or garment (Ps 73:6).[365] "Violence" (*ḥāmās*) also denotes both interpersonal and international infractions (e.g., Amos 3:10; Hab 1:2, 9; Ps 18:48 [MT 49]; 140:1, 4 [MT 2, 5]).[366] Others propose that the imagery of covering signifies the act of taking a wife—that is, spreading the garment is symbolic (Deut 22:30; Ruth 3:9; Ezek 16:8). Covering with violence further signifies that marriage is no longer a protection; rather, marriage to one woman conceals the divorce of a previous one.[367]

The admonition takes a slightly different meaning if the first part of 2:16 is about the Deity's hatred of divorce—*do not act treacherously.* Part of the motivation for guarding oneself is to avoid practices that Yahweh hates

361. Cf. Glazier-McDonald, *Malachi: The Divine Messenger,* 110–11; Hugenberger, *Marriage as Covenant,* 73–76; Floyd, *Minor Prophets 2,* 608–9.

362. Thus Verhoef, *Haggai and Malachi,* 279; R. L. Smith, *Micah–Malachi,* 319; Weyde, *Prophecy and Teaching,* 272; NIV and NRSV.

363. Thus Hill, *Malachi,* 251.

364. Cf. Glazier-McDonald, *Malachi: The Divine Messenger,* 110–13; Hugenberger, *Marriage as Covenant,* 69–75.

365. On the concept of the external manifestation of one's garment, see Prov 31:25 (strength and dignity); Isa 59:17 (vengeance); 61:10 (salvation); cf. Isa 61:3 (the mantle of praise instead of a faint spirit). Cf. Hugenberger, *Marriage as Covenant,* 73–75; Weyde, *Prophecy and Teaching,* 271–73.

366. See also Gen 6:11, 13; 2 Sam 22:3; Zeph 1:9. Contrast Verhoef, *Haggai and Malachi,* 280. He proposes that covering the garment with violence is a cultic practice of putting the blood of the sacrifice on one's garment; to obtain the blood, people did violence to animals.

367. For discussion, see Hill, *Malachi,* 252–53; Glazier-McDonald, *Malachi: The Divine Messenger,* 111–12.

(cf. Deut 12:31; 16:22).[368] The unit 2:13–16 closes with the exhortation not to act treacherously (*bāgad*), further signaling the sustained focus on the issue within this unit (cf. Mal 2:15). The admonition cautions the hearers, the men of Yehud—*do not act treacherously*—denoting a violation of relational terms and expectations. The focus remains on the spousal relationship, and whatever figurative nuance is present is secondary to the warning and admonition.

Given the textual challenges, especially of 2:15–16, the assertions that commentators make and the implications that they draw regarding these verses are tentative at best. Much caution should be exercised, especially considering how these verses have been used on issues of divorce, intermarriage, and alliance. The possibilities identified above offer insights into the meaning of the text and understandings of the possible perspectives.

III. DISPUTATION SEQUENCE: WORDS EXEMPLIFYING BELIEFS (2:17–4:6 [MT 2:17–3:24])

Malachi 2:17–3:24, the third and final macrounit of the book of Malachi, consists of two subunits: 2:17–3:12 and 3:13–3:24. Like the other macrounits, this third unit contains a question-answer schema that is significant to the book's structure and to the cohesion of various units (e.g., 2:17; 3:7–8; 3:13). Nonetheless, they are not decisive regarding the form and function of the macrounits within the whole. Based on the behavior and beliefs that constitute the foci of the accusations, I divide 1:6–3:24 into two parts: First, 1:6–2:16 highlights the behavior that dishonors the Deity by violating the requirements of the covenant relationship. Second, 2:17–3:24 highlights beliefs that challenge the character of the Deity and the purpose of the covenantal relationship. Malachi 2:17 and 3:13, the opening verses of the respective subunits, mention the people's negative "words" toward Yahweh. Notably, the "words" could denote either verbal expressions and sentiments, or ideology played out in behavior or lifestyle, or both (cf. Hag 1:5; Mic 3:10). When the people's or priests' perspectives are identified, the prophet voices them.[369]

368. Other passages attesting things or persons that God hates include Ps 11:5 (violence); Prov 6:16 (six things); Amos 5:21; Isa 1:14 (new moon and appointed feast); Zech 8:17 (evil and false oath); cf. Jer 44:4.

369. Cf. Tiemeyer, "Malachi Interlocutors," 173–92.

A. WORDS SPOKEN AGAINST YAHWEH—YAHWEH'S JUSTICE (2:17–3:12)

That the people have wearied Yahweh with their words is the basic charge of 2:17–3:12. They claim that Yahweh regards evil as good and favors evildoers. Malachi 2:17 reports their specific sentiments or words, followed by Yahweh's response in challenging the validity of their perspectives (in 3:1–12).

1. *Report of a Charge: Misrepresenting God (2:17)*

17 *You have wearied Yahweh with your words. But you say, "How have we wearied*[a] *[him]?" When you say, "All evildoers are good in the eyes of Yahweh and he delights in them; or where is the God of justice?"*

a. For the term *hôgā'ənû,* the *hiphil* perfect first common plural, *BHS* proposes *hôgā'nuhû,* the first common plural plus the third masculine singular suffix. Some modern translations incorporate the object suffix: NIV, NRSV—thus, "wearied him"; for this view, see R. L. Smith, *Micah–Malachi,* 325; Verhoef, *Haggai and Malachi,* 282; and Petersen, *Zechariah 9–14 and Malachi,* 207.

The charge against the people consists of two parts: (1) the declaration of the charge and (2) the people's response to the charge and the Deity's response to their retort. No explicit markers identify the persons or group against whom the charge is brought. Instead, their identity is discerned in the second-person masculine plural verbs[370] and the pronominal suffix on the noun *your* words (*dibrêkem*). Conceptually, the people's words identify them because the words are distinctly theirs.

a. Declaration of the Charge (2:17aα)

17 The reported charge reveals the action that provoked it: the people wearied Yahweh (*hôga'tem*). Used of humans, the verbal form *yāga'* means "to labor or toil" (Josh 24:13; Isa 47:12, 15; 57:10; 62:8; 65:23). It can also mean wearying oneself (Isa 49:4; Ps 69:3 [MT 4]; Prov 24:3) and futile actions that result in weariness (Jer 51:58; Hab 2:13; Job 9:29).[371] Furthermore, the prep-

370. The verbs *hôga'tem* (*hiphil* perfect second masculine plural), *wa'ămartem* (*qal* perfect second masculine plural plus *waw*), and *be'əmārəkem* (*qal* infinitive construct plus second masculine plural suffix and prefixed preposition *bet*).

371. See Lam 5:5 and Eccl 10:15, which use *yāga'* to express being exhausted.

osition *bet* accompanies *yāgaʿ* to indicate the object of someone's weariness (e.g., Isa 43:22, Jacob is weary of Yahweh)[372] or the means by which someone wearies someone else. For example, Isa 43:23 mentions that Yahweh had not "wearied [Israel] with frankincense" (*bilbônâ*). There, the *hiphil* of *yāgaʿ* is used parallel to *ʿābad* (to work) to convey Yahweh's claims not to have wearied the people.[373] The verbs *yāgaʿ* and *ʿābad* are used in parallelism to show that Israel burdened and wearied Yahweh with its sins and iniquities (Isa 43:24).[374] Similarly, Mic 6:3–8 debates whether or how Yahweh has wearied the people. Here too it appears that the people charge Yahweh with wearying (*lāʾâ*)[375] them, and Yahweh responds by asking them to substantiate the charge. Yahweh's list of benevolent acts toward Israel delineates the possible ways Yahweh may have wearied the people; the people's list of possibilities focuses on cultic practices—presumably the activities by which they have been wearied.[376]

In Mal 2:17 Yahweh is not the subject but the object of the verb *yāgaʿ*; the people wearied the Deity. Unlike Isa 43:22–23, where the means of wearying are the cultic practices and other sins, in Mal 2:17, the means are the people's words (*dəbārîm*). It is not the sound of the people's talking that Yahweh found objectionable.[377] In contrast to all the works of their hands, which Yahweh will reject, the prophet identifies the specific words and thoughts as being what wearied Yahweh.[378] Evidently, Yahweh and the people are charging each other with wearying, thus revealing the tension in their relationship. Mostly by design and selection, the charges are paired with a challenge from the one against whom the charge is being made.

372. Yahweh as speaker: "You have wearied of me" (*kî-yāgaʿtā bî*).

373. Together the verbs argue that Yahweh has not burdened or tired the people.

374. "You have burdened me with your sins," *heʿĕbadtanî bəḥaṭṭ(ʾ)ôtêkā*, and "you have wearied me with your iniquities," *hôgaʿtanî baʿăwōnōtêkā*.

375. Jacobs, *Conceptual Coherence.* The verb form occurs in Isa 47:13; Jer 6:11; and 15:6. In Isa 1:14 *lāʾâ* is paired with *śānēʾ*, "to hate," to convey God's hatred and weariness of Israel's sacrifices, which are seen as a "burden," *ṭōraḥ*.

376. Jacobs, *Conceptual Coherence.*

377. Both Amos and Isaiah reflect the idea of Yahweh's weariness with the cultic practices accompanied by sin. Cf. Amos 5:21–23, Yahweh despised the solemn assemblies; Isa 1:12–14, the practices are a burden to God (*ṭōraḥ*, "burden").

378. Cf. Hill, *Malachi,* 261; contrast Glazier-McDonald (*Malachi: The Divine Messenger,* 127), who interprets the words as a reference to chatter.

b. Response/Challenge to the Charge (2:17aβ–b)

(1) The People's Question (2:17aβ)

The narrative formula "but you say" (*wa'ămartem*) in Mal 2:17 introduces the people's thoughts about Yahweh. Like the other charges that depicted an exchange using the prophet's perception of the priests, the people's charge results in the same sort of response (1:2, 6, 7; 2:17; 3:7, 8; 13).[379] The people's charge against Yahweh is appalling, yet the people challenge the way they have been presented.

As in the other occurrences of the competing perspective, *bammâ*, "in what way," signals a challenge to the validity of the charge: *how have we wearied [him]?*[380] In the context of competing perspectives in Ezek 18:19, 25; and 33:20, the speaker offers the desired or valid perspective. Then the competing or dissenting perspective is introduced with *wa'ămartem*, "but you say." The agents in the interchange are at odds with each other, and the confrontations state the reason for the discord. In Mal 2:17, the challenge to the idea of wearying Yahweh asks the speaker to substantiate the charge. The people do not concede the matter; rather, they debate whether they have wearied the Deity. One may note here the psychological weariness of being either discouraged or annoyed. Fundamentally, the people have dishonored Yahweh, and they challenge the Deity to substantiate how they have done this.

(2) The Substantiation of the Charge (2:17b)

The people's words about the Deity are the means by which they have wearied Yahweh. The content of the people's perspective includes a perception that Yahweh requires of people something that the Deity does not require. It includes two interconnected groups of thoughts regarding evildoers and God's justice.

Regarding evildoers, the addressees' perception is about how God relates to all (*kol*) who do evil (*'ōśê rā'*)—*all evildoers are good in the eyes of Yahweh.* Yahweh violates basic principles and is pleased with evildoers. In this perception, Yahweh contributes to the persistence of evil by evaluating evil as good, and the evaluation is comprehensive: *all evildoers* are regarded as good. The good news is that God evaluates all evildoers the same, regardless of their identity, whether priests or laypersons.[381] The bad news is that God

379. Cf. J. D. Hendrix, "'You Say': Confrontational Dialog in Malachi," *RevExp* 84 (1987) 468–70; Tiemeyer, "Giving a Voice to Malachi's Interlocutors," pp. 173–92.

380. See discussion notes above regarding the absence of the pronoun in Mal 2:17.

381. See Verhoef's (*Haggai and Malachi,* 286) overview regarding the various persons who may be included.

does not deem them to be evildoers but considers them to be good. Their references to "those who do wickedness" (*ʿōśê rišʿâ*) in Mal 3:15; 4:1 (MT 3:19) further illustrate their perspective about God's propensity to affirm those who perpetuate evil.

The gravity of the people's perception of Yahweh is underscored by its contrast with texts stating that Yahweh requires good and not evil from the people and indicts those who prioritize evil over good. For example, Amos 5:14, "seek good and not evil"; 5:15, "hate evil and love good"; and the indictment in Mic 3:2 against the leaders for "loving evil and hating good."[382] Although Mal 2:17 does not say how God evaluates good, it suggests that God either evaluates both evil (*rāʿ* or *rāʿâ*) and good (*ṭôb*) as good[383] or that God evaluates evil as good and good as evil. Presumably, God evaluates both good and evil as good. At stake are the Deity's reputation and credibility. If the Deity regards both good and evil the same, then extrinsic motivation (prospect of reward) to do good is also at stake (cf. Mal 3:15; Pss 73; 36).

The formulation *in the eyes of Yahweh (bəʿênê yhwh),* which indicates that a particular view belongs to the named agent, is used to indicate an evaluation of person(s) (2 Sam 15:25), offerings/sacrifices, or behavior.[384] The formulations may also reflect attention to evildoers (cf. Ps 34:15 [MT 16]; Prov 15:3; 22:12; Amos 9:8; Zech 4:10), evaluation of them (Prov 5:21), and their existence in God's presence or awareness.[385] When behaviors are listed and evaluated as either good or evil (cf. 1 Kgs 11:6; 14:22; 15:5, 11, 26; Jer 52:2),[386] the expression "in the eyes of Yahweh" may also suggest that the Deity evaluates using identifiable criteria. The people's perspective about the Deity shows that they too have criteria for monitoring the Deity's deeds and are cognizant of what is good and what is evil. They are therefore capable of evaluating the Deity's and each other's behavior. Armed with this evaluative ability, they per-

382. The recurring concept of one's orientation toward good and evil is seen in the Writings (Ps 34:14 [MT 15]; 37:27) and Prophetic literature. The negative evaluations of those who by their words or actions tend toward evil include Pss 36:4 (MT 5); 37:27; 38:20 (MT 21); 52:3 (MT 5); 109:5; Jer 4:22; 13:23. See Jacobs, *Conceptual Coherence*, regarding Mic 3.

383. Cf. Eccl 9:2: same fate for the good and evil; 12:14: God will judge every deed.

384. Cf. Gen 6:8; 38:7, 10; Num 32:13. The formulation is found in several places in Deuteronomy: to do "good" in the sight of Yahweh (Deut 6:18; 12:28; 13:18–19; 21:9) and to do "evil" in the sight of Yahweh (Deut 4:25; 9:18; 17:2; 31:29). In several instances the individuals are the Israelites or others who are evaluated as having done evil in Yahweh's sight—Judg 2:11; 3:7, 12; 1 Sam 2:17; 12:17; 15:19; 1 Kgs 11:6; 14:22.

385. The concept of the "eyes of God" regarding evaluating something appear in Deut 11:12 ("eyes of Yahweh your God," *ʿênê yhwh ʾĕlōhêkā*); other occurrences include 2 Chr 16:9.

386. Most of the occurrences of *bəʿênê yhwh* are in the book of Kings in the evaluative statements about the kings' reigns. For example, Solomon did evil in the eyes of Yahweh (1 Kgs 11:6; cf. 15:26, 34; 16:7, 19, 25; 2 Kgs 3:2); David did good in the eyes of Yahweh (1 Kgs 15:5; cf. 15:11).

ceive the absence or misuse of Yahweh's ability for the people. Consequently, the people's perception of Yahweh conflicts with the image of the Deity's intolerance for evildoers and favor toward those who do good. For example:

> The *good* obtain favor from the Lord, but those who devise *evil* he condemns. (Prov 12:2)
>
> and
>
> The *eyes of the LORD* are in every place, keeping watch on the *evil* and the *good.* (Prov 15:3)

The charge against the Deity also conflicts with the depictions of the Deity as punishing those who call evil good and good evil (Isa 5:20; cf. Jer 18:20). By saying that God calls evil good (Mal 2:17), the people present God in the same way that God has seen them and their ancestors. In their critique, Yahweh is either blind to the evildoers (not being able to see their evil) or knowingly opts to evaluate the evil as good. If the latter is the case, God would be in the same category as those who return evil for good.[387] Neither of these interpretive options speaks well of the Deity: incapable of accurately evaluating evil and/or deliberately assessing evil as good.

The people thus call into question Yahweh's evaluation about what pleases (*ḥāpēṣ*) Yahweh—*and he delights in them* (cf. Mal 1:10)[388]—and presume that Yahweh delights in evildoers. Yahweh's behavior is an active disregard, ignoring the deeds of evildoers. The people's perspective may come from those who deem themselves to be "good." They want God to execute justice against the evildoers because they do not consider themselves to be among the evildoers. While it may appear that Yahweh does not address evildoers, it may be that Yahweh desires evildoers to reform. The delight then is not in their evil but in the prospect of their turning from their evil:

> Have I any pleasure in the death of the wicked, says the Lord God, and not rather that they should turn from their ways and live? (Ezek 18:23 NRSV)

Consequently, what people perceive as delight with evildoers may be Yahweh's deferred judgment.

387. See instances where someone is depicted as returning evil for good (*rāʿâ taḥat ṭôbâ*), Gen 44:4; 1 Sam 25:21; Pss 35:12; 38:20 (MT 21); 109:5; Prov 17:13.

388. See the other occurrences of the root in Malachi: *ḥăpēṣîm* (adjective, 3:1); *ḥēpeṣ* (noun, 1:10; 3:12); see Isa 1:11 regarding the cultic practices.

The deferred judgment may facilitate the idea of Yahweh's lack of justice; hence the question *or where is the God of justice?* This is the second main part of the people's perspective, the first having to do with how God relates to evildoers. Introduced with the particle *ʾayyê*, "where," the question suggests either that the "God of justice" in fact accepts evildoers[389] or that God has ceased to be the "God of justice"—that is, God no longer cares about or practices justice.[390] The people's question challenges Yahweh to confirm that the Deity executes justice, presumably in the form of an accurate evaluation of deeds. However, one is left with questions about the very formulation of the charge that Yahweh evaluates evil as good. The phrase *in the eyes of Yahweh (bəʿênê yhwh)* suggests Yahweh's criteria. How one individual regards behavior may be inconsistent with how another regards the same behavior. The people did evil in Yahweh's eyes, but on the other hand, they may have done what was right in their own eyes (*bəʿênāyw*, Judg 17:6; 21:25).[391] When each agent/person does what is good or right in his or her own assessment of the actions, the result is usually chaos. Certainly, it indicates that Yahweh's criteria are not identical with the people's criteria. It also indicates that the people, known to be at odds with the Deity, are clear-minded enough to see and recognize evil for what it is.

In Mal 2:17 the word *hammišpāṭ*, "judgment," refers not only to being just but also to practicing justice by judging evildoers. Perhaps *justice* refers to executing it within an appropriate time frame, the day of Yahweh. In that case, the processes on the day of Yahweh will be the response to the charge and question about Yahweh's evaluation of evildoers (cf. Mal 3:1–5).[392] In addition, *hammišpāṭ* includes the broad concept of "justice," the procedure, and the setting for adjudication. Yahweh asked *where is my honor (ʾayyê kəbôdî)* and *where is my reverence (ʾayyê môrāʾî;* Mal 1:6)? And the people in turn ask *where is the God of justice?* Yahweh accuses the people of failing to live up to the expectations of the relationship; the people are just as adamant that Yahweh has failed to live up to the principles that the Deity ought to exemplify.[393] Have

389. Thus Baldwin (*Hag, Zech, Mal,* 242), who sees it as a question about God's existence.

390. Thus Verhoef, *Haggai and Malachi,* 286.

391. As in the expression "each person does what is right in his own eyes" (*hayyāšār bəʿênāyw*).

392. Hill (*Malachi,* 264) argues that *hammišpāṭ* should be translated "judgment" and that it refers to the eschaton (Day of Yahweh). Most often *hammišpāṭ* in Mal 2:17 is translated "justice," for example: the NIV; NRSV; Verhoef, *Haggai and Malachi,* 285; Baldwin, *Hag, Zech, Mal,* 242; R. L. Smith, *Micah–Malachi,* 324; Floyd, *Minor Prophets 2,* 619; contrast "judgment" in the KJV and NJB.

393. Hill (*Malachi,* 264) sees this as a matter of the people's inability to perceive God's judgment because they have not honored or respected Yahweh.

the people themselves been blind to Yahweh's judgment of evil? Apparently, the people have forgotten the judgment of their ancestors (cf. Zech 1:4–6). They are nonetheless cognizant of an apparent misalignment between their expectations about Yahweh and the reality of Yahweh's current presence or apparent absence. By asking *where is the God of justice?* the people are not denying God's existence; instead, they are challenging God's integrity.

2. Yahweh's Response to the Misrepresentation (3:1–12)

The first of Yahweh's responses to the people's perspective about Yahweh is the announcement of judgment (3:1–7). The announcement includes the coming of Yahweh's messenger (3:1–4) and Yahweh's own coming (3:4–7), followed by the rationale for the deferred annihilation of Israel (3:6–7). The second part of 2:17–3:12 begins with 3:7b and urges the people to return to Yahweh (3:7b–12). Although 3:7b–12 differs somewhat from 2:2–3 in form, the two units share a correlation between obedience to Yahweh on the one hand and blessing or curses on the other. Malachi 3:7b–12 clarifies the way to return by identifying at least one way that the people have gone away (strayed) from God—by robbing God. As in 1:6–14 and 2:13, the reference to the offering is noteworthy in Mal 3:8–9. The latter verses mention the offering in connection with the "tithe," thus signaling perhaps a different element from what 1:6–14 alludes to (sacrifices), one that is similar to the offering in 2:13. It is likely that 2:13 and 1:6–14 both refer to sacrifice, while 3:8–9 primarily refers to the tithe and related taxes, though not excluding sacrifices.

Despite the absence of explicit language about honoring the Deity's name, the answer to the question about how to return to Yahweh—to bring the full tithe—implies that the people have dishonored the Deity through their behavior. The implication is that robbing God is as much a dishonor as any of the other ways of dishonoring. The challenge is to test the Deity by bringing the full tithe. This test certainly would encompass the challenge about God's evaluation of evil as good (2:17). The concept of retribution is the framework in which the event sequence is construed. Will God reward obedience? Mal 3:10–11 reflects the blessing-curse dynamics of Deuteronomy, where God shuts the heavens in response to the people's disobedience (cf. Hag 1:10–11). The promise in Mal 3:10–11 is to open the heavens, thus suggesting blessing. Blessing is connected to tithing as a response to obedience. It does not mean that tithes in themselves would generate blessings or the removal of curses for all persons. Rather, inasmuch as malpractice in the area of tithing resulted in the Deity's displeasure, correct practice would result in the Deity's favor. In this respect, the tithe—like sacrifices, instruction, and marriage—is a significant aspect of the covenant relationship. The curse would cease when the malpractice was corrected, and the nations would acknowledge God's favor toward Israel (3:12).

a. Announcement of Impending Judgment (3:1–7aα)

The announcement of judgment is a direct response to the people's perspective about God's evaluation of evil and their challenge that God may have ceased to be a God of justice or has become someone who loves evildoers. Hence, Yahweh responds by sending a messenger and coming to address their perspective and remove any notion that Yahweh indulges evildoers.

(1) Sending and Coming—the Messenger and Yahweh (3:1–4)

1 *"See! I am sending my messenger and he will prepare a way before me.*
Then suddenly he will enter into his temple—the Lord whom you are seeking,
yea, the messenger of the covenant whom you desire.[a] *See! He is coming," says*
Yahweh of hosts.
2 *But who can endure the day of his coming? And who can stand when he*
appears? Because he[b] *is like a smelter's fire and like a launderer's soap.* 3 *He will*
remain a smelter and purifier of silver; and he will purify the sons of Levi and
refine them like gold and silver. Then they will be Yahweh's, those who bring
an offering in righteousness. 4 *Then the offering of Judah and Jerusalem will be*
pleasing to Yahweh, as in the days of antiquity—as in ancient times.

---

a. *BHS* notes that this clause was added: *ûmal'ak habbərît 'ăšer-'attem ḥăpēṣîm hinnê-bā' 'āmar yhwh ṣəbā'ôt*, "and the messenger of the covenant whom you desire." In part, the switch from first- to third-person speech may be indicative of a later addition.

b. The LXX adds *eisporeuetai*, "he enters"; thus the reading "because he enters." This reading clarifies the antecedent of the pronoun—namely, the messenger of Yahweh.

As a response to the question about the whereabouts of the God of justice, 3:1–4 and 3:5 challenge any notion of the unresponsiveness or nonexistence of the Deity. Not only does the Deity exist; the Deity is active and prepared to execute judgment. This unit focuses on the coming of at least two figures and the effects of their coming—that is, the messenger as the forerunner to Yahweh and the effect of the messenger's coming and Yahweh's own coming.

(a) Announcement regarding the Sending (3:1)

1 Regarding the messenger in 3:1, the language and description attest his role and tasks. *See! I am sending my messenger.* The first-person speech indicates

Yahweh as the speaker who announces the intent: *I am sending (šōlēaḥ)*. The particle *hinənî* plus the participle may indicate the commencement, certainty, and immediacy of the action.[394] The formulation *šālaḥ* ("to send") plus an object occurs in two other places in the book of Malachi: 2:2 (about a curse) *wəšillaḥtî*, "will send"; and 4:5 (MT 3:23; about Elijah the prophet) *hinnê ʾānōkî šōlēaḥ, See! I am sending.*[395] In these instances, the subject of the verb *šālaḥ* (to send) is Yahweh. In Mal 3:1, Yahweh (the subject) is sending an agent identified as "my messenger" (*malʾākî*, the direct object of the verb).

The identity of the agent whom Yahweh is sending is vital to addressing the community's idea about how Yahweh relates to evil. Even so, the description of the messenger gives only his functional relationship to the sender without the messenger's name. Consequently, the identity of the agent in 3:1a is debated, and the multiple descriptions of a figure in 3:1 further contribute to the question about "my messenger" (*malʾākî*). Of the several suggestions for the messenger's name, the identity that I explore here highlights the messenger's function, which is the concern of the announcement about his coming.

The purpose for sending the messenger is to prepare the way for Yahweh (the sender)—*he will prepare a way before me*—which entails his preceding Yahweh. The task of preparing (*pānâ*) a way for Yahweh may resemble the preparation for the arrival of a king, including removing obstacles from his path.[396] In Gen 24:31 and Lev 14:36, the occurrences of the verb *pānâ* in the *piel* connote preparation for a subsequent activity. In Isa 57, the preparation may focus on the removal of obstacles or impediments (cf. Ps 80:9 [MT 10]). Zephaniah 3:15 uses *pānâ* to denote the removal of enemies. While Mal 3:1 does not specify what constitutes preparing the way, it may involve readying the people to receive Yahweh. It clearly resembles the formulation in Exod 23:20, "See, I am sending an angel" (*hinnê ʾānōkî šōlēaḥ malʾāk*).

> I am going to send an angel in front of you, to guard you on the way and to bring you to the place that I have prepared. (Exod 23:20 NRSV)

Particular to the exodus out of Egypt, the messenger/angel's role was to protect or guard the way of the Israelites. Their compliance with the messenger/angel would result in Yahweh's protecting them from their enemies in

394. See *IBHS* §40.2.1b regarding the translation of the formulation *hinnê* plus participle (*hinənî šōlēaḥ*). To convey the futuristic dimension of the proclamation, some opt to translate it "I will send": Verhoef, *Haggai and Malachi,* 286; ASV; KJV; "I am about to send": Glazier-McDonald, *Malachi: The Divine Messenger,* 122.

395. See discussion of Mal 4:5 (MT 3:23) below. Note also the formulation in Exod 23:20.

396. Verhoef, *Haggai and Malachi,* 287.

anticipation of Yahweh's annihilation of the Canaanites (Exod 23:23).[397] In addition to the similarity between the functions in Exod 23:20 and Mal 3:1 in anticipating Yahweh's action, Mal 3:1 mentions the specific purpose of the sending with regard to the "way" (*derek*).[398]

The interpretive options about the messenger's identity can be classified into two categories: human messenger and divine messenger. Among the potential human messengers are a prophet, the prophet Malachi himself, and an ideal figure (e.g., Elijah, John the Baptist). This messenger's being a forerunner may signify that he is Elijah, the prophet identified in Mal 4:5 (MT 3:23).[399] On the other hand, the messenger may be a divine agent, an angel. In Mal 3:1 it seems most likely that the messenger is a priest or prophet sent in anticipation of Yahweh's coming.[400]

Continuing the answer to the question about God's justice, the speaker comments on the Deity's entry: *suddenly he will enter into his temple.* Is the Lord not in the temple?[401] The adverb *pit'ōm*, "suddenly," suggests not only a change from nonpresence to presence in the temple, but more importantly, a surprise element in the change and its immediacy. Elsewhere, *pit'ōm* signals the coming of Yahweh in judgment (cf. Isa 29:5; 30:13; 47:11; Jer 4:20; 15:8; 51:8).[402] The Lord's (*hā'ādôn*) entry into the temple is yet to be fulfilled (cf. Hag 2:7) and indicates that the temple is operating without the Deity's presence. Whatever the import of the Deity's presence is for the restoration community, the Deity has not returned to the temple (*hêkālô*; cf. Hag 2:5, 9; Zech 2:14; 8:3). The question "where is the God of justice?" is not absurd; rather, it is a legitimate query concerning the apparent absence of Yahweh from Jerusalem. The announcement validates the question not by confirming the nonexistence but by supporting the nonverified activity of the Deity among those posing the question. Both the questioner and the respondent correctly note at least a reduced involvement of the Deity in the life of the

397. In Exod 33:2 the messenger is to clear the land of the people in preparation for Israel's arrival and occupation of the land. Cf. Durham, *Exodus*; Childs, *Exodus,* 486–88.

398. See Isa 40:3 for the formulation *pannû derek,* "prepare the way": A voice cries out: "In the wilderness prepare the way of the Lord, make straight in the desert a highway for our God" (NRSV).

399. See discussion of Mal 4:5 (MT 3:23) below.

400. Cf. Isa 42:19; 44:26; 63:9; Hag 1:13. Edgar W. Conrad, "Messenger in Isaiah and the Twelve: Implications for Reading Prophetic Books," *JSOT* 91 (2000): 93–94. Conrad notes that the appearance of the messengers in the Book of the Twelve recalls the appearance of the ancestors (cf. Hos 12:2–6 [MT 3–7]).

401. Note that "the temple" would refer to the Second Temple, dedicated in 516/15 BCE.

402. For other instances of the use of the adverb *pit'ōm* to indicate surprise, see Num 6:9; Josh 10:9; 11:7; Isa 48:3; Jer 6:26; 18:22; Prov 6:15; and 24:22. The adverb may also denote immediacy—for example, in Job 9:23 and Prov 7:22.

community. The inability to find Yahweh in the cult reflects the Deity's absence from the cult (cf. Mal 1:10). *His temple (hêkālô)* specifies the Deity's destination without mentioning the place of departure. Elsewhere, Yahweh descends from his temple and treads upon the high places of the earth (cf. Mic 1:3).[403] Here in Mal 3:1, the focus is on the disruption.

Like the identity of the messenger, so the identity of the one who suddenly appears in the temple is a point of discussion. At issue is whether *hāʾādôn*, "the Lord," is the same being as the messenger. In the phrase *the Lord whom you are seeking*, "the Lord" (*hāʾādôn*) appears in the temple. While I am cognizant of suggestions about how the growth of the text impacts our understanding of the identity of the figures in 3:1, I will be focusing on the text's extant form.[404] The various interpretations of "the Lord's" identity include these: the phrase refers to one figure (not Yahweh);[405] there are two figures—the messenger and Yahweh;[406] and there are three figures—the messenger, the Lord, and the messenger of the covenant.[407]

The agent identified as entering the temple is the Lord (*hāʾādôn*). The phrase functions as an extended qualifier of the third-person masculine suffix on *hêkālô*, "his temple." The appositive clarifies that the Lord, rather than the messenger, will enter the temple (cf. Mic 1:2). Further clarified is the identity of the figure with respect to the addressees' inquiry on the whereabouts of the God of justice (Mal 2:17). The one whom they seek is the one who will appear suddenly in the temple. "The Lord" as a designation for Yahweh may also be found in Zech 4:14; 6:5 ("the Lord of all the earth," *ʾădôn kol-hāʾāreṣ*).[408] In seeking (*məbaqšîm*) the Lord, the addressees seek more than a cultic gathering; they want to clarify Yahweh's relation to evildoers and secure the execution of divine judgment on the evildoers in the community (cf. Zech 8:21–22).[409]

403. Other instances of the use of *hêkal* to designate Yahweh's place include 2 Sam 22:7//Ps 18:6 (MT 7); Hab 2:20; Hag 2:15, 18; Zech 6:12–15; 8:9; Ps 11:4; 79:1.

404. For further discussion and bibliography about the growth of the text as related to the identity of the figures, see Weyde, *Prophecy and Teaching*, 285–87; Mason, *Haggai, Zechariah, and Malachi*, 153; Redditt, *Haggai, Zechariah, Malachi*, 176; Petersen, *Zechariah 9–14 and Malachi*, 211.

405. Petersen, *Zechariah 9–14 and Malachi*, 211.

406. Baldwin (*Hag, Zech, Mal*, 242–43) and Verhoef (*Haggai and Malachi*, 288–89) suggest at least two figures. Cf. B. Glazier-McDonald, "*malʾak habbərît:* The Messenger of the Covenant in Mal 3:1," *HAR* 11 (1987): 96–98; R. L. Smith, *Micah–Malachi*, 328.

407. Hill, *Malachi*, 269.

408. The epithet *hāʾādôn yhwh* (the Lord Yahweh) is also found in Exod 23:17; 34:23; Isa 1:24; 3:1; 10:16, 33; 19:4. In Mal 1:6 the form is *ʾădōnîm*, the masculine plural construct form.

409. Hill (*Malachi*, 268–69) argues that they seek Yahweh in order to expedite the judgment. Others argue that the seeking is for cultic gathering—e.g., Glazier-McDonald,

Concerning the clause *yea, the messenger of the covenant whom you desire*, the *waw* in the formulation introduces the appositive that further identifies the Lord (*hāʾādôn*) as the "messenger of the covenant" (*malʾak habbərît*).[410] While the *waw* may be the simple conjunction introducing a third figure—the messenger/angel of the covenant—the presence of a third figure seems unlikely in this context.[411] By identifying the "messenger of the covenant" with Yahweh, one identifies the being as divine rather than human.[412] The enforcer of the covenant in whom the people delight is Yahweh, who will execute justice through judgment. Furthermore, the images of Mal 3:2, usually associated with Yahweh, refer to the effects of the day of Yahweh.[413]

The messenger of the covenant is one who enforces the covenant (*bərît*), which refers to *covenant* in the broadest sense—the binding agreement between Yahweh and Israel.[414] Also included is the specific nuance of the new covenant, in which corporate responsibility is replaced with individual responsibility (cf. Ezek 18; 33:7–20).[415] However, Mal 2:17 gives the impression that there is little or no differentiation between the evildoers and others. The addressees desire (*ḥāpēṣ*) the messenger of the covenant, presumably the one

Malachi: The Divine Messenger, 141–42. Weyde (*Prophecy and Teaching*, 291) notes the occurrences of the phrase "those who seek Yahweh" (*bāqaš*) as being indicative of this interpretation (cf. Pss 40:16 [MT 17]; 69:6 [MT 7]; 70:4 [MT 5]; 105:3; 1 Chr 16:10; 2 Chr 11:16; Ezra 8:22).

410. For a discussion of the epexegetical use of *waw*, see Hill, *Malachi*, 269; *IBHS* §39.2.4. This usage is usually translated in English "that is," or a word that gives an emphatic sense, such as "yea" or "even."

411. Thus Verhoef, *Haggai and Malachi*, 289. While amenable to the idea that the figure may not be a third individual, Baldwin (*Hag, Zech, Mal*, 242–43) suggests that the angelic figure functions much the same as a being who assists in "establishing the Mosaic covenant (Exod 3:2) and the new covenant (Jer 31:31; Ezek 37:26)." In contrast, Hill (*Malachi*, 269) maintains that there may be a third eschatological figure, the angel of the covenant.

412. Usually two interpretive options are provided for understanding *malʾak habbərît*: (1) "angel of the covenant" (a divine being)—e.g., Hill, *Malachi*, 269; Verhoef, *Haggai and Malachi*, 289; (2) "messenger of the covenant" (a human figure)—e.g., Glazier-McDonald, *Malachi: The Divine Messenger*, 122.

413. Thus Glazier-McDonald, "Messenger of the Covenant," 95. Similarly, some scholars identify the Lord and the messenger of the covenant as Yahweh on the basis of the literary features of the text: Verhoef, *Haggai and Malachi*, 288–90; Reventlow, *Propheten Haggai, Sacharja und Maleachi*, 152. Against this tendency to identity the Lord as Yahweh and the messenger of the covenant, Weyde (*Prophecy and Teaching*, 288–90) argues that the covenant designation (messenger of the covenant) refers to the covenant with Levi (Mal 2:4–6) rather than to the covenant with the community—that is, the covenant at Sinai. Accordingly, Weyde contends that the messenger of the covenant is a priestly figure (p. 289).

414. Cf. Verhoef, *Haggai and Malachi*, 289; Hill, *Malachi*, 270.

415. Hill (*Malachi*, 270) argues that the restoration community was doubtful about the new covenant, presuming that it was operative but unable to see its effects.

who will correct the pattern of delighting in evildoers. The people's anticipation presumes that they are not among the evildoers and that Yahweh's coming judgment will negatively affect evildoers only. If they anticipated blessings, their desire for the messenger of the covenant is misinformed by their misconception about the implications of the Deity's coming (cf. Amos 5:18).[416]

The announcement of the coming therefore concludes with a reaffirmation of the coming: *See! He is coming.* The affirmation is a direct response to the query about the God of justice in the restoration community. The affirmation may also target the discouragement about Yahweh's presence in the community and the anticipated exaltation of Jerusalem. Then 3:2–5 presents the implications of the coming.

(b) Effects of the Coming (3:2–4)

2 Malachi 3:2 speaks about the coming of the messenger of the covenant, Yahweh, in a sequence consisting of two questions and the rationale for the questions regarding the messenger: enduring "the day of his coming" (*yôm bô'ô*) and the appearance itself (*hērā'ôtô*).[417] The rhetorical questions imply that no one can endure the coming, neither the evildoers nor the righteous: *But who can endure the day of his coming?* Both Mal 3:2 and Joel 2:11 use the verb *kûl* to convey the idea of enduring.[418] In the context of the day of Yahweh, Joel 2:11 also asks this question:

> Truly the day of the Lord is great;
> terrible indeed—who can endure it?[419]

Likewise, the question occurs in Nah 1:6 regarding Yahweh's anger. In Mal 3:2, the object of the verb *kûl* is the phrase *yôm bô'ô*, "the day of his coming." The futuristic aspect of the day is likewise attested in Mal 4:1, 3, 5 (MT 3:19, 21, 23). The parallel question—*who can stand when he appears?*—is introduced by "who" (*mî*), using the verb *hā'ōmēd* (from *'āmad*, "to stand"),[420] thus sug-

416. Compare Baldwin, *Hag, Zech, Mal*, 243; Hill, *Malachi*, 270–71.

417. The infinitive construct form of *rā'â*, "to see," plus the 3rd masculine singular suffix.

418. The root means "to sustain, provide" (e.g., as with food, Gen 45:11; 47:12; 50:21; 2 Sam 20:3; 1 Kgs 4:7; 5:7; Zech 11:16; cf. Ps 55:22 [MT 23]; Neh 9:21; Ruth 4:15); or "to contain" (e.g., of God, 1 Kgs 8:27; 2 Chr 2:5; 6:18); or "to endure" (e.g., Jer 10:10; Amos 7:10).

419. While the question of surviving or withstanding Yahweh's coming or anger is variously expressed, the common idea is that none are able to do so: *ûmî yəkîlennû* (Joel 2:11); *ûmî yāqûm* (Nah 1:6).

420. Among the various meanings of *'āmad* are "to stand" (e.g., Exod 33:10; 2 Sam 15:2; Hab 2:1; Zech 1:8, 10; 3:3, 4, 5, 7; 4:14; 14:4; Ps 147:17; Dan 11:16), "to survive" (e.g., Exod 21:21), "to endure" (Isa 66:22; Amos 2:15; Nah 1:6; Pss 19:9 [MT 10]; 33:11; Eccl 1:4; cf.

gesting the negative response, "none." The time when the people will not stand is denoted by *bəhērā'ôtô*, "when he appears"—here, the *niphal* infinitive construct plus the third masculine singular suffix. The *niphal* form also occurs in 1 Sam 3:21 and Judg 13:21 with reference to the appearance of Yahweh and an angel.[421] Together with the first question, the text is claiming that two elements are intolerable: the act of coming and the appearance itself, both signifying Yahweh's presence (Mal 3:2). Exodus 33:20 expresses the same idea about the intolerability of seeing the face of God: "for no one shall see me and live." Malachi 3:2 expresses this idea with reference to the presence of God manifested in the coming and the particular appearance.

The *kî* clause provides the rationale for the questions by describing the messenger and his activities, "for he is . . ." (*kî-hû'*). The messenger of the covenant is characterized with two similes using instruments of a purification process: fire and soap. In the first image, *he is like a smelter's fire (kə'ēš məṣārēp)*. Attaching this simile to the previous questions suggests that the coming and appearance will bring about decisive change. The refiner is an active agent of change in metals through the smelting process, which here is applied to humans through adversity (Isa 48:10). As in instances when the metal resists the smelting, sometimes the process with humans proves ineffective in yielding a purer product or reconstituting the product (Isa 1:25; Jer 6:29; Dan 12:10; cf. Zech 13:9; Pss 12:6 [MT 7]; 66:10; Prov 25:4).[422] This simile recognizes the presence of some elements that undermine the whole and maintains that the removal of unwanted elements (dross) is a focused process (Ezek 22:18).[423] The smelter/refiner knows what elements to remove and what, by his standards, will constitute purity of the product. A successful process requires removal of certain elements to achieve the desired quality: refining the troops (Judg 7:4), constituting a group (Dan 11:35).

The second image also uses a simile from the conceptual field of purification: *like a launderer's soap (kəbōrît məkabbəsîm)*. The noun *bōrît*, "soap," refers to the substance used to clean a garment and restore it to an unblemished state (Jer 2:22).[424] The verb *kābas* is used in Lev 14:8 of washing clothes

---

Job 8:15), and "to remain" (e.g., Hag 2:5; Zech 14:12). Modern commentaries vary in their translations of *'āmad* in this second question. Accordingly, Baldwin (*Hag, Zech, Mal,* 243) reads "stand" in the sense of standing one's ground in battle; Verhoef (*Haggai and Malachi,* 290) reads "remain upright"; Hill (*Malachi,* 259) reads "survive."

421. The form *lērā'ôt* is also used in Exod 34:24 and Deut 31:11 to denote the people's "appearance" before Yahweh (Isa 1:12; Ezek 21:24).

422. For further examples of the use of *ṣārap*, see Isa 41:7; Jer 9:7 (MT 6); 10:9, 14//51:17; Judg 17:4; Neh 3:8, 32; of Yahweh, 2 Sam 22:31//Pss 18:30 (MT 31); 17:3; 26:2; 105:19; 119:140; Prov 30:5.

423. Israel will be dross (*sûg/sîg*) to Yahweh. The wicked may be regarded as dross.

424. Used twice—that is, Jer 2:22 and Mal 3:2.

(cf. Exod 19:10; Lev 13:58; 15:17; Num 8:7, 21) and figuratively of cleansing (e.g., Jer 2:22; 4:14; Ps 51:2, 7 [MT 4, 9]).[425] Thus, Mal 3:2 uses two occupations to portray Yahweh's coming and the purpose of the ensuing activities: the smelter and the fuller/launderer represent purification as the vehicle of the judgment (Ps 66:10; Dan 11:35; 12:10).[426]

3 Building on the identification of the instrument of purification in 3:2, verse 3 focuses on the purification through smelting. One can argue either that the "washing" imagery is set aside or that this imagery is sustained through the language of purification (*ṭāhār*).[427] Yahweh will remain committed to the process until achieving the desired results. The idea that the smelter will remain or continue smelting illustrates Yahweh's persistence in the process—*he will remain a smelter and purifier of silver*. The verb *yāšab* has yielded several interpretations of Yahweh's activity. The first interpretation is "then sits like a smelter" and adding *ke*, "like."[428] The second interpretation of *yāšab* is "gets set" denoting that the messenger is getting ready to refine but has not started the process.[429] I favor the third interpretation: that Yahweh remains smelting,[430] further denoting the act of judgment.

In Mal 3:3 and elsewhere, *ṣārap*, "test, refine, smelt," is used of silver or gold (cf. Isa 40:19; 46:6; 48:10; Pss 12:6; 66:10; Prov 25:4). Malachi 3:3 juxtaposes *ṣārap* with two other terms indicating the purification and refining process: *ṭāhār*, "to purify,"[431] and *zāqaq*, "to refine" (cf. Job 28:1; 1 Chr 29:4;

425. The verb *rāḥaṣ*, "to wash," is a synonym: for example, Isa 4:4.

426. Hill, *Malachi*, 273. Hill argues that this is a two-stage process of testing (smelting) and cleansing (washing). In contrast, Glazier-McDonald (*Malachi: The Divine Messenger*, 147–48) contends that the washing imagery is part of the smelting process to remove the dross or unwanted elements.

427. See Floyd (*Minor Prophets 2*, 617), who seems to hold that only the imagery of the smelter is retained.

428. Thus Verhoef (*Haggai and Malachi*, 290) notes that the silversmith sits in front of a furnace to smelt (cf. the NRSV). R. L. Smith (*Micah–Malachi*, 326) reads, "he will sit refining and purifying silver." Weyde (*Prophecy and Teaching*, 299) posits that the verb refers to the act of sitting in judgment as in Joel 3:12 (MT 4:12).

429. Eric M. Meyers and Carol L. Meyers, *Zechariah 9–14: A New Translation with Introduction and Commentary*, AB 25C (New York: Doubleday, 1993), 395.

430. Hill (*Malachi*, 274–75) prefers this reading because it better fits the portrayed arrival and the type of action conveyed by the participles, without the need to supply the *ke* particle of comparison.

431. Not used elsewhere of silver or gold; used in the book of Leviticus of cleaning and purification (e.g., Lev 11:32; 12:7–8; 13:6, 34, 58; 14:8–9). See also Ezek 36:25, 33; and 37:23 for purification especially as related to idols. Weyde (*Prophecy and Teaching*, 298) notes that the verb is used throughout 1–2 Chronicles to denote purification, including purifying Judah and Jerusalem (e.g., 2 Chr 34:3–5, 8; cf. Neh 12:30).

28:18).[432] In so doing, Mal 3:3 pairs the gold or silversmith's refining process with the priests' ritual purification of a diseased or contaminated person. The messenger is assigned the task of purifying the "sons of Levi" (*bənê-lēwî*). The messenger of the covenant will purify (*ṭāhār*) the sons of Levi. Who are they? Why do they need to be purified? Perhaps the more difficult of the questions is who they are. The designation is used in several contexts including genealogies (Gen 46:11; Exod 6:16; Num 3:17; 1 Chr 6:1, 16; 23:24, 27–29; 24:20).[433] At issue is whether in Malachi the sons of Levi are synonymous with the priests. Several passages in the book of Deuteronomy identify the priests as the sons of Levi; hence, "the priests, the sons of Levi" (*hakkōhănîm bənê lēwî*; Deut 21:5; 31:9; cf. Ezra 8:15). On the other hand, some priests were not sons of Levi (1 Kgs 12:31). The Zadokites were a priestly group from among the sons of Levi (Ezek 40:46). According to 2 Chr 29:12–18, the Levites (*haləwiyyim*) consecrated themselves and then went to purify (*ṭāhār*) the temple, the house of Yahweh (cf. 1 Chr 23:26–28).[434] Likewise, the priests and the Levites purified themselves and the people (Neh 12:30; cf. Num 8:21). The sons of Levi in the postexilic community needed to be purified because they were contaminated, or they had corrupted the people and defiled Yahweh.[435]

The second expression makes a comparison to metallurgy: *refine them like gold and silver (kazzāhāb wəkakkāsep)*. Here, the verb *zāqaq* signifies the process and *ʾōtām* identifies the object, the sons of Levi. Typically the expression is silver and gold (*kesep wəzāhāb*);[436] the reverse order, gold and silver, appears in Zech 13:9, also in a context of refining, using the verbs to smelt/refine (*ṣārap*) and test (*bāḥan*). The messenger's activity of performing a refining process means the sons of Levi or the Levitical priesthood will change because of the process. Something will be removed to achieve a particular product, or the best of the Levites will remain while the contaminating agents

432. See other instances where *ṣārap* is used with *zāqaq* (Ps 12:6 [MT 7]). When used with reference to testing, it is also paired with *bāḥan*, "to test, try" (e.g., Jer 9:7 [MT 6]; Ps 26:2). For further discussion of the significance of using the three terms together, see Weyde, *Prophecy and Teaching*, 297–99.

433. See also the mention of the sons of Levi (*bənê lēwî*) in Exod 32:26, 28; Num 16:7; 18:21; Josh 21:10; Neh 12:23. Elsewhere the term *haləwiyyim* is used to designate "the Levites" (e.g., Exod 6:25; Num 1:50; 8:19, 21.

434. Josiah purified the temple (2 Chr 34:1–8).

435. The characterization of the sons of Levi in this manner presumes that "priests" and "Levites" are used interchangeably to refer to the priesthood in the postexilic community. Cf. J. M. O'Brien, *Priest and Levite*, 24–25, 47.

436. Cf. Gen 24:35; Exod 12:35; Num 22:18; Deut 17:17; Josh 6:19; 2 Sam 8:11; 1 Kgs 15:19; 2 Kgs 16:8; Isa 2:7; Jer 10:4; Ezek 7:19; Hos 2:8; 2 Chr 1:15; Ezra 1:4; Ps 105:37; Eccl 2:8; Dan 11:8. The order "gold and silver" (*zāhāb wākesep*) also appears (e.g., 2 Kgs 14:14; Ezek 16:13; Hab 2:19; 1 Chr 29:3; 2 Chr 9:14; Ezra 5:14; Esth 1:6; Ps 119:72; cf. Dan 5:2, 3).

are removed. In postexilic Yehud, the priests mediated Yahweh's presence among the people through teaching and administering the cultic practices.[437] Their contamination would result in the community's contamination; their purification would contribute to the community's purification (cf. Hag 2:14). The simile of the smelter suggests the need of purification for the outcome (cf. Mal 2:9). This imagery thus conveys that some are considered dross (cf. Ezek 22:18–19)—contrary to being the prized possession (*səgullâ*, 3:17). Usually it is the wicked who are regarded as unwanted or worthless (cf. Isa 1:25; Ps 119:119); but in Mal 3:3, some of the sons of Levi are the contaminants (see Hag 2:13–14).

As the result of the purification and presumed legitimation, the Levites *will be* Yahweh*'s* (*hāyû layhwh*).[438] Thus, this purification process identifies those who are truly Yahweh's as compared with those who, although sons of Levi, are not following the commands set for them. A similar expression of possession occurs in Num 3:12, also designating the Levites as distinct from others (e.g., other tribes; *hāyû lî haləwiyyim*, "the Levites shall be mine"). Note that the Yahweh-fearers are also identified as belonging to Yahweh (*hāyû lî*; Mal 3:17; cf. Exod 19:5).[439] Those who are truly Yahweh's are further characterized in Mal 3:3 as *those who bring an offering in righteousness* vis-à-vis those who contaminated Yahweh's table (Mal 1:7). Here, as elsewhere in Malachi, the verb *nāgaš* plus the object offering (*minḥâ*) expresses the idea of bringing an offering (Mal 1:11; 2:12); in 2:12 and 3:3, the preposition *le* indicates Yahweh or Yahweh's name as the intended recipient.[440] The way the offering is presented is *in righteousness* (*biṣədāqâ*) and, by implication, the offering itself is in accordance with the law. Offering a sacrifice in righteousness would correct the practices that dishonored Yahweh (cf. Mal 1:6, 8, 13; 2:2)

4 Further qualifying the nature of the offering, Mal 3:4 specifies the

437. Weyde (*Prophecy and Teaching*, 302–33) argues that the refining process results in a shift within the priesthood: "Mal 3:3 perhaps bears witness to a struggle between apostate Zadokite priests and others, presumably Levites, the latter seeking to restore the community and the temple service on the basis of an earlier ideal from the days of old, from former years" (p. 303). He cites Deut 33:8–11 as evidence of this restoration. Cf. "Levi," *TDOT* 7:483–503.

438. Thus Glazier-McDonald, *Malachi: The Divine Messenger*, 153. Contrast those who interpret the term *layhwh* as an indirect object of the verb *nāgaš*, "to approach, draw near," until they present offerings *to the Lord*—thus modern translations (e.g., the ASV, KJV, NRSV); Baldwin, *Hag, Zech, Mal*, 243; Verhoef, *Haggai and Malachi*, 282; Weyde, *Prophecy and Teaching*, 299–300.

439. Note other instances of the concept of an entity as Yahweh's possession: the earth (Exod 19:5), Israel (Isa 43:1), the firstborn of all of Israel (Num 3:13; 8:17), the silver and gold (Hag 2:8).

440. Weyde (*Prophecy and Teaching*, 300) uses the pattern of the verb plus object to argue for the translation "they will present . . . to Yahweh." This argument is unnecessary since the recipient is indicated in 3:4.

result of the purification. As in Mal 2:6–8, where the good practices of the exemplar Levi result in positive practices in the community, so the purification of the sons of Levi will influence what is offered in the community—*then the offering of Judah and Jerusalem will be pleasing to Yahweh.* The offering (*minḥat*) of the nation, designated by the name of the state and the capital (*yəhûdâ wîrûšālāyim*), is representative of the community's devotion to Yahweh and its loyalty (cf. Mal 2:11).[441] The verse elaborates on the statement that the offering will be pleasing to Yahweh (*ʿārəbâ layhwh*)[442] with reference to earlier times. The offering in the future will be like the offering of the past, *as in the days of antiquity (kîmê ʿôlām)—as in ancient times (kəšānîm qadmōnîôt).*[443] Using the past as an object lesson for the present or future tends to idealize the past or depict it as a monolithic experience (cf. Amos 9:11; Mic 7:14–15). The qualification makes the implicit claim that the ancestors' offerings were pleasing[444] and that the community would also bring an offering that pleased Yahweh. This is an ideal image of the outcome of the purification that ensues from Yahweh's coming.

(2) Yahweh's Own Coming (Further Delineated) (3:5–7aα)

5 *"Then I will draw near to you for judgment; and I will be a swift witness against those who practice sorcery, and against those who commit adultery, and against those who swear falsely, and those who oppress a hired laborer through the wages, widow, and orphan, those who turn aside a sojourner; but they did not fear me," says Yahweh of hosts.*
6 *"Indeed, I, Yahweh, I have not changed; so you, children of Jacob, have not been destroyed.*
7a *Since the days of your ancestors you have turned aside from my precepts and you have not kept [them]."*

This unit continues to address the question of the whereabouts of the God of justice (2:17). It further describes Yahweh's coming by specifying the targets of judgment (3:5), clarifying the reason that the wicked continue to exist (3:6), and declaring the span of time of the persistent disobedience (3:7a).

441. Other occurrences of *yəhûdâ wîrûšālāyim* in the prophets include Isa 1:1; 2:1; Jer 19:7; 27:20; 29:2; Joel 3:1, 6 (MT 4:1, 6); cf. 2 Chr 32:12; 34:3; Ezra 4:6; 5:1; 7:14; 10:7.

442. The verb *ʿārab*, "to be sweet, pleasing," is used of sleep (Jer 31:26; Prov 3:24), of a realized wish (Prov 13:19), of offering (Jer 6:20; Hos 9:4), or of meditations that are/are not pleasing to God (Ps 104:34). The verb *ʿārab* is a synonym of *ḥāpēṣ*, "to delight" (e.g., Ps 51:16, 19 [MT 18, 21]) and *rāṣâ*, "to accept, be pleased with" (Mal 1:8; cf. Mic 6:7).

443. See the use of *qadmōnîôt* in Isa 43:18 and Ezek 38:17. The expression *min-hāʿôlām*, "from of old," occurs in Joel 2:2 (cf. Jer 25:5).

444. Some argue that the time period is the time of Moses: Verhoef (*Haggai and Malachi,* 292) posits that the reference to the past should include, among others, the times of Hezekiah (2 Chr 30–32) and Josiah (2 Chr 34–35). Cf. Weyde, *Prophecy and Teaching,* 302.

(a) The Target of the Judgment (3:5)

5 The transition to the report of Yahweh's coming is signaled by the first-person form of the verb (*wəqārabtî*), a switch from the third-person description in the preceding verses (3:2–4). With Yahweh as speaker, the statement regarding the coming includes the intended recipients, "you," and the purpose of the coming, judgment (*lammišpāṭ*, cf. 2:17).[445] The announced coming tells the community that Yahweh is active in executing judgment and that Yahweh will be a *swift witness* (*ʿēd məmahēr*), that is, rapid and decisive. The role of the witness (*ʿēd)* was to provide evidence in the legal preceding and to substantiate a particular side of an issue. Yahweh serves as witness in several instances (Jer 42:5; Mic 1:2) and may call upon the mountains to be witnesses (cf. Mic 6:1–2).[446] Likewise, the law and other reminders may be witnesses against Israel for its violation of the covenant relationship (Deut 31:19, 26). When used as a modifier, *māhar* may denote swiftness or skill/expertise—as in a scribe skilled in the law of Moses (Ezra 7:6; cf. Ps 45:1 [MT 2]). Here in Mal 3:5 *māhar* may also denote a skilled witness, namely, one who is able to discern the targets of the judgment (3:18) and to apply the criteria for judgment (based on the law).

The judgment will be executed against several categories of people—possibly specifying those included in the "evildoers" (*kol-ʿōśê rāʿ*, Mal 2:17). The particle *be* (against) introduces the four groups, and each group is designated by a participle that conveys continuous action: *those who practice sorcery* (*bamkaššəpîm*), *those who commit adultery* (*bamnāʾăpîm*), *those who swear falsely* (*bannišbāʿîm laššāqer*), and *the hired laborer through the wages* (*bəʿōšəqê*). While the law does not list the groups together, each group can be found in the law.

Concerning *those who practice sorcery*, the verb *kiššēp* denotes the practice of sorcery, which was prohibited (cf. Deut 18:10).[447] A cultic behavior punishable by death, it may include forms of witchcraft yet not be limited to those practices. The remaining three categories do not deal directly with sacrifice or practices specific to the temple; they address issues of interpersonal conduct with societal ramifications.

Concerning *those who commit adultery*, the Decalogue prohibits adultery (Exod 20:14; Deut 5:18), and it is punishable by death (Lev 20:10; Deut

445. Compare Isa 41:1—*lammišpāṭ niqrābâ*, "let us draw near for judgment."

446. Other instances of Yahweh as witness include Gen 31:50 and 1 Sam 20:23. A covenant may also be a witness to the relationship of Yahweh and Israel (Gen 31:44).

447. The sorcerer indicated by the *piel* masculine participle *məkaššēp* or *məkaššəpîm* (Deut 18:10; Exod 7:11; Dan 2:2) or feminine participle *məkaššēpâ* (Exod 22:18 [MT 17]); cf. *kiššēp,* the *piel* perfect third masculine (2 Chr 33:6). The practice *kešep* itself is also condemned, e.g., 2 Kgs 9:22; Isa 47:9, 12; Mic 5:12.

22:22).[448] The third category, *those who swear falsely*, reflects the command against bearing false witness in Exod 20:7, 16; Lev 19:12; Jer 7:9. One may make restitution for this offense (Lev 6:5 [MT 5:24]). The condemned practice occurs with the sin of adultery in Jer 23:14; 29:23 (cf. Hos 4:2).[449] The fourth and final category includes violations against the underprivileged—*and those who oppress a hired laborer through the wages, widow, and orphan, those who turn aside a sojourner.* The laws that prohibit the mistreatment of hired laborers include Deut 15:18; 24:14, 15; and Lev 19:13 (cf. Ezek 18:7). Likewise, the laws prohibit oppressing widows and orphans (*ʾalmānâ wəyātôm*) or depriving them of justice (Exod 22:23 [MT 22]; Deut 27:19; cf. Jer 22:3; Ezek 22:7; Zech 7:10). Concerning *those who turn aside the sojourner or resident alien* (*gēr*), the law stipulates that justice be carried out (Exod 23:9; Lev 19:33; Deut 24:17; 27:19).[450] The last statement of Mal 3:5 further identifies those who oppress the underprivileged: *but they did not fear me* (cf. Mal 3:16),[451] or it summarizes all the categories of people who carry out these proscribed practices instead of fearing God. This final statement thus anticipates Mal 3:6 and implies that those who fear Yahweh do not practice the prohibited behaviors (cf. Ezek 18:5–9, concerning the righteous). The catalog in Mal 3:5 thus includes laws from Exod 22:18–21 (MT 17–20); 23:6–9; and Deut 18:10; 24:17; and 27:19[452] and makes the judgment a concrete event, not simply an unfocused, unsubstantiated threat. The judgment is based on one's own behavior and not determined by affiliation with a group.

(b) The Reason the Wicked Continue to Exist (3:6)

6 Malachi 3:6 depicts the nature of the Deity with a first-person account, *I have not changed (šānāʾ),*[453] an affirmation of the reason Israel continues to survive: the Deity's commitment to sustain Israel and to be faithful to the covenant made with Israel's ancestors remains unchanged. Yahweh's steadfastness is also the reason that Yahweh will act as an expert witness against the evildoers—the Deity is witness both to the covenant and to Israel's behavior.

448. See Ezek 16:38–42 regarding God's punishment compared to that against adultery. Cf. Matt 5:27–28; Mark 10:19; Rev 2:22.

449. Zechariah 5:2–4 (the curse against the thief and those who swear falsely); cf. Matt 19:18; Luke 18:20.

450. Cf. Jacobs, "Theology of the Underprivileged."

451. Most translate the perfect form as "those who do not fear/revere"; e.g., Verhoef, *Haggai and Malachi,* 294; Hill, *Malachi,* 259, 284.

452. Cf. J. M. O'Brien, *Priest and Levite,* 91–92.

453. Lamentations 4:1; Pss 77:10 (MT 11); 89:34 (MT 35); Prov 31:5. In the context of judgment, a similar idea is expressed using *nāḥam,* "to relent," of Yahweh's resolve not to back down (e.g., 1 Sam 15:29; Jer 4:28; 5:15–16; Ezek 24:14; Zech 8:14).

The perspective in Mal 3:6 is similar to Deut 9:4–8—it is not the people's righteousness that kept God from destroying (*šāmad*) them. The deterrent is God's faithfulness. Were the people's lifestyle the sole criterion in Yahweh's decision, they may have fared differently. Even if the people's rebellion became a catalyst for the Deity's decision to punish, the perspective in Mal 3:6 and Deut 9:4–8 is that the people's character is not the determining factor in the Deity's unchanged stance toward them. The change is about behavior and relationship dynamics and by implication anything else affected by those dynamics.

Yahweh has not changed, *so you, children of Jacob, have not been destroyed*. The statement consists of two affirmations: regarding Yahweh's unchangeableness and regarding Israel's existence. Notably, the explanation connects the current addressees, *you (ʾattem),* with the Israel of the past, with the designation *children of Jacob (bənê-yaʿăqōb)*. Elsewhere, the book of Malachi mentions the ancestors (Mal 2:4, 10). Malachi 3:4 makes another reference to the ancestors with the image of past times, when acceptable offerings were presented to Yahweh. In Mal 3:6 the depiction of the ancestors' disobedience is a reminder of the perspective underlying Mal 1:2–4. The ancestors were selected for reasons other than their righteousness, and they are also protected from annihilation for reasons other than their righteousness. Because of God's choosing them, they are not terminated (*kālâ*). The verb *kālâ* is used in Exod 32:10 and 33:3 of Yahweh's intent to destroy the community (cf. Exod 33:5). Likewise, Exod 32:12 conveys the idea that God does not destroy the people because of Yahweh's relationship with the covenant people.[454] In Mal 3:6 the verb *kālâ* speaks of destruction of Israel in the present as well as continued nonexistence in the future. Thus, 3:6 picks up the perspective of Mal 1:2–5 regarding Israel. On the one hand, Edom's existence will be brought to an end (Mal 1:2–4); on the other hand, Israel has not been terminated. Given that both Edom (Esau) and Israel (Jacob) sinned, to annihilate one and not the other reflects preferential treatment and fosters the image of Yahweh delighting in evildoers. If nothing else, Yahweh has a preference and has different criteria for punishing the covenant community—whether the criteria are defined by the relationship, or they determine the timing of the eventual punishment (cf. Mic 2:7). The gracious delay holds open the opportunity for some to continue their sin or to change their perspective about how Yahweh deals with sin (cf. Mal 3:14–15; Hab 1:2–4, 13). The delay also gives occasion for either repentance or confirmation of the Deity's determination to bring punishment.

454. In other instances, the verb *kālâ* is used to denote destroying or consuming the covenant people—for example, Num 16:21, 45; 25:11; Deut 28:11; Zeph 1:18.

(c) The Time Span of the Disobedience (3:7aα)

7 Even when expressing a preference for the children of Jacob, Yahweh draws attention to their sin, thus reaffirming that their sin (although determining the quality of the covenant relationship) is not decisive for the existence of the relationship. The clause *since the days of your ancestors* denotes the temporal parameters of Israel's sins. First, it continues the reference to the former generations by linking the past and the current practices of disobedience (cf. Mal 3:4). The temporal indicator *since the days (ləmîmê)* points to the past[455] and signifies that these actions did not begin recently or resume after a period of absence. Likewise, identifying the ancestors (as a collective, *ʾăbōtêkem*, "your ancestors") signifies that the connection, not to the sins of other nations, but to the sins of Israel's own ancestry is also linked to their present infractions. The temporal indicator specifies the behavior that has persisted from the time of the ancestors to the present, which is their disposition toward the precepts. Notably, two actions depict the people's disregard for Yahweh's precepts: an act of defiance rather than ignorance (*you have turned aside . . .*) and disobedience (*and you have not kept [them]*). The first is expressed positively (what you have done), and the second, negatively (what you have not done).

The positive expression of what they have done, however—*you have turned aside from my precepts*—means to breach the covenant. Active disregard is represented by the verb (*sûr*) plus its prepositional phrase "from my statutes" (*mēḥuqqay*)[456]—referring to Yahweh's statutes (*ḥōq*). The statutes are identified here as the law and the commandments. Elsewhere, the noun "statute" in its masculine and feminine forms (*ḥōq/ḥuqqâ*) is used with the noun "commandment" (*miṣwâ*; Gen 26:5; Exod 15:26); it is also used in the formulation "my statutes and ordinances" (*ḥuqqōtay wəʾet-mišpāṭay*; Lev 18:26). Notably, Israel is not the only nation that has statutes; thus, the people are warned not to follow the ordinances of the Canaanites (Lev 18:3). Yahweh is concerned about the statutes given to Israel, not the statutes of other nations.

The negative expression *and you have not kept [them] (šəmartem)* again specifies Israel's disregard for the statutes.[457] It highlights the imperative to obey with the accusation that the people have perpetually disregarded Yah-

455. See Ps 106: the Torah story and recitation of Israel's misdeeds vis-à-vis God's benevolence.

456. The phrase consists of the assimilated form of the preposition *min* ("from") plus the masculine plural construct form of *ḥōq* (statute) with its first common singular genitive pronominal suffix *-ay* ("my").

457. The verb *šəmartem* is the *qal* perfect masculine plural of the verb *šamar* (to keep). The object may be inferred from the context.

weh's statutes, not because they did not know of their existence, but because of active neglect. The people, consequently, have a choice to remain in their disobedience or to obey God. Both choices have consequences for the present generation just as they had for past generations.

b. Admonition regarding the Impending Judgment— Return to Yahweh (3:7aβ–12)

7aβ *"Return to me that I may return to you," says Yahweh of hosts. "But you*
said, 'How shall we return?' Tithes and offerings. 8 *'Will a person rob*[a] *God?'*
Indeed you are robbing[b] *me. But you said, 'How have we robbed you?'*[c] *The*
tithe and the offering.[d] 9 *You are being cursed with the curse. Yet you are robbing*[e]
me—the entire nation![f] 10 *Bring the full tithe to the storehouse, that there may be*
food in my house. Test me in this [matter]," says Yahweh of hosts, "if I will not
open to you the windows of heaven and pour out to you an abundance of bless-
ing. 11 *I will rebuke for you the devourer and he will not ruin for you the fruit of*
the ground, and the vine of the field will not be barren for you," says Yahweh of
hosts. 12 *"Then all the nations will call you fortunate for indeed you will become*
a 'land of delight,'" says Yahweh of hosts.

---

a. *BHS* proposes *hăyaʿăqôb* ("to defraud, cheat, deceive") based on the LXX *ei pterniei.*

b. *BHS* proposes *ʿōqəʿîm* based on the LXX *pternizete.*

c. LXX *epterníkamēn se*; proposed reading *ʿăqabnûkā,* presuming the root *ʿāqab* and thus fostering a wordplay with the noun *yaʿăqōb* (Jacob) in Mal 3:6.

d. *BHS* proposes the reading *bammaʿăśēr ûbattərûmâ,* including the preposition *bə,* thus reading "in the tithe and offering." Compare the Peshitta, targum, and Vulgate. The proposed reading thus clarifies the mode of the return with "in the tithes and the offerings." Several modern versions follow this proposed change and include the plurals of the nouns: ASV, KJV, and NIV (in tithes and offerings); NRSV (in your tithes and offerings). Cf. Verhoef, *Haggai and Malachi,* 303; Glazier-McDonald, *Malachi: The Divine Messenger,* 173, in contrast to Hill (*Malachi,* 307), who retains the MT.

e. Based on the LXX *pternizete, BHS* proposes *ʿōqəʿîm.*

f. *BHS* notes that *haggôy kullô* is added and proposes that the phrase be emended to *hăgam kullô* and transposed to the end of 3:8. The meaning of this would be "Even all of it?" (see Gen 16:13; 1 Sam 10:11, and 12 for uses of the interrogative particle plus the conjunction *hăgam*).

Malachi 3:7aβ begins the call to return based on a portrayal of the messenger and Yahweh's coming and the ensuing effects of the coming. This call to return is analogous to Mal 2:2–9, more specifically 2:2–4, where the curse's duration is contingent on the addressees' regard for Yahweh's name. The unit 3:7aβ–12 begins with the admonition to return (3:7aβ) and includes repercussions for disobedience (3:9) and obedience (3:10–12).

(1) Declaration of the Admonition (3:7aβ)

The first-person address indicates Yahweh's continued challenge to the people: *return to me that I may return to you.* Malachi 3:7a provided the basis for the challenge: the people have perpetually turned away (*sûr*) from Yahweh's statutes. The verb *šûb* (to return) suggests that at some time the people were with Yahweh, but because they are not keeping the statutes now, the imperative form calls them to return. Even so, the people's separation from the Deity is matched by Yahweh's distance from the people. The conditional aspect of the admonition further suggests that the separation is mutual; the people's disregard for Yahweh's statutes has implications for Yahweh's relationship with them. Consequently, the disobedience indicated by the language of turning away from and not keeping them has redefined the relationship between Yahweh and the people.

Furthermore, the challenge connects the call to return to Yahweh with the promise of Yahweh's return. Yahweh's intended return is contingent on the people's return. The admonition presupposes that Yahweh had departed from the people and would have to return to be with them, whether this refers to a spatial return or restoration of the quality of the relationship. The text provides a clue when speaking about a sudden entry into the temple. The physicality of the return is one dimension; the relational quality is the other dimension. But the promise is conditional: it imposes a prerequisite on the people to prepare for Yahweh's return to the relationship. The adversity that the community is facing serves as a coercive measure to secure their return to the relationship, after which the Deity is ready to remove the adversity and restore the relationship.

However, the call for a return does not signify the absence of a relationship but instead a fractured relationship needing to be restored to a quality relationship. The admonition indicates intention—not necessarily a promise or commitment—to restore the relationship.[458] A promise would not be contingent on the actions of the individuals to whom it is given but would be dependent on the ability of the one who is making the promise. The imperative "return to me . . . and I will return to you" (*šûbû ʾēlay wəʾāšûbâ ʾălêkem*)—appears with the divine-utterance formula *ʾāmar yhwh ṣəbāʾôt.* A similar conditional expression appears in Zech 1:3–4, where the call to return is paired with an admonition not to emulate the ancestors who did not heed the prophets. The object lesson is that Yahweh's commands are enduring, and when Zechariah's audience realized that enduring quality, they returned/repented (*šûb*). Here in Mal 3:7 the call for return is also given in light of the ancestors' behavior.

458. Contrast Weyde, *Prophecy and Teaching,* 328–29. He sees this as a promise.

(2) Expansion of the Admonition (3:7b–12)

The addressees' question is another element of the confrontation. As elsewhere in Malachi, the people's challenges to the Deity are introduced by the formulation *wa'ămartem*, "but you said."[459] The question *how shall we return?* is followed by two interconnected responses: a question (3:8) and a declarative statement (3:10). Yahweh's question to the reported speaker (Mal 3:8) introduces another issue, presumably on a par with divorce—namely, robbing God. God accuses the people of robbing the Deity in the area of tithes and offerings (Mal 3:8) and reiterates the connection between the curses and the people's practice (3:9). Likewise, Mal 3:10–11 continues the language and imagery of Deut 28, where the heavens will be closed as a way of cursing the works of the people's hands, and opened to signify blessings.[460] Malachi 3:10–11 challenges the people to test the equation: disobedience results in being cursed and obedience results in being blessed. Thus the retributive element once again emerges as the basis for the event sequence, much as it does in Mal 2:2–3 (cf. Mal 1:4–5). Malachi 3:12 reintroduces the onlookers as witnesses to Yahweh's action toward a people (cf. Mal 2:9). The role of the witnesses is similar to the role in Mal 1:5 (regarding the reputation of Edom) and in Mal 1:11 (regarding the larger perspective of Yahweh's reputation among the nations).

(a) Report of the People's Question regarding Returning to Yahweh (3:7b)

The people challenge the admonition—*But you said, "How shall we return?"* The verb in the formula is in the imperfect (*nāšûb)* denoting incomplete action and most likely anticipated action—the addressees' return to Yahweh. Moreover, the question to Yahweh introduces doubt regarding the mode and possibility of the people's return. Like the other questions attributed to the addressees, this one requests more than information; it seeks clarification about the underlying issues and the charge against the people. If they have a history of breaching the relationship as demonstrated by their propensity to follow the example of their ancestors in turning away from the Deity, is it likely that they will return to Yahweh willingly ?

459. See table 7. Note the occurrences of the formula and the resulting pattern.

460. Cf. Deut 28:12; Hag 2:2–4, esp. v. 4.

(b) Reported Response to the People's Question (Robbing Yahweh) (3:8–12)

Yahweh's response to the community includes an interchange on the subject of robbing God and a primary focus on the means of returning to God (3:10–12).

(i) Reported Interchanges (3:8)

8 The interchange between Yahweh and the community focuses on the tithe, which is one example of the statutes that the people have disobeyed. The divine inquiry from Yahweh to the community is about robbing God. The charge takes into account the agents involved—any human being vis-à-vis the Deity (3:8). The people's attitude toward the Deity is significant, as are the effects of their actions (3:9). The curse exemplifies the fracture in the relationship between Yahweh and the community rather than causing that fracture.

(a) First Interchange (God) (3:8aα)

The question comes from Yahweh: *"Will a person rob God?"* To rob (*qāba'*)[461] is to take a possession from someone, usually something of great value. Other examples of robbery include taking away from the underprivileged (Prov 22:22; Mic 2:2; 3:2; Ps 35:10), each of these texts using the verb *gāzal*, "to rob or seize" (cf. Mal 1:13).[462] In Mal 3:8, the use of the interrogative particle with the imperfect may indicate a wish or possibility. Whatever one thinks about the possibility of taking from God, the nuance of the question suggests, not so much the possibility, but the reality of robbing God, as indicated in the charge against the community.[463] Whether the question further reflects the

461. The meaning of the verb *qāba'* is disputed. The root occurs in Mal 3:8 (3×), 9; and Prov 22:23 (2×). The ancient witnesses attest at least two traditions: (1) Tradition 1, *qāba'*: The MT reads *qāba'*. The ancient Greek witnesses, Aquila, Symmachus, and Theodotion, read *apostēreo*, "to rob"; the Syriac reads *tlm*, "to defraud." Among those who adopt this reading are Hill, *Malachi*, 30; Verhoef, *Haggai and Malachi*, 302; and modern translations such as the NRSV, KJV, NIV, and ASV. (2) Tradition 2: *'āqab*: The root *'āqab* occurs in several texts where the meaning "to supplant or deceive" fits the context, e.g., Gen 27:36; Jer 9:4 (MT 3); Hos 12:3 (MT 4). The LXX reads *pternizo*, "to betray." Typically the emendation to *'āqab* is suggested on the basis of forming a wordplay with *ya'ăqōb*, 3:6. Among those who suggest the reading *'āqab*, "to betray," in place of *qāba'* are: Rudolph, *Hag, Sach, Mal*, 281, 282; and Vuilleumier, "Malachie," 247. For further bibliography and discussion of 3:8, see Hill, *Malachi*, 303; and Verhoef, *Haggai and Malachi*, 302–3.

462. Other uses of the verb include Deut 28:31; Lev 19:13; Jer 21:12; 22:3; Ezek 22:29.

463. Contrast Verhoef (*Haggai and Malachi*, 302), who contends that "it is unthinkable

incredulity of the community regarding the implications and significance of its actions is another dimension to be considered. The addressees at various points in the book of Malachi are portrayed as either ignorant of their actions or blatantly disregarding Yahweh (cf. Mal 1:7, 12–13).

Might this also be an instance where the community does not fully grasp the ramifications of its actions? What the people consider about a cultic act or community practice has far-reaching and uncalculated implications for the covenant relationship. Thus, the rhetorical question identifies and confirms the possibility and the inadvisability of robbing: should a person, any person, rob the Deity? Should human beings (*'ādām*) unlawfully take from God (*'ĕlōhîm*)?[464] To this question, the answer is no; no one should rob God. The inadvisability lies in the consequences (cf. Mal 3:9).

Yahweh's first-person speech states that the addressees are robbing the Deity—*indeed you are robbing me.* The speech intensifies the focus on human (*'ādām*) versus God (*'ĕlōhîm*) and fosters a contrast between "you" (*'attem*), the robbers, and "me" (*'ōtî*), the robbed. Not only is it possible to rob God, the hearers are executing that action against God. The participle (*qōbə'îm*—robbing) may indicate continuous action, denoting that the robbery is still taking place. This response thus represents the Deity as the victim of their robbery. There is no indication of human victims of the robbery; rather, the sympathy if any is garnered for the Deity. One understands the impact on the community by investigating the stipulations, especially the purpose of the tithe.

(b) Second Interchange (God and the People) (3:8aβ–b)

In typical style, the hearers' response to the charge is in the form of a question: *But you said, "How have we robbed you?"* Introduced with the formula *wa'ămartem bammê,*[465] the addressees' response manifests doubt about the charge or at least raises the possibility that they are not robbing the Deity (Mal 1:2; 3:7). Even so, the question seeks evidence of the charge and places the burden of proof on God. As in the other instances where the people's perspective competes with the Deity's and is refuted, here in 3:8 the people's perspective is set up and refuted. This is not inquiring about the reasons that

---

that a man could rob God" because of the "infinite distance" between man and God. Likewise for Weyde (*Prophecy and Teaching,* 330), this rhetorical question addresses the possibility of robbing God and solicits a negative response (cf. Job 22:2–5—Can a mortal be of use to God? Can even the wisest be of service to him? [v. 2]). However, one would not expect a negative response. Only a misguided people would think that robbing God was impossible and thus reflect a skewed or misinformed perspective.

464. In the book of Malachi, the divine name *'ĕlōhîm* occurs in 2:15; 3:8, 14, 15, 18.

465. *But you say (wa'ămartem) how (bammê) . . . ?*

they robbed God or whether there was a lack of valid priestly instruction.[466] Because of the previous disregard for Yahweh, this should be seen as additional disregard and dishonor—not obeying the ordinances and consequently violating the covenant relationship. Malachi 3:7a sets up the scenario: you and your ancestors have gone astray by not keeping the statutes. The solution is to return to Yahweh by keeping the statutes and ordinances—the commands. However, the response to the inquiry about how to return focuses on *the tithe and the offering*. It is not until Mal 3:14 that the commands are mentioned—that is, keeping what is to be observed (*mišmeret*).[467] The particular statues to which Yahweh is referring are those concerning the tithe and offering; the larger issue is obedience.

The people ask for evidence of the charge against them. Yahweh responds by offering the evidence—*the tithe and the offering (hammaʿăśēr wəhattərûmâ)*—thus positing that the robbery happens in the arena of tithes and offerings. The Old Testament stipulations regarding the tithe (*maʿăśēr*) include the nature of the tithe and its purpose. Abram gave a tithe of all his possessions to King Melchizedek.[468] The term *maʿăśēr*, "tithe," denotes a tenth of all produce or yield that was to be given to Yahweh. According to Lev 27:30–33, all the tithe of the land (*kol-maʿśar hāʾāreṣ*) is to be given to God, including seed and fruit. The types of tithe come from several sources, including the produce of the land and the herds or flocks (*kol-maʿśar bāqār wāṣōʾn*). The tithe thus consists of raw produce (grain), refined products (wine, oil), and livestock. The tithe, along with the contribution/offering (*tərûmat*) and other sacrifices and offerings, were to be given to God (Deut 12:6, 11, 17–18).[469] All persons of the community, including the underprivileged and the Levites, were allowed to eat of the products presented at the designated place.[470]

The types of tithe may also be categorized by their frequency. The annual tithe of the yield of the land and livestock was to be set aside for God at

466. Verhoef (*Haggai and Malachi,* 303) assumes that they are ignorant of their behavior because the priests have failed to give them proper instructions. I argue that, while the community may not fully comprehend the ramifications of its behavior relative to robbery, it may be aware that withholding tithes and offerings is an affront to the Deity simply because of the stipulations regarding the tithes and offerings.

467. Note the use of *šāmar*, "to keep," plus *mišmeret*, "charge, watch," to denote keeping an obligation. The expression usually occurs with commandments, statutes, and laws (Gen 26:5; Deut 11:1; cf. Zech 3:7). It may also be used of performing cultic obligations or responsibilities (Num 3:25, 31, 38; 4:28; Neh 12:45; 1 Chr 23:32).

468. In Gen 28:22 the verb *ʿāśar*, "to tithe," is used of Jacob's vow to tithe to God of everything that God gives to him.

469. In this context, the people are instructed to bring the tithes and offerings along with the burnt offerings (*ʿōlâ*), sacrifices (*zebaḥ*), and votive gifts.

470. Cf. Craigie, *Deuteronomy,* 217–18.

the designated place for community consumption (Deut 14:22–23). In the case of distance from the location, the law specifies that the tithe may be converted to money (*kesep*) and taken to the designated area. Once there, the tither may convert the money to a product and present that product as a tithe for the community to consume. The cited rationale is that through offering and partaking of the tithes, contributions, and other offerings and sacrifices, the community "will learn to fear Yahweh your God" (*tilmad ləyirʾâ ʾet-yhwh ʾĕlōhêkā*).

The third-year tithe was to be the full tithe (*kol-maʿśar*), with the difference being that it was to be stored in various towns rather than at a designated location. As with the annual tithe, the Levites and the underprivileged were to be allowed to partake of the third-year tithe (Deut 14:28; 26:12).[471] Regardless of the economic times, the requirement to bring the tithe remained. Both types of tithe presumed that the Levites had no allotment and were not to be neglected or excluded from consuming the tithes and accompanying offerings and sacrifices (Deut 14:27, 29; cf. 26:12).[472] Another motivation for allowing the Levites and underprivileged to enjoy the tithes and other offerings is that God would bless (*bārak*) the community (Deut 14:29).[473] To neglect the tithe would be to forfeit blessings by failing to honor God. In this respect, we can see the practical and social implications behind the purpose of the tithe.[474]

The purpose of the tithe seems to be threefold: to honor God (Deut 14:27; 26:12); to provide sustenance for the Levites and underprivileged and allow them to participate in a cultic activity (Deut 14:27, 28); and to compensate the Levites for services rendered (Num 18:21–25).[475] Regarding the latter purpose, the rationale for not having a portion (*ḥēleq*) or inheritance (*naḥălâ*) is that the full tithe (*kol-maʿăśēr*) belongs to the Levites. Conceivably, if all of Israel were to give the full tithe, the Levites' possession would exceed that of the Israelites or at least most of the people in the community. Furthermore, the Levites were to give to God an offering (*tərûmâ*) equivalent to the produce of the land (e.g., grain)—a tithe of the tithe (*maʿăśēr min-hammaʿăśēr*; Num 18:26).

471. The third year is also "the year of the tithe" (Deut 26:12).

472. The Levites and the underprivileged may be on the same economic level according to the perspective of Deut 14:22–28; both groups do not have an allotment. Compare with Num 18:21–30.

473. Among the underprivileged identified in Deut 26:12 are resident aliens, orphans, and widows.

474. One may consider the context of Amos 4:4 not as an indication of the frequency of the tithe but as sarcasm regarding the absurdity of the community's practices.

475. See Hill (*Malachi*, 305–6) for a discussion about the relative dates of the Num 18 stipulation vis-à-vis the Deuteronomy perspective.

> You shall speak to the Levites, saying: When you receive from the Israelites the tithe that I have given you from them for your portion, you shall set apart an offering from it to the LORD, a tithe of the tithe. (Num 18:26 NRSV)

In the time of Nehemiah, bringing a "tithe of the tithe" (*maʿăśar hammaʿăśēr*) was part of the stipulations for the Levites (Neh 10:38 [MT 39]); they were to bring the tithe of the tithe to the storehouse (*bêt hāʾôṣār*). They set aside the portion for the descendants of Aaron (Neh 12:47). While it appears that the tithe was being collected at various times in the restoration community, there also appear to have been intermittent periods of neglect. Nehemiah learned that the portion (*mənāyôt*) was not being given to the Levites, resulting in Levites having to work in the field (Neh 13:10–14). The solution was to collect the tithe into the storehouse (*ʾôṣārôt*) and to distribute the tithe to the temple personnel.

Regarding the offering (*tərûmâ*), the stipulations indicate several ways the term is used. The terms *tithe* and *offering* occur together in several contexts: Num 18:24, 26, 28; Deut 12:17; Neh 12:44; and 13:5. First in the broadest sense, *tərûmâ* could be translated as a contribution referring to a portion of a commodity such as a contribution of materials for building the tabernacle (Exod 25:1–7). Included here is the contribution of the first of every product, including the firstling (Num 15:17–21).[476] Second, *tərûmâ* is an offering presented along with the tithes, burnt offerings, and votive gifts (Deut 14:22–26). Thus, fulfillment of the duty to give the tithes and offerings provides the community meal. Third, *tərûmâ* is a particular portion of the tithe—a tithe of the tithe (Num 18:24, 26, 28). In this regard, the *tərûmâ* was a tenth of all the tithes that the Levites received from the community. In addition to the tithe of the tithe, the Levites were to give a contribution (*tərûmâ*) to Yahweh. Continuing this idea of the *tərûmâ* as a segment of something else is Lev 7:14, where the *tərûmâ* may be a quantity of an offering (*qorbān*) or a segment of the sacrifice (*zebaḥ*; Exod 29:27–28). Furthermore, spoils of war were to be given to God and to the priests and Levites (Num 31:25–30). Given the nature of the stipulations, it appears that the *tərûmâ* was also required of the community, especially as it related to tithes, the sacrifices, and spoils of war.

Here in Mal 3:8, tithes and offerings are the specific ways in which the community may return to Yahweh. The understanding is that keeping the commandments regarding the tithes and offerings is just as important as keeping the other commands and ordinances. To violate these ordinances would also incur Yahweh's displeasure and punishment. Primarily, the motivation for giving the tithes and offerings is obedience to God.

476. Cf. Verhoef, *Haggai and Malachi*, 304–5; Hill, *Malachi*, 306.

(ii) Effects of the People's Actions (3:9–12)

(a) Announcement of Judgment regarding Robbing God (3:9)

9 After the mode of robbery is named, the consequences of the action are specified: *You are being cursed with the curse.* The participle *nēʾārîm* denotes the persistence of the action against the addressees, *ʾattem* (you), the second masculine plural independent personal pronoun. The curse is the consequence of violating the stipulations about the tithe and offering, thus addressing the people's past and present actions (cf. Deut 28:15–57). The noun *məʾērâ,* derived from the root *ʾārar,* "to curse," denotes the mode of the action—*cursed with the curse.*[477] In each of the other contexts where *məʾērâ* occurs, it is a result of punishment. Accordingly, in Deut 28:20 it is the result of forsaking (*ʿāzab*) Yahweh. Likewise in Prov 28:27, curses (*məʾērôt*) will result from neglecting the poor.[478] In Mal 2:2 the curse is a consequence of dishonoring God. The curse is the mode of the punishment, and these contexts do not delineate additional adverse events. Although the same is true for Mal 3:9, further information about the curse can be discerned in 3:11: economic challenges resulting from agricultural failure (see discussion below). While God's promised return is contingent on the people's return, the implementation of the curse is not. Rather, the curse is part of the reality defining the community's existence.

Even with the persistence of the curse in their midst, the addressees continue to rob (*qōbəʿîm*) God. *Yet you are robbing me—the entire nation!* Malachi 3:9 repeats the contrast in 3:8 between "you" (*ʾattem*) and "me" (*ʾōtî*). The addressees are further identified as *haggôy kullô, the entire nation.*[479] The text does not explain whether every person in the nation or a group (e.g., leaders, the rich, men, or women) is robbing God. Thus, the accuser (Yahweh) does not distinguish between those who may be oblivious to or innocent of the charge. Similarly, Hag 2:14 identifies the nation (*haggôy*) as the culprit in contaminating Yahweh.[480] The charge against the nation in Mal 3:9 is that it continues to rob God even in the face of punishment, thus failing to recognize and accept God's displeasure with the nation's behavior.

477. Verhoef (*Haggai and Malachi,* 305): "you are greatly cursed"; NRSV: "cursed with a curse."

478. Cf. Prov 3:33.

479. The expression refers to the entire nation; see, for example, 2 Sam 2:9, "all of Israel" (*yiśrāʾēl kullō*); Isa 9:8 uses *hāʿām kullô,* "all the people."

480. The use of the noun for Israel is not an indication of its apostasy but a label for identifying the geographical, political, and social entity. Some interpreters believe that it is used of Israel to equate it with other pagan nations, for example, Hill, *Malachi,* 308; and Verhoef, *Haggai and Malachi,* 306.

A similar call for return appears in Amos 4:6–13 (cf. Hag 2:17).[481] A persistent call with veiled threats is presented here in Mal 3:8–11, including the articulation of a conditional plan for the return; the declaration of an already implemented curse (3:9); and the declaration of intent to remove the effects of the curse (3:11). All these demonstrate Yahweh's efforts to persuade the addressees to conform to Yahweh's desires. As long as the addressees continue to disregard Yahweh, the curse and adversities will remain on the land. To refuse to return is to choose a reality riddled with adversity, putting the community's livelihood and survival at stake. That Yahweh describes a plan for return may mean only that Yahweh is less stubborn. Perhaps Yahweh's inflexibility underlay the call for return because it was issued to people who were reluctantly involved in the relationship and hence were merely compliant with the requirements of the relationship. Faced with the options of perpetual adversity or adherence to relationship obligations, the only way to regain economic vitality is to conform to Yahweh's command.

(b) Command to the People: The Tithe as a Way to Return (3:10)

10 After identifying the mode of the robbery and affirming that God is punishing the nation for the robbery, the focus turns to identifying the mode of return—*bring the full tithe to the storehouse*. This imperative responds to the question in Mal 3:7, *how shall we return?* The answer comes as a command to the community to return and an invitation to test God (3:7). The command proper consists of the imperative (*hābîʾû*) plus the object (*kol-hammaʿăśēr*) and indirect object (*bêt hāʾôṣār*)—*bring the full tithe to the storehouse.* The formulation "the full tithe" (*kol-hammaʿăśēr*) may denote all types of tithes, including: the tithe of the tithe, the tithe of any product (agricultural), the entire quantity, the frequency, or the types. Several passages use "full tithe" (*kol-hammaʿăśēr*) to denote the entire quantity (cf. Deut 14:28; 26:12).[482] Deuteronomy stipulates that the tithe was to be taken to a place God designated (Deut 12:5–7; 14:22–23).[483] Here in Mal 3:10 the designated place is the storehouse (*bêt hāʾôṣār*). This terminology is used in Neh 10:38 (MT 39) of the place—specifically, the chamber of the storehouse where the Levites were to bring the tithe of the tithe.[484] According to 2 Chr 31:11–16, the tithes

481. Jeremiah 3–4; Hos 11.

482. The plural form occurs in several texts, including Num 18:28, *kōl maʿśərōtêkem*, "all of your tithes"; Deut 12:6, 11, *maʿśərōtêkem*, "your tithes." Totality may also be expressed as *maʿśar hakkōl*, "a tithe of everything/all" (2 Chr 31:5).

483. In Deut 12:1–11 the designated place is where the first of each type of produce is to be brought as a remembrance of God's act of benevolence toward Israel. The third-year tithe was to be given to the Levites and the underprivileged in the towns.

484. In Dan 1:2, "the house of the treasury of his god" (*bêt ʾôṣar ʾĕlōhāyw*); see "the

were brought to the chamber in the house of Yahweh (*šākôt bəbêt yhwh*). In these cases, the texts indicate a storage place for the tithes and offerings/contributions. Such storage facilities are identified as "treasuries" or storehouses (*ʾôṣārôt*—Neh 12:25, 44; 13:12, 13) or a large room (*liškâ gədôlâ*—Neh 13:5). The term *ʾôṣār* can also refer to the heavens as the place where Yahweh's treasures are stored (Deut 28:12; cf. Jer 10:13//51:16).

Immediately juxtaposed to the command to bring the full tithe is the rationale—*that there may be food in my house*—or the motivation for the desired action, which further clarifies that the storehouse belongs to the Deity (*bêtî*).[485] The motivation makes no mention of the Levites and the underprivileged, but since the laws about tithes designate them for the Levites and the underprivileged, this imperative alludes to the purpose of the tithe. The purpose clause (*that there may be food*) uses the noun *ṭerep,* which typically means prey, the food for wild beasts, typically lions (Num 23:24; Isa 5:29; 31:4; Amos 3:4; Nah 2:12 [MT 13]).[486] In several instances, including Mal 3:10, it denotes food (i.e., Ps 111:5; Job 24:5; Prov 31:15).

God invites the community to test (*bāḥan*)[487] the validity of God's promise to return: *Test me in this [matter].* At stake are the Deity's credibility and integrity. Does God reward those who are faithful—those who keep the ordinances and commandments (Mal 2:17; 3:14)? The partial oath formula (introduced by *ʾim-lōʾ*) relates how God's promise will be verified: God's action of opening the windows of heaven.[488] Despite what is at stake, the invitation seems to counter the tradition: God tests humans but usually prohibits humans from testing God.

> Do not put the Lord your God to the test [*nāsâ*], as you tested him at Massah. (Deut 6:16 NRSV)

In some instances humans do test or provoke God (Exod 17:2, 7); however, Ahaz's refusal to ask for a sign shows the negative side of testing God:

> But Ahaz said, "I will not ask, and I will not put the Lord to the test [*nāsâ*]." (Isa 7:12 NRSV)

---

treasury of the house of Yahweh" (*ʾôṣar bêt-yhwh*), 1 Chr 29:8 (cf. Josh 6:24). The term *ʾôṣārôt* is used generally of storehouses (not necessarily of places to store the tithes) in: 2 Kgs 20:13, 15//Isa 39:2, 4 (of Hezekiah's treasuries); cf. Joel 1:17.

485. The first common singular suffix personalizes the location as the house of Yahweh, referring to the temple.

486. Note Ps 104:21; Job 4:11, 38:39. See also Ps 124:6; Job 29:17; Ezek 19:3, 6; 22:25, 27.

487. The verb *bāḥan* is also used to denote smelting (of precious metals; Zech 13:9).

488. Weyde (*Prophecy and Teaching,* 333–34) notes the occurrence of "the fragmentary oath formula" and the similarities to Gen 42:14–16 (Joseph's encounter with his brothers).

What is the community invited to do? In the Old Testament, several terms denote the concept of testing: *nāsâ*, "to test, try";[489] *ṣārap*, "smelt, refine, test";[490] and *bāḥan*, "to exam, try."[491] God tests the faithfulness of Israel with adversity (*ṣārap*, Isa 48:10–11); God tests them to determine the extent of Israel's trust in God (*bāḥan*, Jer 11:20; 12:3).

In Mal 3:10 the test involves two parties, the community (the tester) and God (the tested). The community is to test God by bringing the tithe. Their return would fulfill the requirement of returning to God and would secure a blessing from God—the blessing that is contingent on participating in the test. It is as if to say, "You cannot lose by testing me." If you obey the ordinances and bring the tithe, God will return to you, the curse will be lifted, and you will receive an overabundance of blessings.[492] The test is whether to choose to continue in disobedience and the curse or to fulfill the tithing requirements and be blessed. To participate in the test, the community must believe that God is responsible for its misfortune and that God is able and willing to lift the curse.

The second side of the test is God's response—whether God will reward the community for its obedience. The conditional clause *if I will not open to you the windows of heaven* indicates that God's action is contingent on the fulfillment of a condition—the action of the community. The result of the test would be God's opening (*pātaḥ*) the windows of heaven (*'ărubbôt haššāmayim*). The Deity's power is juxtaposed with engagement with the community. The one who desires the community to return has power over the ecology of the region. Just as the invitation to test God is particular to Yehud, so Yahweh's intention is particular to the nation and its situation.

To open or close the windows of heaven means sending or withholding rain (cf. Gen 7:11; 8:2). In Deuteronomy, "opening the windows" is the manifestation of God's blessing on the community for its obedience (Deut 11:11–14; 28:8, 12). On the other hand, "closing the windows" is the manifestation of a curse on the community (Deut 11:17; 1 Kgs 8:35–36//2 Chr 6:26–27; 7:13; Amos 4:7). In Mal 3:10, the test is the people's return, and the effect of the test is opening the windows of heaven. They will not be opened in anticipation of the return[493] but, rather, in confirmation of the return. Unlike Gen 7:11–12 and 8:2, where the windows are paired with rain (*gešem*), Mal 3:10 makes

489. The use of *nāsâ*: of humans testing God (Exod 17:2, 7; Deut 6:16; Isa 7:12); of God testing humans (Gen 22:1; Exod 15:25; 16:4; 20:20; Deut 8:2; 13:3; 2 Chr 32:31); and of humans testing each other (2 Chr 9:1).

490. Used of God testing and refining humans: Isa 1:25; 48:10; Jer 9:7; Mal 3:2–3.

491. The uses of *bāḥan*: God testing humans (Jer 9:7; 11:20; 12:3; 17:10; Pss 17:3; 26:2; Prov 17:3); humans testing each other (Gen 42:15; 1 Chr 29:17).

492. In Exod 16:4 God tested the people to see if they trusted the promise of God to provide for them daily.

493. Thus Verhoef, *Haggai and Malachi,* 308.

no reference to rain. Instead, the opening of heaven is paired with blessing (*bərākâ*);[494] the blessing results from sending rain.

The articulation of the intention continues by identifying the effects of the unfolding actions—*and pour out to you an abundance of blessing*—first the opening (*pātaḥ*) of the windows and next the pouring out (*rîq*) of a blessing. Like Yahweh's intention of returning to God's people, the outpoured blessing is conditional. While in Eccl 11:3 the verb *rîq* is used of emptying the heavens of rain (*gešem*), in Mal 3:10 it is used of pouring out a blessing (*bərākâ*)[495] that is qualified by the phrase *'ad-bəlî-dāy*, the meaning of which is multivalent. The literal translation is "until there is no sufficiency."[496] Other interpretations include "until there is no need,"[497] "a totally sufficient blessing,"[498] and "overflowing blessing."[499] Certainly the phrase *'ad-bəlî-dāy* does not refer to exhausting God's blessing until there is no need for it; rather, it refers to an abundance of blessings received due to God's actions toward the community.[500] Blessings result from opening the windows of heaven to rain on the land (cf. Deut 28:12) in contrast to withholding rain and ensuing devastation (Deut 28:24). This qualifying phrase means that the rain will result in *an abundance of blessing* (Joel 2:23–27; Zech 8:12; 10:1; Isa 30:23–26).[501] The blessing on the community will be physically manifested in the land, and its production will verify the restored relationship between Yahweh and the community. Yahweh's intention to bless the community if it is obedient is particular to the fractured Yahweh-Israel relationship; the text does not promise the Deity's response to everyone who brings a tithe.

(c) Announcement: Promise regarding the Return (3:11–12)

The manifestation of God's blessing on the community continues with the second part of the verification: the first is the opening of the windows of

494. Weyde, *Prophecy and Teaching*, 335. Weyde is dubious that the mention of blessing is an abbreviated form of the expression *gišmê bərākâ*, "showers of blessing" (Ezek 34:26).

495. The verb *rîq* is also used of emptying a sack (Gen 42:35), vessels (Jer 48:12), and a net (Hab 1:17).

496. Hill, *Malachi*, 315. Hill notes that the phrase consists of the preposition *'ad*, the negative particle *bəlî*, and the substantive *dāy*.

497. Weyde, *Prophecy and Teaching*, 337; Glazier-McDonald, *Malachi: The Divine Messenger*, 173, 198.

498. Petersen, *Zechariah 9–14 and Malachi*, 213.

499. Verhoef, *Haggai and Malachi*, 308; NRSV. Other modern translations include the ASV and KJV (cf. NIV): "that there shall not be room enough to receive it."

500. Hill (*Malachi*, 291, 315–16) reads "blessing without measure." He understands the phrase to refer to the abundance of the blessing.

501. Cf. Jer 14:22.

heaven and ensuing blessing, and the second is protecting the agricultural produce and process. This protection ensures the abundance of blessing. Accordingly, the announcement of benevolence includes action (rebuke) against the devourer on the community's behalf. In addition to action, the effects are also noted: the devourer will be ineffective in ruining the crop (negatively stated), and the crops will not wither (a positive result ensuing from the ineffectiveness of the devourer). Notably, God also rebuked the offspring of those who dishonored God (Mal 2:3). Here in Mal 3:11 one should note the instances of the Deity's rebuking (*gāʿar*) the elements of nature (e.g., the sea; see also Isa 17:13; Nah 1:4; Ps 106:9) as examples of Yahweh's power to squelch nature's power or effects.[502] The promised protection emphasizes that Yaḥweh's actions and their effects will be for the community (*lākem*).

11 Pending the people's return, Yahweh's intends to safeguard their efforts: *I will rebuke for you the devourer.* This statement reveals a connection between the adverse events and God's involvement with the people. This specific preventive action will be done on their behalf—*for you (lākem).* In particular, God will overpower the devourer (*ʾōkēl*)[503]—to prevent the devourer from succeeding in its destructive activity. Behind the preventive measures that God intends to take is the image of pests (e.g., locusts, flies, or worms) destroying crops. Whether Mal 3:11 refers to locusts or worms, it depicts an agent or pest that destroys crops. Some thus suggest that God will destroy the dormant locust eggs in dry conditions so that they will not hatch in response to rain.[504] In the context of a curse, the locust (*ʾarbeh*) and worm (*tōlāʿat*) devouring the crop or vine exemplifies God's judgment (Deut 28:38–39). Likewise, in Joel 1:4, 19, the image of various types of locusts completing the others' destruction helps one understand the preventive measure that God will take on behalf of the community.

Consequently, *he will not ruin for you the fruit of the ground.* The name of the devourer is not mentioned, but his activity constitutes his identity. By rebuking the devourer, God will prevent the devastation. Although the priests destroyed (*šāḥat*) the covenant of Levi (Mal 2:8), God will not allow the community's means of sustenance to be ruined (*šāḥat*). The effective prevention means that the devourer will *not ruin (šāḥat) the fruit of the ground*

502. Note Isa 54:9, God's declaration about not rebuking God's people. Elsewhere the verb is used of interpersonal communication to signify a retort: e.g., Gen 37:10; Jer 29:27; Ruth 2:16.

503. Literally, "the one who devours": the *qal* masculine participle of *ʾākal,* "to eat." It may also be used of ravaging or destroying people—e.g., Num 13:32; Ezek 36:13. See Weyde, *Prophecy and Teaching,* 339–40. Weyde contends that while it is possible that the devourer refers to humans and nations in particular, in the context of Mal 3:11 and in light of Ps 78:45 and Jer 15:3, the reference is most likely to animals—for example, locusts, flies, or wild animals.

504. Verhoef, *Haggai and Malachi,* 308–9; Hill, *Malachi,* 316–17.

(pərî hā'ădāmâ), the very product that the community is to tithe (Deut 26:2, 10; cf. Neh 10:35 [MT 36]), and the target of Yahweh's blessing (Deut 28:4, 11; 30:9), curse, or judgment (Deut 28:18, 33, 51; Jer 7:20).[505] In response to the community's obedience, God will bless the land by preventing adverse events such as sterility and barren crops (Deut 7:12–16). Malachi 3:10 echoes this promise of blessing.

The preventive actions continue with the promise that *the vine of the field will not be barren for you,* which will be the result of the devourer's inactivity. The vine (*gepen*) will not be barren (*šākal*).[506] The text portrays fertility. The vine is the source of grapes and thus the possibility of wine. Vines along with fig trees are common images of blessing (Hag 2:19; Ps 128:3) and judgment/curse (cf. Isa 7:23; Jer 5:17; Hos 2:12 [MT 14]; Pss 78:47; 105:33).[507] The promise in Mal 3:11 is that the vine will be productive for the community, *for you (lākem).* Regardless of its productivity for others, it will be fruitful for the Yehud community. The recurrence of the particle *lākem* emphasizes the particularity of the promise for the community. The blessing is not necessarily for all who bring tithes, but for this covenant community, which will be bringing tithes in obedience to God.

The representation in Mal 3:11 of God's intervention, with its agricultural imagery (rebuking the devourer), has two effects like a chain reaction, one contingent on the other. If there are no crops to harvest, the people will have little or nothing to tithe. If they do not tithe, their efforts will be frustrated; but if they tithe, their efforts will be successful. As with the accusation that they are robbing God, so also God's intervention does not distinguish between those who experience frustration and those who experience reward. The community rather than the individual is the focus of this text. It also suggests that God's response to the people's behavior regarding tithing is particular rather than general. When the community fulfills its obligation to Yahweh, the relationship will be restored and the blessings will evidence the restoration. The change in circumstances and the abundance of blessing will allow others to witness the effects of God's intervention. Consequently, the nations will witness the physical abundance of the community.

12 The nations' response upon observing God's benevolence toward Yehud (Mal 3:11) will be positive, in contrast to the nations' ridiculing Judah/Jerusalem or its temple because it appears to be abandoned or destroyed by

505. The phrase occurs elsewhere: Gen 4:3; Ps 105:35. A similar expression, "fruit of the land/earth" (*pərî hā'āreṣ*) also refers to agricultural production, either given as a blessing or withheld as a curse (Num 13:20, 26; Deut 1:25; Isa 4:2; cf. Lev 25:19; 26:20; Jer 2:7).

506. The verb signifies "to deprive or to miscarry." It is used of humans: "to be barren" (Gen 43:14; Exod 23:26; 1 Sam 15:33) or "to miscarry" (Hos. 9:14). It is also used of animals (Gen 31:38; Job 21:10).

507. Cf. Ezek 17:7–8; Joel 2:22; Hab 3:17.

Yahweh (Deut 28:37; Jer 24:9; 2 Chr 7:20; cf. Joel 2:17). In the clause *all the nations will call you fortunate*, the phrase *kol-haggôyim*, "all the nations," can refer to those that are close enough to observe or hear about Judah's status (see map 2). However, the phrase "all the nations" here signifies the totality of the nations that will recognize the status of the restored community and reflects the international effect of the happenings in Yehud and the status of the relationship between Yahweh and the covenant community. Yahweh would exalt an obedient Yehud above all the nations of the earth (Deut 28:1).[508] On the other hand, the interface between Yahweh and a disobedient community would also be witnessed by the nations (Deut 29:24; Ezek 39:21).[509] The prophetic texts attest the collective actions of the nations, including going to the mountain of Yahweh (Isa 2:2//Mic 4:1). The international scope of Yahweh's power is likewise evident in the actions toward the nations (Jer 30:11; Joel 3:2 [MT 4:2]; Hag 2:7; Zech 12:9; 14:2).[510] In the book of Malachi, the collective witness of the nations plays an important role in the relationship between Yahweh and the community—both to indicate Yahweh's universal authority and appeal, and to reflect the universal awareness of Yahweh's particular relationship with the covenant community.

All the nations (kol-haggôyim) will declare the community fortunate (*'āšar*), just as they will declare the king fortunate (Ps 72:17).[511] In both instances, the prosperity in the land directly corresponds to obedience—the people's (Mal 3:10) and the king's (Ps 72). The verb *'āšar* characterizes those regarded positively because of their obedience. Similarly, the reversal of the curse results in the nations' acknowledgment that Yehud is a blessing (*bərākâ*; Zech 8:13).[512] The covenant community may also be a byword, a disgrace, or an "object of horror" because of Yahweh's response to its disobedience (Deut 28:25, 37; 2 Chr 29:8; Jer

508. The totality is represented by "all the nations of the earth" (*kōl gôyê hā'āreṣ*) and refers to the nations' acting in a collective manner or being the collective recipient of the effect of Yahweh's relationship with the covenant community (e.g., Gen 18:18; 22:18; 26:4; Jer 44:8), or it indicates all of the nations of the earth plus their collective action (Zech 12:3).

509. Here it is "all the nations" (*kol-haggôyim*) plus the collective action; see, e.g., Ezek 39:21; Neh 6:16.

510. Compare with the expression "all the peoples of the earth" (*kol-'ammê hā'āreṣ*), which is used in a similar way to denote the role of the witnesses to Yahweh's dealing with the covenant community (Deut 28:10; Josh 4:24; 1 Kgs 8:43, 59–60; Zeph 3:20). "Nations" (*gôyim*) and "peoples" (*'ammîm*) are synonymous (e.g., Ps 96:3; 1 Chr 16:24).

511. In these instances, *'āšar*, "to consider fortunate or call happy," is the verb used, with "nations" (*gôyim*) as its subject. The verb is also used with an individual as object (Leah, Gen 30:13; prudent wife, Prov 31:28; beloved, Song 6:9) or of groups within the community (the arrogant, Mal 3:15). Other occurrences include Job 29:11 and the *pual* form in Ps 41:2; Prov 3:18. Weyde (*Prophecy and Teaching*, 343–44) notes that, in all the occurrences except Gen 30:13, the person considered fortunate is one who keeps the laws.

512. Yahweh's blessing on a person or nation is perceived by others (cf. Isa 61:9).

25:9; 44:12; Ezek 5:15; 22:4; Mic 2:4).[513] This time, the nations will respond to the covenant community because of the perceived prosperity of the community.

The *kî* clause provides the reason that the nations will regard the addressees as fortunate: *for indeed you will become a "land of delight."* The second masculine plural personal pronoun (*'attem*) and verb (*tihyû*) identify the addressees as being synonymous with the land (*'ereṣ*). Thus, the geographical entity and covenant community share the same existence. Yahweh's benevolence toward the people will be manifested physically on the land just as Yahweh's wrath would be manifested in negative effects on the land. The land that was under the curse (3:9) will be transformed into a "land of delight" (*'ereṣ ḥēpeṣ*) because of Yahweh's blessings (3:11) in response to the community's return to Yahweh. Thus, the theme of the interface between Yehud and other nations continues. God's reputation transcends the borders of Yehud, and the effects of the Deity's responsiveness to the restoration community will be known outside the borders of Yehud/Jerusalem.[514] The transformation from not being delighted in (Mal 1:10) to becoming delightful is contingent on the community's obedience to Yahweh. The land may be transformed from pleasant to desolate because of disobedience (Zech 7:14).[515] In Isa 62:4 Yahweh's vindication is the means of transformation, and the change in status is reflected in the name changes from "Forsaken" and "Desolate" to "My Delight Is in Her" and "Married." In addition, the change comes because "Yahweh delights in you, and your land shall be married." Likewise, Judah's identity depends on its relationship to God, and other nations' identities are similarly construed—for example, Edom ("wicked country," Mal 1:4).[516] The return will have the effect of blessing on the land and positive regard from the nations.

B. WORDS ABOUT REWARD FOR SERVING YAHWEH (3:13–4:6 [MT 3:13–24])

Malachi 3:13–4:6 (MT 3:13–24) consists of two sections: 3:13–15 and 3:16–24. On a whole, 3:13–24 picks up on the "words" of the people (from 2:17).

513. Cf. 1 Kgs 9:7. God has also made other nations an "object of horror" or ridicule (e.g., Babylon, Jer 51:37, 43).

514. The reason for being considered fortunate may be twofold: that Yahweh delights in the land and that the nations delight in the land. Thus Verhoef, *Haggai and Malachi,* 310. Hill (*Malachi,* 319) contends that "Israel will finally fulfill its commission as the ensign of Yahweh's light and glory to the nations (Isa 42.6; 60.3; 61.9, 11; 66.19)."

515. From "pleasant land" (*'ereṣ-ḥemdâ*) to a "desolate land" (*šammâ*); see Jer 3:19, "pleasant land" (*'ereṣ-ḥemdâ*).

516. Hill, *Malachi,* 320. Hill notes that Moab is "a vessel of no value" (Jer 48:38).

This time they speak against Yahweh as compared with their earlier words of derision about Yahweh's character relative to evil (Mal 2:17). Specifically, Mal 3:13–15 continues with the concerns of the preceding unit (2:17–3:12). Thus, while 2:17 introduces the thought that Yahweh takes pleasure in the evildoers and may not punish them as the tradition dictates (cf. Hab 1:12–13), Mal 3:1–7 addresses that apparent misconception by identifying the groups of evildoers who will be judged. Likewise, the text equates the people with the evildoers, as descendants of evildoers, and as evildoers themselves. Malachi 3:13–15 is concerned about the connection between obedience and blessing as reward for serving Yahweh. In the people's perspective, it is not worthwhile to serve Yahweh (3:13–15). Clearly this text draws on the wisdom-tradition theme regarding the reason for serving God. The book of Job reflects this in the question "does Job fear God for nothing?" (Job 1:9; cf. 21:15). The people have observed that there is no guaranteed correlation between righteous living and the receipt of blessing; rather, evildoers prosper. Therefore, they perceive that blessings are not exclusive to those who serve God but may come to evildoers (3:15).

The individuals who challenge the value of serving God consider the receipt of rewards to be its value; thus, without the prospect of rewards, there is no reason to serve God. The misconstrued reality underlies this perspective to such an extent that those who adhere to this ideology believe themselves to be deserving of reward, presumably because of their righteousness (cf. Mal 2:17).

Malachi 3:16 offers a counterperspective from some individuals who revere God (cf. Mal 2:4–7) and also introduces the final unit of the book, 3:16–24, in which Yahweh elaborates in response. The unit contains the report about the Yahweh-fearers (3:16) and Yahweh's response to them (3:17–4:6 [MT 3:17–24]); they address each other rather than people confronting the Deity (cf. Mal 3:13–15). In this section the "name" links back to Mal 1:6, 11; 2:5. While the rest of the book of Malachi focuses on issues inside the nation, the last unit, 4:5–6 [MT 3:23–24], focuses on Yahweh's messenger and the anticipation of judgment. Will the messenger succeed in averting the judgment of the community, or is judgment inevitable regardless of the messenger's success? The ideal image of the future is of Yahweh, the God of justice, continuing to execute justice.

1. Words against Yahweh (3:13–15)

13 *"Your words have been strong against me," says Yahweh;*[a] *"but you say, 'How have we spoken against you?'* 14 *You said, 'It is futile to serve God. What profit [is there]? If we kept his charges; and if we walked mournfully*

before Yahweh of hosts? ¹⁵So now we call the haughty fortunate. Not only have those who do wickedness been built up, rather they have tested God and escaped.'"

a. *BHS* proposes the insertion of *ṣəbā'ôt* here; see LXXL.

This unit consists of an accusation or charge against the addressees (3:13a) followed by the addressees' questions challenging the charge (3:13b) and the substantiation of the charge in the form of citing the addressees' words (3:14–15). Like the other sequences, Mal 3:13–15 reveals the tension between Yahweh and the community, and it also furthers the charge in 2:17 by identifying the words and ideas that led to this tension.

a. Charge against the People: You Spoke Harshly against Yahweh (3:13a)

13 In addition to the charge in Mal 2:17, another charge is brought against the people: *Your words have been strong against me.* The addressees are charged with speaking *strong words (ḥāzaq)* against Yahweh. This verse, as does the accusation about robbing God, sets up a contrast between "you" (the community) and "me" (the Deity). The verb *ḥāzaq* occurs here in the *qal* perfect third masculine plural form followed by the prepositional phrase (*'ālay*) and the subject (*dibrêkem*). A similar expression occurs in 1 Chr 21:4, "But the king's word prevailed against Joab" (*dəbar-hammelek ḥāzaq 'al-yô'āb*).[517] In the latter instance, the preposition plus verb has an adversarial tone and signifies "overpowering" the object. The construction in Mal 3:13a may also denote "overpowering" in the sense that the community was attempting to overpower Yahweh with its words, seeking to change Yahweh's behavior by its portrayal of Yahweh—the words defining the character of the Deity.[518]

The verb *wa'ămartem*, "but you say," introduces the response to the charge: *how have we spoken against you?* As seen elsewhere in Malachi, the question constitutes a challenge to substantiate the charge and refute its validity (see table 7). On the one hand, the community challenges Yahweh to prove that it has spoken against Yahweh. This could mean that the community does not deny what it has said about Yahweh; rather, it is daring Yahweh to prove that the community's perspective of Yahweh is wrong (cf. Mal 2:17).

517. See the parallel verse in 2 Sam 24:4. Here too the words of the king overpower Joab.

518. Hill, *Malachi*, 329; Weyde, *Prophecy and Teaching*, 350–51.

In response to the charge describing the character of their words (misrepresenting Yahweh), the respondents' question may be another act of speaking against God that reflects the conflict between their words and Yahweh's character. By asking "how have we spoken against you?" (*mah-nidbarnû ʿālêkā*), the respondents are exhibiting the disharmony between the Deity and themselves,[519] whether their ideas are spoken to God or to each other about God.[520] Ezekiel 35:13–15 reflects the negative consequences for Edom due to its words against Yahweh.

> And you magnified yourselves against me with your mouth, and multiplied your words against me; I heard it. Thus says the Lord God: As the whole earth rejoices, I will make you desolate. (Ezek 35:13–14 NRSV)

Although Mal 3:13a does not include punishment for the community's words, it receives them negatively. However, their words claim that the Deity lacks integrity in dealing with the community. Ambiguity persists regarding whether the error lies in the people's perspective about how God deals with the wicked, or in an actual incongruity between their beliefs about Yahweh and the behavior and practices of Yahweh, or in the lack of predictability or a discernible pattern to God's practices.

b. Challenging the Charge (3:13b–15)

The community is depicted as being contentious throughout Malachi, and that depiction is repeated in 3:13b–15. As in the other instances, here the community voice challenges the Deity to demonstrate the validity of the charge that it has spoken harsh words against Yahweh.

(1) The People's Question: How? (3:13b)

One of the elements of the challenge is introduced with the question *how?*—that is, in what way(s)? Whether the question is intended to deflect from the charge or to obtain clarity about the dynamics of the relationship highlighted, it does not signal acceptance of the charge.

519. The particle *mah,* in this instance, "what have we spoken?"; thus Verhoef, *Haggai and Malachi,* 315; Petersen, *Zechariah 9–14 and Malachi,* 219.

520. The *niphal* form of *dābar,* "to speak" (*nidbarnû*) may be interpreted in the reflexive, "spoken among ourselves"; other instances include Ezek 33:30 (*hannidbārîm bəkā,* "who talk together against you") and Ps 119:23 (*bî nidbārû,* "they plotted against me"). Verhoef, *Haggai and Malachi,* 315; Hill, *Malachi,* 331.

(2) Yahweh's Response: Quoting the People's Words (3:14–15)

The people's words or beliefs are presented to substantiate the charge against them. One can see a connection to the previous dialogue about testing God that puts the integrity of the Deity at stake. Do the words or beliefs of the community accurately reflect Yahweh's practices (quite apart from explanations about the rationale for the practices)? Return to Yahweh would produce tangible effects—blessing on the land (Mal 3:10–11). Likewise, Yahweh's practices would produce tangible evidence—reward or punishment. Yahweh's response cites the people's contention about God's misaligned practices toward the wicked (cf. 2:17): a challenge regarding the reward (3:14) and an observation about the wicked (3:15).

14 The challenge regarding the reward includes two components: a statement regarding the futility (3:14a) and a question about the actual practices (3:14b). The notion that *it is futile to serve God* (*šāw' ʿăbōd ʾĕlōhîm*) contradicts the concept of retribution in which there is a correlation between disobedience and adversity and between obedience and blessing. The people do not observe such a correspondence but, instead, an inverse relationship between adversity and obedience (cf. Mal 3:15). Yet even the representation suggests that the questioners perceive themselves as faithful to God. One cannot help but see the glaring contrast between God's charge that the people are robbing and thus dishonoring God and their perspective about the futility (*šāw'*) of serving God (*ʿăbōd ʾĕlōhîm*). "Futility" refers to a lack of tangible results in spite of effort expended (cf. Jer 2:30; 4:30; 6:29; 46:11).[521] The futility of an effort may include bringing offerings (Isa 1:13). The particle *rîq*, "vanity," is used to express a similar concept, such as the destruction that God will bring on those who disobey (e.g., Lev 26:16, 20).[522] Psalm 73:13 uses *rîq* to represent the futility of seeking to be righteous:

> All in vain [*rîq*] I have kept my heart clean and washed my hands in innocence. (Ps 73:13 NSRV)

Likewise, Job questions the value of serving God, especially when he and the reader observe the prosperity of the wicked and their descendants, who seem to outlive and out-prosper the righteous. They reject God yet prosper.

521. The particle in these texts is *laššāw'*. Hill, *Malachi,* 332.

522. The root functions as the noun "vanity, empty," and the verb "to make empty" (of the heavens; Eccl 11:3; Mal 3:10). Other uses of *rîq* (noun) signifying futile effort include Isa 49:4; 65:23 (with *yāgaʿ*, "to labor or toil"); Jer 51:58; Hab 2:13; Ps 2:1. Note also the synonym *hebel,* "vanity, futility," which is sometimes used parallel to *rîq* (Isa 30:7; 49:4; cf. Eccl 1:2, 14; 4:4).

> Why do the wicked live on, reach old age, and grow mighty in power? . . . They say to God, "Leave us alone! We do not desire to know your ways. What is the Almighty, that we should serve him? And what profit do we get if we pray to him?" (Job 21:7, 14–15 NRSV)

However, people—present and past—commonly have a distorted understanding of the status of their relationship with God. Likewise, people who are blinded to their faults are also blinded to other things—in this case, how their belief and behavior dishonor God, and regarding their erroneous perspective about God (2:17). Even so, questions about God's faithfulness in rewarding the righteous are not farfetched but on track with experience. Although at first glance the people's perspective may seem to dishonor God, the perspective may be an attempt to make sense of the apparent failure of the Deity to perform according to their expectations, however misguided that attempt may be.

Not simply doctrine, the words are at the heart of the people's behavior and view of God. The people's disenchantment appears further in the question about the profit of serving God: whether there is any "gain" (*beṣaʿ*) in keeping Yahweh's charges/commandments (in the broad sense of obligations). Elsewhere *beṣaʿ* refers to "unlawful" gain based on the means and motive of acquiring it (Gen 37:26; 1 Sam 8:3; Isa 33:15; Jer 6:13; 8:10; 22:17; Ezek 22:13, 27; 33:31; Hab 2:9; Prov 1:19; 15:27).[523] In Job 22:3, *beṣaʿ* is used of the benefit to Yahweh:

> Is it any pleasure to the Almighty if you are righteous, or is it gain [*beṣaʿ*] to him if you make your ways blameless? (Job 22:3 NRSV)

Here also the issue is whether there are positive rewards for a practice or state of being (cf. Job 21:15). The group of questioners in Mal 3:14 may consist of both wicked and righteous individuals. The righteous would not perceive themselves to be seeking illegitimate gain; rather, they would want what they perceive to be earned by faithfulness to God. The question itself does not suggest a lack of desire to serve Yahweh; on the contrary, it may suggest a vested interest in the outcome of one's endeavors. No profit, no service—one will invest only where something can be gained. This may be logical to some, but to others it may be sacrilegious. This perspective would more likely be held by those who do not serve God, either because they have not received gain or because they have received gain without serving God. Clearly, this is not an abstract question about the reward for being righteous but a question specific to life practices—tangible rewards for tangible practices.

523. Cf. Exod 18:21; Mic 4:13; Prov 28:16; Pss 30:9 (MT 10); 119:36.

The expression *if we kept his charges (kî šāmarnû mišmartô)* denotes obligation and is sometimes used with commandments, statutes, and ordinances (cf. Lev 8:35; Deut 13:18; 1 Kgs 2:3). "The charge" (*mišmeret*) denotes an obligation or behavior required in particular situations (Lev 8:35; 18:30; 22:9; Num 9:19, 23; 1 Kgs 2:3; Ezek 44:8, 16; 48:11; Neh 12:45; 2 Chr 13:11; 23:6). The invitation to test God implies that there is reward/gain in obeying God's stipulations (cf. Mal 3:9–12). This question focuses not simply on the benefit of a good relationship with the Deity, but on the verifiable gains—a relationship not characterized by punishment and adversity. The people are asking, "What's in it for me?" Inasmuch as Yahweh seeks to show the people the benefit of their service, Yahweh affirms their perspective.

The second area of inquiry about profit in serving God asks, [what profit is there . . .] *if we walked mournfully before Yahweh of hosts?* The meaning of the phrase *hālaknû qədōrannît* is contested because the adverbial particle *qədōrannît* is unique to Mal 3:14.[524] In the context of the laments, the root *qādar* denotes mourning. For example:

> I say to God, my rock, "Why have you forgotten me? Why must I walk about mournfully because the enemy oppresses me?" (Ps 42:9 [MT 10]; cf. 43:2)

The question touches on the idea that there is value in mourning since God secures the well-being of those who mourn (Job 5:11). The people whose views Mal 3:14 represents have doubt about whether God acts benevolently on behalf of mourners—regardless of whether their mourning is due to oppression, other forms of adversity, or penitence.[525] The questioner is distressed that God is unmoved by their keeping the command and their sorrowful expressions (whether genuine or contrived).

15 While they may previously have believed otherwise, *now (ʿattā),* based on their observations, the addressees draw this conclusion about evildoers (*ʿōśê riš'â*) or the arrogant/haughty (*zēdîm*): fundamentally, God has not acted according to expectations. Some may be disenchanted because the wicked receive the same reward as the righteous. However, in Mal 3:14, the more likely concern is that the wicked receive reward while the righteous do not. Typically, the obedient are regarded as fortunate

524. The particle is derived from the verb *qādar*, "to be dark" (cf. Mic 3:6, of the day); Joel 2:10; 3:15 (MT 4:15), of the sun and moon. Another meaning of *qādar* is "to mourn" (Jer 8:21; 14:2; Ps 35:13 [MT 14]; 38:7; Job 30:28).

525. See Hill (*Malachi,* 334) for a discussion of those who base their interpretation on the Arabic *qadara*, "to honor," and thus translate the phrase "walk earnestly" (Glazier-McDonald, *Malachi: The Divine Messenger,* 214); "walked piously" (Petersen, *Zechariah 9–14 and Malachi,* 219).

(*mə'aššərîm*),[526] but here the faithful seem to count the arrogant (*zēdîm*)[527] as the fortunate ones—*so now we call the haughty fortunate.* The arrogant are usually rebuked or cursed (e.g., Isa 13:11; Ps 119:21; cf. Prov 3:33); they oppose and oppress the righteous or those who seek to follow the commandments (Ps 119:51, 78, 85, 122).[528] Are the arrogant fortunate, or is their situation more complex than it appears to be? Psalm 73 depicts a transformed awareness about the wicked: though they appear to have everything, they will be destroyed. Perhaps the sentiment in Mal 3:15 concerns the "here and now." Whatever else happens to them, the idea is that they should not prosper at all—not even for a while.

Why are they considered fortunate? First, those who practice wickedness are built up (*nibnû*).[529] This perspective is discomforting for those who perceive themselves to be righteous because of their belief that the wicked *are or should be* punished. They should receive trouble and adversity (cf. Prov 10:16).[530] In Jer 50:31–32, *zādôn*, "proud," indicates the outcome for the arrogant; those who are insolent and oppose the ways of Yahweh will not be tolerated.

> The arrogant one shall stumble and fall, with no one to raise him up, and I will kindle a fire in his cities, and it will devour everything around him. (Jer 50:32 NRSV)

The way of the evildoers is destroyed (*pōʿălê 'āwen*; Ps 5:5 [MT 6]; Prov 10:29). The boastful/arrogant will not stand because God "hates all evildoers" (cf. Pss 34:16 [MT 17]; 146:9). Consequently, one ought not to envy the evildoers (Prov 24:19; Ps 37:1, 9, 10, 12–13), though that temptation arises when one observes that they sometimes prosper (Ps 73:3, 13). However strong the perspective regarding the demise of the wicked may be elsewhere, in Mal 3:14 the people are aware that reality is more complicated—the wicked do not all meet the same end. One tradition is that God's practices concerning evildoers and the righteous or blameless are clear: God does not side with evildoers or reject the blameless (Job 8:20). Even so, there is also a sense that sometimes evildoers prosper, although they will ultimately be destroyed (Ps 92:7 [MT 8]; cf. 92:9 [MT 10]).[531] Therein lies the disenchantment with Yahweh, who

526. This word is the *piel* masculine plural participle of the verb *'āšar*. Compare with the root in Mal 3:12, "All the nations will call you fortunate" (*'iššərû*).

527. The masculine plural form of *zēd*, "proud, arrogant," occurs in several texts, including Isa 13:11; Pss 19:13 (MT 14); 54:3 (MT 5); 86:14; 119:51.

528. A synonym is *gē'îm* (cf. Ps 140:5 [MT 6]).

529. The *niphal* third masculine plural of the verb *bānâ*, "to build."

530. "The wage of the righteous leads to life, the gain of the wicked to sin" (NRSV).

531. Evildoers (*pōʿălê 'āwen*) and wicked (*rəšāʿîm*) used in parallel. Cf. Ps 101:8.

is responsible for the positive and negative outcomes of the wicked. Contrary to what one believes, not only do the wicked exist, but they thrive—at least for a while (Mal 3:18; 4:1 [MT 3:18–19]).

The second observation is that the wicked test (*bāḥan*) God and escape (*mālaṭ*). Here, as in the first observation, the perspective is simplistic or at least one-dimensional. The perspective assumes that testing God leads to negative outcomes. While this idea has a sound basis (cf. Exod 17:2), it overlooks the possibility of positive consequences. Or perhaps the frustration lies not so much in the fact that someone tested God but in who they were who tested God—*those who do wickedness* (*ʿōśê rišʿâ*; see Mal 3:10 above). They tested God and, as a result of their test, they escaped; they passed when they should have failed. Not only does God deviate from expectations, but the deviation creates anomalous consequences—the wicked are built up. People expect that those who despise and break the covenant will not escape (cf. Ezek 17:15–18, "Can he break the covenant and yet escape?"). Evildoers (whether or not they test God) will not escape punishment (Prov 19:5; cf. Prov 28:26). The wicked will be punished, but the righteous will escape punishment (Prov 11:21).

Fundamentally, however, Mal 3:15 does reflect the same sentiment as found in other traditions: the wicked prosper while the righteous languish.

> There is a vanity that takes place on earth, that there are righteous people who are treated according to the conduct of the wicked, and there are wicked people who are treated according to the conduct of the righteous. I said that this also is vanity. (Eccl 8:14 NRSV)

The speakers are not entirely off course in their assessment of Yahweh's behavior; their perspective may be skewed by their frustration. Consequently, they are unable to see the larger picture. Nonetheless, the speakers' view and frustration are understandable—why serve God if there is no reward? Why serve God if one already has reward without service? Just as understandable is the frustration with those who prosper even though they do not serve God or follow the commands, or even obey merely out of obligation. Whether it is the focal point or a byproduct of the apparent prosperity, the connection between observing the law and prosperity (Mal 3:10–12) is both confirmed by Malachi and challenged by some in Malachi who doubt the integrity of Yahweh to honor that connection (3:13–15).

2. Counterperspective and Yahweh's Response (3:16–4:6 [MT 3:16–24])

Yahweh addresses the community's apparent misconception regarding Yahweh's treatment of evildoers. Yahweh's response takes into consideration both the righteous and the wicked; it affirms Yahweh's justice and clarifies the time of justice.

a. Report concerning Those Who Fear Yahweh (3:16)

16*Then those who feared Yahweh spoke to themselves, each man with his companion; so Yahweh paid attention and listened. Then a book of remembrance was written before Yahweh for those who fear Yahweh and those who esteem his name.*[a]

a. This reading uses the emendation—"those who fear him and esteem his name." Another emendation proposes the verb *ḥāsâ*, "to take refuge," instead of *ḥāšab*, "to think, respect," thus reading "those who fear Yahweh and take refuge in his name"; see, e.g., J. M. P. Smith "Malachi," 78. Modern translations tend to represent the idea of thinking about the name: Baldwin, *Hag, Zech, Mal,* 249—"those who thought on this name"; Verhoef, *Haggai and Malachi,* 312; ASV, KJV, NRSV—"kept his name in mind"; cf. Petersen, *Zechariah 9–14 and Malachi,* 219—"those who ponder his name." Others interpret *ḥāšab* as "to esteem, respect"—e.g., Glazier-McDonald, *Divine Messenger,* 206; R. L. Smith, *Micah–Malachi,* 335; Hill, *Malachi,* 340–41; NIV.

(1) The God-Fearers' Reaction to the Words against Yahweh (3:16a)

16 The particle *'āz* , "then," forms the transition to the counterperspective of the larger group, whose views are cited in Mal 3:14–15.[532] The group who challenged God's dealings with the wicked may not have been homogeneous.[533] Among them were those who feared Yahweh (*yir'ê yhwh*), who—while aware of the disconcerting outcomes of Yahweh's dealings with the wicked—were not settled on holding that perspective. The adverbial particle *'āz* indicates the shift in perspective within the group upon hearing their perspectives voiced. The break in the collective perspectives is marked by the fearers of

532. The LXX reads *tauta,* "this," for the MT *'āz.* Accordingly, the LXX reads, "this those who revered the Lord spoke . . ."—thus J. M. P. Smith, "Malachi," 81. The LXX also assumes that the content of their speech follows in the latter part of 3:16. Most modern translations retain the MT *'āz*—e.g., ASV, KJV, NRSV; Hill, *Malachi,* 326; Verhoef, *Haggai and Malachi,* 312; Weyde, *Prophecy and Teaching,* 356.

533. Hill (*Malachi,* 337) argues that the wicked are also part of the audience. See also Baldwin, *Hag, Zech, Mal,* 249. Others propose a homogeneous group of either the wicked or the righteous. Accordingly, Glazier-McDonald (*Malachi: The Divine Messenger,* 217) suggests that the righteous alone constituted the group. Verhoef (*Haggai and Malachi,* 319) proposes that 3:14–15 represents the perspectives of the evildoers and arrogant, who are a different group from the one in 3:16. R. L. Smith (*Micah–Malachi,* 338) proposes that the group in 3:14–15 consists of skeptics, while the group in 3:16 consists of Yahweh-fearers.

Yahweh (*yir'ê yhwh*)[534] speaking among themselves (*nidbərû*).[535] This is not simple chatter but reasoning together, presumably about the larger attitude regarding Yahweh's actions toward the wicked. The fact that these people fear Yahweh signifies that they are at least circumspect in their behavior and tempered in their approach.[536] Conformity to the ways of Yahweh would be typical of this group; but being a Yahweh-fearer does not necessarily denote unawareness of the reality signaled in the perspectives about the prosperity of the evildoers. Yahweh is benevolent toward the God-fearers—befriends them, shows them goodness, protects, blesses, and provides for them (cf. Pss 25:14; 33:19 [MT 18]; 34:7 [MT 8]; 103:11; 111:5; 145:19; 147:11).

(2) Yahweh's Reception of Their Behavior: The Book of Remembrance (3:16b)

The community includes distinctive groups; simply being part of the covenant community does not make a person a Yahweh-fearer. Those who fear God have a special connection with God manifested in God's responsiveness to them. Accordingly, the actions of the Yahweh-fearers are noted, and they secure Yahweh's response. Yahweh *paid attention (wayyaqšēb yhwh)* to them and *listened (wayyišmā')*.[537] As members of the group who challenged Yahweh's practices, they received a response that addressed their perception of their fate and the fate of the wicked.

A book of remembrance was written before Yahweh. The writing of the book is the second part of the event sequence resulting from the Yahweh-fearers' speaking together. It was written (*wayyikkātēb*), though the recorder(s) are not identified. The verb *kātab* in the *niphal* stem denotes the act of recording (Job 19:23; Esth 1:19; 2:23; 9:32; Ezra 8:34) or being enrolled in a book or registry (Ezek 13:9). The opposite of being enrolled or written is to be blotted out (*māḥâ*; cf. Exod 32:33; Ps 69:28 [MT 29]) or recorded elsewhere other than in God's book (Jer 17:13 in Sheol). Kings kept records of events and situations as a foundation for future actions and decisions. This was not

534. Other occurrences of *yir'ê yhwh* include Ps 61:5 (MT 6; cf. Ps 25:14).

535. Here the reflexive nuance is appropriate and confirmed by the expression "each man to his companion" (*'îš 'et-rē'ēhû*), denoting reciprocity. The *niphal* form of *dābār* also occurs in 3:13 (*nidbarnû*).

536. Also designated as *yir'ê 'ĕlōhîm* (God-fearers), a respected and valued group in the community. Fearing God is one of the qualities of an elder, along with hating dishonest gain (*śōnə'ê bāṣa'*), Exod 18:21. Cf. Ps 66:16; Eccl 8:12.

537. Hill (*Malachi*, 338–39) recommends that *wayyaqšēb yhwh wayyišmā'* be translated "took notice and listened" to guard against the possible nuance of Yahweh's "being a reluctant listener" (cf. the NRSV). Contrast Verhoef (*Haggai and Malachi*, 312): "the Lord heeded and listened."

simply a log of names[538] but may have been purposeful in registering ideas and attitudes. While the label *book of remembrance (sēper zikkārôn)* is unique to Mal 3:16, a similar label occurs in Esth 6:1–2 regarding King Ahasuerus's records (*sēper hazzikərōnôt*), in which Mordecai's good deed was written.[539] As to God's record or book (*sēper*), several Old Testament texts refer to such a record and its uses. Thus Moses challenged God to forgive Israel or to remove him (Moses) from the book; God declared that the sinners would be blotted out of the book (*sēper,* Exod 32:32–33).[540]

The function of the book may be to remind Yahweh of various matters. "Remembrance" (*zikkārôn*) includes bringing to memory the full scope of the events, perhaps including the emotions or reactions associated with the memory.[541] Is their speaking to themselves the cause of God's action to keep an account about their lives? While nothing is said of the lives of the wicked, it is possible that the book of remembrance is focused on the Yahweh-fearers but includes an account of the wicked.[542] God does not forget or overlook anyone; rather, the book is not exclusively about the Yahweh-fearers but is kept on their behalf.[543] It may serve as a reminder that Yahweh is aware of the wicked and has not forgotten those who serve Yahweh.

Specifically, the book was recorded for the Yahweh-fearers (*yir'ê yhwh*) and for *those who esteem "his" name* (*ləḥōšəbê šəmô*). It highlights the contrast between this group and those who despise Yahweh's name (*bôzê šəmî*—Mal 1:6). Interpreting the verb *kātab* in the sense of "enrolling" would mean that

538. In contrast to Baldwin (*Hag, Zech, Mal,* 249), who notes that "the *book of remembrance* recorded not righteous deeds, as in a Persian king's chronicles (Est. 6:1, 2), but the names *of those who feared the Lord and thought on his name.*"

539. Other texts indicating that records were kept include Dan 7:10 ("books," *siprîn*; cf. Acts 10:4—memorial).

540. See. Ps 139:16: God's book as a record of the existence of human beings. Other texts attest a record or the act of recording (*kātab*), Isa 4:3; 65:6. There are also several other types of books: the "book of the wars of Yahweh" (*sēper milḥămōt yhwh*)—Num 21:14; "book of the law" (*sēper hattôrâ*)—e.g., Deut 29:21 (MT 20); 31:26. Like Exod 32:32–33, the NT concept of "the book of life" reflects a tradition in which the good are recorded and sinners excluded (Rev 3:5; 13:8; 17:8; 20:15; 21:27; cf. Phil 4:3; Rev 20:12). Cf. *TDOT* 7:380, "heavenly books."

541. Compare the various uses of *zikkārôn*: a day that commemorates an event (e.g., Exod 12:14); a memory or history (Exod 17:14; Deut 25:19; Eccl 2:16; cf. Ps 34:16 [MT 17]); a symbol or offering used as a reminder (Exod 28:12, 29; 39:7; Num 5:15, 18).

542. Some note that names and an account of the deeds are recorded—e.g., Verhoef, *Haggai and Malachi,* 321.

543. Note Hill (*Malachi,* 340–41), who argues that the Yahweh fearers and those who esteemed Yahweh's name were enrolled in the book. Weyde, *Prophecy and Teaching,* 362. R. L. Smith (*Micah-Malachi,* 338) holds that the words of the Yahweh-fearers are recorded.

Yahweh-fearers were enrolled in the book,[544] which distinguishes them from the evildoers. This interpretation of the book of remembrance reflects the tradition regarding the "book of life" (cf. Rev 3:5; 13:8; 17:8; 20:12, 15; 21:27).[545] The wicked not being found in the book would indicate Yahweh's decision to destroy them; inclusion would be a reminder to reward the Yahweh-fearers.[546] On the other hand, the book of remembrance may not have had this eschatological perspective but was written for the Yahweh-fearers, "to remind worshippers of the traditions concerning Yahweh, so that they will continue to fear Yahweh and reflect on the implications of his reputation."[547] While the book may be a reminder of Yahweh's attention to the ways of all, it also validates the reasons for Yahweh's actions toward the wicked and the righteous, whether in the present or in the imminent or remote future.

b. Yahweh's Extended Response to the Yahweh-Fearers (3:17–4:6 [MT 3:17–24])

Malachi 3:17–24 further consists of 3:17–4:3 (MT 3:17–21) and 4:4–6 (MT 3:22–24). As a whole, 3:17–24 is unified by its attention to the day of Yahweh in its various formulations: day when I will act (3:17); day is coming (4:1 [MT 3:19]); terrible day of Yahweh (4:5 [MT 3:23]). Likewise, the unit picks up the same motif from 3:2–7 regarding the coming of the messenger and Yahweh. As to the distinctiveness of 3:17–4:3 (MT 3:17–21) in comparison with 4:4–6 (MT 3:22–24), 3:17–4:3 (MT 3:17–21) differentiates between the evildoers and the righteous, presumably in response to the preceding claim that there is no reward in serving God. On behalf of those who revere God, they are promised that the distinction will be made clear to them (3:18) by

544. Thus Hill, *Malachi,* 341; cf. Baldwin, *Hag, Zech, Mal,* 249. Floyd (*Minor Prophets 2,* 624) argues that the book was recorded in Yahweh's presence in the sanctuary, not in heaven.

545. See discussion of the book of life: Regarding Rev 20:12, 15, a tradition seems to be preserved about two heavenly books: one records the deeds of the righteous, and the other records the deeds of the wicked (Dan 7:10; cf. Isa 65:6).

546. David E. Aune (*Revelation 17–21,* WBC 52c [Nashville: Thomas Nelson, 1997], 1102–4) notes that Rev 20:15 "means that the only criterion of salvation is to have one's name written in the book of life and it appears to make superfluous the rendering of judgment on the basis of the deeds recorded in the book" (p. 1103).

547. Floyd, *Minor Prophets 2,* 624. He contends that the book's function is to motivate them to repent. He further reasons that the content of the book explicates Mal 3:16b. "The document will serve as a repository of the tradition that needs to be engaged through interpretation in order to live the kind of repentant life that will lead to salvation" (p. 624). Contrast J. Nogalski's (*Redactional Processes,* 209–10) view that the book of remembrance is the book of Malachi.

way of a fire that destroys the evildoers but spares the righteous. Even here, the emphasis is on retribution—the reward for the righteous and punishment for the evildoers.

Nonetheless, the persistent theme of the noncorrelation between evil and curses (cf. Ps 73)—some wicked persons prosper—is not addressed. Rather, an ideal and idyllic image of blessings is presented (3:17–4:6 [MT 3:17–24]) to confirm Yahweh's integrity and to address concerns about Yahweh's regard for the wicked. Fundamentally, some in the community do not trust Yahweh and perceive Yahweh to be unreliable. They have turned away from Yahweh because they perceive no profit in serving Yahweh. Dishonor, then, is a byproduct of their perspective and lack of commitment to Yahweh.

(1) Their Relationship with Yahweh (3:17–4:3 [MT 3:17–21])

17 *"And they will be to me," says Yahweh of hosts, "a valued possession, on*
the day when I act. And I will have compassion on them as a man has compassion
on his son, the one who serves him. 18 *Then you will again distinguish between a*
righteous person and a wicked one, between the one who serves God and whoever
has not served him. 4:1 (3:19) *For behold! The day is coming, burning like an oven,*
when all the arrogant and everyone who does wickedness will be stubble. And
the coming day will set them ablaze," says Yahweh of hosts, "that will leave[a] *to*
them neither root nor branches. 4:2 (3:20) *So a sun of righteousness will rise for*
you—those who reverence my name—healing in its wings; and you will go forth
and prance about like fatted calves. 4:3 (3:21) *And you will trample the wicked,*
for they will be ashes beneath the soles of your feet, in the day when I act," says
Yahweh of hosts.

a. The LXX *hypoleipō* = *yēʿāzēb*.

(a) Yahweh's Special Possession (3:17)

17 Yahweh speaks concerning an impending day of action (*layyôm ʾăšer ʾănî ʿōśê*, "the day when I act"), when a distinction will be made between those who serve God and those who do not. The Yahweh-fearers identified here with the third masculine plural form of the verb (*hāyû*), will be a valued possession (*səgullā*) to Yahweh.[548] The noun *səgullā* refers to the nation, the covenant community (Exod 19:5; Deut 7:6; 14:2; 26:18), the people chosen by God. The election of Israel may constitute its status as a valued possession

548. Most translate the noun *səgullā* as "mine"; e.g., Verhoef, *Haggai and Malachi*, 312; Baldwin, *Hag, Zech, Mal*, 249; modern versions, ASV, KJV, NIV, NRSV. Contrast Hill (*Malachi*, 326): "a prized possession."

(Deut 7:6; 14:2; Ps 135:4); in Exod 19:5 the status is contingent on obedience. Likewise, in Deut 26:18–19, God chose the people to be a valued possession, and they agreed to the terms of the relationship—to be a holy people (*ʿam qādôš*).[549] In Mal 3:17, *səgullā* does not refer to the entire nation but to those within the nation, however few or many, who fear God—the very stance lacking in the priests.[550] The priests' lack of reverence and honor led to the accusation and contributed to the curse on the land. Consequently, while the entire nation may have been deemed God's possession, in the postexilic community that label is used in a restrictive sense of the Yahweh-fearers. Being a member of the covenant community does not guarantee blessing. The narrowed distinction is apparent in this designation of Yahweh's planned action. Whether or not this qualifies the status of the community before Yahweh at the present, the temporal indicator does qualify its status at a specific time—that is, *the day (hayyôm)* when Yahweh acts (cf. Mal 3:19, 21). The temporal indicator may also govern the other promised action: God's future compassion.

The recipients of God's compassion will be the covenant people—in particular, those who fear God—*I will have compassion on them.* Clearly, in this instance the corporate view of the community is secondary. The distinctions between the wicked and the righteous regulate how Yahweh will deal with the community. God will have compassion on (*ḥāmal*) only the Yahweh-fearers.[551] The verb *ḥāmal* usually means "to have compassion" and "to spare," especially in the context of war (cf. 1 Sam 15:3, 15).[552] It may be used in negative formulations to mean not having compassion or sparing people (e.g., Ezek 8:18; Zech 11:5–6), or positively, of having compassion (Joel 2:18). By specifying the recipients of the compassion with the preposition (*ʿălêhem*) "on them," the declaration excludes others—that is, those who do not fear Yahweh.

The declaration elaborates and further narrows the group of recipients by means of a comparison with the action of a father toward his son: *as a man has compassion on his son.* This speaks to the typical nature of the relationship (Mal 1:6); a "man" (*ʾîš*) would have compassion on "his son" (*bənô*).

549. In Deuteronomy, the community is "a people holy to Yahweh" (*ʿam qādôš ʾattā layhwh*); e.g., Deut 7:6; 14:2, 21; 26:19.

550. Accordingly, Hill (*Malachi,* 342) argues that "Malachi narrows the understanding of the *səgullā* from the nation as understood in the pentateuchal citations, to the righteous remnant of Israel—perhaps on the basis of this criterion of 'holiness.'" Cf. Weyde, *Prophecy and Teaching,* 342.

551. The verb *ḥāmal* occurs here with Yahweh as subject. Elsewhere the root may denote "to have compassion" (e.g., Exod 2:6; Jer 13:14; 15:5), "to spare" (2 Sam 21:7; Isa 9:19; Jer 51:3; Ezek 9:5).

552. Most of the modern versions translate *ḥāmal* in Mal 3:17 as "to spare"—ASV, KJV, NIV, NRSV; cf. Verhoef, *Haggai and Malachi,* 312, 323.

> As a father has compassion [*riḥam*] for his children, so the Lord has compassion for those who fear him [*ʿal-yərēʾāyw*]. (Ps 103:13 NRSV)

But a further qualification signifies that only under certain conditions is compassion normative. Compassion is for *the one who serves him.* The clause *the one who serves (ʿābad) him* alludes to Mal 3:14 regarding the possibility of reward for serving God (contrast 2:8). One would expect a servant to serve but a son to love and honor (Mal 1:6). In making this distinction, Mal 3:17 reveals that the promised actions do not apply to all but only to those who serve Yahweh. Not all are the valued possession, and not all will be spared. The idea that the wicked escape is thus addressed even here—they will not be spared if they do not fear and serve God (cf. Mal 3:15). The decisive element in the father's compassion toward his son would be service. Arguably, the father would not have compassion on a son who does not serve him. By comparison, Yahweh would be compassionate toward the Yahweh-fearers—namely, those who serve Yahweh.

(b) Ability to Differentiate between the Righteous and the Wicked (3:18–4:3 [MT 3:18–21])

The focus on the centrality of serving Yahweh continues in 3:18, which reports the people's renewed ability. The time frame continues from 3:17, the day in which Yahweh will act. Here, "to serve" is the decisive criterion in distinguishing the righteous and the wicked. Just as Yahweh is able to distinguish between them, so the people will also distinguish the righteous from the wicked. Presumably, they will not be fooled because they will use the same criterion as Yahweh: serving God.

(i) The Ability Identified (3:18)

18 The ability to differentiate between the righteous and the wicked is both a privilege and a responsibility, for the people will not have any excuse if they misconstrue the criteria for a right relationship with Yahweh. The clause *then you will again distinguish (wəšabtem ûrəʾîtem)* uses the *qal* perfect form of *šûb,* "to return," plus the *qal* perfect form of *rāʾâ*, "to see." The verb *šûb* functions as an auxiliary verb to *rāʾâ.*[553] Although the concern has been about

553. Hill, *Malachi,* 344; *IBHS* §39.3.1b—used adverbially (thus the NRSV and NEB). Several other instances of its use as an auxiliary with the adverbial sense occur in Zechariah: 5:1; 6:1 (*ʾāšûb wāʾeśśāʾ*, "Again I looked"); 8:15 (*šabtî zāmamtî,* "again I have proposed"); cf. Hos 14:7 (MT 8); Mic 7:19. The LXX reads "and you will return, and you will see" (*kai epistraphesesthe, kai opsesthe*). R. L. Smith (*Micah–Malachi,* 339) proposes that *šûb* be inter-

how Yahweh deals with the wicked, the people will be able to discern between the righteous and the wicked (*ṣaddîq lərāšāʿ*). The *ṣaddîq* in this instance are synonymous with the Yahweh-fearers (3:16). On the other hand, the *rāšāʿ* are those who do not serve Yahweh (3:18): the arrogant (3:19), the evildoers (2:17), and doers of wickedness (3:19). The only other place outside the Psalms and Proverbs where the phrase *ṣaddîq wərāšāʿ* occurs is in Ezek 21:3–4 (MT 8–9; cf. Hab 1:4, 13).[554] Fundamentally, the difference is between the one who serves God (the righteous) and *whoever has not served him* (the wicked). Yahweh determines the criteria, not the community. Accordingly, service may be defined as religious observances. Within the Mal 3 context, fulfilling one's obligation to tithe is one means of service. However, if the ability to discern will happen during the "day of Yahweh," what will happen in the interim—until that day?

(ii) Specification of the Contrast (4:1–3 [MT 3:19–21])

The contrast between the righteous and the wicked will be manifested during the day when Yahweh acts. This day will be a day of judgment on the wicked, in which their destruction will be completed (4:1 [MT 3:19]). By comparison, the fate of the righteous will also be manifested; they will be built up and will become the instrument of God's judgment against the wicked (4:2–3 [MT 3:20–21]).[555]

(a) The Arrogant and Evildoers (4:1 [MT 3:19])

1 The declaration—*For behold! The day is coming*—continues the time frame introduced in 3:1, *See? He is coming* (*hinnê bāʾ*). This is also the time frame indicated by "the day" in 3:2 (*the day of his coming*); 3:17; 4:3 (MT 3:21; *on*

---

preted as a verb denoting the first action in the series, thus "you will return and perceive" (thus the ASV and KJV).

554. The occurrences include Ps 11:5; Eccl 3:17; 9:2. In most of these instances, the terms are definite: "the righteous" (*haṣṣaddîq*) and "the wicked" (*hārāšāʿ*). While the terms are indefinite in Mal 3:18, some translate them as definite to indicate the type of people: e.g., Glazier-McDonald, *Malachi: The Divine Messenger,* 206; Verhoef, *Haggai and Malachi,* 312. Of the righteous, see Pss 94:21; 112:6; 141:5; Prov 9:9; 20:7; compare with the plural form—*ṣaddîqîm*, Ps 69:28 (MT 29); Prov 4:18. Of the wicked, see Prov 3:33; 10:3, 30; 12:12.

555. Carroll, *When Prophecy Failed*, 204–5. Carroll argues that the eschatological motif includes the prophetic announcement of the Deity's plan, though divine intervention serves as a bridge between prophecy and apocalyptic. Yahweh is making up for the failure to actualize salvation. It is a transformation resulting from the perceived and real failure of the preexilic prophecies.

the day when I act); and 4:5 (MT 3:23; *the great and dreadful [day]*).[556] The characterization of the day's coming uses figurative language: *burning like an oven* (*bōʿēr kattannûr*).[557] Along with the imagery of the refiner's fire (*ʾēš məṣārēp*) in Mal 3:2–3, this description heightens the decisiveness of the day. Just as one cannot endure the smelting process and remain unaltered, so one cannot endure a burning oven and emerge unchanged. The day itself is the subject of the verb *bāʿar*, "to burn."[558] This day of Yahweh—which verifies Yahweh's integrity as the God of justice (2:17) and corrects the misconception that God does not punish the wicked—will be a day of destruction and annihilation. The horrific imagery of an "oven" (*tannûr*), using a furnace to annihilate people, reiterates that the day of Yahweh is a day of judgment (cf. Ps 21:9 [MT 10]). While that day is particular to the situation, it may also reflect other days that share its characteristics; there are different manifestations of the day of Yahweh and not a single ultimate manifestation. Even so, Mal 4:1 (MT 3:19) provides reassurance for the righteous that Yahweh is engaged in the life and fate of all. By pointing to the future, the righteous are compelled to trust God and wait for the actualization of that future and the confirmation of God's justice against the wicked.

The future manifestation of the day of Yahweh will be characterized by the destruction of all the wicked: a time *when all the arrogant and every one who does wickedness will be stubble.* Unlike other representations of the nations, which identify the whole as the subject of the collective action, this passage distinguishes the wicked from the God-fearers. The preceding verses noted the Deity's response to the God-fearers (i.e., Mal 3:17). Here in 3:19 Yahweh's response clearly indicates that the Deity is neither ignorant of the wicked nor complacent about their deeds. It observes that, regardless of any success the wicked may enjoy, they will not overpower God. The present success (if any) is only a precursor to their demise. Furthermore, none will

556. Cf. Joel 2:1 (the day of Yahweh is coming); Zech 14:1 (a day is coming for Yahweh). Note the discussion of the various temporal indicators in DeVries, *From Old Revelation to New*.

557. The noun *tannûr*, "oven," occurs also in Hos 7:4—like a heated oven (*kəmô tannûr bōʿērâ*) (cf. 7:6). Elsewhere it used with "baked" (Hos 7:4; Lev 2:4; 7:9). In some contexts the imagery occurs using the verb *ʾākal* with the idea of consuming others; e.g., Hos 7:7; Ps 21:9 (MT 10). See Hill (*Malachi*, 346) for his discussion of how the ancient witnesses read 3:19—the LXXG inserts "and it will consume them" after "burning like an oven." The Peshitta includes "my anger" as the subject of the verb (burning).

558. Yahweh's anger burns (*bāʿar*), and fire or burning is used as a means of punishment on the people. Mount Horeb was burning with fire (*bōʿēr bāʾēš*, Deut 4:11; 5:23; 9:15). Cf. Weyde, *Prophecy and Teaching*, 368. Weyde notes that the day of burning is probably a metonymy. The "day as an active force" of Yahweh's judgment is a late development in the idea of the day of Yahweh.

escape, since "all the arrogant" (*kol-zēdîm*) and "everyone who does wickedness" (*ʿōśê riśʿâ)* will be subjected to Yahweh's action.

The total annihilation of the wicked is signaled by the clause *wəhāyû . . . qaš,* denoting a time in the future when they will be "stubble" (*qaš*). The noun *qaš* is used in various contexts with fire as the destructive force—for example, Isa 5:24; 47:14; Obad 18; Joel 2:5 (cf. Exod 15:7).[559] Similarly, *qaš* is used with the wind as the destructive agent—for example, Isa 40:24; Jer 13:24; Ps 83:13 (MT 14); Job 13:25. Psalm 1:4 depicts the fate of the wicked as that of "chaff" (*mōṣ*) driven away by the wind. In all of its occurrences, stubble represents a nondurable, flimsy substance that is easily disposed. So rather than being a refining process, the day will be an annihilation process for the arrogant and wicked. Contrary to 3:15, which notes the prospect of the wicked escaping, here in 3:19 their future is to burn.

The temporal indicator "the coming day" (*hayyôm habbāʾ*) gives the time frame for God's response to the wicked: *and the coming day will set them ablaze.* This temporal indicator aligns with the indicator regarding the Deity's response to the Yahweh-fearers (3:17). "Them" (*ʾōtām*), the object of the verb *lihaṭ*, "to set ablaze,"[560] refers to the total population of the wicked and arrogant. What is Yahweh about to do to the wicked? Yahweh plans to consume them. Other instances of this imagery of using fire to destroy occur in the Old Testament.[561] For example:

> Through the wrath of the LORD of hosts the land was burned, and the people became like fuel for the fire; no one spared another. (Isa 9:19 [MT 18])

Similarly, Ps 83:13–15 (MT 14–16) speaks of destroying God's enemies using fire to consume the forest and flames to set ablaze (*lāhaṭ*) the mountains. God's response, whether imminent or remote, will address both the righteous and the wicked. Because of the delayed action, the wicked appear to have escaped judgment.

The metaphorical language continues, relating the total destruction—*that will leave to them neither root nor branches.* In several instances this imagery denotes nonexistence or the impossibility of rejuvenation. The presence of branches and grounded roots (*šōreš*) indicates the ability to bear fruit—survival

559. The noun *qaš* is also used with *ḥăšaš*, "chaff" (Isa 33:11); *ʿāpār*, "dust" (Isa 41:2). In these contexts, it signifies termination of existence. Other uses include Exod 5:12; Nah 1:10; Job 41:28–29.

560. The *piel* third masculine singular form of the verb *lāhaṭ*. Cf. Joel 1:19; 2:3.

561. Aune (*Revelation 17–22*, 1103) notes the frequency of fire as a motif for punishing the wicked in early Jewish and early Christian texts (e.g., CD II 5; 1QS II 7–8).

and hope (Isa 37:31; Ezek 17:8–9).[562] In contrast, withered roots and branches signal lack of survival, annihilation of the agents, and thus removal of the possibility for descendants (e.g., Job 18:16–21).[563] In Mal 4:1 (MT 3:19), being burned will cause an absence of roots and branches—the nonsurvival of the wicked and their descendants. Just as God will address the priests by humiliating and cursing their descendants (Mal 2:2–3), so God will obliterate the wicked.

(b) Those Who Fear the Name of Yahweh (4:2 [MT 3:20])

2 This verse continues the contrast between the fate of the wicked (3:19) and the fate of the righteous, "who fear my name" (*yirʾê šəmî*; cf. 3:16—"Yahweh-fearers," *yirʾê yhwh*).[564] Malachi 3:20 addresses the Yahweh-fearers in particular, using *lākem, for you.* The future actions on behalf of the righteous in 3:20 correspond with the Deity's response in the rest of the book of Malachi (cf. Ps 112:1).[565] Accordingly, the prophet notes that the priests despised (*bāzâ*) Yahweh's name (1:6) but that the name is great (*gādôl*) and is feared (*yārēʾ*) among the nations (Mal 1:11, 14). The actions are also consistent with Mal 2:2–3, where a curse will come on those who do not give glory to Yahweh's name. The exemplar Levi feared (*yārēʾ*) Yahweh's name (Mal 2:5). Those who fear Yahweh's name are characterized by both their actions and what happens to them. It is their fearing or reverencing of Yahweh that distinguishes them from the wicked and results in Yahweh's benevolence toward them.

Another element of the contrast is what will happen in the day of Yahweh—*so a sun of righteousness will rise for you.* The *sun of righteousness (šemeš ṣədāqâ)* is identified by its actions. First, the sun will rise (*zāraḥ*). *Zāraḥ* is typical Hebrew usage for the sun's appearance (e.g., Gen 32:31; Judg 9:33; 2 Sam 23:4; 2 Kgs 3:22; Jonah 4:8; Nah 3:17; Ps 104:22; Eccl 1:5).[566] The verb *zāraḥ* is also used in Mal 1:11 with the formulation "from the rising of the sun until its setting" to denote continuous activity (cf. Pss 50:1; 113:3; Isa 41:25).[567] The formulation "sun of righteousness," however, is unique to Mal 3:20. Nevertheless, some propose that the imagery of the leader as a solar luminary is not unique. The mode of the rising is depicted with reference to its wings—*healing in its wings (marpēʾ biknāpêhā).* The "healing" (*marpēʾ*) refers to the

562. Note other occurrences of the terms "roots" (*šōreš*) and "branches" (*ʿānāp*): Ps 80:9–10 (MT 10–11). In some instances, the "fruit" (*pərî*) and "roots" (*šōreš*) are used together to refer to vitality or the lack thereof (e.g., 2 Kgs 19:30; Amos 2:9). Cf. Hill, *Malachi,* 348.

563. Terms paired in Job 18:16 are "roots" (*šōreš*) and "branches" (*qaṣîr*).

564. To show the contrast, most translate the *waw* "but"—thus Hill, *Malachi,* 326; Verhoef, *Haggai and Malachi,* 327; modern versions: ASV, KJV, NRSV.

565. Cf. Ps 112:1, "Fortunate is the person who fears Yahweh" (*ʾašrê-ʾîš yārēʾ ʾet-yhwh*).

566. Also used of Yahweh (e.g., Deut 33:2; Isa 60:2).

567. See 3 Macc. 4:15 and Rev 7:2, "rising of the sun."

wings' restorative effect.[568] The healing addresses diseases, disasters, brokenness, and anything that distracts from wholeness. Thus, despair is manifested by lack of healing (cf. Jer 14:19; Prov 6:14–15; 2 Chr 21:18; 36:16). Healing, however, is manifested by prosperity and security (Isa 19:22; 57:18; Jer 30:17; 33:6).[569] The imagery of the sun seems to belong to the Near Eastern "description of the winged sun disk,"[570] which brings to mind the royal figure of the king as the protector of right order and justice (cf. Ps 72).[571] Even so, various Old Testament images of Yahweh as the sun might more readily facilitate our understanding of "sun of righteousness" here in Mal 3:20. For example, in Ps 84:11 (MT 12), Yahweh is *šemeš ûmāgēn*, "sun and shield":

> For the Lord God is a sun and shield; he bestows favor and honor. No good thing does the Lord withhold from those who walk uprightly. (Ps 84:11[12] NRSV)

In Isa 60:19–20 Yahweh will be the people's light so that they have no need for the sun; Yahweh will be their sun.[572]

The wing (*kānāp*) as a place of refuge referring to Yahweh's protection also portrays a clear picture of Yahweh's future acts on behalf of Yahweh-fearers (cf. Pss 17:8; 36:7 [MT 8]; 57:1 [MT 2]; 61:4 [MT 5]; 63:7 [MT 8]; 91:4; Ruth 2:12).[573] Accordingly, one might consider Yahweh to be the sun and the protective imagery as being manifested in healing and restoration.[574] God

568. The occurrences of *marpē'* include Prov 4:22; 12:18; 13:17; 14:30; 16:24; 29:1. The verb *rāpā'*, "to heal," also appears in Gen 20:17.

569. Also note other uses of the verb to denote the removal of various forms of adversity—e.g.: Hos 6:1; 11:3; Pss 6:2 (MT 3); 30:2 (MT 3); 41:4 (MT 5); 107:20; 2 Chr 7:14; 30:20 (cf. Jer 3:22; Hos 14:4).

570. Verhoef, *Haggai and Malachi,* 329–30; Weyde, *Prophecy and Teaching,* 372–74. Note Weyde's discussion about interpretations of the "sun" imagery, including his bibliography; for example, see Mark S. Smith, *The Early History of God: Yahweh and the Other Deities in Ancient Israel* (San Francisco: Harper & Row, 1990), 115–25; J. G. Taylor, *Yahweh and the Sun: Biblical Archaeological Evidence for Sun Worship in Ancient Israel,* JSOTSup 111 (Sheffield: Sheffield Academic, 1993), 212–16.

571. M. S. Smith, *The Early History of God,* 118–19.

572. Some see a connection with the imagery of "shining forth"—thus Verhoef (*Haggai and Malachi,* 328), the righteous shine forth (e.g., Isa 58:8; Ps 37:6). Similarly, R. L. Smith (*Micah–Malachi,* 339) argues that "the rays of the sun must be behind the expression in the priestly blessing" in Num 6:24–26, "make his face to shine upon you."

573. The noun *kānāp* is also used of a skirt or the fold of a garment—e.g., 1 Sam 15:27; 24:11; Hag 2:12; Ezek 16:8. Note Verhoef's (*Haggai and Malachi,* 331) discussion of the interpretation of *kānāp* as edge of the garment.

574. For consideration, see Taylor, *Yahweh and the Sun,* 211–16; Weyde, *Prophecy and Teaching,* 373–74; Hill, *Malachi,* 350–51.

both heals and devastates, depending on the circumstances and the people involved (Deut 32:39; Isa 19:22; Job 5:18). Here in Mal 4:2 (MT 3:20), healing is not for all but for those who fear Yahweh.

The rising of a "sun of righteousness" on behalf of the God-fearers will result in their vitality: *and you will go forth and prance about like fatted calves.* The benefactors of the sun of righteousness will be alive and hopeful. They will not suffer under the weight of adversity but will be vital. They will "go out" (*yāṣāʾ*) and "prance about" (*pûš*). Also used of calves in Jer 50:11, the Hebrew word *pûš* denotes carefree existence and playfulness, rather than subduing another being (cf. Hab 1:8).[575] In Mal 3:20 the Yahweh-fearers will be like young, lively calves (*ʿēgel*). Elsewhere, the noun *ʿēgel* (singular or plural), "calf/calves," is modified by *marbēq* (fatted or stall) to characterize them as "fatted" (1 Sam 28:24; Jer 46:21).[576] In Amos 6:4, the plural form *ʿăgālîm*, "calves," occurs in parallelism with lambs from the flock, suggesting that *marbēq* has the meaning of "stall."[577] In Mal 4:2 (MT 3:20), the language of fatted calves connotes the vitality of the calves and their freedom.

(c) The Wicked (4:3 [MT 3:21])

3 Those who fear Yahweh will subdue the "wicked" (*rəšāʿîm*), a dominance represented as trampling (*ʿāsas*), which is also the language used for the way the underprivileged are treated (Amos 2:7).[578] The Yahweh-fearers will be the instruments of Yahweh's judgment.[579] Additionally, the Yahweh-fearers' action of subduing the wicked will make the wicked "ashes" (*ʾēper*) under their "feet" (*raglêkem*).[580] Both the image of ashes and the location beneath their feet convey insignificance; the wicked are a nonthreat. Their status as ashes follows from their being burned (3:19) and conveys that they are only residual, without any vitality, much like the stubble that is subjected to fire (cf. Ezek 28:18).[581]

So, whereas the God-fearers are enlivened and thrive, the wicked are

575. Contrast Mal 4:5 (MT 3:23), with its image of Yahweh subduing the nations.

576. The singular *ʿēgel-marbēq* occurs in 1 Sam 28:24. The singular *ʿēgel*, "calf," is used figuratively of a nation (Jer 46:20; Hos 10:11).

577. Most interpret *marbēq* as "stall": e.g., Verhoef, *Haggai and Malachi*, 331–32; modern versions: see the ASV, KJV, NRSV. Contrast Hill (*Malachi*, 353), "stall-fed calves"; R. L. Smith (*Micah–Malachi*, 336), "fatted calves."

578. Amost 2:7 uses *šāʾap*, "to trample."

579. Cf. Hill, *Malachi*, 353.

580. Underfoot as a place of submission and inconsequence: Job 39:15; Pss 68:30 (MT 31); 91:13; Isa 14:25; cf. Matt 7:6.

581. The noun also occurs in Gen 18:27; Job 30:19; and 42:6. It is also used in contexts signifying the activities associated with mourning rituals (Jer 6:26; Ezek 27:30; Lam 3:16) or supplication (Isa 58:5; Esth 4:1, 3; Dan 9:3, Jonah 3:6; Job 2:8).

subdued and annihilated. Such images of the fates of the righteous and the wicked signify that the God of justice is attentive to the community, and individuals who perceive the wicked as enduring or even thriving are mistaken. The depiction likewise suggests that the vantage point from which one views the wicked determines one's understanding. This image portrays the ideal that will be realized on the day when Yahweh acts (cf. Mal 3:17). The righteous will have their triumph at the demise of the wicked; however, such triumph must come with destruction. Accordingly, the day of Yahweh does not offer all-inclusive hope for the community. Some will be destroyed, while others will be blessed. Who could rejoice in anticipation of that dreadful day? Since the text focuses on the future realization of the demise of the wicked, it leaves the present open for interpretation. The rejoicing could be that at least for a while the terrible day is unrealized. The unit closes with the picture of the dreadful day even for the righteous, who in that "day" (*bayyôm*) will be God's tool of destruction.

(2) Prescription regarding Averting Judgment (4:4–6 [MT 3:22–24])

4:4 (3:22) *"Remember the Torah of Moses, my servant, which I commanded him at Horeb concerning all of Israel, precepts and ordinances.* 4:5 (3:23)*See! I am sending to you Elijah, the prophet, before the coming of the day of Yahweh—the great and dreadful [day].* 4:6 (3:24)*Then he will turn the heart of fathers to [their] children and the heart of children to their fathers, lest I come and smite the land with a ban."*

Malachi 4:4–6 (MT 3:22–24) is an integral part of the book's perspective. It functions as a preventive measure to address the possibility of Yahweh's cursing the land for its disobedience (dishonoring Yahweh) and holds out the possibility of Yahweh's averting the curse because of the people's repentance.[582] As compared with the preceding unit (3:17–21)—which uses *bayyôm 'ăšer 'ănî 'ōśê*, "day when I act"—4:4–6 (MT 3:22–24) uses *yôm yhwh* to denote the day of Yahweh. The unit continues the idea of the messenger (cf. 3:1), naming the messenger and his specific role.[583]

(a) Prescription: Call to Remembrance—Law of Moses (4:4 [MT 3:22])

4 In light of the future pictured for the wicked and the righteous, the community is admonished to adhere to the covenant stipulations. The call to remem-

582. This is not simply an editorial addition or an appendix to the book of Malachi and the Book of the Twelve.

583. Cf. R. L. Smith, *Micah-Malachi,* 341. Smith sees a shift in the role in that Elijah, the messenger, is assigned the task of turning the people back to God.

ber (*zākar*) reflects the concerns of the book of Deuteronomy (e.g., 5:15; 7:18; 8:2, 18; 9:7; 15:5; 24:9; 32:7).[584] The verb *zākar* is used in Deuteronomy and elsewhere in the Torah story to remind the people of Yahweh's benevolence on their behalf. The reminder serves as a motivation to obey or to conform to Yahweh's expectations (Deut 24:18–22; Isa 46:9; Mic 6:5; cf. Isa 44:21).[585]

> Remember that you were a slave in Egypt, and diligently observe these statutes. (Deut 16:12; cf. 5:15; 15:15)

The collective memory is important for the identity and behavior of the community because it sets the parameters for good behavior, warns against bad behavior (Num 15:39–40; Deut 8:2; 9:7, 27–28; 24:9; cf. 11:2), and defines the relationship with other nations (Deut 7:17–18; 25:17). To "remember" in these instances means actively to employ the memory in decision-making and life practices, not simply to hold a piece of information in mind.

Here Mal 4:4 (MT 3:22) admonishes the people to recall the *Torah of Moses* (*tôrat mōšê*). The laws and statutes have a vital part when the book of Malachi is speaking about the community's responsibility for its behavior. The Torah/law of Moses refers to the specific commandments that Moses wrote or copied and attempted to maintain. Elsewhere the law is also referred to as the book of the law of Moses (*sēper tôrat mōšê*—Josh 8:31; 23:6; 2 Kgs 14:6; Neh. 8:1). In Mal 2:8 the deviant priests mislead the people, so they do not walk in the way of Yahweh. In other instances, deviation from the way indicates disregard for Torah or the law of Moses (cf. Dan 9:11–13). Keeping the law will result in prosperity (1 Kgs 2:3) or at least avoiding punishment. Here in Mal 4:4 (MT 3:22), the community is called to remember Moses, and the identity of Moses is his role in relationship to the community.

Moses's identity is first designated in relation to Yahweh: "Moses my servant" (*mōšê ʿabdî*).[586] He is no stranger to Yahweh; rather, he mediated the covenant with the people. God trusted Moses and reminded the people of the command that Moses "commanded" (*ṣāwâ*) or charged them.[587]

584. Floyd (*Minor Prophets 2,* 624) notes that the book of remembrance includes Deuteronomy (e.g., Deut 5:2–3).

585. Several times in Ezekiel, *zākar* as the act of remembering is the catalyst for further behavior, including self-loathing for the evil committed (Ezek 20:43; 36:31) and being silent out of shame (Ezek 16:63). Cf. Ps 105:5.

586. Other occurrences of the designation "my servant Moses" (*ʿabdî mōšê*) include Num 12:7, 8; Josh 1:2, 7; 2 Kgs 21:8. Note Zerubbabel as Yahweh's servant in Hag 2:23.

587. Several passages speak of Moses's coming to the people or a subgroup of the people, reiterating the laws as they applied to various situations, e.g., Exod 16:24; Num. 34:13; Deut. 31:10, 25; Josh 8:35; 11:15 (cf. Matt 8:4; Mark 1:44; Luke 5:14; John 8:5).

The second marker of Moses's identity is the command Yahweh gave him, including the location, Horeb—*which I commanded him at Horeb*. Yahweh commanded (*ṣāwâ*) Moses concerning the law, thus entrusting him with the task of communicating, safeguarding, and preserving the integrity of the law.[588] The clause—*which I commanded him* (e.g., NIV, NRSV)[589]—modifies the law of Moses, and Horeb designates the place where Moses encountered God and received the law (Exod 3:1; Deut 1:6, 19; 4:10, 15; 5:2; 9:8; 18:16; 29:1 [MT 28:69]).[590] The location is also designated as Sinai (Exod 19:11, 18, 20, 23; 24:16; 31:18; 34:2, 4, 29, 32; Lev 7:38; 25:1–2; Num 3:1, 14; 9:1).[591] The traditions use both names for the place where the law was received.

Coming from Yahweh, the law that Moses commanded also designates the law given to Israel by God (e.g., Josh 1:7; 2 Kgs 21:8). Moses received the law for the larger community, not simply for himself or the religious personnel. Accordingly, the recipients are *all of Israel* (*kol-yiśrāʾēl*), referring most likely to the covenant community. "All of Israel" could refer to the nation, those who according to Exod 19 and 24 were present when God communicated the law to Moses, or to the covenant community, including the descendants and various generations or groups within the covenant community. In reviewing the law, Moses refers to "all of Israel," indicating the entire community (Deut 5:1).[592]

588. The execution of the instruction as Yahweh commanded Moses was crucial to establishing the cult (e.g., Exod 39–40; Lev 7:38; 8:9, 13, 17, 21, 29; 9:10; Num 9:5) and to maintaining a godly way of life and community practices (e.g., Lev 24:23; Num 2:33–34; 27:11; 30:16; 31:7; 2 Kgs 18:6).

589. Other instances of *ṣāwâ* in an *ʾăšer* clause, including a person as object, are noted: Judg 2:20; 2 Kgs 17:13; cf. 1 Sam 2:29. Usually these objects are in the form of a pronominal suffix (Exod 32:8; Deut 9:12; Judg 13:14; Jer 13:6). Glazier-McDonald (*Malachi: The Divine Messenger,* 250) "understands *ʾôtô* reflexively in conjunction with *ʾăšer*." She reads, "which I commanded him"—thus Verhoef, *Haggai and Malachi,* 337; R. L. Smith, *Micah-Malachi,* 340. In contrast, Hill (*Malachi,* 367) interprets *ṣāwâ* with the double object—the person Moses (*ʾôtô*) and the things, statutes, and ordinances (*ḥuqqîm ûmišpāṭîm*). This accounts for the masculine *ʾôtô* and the feminine (*tôrâ*). Thus, he reads, "Moses my servant, whom I commanded at Horeb."

590. Horeb as the location where God gave the law is also mentioned outside the Pentateuch: e.g., in 1 Kgs 8:9//2 Chr 5:10. It is also remembered as the place of apostasy: e.g., Ps 106:19. Horeb and Sinai occur together in Sir 48:7. Cf. Verhoef, *Haggai and Malachi,* 338–39.

591. Sinai also occurs in Deut 33:2, 16. Outside the Pentateuch, references to Sinai include Judg 5:5; Neh 9:13 (cf. Ps 68:8, 17 [MT 9, 18]).

592. See Verhoef (*Haggai and Malachi,* 339), who posits that the reference is to all strata of the community. Deuteronomy 29:1 (MT 28:69) distinguishes between the law commanded at Horeb and that commanded in the land of Moab. The latter "words" were added to the covenant made at Horeb.

The law commanded to Moses is specified as the *precepts and ordinances* (*ḥuqqîm ûmišpāṭîm*; Exod 24:3).[593]

> These are the statutes and ordinances and laws that the LORD established between himself and the people of Israel on Mount Sinai through Moses. (Lev 26:46 NRSV)[594]

When admonishing the people to remember the law, the book of Malachi reminds the people that they too are under obligation to the law because of the scope of its recipients.

(b) Expansion: Yahweh's Provision—Elijah the Promised Prophet (4:5–6 [MT 3:23–24])

The other part of the subunit 3:22–24 promises to send a prophet, Elijah, who will precede the day of Yahweh (4:5–6 [MT 3:23–24]). In mentioning the prophet and his coming, 4:5 (MT 3:23) echoes 3:2–4 and relates the time of the coming to the day of Yahweh and the activity of the prophet to the parent-child relationship. Finally, 4:6 (MT 3:24) announces the purpose of this prophet: to eliminate Yahweh's curse on the land. Even so, the competing image of the curse already active in the land persists (Mal 2:2–3; 3:9), offering the perspective that, even if the prophet succeeds, the land already under the curse will have to endure adversity until the effects of the curse dissipate.

(i) Announcement of the Prophet's Coming (4:5 [MT 3:23])

5 Yahweh announces the intent to send Elijah the prophet, an announcement with several features. First, the announcement includes the prospect of sending and then the identity of the one who is sent. Next, the further clarification of the timing is significant to the function of Elijah as a preparatory agent for the day of Yahweh. Finally, it raises questions about the identity of the messenger in 3:1 and Elijah in 4:5 (MT 3:23) in light of their depictions as forerunners.

The announcement, *See! I am sending to you Elijah, the prophet*, echoes Mal 3:1, where Yahweh announces the intent to send "my messenger" (*mal'ākî*) without naming the messenger. That context highlights the messenger's ac-

593. The designation *ḥuqqîm ûmišpāṭîm* or a similar form occurs throughout the Pentateuch—e.g., Lev 26:46; Deut 4:1, 5, 8, 14, 45; 5:1; 11:32; 12:1; 26:16 (cf. Josh 24:25; Ezra 7:10; Ps 147:19).

594. Cf. Josh 1:13.

tivities and effects.[595] Malachi 4:5 (MT 3:23) also identifies the intended recipients by using *lākem* (preposition plus the masculine plural suffix), and the agent who will be sent is identified by name, Elijah (*ʾēliyyâ*).[596] Elijah in Mal 4:5 (MT 3:23) is further designated by his role: "the prophet" (*hannābîʾ*; cf. 1 Kgs 18:36; 2 Chr 21:12, *ʾēliyyāhû hannābîʾ*). The most common form of the name in 1 Kgs 17–2 Kgs 2 is *ʾēliyyāhû* without an appositive (neither "the prophet" nor "the Tishbite").[597] Elsewhere the prophet is designated Elijah the Tishbite (*ʾēliyyāhû hattišbî*—e.g., 1 Kgs 17:1; 21:17, 28).[598] One can observe several characteristics of Elijah in the Kings' narrative, the most important being that he ascended into the heavens. In 2 Kgs 9:36, Elijah is identified as Yahweh's servant, his servant, and Elijah the Tishbite (*ʿabdô ʾēliyyāhû hattišbî*; cf. Moses his servant, Mal 4:4 [MT 3:22]). In Malachi, Elijah is the prophet who will precede the day of Yahweh and, consistent with other prophets, may represent Yahweh's intention to the people, including the announcement of judgment. In Deut 18:15, Moses is the ideal prophet, but here in Mal 4:5 (MT 3:23), Elijah is the ideal.[599] In mentioning both figures, the text may signal the connection between their functions—one as the law-giver and one as the voice of Yahweh to a sinful people who have broken the law.

Along with the recipients, the sending is further qualified by the time frame, *before the coming of the day of Yahweh.* The temporal indicator is formed by *lipnê* plus the verb *bôʾ* (to come) plus *yôm* (day). The action of sending will be prior to *(lipnê) the . . . day of Yahweh (lipnê bôʾ yôm yhwh),* as compared with Mal 3:1, where the action is qualified in relation to Yahweh, *before* Yahweh (*me—ləpānāy*). While the formulation manifests an eschatological framework for the depicted actions or events, that time frame is remote but not necessarily at the ultimate end of time.[600] As in Mal 3:1–2 and in other instances of the concept, "the day" lies in the future, even though the signs and preparation for that day are manifested now.

Several prophets share the concept of the day of Yahweh, which includes several characteristics, such as the description *great and dreadful (haggādôl wəhannôrāʾ;* cf. Joel 2:31 [MT 3:4]).[601] In both Malachi and Joel, signs precede the coming of the day, including the forerunner (Mal 4:5 [MT 3:23]),

595. See the discussion of Mal 3:1–4 above.

596. Cf. 2 Kgs 1:3, 8 (*ʾēliyyâ hattišbî*) and 2 Kgs 1:4, 12; 1 Chr 8:27; Ezra 10:21, 26 (*ʾēliyyâ*).

597. E.g., 1 Kgs 17:13, 15; 18:1, 15, 25; 19:1; 2 Kgs 1:15, without the appositive "the prophet" or "the Tishbite."

598. The LXX includes *ton thesbiten,* "the Tishbite," possibly recalling *ʾēliyyahû hattišbî.*

599. Cf. Petersen, *Zechariah 9–14 and Malachi,* 230 n. 118.

600. Cf. Hill, *Malachi,* 376.

601. See. the use of the expression in Deut 8:15 (of the land) and 1 Chr 17:21 (of Israel's reputation/name).

the outpouring of God's spirit, and the upheaval in nature (cf. Joel 2:28–32 [MT 3:1–5]).[602] In its various manifestations in the prophetic texts, the day of Yahweh is not a day to anticipate, because it will be a day of judgment rather than of blessing and celebration (Isa 13:6, 9; Jer 46:10; Amos 5:18, 20).[603] That day is inescapable, all-encompassing, and imminent (Obad 15; Joel 1:15; 2:1–11; 3:14 [MT 4:14]; Zeph 1:7, 14).[604]

This concept also raises questions concerning the presence of God. Is the Deity more present during the day of Yahweh than at other times? The difference between the day of Yahweh and other times may be the nature of the Deity's presence. This concept also challenges the idea that the divine presence ensures blessing and security. The fact that the day lies in the future demonstrates the difference between the anticipated and the actualized, the vision and the reality. Malachi's and Joel's representations of the day of Yahweh differ from others' in having a preparatory stage before the depicted reality. Hill argues that the experience of Persian domination resulted in the restoration community's need for nationalistic hope. Part of that hope involved grounding themselves in their traditions, including "the Second Temple, the priesthood, and the Torah of Moses."[605]

The role of the prophet includes disclosing to the community the intent of the Deity according to the message that the Deity gave the prophets. Israel rejected the prophets and continued to break the commandments (2 Kgs 17:13).[606] Similarly 2 Chr 36:15–16 reports the failure of Yahweh's effort through the messengers/prophets:

> The Lord, the God of their ancestors, sent persistently to them by his *messengers,* because he had compassion on his people and on his dwelling place; but they kept *mocking the messengers of God*, despising his words,

602. Cf. Glazier-McDonald, *Malachi: The Divine Messenger,* 264–65.

603. R. E. Clements, *Prophecy and Covenant,* SBT 43 (London: SCM, 1969), 109–10. Clements argues that Amos's proclamations regarding the day of Yahweh diverge from the cultic expectations of a festive day and focus on the judgment, disaster, and possible "dissolution of the covenant." Carroll (*When Prophecy Failed,* 171–27), recognizing the transformation of the tradition (Ezek 7:5–9; Amos 5:18; Zeph 1:7, 14), argues that the tradition is ambiguous and thus allows for dissonance. Is the day coming, has it come, or is it near (Joel 1:15; 2:1)? The ambiguity may have served the prophets in delivering their prophecy. Any delay would have been perceived as a failure, so the ambiguous language may have allowed for interpretation about the onset of the actualization.

604. Joel 2:31 (MT 3:4) speaks of events that will precede the day of Yahweh: "The sun shall be turned to darkness and the moon to blood, before the great and terrible day of the Lord comes."

605. Hill, *Malachi,* 385.

606. Cf. 2 Kgs 24:2; 2 Chr 24:19; Jer 7:25; 25:4; 29:19; 35:15; 44:4.

> and *scoffing at his prophets*, until the wrath of the Lord against his people became so great that there was no remedy. (2 Chr 36:15–16 NRSV)[607]

"Messenger" and "prophet" designate the role of being responsible for conveying the message of repentance to God's people.

Having investigated the occurrences of Elijah's name and function as a preparatory agent for the day of Yahweh, we have only two questions remaining with regard to his identity: Is he the same as the messenger in Mal 3:1? Who is he? Regarding whether the messenger and Elijah are the same, one proposal is that the messenger in 3:1 and Elijah are two different agents, though they both function as forerunners. In this interpretation, they are different figures and preparatory agents for different events.[608] The messenger (3:1) may be the forerunner John the Baptist, and Elijah (4:5 [MT 3:23]) may be the forerunner of Christ's second coming.[609] Or the messenger may be an angel,[610] and the prophet may be Elijah himself.

Another proposal regarding the identity of this figure is that the messenger and Elijah are the same agent.[611] This leaves the question, who is Elijah? The proposals include Elijah himself,[612] John the Baptist,[613] and one in the tradition of Elijah who exemplifies the spirit and purpose of Elijah.[614] This is my interpretation: the messenger and Elijah are the same; both anticipate and prepare for Yahweh's coming.

Along with the identity of Elijah within the text and beyond comes the juxtaposition of the figures Moses and Elijah in Mal 4:4–5 (MT 3:22–23). Notably, the similarity of these two figures and the representation of Elijah as a Mosaic prophet in the 1 Kgs 17–19 context bolster the prophet's reputation and elevate him above other prophets.[615] The similarities include the theophany on Mount Horeb, each associated with the apostasy of the peo-

607. Cf. Jer 35:15.

608. Weyde (*Prophecy and Teaching*, 392–93) argues that they exemplify different tasks: the messenger will restore the sacrificial cult by purifying the descendants of Levi; Elijah will address the impending judgment of God on the community.

609. Verhoef (*Haggai and Malachi*, 340) surveys the perspectives, including those noted above. Cf. Hill, *Malachi*, 383.

610. Cf. Floyd, *Minor Prophets 2*, 619.

611. Hill, *Malachi*, 383; Petersen, *Zechariah 9–14 and Malachi*, 230; Lescow, *Das Buch Maleachi*, 172; Glazier-McDonald, *Malachi: The Divine Messenger*, 263.

612. Weyde, *Prophecy and Teaching*, 392. The New Testament attests the figure of Elijah—see Matt 17:10–11; Luke 1:17; John 1:21; and the Matt 17:12 figure—"but I tell you that Elijah has already come, and they did not recognize him, but they did to him whatever they pleased. So also the Son of Man is about to suffer at their hands."

613. Verhoef, *Haggai and Malachi*.

614. Hill, *Malachi*, 383.

615. Wilson, *Prophecy and Society*, 198–99.

ple.[616] Moses on Horeb receives the law and returns there after the people's apostasy, intercedes for the people, experiences a theophany, and receives the new copy of the law (Exod 32–34).[617]

After denouncing the idolatrous practices of the populace and killing the Baal prophets, Elijah flees to Horeb, haunted by the perception of being alone in his loyalty to Yahweh. There he receives confirmation from Yahweh and learns of the support of people who had not followed Baal (1 Kgs 19:9–18).[618] In both instances, the experience at Horeb is marked by reception of the Deity's instructions and reassurance. Both leaders are set apart from others as God's intermediary to the people. Like Moses, Elijah is an intermediary between God and the people and uses the law as the basis of his critique of the community for breaking Yahweh's covenant by following other gods (1 Kgs 19:10). Malachi 4:4–5 (MT 3:22–23) alludes to both traditions as reminders of the instruments of God's covenant—the law (Moses) and the prophet (Elijah)[619]—affirmations of the message of Yahweh to the people to obey Yahweh.

(ii) Purpose of the Coming (4:6 [MT 3:24])

6 The action of Elijah the prophet is articulated along with the rationale for that action. First, regarding the action, the presumed subject of the verb (*wəhēšîb*) is Elijah.[620] The action is taken toward parents and children—the intergenerational aspect of the community. Each will be "turned" to the other. But what does that mean? Perhaps a reconciliation is in mind.[621] As in other texts, such as Jeremiah, the purpose for sending the prophet to the community

616. Wilson (*Prophecy and Society,* 198) sees Elijah as part of the Ephraimite tradition of prophets. He does not place Malachi in this tradition but sees him as being influenced by both the Judean and the Ephraimite traditions, in which Elijah exhibits signs of being either a central intermediary or a peripheral figure who harshly critiques the priesthood (p. 290).

617. Durham, *Exodus*; Childs, *Exodus,* 586, 589. Cf. G. Rice, *Nations under God: A Commentary on the Book of 1 Kings,* ITC (Grand Rapids: Eerdmans, 1990), 59–60.

618. B. O. Long, *1 Kings: With an Introduction to Historical Literature,* FOTL 9 (Grand Rapids: Eerdmans, 1984), 198–99; Rice, *Nations under God,* 156–61. J. Gray (*1 and II Kings: A Commentary* [Philadelphia: Westminster, 1963], 363, 365) notes similarities between Elijah's and Moses's experiences. He also argues that the theophany in Ezek 19 was intended to teach the prophet not to expect the supernatural but instead the practical means by which the Deity works—despite the violent measures taken against the prophets of Baal on Mount Carmel.

619. Cf. Vuilleumier, "Malachie," 253.

620. The *hiphil* third masculine singular form of the verb *šûb,* "to return."

621. Contrast Ezek 5:10, "Surely, parents shall eat their children in your midst, and children shall eat their parents; I will execute judgments on you, and any of you who survive I will scatter to every wind."

is articulated but not actualized.[622] Elijah is both the same as and different from the other prophets. He is the same in that he also is sent (*šālaḥ*) to the people with a message. Notably, the prophets' effectiveness in turning the people from their sins does not depend on their being sent. In fact, the prophets attest the failure of their message to bring about reform or repentance. Thus,

> I have *sent* to you all my *servants the prophets*, sending them persistently, saying, "Turn now everyone of you from your evil way, and amend your doings, and do not go after other gods to serve them, and then you shall live in the land that I gave to you and your ancestors." But you did not incline your ear or obey me. (Jer 35:15 NRSV)[623]

However, we can also observe that delivering the message and influencing the people to reform constitute different measures of success. Elijah differs from other prophets in that he ascended to heaven without experiencing death. In essence, he is a "super" prophet. If anyone could effect a transformation of the community, surely it would be Elijah. He influenced his community to return to worshiping Yahweh and to abandon Baal worship. Malachi 4:6 (MT 3:24) thus does not anticipate the physical person of Elijah to reappear and again warn the community to repent, but it expects someone with the spirit and effectiveness of Elijah to precede the day of Yahweh's judgment.[624]

The descriptions of his actions and their prospective consequences clarify this second Elijah's purpose. Furthermore, the action and its counterpart use the verb *hēšîb*, "to turn,"[625] with the direct object *lēb*, "heart," of the fathers and the sons. Interestingly, this depiction works in much the same way as the effect of the exemplar Levi (Mal 2:6–7), who "turns" (*hēšîb*) the community from iniquity. Likewise, the prophets seek to return (*šûb*) the people to Yahweh. The verb in these instances is used of changing the course of the people's actions so that their behavior is transformed—from disobedience to obedience (Ezek 14:6; 18:21), from going away from (*sûr*) Yahweh to returning to (*šûb*) Yahweh (Mal 3:7).[626]

622. Cf. David Petersen, *Late Israelite Prophecy: Studies in Deutero-Prophetic Literature and in Chronicles,* SBLMS 23 (Missoula, MT: Scholars Press, 1977), 44.

623. Cf. 2 Chr 36:15–16. Carroll (*When Prophecy Failed,* 196–99) argues that in evaluating the failure of prophecy one must consider that perhaps there is more to the lack of turning back to Yahweh than the people's resistance. Perhaps the "deity's deceiving the people using the prophets, is part of the picture (e.g., Jer 7:31; Ezek 20:25, 26)."

624. Petersen, *Late Israelite Prophecy,* 44.

625. The *hiphil* third masculine singular form *šûb*, "to turn." The Vulgate reads *convertet.*

626. Compare other instances when the people are admonished to return to Yahweh (Jer 4:1–4; Ezek 18:32; 33:11; Joel 2:12; Zech 1:3) or to turn from their evil ways (Jer 18:11; 25:5; 35:15; 36:3, 7; 44:5; Ezek 3:19, 20; 33:9; Jonah 3:8); or they are characterized as not

Here Mal 4:6 (MT 3:24) signals a change not with regard to Yahweh but regarding the human agents: fathers (*ʾābôt*) and sons (*bānîm*). What does it mean to turn the heart (*lēb*) to another person? Both Jeremiah and Ezekiel use the image of transforming the heart as leading to behavioral changes. Thus Jer 24:7 proposes giving the people a heart to know Yahweh. Ezekiel 11:19–21 speaks of removing a heart of stone—the stubborn tendencies of the people—and replacing it with a heart of flesh to indicate the inner transformation implanted by Yahweh (cf. Ezek 36:26). Other texts regard the heart as the source of fearing God (Jer 32:39, 40), of idolatry (Ezek 14:3–7), and of resistance to Yahweh. Likewise, the oneness of the community in its adherence to Yahweh is indicated by the heart transformation—in this case, one heart (Ezek 11:19; Jer 32:39).[627]

Malachi 4:6 (MT 3:24) does not illustrate the turning with reference to the law and replacement of the heart, but by the heart of human agents in relation to each other. Presupposing the context of the restoration community and intermarriage in particular, some scholars have proposed that Elijah's task is to address the family disruptions and influence reconciliation and social transformation. In this interpretation, Elijah's actions form part of the larger eschatological effort to transform the social order by achieving intergenerational harmony. In particular, the effort seeks to correct the sins of the descendants, who have intermarried and thus deviated from the ancestors' covenant with Yahweh.[628] However, one need not assume intermarriage as the basis of the discord; it may be symptomatic of the disintegrating society. Note that family disruption and social disorder abound when abuses pervade a society (Mic 7:1–7).[629] A similar vision of familial discord is depicted in Ezek 5:10. More fitting is the understanding that Yahweh's judgment or curse on a society results in the breakdown of the society—and of the family, in particular (Exod 20:5–6).

The second interpretation, and the one I favor in this discussion, also recognizes familial discord as characteristic of the disintegration of a society. This perspective does not necessarily focus on the intermarriage depicted in Ezra, although intermarriage may be a factor. Instead, the focal point is the relationships within the covenant community. Malachi readily shows the intergenerational or transgenerational connections as the basis for the critique and thus stands with others in their critique of the community's behavior—ei-

---

returning to Yahweh (Jer 3:1–10; 15:7; Amos 4:6–11; Hos 11:5; Hag 2:17); or the return is seen as a transformative process (Jer 24:7). The transformation may also be from righteousness to wickedness (Ezek 18:24, 26; 33:18; cf. Hos 7:16).

627. The concept of one heart (*lēb ʾeḥād*) as indicating unified action appears in 2 Chr 30:12. Here also God gives the community one heart to follow what God commands.

628. Hill, *Malachi*, 387–89.

629. Jacobs, *Conceptual Coherence.*

ther the community has abandoned the ways of the ancestors and gone astray, or the community is following the evil ways of the ancestors and is disobeying (Mal 3:7). The evil of the ancestors impacts their descendants (Ezek 20:18). Malachi looks at the deviation from Yahweh's ways without making any effort to analyze the ancestors' obedience. The ancestors themselves are the exemplar (Mal 3:4). In Mal 4:6 (MT 3:24) the ancestors refer not so much to the immediate living, physical family members as to the transgenerational dimension—the ancestors and their descendants—the continuity between the past and present generations. As exemplars, the ancestors received and affirmed the covenant, but the descendants polluted the covenant. Malachi's tendency to hold up the past as the ideal surfaces again in this presentation of Elijah's purpose.

The turning of the ancestors and descendants conveys the father's receptivity to the children in passing on the legacy, while the children's turning to the father denotes their receiving the legacy. The crucial exchange may explain the representation of both sides. That reciprocity allows for failure on the part of Elijah. Success would mean that the interchange happens and that the descendants hear and affirm, receive and obey the law. To receive and not obey the covenant would be tantamount to failure. One should note the possible aversion of the descendants toward their ancestors because the ancestors' deeds led to the descendants' demise. So why would the descendants want to embrace their ancestors? Again, Malachi appeals to the ideal rather than the particulars of the past.

Why punish the land for the lack of transformation among the people? *Lest I come and smite the land with a ban.* The connection to Yahweh is noted as the contingency signaled by the particle *pen*, "lest."[630] It introduces two prospective actions of the Deity—the coming and the striking, the latter dependent on the former. Even so, the significance of *pen* in the transition to the final clause in the book of Malachi is multivalent, yielding at least two interpretive options, the issue of whether Yahweh comes and the issue of Elijah's success. Some argue that the coming is certain and that the issue is Yahweh's striking the land as the contrary action to Elijah's lack of success.[631] In favor of the suggestion that the particle *pen* introduces the prospect of failure to accomplish the action,[632] some argue that the issue is not the coming of Yahweh but, rather, the action taken upon Yahweh's arrival. In this interpretation,

630. The significance of the particle is noted in the representation of contingencies: if one condition is not met or does not exist, then a particular event is triggered; usually judgment follows the lack of reform or repentance. Cf. Jer 6:8; 21:12; Hos 2:3–4 (MT 4–5); Amos 5:6. A similar pattern occurs in Psalms and Proverbs, usually indicating demise as the contingency, e.g., Pss 13:3 (MT 4); 28:1; 50:22; Prov 25:7–10; 30:5–6.

631. Verhoef, *Haggai and Malachi,* 343.

632. GKC §107q; *IBHS* §31.6.1c.

both Yahweh and Elijah will come. Elijah's coming and success would avert the punitive effect of Yahweh's presence. Even so, one must wonder, if the judgment is averted, what then would be the purpose of Yahweh's coming? It is this question that leads one to consider the possibility of another option.

Some argue that *pen* introduces the conditions for Yahweh's coming: if Elijah comes, Yahweh will not.[633] If Elijah does not come, Yahweh will come in judgment. This interpretation has the further nuance that Yahweh desires to provide the opportunity for repentance so as not to punish. Since coming would bring punishment, Yahweh hesitates and will send Elijah (cf. Ezek 18:23, 30–32).[634] This perspective challenges the role of Elijah as forerunner to Yahweh's coming (Mal 3:2, 5; 4:5 [MT 3:23]). Yahweh intends to come to dispel notions that God does not judge the evildoers.

The action to be executed with Yahweh's coming is indicated as *lest I come and smite the land with a ban.* The two words "earth" and "land" in "smiting the *earth, land,*" are two different legitimate ways of translating the term *hāʾāreṣ* into English—two different nuances of the same term—and both nuances appear at times in the Old Testament. While each offers a different perspective regarding the scope of Yahweh's action and effect, they should not be considered mutually exclusive. First, some suggest that *hāʾāreṣ* here in Mal 3:24 refers to the land and the particular geographical area of the covenant community's existence during the restoration period.[635] In support of this interpretation is the focus of the book of Malachi on the community, whether the community comprises the priests or the people as a whole. However, one must also note the attention given to realities beyond the geographical boundaries of Yehud (Mal 1:5, 11). The second suggestion is that *hāʾāreṣ* refers to the earth and thus the cosmic effect of Yahweh's action.[636] That scope would be consistent with the cataclysmic events of the eschatological age announced in Joel 2. Likewise, the effect of Yahweh's presence in response to the behavior of God's people is variously attested in theophany reports (Mic 1:2–4).

The *ban (ḥērem)* may represent annihilation of the community. This would not be a temporary action with limited results but, rather, a temporal action with enduring effects (e.g., Isa 43:28).[637] The noun is also used in relation to Edom; thus its use provides a link with the idea of Edom's annihilation (Mal 1:2–3; cf. Isa 34:5). Consequently, the *land* here may refer to the geopolitical reality of the restoration community, and striking (*nākâ*) the land

633. Petersen, *Zechariah 9–14 and Malachi,* 232.

634. R. L. Smith, *Micah–Malachi,* 342.

635. Glazier-McDonald, *Malachi: The Divine Messenger,* 258–59; Verhoef, *Haggai and Malachi,* 343–44; R. L. Smith, *Micah–Malachi,* 342; Hill, *Malachi,* 389.

636. Petersen, *Zechariah 9–14 and Malachi,* 232.

637. Compare with Zech 14:11, where Jerusalem will never again be "doomed for destruction."

would then constitute an act of judgment whereby the land is destroyed along with its inhabitants (Jer 6:8; 36:3).

This final verse is therefore a hopeful message and consistent with the overall tone of Malachi. How is it hopeful? God's integrity concerning evildoers and reward for the righteous are being undermined. However, the final message is that, while Yahweh intended to come bringing destruction, Yahweh will first send Elijah as a warning. The hope is that the community will heed the warning and return to Yahweh. The announcement thus addresses the perception of Yahweh's lack of justice and emphasizes that Yahweh is just, yet it provides the community with a chance to return to Yahweh.

Index of Authors

Index of Subjects

Index of Scripture and Other Ancient Sources

APOCRYPHA / DEUTEROCANONICAL